LIVING SYS

LIVING SYSTEMS

Principles and Relationships
Third Edition

JAMES M. FORD

JAMES E. MONROE

SKAGIT VALLEY COLLEGE

Canfield Press ⌀ San Francisco

A Department of Harper & Row, Publishers, Inc.

New York   Hagerstown   London

The cover is a photomicrograph of the human eye, showing blood vessels, retina, and blind spot.

The text was designed by Cynthia Bassett; the cover was designed by James Stockton; the Bio-Topics were written by Abraham Flexer; the copyeditor was Patrick Foley; the biological art was drawn by Cynthia Bassett and Holly Zapp; the graphic art was drawn by Larry Jansen, the photo editor was Kay Y. James. The book was set in Trump Medieval by York Graphic Services, Inc. and printed and bound by R. R. Donnelly & Sons Company. The color separations were prepared by Focus 4.

The color plates on human development following page 416 are from Rugh and Shettles, *From Conception to Birth—The Drama of Life's Beginnings*, Harper & Row, 1971.

Unit I, page 2: Planarians, *Dugesia*. (Courtesy Carolina Biological Supply Company.) Unit II, page 44: Living cells of *Sarcina maxima*. (Dr. Stanley C. Holt, University of Mass.) Unit III, page 128: *Physalia physalis*, Portuguese man-of-war. (Runk/Schoenberger, from Grant Heilman.) Unit IV, page 206: Living human blood cell ingesting a chain of streptococci. (Photo Courtesy Pfizer, Inc.) Unit V, page 282: DNA helix. (Dr. Jack Griffith, Stanford University.) Univ VI, page 380: 40-day human embryo within intact fluid sac (x 2). (Chester F. Reather, Carnegie Institution of Washington.) Unit VII, page 426: Salmon leaping upstream at Selkirk Cauld. (Aerofilms, Ltd.) Unit VIII, page 480: Fossil trilobite from the Devonian Period. (Richard Gross.) Unit IX, page 546: Phytoplankton and zooplankton (x 100). (Runk/Schoenberger, from Grant Heilman.)

Library of Congress Cataloging in Publication Data

Ford, James M   1927–
    Living systems: principles and relationships.

    Includes bibliographies and index.
    I. Biology.   I. Monroe, James E., joint author.
II. Title.
QH308.2.F67 1977   574   76–58034
ISBN 0-06-382697-6

Living Systems: Principles and Relationships, Third Edition
Copyright © 1971, 1974, 1977 by James M. Ford and James E. Monroe

79 10 9 8 7 6 5 4 3

Contents in Brief

Detailed Contents

From the Authors

Given the dynamic quality of contemporary biology, planning the revision of a text begins with a series of choices: what to retain, strengthen, up-date; what to eliminate, replace, rethink? How do the current users—instructors and students—view the book? Why did they decide to use the book in the first place, instead of one of the dozens of alternatives? How are their courses, students, and attitudes changing? How should the text and its supplementary materials be revised and improved to complement these changes?

Our publisher's national survey of instructors, with which we began our planning for this new edition, was both helpful and informative. The increased emphasis on human biology, environmental aspects of biology, biomedical applications of research, and the continuing prominence of evolution as one of the major organizing concepts of the field were reported by instructors around the country. In addition to our strongly felt interest in meeting the needs of this course, we wanted to produce a new edition consistent with our personal views of the text and its goals.

The Concept of the Text

Beginning with the first edition, we have built this book around four basic precepts:

1. Adaptations and natural selection are evident in all aspects of biology.

2. Life's functions are based on chemical and physical reactions.

3. There is a hierarchical structural and functional scheme in the organization of life from atoms to the living community.

4. All organisms must interact with other life and with their physical environment.

Further, we believe that this changing field requires that new material be added and woven into existing information about the living world. This includes the ever increasing information on environmental and molecular biology, human impact on the biosphere, and bioethical considerations.

Despite the major changes that we have made in preparing this third edition, these four precepts have not been compromised or sacrificed. First and foremost, we have integrated these ideas into a book designed and written to stress all the important principles that should be included in a contemporary biology course. Some topics receive more emphasis than others, but this is done because the trends in biology today reside in certain areas. However, no matter what orientation instructors may prefer—cellular, molecular, environmental, organismal, behavioral, or evolutionary—the foundation of the course still can be a general one, based on the major topics and concepts of the discipline. We feel that LIVING SYSTEMS has consistently provided this foundation because the book is designed to be well-balanced and to reflect the experience of our years of teaching.

The Goals of the Third Edition

As you look at the Contents in Brief, one major change will be apparent—the new organization of the text. Although we have retained the approximate topic sequence of previous editions, including later placement of evolution and diversity, we feel that the new organization adds the desired element of increased flexibility to the text. As we discuss in the following section on organization, the book can be readily used both by instructors who prefer (for reasons of course length) a comparatively large number of chapters and by instructors who prefer a select group of conceptual units.

Because biology is a science making extraordinary strides now in the late 1970s, we revised this book to reflect the new excitement and changes in biology. In the creation of timely chapters (Chapter 8, Living Communities: Human Impact and Chapter 21, Human Evolution) as well as special attention to biomedical advances, ethical problems of scientific progress, and environmental deterioration, we feel that we have come a long way toward achieving this goal. These improvements were made possible in part by reducing the historical detail in both text and illustrations.

Bio-Topics, written by Abraham Flexer of the Biological Sciences Curriculum Study in Boulder, Colorado, are yet another component of the contemporary image of the book. Placed appropriately within each chapter, the Bio-Topics provide thought-provoking highlights on scientific research, describe applications of biological principles, and often supply a provocative perspective on the discipline. And of course no revision would be complete or adequate without a thorough re-view and reconsideration of its content. Every page of this book has been edited, carefully rewritten, and developed to make it as complementary as possible with the goals set forth above.

The Organization of the Text

This book is organized into nine units and twenty-four chapters. After the first unit—an introduction to the characteristics, methods of study, and origins of living systems—the remaining eight units represent the principal conceptual areas of biology: structure, living communities, metabolism, regulation, reproduction and development, behavior, evolution, and diversity of life. Even though we regard this organization as most effective in unifying the principles of biology, we realize that there are other ways of presenting the material. The new flexibility and versatility of this organization can facilitate both the learning and the teaching processes because it provides instructors the freedom to select topics and chapters according to differing course lengths and emphases.

There are three significant new features of this organization. First, we begin the book with an overview of living systems, incorporating an early introduction of the concept of evolution, which can be of great use throughout the book. Later, we return to evolution (Unit VIII) to fill in the historical and biological bases of this fundamental concept. Second, we introduce ecology and the environment in the first third of the book, thus providing early coverage of these high interest topics, yet permitting instructors so inclined to treat these topics later as a synthesizing, summary topic. Third, the many living forms are now covered in a new unit, The Diversity of Life (Unit IX). Here the classification, basic structure, function, natural history, and characteristics of the major representative organisms are discussed. This unit can be used as (1) a student reference, (2) a framework for a complete survey of the living world, or (3) as the basis of discussion of selected organisms where appropriate in a particular course.

What to Look For

In rethinking the part structure of the book, we decided to provide some new elements of pedagogical interest. Each chapter opens with an introduction that incorporates the internal section heads of the chapter, tying together the topical structure of the chapter, and giving the student useful clues as to what to concentrate on. Review questions, a chapter summary, and supplementary readings end each chapter, providing maximum reinforcement and review. A glossary concludes the text.

Perhaps there is no way to capture completely the excitement, variety, and wonder of the living world. Fortunately, we live in an age of superb color photography that gives us at least the opportunity to illustrate some of the more dramatic and visually arresting aspects of biology. You will find four photo-plate inserts on Tissues, Biomes, Human Development, and Diversity, following pages 112, 160, 416, and 592 respectively.

To Use with this Text

As with previous editions, three completely revised and coordinated supplements are available for use with this text.

The **Instructor's Manual** includes chapter introductions, suggested performance objectives, audiovisual materials, and chapter quizzes.

The **Study Guide** offers unit and chapter overviews, chapter study goals, learning strategies, study questions, and self-evaluation questions.

The **Laboratory Manual** has been thoroughly up-dated to provide 32 experiments (including 11 new to this edition). In addition, each experiment includes a coordinated Laboratory Report Form.

Because we feel strongly that such aids greatly enhance both the learning and teaching experiences, we have arranged with our publisher to offer the Study Guide at a discounted rate to make it more readily available to all students who would benefit from it. We recommend that both instructors and students avail themselves of the appropriate components of this total teaching system.

This book has been written for and to students. We have constantly strived for a level of clarity and interest which we hope will be effective for our audience of beginning biology students. We welcome feedback and suggestions from instructors and students alike.

James M. Ford

James E. Monroe

Mt. Vernon, Washington

January 1977

Living Systems
Areas of Suggested Emphases for Different Approaches

Chapters	One Quarter or One Semester					Two Quarters			
	General Biology	Human Biology	Environmental Biology	Molecular Biology	Behavioral Biology	General Biology	Environmental Biology	Molecular Biology	Behavioral Biology
1	X	X	X	X	X	X	X	X	X
2	X					X		X	X
3	X	X	X parts	X	X parts	X	X	X	X
4	X	X	X	X	X	X	X	X	X
5	X parts	X parts				X parts			
6	X		X		X	X	X	X	X
7			X			X	X		X
8	X parts		X		X	X parts	X		X
9	X	X		X	X parts	X	X parts	X	X parts
10	X parts	X		X parts		X parts	X parts	X	
11	X parts	X		X parts		X parts	X parts	X	
12	X parts	X parts		X	X	X parts		X	X
13	X parts	X parts		X	X parts	X parts	X parts	X	X parts
14	X	X parts		X		X		X	X
15	X	X			X	X	X parts	X	X
16	X parts	X parts		X		X		X	
17	X		X		X	X	X	X parts	X
18	X parts	X	X		X	X parts	X	X	X
19	X		X	X	X	X	X	X	X
20	X			X		X	X		X
21	X parts	X	X		X	X	X		X
22			X			X	X		X
23			X			X	X		X
24			X			X	X		X

Acknowledgments

The efforts of many people are essential in the production of a textbook. We wish to take this opportunity to gratefully acknowledge the contributions of the people involved in the preparation of the third edition of LIVING SYSTEMS.

Between the second and third edition, the feedback of the many instructors and students who used the book was the foundation of our planning for the revision. The guidance and comments of the Harper & Row field staff brought us useful information from beyond the campus where we were using the book. To the dozens of people who responded to our publisher's national survey of biology instructors, we also convey our thanks.

The following instructors provided critical comment on the plans for the third edition, early in its developmental history: Paul D. Anderson, Massachusetts Bay Community College, Massachusetts; John Buuck, Concordia College, Oregon; Thomas Cole, Phillips County Community College, Arkansas; Bruce Criley, Illinois Wesleyan University, Illinois; Marvin Druger, Syracuse University, New York; Eugene T. Estes, Rend Lake College, Illinois; Rose Feldman, Allegheny County Community College, Pennsylvania; Henry Muschio, Dutchess Community College, New York; Philip Mulvey, Suffolk University, Massachusetts; Richard Nowadnick, Skagit Valley College, Washington; Paul Roby, Riverside City College, California;

James Russell, Georgia Southwestern College, Georgia; Edward Saiff, Ramapo College, New Jersey; Ralph Troll, Augustana College, Illinois; Arnold Van Pelt, Greensboro College, North Carolina; Kathleen Webb, Peirce Junior College, Pennsylvania.

The following instructors reviewed portions of the manuscript as we proceeded with the revision: Marc Bekoff, University of Colorado, Colorado; Carl Brunner, Broome Community College, New York; Valerie Liston, University of Minnesota, Minnesota; Paul Monson, University of Minnesota, Minnesota; Eston Morrison, Tarleton State University, Texas; Andrew Snope, Essex Community College, Maryland; Edward Tisch, Peninsula College, Washington; Carlo Vecchiarelli, Chabot College, California. John Fitch, Michigan State University, provided valuable comments for revision of the Laboratory Manual.

Abraham Flexer of the Biological Sciences Curriculum Study, Boulder, Colorado wrote the stimulating Bio-Topics and provided us with exceptionally useful feedback on the final manuscript. Mark Dubin of the University of Colorado gave us detailed and constructive feedback during the same phase. Bates Brian of Chabot College provided excellent commentary on the laboratory manual and contributed to its revision. The entire project was skillfully and creatively coordinated by Malvina Wasserman. We are thankful for her constant stimulation, essential editorial assistance, and inspiration which are so vital to the completion of a textbook. To our production editor, Patricia Brewer, who so expertly and calmly put together the final volume, we extend our deepest thanks. The personal support and encouragement of R. Wayne Oler of Canfield Press was a vital ingredient in the development of the previous two editions.

John Hendry, a skilled and creative biology editor, did a superb job in developing and polishing the first draft of the manuscript.

Jan Allen cheerfully and efficiently carried the burden of manuscript preparation and other secretarial duties in our offices on campus. Her efforts are greatly appreciated.

Finally, we wish to express our thanks to our families for their patience and understanding throughout the many months required to complete this edition.

J. M. F.

J. E. M.

LIVING SYSTEMS

Unit I
Life and Change

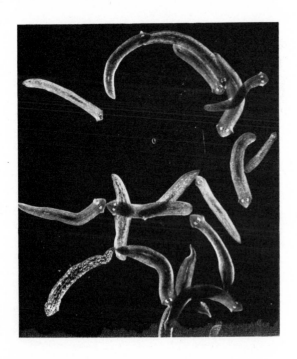

Human beings are curious. We want to know what life is and where it came from. We want to search for a definition of life as well as for characteristics by which we can recognize it. By studying life, we have found that living systems have many characteristics in common: they all reproduce and adapt to their environments; they have a genetic information system that provides for adaptation; they process energy; they are cells or are composed of cells; and they respond to their environment. In our study we need not worry about defining life, but we should recognize these characteristics. Organization is certainly a key concept in our attempt to understand life, because the substances of living matter are no different from those which compose the nonliving world. Since all forms of life have similar characteristics, it is highly probable that they have a common ancestry and origin.

Indeed, one approach to an understanding of life is through a study of origins: the origin of life and of the various kinds of life. When we begin such a study, we are first confronted with the problem of conditions on the primitive earth, and so we must learn something about the beginnings of our solar system and our planet. Then we can proceed to a study of how the molecules necessary for life could have developed from nonliving materials. Once life began, other "origins" occurred to bring about an almost unbelievable variety of living systems.

Evidence indicates that living systems have changed during the many millions of years they have inhabited the earth. Change is an important part of nature—the earth changes, climates change, environments change, and organisms change. Humans attempt to study the living and nonliving parts of our planet through a process known as science. We should know something about this process and how it contributes to our lives. This unit will give you a very general introduction to life, how we study it, and how it may have originated. The remaining eight units will enlarge on these basic concepts.

Chapter 1

Living Systems: Overview

You already know a great deal of biology. Probably in few other courses do you start with such an excellent sense of the subject matter. You are a living system and you live in an environment filled with other living systems. This chapter attempts to organize what you already know about biology and to provide you with some new insights and information.

One of the most dramatic and easily observable characteristics of the living world is its variety. *The Diversity of Life* amounts to almost two million kinds of organisms. To deal with this number, biologists have developed categories and naming systems, which help us isolate specific plants, animals, and other organisms and study their specialized functions.

If we look at the *Living Systems in a Modern World,* we see that our own type—humans—has extraordinary capabilities to alter and interfere with the life patterns of most other species. Part of the problem posed by humans is numerical. *The Problem of Overpopulation* will be explored from several different angles in this book.

Our introduction to biology continues as we look at *Biology as a Science.* There are attitudes and approaches common to all sciences, but we will concentrate on how those principles have been applied throughout the history of modern biology. *The Conquest of Viral Diseases,* through which humanity has been spared the effects of such afflictions as polio and smallpox, tells us a great deal about how biological research can be applied.

What do biologists and other scientists do? How do they approach questions about the natural world? What makes their procedures distinctive? *The Scientific Approach or "Method",* while not a set formula or recipe, is useful as a general explanation of what scientists do and how they verify the "correctness" of their findings.

The scientific approach, though it is a dominant force in our modern society, actually has a very long history. *The Development of the Scientific Attitude* goes back to the ancient Greeks. Starting around the 1600s, it moved out of the range of philosophy and was directly applied in experimental ways.

Biology has a fascinating history, but in this book we are going to spend more time on *Biology Today.* How is this science contributing to our understanding of life, the quality of our ways of life, and the health of our environment?

Life occurs in almost every place on earth. We are well aware that living things need food, excrete wastes, respond to and interact with each other, reproduce, and eventually die. All organisms have definite structure and require energy to carry on their many life activities. In addition, most organisms exhibit some type of *behavior* by responding to their environments in various ways. Although responses are very simple in some types of life such as plants and single-celled forms, others may have complex behavior including communication, territoriality, and social structure. For example, chimpanzees and humans share some behavioral patterns including tool using, maternal care, meat eating, problem solving, and vocal communication. Chimpanzees are capable of expressing their moods and desires through the use of over twenty different calls as well as other activities such as threat displays or mutual grooming (Figure 1–1).

FIGURE 1–1 A five-year-old chimpanzee in Tanzania's Gombe Stream Reserve uses a tool she made herself by stripping down a blade of grass. (Baron Hugo van Lawick, © National Geographic Society.)

Bird nests are a constant reminder that organisms *reproduce.* Many of us have seen eggs in the nests during breeding seasons and a few patient observers among us may have seen the eggs hatch. We all know that young birds grow quickly and develop into adult birds that very closely resemble their parents. *Growth* and *development* then are a part of the life cycle of every living system.

For all these life activities, *energy* is necessary. All living things must process food and use its chemicals to produce energy and to synthesize more material for growth and repair. These chemical processes are all referred to as *metabolism.* Although this chemical activity supports and drives the total organism, the basic processes occur in individual living units known as *cells.* These structural units can be observed when any organism is studied through the use of a microscope. Cellular structure then is a fundamental characteristic of all living things.

The things we have been discussing are characteristics of living systems, or organisms. If we compared a clam with a rock on the beach, it would be obvious that one is living and the other is not. Nevertheless, some biologists think that it is difficult to define life. They point to the definitional problem posed by the particles known as *viruses* (Figure 1–2). Are viruses alive or not? Only when they are inside living cells can they carry out two of the most basic functions of life—reproduction and *adaptation,* the ability to change in order to survive in a specific environment. Viruses possess no metabolic machinery of their own; instead, they take over the metabolic machinery of the cell they infect, directing it to produce the energy and materials they need to replicate (reproduce) themselves. For this reason, some biologists deny that the term "living" applies to viruses.

We can, however, speak of the characteristics of life or of living systems and thus avoid unnecessary debates over definitions of life itself. Living systems do have a particular kind of structure—*cellular structure.* They do release energy through *metabolism,* and they do *respond* to their environment. Furthermore, living systems are capable of *adaptation*—they are

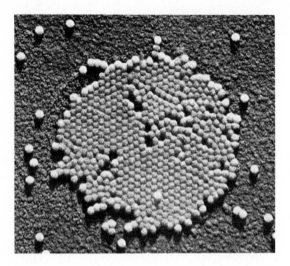

FIGURE 1–2 Living or nonliving? Viruses such as this polio virus can reproduce only within living cells (× 100,000). (Virus Lab, University of California.)

able to adjust to changing environmental conditions. This characteristic has made possible their long-term existence on earth. Both individuals and populations are capable of adaptation; the adaptation of populations takes place over many generations and is therefore an *evolutionary* process.

The importance of cellular structure and of the capacity for adaptation will become clearer as we study living systems. The crucial role of

chemical reactions in the functioning of living systems will also become clear. The characteristics noted above provide the basis for a definition of living systems that is commonly used by biologists: *Living systems are cellular structures capable of self-perpetuation.* As we shall see later, reproduction and adaptation are the two important mechanisms in self-perpetuation (Figures 1–3 and 1–4).

All living systems, then, show similarities in their basic life processes. But it is also quite apparent that organisms differ from one another, so biology must be concerned with differences as well as similarities.

THE DIVERSITY OF LIFE

Living systems exhibit an almost endless variety of size, structure, and specialized function. Some forms live on land, others are found in water, and still others take to the air; some spend different parts of their lives in two of these habitats or even in all three. And the sizes of living systems range greatly. Some are millions of times smaller than ourselves; others are hundreds of times larger.

Traditionally, each living thing has been assigned to either the plant or the animal kingdom. But life is more diverse than this, and a more realistic way to classify living systems is to use at least four kingdoms. Later we shall consider the four-kingdom classification sys-

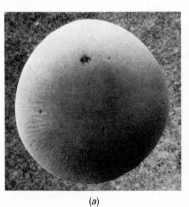

(a)

(b)

(c)

FIGURE 1–3 Reproduction is a characteristic common to all living systems. (L. M. Beidler.)

FIGURE 1-4 Adaptation is a characteristic common to all living systems. Here the insect resembles the leaf on which it rests. (Courtesy of Dr. Asa C. Thoresen.)

tem in some detail. Here, however, we introduce a concept that is essential in dealing with the diversity of organisms on our planet: the concept of *species*.

No one knows how many kinds of organisms there are, but the number identified so far approaches 2,000,000. On color plates XIII–XVI after page 592, some of the 2,000,000 are shown. Some authorities think the actual total may be several times that figure. Each of these kinds is designated as a *species*. (The term *species* is both singular and plural.) All human beings are members of one species, and all chimpanzees are members of another species. The species grouping, which is generally based on external characteristics, forms the very basis of the classification system. But the concept of species has a much greater significance in biology than its role as a classification group. This significance lies in the fact that members of a species reproduce only with others of their kind, that is, they *interbreed* (Figure 1–5). For example, robins may live in an area with many other kinds of birds, but they do not breed with these other birds. Robins breed only with robins, so we therefore speak of robins as an interbreeding group. Definitions of the term *species* always include interbreeding. The classic formulation proposed by zoologist Ernst Mayr, for example, defines a species as "a group of actually or potentially interbreeding populations that are reproductively isolated from other such groups."

The fact that sexual reproduction is involved in the definition of species implies that organisms can be produced which differ from the parents. Consequently, species can change. Although we regard them as fixed units for the purpose of classification, species are really dynamic—that is, changing—groups. As a result of these changes, some members of a group that once interbred may be incapable of mating with other members of the original species. The process by which one species diverges into two is called *speciation*. We shall say more about speciation in Chapter 2 and then examine it in detail in Chapter 20.

The species name for the robin is *migratorius*. However, the species name is always accompanied by a genus name (a genus is a group of related species) and the full, formal designation of the common robin is *Turdus migratorius*. The designation of our own species, *Homo sapiens*, is already familiar to you. Note that the genus name comes first; it is

FIGURE 1-5 These dogs can interbreed because they are all members of the same species—*Canis familiaris*.

capitalized, whereas the species name is not. Note, too, that both names are written in italics. For examples of the complete classification of organisms, see the introduction to Unit IX.

LIVING SYSTEMS IN A MODERN WORLD

Our planet has nurtured living things for a very long time. The fossils give evidence that life has been on earth for at least 3 billion years. During this unimaginably long period, living forms developed into the vast array of plants, animals, and other organisms we see today. The human species has been present for only a tiny fraction of this immense time span; it appeared between 250,000 and 500,000 years ago, depending on whose reading of the fossil evidence one accepts.

During the thousands of millions of years that living systems have been developing, they have faced changing environmental conditions—mountain-building processes, flooding, climatic changes such as the coming and going of ice ages, and so on. However, the most traumatic changes have come about since humans evolved to the point where they could greatly influence the environment. Every species has an effect on the environment and the other organisms living in it. But no other form of life is capable of altering the environment to the extent that humans can. This capability springs mainly from human technology and its applications. In the last two centuries, the effects of industrialization—deforestation, massive urbanization, strip mining, soil erosion, water pollution, the hunting of animal species to extinction, and successes in medical technology, to name only a few—have drastically changed the "natural" state of the earth as living systems formerly experienced it.

The Problem of Overpopulation

In the natural state, most populations of organisms are kept in check by natural processes. But human technology has altered the natural situation. The state of our own species is not "natural" in the same sense that the states of other species are, because natural selection no

FIGURE 1–6   A market street in Cairo. (Paul Almasy/WHO.)

longer controls the reproduction of human individuals or the size of the human population. As a result of human liberation from this natural constraint, the population of our own species has been accelerating at a tremendous rate since the Industrial Revolution began around 1750. In that year there were about 750 million human beings; by 1950 the number had tripled to about 2.5 billion; and today there are more than 4 billion of us (Figure 1–6).

Every single living system in the world is affected by this massive increase in human numbers and by the technology which made it possible. With each passing year, more natural habitats are destroyed and the delicate relationships among plants and animals are further disrupted.

The Problem of Environmental Pollution

One of the greatest problems facing all life is the pollution of the environment caused by

FIGURE 1-7 Four Corners generating plant, Shiprock, Arizona. (EPA—Documerica—Lyntha Scott Eller.)

human technology. As our population, industrialization, and urbanization increase, so does the release of waste materials into the environment (Figure 1-7). In the effort to produce more food for more people, pesticides are pumped onto the land, where they do great harm as well as good before they are washed into rivers, lakes, and oceans—where they do further harm. Smokestacks and auto exhaust pipes pour out noxious fumes which sicken and even kill many organisms, including human beings. Huge amounts of other dangerous waste products are dumped onto the land and into the waters.

The insatiable need of humans for energy to power machines and appliances is not only draining the available fuel supplies but is also causing still another form of pollution: thermal, or heat, pollution. Thermal pollution of rivers, lakes, and streams often kills fish and speeds up the growth of water weeds; it also tends to spread parasites and other disease-causing organisms. Atmospheric thermal pollution can actually affect weather conditions. For example, when it snows over a wide area, the snow over a large industrial city may turn to rain. There is also evidence that industrially generated heat causes fogs, and that these artificial fogs are interfering with airport operations and even contributing to auto accidents.

The Search for Solutions

All these aspects of the modern world—overpopulation, environmental pollution, energy needs—pose problems for all living systems. But we are at last becoming aware of our negative impact on the environment and waking up to the fact that uncontrolled economic, technological, and population growth could lead to worldwide disaster.

Technology (or, more correctly, our chosen use of it) has put us in this predicament, and it may help us get out of it. We may, for example, be able to develop additional biodegradable pesticides and design more efficient filtering devices to protect the air and water from pollutants. We may also be able to slow the increase of thermal pollution by further developing sources of solar, wind, and tidal power.

But a truly satisfactory solution may necessitate some major changes in our way of life. We citizens of the developed countries may have to adapt to fewer material conveniences and less energy consumption. We may have to adjust to different foods. We may even have to develop different ethical and spiritual viewpoints, particularly with regard to nature. We—especially those of us in the Western world—must come to realize that we are part of nature and not the masters of it. We shall examine our negative impact on nature, and some prospects for reducing this impact, in Chapter 8.

BIOLOGY AS A SCIENCE

When we hear the term *science,* we frequently think of one of the natural sciences—physics, chemistry, or biology. But most fields within the natural sciences are interdisciplinary; that is, an understanding of one field requires some knowledge of the others. Oceanography is a good example of an interdisciplinary study. It is concerned not only with the physical structure and chemical composition of the oceans, but also with the life found there.

Biology may be defined as the science of living systems. But matter forms the substance of all living systems, and energy is their driving force. As a result, biology draws heavily on the concepts, data, and methods of the two more fundamental natural sciences, physics and chemistry. Biochemistry, a relatively new interdisciplinary field, studies the chemistry of organisms. Biophysics, a still newer field, deals with such topics as muscle movement and the properties of liquids and gases. In fact, every branch of modern biology requires some background in physics and chemistry.

Biology, then, is a natural science and an interdisciplinary science. But what do we mean by the term *science* itself? As we shall use the term, science is that mode of inquiry which seeks to investigate matter and energy and their properties, and to explain nature in terms of these properties. In other words, science is a particular type of activity whose goal is to formulate meaningful concepts about nature, which can be derived and stated mechanistically.

The concept of *mechanism* holds that all natural phenomena result from the properties of matter and energy; that is, all events can ultimately be explained in physical and chemical terms. Advances have been made in medicine and agriculture, for example, because research in these areas has followed mechanistic procedure. An alternative to the mechanistic viewpoint is the doctrine of *vitalism,* which relies on supernatural explanations. Vitalists refer to a "vital force" as a cause of natural

events or processes. Science rejects such views. Although some natural phenomena cannot yet be explained by science—the causes of certain diseases, how certain minerals are taken in by plants, or how the brain functions, for example—these phenomena cannot simply be ascribed to some mysterious force, because that would really explain nothing and would shut the door to further study.

The Scientific Attitude

Most scientists agree that there is no single method of scientific investigation; some contend that there may be as many methods in science as there are problems. What *is* characteristic of all science, however, is an attitude and a general approach to problems.

The scientific attitude might be best described as one of *rational impartiality.* The term *rational*—characterized by the use of reason—would seem to require no explanation. But what about *impartiality?* Aren't scientists "partial to," or biased toward, what they are trying to discover or do? Surely dedicated investigators feel a sense of commitment to their ideas. Of course they do, just as anyone does who is actively pursuing a goal (Figure 1-8). The impartiality is required *after* the initial creative insight. The scientist T. K. Landauer has put the matter well: "Science is the goal of attaining truth under the strictest possible rules of evidence. . . . Science is not characterized by its method of creation, but by its tests of validity."

Rational impartiality, then, comes into play after a hypothesis is proposed or a theory formulated. A scientist must be both willing and able to subject creative ideas to rigorous testing, to determine whether or not they are valid. The scientist who can do this may be said to possess the scientific attitude. The scientist who cannot meet this test may be an innovative theorist and a brilliant thinker, but is not a good scientist in the strict sense of that term.

The rigorous testing to which every scientific hypothesis must be subjected varies in its details from project to project, but the general approach or method is always the same. We shall cite some examples of scientific research

FIGURE 1–8 This scientist at Brookhaven National Laboratory is removing half of the liver of the mouse to study and test the genetic effects of a specific diet on the liver's regeneration. (Burk Uzzle, Magnum.)

in which this method was successfully used, and then we shall present the central features of the method itself.

The Conquest of Viral Diseases

Such dreaded diseases as smallpox, rabies, and infantile paralysis have plagued our species throughout recorded history (Figure 1–9). Each of these diseases is caused by a virus. The efforts of physicians and scientists to cure and prevent these diseases form an epic in the history of science; they also provide dramatic examples of the application of the scientific approach to problem solving.

Jenner and Smallpox

For centuries, smallpox was not only one of the most infectious and deadly of human diseases, but also one of the most widespread and dreaded. People in many countries had discovered that if a child were brought into contact with a smallpox victim, ideally one with a mild case of the disease, the child would contract smallpox. Usually, however, the induced case would be a mild one; the child would survive and—this was the purpose of the whole proce-

FIGURE 1–9 Yellow fever, another disease caused by a virus, is carried from victim to victim by this species of mosquito, *Aedes aegypti*. (USDA photo.)

FIGURE 1–10   Edward Jenner, 1749–1823. (WHO photo.)

Pasteur and Rabies

Almost 90 years after Jenner developed his smallpox vaccine, the French chemist Louis Pasteur produced a vaccine effective against rabies. Pasteur first infected rabbits with saliva from rabid dogs and then continued to infect more rabbits with material taken from the brains and spinal cords of the rabid rabbits. After many infections in rabbits, the virus became less severe in dogs, but still very destructive to rabbits. Next, Pasteur removed the spinal cord of an infected rabbit and dried it in a flask at room temperature (Figure 1–11). Each day a preparation was made by crushing a bit of this spinal cord in water. This solution was injected into a healthy rabbit to see if it would cause rabies. After the infected spinal cord had

dure—the child would thereby gain lifelong immunity to further attacks.

Later, this treatment was further refined: actual inoculation with a drop of pus from a smallpox victim was made available to those who could afford it. But both modes of treatment were akin to treating fire with fire: they were a dangerous business, causing many fatalities while saving many lives. A safer method of preventing smallpox was urgently needed.

This was where things stood in 1798, when Edward Jenner, an English physician, recognized that milkmaids who had contracted cowpox were immune to smallpox (Figure 1–10). Jenner, who knew nothing of viruses, reasoned that vaccination with fluid from cowpox pustules should give immunity to smallpox. Testing proved him right. Although infection because of nonsterile techniques created many problems and even caused deaths, Jenner's cowpox vaccination proved effective against the smallpox virus. Jenner provided the world with a weapon against smallpox, and in less than two centuries this weapon has virtually eliminated the disease.

FIGURE 1–11   Louis Pasteur (1822–1895) studying a flask containing dried spinal cord from a rabid rabbit. Injections prepared from these cords gave immunity to rabies. (Bettmann Archive, Inc.)

dried for two weeks, injections from it seldom caused rabies. The drying process had severely weakened the virus.

Pasteur next attempted to immunize a healthy dog by reversing the procedure. The dog was injected with rabbit-cord extract each day for 14 days. The dog was given 14-day-old extract the first day, 13-day-old extract on the next day, and so on; on the final day the most infective 1-day-old extract was injected. The dog did not develop any rabid symptoms. Pasteur then decided to take his experiment one step further—he caged his immunized dog with a rabid dog. Although it received many bites and scratches, the immunized dog did not contract rabies.

After this success, Pasteur used his method to immunize many dogs against rabies, but he dared not use it with humans. Finally, a physician sent Pasteur a young boy who had been badly bitten by a rabid dog and who seemed sure to die of rabies. Pasteur used his 14-day procedure on the boy, who survived without showing any symptoms. New methods have since been devised for the preparation of rabies vaccine, but very little change has been made in Pasteur's original treatment procedure.

Jenner and Pasteur both developed successful methods of immunization against unknown, unseen, viral killers. Not until 1935, when Wendell Stanley crystallized the tobacco mosaic virus, were the first virus particles observed. The invention of the electron microscope at about the same time enabled researchers to get a closer look at their enemy. Armed now with knowledge of the structure and chemical makeup of viruses, scientists intensified the fight against viral diseases.

Salk, Sabin, and Poliomyelitis

Although epidemic outbreaks of poliomyelitis (infantile paralysis) had occurred among children and young adults in the United States since the early 1900s, the epidemics rose to an alarming number in the 1920s and 30s. By 1952 paralytic polio was striking about 20 persons out of every 100,000. Young people between the ages of five and twenty were especially susceptible.

Drawing upon historical evidence that the disease might be virally induced and using the newest technology, medical scientists began an immense effort to stop poliomyelitis. Franklin D. Roosevelt, himself a polio victim, established in 1927 a public foundation to support research and therapy, and by 1938 the National Foundation for Infantile Paralysis had been formed. Research teams debated whether to try a weakened live-virus or a dead-virus immunization. A significant breakthrough was the discovery that rhesus monkeys, who are evolutionarily related to human beings, could contract polio and could therefore be used for experimentation. Researchers thought that polio virus weakened by exposure to certain chemicals might induce immunity in humans. On this premise, vaccines were produced and tried first on monkeys and finally on children. The effort was not without failure and tragedy. Vaccines made of weakened polio virus were administered to thousands of children in 1935. In one such trial, 1 out of every 1000 persons vaccinated contracted the disease—an unacceptable risk.

By 1949, several new discoveries and techniques had been incorporated into polio research. New methods of tissue culture made it possible to grow the polio virus outside monkeys. Greater amounts of the virus were thus available for research. Furthermore, it was discovered that there were three different types of paralytic polio virus. Any vaccine would thus have to protect against all three.

Research efforts were increased, and in 1952 the work of hundreds of persons over nearly 50 years finally began to yield results. In that year Jonas Salk (Figure 1–12) prepared a vaccine containing chemically inactivated viruses of all three types. He gave his vaccine first to groups of convalescent polio patients and then to large numbers of children in 1953 and 1954, and the vaccine proved effective. Then, suddenly, tragedy struck the immunization program. Early in 1955 some commercial vaccines were found to be infective; some viruses in the large batches were evidently escaping the chemical treatment. Of the 5 million persons who received the Salk vaccine, only 113 developed polio.

FIGURE 1–12 Jonas Salk, who prepared the first effective and safe polio vaccine in 1953. (WHO photo from USIS.)

Still, that was too high a price to pay, and scientists redesigned the vaccine-producing process and imposed stricter quality controls.

The Salk vaccine emerged successful from this setback, and the incidence of paralytic polio soon dropped to a record low. But this inactivated-virus vaccine was not considered ideal: at least three shots had to be taken, and booster shots were also recommended.

But medical science now had the means to keep polio at bay; with some of the pressure off, other types of vaccines could be considered. Live polio virus, weakened by repeated passages through tissue-culture cells, was found to confer quicker immunity, since it was the result of an actual infection. Extensive testing of an oral, live-virus vaccine developed by Albert Sabin was therefore begun. By 1962 the Sabin vaccine was considered sufficiently safe to be released to physicians for routine immunizations. Thanks to the widespread use of this safe, convenient, and effective vaccine, paralytic polio is practically unknown in industrialized countries today.

The Scientific Approach or "Method"

In the conquests of smallpox, rabies, and poliomyelitis we can see the value of the scientific attitude. Hard work, honesty, critical thinking, and what we have called rational impartiality are all characteristic of it. But besides this attitude there is also a *scientific approach*, a general scheme of inquiry characteristic of scientific endeavor. This general scheme (which is not a single, rigid "scientific method") can be outlined as follows:

1. An unexplained situation is noted. (For Jenner, the problem was: "Does a case of cowpox confer immunity to smallpox?" For later investigators, it was, "Just what causes smallpox?")

2. A tentative explanation, or *hypothesis*, is formulated.

3. Experiments or observations designed to test the hypothesis are set up, and data are collected. (Jenner vaccinated humans with fluid from cowpox pustules.)

4. These data are analyzed.

5. The data either support the hypothesis or they do not. If they do, then further observation or experimentation determines the probability, or degree of certainty, that the hypothesis explains the phenomenon. (Most individuals vaccinated by Jenner did not contract smallpox.)

6. If that probability is high, the hypothesis can be considered a reliable explanation. It then becomes a *theory*.

7. If the hypothesis is found to have a low probability, it is rejected. Then a revised or wholly new hypothesis is formulated and tested by experimentation or careful observation.

Note the emphasis on both observation and experimentation in the general scheme given above. Science is *empirical*: theories can be verified or disproved by observation or experimentation. Because science deals with the material world, a theory proposed by one scientist can be tested, through experimentation or observation, by others.

Note also that the general scheme outlined above says nothing about how a scientist arrives at a hypothesis in the first place. There are two reasons for this omission. The first is that scientific ideas have so many sources that it would be impossible to list them all. The second reason is that in science it *doesn't matter* how the creative idea emerges. It may be the fruit of long, patient, logical thinking. It may be a sudden inspired or "lucky" guess. It may be an insight gleaned from a casual or joking remark by a colleague or friend. How the idea originates is irrelevant to science; all that matters scientifically is how the idea, once conceived, is put to empirical test.

The scientific approach or method, then, is a general scheme for testing a hypothesis after it is conceived. In other words, it is a way of determining validity or invalidity according to "the strictest possible rules of evidence," as T. K. Landauer put it.

Experimentation and Controls

All scientific experimentation requires the use of *controls*. A control is a standard against which the effects of experimental conditions are compared (Figure 1–13). It indicates how much change was produced by the experiment and how much would have happened without experimental treatment. For example, Pasteur used as controls healthy rabbits and dogs living under the same conditions as those receiving injections; the condition of these animals was essential to the accurate interpretation of his experimental results. Using these methods, scientists may eventually conquer other dreaded diseases such as cancer, multiple sclerosis, and muscular dystrophy.

Probability, Hypothesis, Theory, and Law

We have said that science seeks explanations of natural phenomena in terms of probability. The greater the probability a solution to a problem has, the greater its value to scientific prediction. For example, when the Salk vaccine was administered to millions of children, the incidence of paralytic polio decreased mark-

FIGURE 1–13 Example of a controlled experiment on the effects of air pollution. The potato plant on the right was grown in city air, while the plant on the left grew in filtered air. (Courtesy of U.S. Department of Agriculture.)

edly. This high probability of success allowed the prediction that Salk vaccine would eventually control polio.

Besides the term *hypothesis*, you have no doubt heard the terms *theory* and *law*; you may wonder where they fit into the scheme of scientific work. A *hypothesis* is a statement presently supported by insufficient evidence; it is therefore only a tentative explanation. A *theory* is supported by a greater range of evidence and has a greater likelihood of truth—that is, a greater probability of being correct. Finally, a *law* is a statement of order and relation in nature that has been found to be invariable (that is, having a probability of 100% or 1) under the given conditions.

Any explanation or interpretation of natural phenomena must be viewed in the light of available evidence. New evidence may be obtained, either through the use of new instruments and techniques or simply by going back over the old ground more carefully. Of course, the new evidence may confound the existing hypothesis or theory by showing that the old explanation does not hold true. Even the use of the term *law* should therefore be regarded as tentative, since new evidence may show that the relations explained by that law are variable under different conditions. That is, the law might not hold true in all cases after all—its probability as an explanation might not be 100%, or 1.

Models in Science

When scientists seek an explanation of some natural process or event, they often use a physical *model*. Such a model may be very tentative until it is tested further; models thus serve as working hypotheses with varying degrees of probability. A model is often the visual representation of a hypothesis or, with increased probability, a theory. One biological model proposed by James D. Watson and Francis Crick to explain the structure of the hereditary material, DNA, will be presented in Chapter 3. We will encounter other models in our study of biology, such as the one currently used to explain the structure of the cell membrane. In Chapter 4 we will see how models of cell membranes have changed during the past 30 years.

By constructing models and using them to predict what will happen in an experiment, scientists make observations which allow them to keep revising their models until they arrive at a better understanding of nature. Models can be abstract concepts as well as physical structures, as we will see when we study behavior in Unit VII.

THE LIMITS OF SCIENCE. Although many people feel that science and its accompanying field, technology, can solve all the problems of humanity, we must realize that science has limitations. Science deals only with the material world; as such it is descriptive, not prescriptive. It cannot be used to formulate, vali-

date, or invalidate ethical systems or moral principles. Scientific methods can be used to help indicate the consequences of a moral or ethical position or system, but science cannot be used to determine morality or ethics. These are the proper business of philosophy, religion, and politics, not of science. These points will be stressed near the end of the book in Chapter 21, where we discuss ethical questions about artificial insemination, abortion, and euthanasia.

DEVELOPMENT OF THE SCIENTIFIC ATTITUDE

We might say that people first showed interest in biology when they learned to identify the plants and animals they used for food. Much later, people began to breed animals selectively and to cross plant strains in an effort to obtain better crops. The historical records of this activity are so fragmentary that we can conclude only that biology was an essentially practical activity. Since the ancient Greeks left some of the earliest written records of their activity, discussions of biological history usually begin with them. The speculations and interpretations of nature recorded by the Greeks show that they did attempt to see relationships in the natural world.

Driven by curiosity and the desire to observe nature carefully, the Greeks used two types of reasoning to formulate concepts about their natural environment. *Inductive* reasoning involves the formulation of general conclusions from individual facts; *deductive* reasoning is the process of using a general premise to explain a specific case. Both types of reasoning occur in scientific thinking. The Greeks were good observers, but they were primarily philosophers and they arrived at philosophical explanations for many natural phenomena.

Aristotle and Observation

The most accomplished and productive Greek scientist was Aristotle (384–322 BC), a student of Plato. Aristotle was a truly great natural historian who possessed very keen powers of observation. Many of his descriptions of the characteristics and behavior of animals are accurate even by modern standards. For example, Aristotle realized that although most fish lay eggs from which the young hatch, others (the shark group) release live offspring. Further, he knew that these young were not attached to an umbilical cord except in the case of the dogfish shark, in which the young carry a yolk sac for some time after birth. Remarkably, zoologists paid little attention to this observation until it was confirmed about 1850.

Aristotle was also an industrious classifier. He categorized plants as the "lowest form" of life; animals he placed higher on his scale of complexity; and the human being, possessing a "rational soul," he deemed the most complex organism. The Aristotelian system of classification, often known as the "scala naturae" (natural scale), was used for approximately 2000 years (Figure 1–14). In matters concerning the complexity and nature of life, we would call Aristotle a vitalist.

Although Aristotle was a good observer, he relied heavily on second-hand information, much of which was faulty. Thus many of his interpretations and conclusions were incorrect, but most of these were accepted uncritically as late as the 1800s, merely because Aristotle had stated them. For example, he claimed that plants did not have sexual organs. His teachings on the human circulatory system also showed a lack of close observation or experimentation. Aristotle believed that the heart was the center of intelligence and sensations, and that the arteries contained blood and air whereas the veins carried only blood.

Science did not flourish during Roman times, but one biological investigator of that era deserves comment: the anatomist and physician Galen (ca. AD 130–200). Although Galen was considered a great physician in his time, it is doubtful that he went so far as to perform dissections on the human body. Most of his writings were based on his dissections of monkeys. Galen's interpretations of the function of organs such as the heart and lungs were wrong, and these errors were perpetuated for many centuries because of his excellent reputation. He seemed to be preoccupied with the spiritual nature of the blood; for example, he wrote that as the blood is formed it receives "natural" spirits in the liver, "vital" spirits in the left ventricle of the heart, and "animal" spirits in

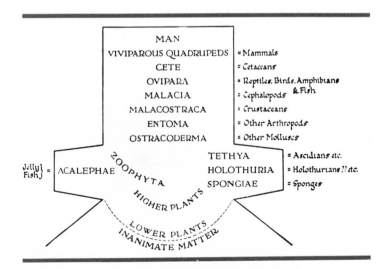

FIGURE 1–14 *Scala Naturae*, or "ladder of life," by Aristotle (384–322 BC), Greek philosopher often called the "father of natural history." (Reproduced from Charles Singer, *A History of Biology*, Third and Revised Edition, Abelard-Schuman, 1959.)

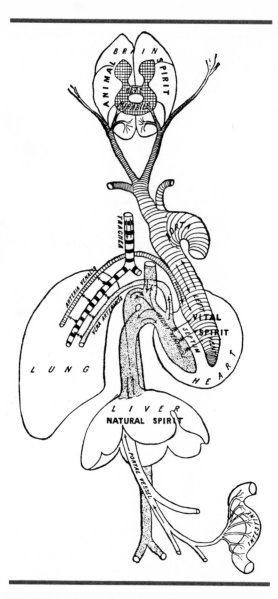

FIGURE 1–15   Physiological system according to Galen (AD 130–200), Greek physician and anatomist. (Reproduced from Charles Singer, *A Short History of Anatomy and Physiology from the Greeks to Harvey.* Copyright © 1957 by Dover Publications, Inc.)

the brain (Figure 1–15). Another erroneous belief of Galen's was that the blood ebbed and flowed, rather than circulated, through the body.

Harvey and Experimentation: The Emergence of Modern Biology

Modern biology began when William Harvey (1578–1657), an English physician and physiologist, traced the pattern of human blood circulation (Figure 1–16). Aristotle's and Galen's incorrect theories about the movement of the blood were still respected when Harvey set out to solve the problem in an experimental manner. He concluded from his calculations that the blood had to travel through the arteries and veins in a circular pattern in one direction only. Harvey was a careful observer. He studied the heart cavities, the valves connecting the cavities, and the vessels entering and leaving the heart. Whereas Galen had believed that the blood passed from the right side of the heart through the wall to the left side, Harvey concluded after careful observation that the blood moved from the right side of the heart to the lungs, and then to the left side, to be circulated through the body. Harvey did not fully understand how the blood passed from arteries to veins; this discovery was to be made later by those who had access to microscopes.

Another pioneer in physiology was the Reverend Stephen Hales (1677–1761) of England. He conducted many experiments on plants and demonstrated such basic functions as the intake of water and its loss by transpiration. Hales was also interested in animal physiology, and he successfully measured blood pressure in mammals. His work was always characterized by a concern for quantitative measurements. This was a new concept in science at this time, but its importance was soon recognized.

The Microscope and a New Dimension

About 1590 the Dutch lensmaker Zacharias Janssens developed the first compound microscope by placing a lens at each end of a long tube. The microscope made possible the observation of cellular structure in larger organisms and the study of minute living organisms such as protozoa and bacteria.

Two men, Robert Hooke (1635–1703), an Englishman, and Anton van Leeuwenhoek (1632–1723), a Dutchman, pioneered the field

FIGURE 1–16 William Harvey demonstrating the principles of blood flow. (Courtesy, Parke, Davis and Company, © 1959.)

of microscopy. It was Hooke who first used the word *cell* to describe the "honeycomb" appearance of a thin section of cork he observed under his microscope. Hooke's many biological studies and drawings demonstrated the great usefulness of the microscope to biology (Figure 1–17). Leeuwenhoek made microscopes that were excellent for his day, and he studiously observed anything that took his fancy. Several of his discoveries were outstanding. He discovered bacteria and differentiated them from other single-celled forms, and he described spermatozoa. Another contribution was his detailed description of the capillary bed connecting arteries and veins. This information filled in the remaining gap in Harvey's description of the circulation of blood.

Many great names and major contributions followed those of biology's formative period. But with the firm establishment of *observation* and *experimentation* as the means of obtaining biological information and validating hypotheses and theories, the essential course of biology as a science was determined. And biology continues on this sound course today.

BIOLOGY TODAY

With the development of new chemical and physical techniques, more refined studies of the chemical composition of life have become possible. New, more powerful electron microscopes have revealed previously unsuspected parts of the cell. Modern genetics is concerned not only with the transmission of heredity from generation to generation but also with the structure and function of the hereditary material. Embryologists are devising experiments to determine how cells differentiate in the development of an organism—that is, why one cell becomes a muscle cell and another a nerve cell (Figure 1–18). The term *molecular biology* is being applied to the investigation of biological structure and function at the molecular level. Learning and memory are now being approached from this direction. Modern medicine continues its fight against cancer and other diseases, using new findings in the health sciences, genetics, and biochemistry.

In addition to the great emphasis on molecular biology, an intense interest in *environmental biology* has emerged. More and more, we

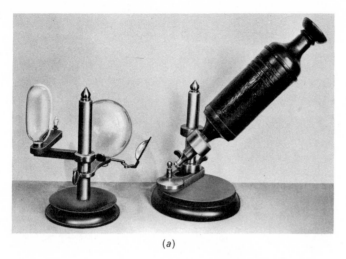

(a)   (b)

FIGURE 1–17   (a) Microscope used by Robert Hooke (1635–1703), English experimental scientist. (Courtesy of Bausch & Lomb, Inc.) (b) Drawing of a flea by Hooke. (Reproduced from Charles Singer, *A History of Biology*, Third and Revised Edition, Abelard-Schuman, 1959.)

are using scientific knowledge—much of it from biology—in the struggle against environmental problems. Perhaps the greatest concern in the contemporary world, apart from disease and the threat of nuclear war, is the danger resulting from human overpopulation and its effects on the environment. How can enough food be produced for the expanding human population? How can we prevent pollution by waste materials, by-products, and pesticides from threatening all living systems? How can we produce enough energy to meet human needs and still maintain a clean world? And finally, how can we preserve (or establish) an environment in which individuals can develop to their fullest potential and still live in harmony with all living systems?

We believe that a fuller understanding of the biological sciences can help solve these pressing problems. All of us must become acutely aware of the relationships and complexities of the living world, and how these affect modern civilization and are in turn affected by it. This book attempts to present a clear picture of contemporary biology. Such a picture should be of interest in its own right. But it is also to be hoped that the picture will convey the all-

important message that we are, all of us, a part of nature. As such, we can aspire to be nature's responsible guardians. But if we lapse into the foolish notion that we are its absolute master, we and all other living systems will suffer for our folly.

SUMMARY

Living systems have certain recognizable characteristics: cellular structure and the capability for metabolism, responding, reproducing, and adaptation. There are many kinds of living systems; each kind is called a species, defined as a group of actually or potentially interbreeding populations that are reproductively isolated from other such groups. All living systems face the problems of changing environments, but the greatest problems have come about since humans began altering the environment. The sheer number of humans and their polluting technology cause the greatest problems for life on earth. But humans, through their science and technology, study the natural world and attempt to solve problems dealing with the material world. The conquest of such viral diseases as smallpox, rabies, and poliomyelitis

(a)   (b)

(c)   (d)

FIGURE 1–18 Sophisticated experiments in embryology are helping us understand the mysteries of development. (a) In one such
experiment, the fertilized eggs of a white salamander (axolotl)
were collected and nuclei removed. (b) Cells from a speckled axolotl were inserted into these eggs in place of the normal nuclei.
Following cell division (cleavage) (c), axolotls of the speckled variety were hatched (d). All three of these axolotls are "cloned" individuals. That is, they were produced asexually from a single parent and therefore have the same genetic makeup. The nuclei of
the speckled cells thus controlled the development of the eggs
from the white species. (Courtesy of Dr. Clarence M. Flaten and
Ann Janice Brothers.)

is an example of the application of science and technology. The scientific approach, or method, stresses observation and experimentation and provides a systematic approach to problems. The results of scientific work can often be stated in terms of probability and can be used for prediction. The development of scientific attitude has followed a pattern from observation and reasoning to experimentation and the use of instrumentation (such as the microscope). In biology knowledge from physics and chemistry has helped us to understand life better. Indeed, we have moved to the molecular level in the study of living systems. We are also greatly concerned about environmental issues as we continue our study of life.

REVIEW QUESTIONS

1. If you were asked to define life, what would your answer be? Similarly, how would you define science?

2. Why were Jenner, Pasteur, and Salk successful in their efforts? Can you see a similarity in the approach each used?

3. Using the scientific approach, design an experiment to test the hypothesis that:
(a) vitamin B_1 is necessary for life.
(b) certain mice are active during the day rather than at night.

4. Why did experimentation in biology have to await certain developments in the physical sciences?

5. Why is it essential to approach the study of medicine in a mechanistic rather than a vitalistic manner?

6. Can the methods of science assist us in the solution of all problems facing humans? Explain.

7. *Science* is often conceived as the area of knowledge that studies relationships and basic principles about the natural world; *technology* is conceived as the application of the theories and laws of science. Which activities below are science and which are technology, and why do you classify them that way?

(a) space study; NASA projects
(b) the study of the structure of cell membranes
(c) the crossing of two types of corn
(d) study of the stages corn seeds go through as they develop

SUPPLEMENTARY READINGS

Bronowski, J., *The Ascent of Man*, Little, Brown, Boston, 1973.   A remarkable work that traces the development of science through our history. This beautifully prepared book provides a perspective, not just on science, but on all civilization as well.

Cartwright, Frederick F., *Disease and History*, Thomas Y. Crowell, New York, 1972.   This well-written book explores the impact of disease on the course of history and traces the influence of disease on civilizations and their people.

Herbert, Don, and F. Bardossi, *Secret in the White Cell*, Harper & Row, New York, 1969.   The story of an investigation of the mechanism by which white blood cells attack and destroy harmful organisms. An inside look at the methods of modern microbiology.

Langer, William L., "The Prevention of Smallpox Before Jenner," *Scientific American*, January 1976.   The early methods used to prevent smallpox are described, and how the inoculation with smallpox itself helped to pave the way for Jenner.

Lanham, Url, *Origins of Modern Biology*, Columbia University Press, New York, 1968.   The main lines of development of biology up to the twentieth century are traced.

Spector, Deborah H. and David Baltimore, "The Molecular Biology of Poliovirus," *Scientific American*, May 1975.   The information that can be gained about cells by the use of viruses, especially poliovirus, is discussed. Poliovirus is described here and some of the information learned in recent years from its study is summarized.

Chapter 2

Living Systems: Origins

As we look at the living world today, we are immediately struck by its complexity and its advanced state of development. The questions: how did life start? is life as found on earth unique in the universe? have been raised by almost all societies and cultures throughout human history. Although the answers put forward have varied greatly, the questions are intriguingly similar.

In the twentieth century, biology and the other sciences have made some fascinating strides in *The Search for Beginnings.* An important contribution has been the evidence presented by astronomers. The universe, they report, is changing constantly. If it is changing now, perhaps we can assume that it changed in the past. As part of that pattern of change, we study *The Evolution of Our Solar System* as a first step in the study of life's origin.

The theories of the "start" and continued evolution of our solar system offer explanation of the *non*living world's origins, but what can science tell us about the probable origin of life itself? As we will see throughout this book, chemistry is closely intertwined with much of what we know about biology. *The Evolution of Biomolecules* explains the transition from simple molecules to more complex ones.

But organisms are more than packets of biomolecules. They are organized into structural units called cells. Cells are so basic to our concept of life that biologists have spent decades researching *The Emergence of Cells*—how the first cells could possibly have developed from unorganized biomolecules.

From ancient mythology to the Viking lander expedition to Mars, we have asked: *Does Life Exist on Other Planets?* If you were in charge of the Viking mission, how would you define life? What would you look for on Mars? Should we expect that any life forms we might find will look like those on earth?

The stepwise change and development of living things on our own planet has not stopped, leaving all organisms the same throughout time. In the nineteenth century the early development of the science of geology offered evidence that living systems have continued to change from the earliest collections of cells. For over a hundred years, scientists have collected and interpreted evidence—in fossils and in structural analysis of organisms as they exist today—which has led to a theory of *The Evolution of Living Systems.*

The story of life began with events unimaginably remote from us in space and time—in the primordial gas cloud from which our galaxy, and then the sun and the planets, evolved during many billions of years.

We know that the physical universe evolved and that the rise of life was part of its evolution. In nature there is no sharp dividing line between "nonlife" and "life." We, not nature, draw such lines as part of our classifying activities. We classify objects and ideas by arranging them in orderly patterns so we can think clearly about them. We often classify the material universe into nonliving material and living systems. This division can be very useful, but it also can be misleading, especially when we recall from Chapter 1 that the prevailing view of science is a *mechanistic* one: ultimately, all phenomena can be explained in physical and chemical terms.

The air, rocks, and waters of the earth are composed of chemical units called atoms. So are all living systems, and living systems contain no kinds of atoms that are not also found in nonliving material. Atoms of carbon, nitrogen, and oxygen found in the earth's crust are indistinguishable from the carbon, nitrogen, and oxygen atoms that compose our flesh and blood. The fundamental laws of physics and chemistry make no distinction between "nonlife" and "life."

Perhaps an analogy would help here. Suppose that bricks are being used to build a house. At some point the structure ceases to be "just a pile of bricks" and becomes "a house." At that point the structure begins to take on features that are different from those of its individual bricks. Not everyone would agree on exactly when the bricks become a house. Yet all would probably agree that the bricks have become a house when *some* level of structure and function had been reached—perhaps at the point when the structure could keep out the wind and the rain, or when it could keep in the heat from a stove or furnace. And no one would argue that at some point a mysterious "house force" had suddenly appeared among the bricks.

Just as people disagree about when bricks become a house, different biologists draw the line between nonliving and living matter on different sides of the curious structures called viruses (Figure 2–1). Some classify viruses as living systems; others classify them as nonliving structures. Most biologists today probably draw the line between the viruses and the cell. This arrangement is convenient and useful because the cell is the smallest structure that can perform many of the functions characteristic of living systems. Further, many structures that are indisputably "alive," such as bacteria, are single-celled organisms. Each of these organisms is a single cell that can exist independently of other cells of the same type.

But biologists never think of this dividing line in terms of a mysterious "life force" that is absent on one side of the line and somehow present on the other. When they think about life in philosophical or religious terms, as many of them sometimes do, they may use concepts

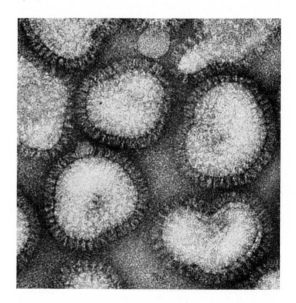

FIGURE 2–1 Viruses are an enigma to those who attempt to classify things as living or nonliving. When outside of living cells, viruses do not seem to be alive. But upon entering cells they assume many of the characteristics of life, such as reproduction and adaptation. This electron micrograph shows an influenza virus ($\times$ 230,000). (Courtesy of Robley C. Williams, Virus Laboratory, University of California at Berkeley.)

that do not require explanation in terms of mechanistic sciences. But when they are doing biology, they must think mechanistically. They do so because as scientists they must rule out forces that cannot be observed and measured. They have no more need in their work for a "life force" than architects or bricklayers have for a "house force."

Smallest among the basic building blocks of living systems are *atoms*, combinations of atoms called *molecules*, and combinations of molecules into still larger molecules, sometimes called *macromolecules* (*macro* = large). These large molecules can organize into recognizable structural and functional units such as membranes and microtubules. Next in order of size and complexity among the building blocks of living systems are *cells*, which are composed of many large and small molecules. Cells in turn form *tissues*, such as the layers of the skin. Tissues form *organs*, such as the heart and the kidneys. And organs form *organ systems*, such as the circulatory and the nervous systems of multicelled animals.

Although biologists do not completely understand how living systems originated or how they function, the mechanistic approach has served well so far. Today they know many important things about living systems that were not known 100, 50, or even 5 years ago. And they have no reason to doubt that this approach will continue to serve them well in the search for knowledge about living systems.

You may find it helpful to keep these points in mind as you read this chapter and those that follow. Science in general and biology in particular have a different approach than philosophical or religious views of life and its origins. Science, philosophy, and religion each seek different kinds of knowledge and ask different kinds of questions. Here we are concerned with scientific questions and answers.

THE SEARCH FOR BEGINNINGS

All scientific hypotheses about the origins of life agree that it arose through a series of events rather than in a single momentous event. They agree on this point because the likelihood that life arose step by step is much greater than the

probability that it sprang forth complete in one event. The evidence supporting any hypothesis about the origins of life is necessarily indirect, because these events occurred billions of years ago, and because the first organisms were probably too soft and small to leave any trace that could be studied today. Scientists must therefore try to imagine what conditions existed on the primitive earth and how life could have begun under those conditions. In the laboratory it is possible to create and experiment with various conditions that might have existed in the beginning. Indeed, many such conditions have been recreated in laboratories.

The fundamental problem in explaining the origin of life in a mechanistic manner lies in the fact that today, so far as we know, only life begets life. Living material no longer evolves from nonliving material. Organisms are composed mainly of organic molecules. But except for those created in the laboratory, virtually all the types of organic molecules on the earth today were synthesized by living organisms. Therefore we must show that at some point in the earth's history, such molecules could have been produced outside living systems. We shall consider the events which led to the origin of life as having occurred in five stages: (1) the evolution of the solar system, including the earth and the formation of small molecules from atoms; (2) the combination of small molecules into large molecules; (3) the combination of these molecules into still larger molecules; (4) the development of very large, self-duplicating molecules; and finally, (5) the development of cellular organization.

THE EVOLUTION OF OUR SOLAR SYSTEM

Stars, such as our sun, are found in large clusters called galaxies (Figure 2–2). It is generally agreed that galaxies began to form when local concentrations of the thin gas (mostly hydrogen) which permeates space condensed into more concentrated masses, or clouds, under the force of gravitational attraction.

It is also generally agreed that stars originated in these galactic gas clouds, or protogalaxies (*proto* = first, early), in much the same way

FIGURE 2–2 The Great Spiral Galaxy in the constellation Andromeda. This galaxy, about 2 billion light years away, is the nearest one to our galaxy. (Hale Observatories.)

that protogalaxies originated from the primordial gas cloud. Within a protogalaxy, the swirling gas concentrated still further, forming clouds which became more and more condensed. At some point the gravitational force within each contracting cloud, or protostar, became so strong that the cloud began to collapse into an extremely dense mass. As this gravitational collapse continued, the dense gas grew hotter, just as the air in a bicycle-tire pump grows hotter as it is compressed by the pump's piston. Normally, a heated gas expands. But if the gas is being compressed by a pump— or by gravitational force—it grows hotter and denser at the same time. Finally the temperature and pressure at the cores of many protostars became so great that the atoms of hydrogen gas there began to fuse into larger helium atoms. This process, called thermonuclear fusion, liberates tremendous amounts of energy. Thus the stars began to give off electromagnetic energy, including light energy.

Most astronomers now believe that the heav-

ier elements, such as carbon, oxygen, silicon, and iron, originated inside the stars and were released into space when some of these stars exploded. And most astronomers believe that the process is still going on. They have accumulated evidence that the galaxies are moving farther apart, new galaxies are forming in the thin gas clouds of deep space, new stars are being "born," old stars are burning out, and the heavier elements are still being created inside stars.

What about our own star, the sun, and its planets? Various hypotheses have been proposed to account for the birth of our solar system. One of the first was put forth by the French mathematician and astronomer Pierre de Laplace in 1796. Laplace proposed that the solar system had formed from a hot, rotating mass of gases and dust that condensed to form the sun. He further proposed that the glowing, spinning mass had thrown off a series of rings, each of which eventually cooled and condensed into one of the planets.

But as time went on, advances in physics and astronomy made Laplace's hypothesis seem less and less likely. Today, the most commonly accepted theory differs from Laplace's mainly in holding that the parental mass of dust and gas was cold rather than hot. It proposes that a cloud of "cosmic dust"—mostly hydrogen gas and tiny dust particles composed of the heavier elements—began to condense about 5 billion years ago, long after the galaxy's earliest stars were born. The central condensation formed the protosun. At the same time, secondary condensations occurred outside the central mass, forming the planets. The protosun then followed the same evolutionary course as other stars, growing denser and hotter until hydrogen nuclei at its core began to fuse. At this point, thermonuclear fusion ignited the "solar furnace" and caused the sun to shine (Figure 2–3).

Unlike Laplace's earlier view, this modern view of the solar system's evolution can properly be called a *theory* (see Chapter 1) because it is supported by a considerable body of evidence. For example, there is a great deal of independent evidence that the sun and the earth originated at about the same time.

FIGURE 2–3   Solar flare on the surface of the sun. Flares are produced by chemical activity in the interior of the sun which erupts to the surface. (NASA.)

THE EVOLUTION OF BIOMOLECULES

Millions upon millions of years of chemical evolution preceded the beginning of biological evolution. This chemical evolution had already begun when the larger earth was forming in a cloud of cosmic dust. It continued as more and larger molecules came into being on the primitive earth. The molecules that make up living systems, some of which are very large, are called *biomolecules*. In addition to these, many small molecules, such as water, are also essential to life. Many of the small and most of the large molecules that we find in living systems came into existence, or evolved, on the earth.

Small Molecules to Large Molecules . . .

As the earth formed and heavy elements such as iron and nickel sank to its center, lighter gases collected in an atmosphere. In 1924 the Russian biochemist A. I. Oparin suggested that this primitive atmosphere contained little or no oxygen but was composed mainly of hydrogen (H_2) and nitrogen (N_2). Some of the earth's oxygen had escaped into space, and the rest was tied up in oxides of metals (such as iron oxide) in the earth's crust. Other investigators now believe that the primitive atmosphere also contained methane (CH_4), ammonia (NH_3), hydrogen cyanide (HCN), and some water vapor (H_2O). (These and other chemical names will be explained in Chapter 3).

In most cases, energy is required to form molecules from atoms; energy is also needed to construct larger molecules from smaller ones. Sources of energy probably available on the primitive earth included ultraviolet light from the sun, cosmic radiation from space, radioactivity, electric discharges (lightning), atmospheric shock waves caused by lightning and by meteors hitting the atmosphere, and intense heat from volcanoes. Oparin hypothesized that the molecules of this early atmosphere, when stimulated by energy from one or more of these sources, combined to form such simple organic—that is, carbon-containing—compounds as amino acids (Figure 2–4). Amino acids are the simple molecules from which proteins are made. Most biologists and biochemists believe that organic compounds had to form in primitive seas before life was possible. It is important to note that the reactions necessary to produce these organic compounds are highly probable when given a long period of time. Although reaction rates were probably slow, the events took place over a span of more than half a billion years.

In 1953, at the University of Chicago, Stanley Miller performed an experiment to test Oparin's hypothesis (Figure 2–5). He circulated ammonia, methane, hydrogen, and water vapor

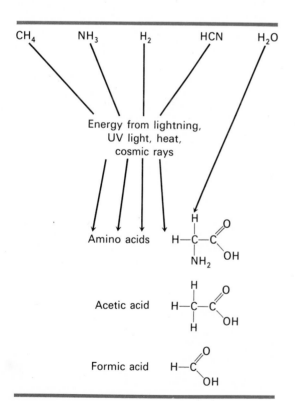

FIGURE 2–4 Formation of simple organic molecules from a hypothetical primitive atmosphere.

through airtight glass tubing and past an electric discharge; then he examined the resulting mixture. Among the products he found were *amino acids*, a *fatty acid*, and *formic acid*—all of them organic compounds found in living systems!

Miller's ingenious experiment proved that the process proposed by Oparin was possible; experiments by other investigators have yielded similar results. In 1970, Sidney W. Fox and Charles Windsor showed that seven different amino acids could be synthesized by heating ammonia and formaldehyde. This was especially significant because these two simple molecules are present in interstellar space. So they could have been present in the primitive earth's atmosphere too, and could therefore have been forerunners of amino acids.

Miller, Fox, and Windsor used heat and electricity to form organic compounds. Recently, Leslie Orgel of the Salk Institute took an opposite approach. He froze a dilute solution of some of the proposed components of the primitive atmosphere very slowly, so that the conversion from water to ice took several days. In the last drop of liquid water, he found organic molecules. One of these molecules was *adenine* (a *purine*), which plays a crucial role in such life processes as heredity and energy transfer. One conclusion we can draw from the work of these scientists is that many of the molecules necessary for life may have originated under a variety of conditions. The probability that these organic molecules formed many different times in many different places is therefore increased. This in turn increases the probability of the mechanistic origin of life.

. . . Large Molecules to Larger Molecules . . .

The next logical step in the formation of molecules required for life would be the production of still larger biomolecules such as proteins. Organisms synthesize proteins from amino acids. Sidney Fox and several of his coworkers at Florida State University have shown that such a process can also take place outside living systems. By subjecting a mixture of amino acids to intense heat (160–200°C) for several

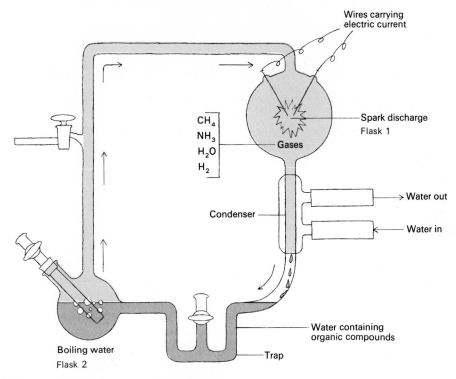

FIGURE 2–5 Laboratory apparatus set up by Stanley Miller to simulate the chemical and physical conditions on the primitive earth. Water vapor produced in Flask 2 is mixed with the gases in Flask 1, passed through an electric discharge, and condensed in the U tube at the bottom. After the gases had circulated for one week, samples of the water were analyzed for organic compounds and several amino acids were found.

hours, they were able to produce very large proteinlike molecules which they called *proteinoids.* Other experimenters have produced similar polymers. (*Polymers* are large molecules formed from chainlike linkages of smaller molecules.)

By pouring water over a mixture of hot proteinoids, Fox produced tiny spherical bodies which he termed "microspheres" (Figure 2–6). These objects are large enough to be seen under the light microscope. And observation with the more powerful electron microscope reveals that microspheres have a double-walled membrane, which is typical of living cells. These microspheres cannot be considered cells, but Fox's experiment shows that proteinoids can form

membranelike structures which are characteristic of cells.

Compounds other than proteins are also necessary for life. Among these are *sugars, purines, pyrimidines,* and *fatty acids.* It seems quite likely that molecules of these compounds could have been produced early in the series of events leading up to living systems. Simple sugars have been produced by irradiating solutions of formaldehyde ($H_2C{=}O$) with ultraviolet or gamma rays, and larger sugar molecules have been produced by heating mixtures of simple sugars. Fatty acids have also been produced under prebiotic laboratory conditions. Fats are formed from one molecule of glycerol (glycerine), and three molecules of fatty acids.

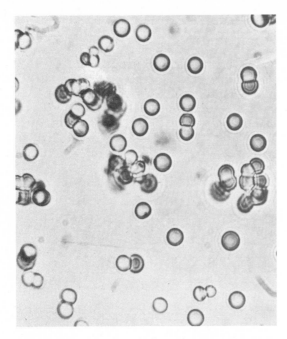

FIGURE 2-6   Microspheres produced by combining water with hot proteinoids. The spheres range in size from 1 to 3 microns. (Courtesy of Institute of Molecular Evolution, University of Miami.)

It is conceivable that on the primitive earth these molecules could have come together in the presence of an energy source to produce large fat molecules, although this has not been done in the laboratory. Pyrimidines, like purines, are compounds of carbon and nitrogen which are essential to the hereditary and reproductive processes of all organisms. The purine adenine has been synthesized in several different ways; in one experiment it was produced when hydrogen cyanide and ammonia were heated together at 100°C. In other experiments, purines and pyrimidines were produced from mixtures of methane, ammonia, hydrogen, and water. Purines have also been produced by the freezing method described earlier (Figure 2-7).

Compounds such as purines and sugars frequently combine within living systems to form even larger biomolecules. These molecules, known as *nucleotides*, are produced when ribose or deoxyribose sugar, a purine or pyrimi-

dine, and phosphoric acid unite as:

$$adenine—ribose—PO_4$$
$$sugar$$

Since nucleotides are inseparably linked with life's functions, these larger molecules must have evolved early in the sequence of events leading to life. Hence this important step in the hypothesized sequence of events would have made further evolution possible. Concentration

FIGURE 2-7   A tube of dilute HCN (hydrogen cyanide) solution was frozen very slowly. The small "bubble" at the top contains a concentrated solution of HCN and organic molecules, of which adenine is one. (D. K. Miller, The Salk Institute.)

processes probably enhanced the synthesis of nucleotides and larger compounds. Dilute solutions of the organic molecules necessary for life, an "organic soup," had to thicken through these concentration processes of evaporation or molecules sticking together on a surface or even freezing. It is not unlikely that some simple molecules acted to speed up these syntheses.

. . . To Self-Duplicating, Coding Molecules

Life requires even larger biomolecules than the nucleotides, and so further polymerization (construction of larger molecules from smaller ones) must have occurred on the primitive earth. We know that in living systems, nucleotides unite to form some of the largest natural molecules known, the *nucleic acids.* As we shall see later, these huge molecules—some of which contain thousands of atoms—are responsible for regulating and controlling all life. Two basic types of nucleic acids are known: ribonucleic acid (RNA), a long single chain of nucleotides, and deoxyribonucleic acid (DNA), a long, usually double chain of nucleotides. The chromosomes of living cells are composed of nucleic acids (mostly DNA) and proteins. Viruses have similar compositions— protein and either RNA or DNA. Some biologists speculate that virus-like structures could have appeared soon after the appearance of nucleic acid and protein molecules.

The important point is that DNA is a long, usually double-stranded molecule that can divide and produce two molecules exactly like itself. DNA also provides a coded system of information that regulates cell processes, including the synthesis of proteins. The information code of DNA is sometimes called the "genetic code." *Genes*, which may for now be defined as the basic units of heredity, are located on chromosomes inside cells. They regulate all cellular processes, including reproduction. That is why the information code of DNA is sometimes called "the code of life." We will take a closer look at the information code of DNA in Chapter 14.

If nucleic acids could be synthesized in the laboratory, another step would be taken toward understanding the origin of life. In 1958, Arthur Kornberg succeeded in doing just this. Kornberg's test tube synthesis was a great advance in biochemistry, and it won him the Nobel Prize in medicine in 1959. The synthetic DNA produced by Kornberg was not, however, exactly like "normal" DNA. Its molecular chains were branched, and they exhibited no biological activity. The next challenge then, was to produce biologically active DNA—DNA which could perform the essential functions of life. In 1967, Kornberg announced a new achievement. In his laboratory at Stanford University, he and his associates had synthesized a viral DNA that could invade bacterial cells to produce a new generation of normal viruses. Kornberg used a virus with circular, single-stranded DNA (Figure 2–8). He was able to

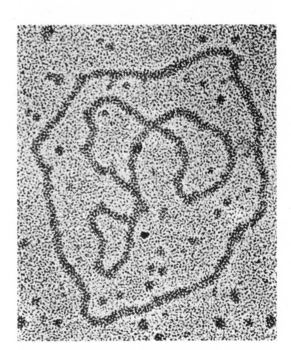

FIGURE 2–8   Electron micrograph of two duplex circles of partially synthetic φ × DNA (× 310,000). One duplex happens to lie inside the other. Each consists of a template of natural virus with a complete synthetic complementary circle. (Reproduced by permission from "The Synthesis of Infective DNA and Its Implications" by Arthur Kornberg, *Hospital Practice*, April 1968.)

isolate the viral DNA, replicate (copy) it in a test tube, and finally copy the copy. This amounted to a complete synthesis of DNA outside the cell. When the artificial DNA was introduced into a specially prepared culture of *Escherichia coli* bacteria, the copy DNA entered the bacteria cells and produced normal viruses. Although in this case the DNA was single-stranded, it was biologically active—and science had moved a step nearer to understanding the genetic mechanisms and the origin of life.

In 1970 Har Gobind Khorana, while at the University of Wisconsin, synthesized the first artificial or "human-made" gene. In this experiment with yeast cells he joined 77 nucleotides into double-stranded DNA that was the code for a type of RNA (another nucleic acid necessary for making proteins). In 1973, after moving to the Massachusetts Institute of Technology, Khorana's research team constructed another test-tube gene. In these experiments on bacteria they synthesized the portion of a bacterial gene that codes for the type of RNA that attaches to the amino acid, tyrosine, and transports it to a site or protein synthesis in the cell. But we now know that in order for a gene to function, additional nucleotides are necessary for regulation. That is, a gene must be instructed when to "start" and when to "stop" its action. In both of these syntheses, Khorana did not make the regulatory parts and therefore the gene could not function. In 1976, however, Khorana's group was able to add these regulatory regions to the bacterial gene, thus producing a fully functional gene. We will discuss this synthesis again in Chapter 14.

THE EMERGENCE OF CELLS

Most of the basic molecules necessary for life have now been discussed, but we know that these molecules function only when enclosed in cells. How then were the first cells formed? Fox's experiments demonstrate one possible way in which cells could have been formed with protein membranes. Other possibilities have been suggested. For example, it would certainly have been advantageous to large molecules of nucleic acids and proteins to be close

to the smaller molecules from which they were formed. Perhaps these smaller molecules stuck to mineral substances such as clay or to globs of accumulated organic material. At this stage, however, we simply do not know how the first cells were formed. We do know that cells have membranes composed of protein and fat and that they possess chromosomes containing DNA, which controls cellular activities. Perhaps the first cells utilized proteins as their informational molecules to control important chemical reactions. But nucleic acids provide for greater control and diversity, because of their coding and self-duplicating capabilities. The kinds of cells found on earth today indicate that various arrangements of cell structure can be successful. Two types of cells are representative of present-day forms: (1) *eucaryotic* cells, which possess a membrane-bound nucleus containing chromosomes, and (2) *procaryotic* cells, which lack a nuclear membrane (Figure 2–9). Perhaps the fundamental problem in understanding the origin of life is explaining

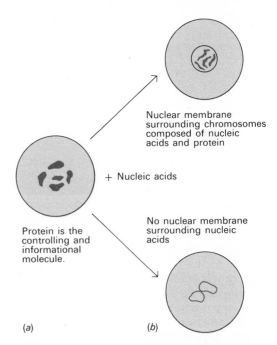

Nuclear membrane surrounding chromosomes composed of nucleic acids and protein

\+ Nucleic acids

Protein is the controlling and informational molecule.

No nuclear membrane surrounding nucleic acids

(a)   (b)

FIGURE 2–9   Probable scheme for the origin of modern cell types from a primitive cell. (*a*) Primitive cell type. (*b*) Modern cell types.

how nucleic acids became associated with cellular structures and how the vital nucleic acid–protein relationship developed. It is highly probable that the very first cells were procaryotic and anaerobic (requiring no oxygen); they probably did not make their own food.

With the development of additional cell structures, the cellular processes of *respiration* (which provides needed energy) and *photosynthesis* (food making) could have evolved. In cellular respiration, oxygen is taken in and used, and carbon dioxide is given off as a waste product. In photosynthesis, the process is reversed: oxygen is released and carbon dioxide is used. These processes were probably significant in the conversion of the primitive hydrogen-rich atmosphere to one containing a considerable amount of oxygen. In fact, most of the oxygen in our present-day atmosphere is believed to be the product of photosynthesis. Once cells were formed with nuclei (*nuclei* is the plural of *nucleus*), proteins, and other cell structures needed for respiration and photosynthesis, the road to life's great diversity was open.

DOES LIFE EXIST ON OTHER PLANETS?

In September 1969 a meteorite fell to earth near Victoria, Australia. The biochemist Cyril Ponnamperuma obtained samples of the Murchison meteorite, as it was called; he found eight amino acids in the samples. In itself, this was not surprising. Several earlier investigators had found amino acids and purines in other meteorites. Meteorites often become contaminated by such compounds from the atmosphere and surface materials of the earth. Indeed, six of the amino acids Ponnamperuma found in the Murchison meteorite occur frequently in earthly organisms.

But the samples also contained two amino acids not ordinarily found on earth. And the Murchison meteorite held another surprise. The atoms of certain molecules can occur in two different structural configurations, each of which is a mirror image of the other. The two forms of these otherwise identical molecules are said to be "right-handed" and "left-handed"

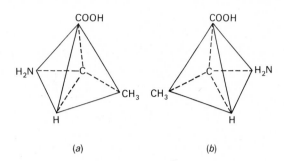

FIGURE 2–10 Two forms of alanine, (a) "left-handed" and (b) "right-handed." Note that they are mirror images of each other. Only left-handed molecules occur in living systems on earth.

(Figure 2–10). Most amino acid molecules on earth are of the "left-handed" variety. But all eight amino acids in the Murchison meteorite contained almost equal amounts of both configurations—a characteristic of compounds produced outside living systems.

Ponnamperuma's two discoveries made it seem highly improbable that all the meteorite's amino acids came from contamination by the earth's atmosphere or surface. The findings pointed to the opposite conclusion: it is very probable that amino acids exist elsewhere in the universe. And if these important building blocks are available elsewhere, it is also possible that life has originated on other planets.

Following this line of reasoning, researchers are now using space flight to study Mars for signs of life (Figure 2–11). As early as 1971 the Mariner 9 space probe indicated that Mars had undergone events similar to those of our primitive earth. We also know that volcanic activity has occurred on Mars, and its permanent polar caps are made of frozen water. We also know that the Martian atmosphere contains some carbon dioxide and oxygen and an inert gas, argon. Ozone (O_3) is also present in minute amounts. A study of the formation of ozone on Mars may help us to understand how it formed on earth, where it serves as a protective filter against harmful ultraviolet rays from the sun. And the river-like nature of the channels on Mars indicates a high probability that water or some similar fluid moved through them at some time in the past.

Bio-Topic: The Ultimate in Long-Range Research

Are there other intelligent beings in our universe? Several attempts to search for radio signals from other civilizations are now under way, but it may be many decades before we can answer the question.

The evolution of intelligent life may be a very rare event, but it is not likely to be unique to our planet. Carl Sagan and Frank Drake, both of Cornell University, estimate that life has evolved on 100 billion planets in our galaxy and that some 1 million planets support civilizations at least as advanced as ours. Sagan and Drake calculate that if these civilizations are randomly distributed in our galaxy, then our nearest "neighbors" are about 300 light years away.

Radio signals have been leaving our planet accidentally since the invention of radio about the turn of the century. This is less than one-third of the time a signal would take to reach a nearest neighbor, and less than one-sixth of the time for a return message to be received by our descendants. So we should not be surprised

that no one has responded to our accidental signals.

What about older, more advanced civilizations that may have been sending signals to us for many centuries? Why haven't we heard from them? Part of the answer is that we have been searching for such signals only since about 1960 and have listened to only about 200 stars in that time. We will have to listen to some 200,000 stars before the odds favor our getting a message.

Communicating with our extraterrestrial neighbors will require an unprecedented amount of patience and commitment. If we were to detect a message tomorrow, some 300 years would elapse before our reply could reach the sender and it would arrive there during the lives of your great-great-great grandchildren. And it would be their great-great-great grandchildren who would receive the next segment of the "conversation." Communicating with extraterrestrials is clearly an enterprise that will need cooperation across many generations.

Earthlings have long wondered whether life exists on Mars. Some of our questions are: Did Mars once have a primitive hydrogen-dominated atmosphere which included some water vapor, similar to the atmosphere Oparin and other scientists have proposed for the primitive earth? Could life have originated in such an atmosphere, and could it have adapted sufficiently to survive the very different conditions found on Mars today? If so, can we expect to find living systems similar to any found on earth?

On July 20, 1976, another earth space probe, Viking 1, landed on the Martian surface. The lander beamed photographs and data on the atmosphere and climate over the approximately 220 million miles of space between earth and Mars. Viking reported the presence of nitrogen and argon in the Martian atmosphere. But the most important data concerning evidence of life came from three separate tests. *Growth:* soil samples were incubated in chambers filled with radioactive-labeled carbon dioxide. After 5 days with Martian sunlight, the samples were incinerated to vaporize any organic material. Some of the labeled carbon had been incorporated into larger molecules in the soil sample. But was this done by a nonbiological process or a biological process, analogous to photosynthesis on earth? *Gas exchange:* soil samples were moistened with water vapor and a nutrient solution, then incubated. Analysis of the gases released indicated a large amount of oxygen (18 times more than expected) and carbon dioxide. Nitrogen, carbon monoxide, and argon were also released. But again, there

FIGURE 2–11 The first photograph ever taken on the surface of the planet Mars. Viking 1 sent this picture to earth minutes after landing on July 20, 1976. (NASA.)

Bio-Topic: Why Viking?

The photographs of the Martian surface are spectacular. The discovery of nitrogen in the atmosphere and water in the polar cap are stunning. The data from the life-detection experiments are tantalizing. But the ultimate question—is there or isn't there life on Mars—remains for the moment, unanswered.

The most encouraging data come from experiments designed to detect photosynthetic Martians, organisms able to convert carbon dioxide to organic compounds. Significant amounts of carbon dioxide were taken up by fresh soil, much less by sterilized soil. If the experiments had been done on earth, they would have given "a weak but definitely positive biological signal," according to Norman Horowitz of the California Institute of Technology, a member of the Viking team.

The least encouraging data came from experiments designed to detect organic compounds in the soil. If there is life on Mars, then there should also be death.

Dead Martians should accumulate in the soil where Viking's instruments would detect them as organic compounds. Instruments capable of detecting minute amounts of organics have detected none. As Harold Klein, leader of the Viking biology team puts it, "There's every sign of life but death. Where are the bodies?"

The basic question may remain unresolved until a Viking 3 is landed, if there is a Viking 3. Why should there be? Why do we want to know if there is life on Mars? Or if there isn't?

Discovering life on Mars would, among other things, help us understand our own origins. Our models for the origin of life here are speculative, and supported by mostly circumstantial evidence. The existence of Martian organisms chemically similar to earth organisms would directly confirm our model and enhance our understanding of living systems. Mars is a laboratory where we hope to find out how we came to be.

might be a nonbiological explanation. *Metabolism:* soil samples were moistened with labeled organic nutrients, incubated, and monitored for radioactive gases released during the incubation period. Such gases, which can indicate life, were indeed released, but the amount soon decreased to a steady level, unlike earth samples would show. No radioactive gases were released from a heat-sterilized sample.

Six weeks later, Viking 2 reported frozen water in the northern polar region of Mars. But the results of Viking 2's biological experiments were similar to those of Viking 1: no evidence of organic matter in the Martian soil. What the Viking experiments do reveal is a chemical activity occurring in the soil that may be very different from that known on earth, activity that is affected by heat sterilization. However, these data do not allow a definite conclusion as to the presence of life on Mars. Further space explorations will make significant contributions to the infant science of *exobiology*, the study of evidence of extraterrestrial life.

THE EVOLUTION OF LIVING SYSTEMS

The first organisms on earth were certainly single-celled and aquatic; they no doubt had to obtain nutrients from smaller biomolecules such as amino acids. But as the supply of organic molecules in the environment dwindled, new sources had to be found. Some developed the ability to synthesize biomolecules from smaller molecules. As the "organic soup" was depleted, autotrophs developed, followed eventually by truly photosynthetic organisms.

But living systems include single cells, colonies, and many-celled forms as well as single cells. After cells originated, some of them may have remained together following division. In this way aggregates (simple colonies) of cells probably evolved. Along with this joining process, cells changed internally and became dependent on each other; they thus established a new way of life. From this development, tissues could have evolved, and further development could have produced organs and organ systems. With the development of complex structures, a division of labor has taken place: different life functions are carried on by different parts. But these developments required an enormous amount of time: they may have occurred over a period of more than a billion years. Once started, however, the events leading to more complex and varied structures of living systems occurred at an increasing pace.

In time, the sea teemed with crawling and swimming creatures. Later, plants invaded the land from the sea; they were followed ashore by animals. Eventually an uncommonly active and intelligent class of animals appeared—the mammals, the class which gave rise to our own mammalian species. As we pursue our discussion of "origins," we are actually considering the formation of new species—not the details or the exact mechanisms involved, but the evidence indicating that species do change.

In discussing the origin of life we have presented primarily indirect evidence for how life could have originated. When we consider the origin of species, we can present direct evidence. In fact, overwhelming evidence indicates that during the course of time new species have evolved and organisms have changed. This can be demonstrated not only from the fossil record but also with living populations under experimental and natural conditions. *Evolution* is often defined as the theory or concept dealing with the changes that occur in living organisms as a result of slight variations through successive generations. This implies that present-day organisms have developed from preexisting forms. The fossil record presents an excellent opportunity for reviewing the history of life as it developed.

Evidence: Fossils

The *fossilization* process has provided us with the remains of living systems that existed on the earth at various stages of its history. This record gives powerful evidence that biological evolution has taken place.

Most fossils are formed when organisms containing hard, mineralized parts—usually skeletal parts or shells—are buried in mud or sand before they have decayed. Once the organism is buried, decay slows down; fossilization can then occur in any of several ways. One type of fossil is the impression or mold formed as the mud or sand hardens into rock (Figure 2–12). Water seeping through this material as it hardens carries away the organism's remains, leaving the fossilized impression. Another type of fossil is formed when hard parts of an organism, such as teeth or bones, are actually preserved. More common are fossils formed when an organism's tissues are replaced by silicates and other minerals dissolved in groundwater. Animals tracks, such as the footprints of dinosaurs, are also part of the fossil record.

Scientists now have techniques for dating fossils quite accurately. Exposed fossil-bearing rocks are thus good sources of information about what ancient living systems were like and where and when they lived.

A spectacular example of such a source is the Grand Canyon (Figure 2–13), created during the last 2 billion years as the Colorado River carved its way through a mile-deep series of rock layers. Here we have an archive of the earth's geological history as well as a record of many organisms that lived at various times.

FIGURE 2–12 Fossil clam shell in a stone fence post in Kansas. (Grant Heilman.)

The oldest rock is found at the bottom of the canyon, where it was originally laid down as mud and sand. Layer after layer was deposited as time went on, so the rock is progressively younger from the bottom to the top. Figure 2–14 is a diagrammatic cross section showing the geological eras and periods represented by the various layers. Typical fossils of each period are listed next to the layers in which they are found. As we might expect, fossils of the simplest living forms are found near the bottom of the canyon, and fossils of more complex organisms are found progressively closer to the top. The fossil record of the Grand Canyon leads to two conclusions: life forms—species—changed over time, and the pattern of change was a development from simple to more complex forms.

The fossil record can also be used to trace the development of particular families of plants or animals. The excellent fossils produced by vertebrates—animals with internal bony skeletons—make those forms a good subject for study. Perhaps the best-known vertebrate fossils are those of the horse family. Many horse fossils of various ages have been found, enabling paleontologists to trace this family back approximately 55 million years. The record shows that the early horses were far different from the horses we know today.

The family tree of the horse as reconstructed by paleontologists is shown in Figure 2–15. Note the progressive increase in overall size, in leg length, and in skull size. Note too the progressive changes in the forefoot from four toes to one. But we should not visualize a straight line of development beginning with *Eohippus*, changing to *Miohippus* and then to *Merychippus*, and culminating in the modern horse *Equus*. There were many lines, many experiments in nature, and *Eohippus* did not completely disappear when *Miohippus* appeared. But as time went on, the frequency of *Eohippus* in the horse population decreased, while that of *Miohippus* increased. This gradual replacement of some horse types by others continued until only the type best adapted to our present environment—*Equus*—remains.

Considerable genetic variation still exists within the modern horse family. Breeders have

FIGURE 2–13   The Grand Canyon. The geological and early biological history of the area is recorded in its rock layers. (George A. Grant, U.S. Department of the Interior, National Park Service photo.)

reported great variations in size and foot structure. They have also managed, by means of selection for primitive characteristics, to produce horses that resemble the forerunners of the modern horse. By this process they have developed varieties that are less than 30 inches tall and have multiple toes.

Evidence: Vertebrate Forelimbs

Although the forelimbs of humans, whales, and birds do not look at all alike, their bone structure is quite similar (Figure 2–16). Thus it appears that the same basic plan was used for the structure of all vertebrate forelimbs, and that each modification is related to the different habits and habitat of its possessor. The fossil record also provides examples of such structural similarities. This phenomenon of structural similarity based on inheritance from a common ancestor is known as *homology*, and the structures so derived are called *homologous* structures. As early as the eighteenth century, comparative anatomists clearly saw these relationships in nature.

Functional comparisons between structures can also be made. For example, the wings of birds and those of insects have different origins

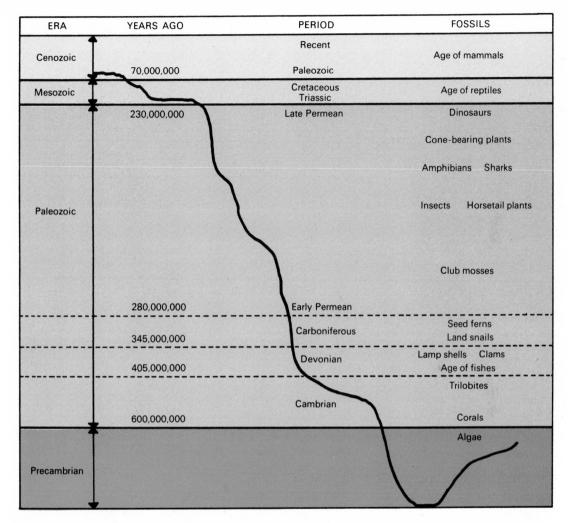

ERA	YEARS AGO	PERIOD	FOSSILS
Cenozoic	70,000,000	Recent	Age of mammals
		Paleozoic	
Mesozoic		Cretaceous	Age of reptiles
		Triassic	
Paleozoic	230,000,000	Late Permean	Dinosaurs
			Cone-bearing plants
			Amphibians Sharks
			Insects Horsetail plants
			Club mosses
	280,000,000	Early Permean	
		Carboniferous	Seed ferns
	345,000,000		Land snails
		Devonian	Lamp shells Clams
	405,000,000		Age of fishes
			Trilobites
		Cambrian	
	600,000,000		Corals
			Algae
Precambrian			

FIGURE 2–14   Section through the Grand Canyon and vicinity showing geologic eras, selected periods, and the common names for some of the fossils.

and therefore different structures, although they serve the same function. Structures that are similar in function but different in evolutionary origin are termed *analogous* structures.

Natural Selection

How has the great diversity of life come about? What caused the changes in the horse family from the ancient *Eohippus* to the modern *Equus?* Why did many once-flourishing living systems disappear from the earth? How did the generalized vertebrate forelimb develop into such specialized forms as the wings of birds and bats, the flippers of whales, and the arms and hands of humans?

The answers to these questions lie in the biological process called *selection,* or—when it

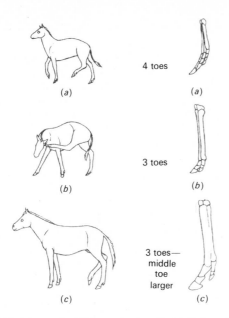

4 toes

(a)

3 toes

(b)

3 toes—
middle
toe
larger

(c)

(a)

(b)

(c)

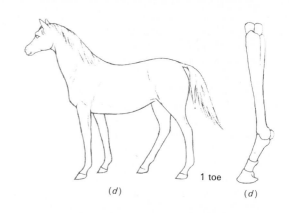

1 toe

(d)

(d)

FIGURE 2–15   Part of the family tree of the horse. The forelegs are shown at the right. (a) Eohippus. (b) Miohippus. (c) Merychippus. (d) Equus.

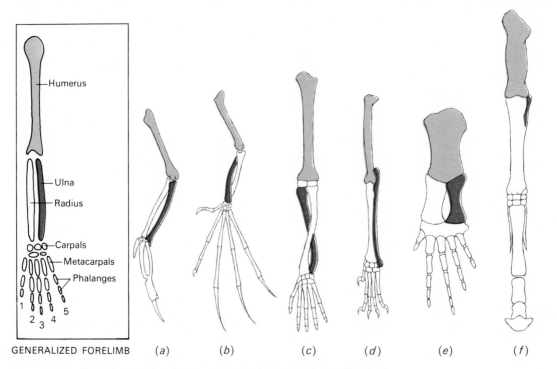

Humerus

Ulna

Radius

Carpals

Metacarpals

Phalanges

1
2 3 4 5

GENERALIZED FORELIMB   (a)   (b)   (c)   (d)   (e)   (f)

FIGURE 2–16   Homologous development of vertebrate forelimbs. The basic plan of organization is shown in the inset as a generalized forelimb. Variations of the plan can clearly be seen in the six examples of vertebrate forelimbs. (a) Pigeon. (b) Bat. (c) Human. (d) Cat. (e) Whale. (f) Horse.

occurs independent of human control—*natural selection*. The development of the selection concept and the recognition of its role in nature are among biology's great achievements. Selection is the primary mechanism of speciation, the origin of species. And speciation, in turn, is the primary mechanism of biological evolution. As we have noted, species can and do change. Once the change has occurred, the members of one new group may reproduce at a faster rate than the others. Groups that reproduce better have more members and might thus have a distinct advantage over other species in that particular community. The less prolific species might, however, fare better in another environment. The process of natural selection explains how some organisms are better able to survive and reproduce than others because of favorable hereditary characteristics. In its simplest form, natural selection is the effect of the environment upon the various characteristics of a breeding group. The process of reproduction may produce individuals with differing characteristics in a specific environment, but only those suited to that environment can live there. Those "favored" individuals can interbreed and produce others like themselves. The "less favored" individuals will eventually die out unless they move to an environment where they can succeed.

Natural selection is the best explanation we have for the many different living systems on our earth. A knowledge of many other biological concepts is required for a full understanding of the process of natural selection, because it is based on the principles of reproduction, genetics, and evolution. These principles will be discussed in detail as we progress in the study of biology. But an awareness of natural selection at the beginning is helpful to a better understanding of biology.

In this unit, we began our exploration of living systems—what they are and how they may have originated. At this point, the view we have of the origins and mechanisms of life is like the view one gets when flying over a new area. We miss a great deal of detail, but we gain a sense of the overall look of things. Now it is time to get closer to the surface and explore its components and contours. What are living systems composed of? What processes—chemical and biological—keep living systems functioning? We will explore these questions in the next few chapters.

SUMMARY

Life originated on earth following physical and chemical developments in the universe which led to our solar system and to further chemical evolution on earth. The proposed chemical events leading to the development first of biomolecules and then of life may be summarized as follows:

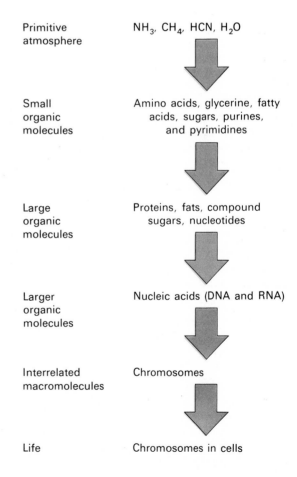

Primitive atmosphere	NH_3, CH_4, HCN, H_2O
Small organic molecules	Amino acids, glycerine, fatty acids, sugars, purines, and pyrimidines
Large organic molecules	Proteins, fats, compound sugars, nucleotides
Larger organic molecules	Nucleic acids (DNA and RNA)
Interrelated macromolecules	Chromosomes
Life	Chromosomes in cells

Once primitive cells had formed, more complex and specialized forms of life could evolve. Multicellular forms of life developed. In time, forms evolved which were capable of producing fossils. These fossils form a record which indicates that many different organisms have lived and changed over the past millions of years. Other evidence also indicates that organisms have changed with time. Natural selection is the primary mechanism that explains the evolution and diversity of living systems.

REVIEW QUESTIONS

1. What chemical and physical developments had to occur on earth before life could develop?

2. In what stages of development do you think Venus and Mars are at the present time? What evidence do you have for your answers?

3. If you were asked to defend the theory that life arose from nonliving matter, how would you prepare your statement? Note experimental evidence that would support your case.

4. Based on what you have studied in this chapter, do you think there is life elsewhere in our universe? Would it be life as we know it?

5. Why do you suppose humans are interested in conducting experiments on the origin of life?

6. How are breeding procedures for specific types of horses similar to natural selection? How do they differ?

7. How is the environment related to natural selection?

8. Why do we say that there is no sharp dividing line between living and nonliving?

SUPPLEMENTARY READINGS

Calvin, Melvin, *Chemical Evolution*, Oxford University Press, New York, 1969. Assuming that there was a period of time in the earth's history between "nonliving" and "living" molecules, the author uses two approaches to discuss the nature of this period: looking back into the historical record and a look at some chemical possibilities which could have led to life.

Carr, Michael H., "The Volcanoes of Mars," *Scientific American*, January 1976. Through this discussion of the extensive and varied volcanic activity of Mars, much information about the history and the mysteries of the planet are revealed.

Lewis, John S., "The Chemistry of the Solar System" *Scientific American*, March 1974. From comparative studies of the planets in our solar system we can learn how our earth and other planets may have originated both chemically and physically.

Orgel, L. E., *The Origins of Life*, John Wiley and Sons, New York, 1973. This small book is designed for the general public and in addition to treating the origin of life, it discusses much general background chemistry, fossils, and extraterrestrial life. It is provocative and presented in a clearly understandable style.

Ovenden, Michael W., *Life in the Universe*, Anchor Books, Doubleday, Garden City, NY, 1962. This well-written and widely used little booklet presents discoveries in biology, chemistry, and physics that give clues to the possibilities of life in our solar system and others.

Unit II
Structure

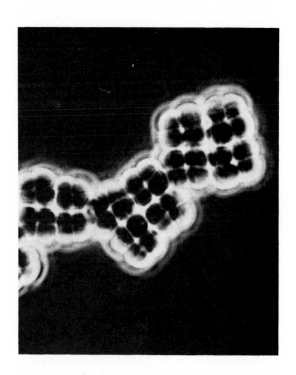

The basic components of living systems are not unique. All the atoms found in living things are also present on the earth and throughout the solar system. What is unique is the organization of these atoms into functional systems of molecules and compounds that comprise the condition we recognize as life.

Atoms such as carbon, hydrogen, oxygen, nitrogen, sulfur, and phosphorus can be combined into a bewildering variety of forms through chemical bonding. We now know a great deal about the chemical structure of life, but we still lack the knowledge and skill necessary to create a total organism in a test tube. We presented several ideas of the origin of life from nonliving materials in Chapter 2, and we hypothesized that atoms first combined to form small molecules, which ultimately gave rise to larger molecules, macromolecules, and cells.

In this unit the properties of the chemicals found in life, their chemical reactions, and their relationship to energy will be explored. Since biological compounds are arranged into a more complex organizational level, the cell, we will examine the cell's microscopic structure and the function of it's various components. Materials must enter and leave cells through cell membranes, and a knowledge of membrane structure and function is important to an understanding of all cell activity.

The ability to reproduce is a fundamental characteristic of living systems. The complex process of cell division allows a cell to produce two daughter cells in a sequence of events known as mitosis, which occurs in all eucaryotic cells.

In the last chapter of this unit we will describe fundamental cell types and show that cells aggregate into functional tissues in plants and animals. At the top of this organizational scheme we find organs and organ systems making up the most complex forms of life—plants and animals.

Chapter 3

Chemistry and Life

In this exciting age of new biological discoveries—on distant planets and within the cell—you will probably appreciate the science of life far more if you can understand the chemical foundations on which it rests.

Chemistry is the science of matter—the "stuff" of the universe—and the changes it undergoes. *Matter and Elements* are closely intertwined concepts because we define elements as the one hundred or so identifiable forms in which we find matter. One of the oldest concepts in science is the idea that matter is organized into indivisible units. Called atoms, they are the basis of the theory of *The Atomic Structure of Matter.*

The parts of the atoms of each element are organized in ways that help explain how each kind of element behaves in the natural world. *Chemical Bonding,* for example, is the process by which atoms of one or more elements combine to form molecules, the structural units of compounds.

From the theoretical definitions, we move to the more immediately interesting side of chemistry, *Compounds in Nature.* We divide all chemical substances into two groups, those which do not contain carbon (the *Inorganic Compounds*) and those which do (the

Organic Compounds). Despite the structural complexity of some of these molecules, everything they do in living systems can be understood in terms of basic chemical concepts.

What *do* these molecules do in living systems? *Chemical Reactions* are the changes that atoms and molecules undergo. Bonds are broken and some are rebuilt to form new compounds. Energy, the ability to do work, is transferred in chemical reactions. In some reactions, energy is stored; in others, energy is released in some measurable form, such as heat or light.

In this chapter we will consider the general processes and conditions under which reactions occur. One of the most important requirements of biological reactions is the presence of *Enzymes: The Catalysts of Life.* Enzymes regulate the chemistry of living systems by making it possible for specific reactions to occur under specific conditions.

Although the chemical side of life seems consistent and well under control, some natural laws of the universe must be obeyed. Systems break down; energy can only be transferred and stored under specific conditions. We will see how *Energy, Entropy, and Living Systems* are interrelated in the last section of the chapter.

The sight of hundreds of blinking fireflies in the summer night is a dazzling experience not soon forgotten. To the curious observer the scene presents several mysteries. The most obvious question is: *How* does the firefly light up? The next question is likely to be: *Why* does the firefly light up—what purpose does it serve? Still another question is: How did the firefly come to have a light in the first place?

Biologists have asked these questions, and they have found some satisfying and useful answers. Biochemists now know a good deal about the chemical processes that cause *bioluminescence*, the production of light by living organisms. Biologists who study animal behavior have confirmed that the firefly's light serves as a signal between males and females, helping them to find each other to mate. Scientists interested in the origins of biological processes can point to evidence that natural selection played a major role in the evolution of the firefly's light.

The nature of the firefly's light, then, raises biological questions of several different kinds, on various levels. In this chapter we shall be concerned with some questions and answers at the *chemical* level of life. Chemistry explains a great deal about life, so a familiarity with some simple chemistry is essential to a full understanding of most biological processes.

MATTER AND ELEMENTS

The first thoughts on the origin and structure of matter are attributed to the early Greeks. As early as the sixth century BC, it was thought that water must be the "mother element" of all matter. Later, air and fire were also suggested as primary substances. About 450 BC, Empedocles of Agrigentum summarized the primary substances as water, air, fire, and earth. This was not the only approach, however. A group generally referred to as the atomists, led by Democritus (460–370 BC), thought that matter consisted of small, indivisible particles called *atomos*. Democritus considered these atomos to be different for each kind of matter. These differences, he thought, determined the varying physical properties of matter.

These and other philosophical speculations by the early Greeks about "the nature of things" were the forerunners of modern science. But Greek scientific thought was hampered by a self-imposed obstacle: a reluctance to experiment and tinker with nature. The Greeks found using tools and performing simple experiments to be degrading work, fit for slaves and not for free men. Some, such as Aristotle, were great theorists and great observers. But with a few notable exceptions, the early Greeks were not experimenters. As a result, their contributions to chemistry did not extend beyond theoretical speculations about the nature of matter.

An interest in the properties of matter survived, however, in *alchemy*—the search for ways to transmute (change) such elements as lead or iron into precious metals. Gold especially was sought after by the alchemists, who considered it the most perfect of metals. From the period of the first century AD through the seventeenth century, the alchemists toiled without success. But their work was not entirely in vain. They transmuted no elements, but their efforts—which involved continual experimentation—were the beginning of modern experimental chemistry. The alchemists discovered and named many elements and compounds, including mercury, sulfur, zinc, lead acetate, nitric acid, sulfuric acid, and hydrochloric acid. They also invented much of the chemist's basic equipment, including beakers, water baths, and distillation apparatus.

ATOMIC STRUCTURE OF MATTER

By the 1600s, the mechanistic view of natural events had become the prevailing one in chemical experimentation, replacing the partly mystical approach of the alchemists. In 1661 the Englishman Robert Boyle defined the known chemical elements as substances that could not be further broken down by chemical means. In 1808 John Dalton, another English chemist, proposed a modern atomic theory; he used the term *atom* after the earlier *atomos* of Democritus. This revived the concept that atoms were tiny, indivisible spheres that could not be destroyed. (We now know, however, that atoms can be broken into parts.)

Bio-Topic: The Modern Alchemy

Gold has long been a fascinating sub-stance. It is beautiful, scarce, workable, and never corrodes. The alchemists of the Middle Ages saw in the purity and stability of gold a clue to the secret of eternal youth. Their goal was to discover the "philosopher's stone," a mythical sub-stance with powers to change—trans-mute—common materials into gold and to prevent aging, disease, and even death.

Supported by hopeful and often aging patrons, alchemists studied and experi-mented with every pure substance their technology could produce. These explora-tions laid the foundations for modern chemistry and for the practice of treating diseases with chemicals. Paracelsus, the most famous of the alchemists, learned in 1527 to use mercury as a cure for the syphilis that was sweeping Europe.

The philosopher's stone remained elu-sive, but alchemy evolved into chemistry, and chemistry led to an understanding of atomic structure. We have learned, nearly 500 years after Paracelsus, to transmute one element into another. We have even achieved the alchemist's dream of making gold from another substance. Gold can today be made by exposing platinum to neutrons. The neutrons combine with the platinum to form heavy platinum which rapidly breaks down to form ordinary gold:

Platinum-196 + Neutron →
   Platinum-197 →
     Gold-197 + electron + neutrino

The catch is that this particular trans-mutation occurs only in atomic piles that are expensive to build and maintain. The cost of gold made from platinum is thou-sands of times greater than the cost of gold mined from the earth.

And the philosopher's stone is not among the products.

Atoms and Molecules

The smallest building blocks of nature that can be studied practically are the components of atoms; and we refer to these as *subatomic particles*. We are concerned here with the particles called *electrons, protons,* and *neutrons* (Figure 3-1). Many other subatomic particles have been discovered, but they are not essential to an understanding of the chemical properties of the atom.

We cannot say for sure what these subatomic particles, or the atom itself, would look like if we could see them. Scientific models of the atom have changed and will continue to change as physics and chemistry advance. But we may imagine protons and neutrons as very dense spheres arranged in a compact mass, called the atomic *nucleus*, at the atom's center. Electrons may be visualized as tiny, negatively charged particles moving around the nucleus at great speed.

A collection of atoms with identical chemi-cal properties is known as an *element*; thus, we speak of the elements hydrogen, helium, car-bon, oxygen, iron, and so forth. More than 100 elements have been identified, ranging in com-plexity from hydrogen with 1 proton and 1 electron to lawrencium with 103 protons, 154 neutrons, and 103 electrons. Most elements, however, play no known role in living systems. Only 11 are found in abundance in living sys-tems, although most organisms contain several other elements also (Figure 3-2). Just four ele-ments—hydrogen, carbon, nitrogen, and oxy-gen—make up 96 percent of the human body's

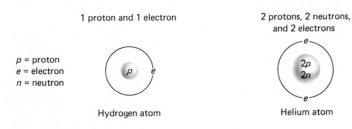

1 proton and 1 electron

p = proton
e = electron
n = neutron

Hydrogen atom

2 protons, 2 neutrons,
and 2 electrons

Helium atom

FIGURE 3–1   Subatomic components of the two simplest atoms, hydrogen and helium. A proton (p) possesses one positive charge; a neutron (n) has no charge; and an electron (e) has one negative charge.

weight; these four, together with phosphorus and sulfur, are the main atomic "building blocks" of living systems.

When atoms of two or more different elements unite, they form a *compound*. The fundamental unit of a compound is called a *molecule*. For example, four hydrogen atoms may combine with one carbon atom to form the compound methane (CH_4). A molecule of methane is thus composed of five atoms, four hydrogen and one carbon. Molecules may also be formed by atoms of just one element, such as O_2 and H_2.

Protons, Neutrons, and Electrons

Most of the mass of an atom is squeezed into a small, dense central nucleus that carries a positive electrical charge. For all elements except hydrogen, atomic nuclei are composed of positively charged protons and uncharged neutrons. Hydrogen, the simplest element, has just one proton and no neutrons. Protons and neutrons possess nearly equal mass, and thus each is assigned a *mass unit* of 1. Hydrogen, with its single proton, has an atomic mass of 1, whereas helium, which has 2 protons and 2 neutrons, has an atomic mass of 4 (Figure 3–1).

The number of positively charged protons in the nucleus of an atom determines the number of negatively charged electrons characteristic of that atom. The atom itself is electrically neutral, because it has an equal number of positively charged protons and negatively charged electrons. Neutrons contribute only to the mass

of the atom, not to its charge. Since the mass of a proton or a neutron is about 1840 times greater than that of an electron, the total mass of the atom depends almost exclusively on the number of protons and neutrons in the nucleus. This mass is also called the *atomic weight* of the atom. The atoms of each element are also assigned an *atomic number*, which is simply the number of protons in the nucleus.

For easy reference in scientific work, chemical elements are arranged in a *periodic table* on the basis of their atomic numbers and chemical properties. But the periodic table is not merely a convenience. The periodic table is to chemistry what the theory of evolution is to biology: an insight into the workings of the universe.

Notice in Figure 3–2 that the atomic weights given below each chemical symbol are not whole numbers, as we might expect. There are several reasons for this. One is that the atomic weights are *relative* weights, not actual weights such as one might obtain by weighing an object on a scale. One element has been assigned a certain weight arbitrarily, and all other elements are compared with this reference weight. Another reason is that not all atoms of an element have exactly the same weight. Atoms of the same element may have various numbers of neutrons and thus various atomic weights. Atoms with the same number of protons but varying numbers of neutrons are called *isotopes*. For example, there are seven known isotopes of the element carbon—carbon 10, 11, 12, 13, 14, 15, and 16. All these isotopes have six protons and six electrons, but they differ in the

Main table

Ia	IIa	IIIb	IVb	Vb	VIb	VIIb	VIIIb	VIIIb	VIIIb	IB	IIB	IIIa	IVa	Va	VIa	VIIa	O
1 H 1.008																	2 He 4.00
3 Li 6.94	4 Be 9.01											5 B 10.81	6 C 12.01	7 N 14.00	8 O 15.99	9 F 18.99	10 Ne 20.18
11 Na 22.99	12 Mg 24.31											13 Al 26.98	14 Si 28.09	15 P 30.97	16 S 32.06	17 Cl 35.45	18 Ar 39.95
19 K 39.10	20 Ca 40.08	21 Sc 44.96	22 Ti 47.90	23 V 50.94	24 Cr 51.99	25 Mn 54.94	26 Fe 55.85	27 Co 58.93	28 Ni 58.71	29 Cu 63.54	30 Zn 65.37	31 Ga 69.72	32 Ge 72.59	33 As 74.92	34 Se 78.96	35 Br 79.91	36 Kr 83.80
37 Rb 85.47	38 Sr 87.62	39 Y 88.91	40 Zr 91.22	41 Nb 92.91	42 Mo 95.94	43 Tc (99)	44 Ru 101.07	45 Rh 102.91	46 Pd 106.4	47 Ag 107.87	48 Cd 112.40	49 In 114.82	50 Sn 118.69	51 Sb 121.75	52 Te 127.60	53 I 126.90	54 Xe 131.30
55 Cs 132.91	56 Ba 137.34	see below 57–71	72 Hf 178.49	73 Ta 180.95	74 W 183.85	75 Re 186.2	76 Os 190.2	77 Ir 192.2	78 Pt 195.09	79 Au 196.97	80 Hg 200.59	81 Tl 204.37	82 Pb 207.19	83 Bi 208.98	84 Po (210)	85 At (210)	86 Rn (222)
87 Fr (223)	88 Ra (226)	see below 89-103	104 Rf (261)	105 Ha (260)													

Lanthanides

57 La 138.91	58 Ce 140.12	59 Pr 140.91	60 Nd 144.24	61 Pm (147)	62 Sm 150.35	63 Eu 151.96	64 Gd 157.25	65 Tb 158.92	66 Dy 162.50	67 Ho 164.93	68 Er 167.26	69 Tm 168.93	70 Yb 173.04	71 Lu 174.97

Actinides

89 Ac (227)	90 Th 232.04	91 Pa (231)	92 U 238.03	93 Np (237)	94 Pu (242)	95 Am (243)	96 Cm (247)	97 Bk (247)	98 Cf (251)	99 Es (254)	100 Fm (253)	101 Md (256)	102 No (254)	103 Lw (257)

FIGURE 3–2 The periodic table of the elements. The most important elements for living systems are shown in the dark color, and trace elements are shown in the light color. The number above each symbol is the atomic number; the number below represents the atomic weight.

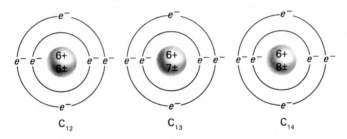

FIGURE 3–3   Three isotopes of carbon. Each proton (+) and neutron (±) represents one mass unit. Note that only the number of neutrons changes.

number of neutrons. Three of the isotopes are shown in Figure 3–3. The atomic weights given in the chart are arithmetic averages of weights of all the naturally occurring isotopes of a given element.

As we noted earlier, the atomic weights of all elements are compared to the atomic weight of one reference element. In the system used today, the reference unit is the most abundant isotope of carbon, carbon-12. Some isotopes are unstable, and may be in the process of breaking down into a more stable state—that is, they may give up a neutron by emitting it in the form of energetic particles. Isotopes of this type are said to be *radioactive*.

Electron Distribution in the Atom

A helpful "picture" of atomic structure for understanding the distribution of electrons and chemical bonding is the *Bohr model.* In 1913 the Danish physicist Niels Bohr proposed this "planetary" model, in which the electrons move around the nucleus in orbits. These orbits correspond to specific energies possessed by the particular electrons. Each orbit, also called a *shell* or an *energy level,* can accommodate only a certain number of electrons.

The Bohr model is not a completely adequate description of the atom; it has been replaced by other models that are more accurate and more useful for certain purposes. We now know, for instance, that electrons do not actually travel around the nucleus in specific orbits but are located in certain areas called *clouds.* The reported distances of electrons from the nucleus

are based on the highest probability of finding the electrons at that distance. (If you have trouble visualizing all this, you're not alone. Physicists and chemists have the same trouble. Verbal descriptions are unsatisfactory ways to picture these phenomena; they must really be described mathematically.)

Despite its shortcomings, the Bohr model is still very helpful in gaining a basic understanding of electron distribution and chemical bonding, so we shall use it here. To keep this discussion brief, we will give the arrangement of electrons only for the first 12 elements in the periodic chart (Figure 3–4). In the Bohr model, there are seven principal energy levels or shells.

Element	Symbol	Atomic Number	Electron Distribution in Shells		
			1	2	3
Hydrogen	H	1	1		
Helium	He	2	2		
Lithium	Li	3	2	1	
Beryllium	Be	4	2	2	
Boron	B	5	2	3	
Carbon	C	6	2	4	
Nitrogen	N	7	2	5	
Oxygen	O	8	2	6	
Fluorine	F	9	2	7	
Neon	Ne	10	2	8	
Sodium	Na	11	2	8	1
Magnesium	Mg	12	2	8	2

FIGURE 3–4   Electron distributions of the first 12 elements in the periodic table.

FIGURE 3–5 (a) Electrovalent bond of sodium and chlorine. When the lone electron from the outer shell of sodium is transferred to the outer shell of chlorine, each atom has eight electrons, a stable number, in its outer shell. The result is the compound sodium chloride (NaCl). Sodium, which has lost an electron, now has one more proton than it has electrons; thus it has a positive (+) charge. Chlorine, which received the electron, now has an additional electron; it thus has a negative (−) charge. Since the ions are of opposite charge, they are attracted to each other. (b) Each of the two electrons in the outer shell of magnesium may be transferred to a chlorine atom. One atom of magnesium thus combines with two atoms of chlorine. Since magnesium has lost two electrons, it has two positive charges (+ +).

None of the biologically important elements have more than four principal electron shells, but larger, heavier elements may have up to seven. Each principal shell can accommodate only a certain number of electrons.

The electrons in the outer shell of an atom are of greatest interest chemically. The stable number of electrons in the outer shell of any element appears to be eight, except helium, which is stable with two. Stability, as used here, refers to the chemical inactivity of an atom. All the chemically unreactive elements—the so-called "inert gases"—have eight electrons in their outer shells. An atom with fewer than eight electrons in its outer shell may react with another atom in one of two ways: (1) it may lose electrons to, or gain electrons from, another atom; or (2) it may share electrons with another atom to complete its outer electron shell. Either way, both atoms achieve a stable configuration which provides a strong force of attraction between the atoms.

CHEMICAL BONDING

Atoms have the ability to combine to form molecules. Whenever two or more atoms combine, they are held together by a chemical bond. There are several kinds of chemical bonds, but they all depend on the number of electrons in the outer, or *valence*, electron shell of each atom. The electrons in the valence shell are called *valence* electrons.

Electrovalent Bonds

When atoms of two or more elements combine to form a compound by an exchange of electrons, they are held together strongly by an electrostatic force. Such a bond is termed an *electrovalent bond*. Sodium chloride—the "table salt" found in every kitchen and an important component in living systems—provides an excellent example of electrovalent bonding (Figure 3–5a). The atomic number of sodium is 11; it thus has 11 protons and 11 electrons. We see that when these electrons are distributed in the shells, the valence shell contains only one electron. Chlorine, atomic number 17, has seven electrons in its valence shell—one less than the number required for a complete shell. When sodium and chlorine come into close contact, one electron is transferred from the sodium atom to the chlorine atom. This leaves sodium positively charged, since it now has one less electron than protons; the chlorine atom has a negative charge, since it has gained an electron. The resulting charged particles are called *ions*. Both ions now have a stable electronic configuration, and there is an attraction between them because positive and negative charges are formed. This force forms an *electrovalent* or *ionic* bond. As another example of ionic bonding, one atom of magnesium, with two electrons in its outer shell, will combine with two atoms of chlorine (Figure 3–5b). The resulting compound is called *magnesium chloride*. Atoms with more than four

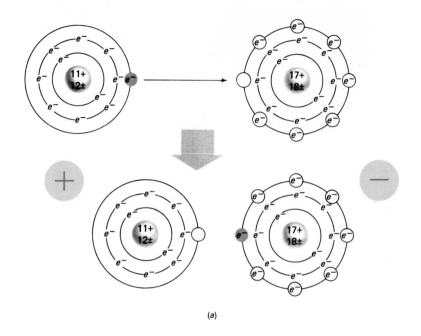

(a)

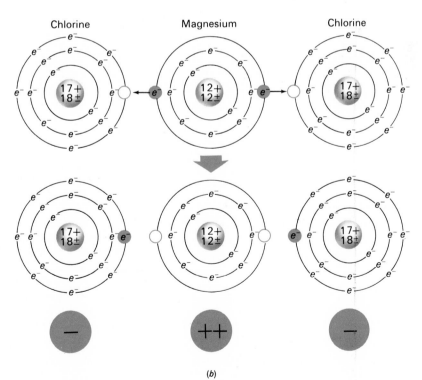

(b)

valence electrons tend to take electrons, whereas atoms with fewer than four outermost electrons generally give away those electrons in bonding reactions. The number of electrons in the valence shells thus determines which atoms will react with one another.

Covalent Bonds

Electrons can also be *shared* between atoms; the strong bond resulting when this occurs is called *covalent*. The valence shell of carbon contains four electrons, just one-half the number required for completion. It is possible, then, for carbon to share its four electrons with the four electrons of four hydrogen atoms to form methane, CH_4 (Figure 3–6). Two carbon atoms may share two pairs of electrons between them; this is called a *double covalent bond* (Figure 3–7). Covalent bonds are the most common bonds found in the molecules of living organisms.

Hydrogen Bonds

A bond weaker than the ionic and covalent bonds is formed when hydrogen is bonded simultaneously to two other atoms. This occurs when the positively charged proton of an already bonded hydrogen atom attracts a negatively charged atom such as oxygen or nitrogen. This attraction, produced by an uneven distribution of charges, is known as a *hydrogen bond*; it is responsible for the association of water molecules (Figure 3–8). Hydrogen bonding helps explain some of the properties of water, such as its resistance to temperature change and its ability to exist in three states— as a liquid, a solid (ice), and a gas (water vapor). Hydrogen bonds are also involved in the complex structure of proteins and nucleic acids.

Electrolytes and Nonelectrolytes

Many ionically bonded compounds, such as sodium chloride, readily separate into charged particles in water. These are called *electrolytes* because, as charged particles, they readily conduct an electric current. Electrolytes play an important role in such living processes as muscle contraction, conduction of nerve impulses, movement of water into and out of cells, and many others. Generally, covalently bonded

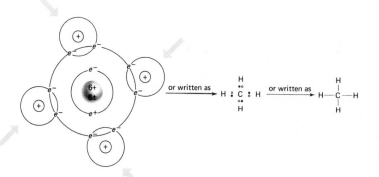

FIGURE 3–6   Covalent bonding of four hydrogen atoms to one carbon atom. Each hydrogen atom shares a pair of electrons with carbon to complete the shell of each atom. The resulting molecule is called *methane;* its chemical formula is CH_4. Two ways to write the *structural* formula of methane are shown above. Each pair of dots (center) or each single line (right) represents a single covalent bond.

H H
| |
H—C—C—H   or   CH₃—CH₃
| |
H H

(a)

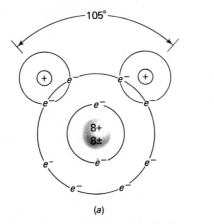

or   CH₂=CH₂

(b)

FIGURE 3–7 Two carbon and hydrogen compounds showing covalent bonds. (a) Ethane. (b) Ethylene with one double bond.

compounds such as sucrose (table sugar, $C_{12}H_{22}O_{11}$), do not dissociate in water to any appreciable degree. Sucrose therefore is a *nonelectrolyte*.

COMPOUNDS IN NATURE

Chemical compounds that contain the element carbon are called *organic* compounds; all others are classified as *inorganic*. The early chemists were convinced that carbon compounds could be produced only by living organisms, but we now know that organic compounds can be synthesized. For example, all of the modern synthetic fabrics and plastics are organic compounds.

Inorganic compounds are also essential components of living systems. We shall consider some inorganic compounds first.

Inorganic Compounds

Although many inorganic compounds are essential to life, they do not compose the fundamental structure of living systems; this is the role of carbon compounds such as proteins and fats. The inorganic compounds we will consider here are water, acids, bases, and salts. As we will see throughout the study of biology, inorganic compounds and ions are necessary for water and acid-base balance, enzyme function, and the activity of cell membranes.

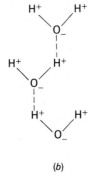

(a)

(b)

FIGURE 3–8 Water molecules. (a) The molecular structure of a water molecule. Because the electrons of hydrogen are associated primarily with the oxygen atom, the molecule is polar, with negative and positive ends. (b) Hydrogen bonding between water molecules. The dashed lines represent hydrogen bonds. Since the electrons of hydrogen are associated with the oxygen valence shell, the positive charge of the proton attracts the negatively charged regions of other water molecules, forming the hydrogen bond.

Water

Water is an important component in living systems. Exact water content varies greatly from one organism to another. Jellyfish are made up of nearly 99 percent water; the human body is composed of about 65 percent water. Within a given organism, some tissues contain more water than others; for example, the gray matter of the brain is about 80 percent water, but compact bone contains only 25 percent. Most chemical reactions occurring in living systems take place in water solution and we know that water is associated with the structure and function of proteins and other cellular components.

Water (H_2O) can dissociate, or separate, into hydrogen ions (H^+) and *hydroxyl* ions (OH^-):

$$H_2O \rightleftharpoons H^+ + OH^-$$

Only a small number of water molecules actually dissociate into these ions. The relationship $\rightleftharpoons$ shown here represents a reversible chemical reaction. The dynamics of chemical reactions will be studied later in this chapter, but we will note some simple chemical changes as we proceed.

Ionic concentrations are often expressed in terms of the *gram–atomic weight* of the ions present in one liter of solution. (One liter equals 1000 cubic centimeters.) A gram–atomic weight is simply the atomic weight of the individual elements of the substance measured in grams. Another unit often used for expressing the amount of a substance is the *mole*. One mole is the amount of a substance equal to its *molecular weight* in grams. Molecular weight is the sum of the atomic weights of all atoms in a molecule. For example, the molecular weight of sodium chloride is 58 (Na = 23, Cl = 35; 23 + 35 = 58); glucose has a molecular weight of 180 (C_6 = 72, H_{12} = 12, O_6 = 96; 72 + 12 + 96 = 180). A *molar solution* is one that contains the molecular weight in grams, that is, one mole of a substance dissolved in a solvent such as water to yield a total volume of one liter. Careful measurements have shown that one liter of pure water contains 0.0000001 (or expressed as 10^{-7} since .0000001 = 10^{-7})

mole of hydrogen ions. Since the ratio of hydrogen ions to hydroxyl ions in water is one-to-one, there is also 10^{-7} mole of hydroxyl ions. Pure water is considered neutral, since it has an equal number of hydrogen and hydroxyl ions. If a solution contains more H^+ than OH^- ions, it is *acidic*; if more OH^-, it is *basic* or *alkaline*.

Acids and Bases

Acidic and basic substances are very common in living systems. Familiar acidic solutions found in or produced by organisms include citrus fruit juice (citric acid) and vinegar (acetic acid). One very common basic compound in organisms is sodium bicarbonate, $NaHCO_3$. Human blood is slightly basic.

To describe the acidity or alkalinity of a solution, we need only state the hydrogen-ion concentration, $[H^+]$. This concentration is commonly expressed in terms of pH, which is defined as:

$$pH = \log \frac{1}{[H^+]}$$

Since pH is a reciprocal number (a number divided into one), *lower* pH values stand for *greater* H^+ concentrations (Figure 3–9). The acid range is thus located between 0 and 7 on the pH scale. For example, if the H^+ concentration of a solution is 10^{-4} gram per liter, the pH is 4. Since pH is expressed on a logarithmic scale, the numerical values are based on powers of 10: pH 3 represents 10 times more H^+ than pH 4, and pH 2 represents a hundred times more than pH 4. The alkaline or base range is between 7 and 14 on the pH scale. The neutral point, pH 7, represents the H^+ concentration of pure water. The pH values of some familiar substances are given in Figure 3–10.

The strength of an *acid* or *base* is proportional to the amount of its dissociation. Compared to such strong inorganic acids as sulfuric acid (H_2SO_4) and hydrochloric acid (HCl), the organic compound acetic acid (CH_3—COOH) is quite weak. The hydrogen covalently bonded to oxygen in the COOH part of the molecule does not dissociate as freely as the H^+ in hydrochloric or sulfuric acid:

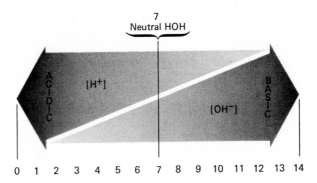

FIGURE 3–9 The pH scale. Equal concentrations of [H⁺] and [OH⁻] are considered to be neutral and are represented by pH 7.

$$HCl \rightleftharpoons H^+ + Cl^-$$
(great dissociation)

$$CH_3\text{—}COOH \rightleftharpoons CH_3COO^- + H^+$$
(little dissociation)

There are also compounds that show basic properties even though they contain no hydroxyl ions. One such substance is ammonia (NH_3), which accepts a proton (H^+) to form NH_4^+. This fact suggests a slightly different definition for both acids and bases. An acid is any compound that can *donate* protons to a solution; conversely, a base is any compound that can *accept* protons. These protons are hydrogen atoms that have lost electrons. The OH^- group is a very strong proton acceptor, and the addition of a single proton to an OH^- ion forms neutral HOH. This reaction is called a *neutralization reaction*.

Salts

A salt is a compound containing a positive ion other than H^+ and a negative ion other than OH^-. The reaction between a strong acid and a strong base produces a salt and water.

$$HCl + NaOH \rightarrow NaCl + H_2O$$

$$acid + base \rightarrow salt + water$$

Salts have several important functions in living systems. Water-insoluble calcium salts, for example, are largely responsible for the strength and rigidity of bones; they are also found in the shells of such animals as snails and clams. Sodium and potassium ions freed by the dissociation of water-soluble salts containing these elements are essential to the functioning of nerves and contraction of muscles.

Buffers

As we shall discuss in Chapter 12, pH values in living systems must be maintained within strict limits. If the blood becomes too acidic, for instance, certain chemical reactions in the cells will cease to take place and the equilibrium of the body will be upset. Compounds known as *buffers* found in the animal bloodstream help to combat sudden increases in acidity or alka-

Substance	pH	
		0 Most acid
Lemon juice	2.0	
Stomach acid	1.0–3.5	
Aspirin	2.9	
Vinegar	3.0	
Oranges	3.0–4.0	
Coffee	5.7	
		7.0 Neutral
Human blood	7.3–7.5	
Human saliva	6.5–7.5	
Eggs	7.6–8.0	
Milk of magnesia	10.2	
Household ammonia	11.0	
Oven cleaner	13.8	
		14 Most basic

FIGURE 3–10 The pH values of some familiar substances.

linity. As their name implies, buffers act as cushions for pH changes. One of the most common buffering compounds in living systems is sodium bicarbonate ($NaHCO_3$), which dissociates into Na^+ (sodium ions) and HCO_3^- (bicarbonate ions). When excess hydrogen ions (H^+) are present in the blood plasma, they combine readily with bicarbonate ions to form a weak acid, carbonic acid (H_2CO_3). Through the buffering action of the bicarbonate ion on hydrochloric acid, a strong acid is converted into a weak acid and a salt:

$$NaHCO_3 + HCl \rightarrow NaCl + H_2CO_3$$
$$\text{(strong acid)} \qquad \text{(weak acid)}$$

On the other hand, when excessive hydroxyl ions, (OH^-), are present, buffers release H^+ ions to help neutralize the solution.

Carbonic acid is an important substance in living systems since it can be formed in a buffering reaction or by the combination of carbon dioxide and water.

$$CO_2 + H_2O \rightleftharpoons H_2CO_3 \rightleftharpoons H^+ + HCO_3^-$$
$$\text{(carbonic acid)} \quad \text{(bicarbonate ion)}$$

These simple reactions, which provide a source of bicarbonate ions, are involved in such important biological processes as gas exchange and photosynthesis.

Organic Compounds

The chemistry of life is largely the chemistry of compounds containing carbon, or *organic* compounds. As we have just seen, inorganic compounds are essential in living systems. But carbon is the main structural element in living systems, and it is crucial in thousands of biological processes.

What characteristics of carbon enable it to play such an important role—we may say the central role—in the chemistry of living systems? Two characteristics stand out: (1) carbon is one of the most chemically versatile elements; and (2) carbon is able to form strong, stable bonds with itself and with other elements at the same time.

The key to carbon's chemical versatility is its outer electron-shell configuration. Recall that the most stable number of outer-shell, or valence, electrons is eight. Carbon has just four valence electrons, so that it would have to gain, lose, or share four electrons for complete stability. Carbon cannot attain a stable outer electron shell by losing its four electrons to an ion or gaining four electrons from an ion, because carbon does not ionize under conditions conducive to life. Instead, it must attain stability by sharing electrons with other atoms—that is, by forming covalent bonds. And since it has four valence electrons, carbon can form a variety of covalent bonds. It can form four single covalent bonds with various atoms—as with hydrogen to make a molecule of methane (Figure 3–6). It can form covalent bonds with itself and with other atoms at the same time, creating the long, chainlike molecules called *polymers*, some of which were mentioned in Chapter 2:

It can form double covalent bonds with other atoms and with itself, and it can form triple covalent bonds with itself. It can form branchlike molecules and ring shapes such as this benzene molecule:

And it can form molecules that combine the straight-chain, branched, and ring configurations. In fact, carbon can form molecules of almost every conceivable size and shape—from small ones containing only two atoms, such as carbon monoxide (CO), to huge ones with thousands of atoms, such as certain protein molecules.

The key to the great *stability* of many carbon compounds lies mainly in the carbon atom's size: it is relatively small among atoms, with only two principal electron shells. This means that the carbon atom's four valence electrons are quite close to its positively-charged nucleus. These four electrons are strongly attracted to the nucleus, which in turn means that the covalent bonds they make with other atoms are quite strong.

Carbon, then, is both a very chemically active element and one whose chemical bonds are strong. The degree to which it possesses both these properties is unique among the elements. Taken together, these properties enable carbon to form nearly a million kinds of compounds —more than those formed by all the other elements put together. Many thousands of these carbon compounds are found in living systems.

We shall now examine the chemical structures and functions of five classes of organic molecules found in living systems: carbohydrates, fats, proteins, nucleotides and nucleic acids, and porphyrins.

Carbohydrates

Carbohydrates are important energy sources for living systems. They also play important structural roles, especially in plants: cellulose, which stiffens plant cell walls, is a carbohydrate. Among the most important carbohydrates are the sugars. The simple sugars or *monosaccharides* are the building blocks of carbohydrates. Monosaccharides are composed of carbon, hydrogen, and oxygen in a ratio of $1:2:1$ (CH_2O). These simple sugars may have as few as 3 carbons ($C_3H_6O_3$) or as many as 8 ($C_8H_{16}O_8$).

Glucose, a monosaccharide and an important source of biological energy, contains six carbon atoms arranged with hydrogen and oxygen in the following way:

If we count the components in this structural formula, we obtain the formula $C_6H_{12}O_6$. In the structural formula, the heavy lines are used to help us visualize a three-dimensional model.

At this point a few words about structural formulas might be helpful. The formula for glucose shown above is a kind of "perspective" drawing in which the three-dimensional structure of the molecule is represented on the two-dimensional space of the book page. The connecting lines between the symbols of the atoms all represent chemical bonds. The six-sided carbon ring shown above should be visualized as a plane (flat) structure much like the outline of a tabletop. The edge closest to the viewer is represented by the uniformly thick horizontal line; the thick tapering lines represent edges of the ring structure that recede from the front edge. And the uniformly thin lines represent the back (most distant) edges. The vertical lines, such as those leading from the carbon atoms to the hydrogen atoms (H) and hydroxyl ions (OH) at the front edge of the ring, represent bonds between atoms in the ring and structural units above or below it.

Ribose, a five-carbon sugar ($C_5H_{10}O_5$), may be written similarly:

Ribose is an important component of compounds involved in energy processes (ATP) and heredity (DNA). Both ATP and DNA will be discussed in more detail later. Six-carbon sugars are commonly used as fuel molecules; five-carbon sugars are involved in the structure of such molecules as the nucleic acids.

Two monosaccharides linked together form a *disaccharide* ("double sugar"); a compound of more than two linked monosaccharides is known as a *polysaccharide*. Maltose is a disaccharide formed by the union of two glucose molecules (Figure 3–11).

In this *synthesis*—the process in which two molecules of glucose join to form maltose—one

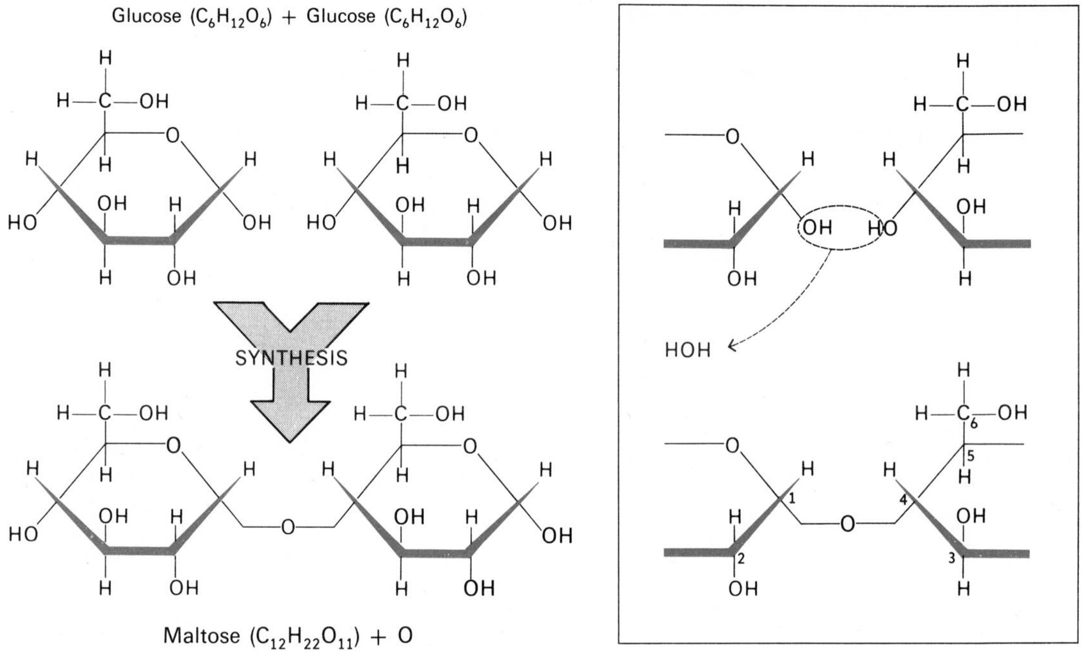

Glucose ($C_6H_{12}O_6$) + Glucose ($C_6H_{12}O_6$)

Maltose ($C_{12}H_{22}O_{11}$) + O

FIGURE 3–11   (a) Synthesis of the disaccharide maltose from two glucose molecules. The linkage formed by the oxygen bridge is an alpha 1,4 glucoside. (b) The inset at the right shows the formation of the water molecule.

molecule of water is produced. Since water is given off in this reaction, it is known as a *dehydration synthesis;* the resulting formula for maltose is $C_{12}H_{22}O_{11}$. The link between the number 1 carbon of one molecule and the number 4 carbon of the other is simply an oxygen bridge (C—O—C). In maltose, the specific linkage is described as an *alpha 1,4 glucoside. Alpha* is used here to indicate that the two hydrogen atoms attached to the oxygen bridge are in the same plane. If many glucose units are linked in this manner into a long chain, they form *starch,* a polysaccharide (Figure 3–12). The human liver forms a glucose storage product called *glycogen,* which is structurally similar to starch in that it is linked by alpha 1,4 glucosides. However, it also has alpha 1,6 glucoside linkages that give the molecule a branched structure. Glycogen provides a ready source of glucose for the blood.

Another important polysaccharide, *cellulose,*

is found in plant cell walls. In cellulose, the 1,4 glucoside linkage is formed in a slightly different manner. Alternate glucose molecules are rotated 180° to form "twisted" configurations called *beta linkages* (Figure 3–12). One important result of this different linkage is that human digestive juices, which split starch into glucose units, do not work on cellulose. But some organisms, including bacteria, digest cellulose. When starch and cellulose are broken down into glucose molecules during digestion, water is added at the linkage. This hydration reaction, called *hydrolytic cleavage,* is the opposite of synthesis. We will examine this process in Chapter 10.

Fats
Fats are members of a group of compounds called *lipids.* They are important to living systems because they store energy and provide protective cushioning for internal organs; in

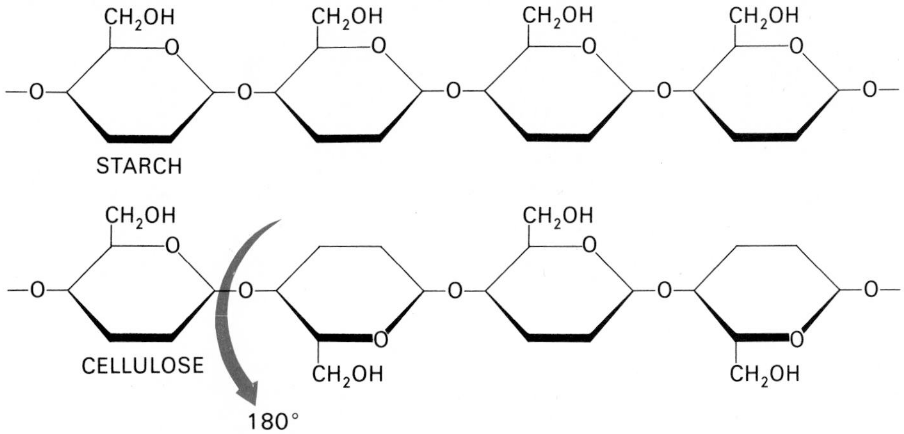

FIGURE 3–12 Comparison of the alpha glucoside linkages of starch with the beta glucoside linkages of cellulose. Note the alternate 180° rotation of the glucose molecules in cellulose.

addition, they are essential constituents of more complex molecules. The two components of a fat molecule are *glycerol* and *fatty acids*. Glycerol is a three-carbon molecule that contains three hydroxyl (OH) groups (Figure 3–13). Fatty acids are straight chains of carbon with most of their bonding sites occupied by hydrogen. If some of the hydrogens of a fatty acid are removed, the carbon atoms may share two or even three pairs of electrons to form —C=C— or —C≡C— bonds (double or triple bonds). A fatty acid in which all available bonding sites are occupied by hydrogen is said to be *saturated* with hydrogen; when some hydrogen is removed, the molecule is *unsaturated*. You may be familiar with certain brands of vegetable oil advertised as *polyunsaturated*; this means that the carbons share many of the available bonds, and very few hydrogen atoms occur along the chain. There is evidence that the ingestion of saturated fats (animal fat) causes increased production of cholesterol in humans. In *arteriosclerosis*, or "hardening of the arteries," deposits of cholesterol are formed within the arteries. This condition is dangerous because it reduces the flow of blood through the arteries. In many health diets, margarine (which contains unsaturated vegetable fat) re-

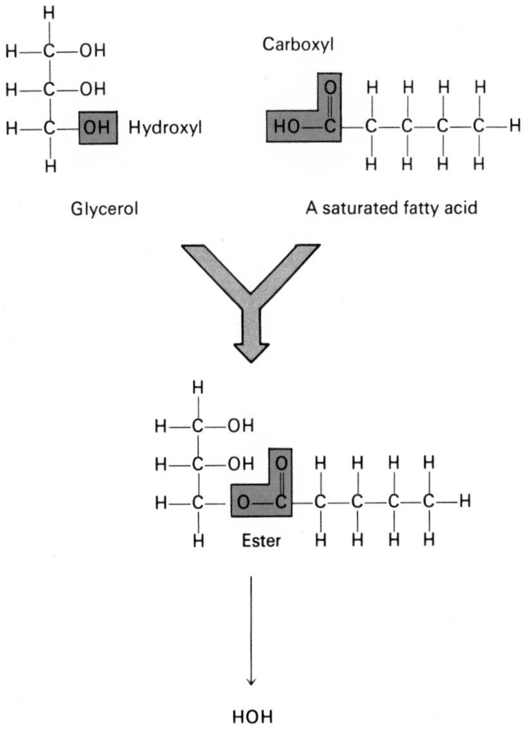

FIGURE 3–13 Formation of an ester linkage between a fatty acid and glycerol.

places butter, and fish replaces beef, which contains large amounts of saturated fats.

One end of the fatty-acid molecule contains an acid or *carboxyl* group, in which carbon shares two pairs of electrons with oxygen to form a double bond and one pair of electrons with a hydroxyl. A carboxyl group is acidic because the hydrogen dissociates in solution to donate a proton. The carboxyl end of the fatty acid may be linked to one of the hydroxyls of glycerine to form an *ester* linkage (Figure 3–13). Water is removed in this synthesis in much the same way as in the formation of maltose and starch. Three fatty acids attached to a glycerol molecule form a fat.

Proteins

Proteins of many sizes and shapes are produced in every living cell. They serve many essential functions in living systems. Proteins are the major structural components of muscle, skin, ligaments and tendons, hair, fingernails and toenails, feathers, fish scales, and animal horn. They also have a structural role in bone and in the cell membranes of all organisms. Enzymes—biological catalysts essential to most chemical reactions in living systems—are proteins. So are many of an organism's "chemical messengers," its hormones.

All protein molecules are large, and some are very large indeed. The chemical formula of one protein molecule found in milk is $C_{1864}H_{3012}O_{576}N_{468}S_{21}$—quite a bit larger than an H_2O molecule! But even this giant is dwarfed by some protein molecules that contain literally millions of atoms.

Each cellular protein fulfills a specific function; it is synthesized according to the heredity of the cell. All proteins are composed of smaller units called *amino acids*. These are carbon compounds with a carboxyl group and an amino group containing nitrogen attached to the same carbon.

There are about 20 different kinds of amino acids found in proteins. The two simplest are glycine and alanine. Histidine and tryptophane, whose molecular structures include rings, are more complex amino acids (Figure 3–14). Some amino acids also contain sulfur.

When amino acids are linked together, the

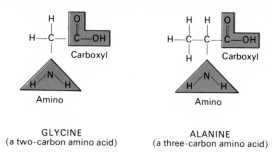

GLYCINE
(a two-carbon amino acid)

ALANINE
(a three-carbon amino acid)

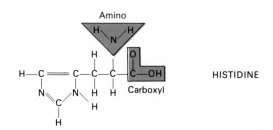

HISTIDINE

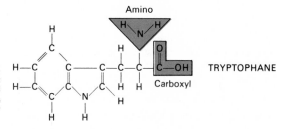

TRYPTOPHANE

FIGURE 3–14 Four kinds of amino acids: glycine, alanine, histidine, and tryptophane.

linkage is called a *peptide*. Two amino acids linked by one peptide form a *dipeptide;* more than two linked amino acids produce a *polypeptide*. The peptide linkage is formed by an interaction between the amino group of one amino acid and the carboxyl group of another (Figure 3–15). The nitrogen of the amino group unites with the carbon of the carboxyl; one water molecule is formed in the process.

In cells, proteins provide the fundamental structure for all major structural components. Simple proteins are composed only of amino acids. But proteins can also combine with other such substances as carbohydrates, fats, or inorganic ions; such proteins are said to be *conjugated*. Conjugated proteins are found in brain

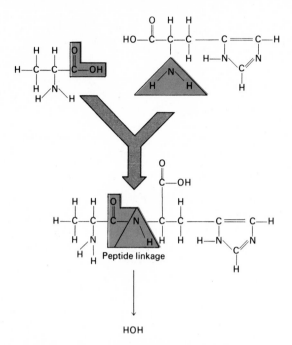

FIGURE 3–15 Synthesis of the dipeptide alanyl-histidine. Note that the structure of histidine here is reversed from that shown in Figure 3–14.

and nerve tissues, mucous secretions, and egg white.

Amino acids joined by peptide bonds form the *primary*, or first-level, structure of a protein (Figure 3–16). Some of these polypeptide chains fold into sheetlike patterns; others coil into helical (spiral) configurations that often assume rodlike overall shapes. Helical structures are common, occurring for example in the keratin of hair and in the globin part of hemoglobin, a major component of blood. These sheetlike and rodlike forms constitute the *secondary*, or second-level, structure of proteins. Secondary structures results from hydrogen bonding between carbon and amino groups of nearby peptide linkages. Secondary structures, in turn, fold upon themselves in complex patterns, the exact configurations depend on the number and location of chemical bonds called *disulfide bridges* (—S—S—) formed between certain sulfur-containing amino acids of the polypeptide chain. The resulting patterns

form the *tertiary*, or third-level, structure of proteins. The most complex structural level of protein is reached when two or more polypeptide chains intertwine; this is called the *quaternary*, or fourth-level, structure. Disulfide bridges are also necessary for the maintenance of quaternary structure. The function of a particular protein depends principally on its quaternary structure.

Nucleotides and Nucleic Acids

Nucleotides and nucleic acids are indispensable components of every living cell; they are important in hereditary mechanisms, protein synthesis, and general metabolic processes. Nucleotides are always composed of three basic parts: first, a nitrogenous base, either a purine or a pyrimidine (Figure 3–17); second, a five-carbon sugar, either ribose ($C_5H_{10}O_5$) or deoxyribose ($C_5H_{10}O_4$), which is similar to ribose but has one less oxygen atom; and third, phosphoric acid. The composition of an adenine nucleotide is diagrammed in Figure 3–18. The nucleotide adenosine triphosphate (ATP) contains two additional phosphate ester groups (see Figure 9–1). ATP is involved in practically all energy transformations in cells; it is found wherever biological activity occurs. Energy can be stored in, and released from, ATP because of the chemical bonds connecting its three phosphate groups. This topic will be discussed in Chapter 9.

Nucleotides may be strung together (polymerized) to form long chains known as nucleic acids. As we noted in Chapter 2, nucleic acids are essential to all living systems because their structure provides the coded information which directs the heredity and protein synthesis of every living cell. Two types of nucleic acids are known: *ribonucleic acid* (RNA) and *deoxyribonucleic acid* (DNA).

Involved in the structure of nucleic acids are five nitrogenous bases. Two are purines, adenine and guanine; the other three—thymine, cytosine, and uracil—are pyrimidines. Adenine, guanine, cytosine, and thymine are present in DNA, but uracil is not. RNA lacks thymine but contains uracil. Since uracil is found only in RNA, researchers often use it as a "marker base" to determine the location of

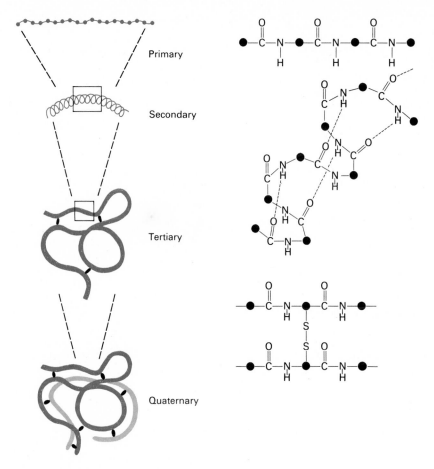

FIGURE 3–16   Four levels of protein structure. Primary: peptide
linkages between amino acids form a chain (polypeptide).
Secondary: one polypeptide is held in a coil by hydrogen bonds
between peptide linkages. Tertiary: a coiled polypeptide is held in
a folded structure by disulfide linkages. Quaternary: several polypeptides are held together by disulfide linkages.

RNA in a cell. In a similar way, thymine can be
used to identify the presence of DNA.

STRUCTURE OF RNA   Each RNA nucleotide
is composed of a ribose, a phosphate group, and
one of four nitrogen bases—adenine, guanine,
cytosine, or uracil. The nucleotides are linked
into a long chain by simple phosphate ester
linkages between the sugars (Figure 3–19). RNA
is basically single-stranded, but many RNA
molecules contain double-stranded regions.

There are several different types of RNA,
which will be discussed in Chapter 14.

STRUCTURE OF DNA   Nucleotides of DNA
are similar in form to those of RNA, except that
DNA contains deoxyribose sugar and thymine
rather than ribose and uracil. Four kinds of
DNA nucleotides thus occur—those containing adenine, guanine, cytosine, or thymine. In
the structure of DNA, purine nucleotides always pair with pyrimidine nucleotides to form

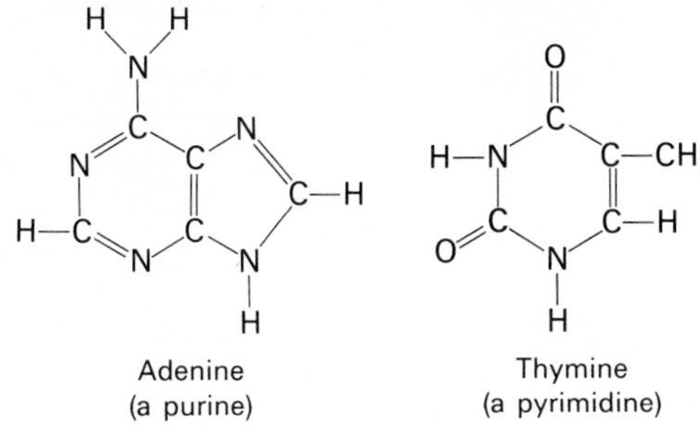

FIGURE 3–17   Two nitrogen bases, adenine and thymine, illustrating purine and pyrimidine structures.

a long *double-stranded molecule.* The pairings of purines and pyrimidines are very specific: adenine (a purine) pairs only with thymine (a pyrimidine), and guanine (a purine) pairs only with cytosine (a pyrimidine) (Figure 3–20). The joining of adenine with thymine and of guanine with cytosine is called *base pairing.* The significance of base pairing in genetic coding and protein synthesis will be discussed further in Chapter 14.

In 1953 two molecular biologists, F. H. C.

Crick of Cambridge University and the American J. D. Watson, proposed a model of the DNA molecule. This model was based on chemical analyses and on the x-ray diffraction studies of the Irish biophysicist M. H. F. Wilkins and his coworkers. Crick and Watson's model accounts not only for the structure of DNA but also for its unique activities, such as reproduction and coding of hereditary information. The double-stranded molecule is believed to be twisted into a spiral or helical shape often referred to as a "double helix" (Figure 3–21). If it were not twisted, the molecule would look something like a ladder; the rails of the ladder correspond to the sugars and phosphates, and the steps are the sequence of paired nitrogenous bases. For their discovery of DNA's molecular structure, Watson, Crick, and Wilkins were awarded the Nobel Prize in 1962.

As we noted in Chapter 2, one important characteristic of DNA is its ability to replicate itself. When the hydrogen bonds holding the two strands together are broken, two distinct halves result. Since adenine pairs only with thymine and guanine pairs only with cytosine, each original strand is a pattern for producing a

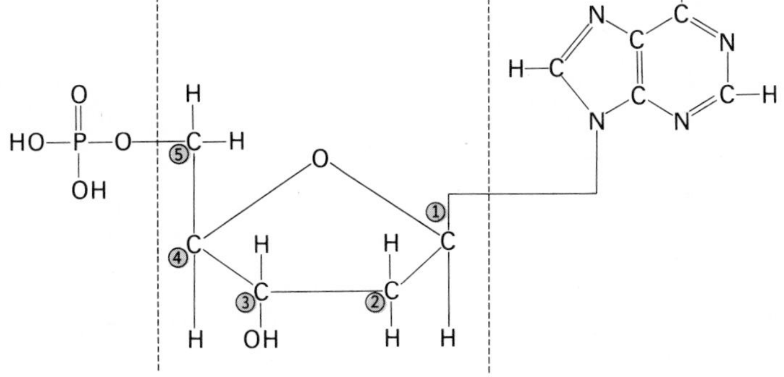

FIGURE 3–18   Structural diagram of an adenine nucleotide showing the three basic components: adenine, deoxyribose sugar, and phosphate.

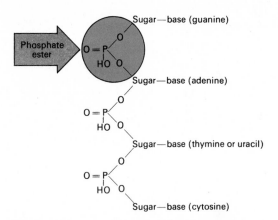

FIGURE 3–19   The phosphate ester linkages that bind sugars and nitrogen bases into nucleic-acid chains.

new half exactly like the other one. So each half of the molecule produces a new complementary polynucleotide chain (Figure 3–22).

Porphyrins

Porphyrins are the fundamental structural units in such pigments as chlorophyll, hemoglobin, and various cytochromes (used to transfer electrons in energy production). In one form or another, porphyrins are essential to the energy processing of all living systems. The basic porphyrin structure is a unique configuration of carbon, nitrogen, and metallic ions. This basic structure is composed of four *pyrrole rings* and is commonly called a *tetrapyrrole-ring compound* (Figure 3–23). Each carbon atom at the edge of the tetrapyrrole structure may be bonded to specific side chains, such as alcohols or proteins. For living systems, the most important property of porphyrins is their ability to gain or lose electrons. This property results from the presence of metallic ions, magnesium in chlorophyll and iron in cytochromes. In the process of trapping and transferring energy, chlorophyll and cytochromes provide a mechanism for transfer of

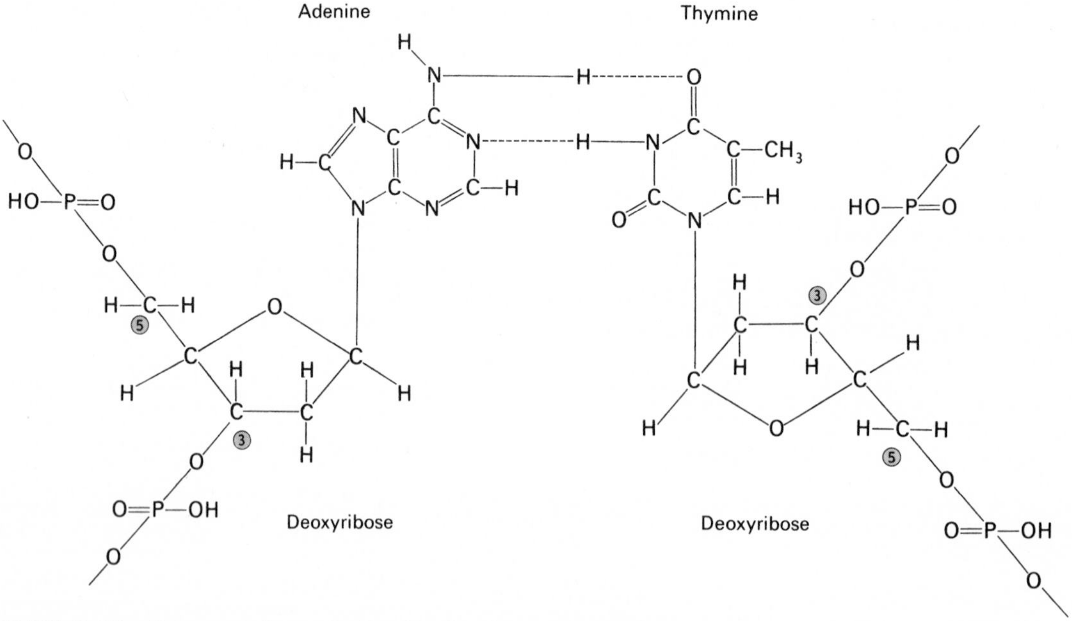

FIGURE 3–20   Structure of an adenine-thymine base pair. Note the hydrogen bonds (dashed lines) and the 3–5 phosphate esters that link the sugars into a polymeric chain.

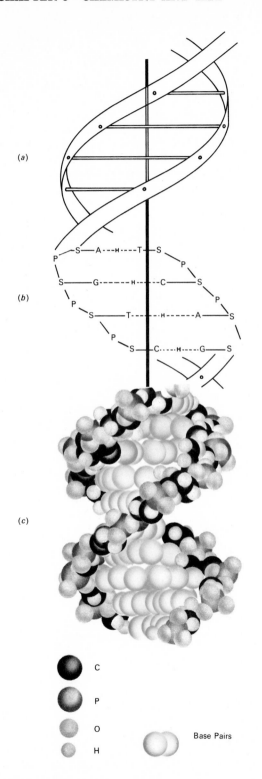

(a)

(b)

(c)

C

P

O

H

Base Pairs

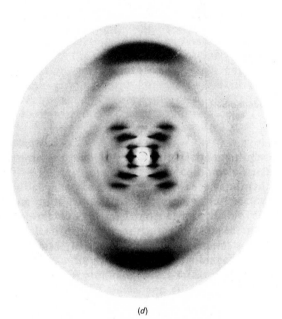

(d)

FIGURE 3–21   The helix of DNA, with the molecular arrangement represented in three different ways. (*a*) General picture of the double helix, with the phosphate-sugar combinations making up the outside spirals and the base pairs the crossbars. (*b*) A somewhat more detailed representation: phosphate (P), sugar (S), adenine (A), thymine (T), guanine (G), cytosine (C), and hydrogen (H). (*c*) Detailed structure, showing how the space is filled with atoms: carbon (C), oxygen (O), hydrogen (H), phosphorus (P), and the base pairs. The x-ray diffraction of semicrystalline β-DNA is shown in (*d*). (Professor M. H. F. Wilkins, Biophysics Dept., King's College, London.)

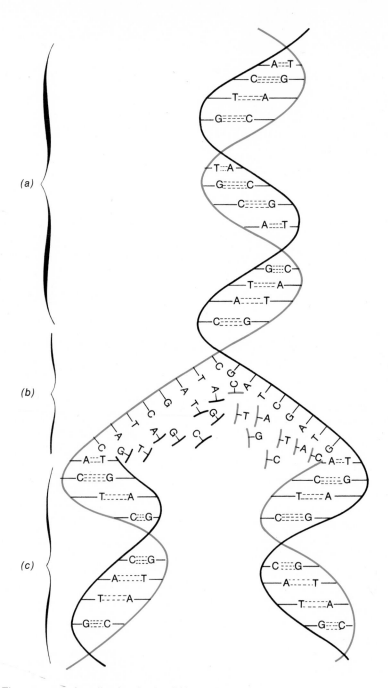

FIGURE 3–22 The process of replication in the DNA molecule.
(a) Portion of original DNA molecule. (b) Area of uncoiling and
breaking of hydrogen bonds between nitrogen bases;
A = adenine, T = thymine, G = guanine, C = cytosine. (c) Area
of synthesis of two identical DNA molecules by pairing of complementary nucleotides and formation of hydrogen bonds.

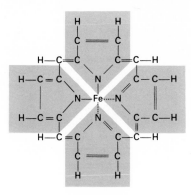

FIGURE 3–23 Basic structure of an iron-containing porphyrin. The colored areas represent pyrrole rings.

electrons in living systems. This is the means of obtaining and processing the energy that supports all life.

CHEMICAL REACTIONS

Chemical compounds may react with one another to form new compounds. For new compounds to be formed, chemical bonds must be broken and reformed; this rearrangement of bonds always involves energy changes. Some chemicals react spontaneously, without external energy. Such spontaneous reactions are called *exergonic*, and they generally produce heat. One such reaction occurs when metallic sodium comes into contact with water: this reaction is rapid and violent, producing both heat and light. Reactions that require external energy to activate them are known as *endergonic*. But some exergonic reactions require inputs of energy to get them started. Light, heat, and pressure may be sources of the *activation energy* needed to start a chemical reaction. Once started, a reaction may or may not be self-sustaining. If it is not, small amounts of *continuation energy* may be needed to keep it going.

Reaction Direction and Reaction Rate

When a chemical reaction does not go to completion, for one reason or another, the products formed may react in a reverse direction as their concentration increases. Such a reaction is known as a *reversible chemical reaction*; and may be stated generally as follows:

$$A + B \rightleftharpoons C + D$$
(reactants)   (products)

As the reaction proceeds and the products accumulate, the rate of the reaction from left to right is slowed down, and an equilibrium may finally be established. The *law of mass action* states that the rate of a reaction is directly proportional to the concentration of the reactants. In the case of hydrogen and iodine, the reaction

$$H_2 + I_2 \rightleftharpoons 2\,HI$$

proceeds from left to right until the concentration of the product is in equilibrium with the concentration of the reactants. The addition of more hydrogen and iodine, however, will speed up the reaction from left to right to produce more HI.

In some chemical reactions, the product is continually removed because it is an insoluble precipitate or a volatile gas. In the reaction between silver nitrate and sodium chloride, for example, the precipitated silver chloride does not take part in a reverse reaction:

$$AgNO_3 + NaCl \xrightarrow{H_2O} \overset{\text{precipitate}}{AgCl\downarrow} + NaNO_3$$

silver nitrate   sodium chloride   silver chloride   sodium nitrate

(Note that in this case the arrow between the reactants and products points in one direction only, indicating that the reaction proceeds mainly to the right.) The law of mass action thus enables us to predict not only the rate of a reaction but also its direction and duration. In living systems, however, the direction and rate of most chemical reactions are influenced by enzymes. And, as we will see, enzymes often "violate" the law of mass action.

Enzymes: Catalysts of Life

Chemical reaction rates can generally be speeded up by increasing the concentration or the temperature of the reactants. Another means of increasing the reaction rate is to add a catalyst which reduces the amount of energy required. Thousands of different reactions that take place continually in living systems could ordinarily take place outside those systems only at temperatures high enough literally to burn up living cells. But special biological catalysts called *enzymes* are found in every living system. Enzymes permit these reactions to proceed in organisms without destructive effects. Enzymes are protein molecules and groups of protein molecules that do for biochemical reactions what catalysts do for chemical reactions generally: they reduce the activation energy needed for a given reaction to proceed.

Enzymes are amazingly efficient catalysts; tiny amounts can make reactions take place thousands or even millions of times faster than they otherwise would. The biochemist G. R. Stark has calculated, for instance, that if just one molecule of the enzyme urease were added to 60,000 molecules of urea (an animal waste product) in a water solution under the right laboratory conditions, 30,000 of the urea molecules would be broken down into carbon dioxide and ammonia in just one second. In the absence of that single enzyme molecule, the same process would take 3 million *years*. Since organisms cannot tolerate high reaction temperatures or wait patiently for years for their biochemical reactions to take place, enzymes are a neat solution to a serious problem. In the example just given, the single enzyme molecule would be catalyzing thousands of reactions per second; we now know that some enzyme molecules in living systems can catalyze their reactions even faster—millions of times each minute.

Enzymes, then, make many essential biochemical processes possible—in other words, they make life possible. How do enzymes work? Although our answer is not complete, we do know that the polypeptide chains of these protein catalysts are linked together in various ways to form a great variety of specific structures, each of which catalyzes a particular reaction. More than 1000 enzymes have been identified; each type appears to fit the reactants physically into its structure. This brings the reactants closer together and thus increases the probability of the reaction. An enzyme can thus serve as a substitute for intense heat, because like heat it gets the reactants together.

Active Sites and Enzyme Structure

The catalytic action of enzyme molecules is located at specific *active sites* in their structure; these sites interact with specific regions of the reactant molecules. The exact geometry of each active site is therefore important, and any molecular change that alters active site structure will change or possibly inactivate the enzyme. Figure 3–24 shows a hypothetical synthesis catalyzed by an enzyme; note that the enzyme does not appear in the product and is thus free to participate in further reactions.

Ribonuclease, an enzyme which catalyzes the hydrolysis of nucleic acids, was one of the first enzymes for which the amino-acid sequence was determined (Figure 3–25). Ribonuclease is structured in a long, folded chain of 124 amino acids of 19 different types. Disulfide linkages at four spots along the folded molecule hold it in its specific shape. Scientists at Rockefeller University and at Merck, Sharp and Dohme Research Laboratories have synthesized active forms of ribonuclease. This is not only the first enzyme to be synthesized, but it is also the largest protein thus far assembled outside a living system.

Influences on Enzyme Action

Enzyme action is influenced by pH, temperature, and enzyme concentration; optimal activity for each enzyme depends on an appropriate combination of these. In general, an increase in temperature or enzyme concentration increases the reaction rates, whereas a lower temperature slows down the reaction. Deviation from the optimum pH also slows a reaction. Extreme deviation from the normal temperature of pH may cause *denaturation* of protein. This is a structural change caused by the breaking of

Bio-Topic: Enzymes: Historical Identity Crisis

The history of enzymes is punctuated by controversy among strong personalities and by scientific conservatism. In 1835 J. J. Berzelius developed the concept of catalysis, the idea that inorganic reactions can be speeded up by tiny amounts of chemicals that are not used up in the reactions. Berzelius and his student Frederick Wöhler later extended this concept to the fermentations known to brewers and winemakers. They argued that fermentations are caused by nonliving chemicals they called "ferments" and that living organisms are in no way involved. Justus Liebig, another chemist, suggested that living organisms might be indirectly involved in fermentations. He suggested that as yeasts decay they induce instabilities in grape sugar, converting it to alcohol and carbon dioxide. The personalities of these three chemists dominated the scientific thought of their day.

When Theodore Schwann and other biologists argued that fermentations are caused directly by the activities of living organisms, Liebig and Wöhler published (under false names) a stinging satire. They wrote that Schwann's yeasts

. . . had a suctorial snout with which they devoured sugar, a stream of alcohol issued from the anus at the same time that

carbon dioxide bubbled forth from enormous genital organs . . .

Louis Pasteur, chemist turned biologist, entered the controversy in the 1850s. He presented considerable experimental support for his assertion that fermentations are caused by living organisms (a contradiction of Berzelius) and that organic materials serve as food for the organisms (a contradiction of Wöhler). Pasteur's ideas were not widely accepted, partly because of the enormous influence of Berzelius, Wöhler, and Liebig, and partly because Pasteur could not explain how organisms cause fermentations.

Chemists continued to reject the role of living organisms in fermentations and biologists continued to reject the involvement of nonliving catalysts. As is often the case in science, both sides were partly right. But the controversy continued until 1930 when American biochemist John Northrup crystallized the enzyme pepsin. Northrup presented overwhelming proof that pepsin is a catalytic protein (proving the chemists right) and the product of a living organism (proving the biologists right). Enzymes had finally been accepted by the scientific community.

Scientists, like all people, are slow to trade familiar ideas for new ones.

hydrogen bonds and disulfide bridges; it produces a disorganized protein incapable of functioning (Figure 3–26).

We shall summarize our discussion of chemical compounds and reactions by returning to the example of the firefly given at the beginning of this chapter. Bioluminescence results from a series of chemical reactions involving at least three organic compounds—ATP, luciferin, and luciferase. Luciferin is an organic compound produced by the firefly (and many other bioluminescent organisms), and luciferase is the principal enzyme involved. The first reaction in this process apparently links luciferin

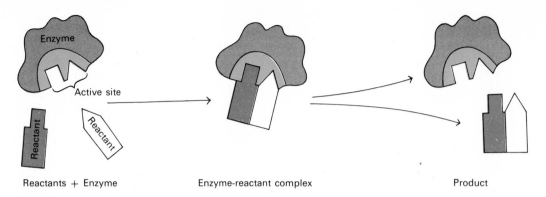

Reactants + Enzyme   Enzyme-reactant complex   Product

FIGURE 3–24 Proposed model for the action of an enzyme in a synthesis reaction. The reactants form a complex with the active sites of the enzyme, complete their reaction, and then are released as product. The model is highly schematic; it does not show what the reactants, enzyme, or product would really look like.

and ATP. Light energy can then be released when a solution of luciferase and an inorganic ion, such as Mg^{++}, is added to the luciferin-ATP complex in the presence of oxygen. The final reaction in the process may be summarized as follows:

$$\text{Luciferin-ATP} \xrightarrow[\substack{Mg^{++}, O_2 \\ H_2O}]{\text{luciferase}} \text{light} + \text{luciferin} + \text{ADP} + \text{P}$$

(Note that ATP is changed to ADP in this reaction. The reason for this will be given in Chapter 9 when we discuss energy.)

When we observe a blinking firefly, then, we are seeing one product—light energy—of a chemical change that is accelerated by an enzyme.

ENERGY, ENTROPY, AND LIVING SYSTEMS

Living systems require inputs of energy to drive the chemical reactions which create and maintain their highly ordered structures, their internal processes, and their behaviors.

Available (Free) Energy

Earlier, we mentioned the activation energy needed by living systems to start certain chem-

ical reactions and the continuation energy needed to keep many of these reactions going once they start. Both these types of energy are forms of *free energy*, which may be defined as energy available to do work. It is important to distinguish between energy that is available to do work and energy that is unavailable for that purpose. For example, an electric-power generating plant burns coal to transform its chemical energy into heat energy in order to do work (generate electricity). Much of the heat energy converts water into steam. Much of the heat energy in the steam is then transformed into kinetic energy, or energy of motion, which turns a generator's turbine fan. Finally, the turbine converts much of the kinetic energy into electrical energy.

Unavailable Energy

But notice that in our power plant example, some free energy is lost at every transformation along the way. Some of the heat from the burning coal goes up the smokestack instead of into the steam. More is lost when the steam condenses, releasing its stored energy as heat energy again; this heat energy is dissipated into the surrounding environment. Still more energy is lost to the environment when some of the turbine wheel's kinetic energy is trans-

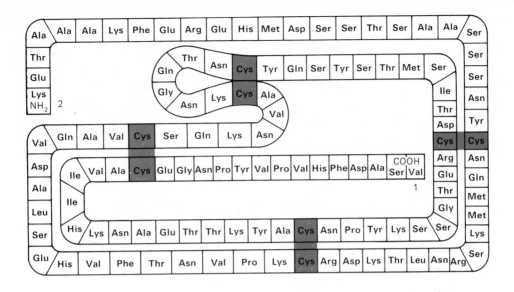

THE BUILDING BLOCKS—19 AMINO ACIDS

Ala —Alanine	**Gln**—Glutamine	**Leu** —Leucine	**Ser**—Serine
Arg—Arginine	**Glu** —Glutamic acid	**Lys** —Lysine	**Thr**—Threonine
Asn—Asparagine	**Gly** —Glycine	**Met**—Methionine	**Tyr**—Tyrosine
Asp—Aspartic Acid	**His** —Histidine	**Phe** —Phenylalanine	**Val**—Valine
Cys —Cysteine	**Ile** —Isoleucine	**Pro** —Proline	

COOH—Carboxy group   NH₂—Amino group

FIGURE 3–25 The amino-acid sequence of ribonuclease. Colored blocks between cysteine molecules indicate disulfide bridges (—S—S—). In the synthesis of this enzyme by Merrifield and Gutte, reported in 1969, the carboxy-terminal amino-acid valine (1) was attached to a solid polymer resin. Then the other 123 amino acids were coupled one at a time, the last one being the amino-terminal lysine (2). (Courtesy of Bernd Gutte.)

formed into heat by the friction of moving parts. These and all other losses of usable energy are described by the *second law of thermodynamics,* which may be stated as follows: *No process is completely efficient in its use of energy; some energy is always lost in the form of heat that is thereafter unavailable to do further work.*

The second law of thermodynamics applies to the energy processes of all systems. Your own body, for example, continually radiates heat energy released in the chemical reactions of your metabolic processes. (Of course, some metabolic processes are designed to do this, in order to keep the body warm. Nevertheless, energy released as "body heat" is soon lost from your system and unavailable for further work.)

We have seen that living systems require free energy to maintain their highly ordered structures. When an organism's energy input slows down or stops, the organism's structures literally begin to break down. If you are cut off from your source of chemical energy (food), you die (cease to function as a living system)

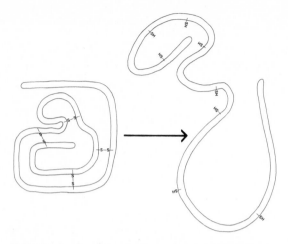

FIGURE 3-26   Denaturation of ribonuclease.

and decompose (become more and more structurally disordered).

The Tendency toward Disorder: Entropy

But this trend toward disorder does not affect only living systems. Every physical structure and system in the universe is subject to it. The most carefully preserved painting or photograph fades. The hardest rock erodes. Eventually, even the majestic orbital organization of a planetary system deteriorates. Unlike living systems, nonliving objects and systems cannot repair themselves; they have no provision for using energy inputs to maintain their structures. A granite mountain breaks down more slowly than a tree or a human, but eventually tree, human and mountain all move from a state of higher structural order to a lower state. This universal "downhill" tendency can be described by a restatement of the second law of thermodynamics: *All processes and systems in the universe are moving toward disorganization and a state of complete disorder.*

The extent of disorder in a system may be measured and expressed mathematically as *entropy*. A low entropy value indicates a high level of organization; progressively higher entropy values represent progressively more and more disorder in a system. The entropy (disorder) of the universe is continually and irreversibly increasing.

Bucking the Trend: Open vs. Closed Systems

But living systems repair themselves, grow, and reproduce. They maintain and even increase their levels of structural organization and replace themselves with more of their kind. Do living systems somehow defy the second law of thermodynamics and the trend toward complete disorder? The answer to this puzzle is No, and its explanation lies in the difference between an *open system* and a *closed system*.

Strictly speaking, the second law of thermodynamics applies only to closed systems. Systems exhibit varying degrees of closure; living systems, for example, are quite open. They receive considerable inputs of energy and matter from their environments. They also release material wastes and waste energy in the form of heat. Living systems do not really defy the second law or the tendency toward greater entropy, because they are open systems. They obtain from outside themselves the free energy needed to maintain their structural order—that is, to maintain low entropy. Note, however, that the free energy gained by an organism is lost from the larger system of which it is a part: the organism takes from its environment energy capable of doing considerable work. It returns to that environment the same amount of energy, but the returned energy is in "degraded" forms which are capable of doing less work. The food you had for breakfast contained considerable chemical energy. Some of that energy was used to move you around today; that energy eventually returned to the environment as heat energy incapable of doing further work (Figure 3-27).

The earth as a biological system—the biosphere—is a more closed system with respect to matter but not to energy. There are no material inputs or outputs. But the system does receive energy in the form of solar radiation, and it releases excess heat energy into space.

The solar system comes closer to being a

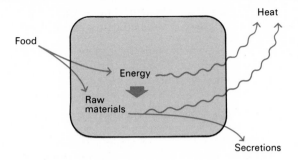

FIGURE 3-27 In a secreting cell, food is converted to energy; this energy is used to transform raw materials into secretions. At each step some energy is lost as heat. Energy must therefore be constantly supplied to the cell.

fully closed system, since it receives no energy from outside itself except for a little starlight. But the solar system does have an energy output: eventually all the energy it generates (most of it originally from the sun) is radiated out into interstellar space.

Apparently, there is only one completely closed system: the universe itself. By definition, a truly closed system has no inputs or outputs Also by definition, there is nothing and no place "outside" the universe. It can thus have no energy inputs or outputs, and so it is a closed system.

The Trend Wins Out

Since the second law of thermodynamics states that a closed system must tend toward disorder (high entropy), we are forced to conclude that the universal "system" is slowly but irreversibly running down. Eventually the universe is condemned to a "heat death." This point will be approached as the total amount of energy in the universe (which never changes) is distributed more and more evenly—in the form of radiant energy throughout the vast reaches of interstellar space, and in the form of heat energy throughout all matter everywhere.

Long before this point of total disorder is reached, the sun and other stars will have grown cold and ceased to shine. And some time

before that, living systems will have ceased to exist anywhere. Organisms have been on this planet for 3 to 4 billion years. Our own actions permitting, they will continue to exist and evolve for a while longer. But nonetheless, life is just an interlude of order in the long journey to disorder.

We have now seen that energy, entropy, and biological organization are closely interrelated, and that this interrelationship must be understood at the chemical level. In the next chapter we shall examine the structure of the cell—the living unit in which the chemistry of life takes place.

SUMMARY

All the material substance of the universe is known as matter; each element is a pure substance composed of just one kind of atom. The atom, the fundamental unit of matter, is composed principally of protons, neutrons, and electrons. One of the most useful models of the structure of the atom is the Bohr model, which depicts a dense, central nucleus with the electrons moving about it in shells corresponding to their specific energies.

Chemical bonds are the forces that hold atoms together to form molecules and compounds. The most common bonds are electrovalent or ionic, covalent, and hydrogen. Compounds may be divided into two groups, inorganic and organic. Inorganic compounds include water, acids, bases, salts, and buffers.

Organic compounds always contain the element carbon; they frequently contain hydrogen, oxygen, nitrogen, and phosphorus as well. Other elements, such as iron and sulfur, also occur in the organic compounds of living systems. Common organic compounds of life include carbohydrates, fats or lipids, proteins, nucleic acids, and porphyrins.

Chemical reactions result when atoms or compounds react to form new compounds called products. These reactions always involve energy changes and the rearrangement of chemical bonds. In living systems, practically all chemical reactions are accelerated by protein molecules called enzymes. The activity of enzymes is influenced by pH, temperature, and concentration.

Living systems require a continual input of energy to drive chemical reactions and to maintain their highly ordered structures and cellular processes against increasing disorder (entropy). Living systems require energy that is available to do work, called free energy. A living organism is an open energy system which takes in high-energy fuels from its environment and degrades them to lower forms of energy. The organism uses the energy thus gained in all its life processes.

REVIEW QUESTIONS

1. How are matter and chemical bonding related to living systems?

2. Draw Bohr atomic models for hydrogen, carbon, sodium, and chlorine.

3. How does atomic structure determine bonding potentials? Show how hydrogen and carbon form methane (CH_4) and how sodium and chlorine form salt (NaCl).

4. Why are inorganic acids stronger than organic acids?

5. How do electrovalent bonds differ from covalent bonds? Give an example of each type.

6. How is the pH of human blood maintained at a near constant 7.35?

7. Describe how the enzymes in your mouth convert starches to glucose.

8. What are the two major components of a fat? How are they bonded together?

9. What three chemical components make up a nucleotide?

10. How does the structure of RNA differ from that of DNA?

11. What is the function of an active site in a reaction catalyzed by an enzyme?

12. What is the relationship between free energy and entropy? Why is free energy essential to living systems?

SUPPLEMENTARY READINGS

Chedd, Graham, *The New Biology*, Basic Books, New York, 1972. A factual presentation of the discoveries that form the basis for modern biology.

Farago, Peter and John Lagnado, *Life In Action*, Alfred A. Knopf, New York, 1972. An explanation of the principles of biochemistry written for the interested individual with little or no science background.

Giddings, J. Calvin, *Chemistry, Man, and Environmental Change*, Canfield Press, San Francisco, 1973. For nonscience students who wish to know more about the principles of chemistry and the chemical origins of some major environmental problems.

Roller, Ann, *Discovering the Basis of Life*, McGraw-Hill, New York, 1974. The essentials of molecular biology are presented with reference to cellular function. A short history of each important discovery is woven into the text.

Sharon, Nathan, "Glycoproteins," *Scientific American*, May 1974. Combinations of protein and sugar molecules produce glycoproteins, which have many important body functions in blood chemistry and metabolism.

White, Emil D., *Chemical Background for the Biological Sciences*, 2nd edition, Prentice-Hall, Englewood Cliffs, NJ, 1970. A brief outline of chemistry for biology students. It contains treatments of inorganic and organic chemistry necessary for an understanding of modern biology.

Chapter 4

Units of Life: Cells

With our background in the chemicals of life, we move to the ways in which these substances are organized into the biological units called cells. **The Cell and Its Parts** is our entry point into the distinctly *living* world. As we move through this chapter, we will classify these parts both according to their function in the cells and in terms of the kinds of cells in which they are found. Not all of these structures occur in all cells.

A structure found in all cells is **The Cell Membrane.** This seemingly simple outer boundary is actually a complex series of layers, and biologists have been studying how it handles the difficult task of regulating **The Movement of Materials Into and Out of Cells.**

What do we find inside the cell membrane? The general class of material inside the membrane is referred to by the broad name of cytoplasm. **The Structure of Cytoplasm** is actually all the nonmembrane structures and dissolved substances which carry on the life processes within the cell. As we survey these microscopic structures, we get our first look at the wide variety of tasks cells must carry out to stay alive.

These tasks are all regulated by **The Nucleus,** the control center of the cell. The nucleus directs the daily chemical functions of the cell while it also maintains the cell's link with its next generation in the form of the heredity material organized in its **Chromosomes.**

From the long-term view most dramatically stated in the theory of evolution, a cell—or for that matter, an organism or species—that cannot reproduce and form more individuals like itself really has little biological significance. At the cellular level, the process of **How Cells Divide** reveals the mechanism of the transfer of vital information between generations. In both plants and animal cells, the hereditary data must be duplicated and correctly distributed to the newly formed cell to assure the existence of the next generation. Biologists have divided the process of mitosis into stages, which make it possible for us to observe how this transfer of information takes place.

As we end the chapter, we survey the **Cellular Interrelationships: Structure and Function.** The study of the parts of the cell gives us some grasp of the extraordinary range of tasks each organism from the simple *Amoeba* to a human being actually carries out.

Cells have sometimes been compared to bricks. The range of sizes, shapes, and strengths of bricks permits the design of many different functional structures; although individual, bricks may differ, they are still easily recognized as bricks. This is also true of living cells.

For decades, biologists have labored to understand life and its processes mainly by studying the structure of cells with microscopes. But microscopy alone yields only structural information. As the study of cells continues, however, important new functional information is being acquired through a combination of microscopy and biochemistry. Cells can be broken down and their many components isolated and identified for biochemical study. When we find that certain chemical reactions occur in specific cell components, we understand better the functions of individual cells and their subparts. Although microscopists are still gathering information about cell structure, the focus of modern cell biology is primarily on *function*.

Much of the effort to understand cell functions is "basic research"—research aimed at increasing our scientific knowledge of cells and the living systems they compose. But it is difficult to say exactly where basic research leaves off and applied research begins. Many research biologists are deeply concerned with applications. Some cell biologists, for instance, are involved in fighting human, animal, and plant diseases. Others are striving to discover how plant genetics can be used to increase crop yields for a hungry world. A fuller understanding of the structures and functions of cells, then, has practical as well as scientific value.

The term *cell* was first used by Robert Hooke in 1665 to describe the small chambers he observed in cork. Much later, in 1838, the German botanist M. J. Schleiden recognized cells in *tissues* of plants. This observation was extended to animals and developed more fully about a year later by Theodor Schwann, a German zoologist. The cell theory proposed by Schleiden and Schwann became a basic concept in biology; it is one of the most significant generalizations in the biological sciences. According to this theory, all living systems are composed of cells, and the cell may be considered the fundamental unit of all life.

THE CELL AND ITS PARTS

Exploration of cellular anatomy began more than 300 years ago with Hooke's description and drawings of cork's "microscopical pores," as he called them. But the efforts of early explorers were hampered by their primitive microscopes. As late as 1835, the contents of certain protozoa were described as "a perfectly homogeneous, elastic, contractile, diaphanous, gelatinous substance, insoluble in water and without traces of organization." And in 1839 the term *protoplasm* ("first substance") was adopted for the substance thought to be "perfectly homogeneous."

Today, thanks to powerful microscopes, we know that cells are structurally complex and very highly organized. In fact, the many substructures of a cell are themselves complex and highly organized. So today we use the term "protoplasm" only as a generalized description of living materials. *Cytoplasm* (*cyto* means "cell") is another general term used to describe the living material between the outer limit (membrane) of the cell and the nucleus.

By 1900 the structures shown in Figure 4–1 had been observed and described. Once adequate microscopes had become available, significant cell discoveries had come rapidly. Over a period of about 100 years, most of the cell structures that can be seen with a light microscope were described. Robert Brown discovered the nucleus in 1831 while examining orchid cells. He described it as an opaque spot and demonstrated its presence in most of the plant's cells. Actually, the nucleus and the nucleolus, the smaller body within it, had been seen as early as 1781. But it was Brown who proposed that these structures are found in all cells. Later, about 1882, it was reported that the nuclear material produced long threads which split lengthwise during cell division and passed into the daughter cells. Six years later these threads were named *chromosomes*, or "colored bodies," because they became much more visible when dyes were applied to the cell.

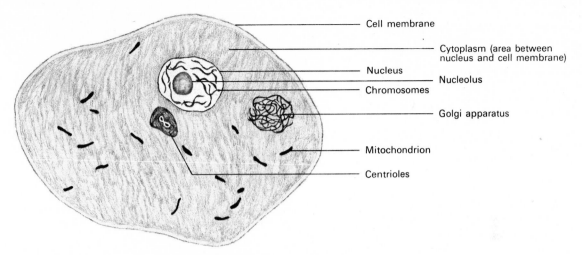

Cell membrane

Cytoplasm (area between
nucleus and cell membrane)

Nucleus

Nucleolus

Chromosomes

Golgi apparatus

Mitochondrion

Centrioles

FIGURE 4-1   Summary of cell structures known before introduction of the electron microscope. Special stains are required to
observe some of these parts.

Richard Altmann suggested, in 1886, that the long filaments he observed in the cytoplasm under a light microscope might have something to do with cellular energy production. We now call these filaments *mitochondria,* and biochemists have proved that mitochondria produce ATP molecules for storing and delivering energy. In 1898 Camillo Golgi reported in nerve-cell cytoplasm a network of material that stained darkly with silver nitrate. Some biologists argued that the *Golgi apparatus* was produced by the staining process itself and did not exist as such in normal cells. But after many years of controversy, Golgi was proved right. Today we know that these structures perform an important function in cellular secretion.

The cytoplasm of every animal cell and of some cells of "lower" forms contains two small structures called *centrioles* that function in cell division. The role of the centrioles in cell division will be discussed later in this chapter.

As improved lenses became available, the limiting factor in light microscopy became the wavelength of light itself. No matter how carefully it is designed and built, a light microscope has limited resolution (sharpness and separation of details). It cannot produce clear, sepa-

rate images of objects closer together than about 0.25 *micron,* or about 1/4000 mm. (A micron is 1/1000 mm.) This is about 500 times better than the naked eye can do. But it is not anywhere near good enough for exploring the fine structure of a cell.

In 1940 a revolutionary new microscope was produced. It utilized a beam of high-speed electrons of extremely short wavelength; electromagnetic "lenses" focused the electrons onto a photographic plate. Electrons are not bent by glass lenses, but since they are negatively charged their paths can be altered by a magnetic field. Today electron microscopes permit resolutions to less than 3 *angstrom units* (1 Å = 1/10,000 micron), and magnification reaches 400,000 times. This greater resolution has led to the discovery of many cellular components in recent years. And a more thorough investigation of the structure of all parts of cells is now possible. Measurements in microscopy have traditionally been made in *microns,* *millimicrons* (1/1000 micron), and *angstrom units.* Today, an international system including *micrometers* (formerly called microns) and *nanometers* (1/1,000,000 mm) is being used.

In electron micrographs (Figures 4-2 and

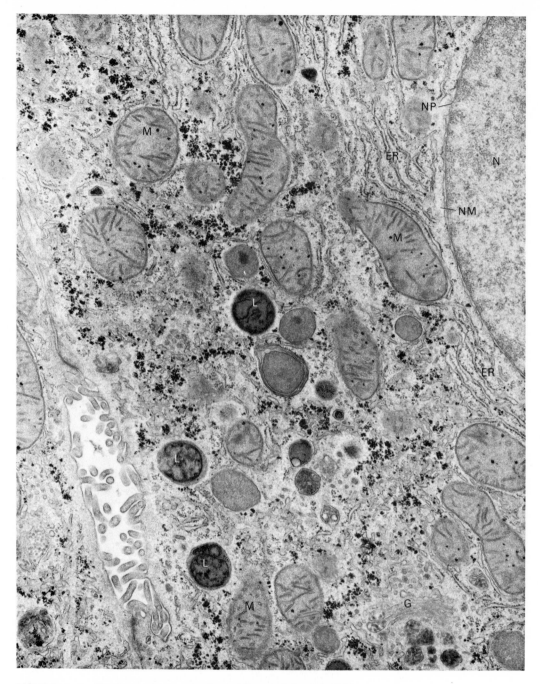

FIGURE 4–2   Electron micrograph of a rat liver cell (× 14,400):
nucleus (*N*), nuclear membrane (*NM*), nuclear pore (*NP*), mitochondria (*M*), endoplasmic reticulum (*ER*), Golgi apparatus (*G*),
lysosomes (*L*). (Courtesy of Keith R. Porter.)

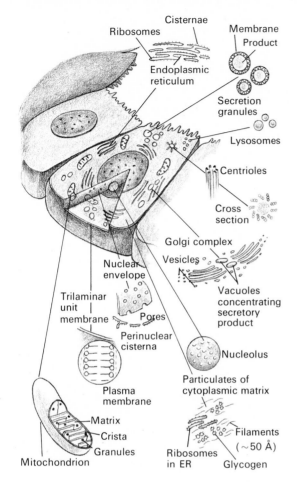

FIGURE 4–3   Three-dimensional diagram of a generalized animal cell based on electron micrographs. The structures of the cellular features are enlarged.

4–3), several structures such as the *endoplasmic reticulum*, *ribosomes*, and *lysosomes* can be seen in addition to the components noted previously. The ability to observe subcellular components in almost molecular detail and to perform biochemical analyses has enabled scientists to formulate hypotheses about the function of each part of the cell.

THE CELL MEMBRANE

Common to all living cells is a *cell membrane* (often called a *plasma membrane*); it is the molecular boundary between a cell and its immediate environment. This living membrane physically contains the cell and provides a large surface area on which many chemical reactions occur. The Danielli-Davson model of cell membranes (Figure 4–4) is an early theoretical molecular arrangement of proteins and lipids that generally agrees with biochemical and electronmicroscope observations. The structure is essentially a sandwich of proteins and lipids with two protein layers enclosing a bilayer (double layer) of lipids.

Three types of lipid molecules are commonly found in cell membranes: (1) triglycerides (fats); (2) phospholipids, which are similar to triglycerides but contain a phosphate and nitrogen component in place of one fatty acid), and (3) steroids such as cholesterol. The key to membrane structure is apparently the phospholipids. These molecules are hydrophilic (attracted to water). In a water medium, phospholipid molecules tend to aggregate into bilayers (sheets two molecules thick), with the hydrocarbon tails attracted inward and the hydrophilic ends oriented outward. In the Danielli-Davson model, the hydrophilic ends are closely associated with protein layers.

The Danielli-Davson model, conceived about 1935 from biochemical and microscopic evidence, is the basis for more modern concepts of the membrane. Recent evidence indicates that there are many different cell membrane structures. Newer models suggest that proteins may be gathered in several positions along a lipid bilayer, forming a mosaic pattern with protein patches serving various functions. Some proteins may be bound to the surface of the lipid, whereas others may be embedded in the lipid layers. Thus we may speak of external and internal protein molecules. Internal proteins may be partially embedded in a lipid layer with an end protruding to the inside or the outside. Or they may be embedded entirely within the membrane or extend completely through the membrane (Figure 4–5). Different regions of a membrane containing different proteins may thus fulfill different functions.

Evidence of these structures has been obtained by freeze-fracture and freeze-etching electron microscopy. Suitable cells, such as red

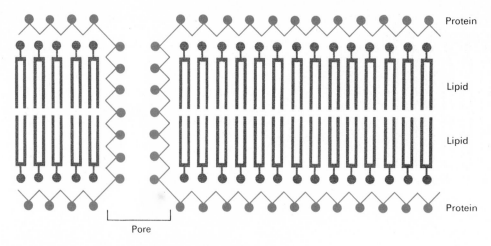

Protein

Lipid

Lipid

Protein

Pore

FIGURE 4–4   Membrane structure according to the Danielli-Davson model. The general structure shown in this model is still valid, but more has been learned about the organization and the arrangement of protein in the membrane. As a result, more detailed models have been proposed (see Figure 4–5).

blood cells, or cellular fragments are quick-frozen in liquid nitrogen. The solidified cell material is then split by a sharp blow with a specialized knife. Membranes often fracture down the center of the bilayer, exposing the protein molecules. After the ice crystals left by the freezing process have been evaporated, membrane fragments are showered with platinum or carbon atoms from one side. This coats the proteins and makes them show up clearly under an electron microscope.

As we shall see, cells contain many specific structures called "organelles" that are composed of membranes and their associated proteins. Many variations of membrane structure probably exist in all types of cells, and these variations may be closely related to the functions of each organelle and cell type.

The Movement of Materials Into and Out of Cells

All living cells require that water, minerals, and organic molecules be able to enter and leave them. If the cells are so securely bounded by membranes, how do these materials get in and out?

Since the lipid bilayer of the cell membrane prevents water and certain ions from passing into and out of cells, cell membranes probably contain pores through which water and ions can pass. It is also probable that these pores are protein-lined. Since the free amino and carboxyl groups of amino acids can take either negative or positive charges, and since like charges repel, specific charged ions could be attracted or repelled according to the immediate physiological state of a cell. This hypothesis helps to explain the great selectivity of these semipermeable membranes for certain ions, even when others may exist in greater concentrations. A semipermeable membrane allows certain materials to pass through but excludes others. Membranes are permeable to water in either direction but may vary in their permeability to other substances.

It is also possible that the ability of a substance to penetrate a cell membrane depends largely on its solubility in lipids. For instance, many large molecules that are highly fat soluble pass with relative ease into cells.

Phagocytosis and Pinocytosis

Most cells can actively ingest nutrients. We can easily see this process when the single-celled *Amoeba* engulfs solid materials, a process

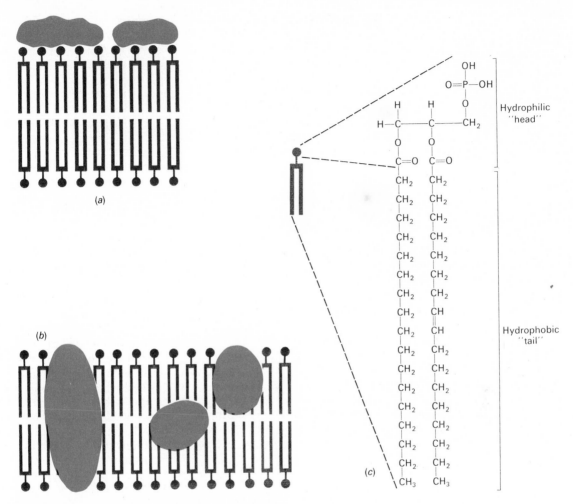

FIGURE 4–5   A modern concept of cell membranes.
(a) Phosopholipid bilayer with external protein. (b) Some possible
locations of internal proteins. (c) Structure of a phosphoglyceride
showing hydrophilic "head" and hydrophobic "tail."

called *phagocytosis* ("cell eating"). Human
white blood cells, for instance, use phagocytosis
to rid the body of bacteria and waste (Figure
4–6). Another process is *pinocytosis* ("cell
drinking"). In both phenomena the cell membrane encircles the particle or droplet and
forms a small membranous pouch. Once inside
a cell the droplet is pinched off to become a
pinocytotic vesicle or, more commonly, a *vacuole*. However, not all vacuoles observed in
cells are produced in this particular manner.

Diffusion and Osmosis

From a chemical point of view, fluids containing particles are of three types: simple suspension or mixture, true solution, and colloidal
suspension. Larger particles that settle out of a
mixture in a very short time—such as fine sand
grains in water—form a simple suspension. In a
true solution, very small particles such as table
salt or sugar (the solute) remain suspended in
water (the solvent) indefinitely. There are limits to solubility. For example, 100 ml of cold

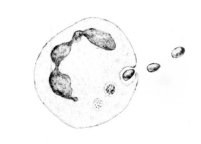

FIGURE 4-6   Phagocytosis: white blood cell engulfing bacteria.

water holds only about 36 grams of NaCl. If more is added, salt crystals form on the bottom of the container.

A *colloidal suspension* is formed when relatively large particles remain suspended in a medium over a long period. In a colloidal suspension the fluid part of the system (usually water) is termed the *dispersion phase*, and the suspended particles are collectively termed the *dispersed phase*. The most important factors determining dispersions are the size and charge of the suspended particles. In general, the larger the particles are, the faster they settle. Droplets of water suspended in air to form clouds are a colloidal suspension. Homogenized milk, in which fat droplets are extremely small, is also a type of colloidal suspension.

Colloidal suspensions exist in two forms—the watery, fluid state called sol, and the more solid state known as a gel (Figure 4-7). In some cells such as an amoeba, temporary reversible changes occur frequently and naturally. In other cases the change from sol to gel is irreversible, as when an egg white is fried. The fluid portions of living cells are both true solutions and colloidal suspensions. Because of this, cell contents do not "settle out" when an organism is inactive.

In 1827 Robert Brown noted that tiny particles suspended in water collide with one another and move in random zigzag patterns. Brown concluded that the plant spores he had observed under the microscope were capable of

independent movement, but other scientists soon demonstrated that a similar movement occurred with nonliving particles. This phenomenon, known as *Brownian motion*, has been observed in all states of matter—solid, liquid, and gas. It results from the movement of much smaller solvent particles, which propel the larger colloidal particles. The kinetic theory, which states that all matter is in constant motion, is the measurable result of this bombardment among atoms and molecules.

Traditionally, the study of the interchange of substances between a cell and its environment was approached as an aspect of diffusion or osmosis. But these processes are not specifically cellular mechanisms, and they do not explain how all materials get into and out of cells. *Diffusion* is the movement of particles through a medium from an area of greater concentration toward a lesser concentration. If, for example, a bottle of ammonia is opened in a classroom, the first students to detect the odor are those seated nearest the demonstration. Soon, however, the molecules disperse so that even those in the back row can smell the ammonia.

Particles in a water medium can diffuse through a membrane if they are small enough to pass through the membrane's pores. In Figure 4-8a, the particles on the left side of the membrane are in constant motion. They pass

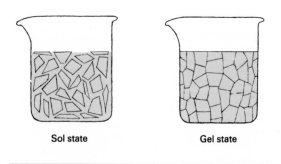

Sol state   Gel state

FIGURE 4-7   Dispersed and dispersion phases of a colloid in sol and gel states. Protein molecules are represented by irregular blocks, water by shading. This is what occurs in the firming up of gelatin desserts.

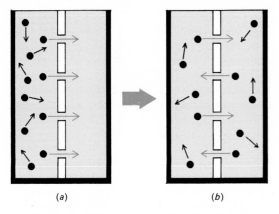

(a) (b)

FIGURE 4–8 Diffusion of particles through a membrane. Most particles move from a greater to a lesser concentration, as shown in (a), until an equal number of particles is present on each side of the membrane, as in (b). The short arrows indicate random movement.

through the pores of the membrane from a greater to a lesser concentration until equal numbers are moving back and forth across the membrane (Figure 4–8b). At that point, the solutions on either side of the membrane are in *equilibrium.*

The term *osmosis* refers to the passage of water across a semipermeable membrane from a region of greater concentration of water to a region of lesser concentration of water. The side of the membrane with the greatest number of dissolved particles bordering it is the side with proportionally less water. Thus the passage of water depends on the concentration of dissolved particles on either side of the membrane.

Figure 4–9 illustrates three conditions that affect the osmotic process. In this demonstration, cellulose sausage skins were used as semi-

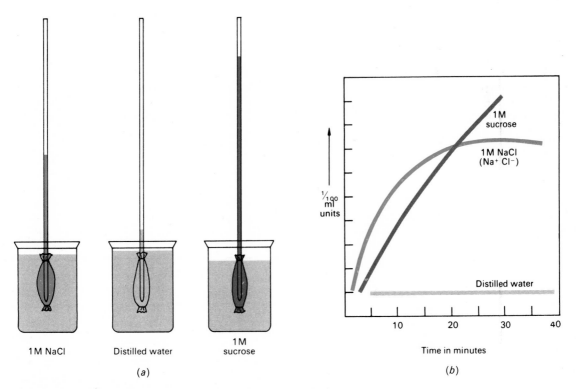

FIGURE 4–9 Demonstration of osmosis across semipermeable membranes using sausage-skin bags. (a) The bag at the left contains 1 M NaCl; the center bag, distilled water; the right bag, 1 M sucrose. (b) Graph of the results.

permeable membranes. Cellulose contains many small holes that permit water molecules to pass through it but block the passage of large particles such as sucrose molecules. Three such bags were prepared and filled with the following solutions: (1) 1 M NaCl, (2) distilled water, and (3) 1 M sucrose. Each bag then was tied tightly to a pipette that extended into the bag. Next, each bag was immersed in a beaker of distilled water. Within a few minutes the NaCl solution in the first pipette was rising rapidly. But after about 25 minutes the sucrose solution in the third pipette had risen as high as the NaCl solution. The rise of the NaCl solution slowed and finally stopped, but the sucrose solution kept rising and eventually spilled over the top of the pipette.

Since NaCl ionizes in solution, nearly twice as many particles were present in the NaCl bag as in the sucrose bag. For this reason water moved into the NaCl bag faster than into the sucrose bag. But the small particles of dissociated Na^+Cl^- eventually passed out through the holes in the semipermeable membrane, and the solutions on the two sides of the membrane reached equilibrium. But sucrose molecules are too large to move through such tiny holes, so equilibrium could not be reached in that case. In the bag containing distilled water equilibrium was present from the beginning, with an equal number of water molecules moving into and out of the bag. Thus the distilled water bag served as a "control" in this experiment.

A living cell must balance the osmotic conditions inside and outside its cell membrane. Excessive amounts of water cannot be allowed to enter or leave. An experiment with *Elodea*, a common aquarium plant, dramatically demonstrates the effect of increasing the salt concentration of the external environment—and thus decreasing its relative water concentration. When a leaf is placed in a 5 percent NaCl solution, water moves out of the cells, leaving their contents in a shrunken state (Figure 4–10). This condition is called *plasmolysis*. As we shall see, however, organisms do not depend entirely on osmosis for the concentrations of ions and other materials they need.

Active Transport

The movement of materials into certain cells does not always follow the principles of diffusion and osmosis. Absorptive cells in the small intestine, for example, can take in large amounts of glucose liberated in digestion. The bloodstream may contain many more glucose molecules than are found inside the intestine, but glucose still moves from the intestine into the bloodstream. According to the principle of diffusion, such movement should not occur. How does it happen? The difference in amount of dissolved solute between the two solutions is called the *concentration gradient*. Moving molecules against this gradient is like moving a stone uphill in that work must be performed on the system. This necessary process is called *active transport*, and it apparently requires the expenditure of energy by the cell. It is the only means by which some substances may enter a cell. For example, vitamin B_6 is known to aid in the active transport of some amino acids which are too large to enter otherwise. A deficiency of vitamin B_6 could therefore lead to a protein deficiency.

The mechanisms of active transport are not yet understood, but experiments have shown that energy and a protein carrier molecule are usually involved. Figure 4–11 illustrates the movement of glucose across the intestinal cells into the bloodstream against a high concentration gradient. A transport mechanism to account for this movement is shown in Figure 4–11c. The carrier molecule (C) is released when glucose is "delivered" to the bloodstream. The energy required is supplied by ATP. In all cases of active transport that have been studied, the addition of a poison to stop the production of ATP inhibits the transport mechanism.

Large molecules such as glucose are not the only materials that may be brought into cells against a concentration gradient. Ions such as sodium (Na^+), potassium (K^+), calcium (Ca^{++}), chloride (Cl^-), and sulfate ($SO_4^=$) are also transported by cell membranes. The cells that line the tubules of the kidneys, for example, actively reclaim ions and glucose from the forming urine. The freshwater alga *Nitella* concentrates large amounts of certain ions in

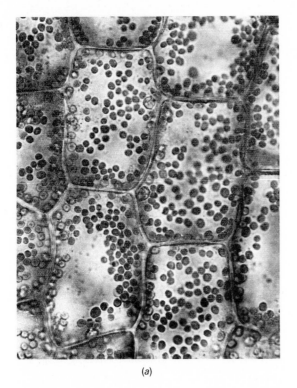
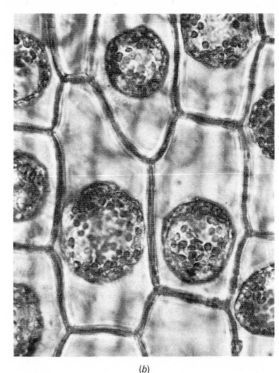

(a)   (b)

FIGURE 4–10   Osmotic effects in *Elodea* leaf cells ($\times$ 400).
(a) Cells from a leaf in a freshwater aquarium; note the even distribution of cell contents. (b) Cells from a leaf placed in a 5 percent salt solution; note the shrinking of cell contents from loss of
water by each cell. (Courtesy of Runk/Schoenberger, from Grant
Heilman.)

its sap. Figure 4–12 compares the ionic concentration in the sap and in pond water. The concentration of chloride ion (Cl^-) in the cell sap
can be a hundred times greater than in pond
water.

The primary mechanism to account for the
ability of living cells to selectively retain certain ions (potassium) and keep out others (sodium) has been attributed to "ion pumps" in
cell membranes. An example of how these
pumps might function in the retention and
exclusion of potassium and sodium ions during
nerve impulse transmission is given in
Chapter 12. It is believed that these pumps use
energy to accomplish the work of transporting
ions in and out of cells (thus the term *active*

transport). It is important to note, however,
that other mechanisms have been proposed to
account for this selective movement of ions
into and out of cells. One recent theory regards
the cell as an ion exchange unit in which the
large organic molecules within a cell act as
negatively charged sites where sodium and potassium ions can associate. Since potassium
binds more readily to these sites, they are retained within the cell and sodium remains
outside. Another aspect of this theory is the
presence of "structured water" (a state somewhere between ice crystals and liquid water)
believed to exist inside cells. Since ions are
generally not soluble in structured water, they
are not retained inside a cell unless the nega-

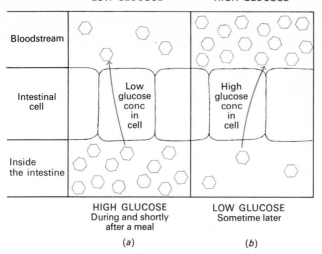

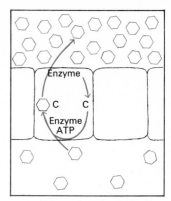

LOW GLUCOSE   HIGH GLUCOSE

Bloodstream

Intestinal cell

Low glucose conc in cell

High glucose conc in cell

Inside the intestine

HIGH GLUCOSE
During and shortly after a meal

LOW GLUCOSE
Sometime later

Enzyme

C   C

Enzyme
ATP

Proposed mechanism
to explain situation in (b)

(a)   (b)   (c)

FIGURE 4–11 Absorption of glucose from the intestine into the bloodstream. (a) Shortly after a meal, a high concentration of glucose is inside the intestine, and diffusion and active transport occur. (b) As glucose movement continues, a higher concentration in the bloodstream results. At this stage, glucose is moving from a region of low concentration to a region of high concentration. (c) A hypothetical mechanism to explain the movement of glucose against the concentration gradient. A carrier molecule is represented by the letter C. Energy, in the form of ATP and enzymes, is also required.

tively charged sites available for binding are free. Since potassium associates more readily with the charged sites, sodium concentration inside a cell is generally very low. As we will note in Chapter 12, changes occur in cells, such as the stimulation of nerve cells. These changes are thought to produce changes inside the cell involving water structuring and preferences of the binding sites for sodium over potassium ions. Although most biologists employ the concept of pumps to explain most active transport and transmission events along a nerve, the ideas of ion exchange and the structure of water inside cells must also be studied further.

THE STRUCTURE OF CYTOPLASM

The term *protoplasm*, once used to define all living substance collectively, has become inadequate since biochemical and electron micrographic studies have permitted us to distin-

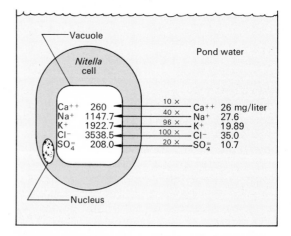

FIGURE 4–12 Comparison of ionic concentrations in the vacuolar sap of *Nitella* and the pond water in which it lives. The higher concentrations in the cell sap result from active transport. The data are expressed in milligrams per liter; the degree of concentration by the cell is shown on the arrows.

Bio-Topic: Immortality in a Test Tube

A woman who died of cancer a quarter century ago has been working in research laboratories all over the world. There is some question whether her name was Helen Lane, Helen Larson, or Henrietta Lacks. Cell biologists know her by her initials, HeLa.

Concerned about irregular vaginal bleeding, HeLa consulted gynecologists at the Johns Hopkins Hospital in Baltimore early in 1951. A biopsy revealed cancer of the cervix which eventually cost HeLa her life. But in a very real sense, she lived on.

In the years before 1950, cell biologists had learned to grow isolated human cells in test tubes. Supplied with nutrients such as sugars, amino acids, and vitamins, and kept under controlled conditions of temperature and acidity, cultures of human cells could be maintained and·studied. About 1950, cancer researchers were trying, mostly unsuccessfully, to grow human cancers in the laboratory.

They hoped that by studying cultured human cancers they could learn more about the disease and how to cure it.

One of the biopsy samples taken from HeLa was sent to George Gey of Johns Hopkins University, one of the leaders in the attempt to culture human cancers. Cells from the biopsy grew well in culture and Gey was soon able to start new cultures from the first one. Subcultures were sent to other laboratories, and within a decade HeLa had become one of the standard research tools of cell biologists around the world.

Studies of the HeLa cell line have, sad to say, not yet led to a cure for cancer. But HeLa cells have shed much light on the biology of the cell and have been used to determine the biological effects of new drugs, plastics, x-rays, pollutants, and other environmental hazards.

HeLa has lived on, serving science, since the death of her body. She is, in a sense, a potentially immortal person.

guish various parts. The portion of cell between the nuclear envelope and the cell membrane is known as the *cytoplasm;* it contains many different dissolved and colloidal substances. Of special interest among these inclusions are fibrillar proteins. Since long, unbranched microtubules were discovered in the cytoplasm of nerve cells in 1953, microtubules and smaller, nontubular microfilaments have been observed in many cell types. These tubules and filaments are now known to have contractile properties important in cell division, the streaming of cytoplasm within cells, amoeboid movement, and muscle contraction (Figure 4–13). The movement of pseudopods in amoebae is apparently due to contraction produced by associations between microfilaments. During the process of movement, these filaments are constantly forming, breaking up, and reforming.

Endoplasmic Reticulum and Ribosomes

Early electron micrographs clearly showed an extensive system of tubules and membrane-bound cavities extending throughout the cytoplasm. These structures, known as the *endoplasmic reticulum* (ER), usually have small particles called *ribosomes* attached to their surfaces. If the ER has no ribosomes, it is called *smooth ER.*

Endoplasmic reticulum is continuous with cell membranes and is closely associated with the nuclear envelope and Golgi apparatus (Figure 4–14). The full significance of endoplasmic reticulum is not yet understood, but this complex internal system of flattened sacs and tubules does increase the available surface area in cytoplasm. It provides a greater "work surface" for producing and channeling materials.

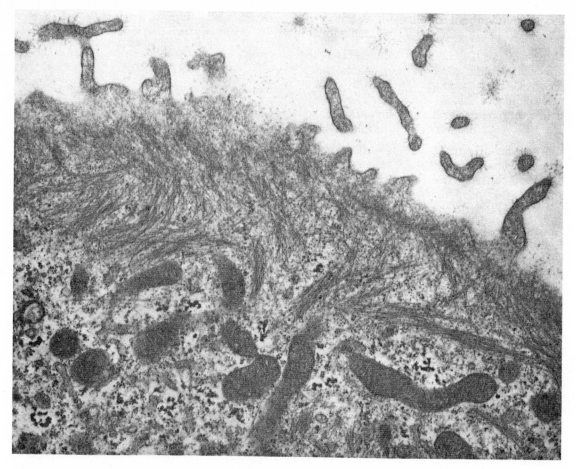

FIGURE 4–13 Electron micrograph of microfilaments beneath
the plasma membrane of an epithelial cell in a salamander
(× 27,000). These contractile filaments may provide for cellular
movement. (Courtesy of Conly Rieder.)

Ribosomes were discovered in 1955 by George Palade of the Rockefeller Institute, who also found that they contain protein and RNA. The rough ER, with its associated ribosomes, is the site of the assembly phase of protein synthesis. Proteins produced for export from the cell move into spaces formed by the double membranes (cisternae). They are then transported to a Golgi apparatus where they are concentrated and stored prior to release. Smooth endoplasmic reticulum most likely provides the connection between rough ER and the Golgi apparatus.

Golgi Apparatus

The basketlike system of silver-stained fibers observed by Golgi is actually a series of membranous, laminar (layered) sacs closely related to endoplasmic reticulum. No ribosome particles occur on their surfaces, however. The Golgi apparatus stores and releases cellular secretions. Cells that actively produce secretions always contain large amounts of Golgi structure (Figure 4–15). The larger lamellae (flattened sacs) appear to break up into smaller vesicles that are eventually expelled through the cell membrane as secretion droplets. Cells

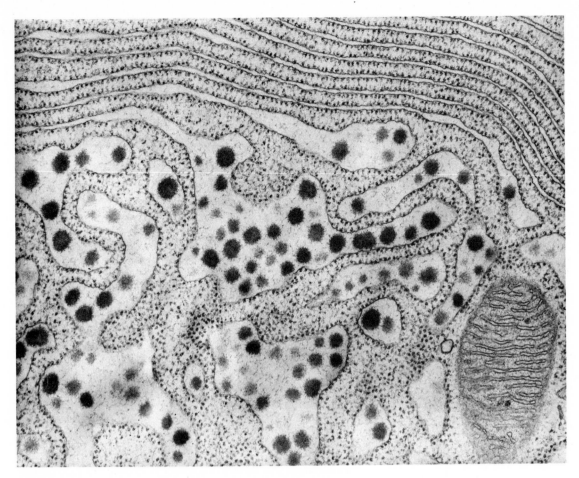

FIGURE 4–14 Electron micrograph of the pancreas of a guinea pig (× 32,000). The long channels in the upper part are endoplasmic reticulum lined with ribosomes (known as *rough ER*). The large, dark-stained droplets are products of protein synthesis. Note the mitochondrion in the lower right portion. (Courtesy of Keith R. Porter.)

of the pancreas, which secrete digestive enzymes, are an excellent example of this process. Since enzymes are proteins, scientists have used radioactive-labeled amino acids to trace the formation, storage, and release of cellular secretions.

Mitochondria and Plastids

The name *mitochondrion* refers to the two principal shapes that have been observed (*mito* means "thread", *chondrion* means "granule"). Through biochemical studies and electron microscopy, we know today that mitochondria are found in practically all eucaryotic cells. They are the principal sites of energy production. A look at an electron micrograph (Figure 4–2) shows that a mitochondrion is also made up of two membranes: a relatively smooth outer membrane and an inner membrane with many folds called *cristae*. The increased surface area provided by the cristae is believed to

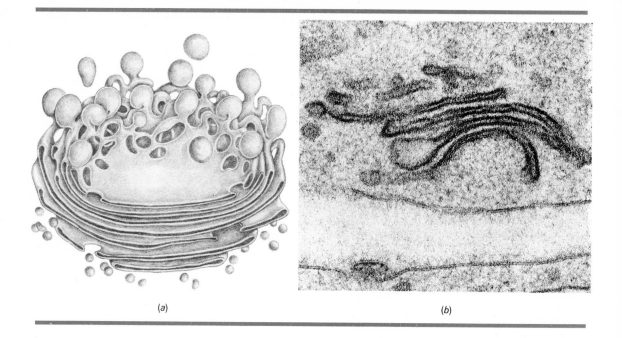

(a)   (b)

FIGURE 4–15   (a) Three-dimensional drawing of a Golgi apparatus showing the formation of secretory vesicles. (Redrawn, courtesy of Dr. C. P. Leblond.) (b) An electronmicrograph of a Golgi
apparatus ($\times$ 113,000). (Courtesy of Herbert W. Israel, Cornell
University.)

permit the attachment of extensive enzyme
systems (Figure 4–16).

Energy-rich compounds such as ATP are produced within the mitochondrion by two processes, both catalyzed by enzymes. The enzymes
for the first series of reactions (the Krebs cycle,
Chapter 9) are located in the mitochondrial
fluid between the cristae. The enzymes for the
second series (electron transport) are attached
to cristae membranes.

When mitochondria are removed from cells,
the energy-producing reactions still operate.
Even if mitochondria are broken up into small
fragments, some fragments are still capable of
producing energy if incubated in the proper
medium. The cristae must thus contain many
separate functional areas along their surfaces.

Three types of *plastids*—cytoplasmic bodies
somewhat similar to mitochondria—occur in
plant and algae cells. *Leucoplasts* contain no
pigments and are the site of starch formation
and storage; *chromoplasts* contain pigments
other than chlorophyll; *chloroplasts*, are complex laminar structures that contain chlorophyll. Chloroplasts, highly specialized for photosynthesis, consist of a parallel array of
platelike membranes called *lamellae*. Electron
micrographs show that at various points along
the plates the membrane is expanded into
thickened, disk-shaped areas (Figures 4–17 and
4–18). These disks are closely packed like
stacks of poker chips within the chloroplast;
each stack is called a *granum*. These double
protein-lipid membrane structures contain all

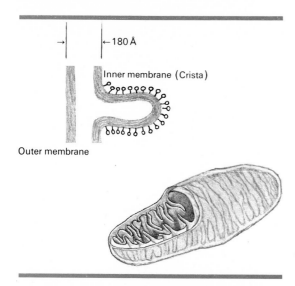

<- 180 Å

Inner membrane (Crista)

Outer membrane

FIGURE 4-16 Cutaway view of a globular mitochondrion showing the relationship between the
inner cristae membrane and the outer membrane.
An enlargement of these membranes is shown at
upper left. The attachments to the inner membrane are the enzyme ATP ase.

the pigments and enzymes necessary for photosynthesis.

Researchers have tried to describe the arrangement of molecules within the grana disks.
The current model indicates that the essential
pigments and enzymes are situated in definite
patterns along the inner membrane surfaces.
The lamellae of chloroplasts provide still another example of the important role of membrane surfaces in biochemical reactions.

It has been discovered that mitochondria
and plastids contain small amounts of DNA
and RNA and so have the systems necessary to
produce proteins. This DNA occurs as circular,
naked fibers. The information necessary for
synthesis of most enzymes in mitochondria
and plastids may be contained only in nuclear
DNA. But the nucleic acids occurring in these
organelles are apparently responsible for the
synthesis of some proteins necessary for their
structure and function.

It has long been known that mitochondria
and plastids are capable of dividing; the discovery of circular, naked DNA fibers in them has
raised questions about their origin. One hy-

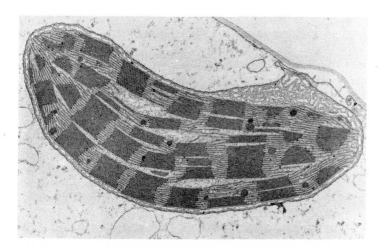

FIGURE 4-17 Electron micrograph of a chloroplast from a corn
leaf. The lamellar structure of the grana can be seen very clearly
(× 13,000). (Courtesy of Dr. L. K. Shumway, Program in Genetics and Department of Botany, Washington State University.)

FIGURE 4-18   Electron micrograph of a granum from a chloroplast of a spinach leaf. The small subunits in the exposed area, known as quantasomes, contain chlorophyll. (Courtesy of Roderic B. Park.)

pothesis suggests that they originated from free-living organisms similar to modern bacteria—which, in fact, do not have mitochondria. These organisms may have entered other cells and become part of the host cell's machinery in a mutually beneficial relationship (Figure 4–19).

Centrioles

The area in most eucaryotic cells that includes centrioles is called the *centrosome*. Through a light microscope, centrioles appear as two dark granules embedded in a heterogeneous matrix; electron micrographs show their structure in much greater detail (Figure 4–20a). They are cylindrical and contain numerous microtubules arranged in a very precise pattern. Nine sets of three tubules are spaced around the periphery of the cylinder.

The basal parts of *flagella* and *cilia*, which are organelles specialized for locomotion, have a similar structure. This similarity suggests that centrioles, flagella, and cilia are very closely related. In cilia and flagella two additional tubules appear in the center; this pattern is known as the 9 + 2 tubular arrangement (Figure 4–20b), whereas the centriole pattern is described as 9 + 0.

During cell division, centrioles leave the centrosome and move to opposite sides of the nucleus. By this time protein fibers have radiated from each centriole to form a star-shaped structure called an *aster*, and other fibers have connected centrioles to the chromosomes. These contractile microtubules (or "spindle fibers," as they are commonly known) are thought to contribute to the separation of chromosomes and the formation of daughter cells (Figure 4–21).

Centrioles reproduce themselves before cell division. Most algae and "higher" plants, however, do not have centrioles. In these species the spindle fibers form just before separation of the chromosomes. Since spindle fibers may form in the absence of centrioles, the relationship between the two is still uncertain.

Lysosomes

Contained in a single membrane, the *lysosome* ("splitting body") appears in electron micrographs as a nearly homogeneous vacuole. The name *lysosome* describes the great hydrolytic power of the enzymes it contains. Enzymes present include those that digest protein, polysaccharides, and nucleic acids, and those that permit the release of energy from ATP. If released into the cytoplasm, these enzymes can be very destructive to a cell. We do not yet know how these enzymes are retained within the membrane. Lysosomes often digest cells that are injured or diseased, and they have an important function in digestion of materials taken into individual cells through the cell membrane (Figure 4–22). Lysosomes may also digest dead structures within a cell.

One interesting example of lysosome action is the absorption of the tadpole tail during frog development. Lysosomes digest entire cells in a

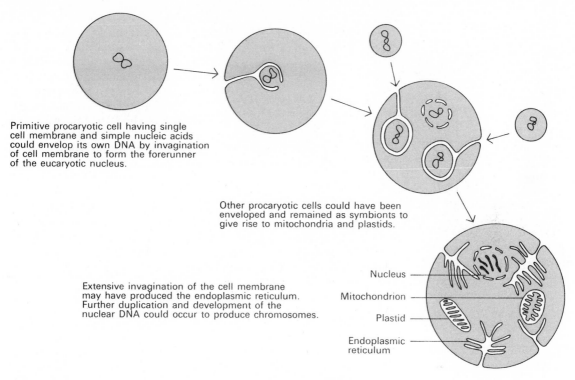

Primitive procaryotic cell having single cell membrane and simple nucleic acids could envelop its own DNA by invagination of cell membrane to form the forerunner of the eucaryotic nucleus.

Other procaryotic cells could have been enveloped and remained as symbionts to give rise to mitochondria and plastids.

Extensive invagination of the cell membrane may have produced the endoplasmic reticulum. Further duplication and development of the nuclear DNA could occur to produce chromosomes.

Nucleus

Mitochondrion

Plastid

Endoplasmic reticulum

FIGURE 4–19   Evolutionary hypothesis for the origin of eucaryotic organelles from symbiont procaryotic cells. Explanation for each stage is given in the illustration.

controlled manner until the tail disappears. The products of this digestion are moved to other areas of the developing frog, where they are used to fabricate new tissue.

THE NUCLEUS

Up to this point we have been concerned mainly with the membranes and the membranous organelles of the cytoplasm. The nucleus, with its inclusions, is also extremely important to the functions of a cell. As we shall see in Chapter 5, some cells lack a well-defined nucleus. But even those cells have DNA that functions much like that in the chromosomes of more complex organisms.

A cell cannot survive long without its nucleus. With a very fine glass needle mounted on a microscope, the nucleus of an amoeba can be

removed. The resulting enucleate cell is incapable of reproduction or digestion and can make only sluggish movements. an enucleate amoeba usually dies within three weeks. If a new nucleus from the same species is transplanted into the cell within a few days, however, the amoeba will again function normally.

An enucleate amoeba cannot digest foods. Digestion requires enzymes, which are specific proteins; without these proteins, digestion cannot take place. This supports the hypothesis that the nucleus contains information necessary for the cell to synthesize specific proteins.

The nuclear membrane contains many small pores (Figure 4–23). These are passageways for the exchange of materials between nucleus and cytoplasm. These pores, roughly 20 nanometers or 200 Å in diameter, appear to be distributed evenly over the membrane.

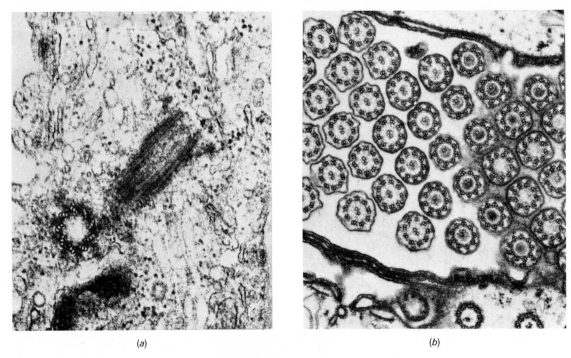

(a)   (b)

FIGURE 4–20   Electron micrographs of centrioles from rat kidney. (a) Longitudinal and cross section ($\times$ 73,000). Note the nine sets of microtubules in the cross section. (b) Cross section of cilia from the ciliate *Trichodina* ($\times$ 35,000). (Courtesy of James D. Newstead.)

The Nucleolus

In most cells, the nucleus contains one or more smaller bodies called *nucleoli*, which contain large amounts of RNA (Figure 4–24). Each *nucleolus* is produced by a specific chromosome after cell division. The function of the nucleolus was not understood for more than 100 years after its discovery. Today we know that the nucleolus is the site of the conversion of ribosomal RNA into subunits of ribosomes, which are then transported to the cytoplasm to function in the synthesis of specific proteins.

Chromosomes

The nucleus contains a fluid called nucleoplasm, similar to the watery, nonmembranous component of cytoplasm. Long threadlike structures composed of DNA and protein are suspended in this nuclear sap. These structures are called *chromosomes*. Under a light microscope, the chromosomes appear to be a network of fibers; the original term "chromatin network" was based on this observation. This term is still used occasionally, but we now know that the DNA-protein threads are simply uncoiled chromosomes.

The protein coating of chromosomes is of two types—*histones* and *nonhistones*. Histones are attached directly to the DNA, since they are positively charged and DNA is negatively charged. Because of their close association with DNA, histones are believed to be involved in genetic regulation. Nonhistones, on the other

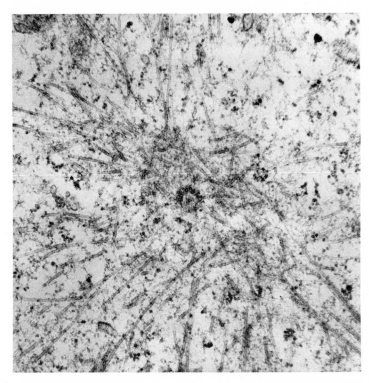

FIGURE 4–21 Electron micrograph of the astral region of a dividing cell (× 46,000). Note the tubular structure of the spindle microtubules. Also note the centriole in the center from which the microtubules radiate. (Courtesy of Conly Rieder.)

hand, are negatively charged; they vary greatly in structure and position in the nucleus.

Chromosomes contain the genetic information necessary for the development and maintenance of each of an organism's cells. Chapter 13 will discuss the genetic mechanism of inheritance in more detail. At this point it is important to know only that the DNA in the chromosomes contains coded information that assures proper cell organization and continuation of life processes.

HOW CELLS DIVIDE

In normal body cells, chromosomes occur in pairs. Cells which contain two of each type of chromosome are called *diploid* cells; they are said to have chromosome number 2n. The two members of a chromosome pair are similar in size and shape, and both carry inheritance factors influencing similar traits. Chromosomes with these similarities are often called *homologous pairs*.

Two types of cell division occur in most plants and animals: (1) *somatic*, or body-cell, division, and (2) *gametic*, or sex-cell, division (gametes are eggs and sperms). Somatic division is known as *mitosis*; gametic division is called *meiosis*. In mitosis both the nucleus and the cytoplasm divide to form two daughter cells, each with the same number and types of chromosomes as the original cell. Meiosis, which will be explained in detail in Chapter 13, is a more complex process in which the chro-

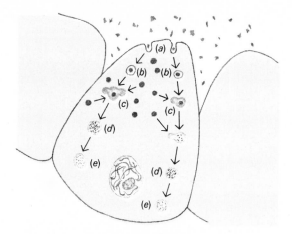

FIGURE 4-22 Functional stages of lysosome action in the digestive gland of a snail. (a) Small bits of food are taken into the cells by pinocytosis. (b) Lysosomes (dark) unite with food vacuoles and contribute hydrolytic enzymes. (c) Food products are absorbed into the cell. (d) and (e) After digestion, large excretory vacuoles are found near the base of the cell.

mosome number in each gamete is halved in preparation for fertilization. Gametic cells thus have only one of each type of chromosome; they are *haploid* or *n*.

Growth and development of every multicelled organism depends upon cell division. Even after growth is completed, cell division is necessary to replace injured cells and those which no longer function. In many singlecelled forms of life, reproduction is the direct result of cell division. Through the process of cell division, the material of one cell is divided equally between two daughter cells.

The nuclear events that occur during cell division were observed for many years before any relationship between chromosomes and cell division was seen. Division was observed in protozoa as early as 1744, even though they were not recognized as cells. In about 1824 the cleaving of frog eggs was finally recognized as multiplication by cell division. In 1888, in a classic paper on the division of fertilized *Ascaris* (roundworm) eggs, Thedor Boveri accurately diagrammed the distribution of nuclear material during cleavage.

Before a cell can undergo mitosis, its chromosomes must duplicate. The DNA of each chromosome duplicates itself according to base-pair specificity—adenine to thymine and guanine to cytosine.

Mitosis in Animals

Mitosis takes place in a series of steps or phases. From beginning to end these phases are: (1) *interphase;* (2) *prophase;* (3) *metaphase;* (4) *anaphase;* and (5) *telophase* (Figures 4-25 and 4-26).

Interphase

During this stage the nuclear membrane is intact and the centrioles are located in the cytoplasm near the nucleus. Chromosomes

FIGURE 4-23 Freeze-etch electron micrograph of nuclear membranes, showing pores. (Student's Collection of Electron Micrographs, J. J. Head. Carolina Biological Supply Company.)

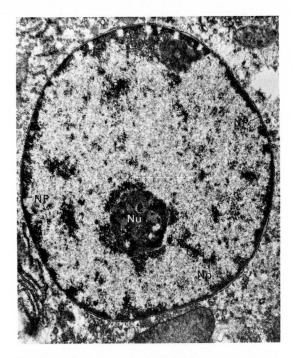

FIGURE 4–24 Electron micrograph of a cell nucleus showing a large nucleolus (Nu). Parts of chromosomes (Ch) are also visible, scattered throughout the nucleus and along the inner edge of the double nuclear membrane. Note the nuclear pores (NP) along the membranes ($\times$ 9,000). (Courtesy of David E. Comings and Tadashi A. Okada.)

within a nucleus are long and threadlike, indistinguishable from one another. Darkly staining areas called *chromomeres* appear at specific points along each chromosome. These thickened regions are concentrations of DNA produced by localized coiling.

For many years after the discovery of mitosis, the chromosomes were thought to duplicate during metaphase, about halfway through the division process. When radioisotopes of phosphorus (P^{32}) and hydrogen (H^3, tritium) became available, tritiated thymine nucleotides were added to the medium of dividing cells. Thymine nucleotides were found to be incorporated into the chromosomes during interphase, so chromosome duplication occurs at that time.

The important events occurring during interphase can be illustrated as in Figure 4–27. Following mitosis, the interphasic nucleus of each daughter cell enters a so-called gap phase, G_1, during which only RNA and protein are synthesized. This is a period of general growth and synthesis of cell organelles. Next, during the S (synthesis) phase, chromosomal DNA and histones are replicated. Finally a second gap phase (G_2) occurs, during which RNA and protein are synthesized to form structures necessary for cell division, such as spindle fibers. After a time which varies according to cell type, mitotic events are again initiated. Nerve cells, for example, divide very rarely, whereas epidermal cells producing skin and intestinal lining may divide every few days. This is why nerve damage is often irreversible—serious damage to the optic nerve, for instance, usually results in permanent blindness. In contrast, destruction of many hundreds of skin cells usually has no permanent disruptive effect. The damaged cells are all soon replaced.

Prophase

In this early phase of mitosis, each long thread-like chromosome begins to coil upon itself, much like the twisting of a rubber band. During this stage the chromosomes become shorter, thicker, and more clearly visible. The nucleoli disappear and do not reappear until telophase, when the nuclear material reorganizes into the nuclei of the daughter cells. Near the end of prophase, the nuclear membrane begins to break down and finally disappears. The centrioles move slowly away from each other to opposite sides of the nucleus to form poles for the division; radiating protein microtubules called *asters* form near each centriole.

Metaphase

When the centrioles have reached opposite positions across the nuclear area, protein microtubules called *spindle fibers* are synthesized between them. Some spindle fibers attach to *centromeres*, specific regions on the chromosomes. Little is known about the mechanics of spindle-fiber attachment or the molecular structure of centromeres. We do know that each chromosome has one centromere, which

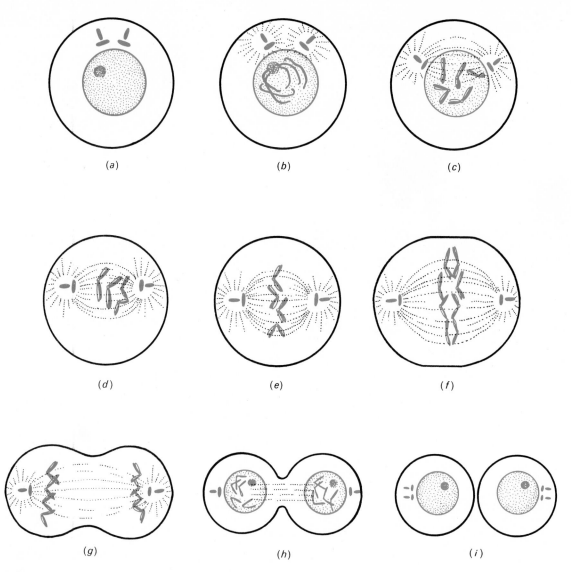

FIGURE 4–25 Interphase and successive stages of mitosis in an
animal cell. (*a*) Interphase: chromosomes indistinct, nucleolus
visible. (*b*) Early Prophase: chromosomes begin coiling, centrioles
begin movement to poles. (*c*) Middle Prophase: chromosomes
very distinct, nucleolus disappears. (*d*) Late Prophase: chromosomes shorter and thicker, nuclear membrane disappears, spindle
fibers in position, centromeres attach to spindle fibers. (*e*) Metaphase: chromosomes line up on equatorial plane. (*f*) Early Anaphase: chromatids separate and move to poles. (*g*) Late Anaphase:
cleavage furrow developing, chromosomes near poles.
(*h*) Telophase: chromosomes uncoil, nucleoli reappear, nuclear
membranes form, cytokinesis nearly complete. (*i*) Two daughter
cells result.

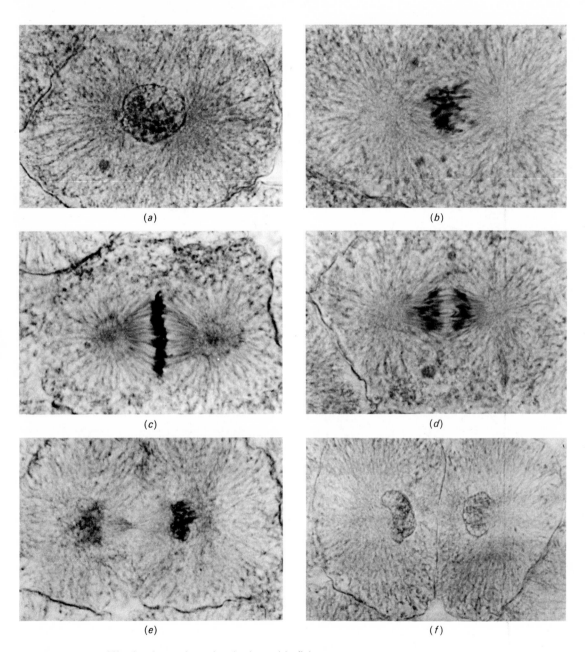

FIGURE 4–26   Mitotic phases in a developing whitefish egg.
(a) Interphase. (b) Prophase. (c) Metaphase. (d) Anaphase.
(e) Telophase. (f) Daughter cells. (Courtesy Carolina Biological
Supply Company.)

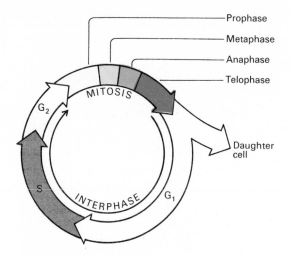

FIGURE 4–27 Cyclic time-sequence of mitosis. G_1 is first gap phase, a period of growth and synthesis of cell organelles; S is synthesis of DNA and nuclear histones; G_2 is second gap phase, when structures necessary for cell division are formed.

is always at the same spot on a specific chromosome. After chromosomes have duplicated they appear thicker and larger. Each half, clearly visible at this stage, is called a *chromatid*.

During metaphase, chromosomes attached to spindle fibers move about until they align on an equatorial plane perpendicular to the centriole poles. The centrioles, spindle fibers, and chromosomes collectively are called the *mitotic apparatus*.

Anaphase
During anaphase the duplicated chromosomes separate and move apart. A chromosome will not move during anaphase unless its centromere is attached to a spindle fiber. Microtubules do not appear to make direct connections between chromosomes and centrioles. Rather, microtubules attached to centromeres have their free ends pointing toward the poles of the spindle. Other microtubules are attached to the centrioles, with their free ends pointing toward the chromosomes. Microtubules of these two types overlap but are not continuous. There is also probably a third type of microtubule, free

at both ends, lying parallel to the two attached types. The movement of the chromosomes toward the poles may be due to a sliding movement among the various microtubules. At this time, however, the mechanism and the motive force by which chromosomes move during cell division are not known.

Separation of the duplicated chromosomes marks the beginning of nuclear division, or *karyokinesis*. By late anaphase, the entire cell begins to divide—that is, a cleavage furrow forms at the center of the spindle.

Telophase
The last phase of division is marked by *cytokinesis*, cleavage of the cell into daughter cells. Usually, some spindle fibers are still visible between the cells. The tightly coiled chromosomes now begin to relax and uncoil; the nuclear membrane and nucleoli reappear. The aster and spindle fibers disappear, and centrioles are usually duplicated during late telophase. Each cell receives one pair of centrioles in the division process. These events complete a normal mitotic cycle, to form two daughter cells with the characteristics of the G_1 portion of interphase.

Mitotic cell division in animals may require from 30 minutes to several hours. In mammalian cells the time is usually about one hour. In mouse spleen cells in culture, prophase lasts 20–35 minutes, metaphase 6–15 minutes, anaphase 8–14 minutes, and telophase 9–26 minutes. Prophase and telophase generally take longer than metaphase or anaphase; in many cases anaphase is extremely short.

Mitosis in Plants

One significant difference between plant and animal cells is the rigid plant cell wall. In animal cells, cleavage of the flexible cell membrane permits formation of two daughter cells. But how are new cell walls formed in plants? Small cell plates believed to originate from the Golgi apparatus form in the midspindle region during anaphase. These coalesce to form part of the new cell wall separating the daughter cells.

Another difference between the mitotic ap-

Bio-Topic: Variations on a Theme

Mitosis is one of the basic common denominators of living systems. Nearly all cells with true nuclei are formed by mitosis from other cells. How did mitosis evolve? What were the first cells able to carry out mitosis? Has mitosis changed through evolutionary history? In what ways?

These questions seemed unanswerable until recently, largely because the first mitotic cells left no traces in the fossil record. The invention of the electron microscope revealed new information about mitosis in modern organisms and may soon answer questions about the evolution of mitosis. Electron microscopy has confirmed that the cells of all higher animals carry out mitosis in essentially one way. The same is true of the cells of higher plants, although mitosis in higher plants does not involve centrioles.

Electron microscopy also revealed an unexpected and almost embarrassing variety of mitotic patterns among the simpler organisms with true nuclei: the algae, fungi, and protozoa. In some of these organisms, mitosis involves centrioles; in others, it does not. In some organisms, the nuclear membrane breaks down during mitosis; in others, the nuclear mem-

brane remains intact; and in still others, the nuclear membrane develops large openings but does not break down. The chromosomes of some organisms are moved about by a recognizable mitotic spindle, but in others, there is no spindle and the chromosomes are attached to and moved about by the nuclear membrane.

These and other variations in such a basic cell function as mitosis surprised and confused scientists at first. Early in the 1970s, Jeremy Pickett-Heaps of the University of Colorado suggested that the variations might provide clues about the evolution of mitosis. He speculated that the variations reflect different stages in an evolutionary sequence and that different groups of modern organisms had "stopped" evolving at different stages in the sequence. Mitotic patterns of modern organisms might be the equivalent of individual frames of a movie of the evolution of mitosis.

Pickett-Heaps' idea is consistent with most of what is now known about the evolution of the algae, fungi, and protozoa. Many new lines of inquiry to test his idea have been suggested. We may soon understand the evolution of one of the most basic of all cellular processes.

paratus of plant and animal cells is that plant cells lack centrioles and astral fibers. We still do not understand thoroughly how spindle fibers form in plant cells or what their function is. The mitotic process in an onion-root tip is shown in Figure 4–28.

CELLULAR INTERRELATIONSHIPS: STRUCTURE AND FUNCTION

Microscopists and biochemists have gathered a vast body of knowledge about the cell's anat-

omy. Each of these tiny living units is more complex than most manmade machinery. For example, most cells are structurally and functionally more complicated than an automobile. An auto has several thousand parts; some individual cells have several thousand mitochondria! And as we have seen, a mitochondrion is itself a complex structure.

Microscopists, biochemists, and other scientists have demonstrated many connections among cellular structures and cellular functions. Their findings emphasize two funda-

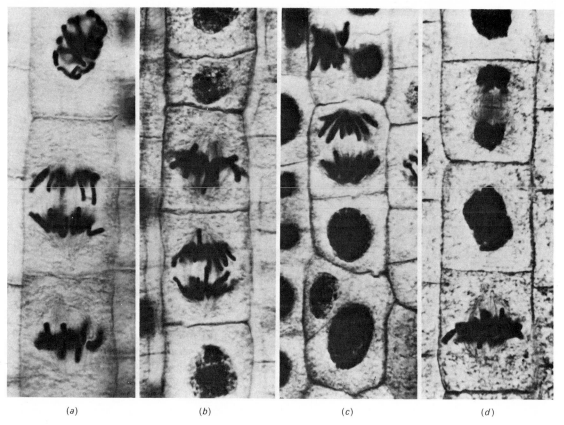

(a)   (b)   (c)   (d)

FIGURE 4–28   Sections of onion-root tip showing various stages
of mitosis. (a) From the top: prophase, anaphase, metaphase.
(b) From the top: two daughter cells, metaphase, anaphase, early
prophase. (c) Just above center: anaphase. (d) Second from top:
telophase. (Courtesy of Carolina Biological Supply Company.)

mental points: (1) cells must continually be
supplied with energy and other raw materials;
(2) cells must be able to process these raw
materials in an orderly, efficient manner. If a
cell's inflow of raw materials is cut off or if its
processing operations are disrupted, it deteriorates and eventually dies.

Within each cell of any organism, a continual state of cooperation is essential. For example, mitochondria function in cooperation with
the cytoplasmic fluids to store the energy
needed for practically all cellular functions.

Perhaps the most striking example of the
interrelationships among cellular structures is

provided by protein synthesis. All cells must
produce proteins—enzymes, structural proteins
for growth and repair, antibodies, and hormones, to name just some of them. Certain
cells, such as those of the pancreas, are highly
specialized for the synthesis and secretion of
enzymes.

In protein synthesis, polypeptides—chains of
amino acids—are produced on the rough endoplasmic reticulum. Then they are carried by
the rough and the smooth ER channels to the
Golgi apparatus, where they are concentrated
and stored for release. The details of protein
synthesis, which is directed by nuclear DNA

and also involves RNA and ribosomes, will be presented in Chapter 14. But the basic sequence of this synthesis should be noted now:

DNA → RNA → protein

The information needed to produce a particular protein is transferred from a segment of DNA to an RNA molecule, which carries this information to the cytoplasm. In the cytoplasm other types of RNA and ribosomes cooperate in the synthesis of the specified protein.

An amoeba, which is at once a cell and a complete organism, performs all the functions of a living system. But multicellular organisms depend on the cooperation of many cells. A human being, for example, contains several billion cells of many different types. Cells of each type perform the basic life processes; many of them are also highly specialized for specific functions. Now that we have a working knowledge of cell structures and processes, we can proceed with our study of the various types of cells.

SUMMARY

All organisms are composed of individual units called cells. A cell has two major regions, the cytoplasm and the nucleus. The cytoplasm includes all the material between the cell membrane and the nuclear membrane. Common cytoplasmic structures include Golgi apparatus, mitochondria, endoplasmic reticulum, lysosomes, ribosomes, centrioles, and chloroplasts. The nucleus contains chromosomes and nucleoli.

The structure of the cell membrane may be thought of as a sandwich of protein-lipid-lipid-protein, but proteins are also found inside the lipid layers. The movement of materials into cells may occur in several ways: phagocytosis, pinocytosis, diffusion, osmosis, and active transport.

The nucleus is the control center for all cell activities. The DNA of the chromosomes provides the information necessary for the production of specific proteins, some of which function as enzymes. The actual synthesis of proteins occurs in the cytoplasm, involving the rough endoplasmic reticulum and ribosomes.

The sequence of nuclear and cytoplasmic events in mitotic cell division has the following phases:

1. Interphase: chromosomes are extended and uncoiled; DNA is replicated.

2. Prophase: chromosomes shorten by coiling, centrioles move to the poles, asters form, nucleoli disappear, and the nuclear membrane breaks down.

3. Metaphase: spindle fibers are attached to chromosomes and chromosomes align on an equatorial plane.

4. Anaphase: chromosomes move to opposite poles.

5. Telophase: cell membrane constricts in animals (in plants, a cell wall develops) to form daughter cells; chromosomes and nucleus return to interphasic condition.

The various parts of a cell must all function cooperatively. Cell division, enzyme action, and protein synthesis, for example, depend on the production of energy, which in turn depends on the cell's ability to take in and process raw materials.

REVIEW QUESTIONS

1. How does the function of a mitochondrion differ from that of a chloroplast? How are the two structurally similar?

2. What are some differences between basic and applied research? How does each type of research benefit humanity?

3. In what structural and functional ways are centrioles, flagella, and cilia related?

4. How does the current cell membrane model differ from the Danielli-Davson version? What may be some functions of the membrane proteins?

5. What are some functions of lysosomes?

6. Why has the electron microscope become such an important tool in biology and medi-

cine? What advantages over the light microscope does the electron microscope offer?

7. List four ways that materials enter cells; give an example of each process.

8. List the principal phases of mitosis and give one important event that occurs in each stage.

9. When sea urchin eggs are placed in distilled water they swell and burst. Explain why.

SUPPLEMENTARY READINGS

Capaldi, Roberick A., "A Dynamic Model of Cell Membranes," *Scientific American*, March 1974. Protein molecules in cell membranes are shown to be distributed in asymmetric positions and involved in many important cell functions.

Luria, Salvador E., "Colicins and the Energetics of Cell Membranes," *Scientific American*, December 1975. Colicins are antibiotics produced by bacteria and have been found to be useful in the study of the functions of cell membranes.

Mazia, Daniel, "The Cell Cycle," *Scientific American*, January 1974. This article discusses the events that occur in cells between divisions. These events include the duplication of chromosomes and other preparations which enable the cell to divide again.

Novikoff, Alex B. and Eric Holtzman, *Cells and Organelles*, Holt, Rinehart and Winston, New York, 1970. A clearly written and well-illustrated description of cell types and the structure and function of organelles.

Satir, Birgit, "The Final Steps in Secretion," *Scientific American*, October 1975. Recent evidence suggests that proteins produced for export from a cell are packaged in membranous vesicles that fuse with the cell membrane at the moment of release.

Satir, Peter, "How Cilia Move," *Scientific American*, October 1974. The movement of cilia is proposed to be the result of adjacent microtubules sliding past one another.

Chapter 5

Cells, Tissues, and Organs

If we look at life only at the cellular level, we miss many of the attributes that make living systems so interesting. Think of most of the organisms in your own environment, including your fellow humans. They are composed not of one cell, but rather of millions or billions of cells. Multicellular organisms are more than collections of cells. They are organized into groups of specific kinds of cells, each kind carrying out a specific function.

One of the ways biologists organize cells is according to the level of complexity of the organisms they comprise. *The Fundamental Cell Types* reflect this kind of classification. We begin with the comparatively simple kingdom, *The Monera.* These cells are procaryotes; that is, they do not have a true nucleus. They generally exist as single-celled organisms. *The Protistan Cells,* on the other hand, have nuclei; they are eucaryotes. The protists are of interest to us in this chapter because some of them form simple multicellular organisms. The two other kinds of cells are *The Plant and Animal Cells,* characteristic of the two kingdoms so prominent in the biosphere.

At the plant and animal level we find *Tissues: The Organization of Cells.* The rela-tionship of structure and function of cells and tissues is dramatically demonstrated in the organization of *Plant Tissues.* Support, internal transport of materials, growth, protection, and exchange of materials are each handled by recognizable types of tissues.

Although somewhat more varied, the principle is the same as it applies to *Animal Tissues.* The maintenance of a system as complex as a human being requires dozens of kinds of cells organized into tissues.

Just as individual cells are not the entire story of the organization of a multicellular living system, neither are tissues a complete explanation of that system's ability to function. Tissues are organized into *Organs: Cooperating Tissues.* Organs, in turn, are organized into organ systems. And in turn, we come to the concept of *Organisms: Independent Living Systems.*

In this chapter we will see how a single red blood cell, designed to carry vital oxygen and yield it to other cells that require it, is a basic unit of the tissue we call blood. As a connective tissue, it forms part of the organ system called the circulatory system and helps maintain the organism in which it functions.

In Chapter 4 we sought a general understanding of the structure and function of the living cell. But of course there is no such thing as a "typical" living cell. We saw this when we noted that plant and animal cells have differences as well as similarities in their structures.

But the distinction between plants and animals is not the most basic difference among living systems. The most fundamental distinction is between *eucaryotic* and *procaryotic* organisms. This is a difference at the cellular level. A eucaryotic cell is one with a true nucleus; its nuclear material is separated by a nuclear membrane from the surrounding cytoplasm. Procaryotic cells are more primitive; they lack true nuclei. Procaryotic cells are

thought to have appeared on earth before eucaryotic cells did, and eucaryotes probably evolved from procaryotic forms (Figure 5-1). One method of classifying the living world is to begin with a primary, fundamental division between the procaryotes and the eucaryotes.

FUNDAMENTAL CELL TYPES

Procaryotic and eucaryotic cells are not completely dissimilar. Both have cell membranes; both utilize DNA and RNA as informational molecules; both have a similar genetic code. But the gulf between them is nonetheless profound, as we shall see in this chapter and in Chapter 22. One implication of the procaryotic/eucaryotic distinction is that in certain re-

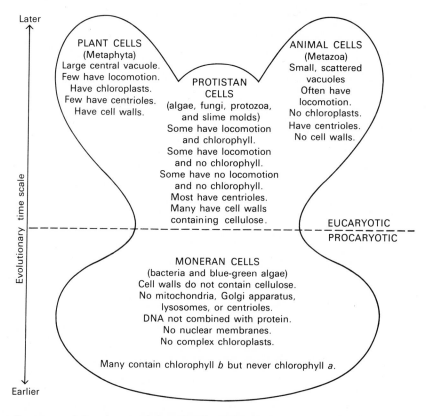

FIGURE 5-1   Summary of the characteristics of cells of the four kingdoms of organisms and their probable evolutionary relationships.

spects human cells have more in common with green algae than green algae have with blue-green algae.

Moneran Cells

Bacteria and blue-green algae are procaryotic organisms; as such, they differ from other organisms in several fundamental respects. In the first place, their genetic material is composed only of nucleic acid, whereas the genetic material of eucaryotic cells is contained in chromosomes composed of nucleic acid and protein. Further, photosynthetic procaryotes never contain chlorophyll *a* or chloroplasts. In addition

to nuclear membranes, these cells lack mito-chondria, Golgi apparatus, lysosomes, and cen-trioles. The flagella of procaryotes do not have the 9 + 2 microtubule pattern shown by the cilia and flagella of nucleated cells (Figure 5–2).

Procaryotes are often classified as the king-dom *Monera*, whereas all eucaryotic organisms are placed in three kingdoms—*Protista, Metaphyta* (plants), and *Metazoa* (animals). We use this classification system in this book.

Protistan Cells

Many eucaryotic organisms, such as *Euglena*, exist as single cells. Other eucaryotic organisms

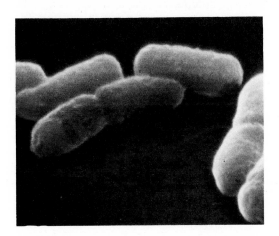

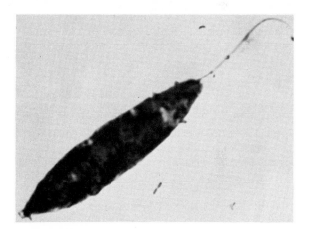

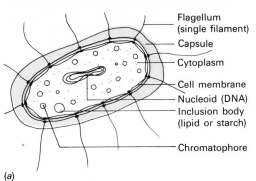

Flagellum (single filament)
Capsule
Cytoplasm
Cell membrane
Nucleoid (DNA)
Inclusion body (lipid or starch)
Chromatophore

(a)

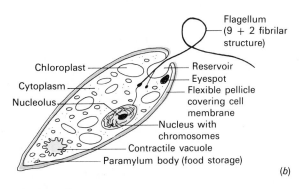

Flagellum (9 + 2 fibrilar structure)
Chloroplast
Cytoplasm
Nucleolus
Reservoir
Eyespot
Flexible pellicle covering cell membrane
Nucleus with chromosomes
Contractile vacuole
Paramylum body (food storage)

(b)

FIGURE 5–2 A comparison of the structure of procaryotic and eucaryotic cells: (*a*) bacterium and (*b*) *Euglena*. Note the greater complexity and organization in the eucaryotic cell. The procaryotic cell lacks an organized nucleus and has no membranous organelles. Flagella in a procaryotic cell do not have 9 + 2 microtubule structure. (Courtesy of Dr. David Greenwood and Carolina Biological Supply Company.)

are simply aggregations or colonies of similar cells—*Volvox* is one example. And fungi and most brown, red, and green algae are eucaryotes composed of a group of nearly identical cells. The cells in all these organisms have a mixture of characteristics we generally associate with plant cells or with animal cells. In other words, this large group of living systems cannot be called true plants or animals. For convenience and for a clearer understanding of evolution, these organisms are classified as Protista.

A good example of a protist is the green, one-celled *Euglena* (Figure 5–2). It moves with a whiplike flagellum and sometimes ingests food like an animal cell. But since *Euglena* contains chlorophyll, it can synthesize food like a green plant. Most authorities agree that flagellate protistans are living examples of early forms of life.

Plant and Animal Cells

At higher levels of development, organisms are commonly classified as either plants or animals. Plant cells generally lack centrioles but have cell walls and large central vacuoles; and in addition, they usually contain chlorophyll. Animal cells contain centrioles and lack cell walls and chlorophyll; in addition, many animal cells are capable of locomotion. At some point in their evolutionary development, animal cells lost chlorophyll and, with it, the ability to make their own food. Plant cells lost centrioles and, in most cases, the ability to move (Figure 5–1).

Plant cells commonly have nonliving outer walls that are hardened and porous. Unlike cell membranes, plant cell walls have no selective permeability. Since cell walls are porous, most substances pass through them. They are composed of two layers: an outer primary wall, which is the first to be formed, and an inner secondary wall. The major structural component of these walls is cellulose. An additional lamella (layer) may be formed between the primary walls of adjacent cells. This middle lamella, which is important in holding cells together, is composed of a colloidal substance called *pectin*. Pectin, a polymer of the six-carbon sugar galactose, is added to fruits to make

jellies. In older tissues soft pectin may become hardened by the accumulation of calcium to form calcium pectate. In woody plants a tough, gluelike substance called *lignin* is impregnated in cellulose walls to help bind wood-fiber cells together to form a solid material.

A central vacuole (Figure 5–3) is very common in plant cells; it functions in the cell's water balance and waste removal. Since the nonliving cell wall forms a rigid framework, cells cannot swell to accommodate changes in osmotic conditions. The central vacuole therefore regulates osmotic balance by losing or gaining water. The vacuole contains a slightly viscous colloid which may include salts, mineral ions, proteins, sugars, and pigments. The central vacuole can also act as a "dump" for wastes, since plants have no excretory system.

TISSUES: THE ORGANIZATION OF CELLS

In the preceding chapter we drew an analogy between cells and bricks as building blocks. Like individual bricks in a building, cells in a

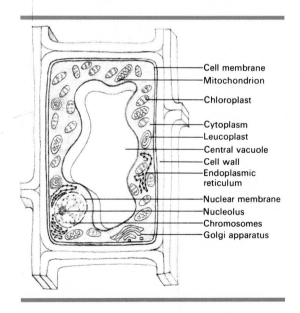

FIGURE 5–3   **Leaf cell of *Elodea*, a common aquarium plant, showing the major organelles.**

multicellular organism are organized into functional structures. Groups of similar cells working together to perform specific functions are called *tissues.*

Because the fossil evidence is inadequate, we have only hypotheses about the origin of multicellular organisms. Certain single-celled green flagellates, which are among the oldest known eucaryotic forms of life, appear to have structures common to both plants and animals. According to one hypothesis, these unicellular organisms gave rise to the great variety of multicellular organisms. But a green flagellate is a complete organism. This hypothesis suggests that groups of similar cells formed cellular *colonies* in which the individual cells were not completely independent. (Many eucaryotic colonial forms, such as certain green algae and sponges, exist today. Procaryotic colonial forms—certain blue green algae—also exist.)

As organisms with more cells developed, their cells became more dependent on one another. Eventually, various essential functions were assumed by specialized cells within an organism. Finally, according to this hypothesis, similar specialized cells came together to form the functional groups we call tissues. In both plants and animals, tissues provide protection, support, circulation, growth, reproduction, and other requirements. But plant and animal versions of these tissues are structurally and functionally so different that we shall consider them separately.

PLANT TISSUES

Plant tissues are identified and named according to location and function. The four basic types of plant tissues and their functions are *meristematic* (growth), *vascular* (conduction), *fundamental* (storage and support), and *epidermal* (protection). Before discussing specific examples of plant tissues we must note that there are several basic types of plants, including mosses, ferns, and seed plants. The arrangement of tissues in plant organs varies widely. For example, stem and leaf structure differ markedly in the two main groups of seed plants.

The complexity of tissue organization increases from mosses through ferns to conifers and flowering plants. We will limit our detailed discussion of plant tissues to those of the seed plants—the *gymnosperms* (conifers) and *angiosperms* (flowering plants). All seed plants are members of a larger grouping, the *vascular* plants. These are the plants with specialized conducting (vascular) tissues organized into true roots, stems, and leaves.

Angiosperms may be further divided into the orders *Dicotyledonae* (dicots) and *Monocotyledonae* (monocots). Dicots may be herbaceous (lacking lignin) like a pansy, or they may be woody like an apple tree. Typical examples of monocots are lilies, grasses, corn, and palms.

Meristematic Tissue

Meristematic tissues in plants provide for growth. All primary tissues of seed plants differentiate from a group of rapidly dividing cells known as *apical meristems*, located at stem and root tips. Cell division in these areas causes increase in the plant's length and gives rise to the epidermis, cortex, pith, and some portions of the vascular tissues. The subsequent thickening and growth of a maturing plant results primarily from cell divisions in the lateral vascular and cork cambiums (Figure 5-4). The cellular regions of a growing root and an apical meristem are illustrated in Figure 5-5.

The cambium layers, present as complete rings of tissue in gymnosperms and woody dicots, give rise to vascular tissues. This cambium sheath is poorly developed in herbaceous dicots and is always absent in monocots.

Vascular Tissue

Vascular tissues composed of tubelike cells provide for the transport of certain fluids within an organism. The vascular tissues of plants are called *xylem* and *phloem.* The stem of an herbaceous monocot stem such as corn gives a graphic example of the location of xylem and phloem. Vascular bundles, which are groups of xylem and phloem, are scattered throughout the supportive tissues of the stem. The arrangement of each vascular bundle resembles a monkey face. The forehead is composed of a patch of thin-walled phloem cells (sieve tubes) and

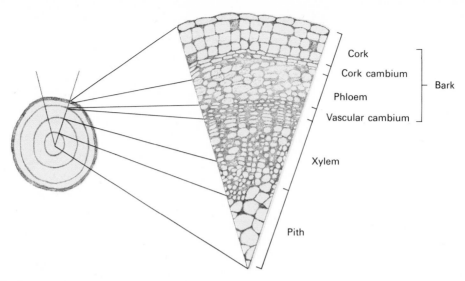

FIGURE 5–4 Location of tissues in the woody stem of an elder-
berry, an angiosperm. Note the two layers of xylem—the larger
cells near the center are produced in the spring of the year, and
the smaller xylem cells are produced in summer.

companion cells, and the eyes and nose are
vessel tubes of xylem. What appears as the
mouth is an air space formed by the rupture of
a rapidly-growing xylem vessel (Figure 5–6, on
the color plate adjacent).

In woody plants the vascular cambium produces rings of xylem and phloem (Figure 5–4).
Each year, after spring and summer growth, the
old phloem layer dies and is pushed outward by
new phloem; it becomes part of the bark.
Xylem layers to the inside of the vascular cambium are left as wood; they provide support to
the stem as well as conduction. Thus the rings
of xylem present in a stem indicate the age of a
tree. A year's growth of xylem actually shows
two bands—an inner band of large conducting
tubes known as spring wood and an adjacent
outer band of smaller tubes known as summer
wood. The greater availability of soil moisture
in the spring leads to faster growth and formation of larger cells than during the summer.

Xylem
Water and minerals are conducted upward
from the roots through xylem. In this way
leaves receive raw materials for use in photo-

synthesis. In the winter and early spring sugars
are found in the xylem of some trees. These
sugars usually result from the conversion of
starch to sugar in the storage tissues.

There are two types of xylem tissues: the
conducting tubes called *tracheids* and those
called *vessels*. Conifers and other softwoods
possess only tracheids, whereas hardwoods
contain both tracheids and vessels. Tracheids
are elongate cells tapered at both ends. At maturity, the cell contents of both tracheids and
vessels die, leaving a large empty cavity. Thin
areas called *pits* along the cell walls allow water
and minerals to pass from one cell to the next.
Thickenings of lignified cellulose called *secondary thickenings* form annular, reticulated,
or spiral rings along the cell walls (Figure 5–7).

Although vessel cells of herbs and hardwoods
also contain pits, they have additional openings
or pores at the cell ends to form a continuous
open tube. Vessels have a larger diameter than
tracheids, so they allow easier passage of fluids.
Not all cells in the xylem are dead. Young,
living xylem cells are located in rays throughout the wood; they store food and function in
lateral conduction.

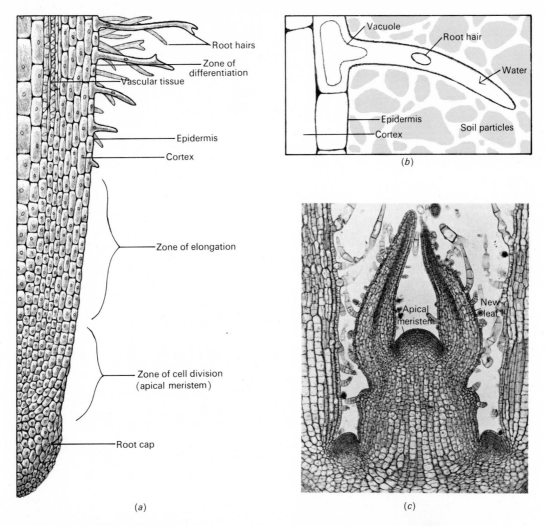

(a)

(b)

(c)

FIGURE 5–5 Cellular regions of a growing root and stem tip.
(a) Longitudinal section of a growing root. Note the proliferation of
cells forming the root cap. (b) Root hair in soil. (c) Growing stem
tip of the common houseplant *Coleus*, showing meristematic tissue. (Courtesy of Triarch, Inc., Ripon, Wisconsin.)

Phloem

Living phloem tissue can be easily observed; it
is the slick, glistening layer on the inner surface
of tree bark. The cells of these food-transport-
ing tissues are unique in that their end walls,
called *sieve plates*, are perforated with many
small openings (Figure 5–7). Phloem cells,
stacked end-to-end like xylem cells, are known
as *sieve tubes*. But unlike xylem cells, phloem
contains slimy strands of protoplasm that
stretch from cell to cell through the pores of
sieve plates. Phloem cells which have no nuclei
at maturity are thought to be controlled by
adjacent, nucleated companion cells through
cytoplasmic connections. Sugar and other organic compounds move downward in the

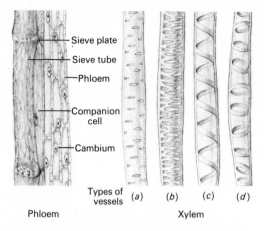

FIGURE 5-7   Conducting structures of angio-sperms. Left: longitudinal section of phloem and cambium. Right: longitudinal section of xylem vessels. (*a*) Pitted. (*b*) Reticulated. (*c*) Spiral. (*d*) Annular.

phloem to nourish the actively absorbing and growing roots. Nutrients especially in the spring, may also be transported upward in the phloem to nourish developing buds and flowers.

Fundamental Tissue

In a young plant stem, regions utilized specifically for support and storage are *pith* and *cortex*, which are composed primarily of fundamental tissues. As we will see, fundamental tissues are specialized to provide this support and storage. Although xylem is obviously an important supporting tissue in woody plants, its primary function is conduction. The three tissues that are collectively termed *fundamental* include *parenchyma, collenchyma,* and *sclerenchyma* (Figure 5–8). The cortex of a plant often includes all three types, whereas pith is composed only of parenchyma.

Parenchyma

Parenchyma is a living tissue found in unspecialized regions of all parts of a plant. Parenchyma cells vary in shape, generally contain a central vacuole, and retain their capacity for cell division. Their uniformly thin walls push

against one another like soap bubbles. The functions of parenchyma cells include food making, storage, and support. The soft parts of apples, potatoes, and melons are parenchyma.

Collenchyma

Collenchyma is a living tissue with tough cell walls that are unevenly thickened in the "corners" where adjacent cells meet. Chloroplasts are often present in the cytoplasm. Pectin compounds in the cell walls give collenchyma strength and elasticity. The cortex cylinder of growing stems and roots often contains this support tissue. The tough, stringy fibers in the ridges of celery are produced by collenchyma.

Sclerenchyma

Sclerenchyma is much less flexible than collenchyma. The secondary cell walls of sclerenchyma become very thick and hard at maturity. At that time the cells die and lose their cytoplasm. Both collenchyma and sclerenchyma may occur in long bundles or sheaths in cortex and pith. The hard shells of nuts and peach pits are made of sclerenchyma cells.

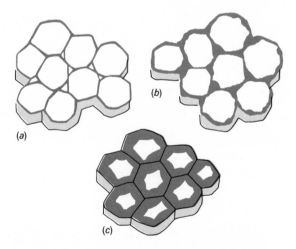

FIGURE 5-8   The three types of fundamental plant tissues in plants. (*a*) Parenchyma. Note the thin walls and many-sided cells. (*b*) Collenchyma. Note the thickened walls, especially at the corners of the cells. (*c*) Sclerenchyma. The cell walls are greatly thickened and often very hard.

Epidermal Tissue

The protective outer covering of young plants is called the *epidermis* (from the Greek *epi*, "outer", and *derma*, "layer"). It is generally a single cell layer thick and is organized into a thin sheath. Epidermal cells are flattened and many-sided.

The epidermis of leaves shows several functional adaptations. Both the upper and lower epidermis of a leaf usually have a secreted cuticle of a waxy substance known as *cutin*, which helps the leaf retain water. This cuticle is particularly thick on the leaves of desert plants. Many stems and leaves also possess tiny hairs which are outgrowths of epidermal cells. Perhaps the most interesting epidermal structures are the tiny openings that regulate the exchange of water and gases with the environment. These openings, called *stomata*, are controlled by the swelling or shrinking of two adjacent guard cells (Figure 5–9, on color plate following p. 112).

The action of guard cells appears to be controlled by osmotic pressure. Production of sugar by guard cell chloroplasts during daylight causes increased osmotic pressure and swelling. When water moves into guard cells because of this high osmotic pressure, the stomata open. At night osmotic pressure decreases as sugar is used for energy and converted to larger starch molecules. Loss of water to adjacent epidermal cells causes the guard cells to become limp and the openings to close. (Recall that osmotic conditions are determined by the number of dissolved particles.)

In mature woody stems, the original epidermis has been replaced by developing bark. This complex of cork and old phloem is continually being pushed outward and eroded as the plant ages.

We have seen that plants possess tissues related to their particular needs: epidermal tissues for protection, meristematic for growth, fundamental for support, and vascular for conduction. Not all plants contain all these tissues; nor do various plants contain them in the same ratios. For example, the simplest land plants, such as mosses and liverworts, do not contain vascular tissues at all.

ANIMAL TISSUES

Animals are functionally different from plants in some striking ways. The energy requirements of such active animals as hummingbirds are certainly much greater than those of sedentary plants. This and other differences in what might be called "strategies of survival" are based on structural differences involving cells and tissues. We considered some of the cellular differences earlier in this chapter.

Most animals move; this movement helps them obtain food and avoid predators and other dangers. The movements of most animals are accomplished by *muscle* tissues. Efficient animal movement depends on internal coordination of muscle, bone, and other tissues. It also depends on the ability to obtain and process information about the external environment: the animal must know what to move toward or away from.

Most animals have developed *nerve* tissues to meet these coordinating and information-gathering requirements. The ability of some simple animals to move and to process information is primitive by mammalian standards, because their muscle and nerve tissues are primitive by mammalian standards. But although their structural details and degrees of complexity differ, these specialized tissues serve the same general purposes in all animals.

Besides muscles and nerve, basic animal tissues include *epithelial* tissues (for protection) and *connective* tissues (for support and circulation).

Epithelial Tissue

Epithelial tissues cover the exterior surfaces of an animal's body and line its cavities. Cells of epithelial tissues may also function in secretion or absorption. Intestinal glands, for example, empty secretions into the gut through special ducts. Nutrients provided by the action of digestive enzymes are absorbed into the circulatory system through the intestinal lining. The primary function of epithelial tissues, however, is protection. Epithelial cells may have various shapes: *squamous* (flat, scalelike), *cuboidal*, or *columnar* (Figure 5–10).

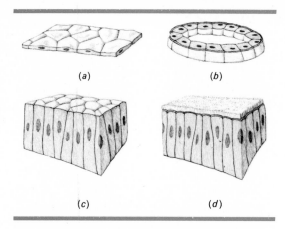

FIGURE 5–10   Examples of epithelial types. (a) Squamous. (b) Cuboidal. (c) Columnar. (d) Ciliated columnar.

Squamous Cells

Squamous or "pavement" epithelium is composed of extremely thin cells. These cells are usually so thin that the nucleus bulges out when they are viewed from the edge. This type of tissue lines the inside of the mouth and the body cavities; it also covers the body as skin epidermis. In the skin, these cells are stacked in thick layers called stratified squamous epithelium (Figure 5–11, on color plate following p. 112).

Cuboidal Cells

In vertical profile, individual cells of cuboidal epithelium are cube-shaped. A surface view of a sheet of these cells, however, often shows a hexagonal pattern. Cuboidal epithelium is found in many glands and gland ducts, as in the urine-collecting tubules in kidneys (Figure 5–12), on color plate following p. 112).

Columnar Cells

Columnar cells are taller than cuboidal cells; they form the lining tissue of such organs as the small intestine (Figure 5–13, on color plate following p. 112). Both columnar and cuboidal cells may possess tiny hairlike structures called cilia (Figure 5–10). Cilia have the ability to move in a whiplike, rhythmical motion. Ducts that require continuous clearing of foreign par-

ticles, such as the nasal passages and the trachea, contain many ciliated cells. Research suggests that ciliary movement occurs when microtubules in the cilium slide past one another.

Connective Tissue

Tissues responsible for support in animal bodies fall into several categories: (1) loose or areolar; (2) dense, such as tendon, cartilage, and bone; and (3) fat-storing adipose tissue. Connective tissues contain tough fibers of a protein called *collagen*; they may also have yellow elastic fibers of a protein called *elastin*. Depending on location and function, connective tissues may be loose, as in mesenteries which support internal organs, or more compact, as in the layers underlying the skin. Loose connective tissue allows for movement and pliability. This is especially important in the digestive tract, where food must be moved by rhythmic muscular contractions (peristalsis). Dense connective tissues such as tendon, cartilage, and bone occur where structural strength is required.

Besides these tough support tissues, a unique fluid tissue—blood—is essential to the life processes of higher animals. Although blood is not connective in the same sense as bone, cartilage, or tendon, it is a tissue. (Recall the definition of a tissue given at the beginning of this chapter: *a group of similar cells working together to perform a specific function.*) Blood is usually classed as a connective tissue because it provides communication among all cells of the body. Blood cells are derived from the same embryonic cells (the mesoderm) that form all other connective tissues. We shall discuss blood more closely later in this chapter; the differentiation of embryonic cells into basic tissues will be discussed in Chapter 16.

Loose or Areolar Tissue

This type of tissue occurs under the dermis of skin; through its elastic properties it helps hold the skin to muscles. Most common in this tissue are undifferentiated cells called *fibroblasts*, which synthesize collagenous and elastic fibers. Next in number are large phagocytic

Bio-Topic: The $6,000,000 Person

Some years ago, a chemist calculated that the elements in a human body were worth about 97 cents. To be sure, inflation has raised this price a bit over the years. But this narrow chemical viewpoint overlooks the fact that in humans and in all living systems the elements are organized into enormously information-rich assemblies: vitamins, hormones, enzymes and other proteins, nucleic acids, organelles, cells, tissues, organs.

Let's start at the molecular level. Hemoglobin can be purchased from a biochemical supply company at about $3 a gram. A gram of insulin goes for just under $50. If these prices seem trivial, consider crystalline DNA at $768 per gram or a gram of acetate kinase at an even $8660. For the really big spender, there is follicle-stimulating hormone at $4,800,000 a gram or prolactin at a current price of about $17,500,000 the gram. (Read about these two in Chapter 12.)

Harold Morowitz of Yale University added figures like these together recently and calculated that the organic molecules and macromolecules in a person of average weight (75 kg, 165 lb) are worth about $6,000,000 at current prices. But these are bargain basement prices. What might be the cost of a gram of endoplasmic reticulum or cilia or other organelles? And the street price of a gram of artificially assembled cells might approach the size of the national debt—if we knew how to assemble cells. Even that's not the end. We can't even begin to estimate the cost of an assembled liver or spleen, let alone an eye or, the ultimate, a brain.

The point of Morowitz's calculations is that living systems are incredibly information-rich, and information costs. Living systems achieve and maintain their information-dense condition by investing energy obtained from the nutrients that sustain them. To duplicate this investment in the laboratory—even if the resources were available—is presently beyond our wildest imagining.

Dr. Frankenstein was a piker.

cells known as *macrophages*, which ingest foreign substances.

Tendon

Tendons connect muscles to bones; the Achilles tendon above the heel is a common example. Tendons are composed of a compact arrangement of collagenous fibers. The fibroblast cells which secrete these fibers are squeezed in among them. The major portion of the tendon is nonliving (Figure 5–14, on color plate following p. 112).

Cartilage

The function of cartilage is to give firm support without rigidity. There are various types of cartilage, but they are basically similar in cellular detail. Living cartilage cells, *chondrocytes*, secrete around themselves a semisolid *matrix* material composed of polysaccharide and protein. All cartilage contains protein fibers to a greater or lesser degree. Hyaline cartilage which lines the joints and forms the end of the nose and the rings of the trachea, is tough but flexible. In contrast, the outer ear cartilage, called elastic cartilage, contains more flexible, springy elastic fibers (Figure 5–15, on color plate following p. 112). A very strong cartilage, fibrocartilage, contains a dense network of protein fibers. It is found between the vertebrae as intervertebral discs.

Bone

We are all familiar with bone and its function, structural support. A thin section of bone shows a complicated pattern of cells and canals (Figure 5–16, on color plate following p. 112). Living bone cells, *osteocytes*, are located in tiny chambers called *lacunae* in compact, calcified bone. These cells are connected to one another and to the central marrow cavity by a network of tiny canals called *canaliculi*. All nutrients reaching these cells must pass through these tiny channels from a main nutrient canal, the *Haversian canal*, which brings blood and nerves into compact bone from the outer covering.

There are two basic types of bone: one develops from a cartilage "model" (endochondrial ossification), and the other replaces a membrane (intramembranous ossification). The long bones of the arms and legs, for example, develop slowly from cartilage, whereas some bones of the cranium form within a special membrane.

In either case, bone tissue is originally organic material. The original matrix undergoes *calcification*—replacement by inorganic calcium salts—to form the hard, nonliving material. But even mature bone tissue is not completely dead. It contains many living osteocytes in the lacunae of calcified bone. Even the calcified material is continually replaced as calcium salts are removed from and returned to the bone matrix.

Adipose Tissue

Adipose tissue is composed of special cells that store fat. The nuclei of the mature cells are pushed up against one side of the cell membrane by the accumulation of fats in the cytoplasm (Figure 5–17, on color plate following p. 112). Besides storing food, adipose tissues function as packing for support and as protection for internal organs. Adipose tissue is found in the subcutaneous layer of skin (Figure 5–29) and in and around many organs.

Blood Tissue

Earlier we saw that cells must take in raw materials and release waste products. And we have seen that tissues are made of cells. Blood, itself a fluid tissue, brings nourishment to the cells of animal tissues and removes their wastes and other products. In this process, blood transports various materials, including food, vitamins, and gases. It also transports chemical signals in the form of *hormones*, the "chemical messengers" of organisms. Blood is composed of several cell types floating in a fluid matrix or *plasma*. Pigments that transport oxygen occur in the blood, either dissolved in plasma (as in the earthworm) or contained in cells (as in mammals).

In humans, cellular components make up about 45 percent of the blood (Figure 5–18, on color plate following p. 112); the remaining fluid is plasma. Noncellular plasma contains water, dissolved salts and nutrients, hormones, gases, and antibodies. Certain proteins are also present in plasma. These include serum albumin, serum globulin, fibroginen (which is necessary for clotting), and complement (which works with antibodies to destroy foreign cells).

RED BLOOD CELLS (RBCs). In vertebrates the oxygen-carrying cells are called red blood cells (RBCs) because the oxygen-carrying substance is the red pigment *hemoglobin*. RBCs are also called *erythrocytes*. Not all erythrocytes are the same size or shape. For example, the nucleated erythrocytes of amphibian blood are very large and elongated compared with those of a mammal (24 microns for a frog to 7.7 microns for a human). Human red blood cells, produced in red bone marrow, are small discs which lose their nuclei when they mature (Figure 5–19). Because an RBC lacks a nucleus and has lost its ability to synthesize proteins, its average life span is about 120 days. After that period it is destroyed in the spleen or the liver. Red blood cells of all vertebrates except mammals possess nuclei.

WHITE BLOOD CELLS (WBCs). The blood of humans and other vertebrates also contains colorless cells called white blood cells (WBCs), or *leucocytes*. Leucocytes are larger than erythrocytes (10 to 12 microns); they can be identified by their large, characteristically shaped nuclei. Leucocytes ingest bacteria and waste particles by means of *phagocytosis*. They also

FIGURE 5-19   Scanning electron micrograph of a human bioconcave red blood cell (RBC) enmeshed in fibrin of a clot. A red blood cell is about 7.7 microns in diameter. (Courtesy of Emil Bernstein and Eila Kairinen, Gillette Company Research Institute, Rockville, MD.)

produce antibodies. The number of white cells varies; it may increase greatly when the body is infected. Leukemia, a malignant disease of the blood and blood-producing tissues, occurs when the production of white blood cells goes out of control. This uncontrolled, abnormal growth is currently thought to be caused by viruses.

Most leucocytes are produced in red bone marrow. They are classified in two general groups, granular and agranular, according to the presence or absence of stainable granules in their cytoplasm. Granular leucocytes include *neutrophils* (which are phagocytes), *eosinophils* (which remove toxic substances produced in immunity reactions), and *basophils* (which release an anticoagulant). Agranular leucocytes include *lymphocytes* (which produce antibodies) and *monocytes* (which are phagocytes).

PLATELETS.   Platelets are fragments of large cells (megakaryocytes) produced in bone marrow. These fragments contain the enzyme *thromboplastin*, which is essential to blood clotting (Figure 5-20). A blood clot is a mesh of insoluble fibrin that traps all the nearby blood cells and platelets. The fluid remaining after a clot is formed is called *blood serum*.

Muscle Tissue

There are three types of muscle tissue: smooth, skeletal, and cardiac. Although the main function of all three is contractile, each is highly specialized.

Smooth Muscle

Smooth muscles are sometimes called *involuntary* muscles because their action is usually not under conscious control. They are located in visceral organs and are responsible for such movements as *peristalsis*. Smooth muscle fibers also occur in the walls of blood vessels and the uterus.

Smooth muscle tissues have the simplest cells of the three muscle tissue types. An individual muscle cell, called a *fiber*, is capable of independent contraction (Figure 5-21, on color plate following p. 112). The muscle cytoplasm, or *sarcoplasm*, of each spindle-shaped cell contains contractile protein fibers called *myofibrils*. A smooth muscle is composed of many cells grouped into a bundle.

Skeletal Muscle

Movement of skeletal, or *striated*, muscle tissues is primarily under conscious direction. Striated means banded or lined; under the microscope, many crossbands can be seen along the fibers of skeletal muscle. Careful observation with the electron microscope coupled with chemical analysis has demonstrated that the striations are produced by specific arrangements of two protein fibrils—actin and myosin

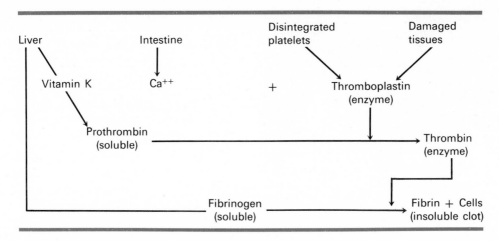

FIGURE 5–20 Interacting substances and their sources in blood clotting. Prothrombin and fibrinogen are soluble blood proteins produced in the liver. Vitamin K is necessary for the synthesis of prothrombin. A deficiency of vitamin K produces symptoms similar to bleeder's disease (hemophilia).

(Figure 5–22, on color plate following p. 112). As in smooth muscle, myofibrils compose the contractile elements of the skeletal muscle fiber. Striated muscle cells each contain several nuclei, all of which are located near the membrane; they are *multinucleate*. The contractile myofibrils within each fiber show a definite banded pattern of striations, set off by dark-staining bands called *Z lines* (Figure 5–23). The banded area between the Z lines is termed a *sarcomere*. The overlapping arrangement of myosin (thick filament) and actin (thin filament) proteins produces the bands of varying density within the sarcomere. In cross section, the filaments appear in hexagonal patterns.

So far we have discussed the muscle as a tissue at rest. What happens when a muscle contracts? Depending on the strength of the stimulus, a nerve impulse or a mild electric shock will cause a certain number of muscle fibers to contract. Physiological studies have shown that increasing the strength of the stimulus causes a corresponding increase in the strength of muscle contraction. In vertebrate muscle, each fiber contracts to its greatest extent when stimulated; muscle contractions of varied strengths thus depend on the number of fibers that are stimulated.

When contraction occurs, the thin actin filaments move together between the thick myosin filaments with a sliding motion. This action changes the pattern (Figure 5–23) as follows: the Z bands are brought closer together, since the actin filaments are anchored to them, and the H zones—which represent the spaces between the actin filaments—disappear. Because this shortening involves thousands of end-to-end groups of filaments throughout the entire muscle, a great contraction can occur and considerable force can be exerted. When the muscle relaxes, the actin filaments return to their original condition.

The thick filaments (myosin) have projections called *cross bridges* which extend to touch the actin filaments. Each crossbridge ends in an enlargement, or head, where it touches an actin filament (Figure 5–24). During contraction the action is primarily in the region of this head, where ATP is hydrolyzed to provide the energy for contraction. The mechanism by which ATP energy causes the sets of interlayered filaments to slide along one another is now a subject of intense research. Although we have some clues about this process, the molecular mechanism is not completely understood.

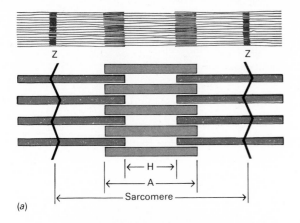

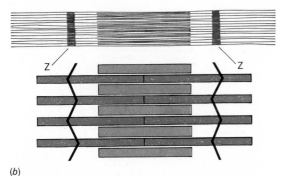

FIGURE 5-23   Model of striated muscle. Myosin is shown in gray. (*a*) The regions of crossbanding are lettered as they appear in relaxed muscle. (*b*) The contracted state.

We know that contraction of a muscle is initiated by a change in the permeability of a muscle-cell membrane to calcium after the arrival of a nerve impulse. The small amount of calcium which enters the muscle fiber reacts with a special regulatory protein called *troponin*, located on the thin filaments. In the absence of calcium, troponin inhibits the interaction of thin and thick filaments. But in the presence of calcium, interaction between the filaments occurs and contraction results.

Cardiac Muscle

Cardiac or heart muscle is a striated muscle that begins regular rhythmic contractions during embryonic development and continues to beat throughout the lifetime of an organism. In vertebrates, the heartbeat rhythm is controlled principally through nerve impulses originating in the *medulla* of the brain. Contractility appears to be inherent in the muscle tissue itself, that is, it contracts without stimulation. The fine structure of the myofibrils of cardiac muscle is similar to that of skeletal muscle. The nuclei of cardiac muscle cells, however, are located in the center of the fiber rather than along the outer membrane.

Cardiac muscle is arranged in overlapping sheets surrounding the heart cavities. Individual fibers are broad and many-sided in shape; that is, the cell membranes are irregular and branching.

Nerve Tissue

The animal tissues that provide for control and communication are found in the brain, spinal cord, nerves, and nerve endings. The fundamental element of nerve tissue is the nerve cell or *neuron*. Several other specialized cell types are also found in this tissue, but the neuron is the "functional unit."

A typical neuron is composed of a cell body and long, slender extensions. These filaments associate with similar ones from other neurons to form a communication network (Figure 5-25, on color plate following p. 112). The cytoplasm of a neuron contains a nucleus, nucleolus, mitochondria, Golgi apparatus, and many small particles of RNA and protein known as Nissl bodies (Figure 5-26). Cellular structures called *axons* and *dendrites* extend from the cell body. Certain animal axons are more than a meter long—an impressive length for a structure that is a part of a single cell!

The formation and propagation of nerve impulses will be explained in detail in Chapter 12, but we will summarize very briefly here. A bioelectrical nerve impulse produced by chemical events travels along the cell membrane from a dendrite toward the axon. In this manner the axon of one cell excites one or more dendrites of an adjoining cell, and the impulse is carried the length of the neuron "chain." Notice that the nerve impulse travels *toward* the cell body along dendrites and *away* from the cell body along the axon. At the tips of the

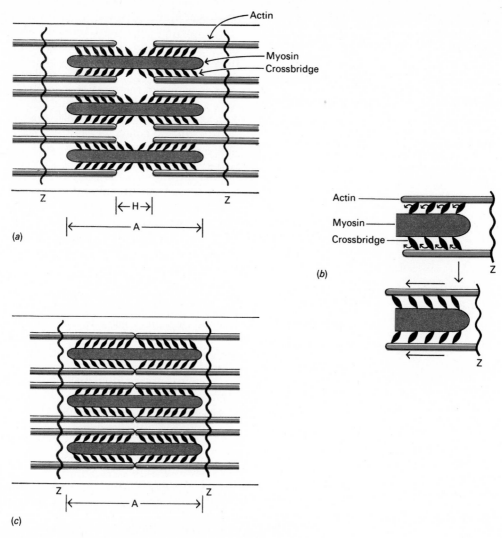

FIGURE 5–24 A proposed model to explain the sliding filament mechanism of muscle contraction. (*a*) Myosin with crossbridges attached to actin filaments in relaxed condition. (*b*) Myosin crossbridges tilt to produce a ratchetlike relative movement of actin and myosin. The Z-lines are thereby moved closer together and the muscle shortens. (*c*) Contracted state, showing disappearance of the H zone and shortening of the distance between the Z lines; the A band, represented by myosin, always remains the same.

axons are small bulbous structures called *synaptic knobs* (Figure 5–27). These tiny structures come very close to, but do not quite touch, the tips of the dendrites belonging to adjacent neurons. A small space of approxi-

mately 200 Å, called a *synaptic cleft*, lies between these endings. The terminal portion (synaptic knob) of an axon is called the presynaptic component. The region of a dendrite adjacent to the end of the axon is called the

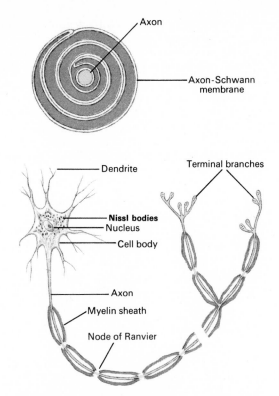

Axon

Axon-Schwann membrane

Dendrite

Terminal branches

Nissl bodies
Nucleus

Cell body

Axon

Myelin sheath

Node of Ranvier

FIGURE 5–26   Myelinated neuron. At upper left is a greatly enlarged cross-sectional view of an axon and its myelin sheath.

correspond to the ribosomal parts of other cells. Nissl bodies provide the concentrated complex of protein-producing organelles these cells need to sustain large amounts of cytoplasm and intense activity.

In vertebrates, the central area of the spinal cord is gray in color because it is composed of nerve cell bodies which have no myelin. Peripheral areas of the cord, however, are composed of white, glistening nerve tracts known as white matter. The white color comes from fatty *myelin sheaths* that surround axons (Figure 5–26). There are gaps in the myelin coating called *nodes of Ranvier*. Myelin is formed into a sheath around an axon by nearby Schwann cells. During development, these cells wrap themselves around the axon to form a spiral layer of membrane and myelin.

The speed of impulse transmission in myelinated nerves is about four times as great as in nonmyelinated nerves. The fatty sheath was first thought merely to protect the cell membrane as insulation protects an electric wire, but it has been found that the impulse actually

postsynaptic component (Figure 5–27). The traveling nerve impulse triggers tiny vesicles in the synaptic knob to secrete *acetylcholine*, which in turn excites the adjacent dendrites. Chemical reactions at a synapse keep nerve impulses flowing from axons to dendrites.

Immediately after acetylcholine is produced, an enzyme called *cholinesterase* splits the chemical into nonreactive components. The synapse is thus prepared to transfer a new impulse. The apparent function of acetylcholine is to change the ionic permeability of the postsynaptic membrane.

Nissl bodies, first described in 1876, were thought to be related to the nuclear material, since they were stained by nuclear dyes. It was supposed that the Nissl substance somehow supplemented nuclear function during nerve activity. The Nissl substance is now known to

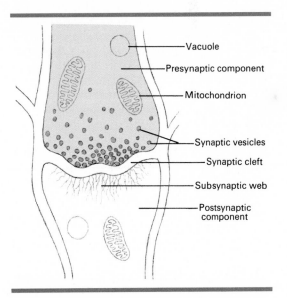

Vacuole

Presynaptic component

Mitochondrion

Synaptic vesicles

Synaptic cleft

Subsynaptic web

Postsynaptic component

FIGURE 5–27   Synaptic region between an axon and a dendrite, showing a synaptic cleft and a synaptic knob.

travels through the intercellular fluids from node to node. Thus the impulse does not have to pass through the entire length of an axon membrane, and the time required to reach the synapse is greatly shortened. The biologist DeForest Mellon, Jr. has described the "speedup" process this way: "The situation is rather analogous to the passage of a telegraph message over two different pathways, each of which is 100 miles long. If the message over one pathway is received and retransmitted at two relay points, it will reach the terminal telegraph station much faster than over a second pathway where it must be received and passed on at each of ten relay points." In this analogy, the two-relay pathway is a myelinated nerve; the ten-relay pathway is a nonmyelinated nerve.

ORGANS: COOPERATING TISSUES

To continue our earlier analogy between biological structure and architecture, we now turn our attention to structures that are formed by the association of various types of tissues. Functional structures made up of several different tissues are called *organs*. In vertebrates, the small intestine, heart, lungs, and brain are all organs. A photograph of a cross section of the small intestine of a monkey, for example, shows four major regions: *mucosa, submucosa, muscularis,* and *serosa* (Figure 5–28).

The mucosa consists of a columnar epithelial lining, glands, and loose connective tissue supporting the villi (fingerlike projections on the inner surface of the intestine). Immediately below the mucosa lies the submucosa, a region containing closely packed connective tissues, intestinal glands, arterioles and venules, lymphatic vessels, and nerve fibers. The muscularis consists of an inner layer of circular smooth muscle and a thinner, external band of longitudinal muscle fibers. The organ is covered externally with the serosa, a thin layer of squamous epithelium.

Organs clearly illustrate the principle of *division of labor*, because each tissue has a specific function in that organ. For example, the epithelial cells of the mucosa layer of the intestine form a lining, and the muscle tissue of the muscularis provides for movement of the organ. An organ is thus capable of doing a job which could not be accomplished by each tissue functioning independently.

The skin of a mammal is composed of several tissue types; it also contains elements of the blood vascular organs (Figure 5–29). The outer layer of skin, the epidermis, is composed of stratified squamous epithelium. Squamous cells are constantly being formed at the base of the epidermis and pushed toward the surface where they become hardened, die, and are finally sloughed off. Cells in the deeper layers of the epidermis produce pigments which give color to the skin. The layer beneath the epidermis, the dermis, consists principally of connective tissue, blood vessels, nerve endings, hair follicles, sweat glands, and sebaceous (oil) glands. Sweat glands, sebaceous glands, and hairs are derived from the epidermis as invaginations into the dermis. A relatively loose attachment to the underlying muscles is provided by a subcutaneous layer of fat and connective tissues.

Plant leaves, stems, and roots are also organs. Leaves, for example, are composed of upper and lower epidermis, parenchyma tissue, and vascular tissues (xylem and phloem). Together these tissues form an efficient food-making organ. Leaf anatomy is discussed in Chapter 9 in connection with photosynthesis and food production.

ORGANISMS: INDEPENDENT LIVING SYSTEMS

Our concept of biological architecture finally leads us to recognize that organs can be organized into functional *systems*. In humans, for example, the mouth, esophagus, stomach, small intestine, and large intestine form the digestive system. Other systems include the respiratory, circulatory, reproductive, excretory, muscular, skeletal, endocrine, and nervous systems.

Some organs may contribute to more than one system. The liver, for example, participates in digestion, excretion, and circulation. All systems are integrated into a functional *organism* by nervous and hormonal control. The success of an organism thus depends on the orderly coordination of all organs as they func-

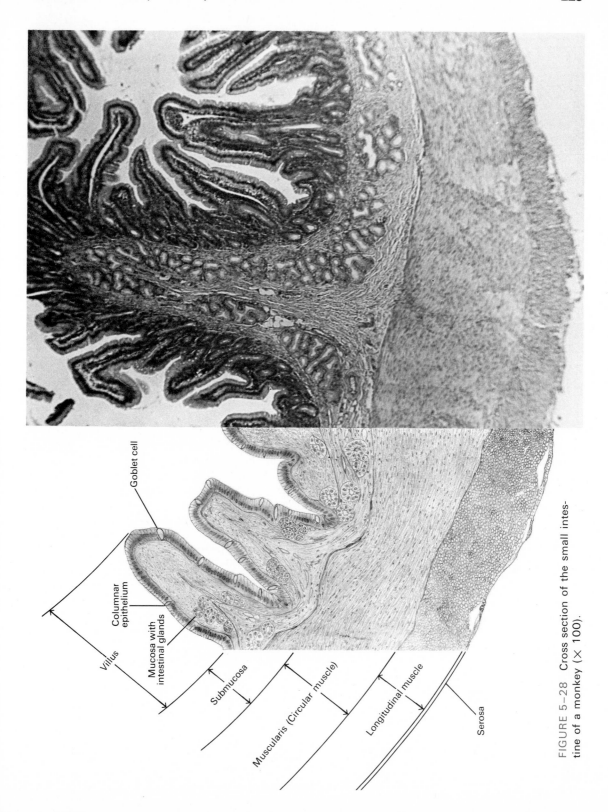

FIGURE 5–28 Cross section of the small intestine of a monkey ($\times$ 100).

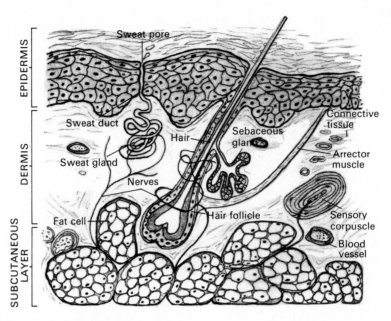

FIGURE 5–29 **Cross section of skin.**

tion together to meet the demands of the environment.

Organisms are the independent living units in nature. As we have seen, there are unicellular organisms, colonial organisms, and multicellular organisms with integrated organ systems. The rest of this book will deal with the structure, function, interaction, and diversity of organisms.

SUMMARY

The most basic distinction among living systems is whether the cells of an organism are eucaryotic or procaryotic. Bacteria and blue-green algae are procaryotes; that is, they lack a true cell nucleus. All other types of life are eucaryotes. Eucaryotes are thought to have arisen through cooperative combinations of procaryotic cells.

Procaryotes are placed in the kingdom Monera; all other cells are classified as Protista (single cells or aggregations of simple cells), Metaphyta (plants), or Metazoa (animals). Plants and animals are composed of tissues, groups of cells which perform specific func-

tions. Functions common to both plants and animals include support, circulation, growth, and reproduction.

The principal plant tissues are: meristematic (cambium); vascular (xylem and phloem); fundamental (parenchyma, collenchyma, and sclerenchyma); and epidermal (epidermis). The basic animal tissues include: epithelial (squamous, cuboidal, and columnar); connective (areolar, tendon, cartilage, bone, adipose, and blood); muscle (smooth, skeletal, and cardiac); and nerve.

Functional structures composed of more than one tissue are called organs. In humans, organs such as the heart, lungs, pancreas, and intestines have components of nearly all tissue types. The principle of division of labor is evident in organs, since each tissue performs specific functions. Organs are interrelated in functional organ systems which comprise the organism.

REVIEW QUESTIONS

1. How is a bacterium different from an amoeba? In what ways are they similar?

2. If a single cell from a frog's intestine is placed in pond water, it will soon die. Why?

3. What tissues would you expect to find in a mature tree stem? What are the principal functions of each?

4. Skeletal muscles show striated patterns that change during contraction and relaxation. How are these changes in pattern related to muscle structure?

5. How do nerve impulses pass across a synapse?

6. List one function for each of the following blood cells: erythrocyte, eosinophil, basophil, neutrophil, monocyte, and lymphocyte.

7. What is the structure of a clot? How is clotting initiated by platelets?

8. What tissues are commonly present in human skin? What is the function of each of these tissues?

SUPPLEMENTARY READINGS

Albersheim, Peter, "The Walls of Growing Plant Cells," *Scientific American*, April 1975. Plant cell walls not only contain cellulose which provides protection and support but also a number of sugars and proteins that participate in many cell wall functions.

Axelrod, Julius, "Neurotransmitters," *Scientific American*, June 1974. The mode of action of neurotransmitter substances such as acetylcholine and noradrenaline at the synaptic junction is examined. The effects of certain drugs are also discussed.

Cohen, Carolyn, "The Protein Switch of Muscle Contraction," *Scientific American*, November 1975. Calcium ions appear to trigger muscle contraction by combining with a muscle protein complex called troponin.

Freeman, W. H. and Brian Bracegirdle, *An Atlas of Histology*, 2nd edition, Dover Publications, New York, 1966. A good source of light microscope micrographs and labeled line drawings of human tissues.

Leeson, C. R. and T. S. Leeson, *Histology*, W. B. Saunders, Philadelphia, 1966. A general histology text dealing primarily with human cells and tissues.

Unit III
Community and Environment

No living system lives alone. Many organisms, of course, have only periodic contact with their own kind. Various animals, for example, are relative loners except during their mating seasons. An extreme example is that human loner, the hermit, who generally shuns other humans during all seasons. Nevertheless every organism is part of a community: *a varied group of organisms inhabiting a common environment and interacting in complex ways.* Hermits shun all human companionship. But even hermits interact with the plants that provide them with food, oxygen, and shade, and with the parasites and beneficial organisms that inhabit their bodies. A community almost always contains plants, animals, and microorganisms, because each type contributes to the survival of the others.

But the nonliving part of the environment is also important to organisms, because they derive their energy and inorganic nutrients from it. Many interactions take place between living systems, the biotic community, and the nonliving environment, the abiotic. Together, the biotic and abiotic realms form ecosystems. A forest with its lakes and meadows can be considered an ecosystem. So can a desert or a grassland, a small pond, a rotting tree stump, or even a tabletop aquarium. Ecosystems exist at various levels of size and complexity, and they can be studied at these different levels. We shall examine some of these in the chapters that follow.

Some interactions in an ecosystem are complex and difficult to determine, but we do understand the fundamental relationships of energy flow, chemical cycling, and productivity. We have also come to realize what can happen when an ecosystem is disturbed or parts of it destroyed. The characteristics and dynamics of living populations are also becoming better understood as we study the living communities of the world. Many of the characteristics and relationships of the major living communities—the tundra, boreal forests, deciduous forests, tropical forests, grasslands, and deserts—are now known.

Humans have had a tremendous, and usually detrimental, impact on the ecosystems of the world. It is the balance between human technology and the natural communities which will ultimately determine the fate of all life on earth. We should be aware of the consequences of human activity and attempt to find solutions that will allow us and other organisms to live in harmony with our environment.

Chapter 6

Living Communities: Basic Relationships

As you have seen in the first two units of this book, life—from the atomic to the organism level—is a series of relationships. For convenience of study, biologists like to organize these relationships in order of increasing complexity. We come then to the relationships between organisms and their environment.

Our daily lives are giving us constant and dramatic evidence of the importance of these relationships. We are finding out that some of them are delicate and easily damaged. We are placing burdens and stresses on our environment that can have serious consequences for us and all other organisms sharing this planet.

Chapter 3 gave us an introduction to chemistry and the laws regulating the movement of energy in the physical world. **Energy Flow and Chemical Cycling** is the broad category under which we group the components of the various organism–organism and organism–environment relationships. These two groups of interactions are the bases of ecosystems. Like any other system, an ecosystem can be described in terms of the **Energy Flow** and transfer of materials which occurs within it. In the living world, energy transfer occurs through

Food Chains and Webs, the links of organic materials between levels of the biosphere. In addition to the one-directional (lower to higher) transfer of energy through the food chain is the movement of equally essential—but chemically simpler—substances through the **Chemical Cycles.**

After surveying the relationships between species and their environments, we will look at groups of individuals of the same species, called **Populations. Population Growth,** for example, is directly regulated by biological and nonbiological factors. There is a great deal of interest today in the artificial regulation of the human population, but there are natural mechanisms of **The Regulation of Populations** that are equally important.

The Relationships between Species brings us to the end of the chapter. Having seen the chemical and biological requirements of individuals and populations, we can appreciate the kinds of relationships that members of different species form. In some of these links, both organisms benefit; in others, one benefits while the other is directly harmed or is unaffected.

A good example of an ecosystem can be found in an ocean tidepool. Patient observation over several days or weeks would give us an appreciation of the variety of life found there and the complexity of its interaction. Before long we might spot a sea anemone—an invertebrate animal about the size of a coffee cup—devouring a small fish it had seized with its many tentacles. The fish had probably been feeding on tiny crustaceans when it was captured. These crustaceans had in turn dined on algae cells that manufacture their own food by trapping sunlight and extracting inorganic raw materials from their watery environment.

Peering closely, we might see a snail scraping algae from a submerged rock. We might also notice that mussels attached to the rock were quietly pumping water into their shells and filtering it over their gills to remove tiny suspended food particles. Upon further study, we would probably find rockbound barnacles rhythmically beating their feathery appendages as they capture their food. And we would find worms and perhaps crabs in temporary homes under rocks and in large filaments of slippery algae.

One day we might spot some newcomers to this community, such as two or three snails of a particular species. If we came back often enough, we might see the *population* of this species increase—slowly at first, then more rapidly, until the snail population stabilized at a certain level. At this point, the snails would have filled their ecological *niche:* their particular place in the *habitat,* or general environment, of the tidepool and in their relationship with other members of the tidepool community.

After several visits we would notice that on warm, sunny days nothing much seemed to be happening in our tidepool community. On sunny days the still, shallow water in the pool becomes several degrees warmer between tides and during this intertidal period visible activity may virtually cease. When the tide flows again, it brings cooler water, oxygen, and chemical nutrients. The tideflow also transports certain organisms into and out of the community.

If we examined water samples under a microscope periodically, we might detect sex cells from some of the organisms, including the sea anemones. These cells appear in the water at approximately the same time each year; some of them unite to produce new organisms.

Though the community continues, sooner or later all individual members of it die. Parts of their bodies are eaten by community scavengers, such as crabs. Then bacteria assist in the decomposition process.

Thus the tidepool community—like all others—shows a definite organization, with each organism contributing in an indispensable way. Cyclical patterns such as tidal and seasonal cycles are also evident. We have noted a few interactions in our tidepool example, but the interaction patterns of any community are far more complex than this. Seasonal and tidal cycles are easily observed, but there is more to them than the untrained eye notices. And chemical cycles are less obvious but no less important. We can gain a better understanding of any community by examining some of its associations and processes in detail. The interdisciplinary science dealing with the relationship of organisms to one another and to their environments is known as *ecology.*

ENERGY FLOW AND CHEMICAL CYCLING

Each living community, like each living cell and living organism, depends on inputs of energy and chemicals. The general energy and chemical relationships in all communities are similar. Energy flows from organism to organism, always in one direction; eventually the energy is all lost from the community, mostly in the form of heat. Chemical materials, however, move in cycles. Some are lost to the community through water erosion and other processes, but much of this loss simply provides material to communities elsewhere. Chemical cycles involve not only living systems but also the abiotic environment. It is through these integrated systems, *ecosystems,* that energy flows and chemicals are cycled.

Energy Flow

In any ecosystem, chemicals must be converted into living materials. Large molecules such as

Bio-Topic: Your Body Is an Ecosystem

The human body is the normal habitat for many kinds of bacteria and fungi. In a healthy person eating a normal diet, the relationship is usually commensal or mutualistic. But drugs, a change in diet, or infection by some viruses may allow these organisms to become pathogenic.

During and after birth, our bodies are exposed to many sources of microorganisms. Our skins are inoculated during passage through the birth canal. The air we breathe contains spores of bacteria and fungi that lodge in our throats and nostrils. Other microorganisms arrive on flakes of skin shed by those around us.

Various parts of our bodies provide ideal conditions for specific organisms that stay with us throughout our lifetimes. Some bacteria inhabit sweat glands; others, the throat, intestines, or vagina. Certain fungi inhabit the mouth and there is a mite that lives on the hair follicles of most adults. We provide these

inhabitants with nutrients and protection. Some of the inhabitants do nothing for us (the commensals), others provide us with protection from disease (the mutualists) by preventing dangerous microorganisms from becoming established.

The balance can be shifted all too easily. Bacteria that normally inhabit the vagina produce acids that prevent the growth of other organisms. Antibiotics taken to treat other infections can kill enough of these bacteria to lower the acidity. This in turn may allow yeasts or other organisms to invade and cause infections. Certain antibiotics may kill enough normal intestinal bacteria to allow pathogenic bacteria to invade the bloodstream, causing serious illness.

The human body is an ecosystem made up of a human and other organisms. Like all ecosystems, the relationships within it are delicately balanced and can be accidentally disturbed.

$C_6H_{12}O_6$ (glucose) are generally synthesized from smaller molecules found in soil, air, and water. Organisms capable of performing these syntheses are referred to as *producers;* they include plants on land and plants and algae in aquatic environments. Note that the flow of energy is not cyclical in a community, but that the sun provides a continuing source of energy.

All producers or *autotrophs* (self-feeding organisms) contain chlorophyll or other light-trapping compounds that enable them to use the sun's energy. *Photosynthesis* (Figure 6–1) is the basic process in which solar energy is converted to chemical energy in the form of ATP and simple carbohydrates such as glucose. Metabolic processes then convert these simple sugars into more complex sugars, proteins, and fats. Eventually, energy and materials stored by producers are transferred to *consumers*—first

to plant-eating herbivores and then through them to carnivores. These *heterotrophs* (organisms which feed on others) are also known as *primary* and *secondary consumers.*

The sun provides a constant source of energy, but chemical materials are not in such constant supply. Therefore a very important component of any ecosystem is the *decomposers*, bacteria and fungi that break down dead organisms. It is through decomposition that chemical nutrients are returned to the environment; without it, all life would eventually cease. Decomposers are found in the soil and at the bottom of ponds, lakes, and oceans.

Thus we see within an ecosystem a structural and functional organization that begins with producers, which provide food (and energy) for consumers. Consumers (and many producers) are broken down by decomposers,

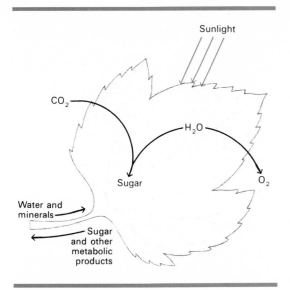

FIGURE 6–1   Basic scheme of photosynthesis.

which return raw materials to the producers (Figure 6–2). In this chain of events, each group of organisms in the community derives energy from the group preceding it. These groups of organisms represent *trophic levels* (Figure 6–3). In the conversion of food to energy from one trophic level to another, the efficiency achieved is nowhere near 100 percent; much energy is lost along the way. For example, a given *biomass* (amount of living material) of plants will support only a much smaller biomass of herbivores, and the biomass of carnivores supported by the herbivores will be smaller still. A pyramid is frequently used to show the relative masses of the various components of an ecosystem (Figure 6–4).

Food Chains and Webs

The flow of energy from one trophic level to another is called a *food chain.* For example, the following food relationship in forests is important to game management experts:

Plants → Deer → Cougars

Many farmers are familiar with another food chain:

Crops → Field mice → Hawks

Some food chains are longer than others. Oceanic food chains can be quite long:

Algae and green plants →
    Animal plankton → Small fish →
Larger fish → Very large fish/whales/humans

The huge energy losses that occur at successive levels of a freshwater ecosystem are shown below:

Trophic Levels	Net production in kilocalories/ square meter/year*
Producers (photosynthesizers)	8833
Primary consumers (herbivores)	1478
Secondary consumers (small carnivores)	316
Tertiary consumers (large carnivores)	15

*After H. T. Odum, *Ecological Monographs, 27*:55–112, 1957.

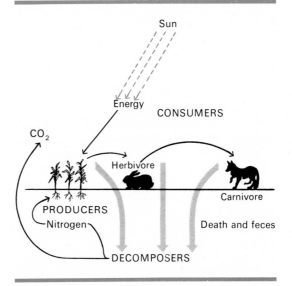

FIGURE 6–2   Relationships among members of an ecosystem.

Bio-Topic: Superbugs

Recent developments in bacterial genetics make it possible to produce tailor-made strains of bacteria that can do very specific jobs. Anandra Chakrabarty, a biologist with the General Electric Corporation, has developed a strain of bacteria that may help to clean up oil spills.

Chakrabarty started with several strains of bacteria. Each strain was able to digest one of the main components of crude oil, but only one, into nonpolluting compounds. Using the techniques of bacterial genetics, Chakrabarty combined parts of the genetic material of four strains into a single "superbug" that alone can digest most of the components of crude oil. Testing and evaluation are not yet complete, but it may be that future oil spills will be cleaned up by pouring a few barrels of superbugs on the spill.

Bacteria are now used in many industrial processes for the production of economically important organic compounds.

With Chakrabarty's example to follow, it may be possible to develop new strains of bacteria that can carry out not just a single reaction, but a series of reactions that convert a raw material into some desired product.

Such tailor-made strains would obviously be of economic importance. But there are risks to this approach. Combining the genes of different organisms results in an entirely new organism with properties that can be predicted to a large extent, but not with absolute certainty. It is at least conceivable that efforts to create a superbug could lead to the accidental creation of bacteria that are somehow harmful to other organisms.

Genetic engineering aimed at creating superbugs will no doubt become more common. But we will need to proceed cautiously and maintain adequate safeguards against the accidental creation of a monstrous species.

When one part of a food chain is disturbed, the results can seriously affect the whole chain. If a bounty encourages excessive cougar hunting, for example, a deer population may increase until sufficient food is not available to sustain the herd. Overcrowding and nutritional problems follow. Many deer starve, and many of the survivors are weak, emaciated, or diseased. Or if the coyotes in a farming area are poisoned by humans to reduce the threat to sheep, the population of field mice may increase so much that the grain crop is severely damaged. This may take a far greater toll of sheep than the coyotes did.

Humans have often imported predators to control such nuisance animals as rats. But after thinning out the pest population, these predators have often turned to other, more valuable animals. We must realize that we can change—and damage—a whole series of ecological relationships by tampering with just one element of a particular ecosystem.

Most animals rely on not one but several species for food. A hawk, for example, eats squirrels, mice, rabbits, and large insects. Because consumers do not rely solely on one plant or animal for food, food chains are not separate but interrelated. These make up a *food web*, which can be very complex (Figure 6–5).

Chemical Cycles

We have seen that life depends on the flow of energy through the ecosystem. But life also depends on nutrients and other chemical compounds that are cycled from the soil, through

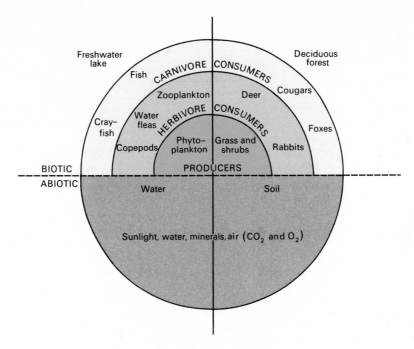

FIGURE 6–3   Principal trophic levels in freshwater and terrestrial ecosystems.

the atmosphere and living organisms, and back to the soil. The best-known and most studied of these cycles involve water, oxygen, carbon, nitrogen, phosphorus, sulfur, and calcium. Some of these will be discussed here to show how the materials are made available to living organisms.

The Oxygen Cycle

Besides being a structural component of sugar, fat, and protein molecules, oxygen is also a necessary agent for the release of energy from foods. We know that as green plants manufacture food, oxygen is released into the atmosphere. It can be demonstrated that this oxygen comes from water taken in by the plant. Organisms use oxygen from the atmosphere (or dissolved in water, in the case of aquatic forms) in the process of respiration (energy production). Within cells, oxygen unites with hydrogen from sugar molecules to produce water. This water can be used again by green plants in photosynthesis and the cycle continued. The

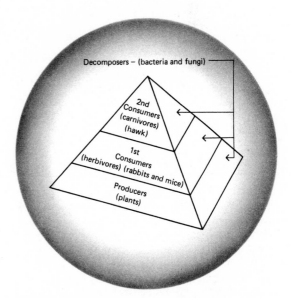

FIGURE 6–4   The biomass relationships in an ecosystem. Fungi and bacteria decompose dead organisms and make the decay products available for reuse.

FIGURE 6–5   **Part of a food web in a forest community.**

details of photosynthesis and respiration will be discussed in Chapter 9.

The Carbon Cycle

Carbon moves from the atmosphere to green plants, where organic carbon compounds are produced. These compounds are used by both plants and animals. Carbon then moves back to the atmosphere as a by-product of respiration from plants and animals (Figure 6–6). Carbon

dioxide (CO_2) is the form in which carbon is taken from the atmosphere by green plants for photosynthesis. It is also the form in which carbon is returned to the atmosphere when dead organisms decompose and plants and animals respire. Carbon is stored in coal and other fuels; the burning of these fuels releases considerable carbon (again in the form of CO_2) into the atmosphere. In addition, carbon is stored and transported as carbonates ($CO_3^=$ or HCO_3^-). Note in Figure 6–6 that the carbon

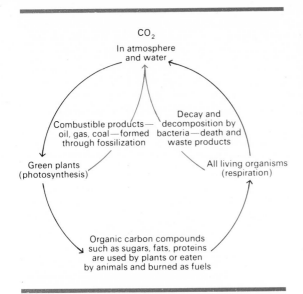

FIGURE 6-6　The carbon cycle.

used by green plants must come directly from CO_2 in the atmosphere or in water.

The Nitrogen Cycle

The process by which nitrogen becomes available to living systems is somewhat more complex than the oxygen and carbon cycles. Nitrogen is an essential element in amino acids, purines, and pyrimidines. These compounds are usually produced first in green plants and then made available to animals. Nitrogen makes up 78 percent of the atmosphere, but it is not directly available to the majority of organisms since much of the nitrogen used by green plants must be fixed in the form of nitrates. A little direct *nitrogen fixing* does take place, however, in a few organisms, such as some bacteria, blue-green algae, and fungi. Lightning can also fix a small amount of nitrogen. Most of the nitrogen used by living systems is made available to them by two principal routes: (1) through the production of *nitrate*, and (2) through the action of nitrogen-fixing bacteria in nodules on the roots of certain plants (Figure 6-7).

Some free-living bacteria in the soil and in water can convert atmospheric nitrogen to am-

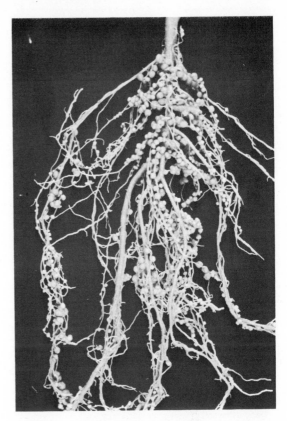

FIGURE 6-7　Roots of birdsfoot trefoil, a legume, with nodules containing nitrogen-fixing bacteria. (Courtesy of Nitragin Co., Inc., Milwaukee.)

monia (NH_3). Another group of bacteria can convert ammonia to *nitrite* (NO_2), and a third group can convert nitrite to *nitrate* (NO_3). In this form, nitrogen can be used by green plants. The ammonia, nitrites, and nitrates are usually present as ions (NH_4^+, NO_2^-, NO_3^-) which can unite with other ions of opposite charge to produce salts. The ammonia produced in animal urine and in decomposition is also utilized by nitrite-forming bacteria. This sequence may be summarized as follows:

Decomposing organisms

$$N_2\text{-fixing bacteria} \rightarrow NH_3 \rightarrow NO_2 \rightarrow NO_3$$

Waste products ⎯⎯⎯⎯⎯⎯⎯

(available to green plants)

We have noted that bacteria attached to nodules on the roots of certain plants can take free nitrogen directly from the soil and convert it into organic nitrogen (Figure 6–7). This nitrogen can be passed in the form of amino acids into the plants possessing these nodules. Thus legumes and alder trees can grow in soil lacking usable nitrogen. Farmers are well aware of the nitrogen-fixing properties of legumes. Forage crops of alfalfa and other legumes are doubly valuable: They contain more protein than non-legumes and they thrive in poor soils where nonlegumes do not.

Some bacteria, then, supply usable nitrogen to living organisms. But others are responsible for an opposite process known as *denitrification*. These bacteria convert ammonia, nitrites, and nitrates to free nitrogen and release it to the atmosphere. Figure 6–8 summarizes circulation of nitrogen in an ecosystem.

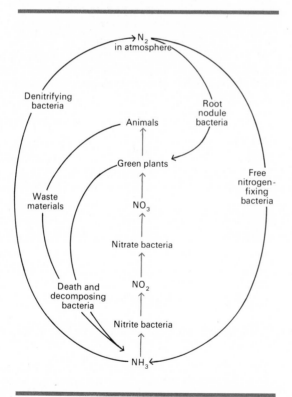

FIGURE 6–8   **The nitrogen cycle.**

The Phosphorus Cycle

The major reservoirs of phosphorus are the rock formations of the earth's crust. Slowly, through the processes of weathering and leaching (dissolution in groundwater), phosphate is returned to soil and the sea. Dissolved phosphate is incorporated into living organisms, usually first into plants and then into animals (Figure 6–9).

Phosphorus in the form of phosphate is essential to energy transfer, the metabolic processes that convert food to usable energy, and the structure of the hereditary material. It is also a major component of bones and teeth. In some aquatic environments, the availability of phosphate may be the limiting factor on growth and reproduction at certain times of the year. Since phosphorus is gradually leached out of soil, phosphate is often added to lawns and farmland when soil has become depleted.

When organisms excrete or decompose, phosphate is put back into circulation. Some phosphate, however, is deposited in sediments on the ocean floor. If the sediments underlie shallow water, enough phosphate and other minerals can be dissolved from the bottom and circulated in the water to support great quantities of marine life. The shallow waters of the North Sea and the Grand Banks, for example, are among the world's most productive fisheries. But phosphate sediments in deep water are usually lost to organisms until an upheaval occurs. Eventually much of this phosphate is returned to the cycle, although some scientists fear that we are slowly but permanently losing more phosphate to the deep sediments. Land-dwelling organisms contribute to the available terrestrial phosphate and thereby assist in maintaining the cycle. By eating fish, humans and birds help to return phosphorus from the sea to land.

POPULATIONS

We noted earlier that individuals do not live alone but are members of a *population*. All members of a species found in a particular community form a population in that community. The concept of population is important in

Bio-Topic: Life in a Closed System

Many kinds of microorganisms obtain their energy and nutrients by attacking the corpses and wastes of other organisms. In natural ecosystems, these decomposers recycle the large polymers left behind by producers and consumers, returning small molecules to the ecosystem. In urban and suburban ecosystems, these same microbes are employed to purify the wastes we and our culture produce. In nearly all municipal waste treatment plants in this country, sewage is treated by systems that rely on the growth and metabolism of microorganisms.

Sewage is pumped into large vats or tanks containing sludge—a mass of actively growing microorganisms. These microorganisms grow at the expense of the organic materials in the sewage. The products of this kind of biological waste treatment are relatively clean water and more sludge. A waste treatment plant in a large city may generate many tons of sludge each week.

What becomes of the sludge? Until recently, sludge was simply burned, dumped at sea, or buried. As time passed and populations and the resulting quantities of sludge increased, the ecological impact of all three methods of disposal became clear and unacceptable. Burning causes air pollution, dumping at sea disrupts a large but delicate ecosystem, and burial uses up vast amounts of precious land. The sum of these ecological costs became acute several years ago, and a search for alternative ways to dispose of sludge began in earnest.

One of the most promising alternatives was to use sludge as fertilizer. Sludge is, after all, little more than a mass of microorganisms—obviously a rich source of nitrogen, phosphorus, and other important nutrients. The application of sludge to experimental plots of grasses reinforced the initial promise. Grasses grew well, soil texture improved, and so did the prospects for a solution to the problem.

But there is no such thing as a free lunch, particularly in a closed biosphere. It now appears that, as the sludge microorganisms extract nutrients from sewage, they also extract such toxic heavy metals as mercury, zinc, and cadmium that are present in minute quantities. Repeated applications of sludge to soil results in the accumulation of these elements to levels which inhibit certain crops. Crops that are not inhibited seem to incorporate these elements into their tissues, making them potentially hazardous to consume.

Living in a closed ecosystem means that we can't escape the consequences of our actions. The problem of dealing with mountains of sludge remains to be solved —along with many others.

---

the study of ecology, behavior, reproduction, and evolution.

Populations possess certain characteristics, such as birth rate, death rate, relative age structure, density, and distribution pattern. These characteristics differ for various species, and they usually vary from year to year depending on changes in the environment and other factors.

Population Growth

If conditions remain favorable, a population once established in a given habitat undergoes a growth pattern that is similar for all species. Favorable conditions include the presence of an initially adequate food supply and the absence of a strongly competitive species. Although population growth may be slow at first, it soon

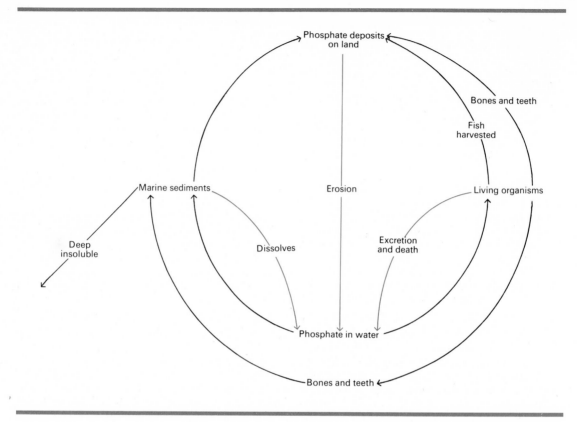

FIGURE 6–9   The phosphorus cycle.

increases as more individuals mature and reproduce (Figure 6–10). Expansion is very rapid and fairly steady until the *carrying capacity* of the environment for that species is reached. This capacity of a habitat depends not only on the amount of food available but also on its nutritional value. Food value, in turn, depends on the nature of the soil and the adequacy of the water supply. The shelter, or cover, available for animals in a habitat is another aspect of carrying capacity. When limits to carrying capacity have been reached, population density usually fluctuates about this level (Figure 6–10). If carrying capacity is exceeded and the population of a plant, animal, or microorganism becomes too dense, harmful physiological and psychological effects may occur.

Bacteria offer a striking example of population growth and decline in an environment with a limited carrying capacity. Because bacteria reproduce so rapidly, dramatic population changes in a bacteria colony can be observed during a short time. When a colony is placed in a fluid growth medium with adequate nutrients and optimum pH and temperature levels, growth is slow for the first few hours (Figure 6–11). But population growth soon accelerates. After about 24 hours the growth rate slows, and for a brief time the reproduction and death rates are about equal. Soon, however, the population begins to decline—gradually at first, then rapidly—as more bacteria die than are produced. Why the decline? Because the carrying capacity has been reached and then exceeded. The food supply has diminished and waste products have increased to a toxic level. What

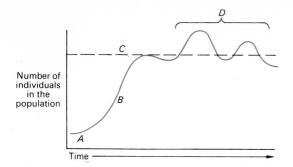

FIGURE 6–10   Growth curve of a population. At *A* the population is growing slowly because few members are present for reproduction. Soon, however, numbers have increased to *B*, the point at which many mates are present, and a rapid increase occurs. Line *C* represents the carrying capacity of the environment. At *D* the population has reached a plateau, since the carrying capacity has been exceeded; no food and shelter are available to support any further increase in population.

we are discussing here is the *environmental resistance* imposed on the growth of any population. Constraints upon food supply, shelter, and space bring an inevitable end to the rapid growth phase of a population.

If we added food and space to our bacteria colony's habitat, and if we removed dead bacteria and other wastes, the population of the colony could continue to grow, though perhaps at a lower rate. From studies such as this one we could learn about populations in general: their patterns of growth, the causes of environmental resistance, and how we can influence growth rates.

Many studies have been conducted on populations, and we are increasing our knowledge of population dynamics. *Natural* populations reach a balance based largely on the carrying capacity of the environment, although other factors also affect population dynamics. Reproduction and behavior, which are important in population dynamics, will be discussed in subsequent chapters.

Regulation of Populations

Populations are regulated by natural forces in either the abiotic or biotic realms. Abiotic reg-

ulating conditions include mineral cycling, shelter availability, and weather. Biotic regulation centers upon the food supply, relationships among members of a species, and relationships with members of other species.

Crowding and Stress

In 1962, J. B. Calhoun reported in *Scientific American* that rats living in crowded conditions developed very abnormal behavior patterns. He also reported that these "stressed" animals had reduced reproductive capabilities. Two years later, F. H. Brown reported on another crowding experiment. He found that overcrowded mice became aggressive and fought a great deal, and that the adrenal glands of these stressed animals were abnormally large. He also found that increased adrenal secretions caused imbalances in other body chemicals and eventually affected the functioning of other glands and organs.

Many subsequent studies of rat and mouse populations have shown that increased population densities cause increased aggressive behavior and lowered fertility rates. Not only do

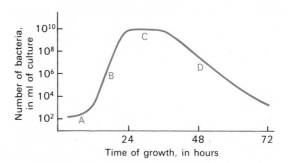

FIGURE 6–11   Growth curve in bacteria (*E. coli*) at about 20°C in a medium containing food for optimum growing conditions. Note the initial phase of slow growth (*A*), then the period of rapid growth (*B*), the slowing and stationary growth to produce a plateau (*C*), and finally, decline of the population (*D*). Since the numbers of bacteria are very large, they are reported on the graph in logarithmic notation; for example, $10^6 = 1,000,000$ (1 million) bacterial cells. The logarithmic phase of population growth is the period represented by B on this graph.

fewer adults mate, but fewer normal, healthy offspring are produced.

Some recent studies of humans living in crowded conditions indicate that the effects of crowding may not always be negative. This finding might not seem very surprising, given that many people live happy, healthy lives in crowded cities. But other recent studies suggest that crowding *can* have bad effects on humans.

With plants, high-density populations apparently exhibit so much stress that individual plant growth is decreased and the death rate increases. These experimental findings are not surprising either; all home gardeners know what to expect if they plant their seeds too close together and do not thin out the young seedlings.

Predation

Crowding is an internal factor controlling populations. One important external controlling force is predation, in which one organism (prey) is eaten by another (predator). In some forest communities, for example, deer are the preferred prey of cougars or dogs (Figure 6–12). Predation forms a relationship between the population sizes of the two species involved. For example, the snowshoe hare of the tundra falls prey to the lynx, and the population cycles of both animals reflect this relationship. The snowshoe hare population decreases as the lynx population increases, and vice versa.

The general fluctuations in population density of predator and prey are shown in Figure 6–13. The situation is usually more compli-

FIGURE 6–12   Dogs have replaced cougars as predators of deer in some areas. (Courtesy of Michigan State Department of Natural Resources.)

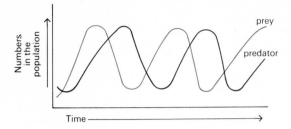

FIGURE 6–13 Fluctuations in population density of a predator and its prey. Note that the predator population reaches a peak after the population of prey attains its peak.

cated than the simple relationships shown, however, since most organisms are part of a complex food web.

Migration

Immigration and emigration of individual members of a population may help regulate its density. An interesting example of this aspect of migration is afforded by the peculiar behav-

ior of lemmings, mouselike rodents that inhabit Scandinavia. Lemming populations undergo cyclical increases and decreases. In most lemming groups, fluctuations occur every three to four years. Ample food and large litter size appear to cause the increased population.

At the peak of the population cycle, large numbers of lemmings leave their home territory in mass migrations; many drown in streams and in the sea. For many years these "suicide marches" were believed to be simply quests for food. But studies by Garrett Clough indicate that these migrations may have additional causes. Field observations by Clough in 1963 and 1964 indicated that lemmings show unusual intolerance for others of their species. As population and social stresses increase, fighting and avoidance may trigger migrations (Figure 6–14). According to Clough, middle-sized lemmings depart from the home territory first, leaving the older breeding population and the young behind. Many move into less favorable marsh and field areas, where they usually

FIGURE 6–14 Early stage in a lemming fight. (Courtesy of Garrett C. Clough.)

perish during the first winter. Very aggressive lemmings also seem to move away from high-density areas. Some scientists believe that this reaction to social stress is an innate mechanism to keep these rodents from eating all the available food in an area and thus destroying the entire species through starvation.

Territoriality

Most wild animal populations show distinct behavioral patterns directly related to the "ownership" of particular areas. In establishing a territory, an organism competes only with members of its own kind. Robins, for example, compete with other robins for space this species can inhabit. This *territoriality* has been noted among both vertebrate and invertebrate animals, and it is now well established that the claiming and defense of territory is an important factor in regulation of animal populations.

Territoriality will be discussed further in Chapter 17.

RELATIONSHIPS AMONG SPECIES

Very close relationships involving two or more species can be found in most communities. These intimate associations are said to be *symbiotic; symbiosis* means "living together." There are three types of symbiosis: *commensalism, mutualism,* and *parasitism.*

Commensalism is a relationship between two organisms in which one member of the pair benefits and the other is neither benefited nor harmed (Figure 6–15). When certain species of barnacles attach themselves to whales, they are geographically dispersed and transported to new feeding grounds. So far as is known, these hitchhikers do no harm to the whales. Another example is a tropical fish that

FIGURE 6–15 Commensalism. As insects are stirred up by grazing cattle, egrets follow and feed on the insects. (Bureau of Sport Fisheries and Wildlife.)

lives in the intestine of a sea cucumber. Apparently the sea cucumber is not affected, and the fish gains a safe home.

Mutualism is a relationship in which two organisms benefit from each other (Figure 6–16). Many such associations are found in nature, and often it is not clear how much benefit each obtains. A lichen, for example, is made up of an alga and a fungus living in a mutualistic relationship: the alga produces food for both, and the fungus obtains and holds water (Figure 6–17). Protozoans capable of digesting the cellulose of wood live in the gut of termites. The termite provides shelter and food for the protozoans, which help the termite digest its food.

Parasitism is a relationship in which one member benefits and the other is harmed (Figure 6–18). Parasites that inhabit the outer surfaces of their hosts are called *ectoparasites;* those that live within the host organism are *endoparasites.* Ectoparasites include fleas and ticks that suck blood from their hosts. Endoparasites, such as tapeworms and liver flukes, have structural and physiological adaptations necessary for their way of life. The tapeworm, for example, has evolved attachment devices such as hooks and suckers on its anterior end to prevent dislocation from a host's intestine (Figure 6–19).

During the life cycle of the beef tapeworm (Figure 6–20), a cow eats grass infected with tapeworm eggs from human feces. Upon entering the cow's intestine, the eggs rupture and release many six-hooked larvae. These larvae

FIGURE 6–16 Mutualism. The small birds on the back of this African Cape elk obtain food by eating insect parasites. The obvious benefit to the elk is the removal of parasites. (Grant Heilman.)

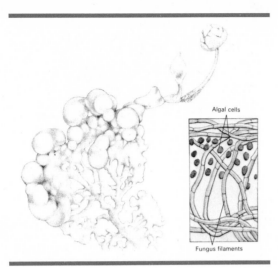

FIGURE 6–17   Mutualism in a lichen. The inset shows algal cells among the fungus filaments.

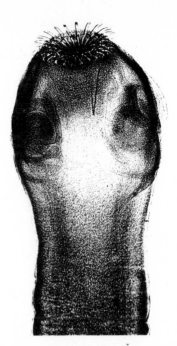

FIGURE 6–19   The anterior hooks and suckers of a mature dog tapeworm. These devices attach the tapeworm to the intestinal lining. (Courtesy of Carolina Biological Supply Company.)

FIGURE 6–18   An ectoparasite: a sea lamprey attached to a fish. (Courtesy of Ontario Department of Lands and Forests.)

bore through the intestinal wall into blood or lymph, which carries them to skeletal muscles. There they encyst and remain inactive in a bladder until they are eaten by a human. When a person eats an infested piece of rare beef, the bladders turn inside out to expose the head, which then attaches by suckers to the intestinal wall. Sexual segments known as *proglottids* mature and break off at the posterior end of the worm to release fertilized eggs which are passed in human feces. In this case the human is the primary host, since the sexual reproduction phase of the tapeworm's life cycle occurs there. The cow is the intermediate host, since it harbors the larval forms. The Chinese liver fluke undergoes a more complicated life cycle: the larvae develop in a snail and then encyst in fish muscle before becoming sexually mature adults in the human liver.

Plants may also be parasites. Mistletoe, which lives on oak and some other trees, is a common plant parasite (Figure 6–21). It actually sends

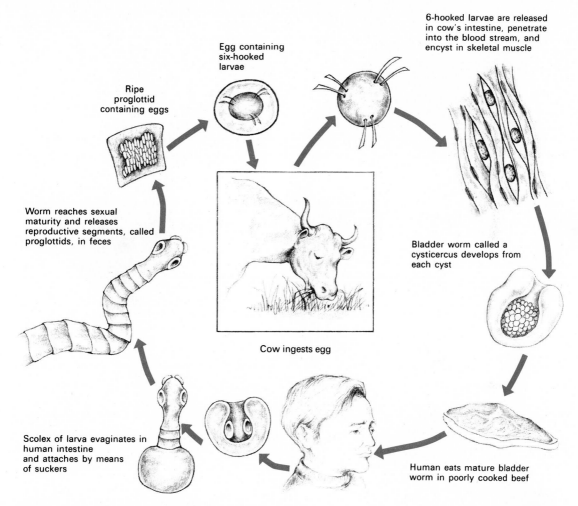

6-hooked larvae are released
in cow's intestine, penetrate
into the blood stream, and
encyst in skeletal muscle

Egg containing
six-hooked
larvae

Ripe
proglottid
containing eggs

Worm reaches sexual
maturity and releases
reproductive segments, called
proglottids, in feces

Cow ingests egg

Bladder worm called a
cysticercus develops from
each cyst

Scolex of larva evaginates in
human intestine
and attaches by means
of suckers

Human eats mature bladder
worm in poorly cooked beef

FIGURE 6–20   Life cycle of a beef tapeworm, a parasite.

rootlike structures into the tree's vascular tissue and taps its nutrient supply. A plant parasite more serious than mistletoe is the fungus
that causes a late blight of potatoes. This disease produced the potato famine in Ireland
from 1843 to 1846, which led to starvation, and
a mass migration to the United States. As part
of a complex life cycle, spores attack both
leaves and tubers of the potato, killing the
leaves and rotting the tubers. Tomatoes are also
susceptible to this fungus, and epidemics of late
blight have occurred in the United States.

Note that a successful parasite must not de-

stroy its host—at least until after it has reproduced. Well-adapted parasites may weaken
their hosts, but they seldom cause immediate
death.

The three symbiotic groups discussed here
are somewhat arbitrary. Not all biologists agree
on the placement of a particular symbiotic
association into one of these three categories.
Some commensal relationships may be evolving
toward parasitism. It is easy to imagine how a
harmless commensal could eventually become
a parasite. Perhaps mistletoe once used the oak
tree only for support, much like the commen-

FIGURE 6–21   A plant parasite: mistletoe growing on a mesquite tree. (Grant Heilman.)

salism between some tropical plants. But the mistletoe then evolved structures that could penetrate into the tree's vascular system, and a parasitic relationship was established.

With this background in the basic principles of ecology, we are prepared to investigate the major living communities of the world (Chapter 7) and to discuss human ecology (Chapter 8).

SUMMARY

A biotic community consists of all the organisms living and interacting within a particular area; if we consider the nonliving components of such an area as well, we speak of an ecosystem. Every ecosystem, such as a lake or forest, shows a definite organization and depends on energy flow and chemicals. Energy through an ecosystem flows in one direction, from the producers to the consumers to the decomposers. Materials such as water, oxygen, carbon, nitrogen, and phosphorus move in a cyclic pattern. Producers are autotrophic, converting solar energy to chemical energy through the process of photosynthesis. Heterotrophs are the consumers; they feed on the autotrophs or other heterotrophs. Energy flows from one trophic level to another in a food chain.

All members of a species in a particular community form a population. Only a limited population can be supported by the carrying capacity of the environment. All populations show a similar growth pattern, and all are regulated naturally by such forces as crowding and stress, predation, migration, and territoriality.

In most communities very close relationships known as symbiosis exist between two or more species. There are three types of symbiotic relationships: commensalism, mutualism, and parasitism.

REVIEW QUESTIONS

1. Define the following terms: *biotic community, abiotic, population, ecosystem, niche,*

habitat, producers, consumers, decomposers, and ecology.

2. Select a living community near your home or college. Describe its organization, noting the organisms and the relationships among them. Which are the producers and the consumers? Are any symbiotic relationships apparent?

3. Why are there laws to protect such birds as sea gulls, hawks, and owls, even though there appear to be plenty of them around?

4. Legumes such as peas and beans contain large amounts of protein even though they may grow in nitrogen-poor soils. Explain.

5. Control of hunting and predators has had little effect on the decreasing caribou population of British Columbia. Logging and forest fires, however, have proved to be the major causes of this population decline. Can you explain why?

6. Would it be possible to alter the natural growth pattern (such as the one described for bacteria) of any population? Explain how.

7. In the 1870s starlings were introduced to the United States from Europe; they gradually spread throughout the country. Based on your knowledge of population dynamics, construct a population curve to predict the growth rate and survival of this species in the United States.

8. Certain crabs have large colonies of sponges on their backs. What do you think is the symbiotic relationship between these two organisms? Give reasons for your answer.

SUPPLEMENTARY READINGS

Emmel, Thomas C., *An Introduction to Ecology and Population Biology*, W. W. Norton, New York, 1973. Basic ecological processes and principles of population biology and the need for understanding and preserving our environment are explained.

Freedman, J. L., *Crowding and Behavior*, W. H. Freeman, San Francisco, 1975. An extensive but popularly written study of crowding in animals, especially in humans. It presents the optimistic view that crowding may not be generally bad but may have good effects, depending on the situation.

Kormondy, Edward J., *Concepts of Ecology*, Prentice-Hall, Englewood Cliffs, NJ, 1969. An excellent presentation of the fundamental concepts of ecology. The structure and function of ecosystems, energy flow, nutrient cycling, and population dynamics are covered.

Meyers, Judith H. and C. J. Krebs, "Population Cycles in Rodents," *Scientific American*, June 1974. Populations of many small rodents fluctuate in cycles of three or four years and although the length of these cycles is not completely understood, this article discusses why the cycles occur.

Whittaker, Robert H., *Communities and Ecosystems*, 2nd edition, Macmillan, New York, 1975. The principles necessary for an understanding of basic ecology are presented in this book written for beginning students. The structure and functions of natural ecosystems are covered.

Chapter 7

Living Communities: Natural Patterns

In the course of your lifetime, you may have the opportunity to return to an area after a period of decades. Even in the absence of human impact or interference, you will see definite changes in the locale. Whether it is a coastline, a forest, or a pond, the evidence of *Changes in a Community: Succession* can be seen, if we know how to look for it. Both primary and secondary patterns of change can be found in *The Major Land Communities.*

When we recall the scenery of a distinctive area we have visited, we are really thinking of the *Biome* in which that area is located. A biome is one of the six primary kinds of biological, climatic, and geological regions of the world. Examples of each kind of biome can be found in North America.

Biomes are one way of classifying the natural patterns of living communities—by moving across the earth's surface. If we move vertically up or down from the earth's surface, we find *Life Zones* marked by changes in altitude. In *The Freshwater Environment,* for example, we see how temperature, availability of dissolved oxygen and other food materials, and the ability of light to penetrate according to depth all contribute to distinct horizontal environments with their own characteristic organisms.

The Marine Environment, composed of the oceans and seas, is the largest one on our planet. As in the freshwater environment, depth from the water surface, temperature, and the availability of food materials combine to create specific marine communities. Further complicating life in the oceans is the high concentration of dissolved substances such as salt. Marine organisms are specifically adapted to the pressure and chemical demands of their environment.

Biologists have long recognized that the continents can be divided into major regions according to the plants which grow there. They have also recognized that each major region has its own characteristic variety of animals, which are dependent on the plant types of the region. The oceans can also be divided into various zones, each with characteristic life forms. In this chapter we shall look at these major biotic areas of the world. But first we shall consider some of the factors leading to the formation of distinct communities of plants and animals.

CHANGES IN A COMMUNITY: SUCCESSION

All environments change constantly. Besides the many daily and seasonal changes, every ecosystem undergoes a characteristic series of biological changes. These changes are deter-mined by such factors as its climate and weather, the nature of its soil-producing rock substrates, and the variety and interaction of its organisms. Home gardeners, for instance, know that weeds will soon overtake their gardens if left unattended.

In certain regions of the western United States, the swath cut through evergreen forests for power lines is a familiar sight (Figure 7–1). All vegetation is removed from a strip 50 to 100 feet wide which may extend for miles. Within a short time herbaceous plants such as grasses and fireweed cover the strip. These are soon followed by blackberry, salmon berry, currant, and other shrubs. Mingling with these plants and eventually replacing them are deciduous alder and willow trees. But after a few years these shrubs and trees will be crowded out by evergreen species such as Douglas fir, western hemlock, or western red cedar—the species that occupied the area before it was cleared.

FIGURE 7–1 The successive reforestation of an area. The right-of-way beneath this power line was cleared of all vegetation. (Grant Heilman.)

Over a period of years, then, one community replaces another until a stable community—the evergreen forest—again inhabits these strips.

These events occur in an orderly, sequential pattern which would repeat itself if the vegetation were again removed. Such a series of vegetational changes through several uniform stages is known as ecological *succession*. The final occupants of an area make up a stable, self-reproducing community called the *climax*. One group of plants prepares the way, chemically and physically, for the next group, until this climax is attained. The reforestation just described is an example of *secondary* succession, so called because the land was previously occupied by plants. Succession in a new environment, or in any area devoid of organisms, is called *primary* succession. Here we are concerned mainly with the plants involved in succession. But we must not forget that the microorganisms in a particular area help determine plant succession, and that the kinds of animals living in an area depend largely on the plants found there.

Primary Succession

One site of primary succession is bare rock. Succession there is generally a slow process; its rate depends on the hardness of the rock and the amount of available water. The first plant occupants of such a site are usually lichens and mosses, which help to break down the rock and prepare the area for later colonization by other organisms (Figure 7-2). Soil—a mixture of rock particles and decomposed organic matter (humus)—collects in crevices, permitting seeds from nearby herbaceous plants to grow. Grasses then can move in, followed by small shrubs, then larger shrubs, and eventually trees (Figure 7-3). Along the western coast of the United States, broad-leaved deciduous trees usually move in first, to be succeeded later by cone-bearing evergreen trees. In other parts of the United States the climax vegetation varies, depending on the soil, the climate, and the particular plants available to colonize these areas. These climax communities will be discussed later in this chapter.

Another succession pattern is that of a lake or pond. All lakes are being converted to land by a process which may take varying amounts of time. As streams carry soil into a lake, its bottom begins to build up. Plants such as tussock sedges, cattails, rushes, or sphagnum moss may grow out from the shore over the water's edge to form a mat. The intertwining roots of these plants collect soil and hold humus material in place. Soon the way is prepared for other plants, such as shrubs of the heath family, to gain a foothold. Meanwhile the pond bottom builds up as the deposition of soil and dead plants and animals continues. Eventually larger

FIGURE 7–2   Early stage of primary succession, in which rock is broken into soil by plants. The plants are primarily lichens and mosses. (Russell K. LeBarron; courtesy of U.S. Department of Agriculture, Forest Service.)

Pioneer colonizers in the form of lichens and mosses begin the succession on a rocky hillside. They begin the process of soil formation by breaking the surface rock into small particles and adding organic material.

More soil is produced and larger plants (herbs) can move in.

Next, shrubs requiring more soil can grow here.

Finally, deciduous, broad-leaved trees inhabit the area.

FIGURE 7–3 Ecological succession on a rocky hillside.

shrubs and trees can move into this newly formed land area (Figure 7–4). Peat bogs in the northern United States and Canada are created by this type of succession (Figure 7–5, on

color plate following p. 160.) If you have a chance to visit a peat bog, you should do so. The quaking, resilient floating border of the bog is a unique environment. Because of incomplete decay of submerged organic matter, usable nitrogen is insufficient to sustain many forms of plant life found elsewhere. Insectivorous plants such as sundew, pitcher plant, and Venus flytrap inhabit bog communities. These plants trap insects to obtain nitrogen from their proteins.

Although the basic patterns of succession are similar, different plant species occur in various geographical areas. For example, a succession which begins on bare rock in the eastern United States may end in a climax vegetation of deciduous forest; in the west such a succession may end in a forest of coniferous (cone-bearing) trees.

Probably the most forbidding environments ever colonized by living systems were the land areas of the primitive earth. These were completely abiotic at first. Perhaps as long as a billion years ago, algae-like organisms gained a foothold on the bare rock of the land's coastal edges. Since they were photosynthesizers, these first terrestrial colonists needed only air, a little moisture, and minerals from the rock to survive. Soon their life activities began to break the surface rock down into smaller particles. At the same time, dead and decomposing algae added organic material to these rock particles to form the first thin soil. Later, other plantlike forms from the sea probably joined the algae on land. Eventually true land plants evolved; these produced more life-sustaining soil and led to further plant evolution and succession.

In the long-range evolutionary time scale, there is no such thing as a climax community. Every species and every colony is eventually succeeded by others. The formidable dinosaurs, for instance, disappeared entirely.

In a shorter evolutionary perspective—over time measured in many thousands or a few millions of years—certain communities of plants and animals become established and maintain their climax positions for extended periods. But sooner or later, climatic or other environmental changes on a large scale cause these climax communities to be succeeded by

Deposition begins and sphagnum moss, the pioneer colonizer, encroaches
from the edges.

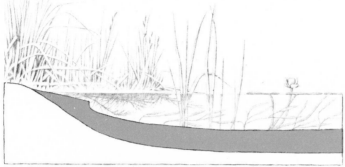

Deposition continues and a thick, sediment-trapping mat of moss, sedges,
and trailing heaths forms.

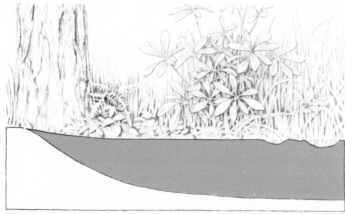

The lake has been completely succeeded by a bog; as deposition continues
and the lakebed fills with firmer soil, the bog plants will be succeeded by
shrubs and trees.

FIGURE 7–4 Succession of a lake by land.

others better adapted to the changed environmental conditions.

Secondary Succession

When humans interfere with the environment,
certain stages may be speeded up or slowed
down in a successional series. Mining, farming,
and logging, for example, may seriously alter
some environments. The clearing beneath
power lines noted earlier is an extreme case of
successional disruption. Although such disruptions remove plant species from a stable community, successional stages eventually return

climax vegetation to the area. This process is known as *secondary succession*. It follows such natural events as fires and avalanches as well as disruptions caused by human action.

We shall next consider some of the major climax vegetation areas of the world—particularly of North America—which have been produced by successional processes.

THE MAJOR LAND COMMUNITIES

Many systems have been suggested for classifying the world into biological regions. The more successful schemes recognize the fact that animals are dependent upon plant life. The terrestrial regions of the earth can therefore be classified mainly in terms of their climax plant communities. Each area with a characteristic climate, group of climax plants, and related group of animal species, is called a *biome*.

Climate changes significantly when one moves north or south of the equator. The general trend is tropical near the equator to more temperate regions, and finally to arctic (very cold). Climate and vegetation also vary with altitude. In mountainous regions, therefore different communities may be quite close, but at different elevations.

Biomes: Climax Regions

Six principal biomes have been identified: tundra, boreal forest, deciduous forest, tropical forest, grassland, and desert (Figure 7-6). This classification is useful, but remember that there are variations of these six basic types. Further-

Bio-Topic: Fire and Ecological Succession

We usually think of fire as a threat and a disaster. In fact, fire is an important shaper of natural communities. There is even a species of pine that is adapted to benefit from periodic fire.

The anatomy of grasses makes them more fire-resistant than the woody shrubs that often succeed them. In dormant grasses, the growing points are underground and safe from fires. The growing points of dormant woody shrubs are well above ground and are killed by fires. Grasses also make seeds within a year or two, while most woody shrubs require several years longer. In a mixed grass–shrub community, a winter fire tips the ecological balance in favor of the grasses. The grasslands of North America may actually be maintained by periodic fires.

The jack pine forests of the western Great Lakes region may also be the result of fire. The first lumberjacks in the area

found mixed forests of white pine, hardwoods, and jack pine. Over the years, intensive harvesting of the white pines left behind tons of debris that dried and eventually caught fire. The fire destroyed the trees and seeds of most species. But not the jack pine. The cones of this species remain tightly closed for many years and the seeds remain viable inside. When warmed by fire, the cones open slowly and release seeds into the cooling ashes that remain from what was once a mixed forest. Fire not only eliminates all competing species, but also provides ideal conditions for the germination and growth of the surviving jack pines. The result is a pure forest of jack pines.

Forest and range managers have begun to recognize the ecological importance of fire and are relaxing earlier policies of suppressing all fires. Smoky The Bear has a two-sided job.

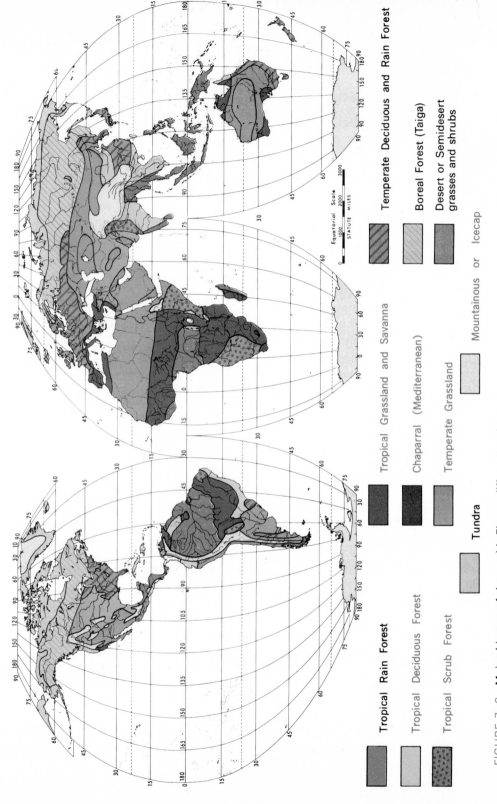

FIGURE 7-6 Major biomes of the world. Eleven different regions are shown, but five are variants of the six basic biome types (with titles in color). (Map by Robert Winter.)

Tropical Rain Forest

Tropical Deciduous Forest

Tropical Scrub Forest

Tropical Grassland and Savanna

Chaparral (Mediterranean)

Temperate Grassland

Tundra

Temperate Deciduous and Rain Forest

Boreal Forest (Taiga)

Desert or Semidesert grasses and shrubs

Mountainous or Icecap

Equatorial Scale
0   1000   2000   3000
STATUTE MILES

more, each biome contains many distinct communities. For example, there are several types of tropical forests and various kinds of deserts. Moreover, one biome can merge almost imperceptibly into another; boundaries are not always distinct. Another problem of classification by biomes is that the climax species in a region are not determined by its climate alone. Soil type and topography (which influences climate) are also important factors. Thus different species may occupy areas which have similar year-round temperatures but different patterns of rainfall. Broadly speaking, however, similar types of plant and animal life are found in similar environments even though the environments may be widely separated geographically. Coniferous forests, for example, stretch across both North America and much of the Eurasian continent. And deserts are found on every continent.

Thus the biome concept is both helpful and convenient in studying the distribution of living systems. In discussing the six major biomes, we shall focus on North American examples (Figure 7–7).

Tundra

This biome stretches across the northern continents, mainly above 60° north latitude. Since the tundra is characterized by snow, ice, and frozen soil most of the year, the plants and animals that live here must be able to resist the cold. The tundra is virtually treeless; its plants are primarily lichens, mosses, sedges, heaths, dwarfed willows, and a few grasses. Seasonal thawing of the frozen ground is an important factor in plant distribution in the tundra. A frozen tundra soil usually thaws from only a few inches to a few feet; therefore, only shallow-rooted plants can survive. Moreover, the flat terrain combined with the frozen subsoil produces plentiful surface water and shallow summer bogs. Caribou, arctic hares, foxes, lemmings, and migratory birds are common (Figure 7–8, on color plate following p. 160.)

Boreal Forest (Taiga)

Characterized by coniferous trees, the boreal forest (or taiga) forms a band across North America and Eurasia south of the tundra. Although spruces, firs, and tamarack are by far the most common, some deciduous trees such as paper birch also occur here (Figure 7–9, on color plate following p. 160). Also characteristic of these northern forests are numerous lakes and sphagnum peat bogs (Figure 7–5). Most of these lakes and bogs occupy holes gouged out by moving glaciers. Though the climate here is almost as severe as in the tundra, the growing season in the boreal forest is longer and warmer. A greater variety of plants is found here, but these plants must be able to withstand subzero temperatures and heavy snowfalls. Some animals common here are wolves, wolverines, lynx, black bears, and moose.

The borders of a boreal forest are not always sharply defined; various transition zones are found along its southern border. In eastern North America the transition is into a hardwood–conifer complex. In the west, the boreal forest merges with other coniferous forests, the Coastal Forest and the Rocky Mountain Forest. These forests are different in many respects, but they also have similarities. Common evergreen trees in these forests are various species of spruce, true fir, pine, cedar, and hemlock (Figure 7–10, on color plate following p. 160). Douglas firs, which are not true firs, are found in the western United States and in western Canada. In some areas conifers grow so densely that little light reaches the forest floor; few shrubs are found in these areas. But several shade-tolerant broadleaf species such as vine maple do well in the boreal forest, and spring wildflowers are common. Climax vegetation varies throughout these coniferous forests because of differences in climatic conditions. In mountainous areas, different species of conifers dominate at various elevations. In coastal regions, the amount of rainfall helps determine the type of plant life. The growing season in these forests varies from three or four months in the coldest areas to almost a full year along the Pacific coast, where the ocean moderates the climate. Coniferous forests are excellent habitats for elk, deer, grouse, rabbits, squirrels, mountain lions, and birds. In areas such as Washington's Olympic Peninsula and eastern

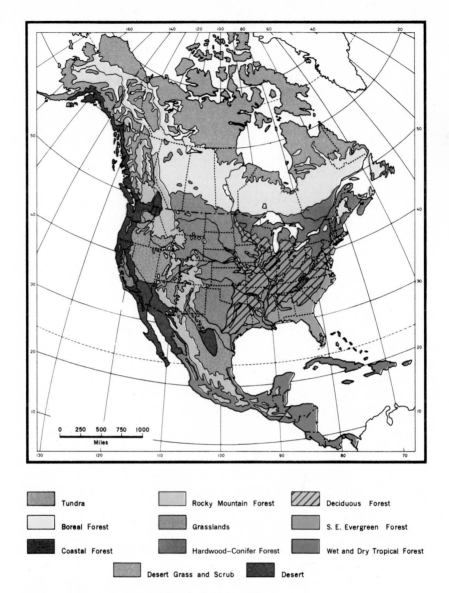

Tundra

Boreal Forest

Coastal Forest

Rocky Mountain Forest

Grasslands

Hardwood–Conifer Forest

Desert Grass and Scrub

Deciduous Forest

S. E. Evergreen Forest

Wet and Dry Tropical Forest

Desert

FIGURE 7–7 Climax vegetation zones of North America. Note that specific types of vegetation develop in specific climatic zones. (Map by Robert Winter.)

Asia, high annual rainfall allows the growth of lush vegetation. In these *rain forests* precipitation as high as 140 inches per year produces the humid conditions necessary for lush growth of mosses and ferns (Figure 7–11, on color plate following p. 160).

Deciduous Forest

Deciduous hardwood trees are the climax vegetation in the deciduous forest. These forests are found principally in north-central Europe, eastern Asia, and the eastern United States. Hickory, oak, elm, beech, and maple are typical broad-leaved species in the United States. Annual precipitation of 30 to 60 inches and a temperate climate are critical factors in this biome. When temperatures drop in the autumn, most trees and shrubs shed their leaves.

The deciduous forests of the eastern United States are quite complex because of varying altitudes, rainfall patterns, and soil types. In the Appalachian and Great Smoky mountains, for example, northern hardwoods may be bordered closely by and mixed with stands of hemlock, spruce, and fir. Further to the south lies the Southeast Evergreen Forest, composed chiefly of southern pine. The open stands of southern pine are actually subclimax forests; if they are not perpetuated by selective cutting and burning, they will be succeeded by magnolia and live oak trees.

In the northern reaches of the deciduous biome on the North American continent, temperatures range from 109°F to below −20°F and annual precipitation averages about 30 inches. Common trees of this region, the Hardwood–Conifer Forest, are spruce, hemlock, white pine, sugar maple, basswood, oak, and birch. Sphagnum peat bogs are also characteristic of this area. Frogs, salamanders, turtles, snakes, lizards, squirrels, foxes, songbirds, rabbits, deer, and raccoons are representative animals (Figure 7–12, on color plate following p. 160).

Tropical Forest

Tropical forests are characterized by high rainfall (more than 100 inches) that occurs during most of the year. We generally refer to these areas as *jungles*; they are found in central Africa, southern Asia, the Amazon Basin, and northern Central America. On the southern tip of Florida a trace of tropical forest also occurs. The warm, humid climate supports broad-leaved evergreen plants. In the jungle the trees are stratified into an overstory and usually two understory levels. The tallest trees (about 120 feet) form an open canopy, but the second and third crown levels block so much sunlight that the jungle floor is usually in deep shade. Ferns and herbaceous plants are common on the jungle floor. Jungle animals include monkeys, snakes, anteaters, birds, and large carnivores such as lions, tigers, and leopards (Figure 7–13, on color plate following p. 160).

Grassland

Grassland covers much of the world's land. It extends through north-central Eurasia, north-central and southern Africa, the central United States (Figure 7–14, on color plate following p. 160), central South America, and the northern half of Australia. Rainfall in grassland regions is often irregular but averages between 10 and 30 inches annually. Strong winds, common throughout grassland areas, dry the soil and air and discourage the establishment of trees.

The western border of the Great Plains in the United States receives much less precipitation than its southern and eastern regions. Because of this difference in rainfall, short grasses are found in the western regions, and longer grass species predominate in the east. Large herds of bison and antelope once roamed the grasslands. As the area became settled, however, the herds were destroyed by hunters. Early efforts at farming left much of the prairie devastated; plowed land, stripped of its grass cover, became badly eroded by wind and water. Farmers using contour plowing, crop rotation methods, and windbreaks of trees and shrubs now have most of the prairie under cultivation or grazing.

Grazing animals dominate in this biome. Common species include jackrabbits, antelope, and prairie dogs. The grasslands of Africa, commonly known as *savanna*, receive ample rainfall in their wet season. But severe drought for several months each year discourages the establishment of trees. A great variety of animals occur in the savanna; large herbivores such as antelopes and zebras are preyed upon by lions and cheetahs.

Although not a grassland, another biome type is found at latitudes where grasslands are common. This is the *chaparral*, characterized by evergreen shrubs with stiff, thick leaves. In the United States chaparral occurs in California, Arizona, and New Mexico. The vegetation becomes very dry and is susceptible to fire.

Desert

Deserts are characterized by extremely low rainfall, generally less than 10 inches per year.

In most deserts rainfall is not only sparse but uneven, and average rainfall figures can be misleading because of spring and summer flash floods. More than an inch of rain may fall to produce a flash flood, but most of that water is unavailable to plants because of rapid runoff or high evaporation rates. Major deserts are found in North Africa, Australia, southwestern United States, and Mexico. A strip of desert is located along the ocean borders of Chile and Peru in South America, and another is found in the interior of Argentina (Figure 7–6).

North American deserts are often classified as cool or hot. The Great Basin Desert, located in parts of Washington, Oregon, Idaho, Wyoming, Utah, and Nevada, is mostly above 3000 feet elevation. The annual rainfall of this cool, high desert varies between 8 and 15 inches. Maximum temperatures average about 105°F, and early morning dew is not uncommon. Winter temperatures may drop to −30°F in many areas. Sagebrush, cheatgrass, and saltbrush are the major plants. Some deserts, such as the Washington and Oregon Great Basin areas, result from a "rain shadow." The high mountain ranges bordering these deserts cause the cool, moist air from the ocean to drop much of its water load on the coast side, thus reducing the rainfall on the interior side.

The Mohave Desert in southern Nevada, eastern California, and the northwest part of Arizona is hotter than the Great Basin Desert, sometimes reaching 115°F. Annual rainfall is lower and more uneven (4 to 8 inches). Common plants of this region include creosote bush, yucca, joshua trees, and various small cacti. Two more hot desert areas occur to the south of the Mohave—the Sonoran, principally in southern Arizona and California, and Baja California and Sonora, Mexico; and the Chihuahuan of central New Mexico and the Mexican Plateau. Here the temperatures may soar to 125°F. Annual rainfall is meager, except in some areas near the Mexican border where 10 to 16 inches is common. A cactus found in both the southern Mohave and Sonoran Deserts is the giant saguaro, which may attain a height of 40 feet and weigh nearly 10 tons (Figure 7–15, on the color plate adjacent). The hot deserts also support smaller cacti such as pincushion, prickly pear, and barrel; green-barked paloverde trees; creosote bush; mesquite; and a few hardy grasses and flowers.

Of particular interest are the adaptations of both plants and animals to these hostile conditions. Some plants, such as paloverde, lose their leaves during the hottest months; others have small, waxy, or hairy leaves which retard evaporation. Most flowering plants are perennial and therefore able to survive even though their seeds may not germinate due to dry conditions. Deep taproots and extensive, spreading root systems are common. Some animals have such efficient kidneys that they get all the moisture they need from seeds and other food; they never need to drink water. The kangaroo rat is one of these. Animals typical of the desert biome include insects, rabbits, quail, doves, rattlesnakes, scorpions, lizards, and coyotes.

Life Zones: Changes with Altitude

Besides biomes, another classification system for the distribution of plants and animals is sometimes used. This system is especially useful in such mountainous regions as western North America, where patterns of plant life vary with altitude. Such regions are termed *life zones;* they result from changes in temperature, rainfall, and soil types.

Whichever concept—biomes or life zones—is used, patches of vegetation characteristic of northerly regions are found in more southerly areas along mountain ranges that run north-to-south. For example, arctic-alpine zones on high peaks in the Cascade and Rocky Mountains are similar to the arctic and tundra of the far north. Arms of the northern boreal forest, too, may reach southward in the higher elevations of these mountains. Just as we observe a series of biomes while traveling from south to north, then, we would observe similar ecological transitions as we move vertically up the side of a mountain (Figure 7–16).

THE FRESHWATER ENVIRONMENT: LAKES AND PONDS

Lakes and ponds occur in practically every biome (Figure 7–17, on the color plate adja-

PLATE V

FIGURE 7–5   The edge of a bog in Oregon, showing sphagnum moss, sedges, and a floating border of water lilies.

FIGURE 7–8   Tundra of northern Alaska, showing low-growing shrubs typical of this biome. (EPA—Documerica.)

FIGURE 7–8

FIGURE 7–5

FIGURE 7-9   Boreal forest. (Richard Frear, National Park Service.)

FIGURE 7-10   Northern coniferous forest. (EPA—Documerica.)

FIGURE 7-11   Rain forest in Olympic National Park. Note the lush moss growth. (National Park Service.)

FIGURE 7-12   Deciduous forest in Shenandoah National Park. (Richard Frear, National Park Service.)

FIGURE 7-13   Tropical forest in Puerto Obaldia, Puerto Rico. (Foto Hetzel.)

FIGURE 7-14   Grassland savanna in Kenya, Africa. (Audrey Ross.)

FIGURE 7-9

FIGURE 7-12

FIGURE 7-10

PLATE VII

FIGURE 7-11

JRE 7-13

FIGURE 7-14

PLATE VIII

FIGURE 7-15   Saguaro cactus in a southern Arizona desert. (Fred Mang, Jr., National Park Service.)

FIGURE 7-17   Crater Lake in southern Oregon, a deep oligotrophic lake. (W. S. Keller, National Park Service.)

FIGURE 7-15

FIGURE 7-17

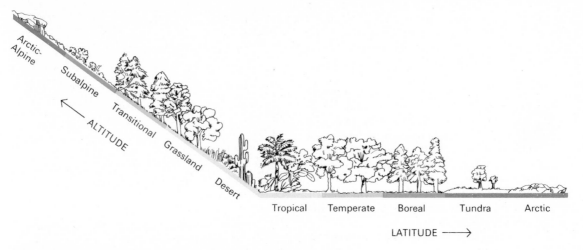

FIGURE 7-16 Comparison of vegetational zones of north-south (latitude) distribution with zones encountered with increasing altitude. The vertical or altitudinal regions are often called life zones. The arctic-alpine life zone corresponds to tundra and arctic conditions, subalpine corresponds to boreal, and transitional to temperate, since both have conifer and deciduous species.

cent). They vary in size from less than an acre to many thousands of square miles, and in depth from several feet to more than a mile. Lakes may be created by several processes. Some are the result of glaciers, whereas others are formed from parts of meandering rivers, cut off from the main stream. Lakes are often classified on the basis of the amount of organic matter they contain. *Eutrophic* lakes are relatively shallow, with a rich accumulation of organic products. *Oligotrophic* lakes, on the other hand, are generally deep and often have rocky, steep sides. The supply of circulating nutrients such as phosphates is often low in these lakes, and the ratio of organic materials to the volume of water is also low.

Almost every biology class has access to a body of fresh water for observation. It's an excellent way to learn biology.

Light in Lakes

The energy producers need to make food by photosynthesis is supplied by sunlight. How much a lake's producers (algae) can photosynthesize depends on how much light enters the lake and how deep it penetrates. The amount of organic matter in a lake affects the depth to which light penetrates. Inorganic particles such as silt and mud also affect the clarity of water. In oligotrophic lakes light may be detected as deep as 50 feet. On the other hand, lakes abounding with algae permit light penetration to only a few feet. In eutrophic lakes where great algae growth screens out light in the first several feet, much of the algae and many fish may ultimately die. Their death may result not only from lack of light but also from lack of oxygen, because of bacterial action causing the decay of dead algae.

Temperature of Lakes

The temperature of a lake is affected by solar radiation. In temperate latitudes, every lake deep or shallow, undergoes a yearly cycle that parallels the changing seasons. In late winter or early spring, the ice layer covering the lake melts and the upper waters warm slightly. As the top layer approaches 4°C it sinks to the bottom, because water reaches its maximum density at this temperature. Ice, always at 0°C or colder, is less dense than liquid water at any temperature. Thus it floats on the surface, and thus a natural body of water always freezes from the top down. This fact is crucial to living systems.

If ice were denser than liquid water, it would sink to the bottom, and lakes would freeze from the bottom up. During especially cold winters, lakes and ponds in high latitudes and in middle latitudes would freeze solid. But because ice floats, lakes and ponds freeze from the top down. The ice cover helps to insulate the water beneath it against subzero atmospheric temperatures, so only extremely shallow bodies of water ever freeze solid.

In the spring, water currents and waves generated by the wind bring about a thorough mixing of the water in the lake. This is called the *spring turnover.*

Higher summer temperatures warm the surface water of the lake. Since this warm water is less dense than the cooler water below, it floats on the cooler water and resists mixing with it. Because of this *layering* phenomenon, the temperature of many lakes during the summer drops sharply at a particular depth. The layer in which this rapid temperature drop occurs is known as the *thermocline.* In a deep lake the thermocline may lie between 30 and 45 meters; in a shallower lake it may occur between 3.5 and 4.5 meters (Figure 7–18). The layer of water above the thermocline is called the *epilimnion;* the layer below is the *hypolimnion.* The thermocline prevents mixing of these two layers of water and thus causes a summer stagnation.

Autumn brings cooler temperatures and the surface waters begin to cool; this brings about a uniform temperature structure once more. Mixing as a result of wind-driven currents and waves can again take place. This mixing produces an *autumn turnover.* As winter begins, an ice layer may form, leading to a winter stagnation period. If ice does not form, some mixing of water may continue throughout the winter, because the water temperature remains fairly uniform from top to bottom. Figure 7–19 summarizes the sequence of temperature changes throughout the year.

If water did not move from top to bottom in

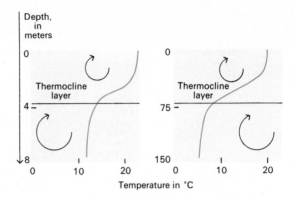

FIGURE 7–18   Summer temperature structures in two different lakes in Washington. (*a*) Cranberry Lake. (*b*) Lake Chelan.

a lake, materials could not be circulated throughout the whole body of water. Seasonal turnovers cause mixing, which in turn moves nutrients up from the bottom and carries oxygen to lower layers. Mixing also distributes organisms throughout the lake.

Oxygen in Lakes

The oxygen content of lake water at various depths provides an indication of the productivity of that lake. By *productivity* we mean a lake's ability to produce organic material from inorganic substances. The upper part of a lake is usually the region of autotrophism; heterotrophism occurs in the lower part, where light does not penetrate.

The oxygen content of lake water can be determined by taking samples from various depths and subjecting them to chemical analysis. Oxygen levels are usually expressed in milliliters or milligrams of oxygen per liter of water (ml/l or mg/l). The temperature structure of a lake may have a great deal to do with its oxygen content at various depths, especially during the summer when the hypolimnion does not mix with the epilimnion. Whether a lake is oligotrophic (with a low rate of photosynthesis) or eutrophic (with a higher rate) also affects the amount and distribution of available oxygen (Figure 7–20).

Dissolved oxygen in bodies of water has two

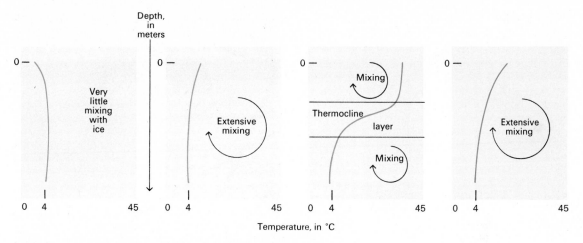

FIGURE 7-19 General temperature structure of most lakes throughout the year. (*a*) Winter. (*b*) Spring. (*c*) Summer. (*d*) Fall.

sources: (1) the atmosphere, by mixing when surface disturbances occur; and (2) photosynthesis by producers (algae). Winds or other events that enhance mixing will increase a lake's oxygen content. Water temperature is also a factor, since cold water can hold more oxygen than warm water.

Other Chemical Compounds in Lakes

Some of the carbon dioxide in a lake is present as part of the bicarbonate ion, since CO_2 read-

ily unites with water. The relationship is:

$$CO_2 + H_2O \rightleftharpoons H_2CO_3 \rightleftharpoons HCO_3^- + H^+$$

Large amounts of dissolved CO_2 thus can increase the acidity of a body of water. Acidity is greater during those times of year when consumer organisms increase in number and release large amounts of CO_2 through respiration.

Nitrates and phosphates are important to the productivity of all ecosystems, including lakes. Since ammonia is the chief product of plant and animal protein decomposition, it can be a source of nitrates if nitrogen-fixing bacteria are present. Phosphates can be scarce, especially in oligotrophic lakes where they may be insoluble and unavailable. Some algae can concentrate phosphorus in their systems by active transport, even when its concentration in the water is extremely low.

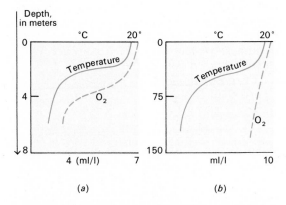

(*a*)   (*b*)

FIGURE 7-20 Summer temperatures and oxygen levels in two different lakes in Washington. (*a*) Cranberry Lake is eutrophic. (*b*) Lake Chelan is oligotrophic.

Freshwater Food Relationships

The same food relationships exist in an aquatic community as in a terrestrial system:

Producers → Consumers → Decomposers

A large and varied group of organisms found only in aquatic environments is *plankton*,

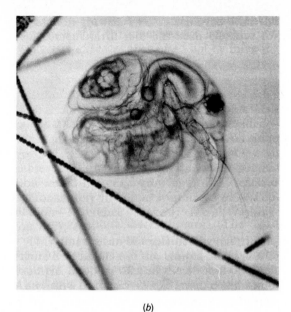

(a)   (b)

FIGURE 7–21 Some examples of freshwater plankton. (a) The spindle-shaped organism at the upper left is the dinoflagellate *Ceratium;* the fork-shaped organism is the rotifer, *Keratella;* the comb-shaped and rod-shaped organisms are diatoms ($\times$ 280). (b) The water flea *Bosmina.*

which are usually small, free-floating organisms. The *phytoplankton* contain chlorophyll and so are capable of synthesizing food. All aquatic algae are phytoplankton. The *zooplankton* depend on phytoplankton as their food source. Plankton are essential members of all aquatic food chains, since they are the producers and primary consumers. One chain commonly found in lakes and oceans is:

Phytoplankton $\rightarrow$ Zooplankton $\rightarrow$
                    Small fish $\rightarrow$ Large fish

Diatoms are among the most important algal members of the phytoplankton of any body of water. Some common plankton forms found in lakes are shown in Figure 7–21.

THE MARINE ENVIRONMENT

Today more and more attention is being focused on the sea, not only as a huge biome of interesting plants and animals but also as a source of food, minerals, and petroleum, and even as a potential habitat for our booming population. *Oceanography*, the study of the sea, draws upon all branches of science.

The oceans are *saline* (salty): their waters contain high concentrations of salt and mineral ions. The most abundant ions in seawater are sodium and chlorine, followed by sulfur, magnesium, and calcium. Every naturally occurring element known is found in the sea.

The most common ions occurring in seawater and their concentrations (in grams per kilogram of seawater) are listed below:

		grams/kilogram
Chloride	Cl^-	19.4
Sodium	Na^+	10.7
Sulfate	$SO_4^=$	2.7
Magnesium	Mg^{++}	1.3
Calcium	Ca^{++}	0.4
Potassium	K^+	0.39
Bicarbonate	HCO_3^-	0.14
Bromide	Br^-	0.065

Dissolved ions occur in very stable proportions in seawater, so total salinity is often calculated on the basis of chloride-ion concentration alone. Salinity of the oceans average 35 parts per thousand (g/kg). Salinity varies most in surface water, which is affected by land runoff, precipitation, evaporation, and melting polar ice. Salinity is highest in tropical regions, where the rate of evaporation is greatest.

Depth Zones

The five major oceans of the earth are the Pacific, Atlantic, Indian, Arctic, and Antarctic. Generally speaking, the cross section of an ocean is shaped like a wash basin. The rim of the basin represents the continental shelf (the edges of the continents). A relatively shallow area of water called the *neritic province* covers the continental shelf. The *oceanic province*, the deeper region of the sea, lies off the continental shelf—it fills the main portion of the wash basin in our analogy. Continental shelves extend out from shore an average of 100 miles to form the *continental slope*, which descends gradually to the ocean bottom. Profiles of the Pacific and Atlantic ocean floors show an irregular topography of ridges, basins, and deep trenches. The Mariana trench, believed to be the deepest, is located east of the Philippine Islands in the Pacific. In 1960 the manned bathyscaphe *Trieste II* descended to a depth of 35,802 feet. There are several deep trenches, but the average depth of the oceans is 2½ miles (12,000 feet).

Since the rate of photosynthesis depends on

Bio-Topic: Life at the Limit

Most communities on our planet are made up of producers, consumers, and decomposers interacting in a complex and delicate balance. A few unusual communities, however, contain no producers, yet they persist. How?

The common feature of such producerless communities is total and unending darkness. An example of such a community is the collection of organisms that live in the icy deep ocean trenches 16,000 feet below the surface. These organisms live in a world where the temperature hovers near freezing and the pressure is a crushing 10,000 times greater than at sea level. Most of the inhabitants of this forbidding world are close relatives of organisms that live nearer the surface. They have adapted to life at the limit by evolving ways to tolerate extraordinary pressures and a Spartan diet. These bottom dwellers are usually pale and blind, as are the inhabitants of deep caves—another producerless community.

If no light penetrates to these depths and there are no producers, where do the denizens of the deep obtain the energy and nutrients to sustain themselves? One possibility is that they eat the carcasses of animals from the surface that float down after dying. This does happen, but the carcasses are often devoured by fish and other animals on the way down. The food that does reach the bottom is a mixture of the wastes from all the creatures that live nearer the surface, along with skins cast off by crustaceans and an occasional morsel overlooked on the way down.

This steady rain of debris serves as food for bottom bacteria which in turn end up as food for the larger bottom dwellers. The energy and nutrients that sustain the bottom community began as sunlight and minerals at the surface and passed through the bodies of perhaps dozens of other organisms on the way down.

the amount of light available, the ocean is often classified into zones according to light penetration (Figure 7–22). The upper 600 feet, the *photic* zone, contains the largest number of organisms; plankton are especially abundant. In marine environments the most numerous phytoplankton are diatoms and dinoflagellates. Zooplankton species include representatives of many animal phyla, but crustaceans predominate both in number of species and in total individuals. Another broad category of organisms, the *nekton*, consists of free-swimming organisms such as fish, squid, and whales. These live not only in the photic zone but in all parts of the ocean.

Although the upper 600 feet of an ocean are generally called the photic zone, some light penetrates as deep as 1200 feet. But because the light below is insufficient for photosynthesis, the area below 600 feet is called the *aphotic zone*. Below 1200 feet is the *dark open-water zone*, a region of perpetual darkness. The animals living here, mostly predators that feed on smaller forms, exhibit interesting adaptations. Some, such as the viperfish and pelican fish, possess enormous jaws and sharp teeth; others have luminescent organs to attract prey. Below 6000 feet is the bottom, or *benthic*, zone. Samples brought to the surface from this depth by dredging and net trawling include bacteria,

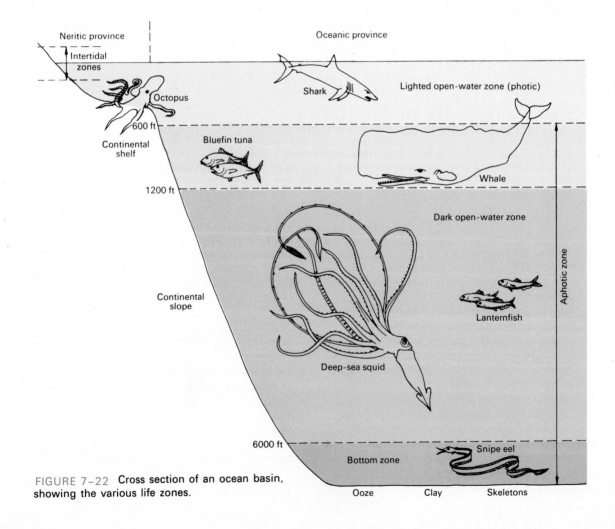

FIGURE 7–22 **Cross section of an ocean basin, showing the various life zones.**

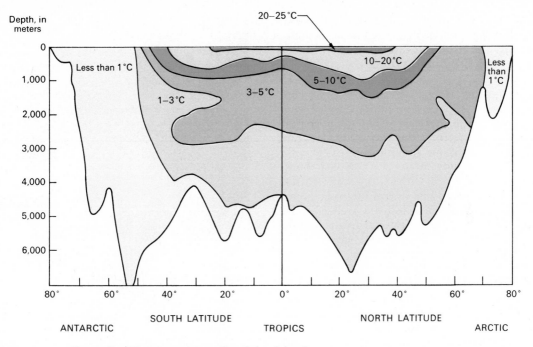

FIGURE 7–23 Generalized temperature profile of the Atlantic Ocean.

siliceous sponges, sea cucumbers, bivalves (mollusks such as clams), polychaete worms, various crustaceans, and brittle stars. A very efficient method of surveying benthic life developed recently involves closed-circuit television.

Ocean temperature also limits the growth and respiration of both plants and animals. Many organisms are distributed according to their ability to withstand extreme temperatures. Ocean temperatures, however, are much more uniform than land temperatures. Therefore adaptation to great temperature changes is not a requirement for oceanic life.

The major temperature variations in the ocean occur in the upper 3000 feet. The Arctic and Antarctic regions are always near 0°C; the Antarctic is somewhat colder. Although surface temperatures of certain seas such as the Red Sea reach 30°C or more, the major expanse of ocean surface ranges from 15 to 27°C. Since seawater freezes at −1.9°C, the temperature range of surface water is approximately −1.9°C

to 30°C. Even at the North and South Poles, water below 6000 feet varies only 2 to 3 degrees throughout the year. These temperature relationships are illustrated in Figure 7–23, which represents a vertical section of the Atlantic Ocean between the Arctic and Antarctic.

Seasonal thermoclines can exist in the oceans, but they are less pronounced than in freshwater lakes. Factors that influence the formation and duration of thermoclines include: (1) warm or cold currents; (2) geographical location (tropical, temperate, or polar); and (3) mixing produced by wave action and upwelling, the rise of deeper water to replace surface water which has been carried away from a coast by wind action or which sinks because it is colder and more dense. Because surface water in tropical regions is consistently warm, little mixing occurs there, and a thermocline persists throughout the year. In temperate and polar latitudes, where surface cooling does occur, temperature profiles are cyclic like those of freshwater lakes. Vertical mixing recirculates minerals necessary to maintain phytoplankton. The greatest amount of plankton—and therefore the best fishing—is thus found in higher northern and southern latitudes.

Intertidal Zones

Tide refers to the vertical rise and fall of coastal waters resulting from the gravitational attraction of the moon and sun. In contrast, *currents* are horizontal movements of water as a consequence of tide, wind, temperature, and salinity. Plants and animals that live in intertidal zones are repeatedly covered and uncovered as the tides rise and fall. The intertidal area is usually divided into life zones: (1) spray zone; (2) high-tide zone; (3) mid-tide zone; and (4) low-tide zone (Figure 7–27). (Tides are measured from a zero point which is the average level of low tides and this average is indicated as zero on a tide table. Levels above zero are plus tides; those below are minus tides.) The spray zone is never covered by water except during storms. The high-tide zone is above tide zero; the mid-tide zone represents the normal zero range; and the low-tide zone is uncovered only by minus tides.

The physical nature of a beach determines which species of plants and animals can survive there. The most common beach types are rocky, sandy, and mud flat (Figures 7–24, 7–25, 7–26). In some areas, nearby freshwater sources produce brackish, or estuarine, conditions. Organisms living in estuarine habitats must be able to withstand wide fluctuations in salinity. Some of them adapt by regulating their internal salt content; these *osmoregulating* organisms will be discussed in Chapter 11. Other factors determining what organisms are found on a particular beach include the amount of protection available from the pounding surf and the length of exposure when the tide is out.

Animals living in intertidal zones show definite zone preferences; many have special physiological adaptions for living in particular zones. On rocky, unprotected beaches in the Pacific Northwest, for example, an air-breathing isopod (*Ligyda*) and the small periwinkle snail (*Littorina*) live on the rocks and in crevices in the spray zone; the acorn barnacle (*Balanus*)

FIGURE 7–24   East Coast rocky coastline in Acadia National Park in Maine. (National Park Service.)

and shore crabs (*Hemigrapsus*) inhabit the high-tide zone; purple and green sea urchins (*Strongylocentrotus*), the green anemone (*Anthopleura*), and the black turban snail (*Tegula*) are common in the mid-tide zone; the giant red sea urchin (*Strongylocentrotus franciscanus*) and the gum boot chiton (*Cryptochiton*) live in the low-tide zone (Figure 7–27a).

Rocky beaches support by far the greatest number and variety of plants and animals. Fragile organisms such as worms and sea cucumbers find shelter in crevices and under large rocks. Sea urchins and piddock clams actually burrow into hard sandstone in the tide pools left by the receding water. Hardy barnacles, mussels, starfish, chitons, snails, and anemones cling to rocks and withstand the full force of the surf.

On sandy beaches, the distribution of life is

FIGURE 7-25   West Coast beach, showing rocky headlands and sandy beach. (National Park Service.)

limited by lack of shelter, attachment sites, and permanent tide pools. Burrowing animals are best suited to this environment. Sandy beaches support clams, worms, sand dollars, and certain crabs (Figure 7-27b). Zonation is evident on these beaches too. On the Atlantic and Gulf coasts, the ghost shrimp and ghost crab can live quite high on the beach. The entire beach usually abounds with the variable clam (*Donax*). Other common forms include edible Venus clams (*Mercenaria*), cockles (*Dinocardium*), arc shells (*Arca*), jackknife clams (*Ensis*), scallops (*Aequipecten*), and edible blue crabs (*Callinectes*). On the West Coast, sandy beaches support such edible varieties as razor clams (*Siliqua*), butter clams (*Saxidomus*), steamer or little-neck clams (*Prothaca*), and scallops (*Pecten*).

In mud-flat habitats, even minor tidal fluctuations may expose large expanses of mud and green eel grass. Clams, worms, snails, crabs, shrimps, and isopods are the most common organisms. The muddy bottom is characteristic of shallow, protected bays that lack circulation and wave action. When the tide is out, a rotten-egg stench of hydrogen sulfide from decaying organic matter is quite common. The mud is mixed with fine organic debris which provides excellent food for burrowing filter feeders and scavengers. On West Coast sand and mud flats the large, edible geoduck clam (*Panope*) sometimes reaches a weight of six pounds. The Dungeness crab (*Cancer*), important for food, also thrives here.

So far, we have considered various communities as if they existed independently of

FIGURE 7–26   East Coast mud flat. Oysters and mud snails are easily seen when the tide is out. At high tide the entire area is covered with water. (Jack Dermid.)

human influence. But humans are members of most of the major terrestrial communities, and their activities affect *all* communities, terrestrial and aquatic. So there is really no such thing as a natural community if "natural" means "undisturbed by humans." Still, our approach in this chapter has been sound; for purposes of analysis it is both possible and helpful to consider many aspects of living communities independently of human influence on them.

But our study of living communities would be far from complete—and hopelessly naive—if it stopped here. The human impact on the world environment and its living communities is great. It is largely destructive, and it increases with each passing day. In Chapter 8 we examine some of the disturbing problems and prospects of human impact on nature.

SUMMARY

All environments change. Every ecosystem undergoes a characteristic series of changes determined by climate, soil type, and the types and interactions of organisms. This series of changes, or succession, occurs until a group of organisms (the climax) is established which can live and reproduce most successfully in the area. Primary succession occurs in areas which are devoid of life, such as bare rock. When development in an area is disrupted, secondary succession takes place.

Successional processes have produced the major land communities of the earth. Each area, or biome, has characteristic plant and animal species. The six principal biomes are: tundra, boreal forest, deciduous forest, tropical forest, grassland, and desert. In mountainous

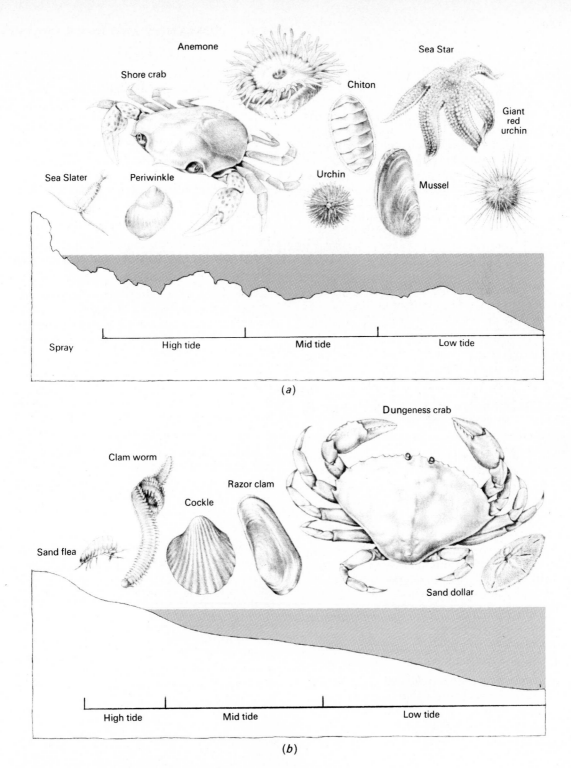

FIGURE 7–27 **Representative animals found in intertidal zones on the West Coast.** (*a*) Rocky beach. (*b*) Sandy beach.

areas, altitudinal zones (life zones) occur. The sequences of life zones on a mountain corresponds to the latitude sequence of biomes.

Freshwater lakes can be rich in organic matter (eutrophic) or low in nutrients (oligotrophic). The physiological and chemical aspects of lakes include light, temperature, oxygen, chemical compounds, and food relationships. These same characteristics are important in marine environments. In addition, depth and tidal considerations are important in studying the oceans.

REVIEW QUESTIONS

1. Blackberry pickers know that wild blackberries can be found in burned or logged forest areas. Why do berries grow best in these areas?

2. If a volcanic eruption suddenly created a new island 50 miles off the coast of California, what successional changes could you predict during the next few hundred years?

3. What are the major characteristics of biomes? Compare the characteristics of a desert biome to those of an eastern hardwood forest.

4. Find out what the climax vegetation is in your area. Next, find a piece of land that has been cleared or altered. Describe the changes that will probably take place in reestablishing the climax.

5. On San Francisco Peaks near Flagstaff, Arizona, alpine fir grows at about 12,000 feet. In the Cascade Mountains of western Washington, this same species may grow at 5000 feet. How can you explain this difference?

6. What could be some of the consequences of a late summer "bloom" (explosive growth) of phytoplankton in a lake? Consider temperature, oxygen, and zooplankton interrelationships.

7. Explain the importance of each of the following compounds to the support of fish in a

lake: dissolved oxygen, dissolved carbon dioxide and bicarbonate ion, phosphates, and nitrates.

8. Compare the physical and biological characteristics of the benthic and intertidal oceanic zones.

SUPPLEMENTARY READINGS

Costello, David F., *The Prairie World*, Thomas Y. Crowell, New York, 1969. Treats the interrelationships of plants and animals of the grasslands in a sensitive and scientific narrative.

Farb, Peter, *Face of North America: The Natural History of a Continent*, Harper & Row, New York, 1963. An ecological interpretation of the diverse features and wildlife from Florida to the Pacific Ocean.

Fell, Barry, *Introduction to Marine Biology*, Harper & Row, New York, 1975. A survey of the distribution of the common organisms of the oceans along with a limited discussion of physical oceanography and ecology.

Freuchen, Peter and Finn Salomonsen, *The Arctic Year*, G. P. Putman's Sons, New York, 1958. A month by month description of the dynamics of the Arctic biome written by an explorer and a naturalist.

Horn, Henry S., "Forest Succession," *Scientific American*, May 1975. The development or regeneration of a forest goes through stages known as succession and the pattern of how one community replaces another is discussed in this article.

Isaacs, John D. and R. A. Schwartzlose, "Active Animals of the Deep-Sea Floor," *Scientific American*, October 1975. The many populations of fishes and other scavengers, their adaptations, and how they are studied are discussed in this interesting article.

Chapter 8

Living Communities: Human Impact

The daily headlines contain a great deal of applied biology. In this chapter, we will see how the ecological principles of Chapters 6 and 7 are directly demonstrated in the relationship between human beings and their environment.

As a species, we have a serious impact on our environment in many ways. Perhaps foremost among them is *The Human Population.* In addition to the natural factors described in Chapter 6, political and economic factors come into play when we are *Analyzing Population Trends. The Industrial Revolution,* the improvement of modern agriculture, and new discoveries in medicine have made possible declines in overall death rates and infant mortality while at the same time increasing the carrying capacity of our planet. But there are limitations on our ability to increase our population and keep it healthy. The two alternatives of *Population Control: Planned or Catastrophic* really offer a choice between disastrous control by famine and disease or planned control through government incentives and improved contraceptive techniques.

The relationship between *Food and Population* has been studied scientifically since the time of Malthus in the late eighteenth century. The most severe problem posed by the increasing world population is the need to maintain an adequate food supply. Maintaining our present agricultural systems will not do the job; at the same time, many modern agricultural practices are dangerous to the long-term health of the land. Agricultural planning in the future will probably involve *Matching the Crop to the Ecosystem* in which it is grown. Further, you might recall that each successive step in a food chain involves a loss of available energy from the preceding level. Thus, *Reducing Food-Chain Lengths* is essential if we are to make food production more energy-efficient.

Increasing world population and the development of modern technology have combined to create an additional hazard—*Environmental Pollution.* As countries strive to provide their populations with a suitable standard of living, they continue to drain the world's natural resources of materials and energy while at the same time creating wastes and by-products that can be dangerous when released into the environment. At the end of this chapter we survey some of these classes of pollutants.

173

We members of the species *Homo sapiens* may be "mere mortals." But the fate of this planet's *biosphere,* the total area of the earth in which organisms live, which we share with millions of other species, is largely in our hands. So far, the record of our stewardship has not been good. We have reproduced ourselves until our numbers place a heavy and growing burden on the biosphere's carrying capacity. We have acquired the power to control the life situations of other organisms and to alter the natural environment intentionally. We have used this power with devastating results, including the unintentional extinction of many species.

Technology has made possible environmental destruction as well as human progress. We all hope that technology also holds solutions to many of our self-inflicted problems. But if we are to solve the many environmental problems, we must develop new attitudes toward our environment as well as new technological solutions. Since the runaway growth of the human population is at the root of many of our problems, we shall consider it first.

THE HUMAN POPULATION

More than 4 billion people live in the world today. Tomorrow—literally tomorrow—there will be 200,000 more of us. Each day approximately that number—the population of a good-sized city—is added to the human community.

Tomorrow 200,000 more; next year, perhaps 80 million more; and by the year 2010, between two and four billion more, if the present annual rate of world population growth (1.9 percent) continues. By the year 2010, you will be sharing this planet with 6 to 8 billion other people.

These figures, unprecedented in human history, are the reason why the term "population explosion" is used so often. The word *explosion* may be defined as "a rapid and expansive change of state." This describes precisely what has been happening recently to the human population.

Relative to the million-year history of our species, the "explosive" phase of our population growth has been very brief indeed: it has taken place almost entirely within the last 250 years.

What accounts for this tremendous growth and this rapidly accelerating growth *rate?* Obviously, people are being born faster than they die. But the situation is somewhat more complex than that. We shall see how this explosive growth rate came about, why it will probably continue for the next few decades, and why it cannot continue for much longer than that. We shall also consider what must be done if a global human catastrophe is to be avoided.

Analyzing Population Trends

Like any population, the world's human population will grow if the number of births (b) exceeds the number of deaths (d) in a given period of time. In other words, birth rate minus death rate equals growth rate. If b is greater than d, the population is increasing (positive growth rate); if b is less than d, the population is shrinking (negative growth rate); if $b = d$, the population size remains constant (zero growth rate).

The terms *birth rate* and *death rate* as used above are more properly called the *crude birth rate* and the *crude death rate;* they refer to the annual number of births or deaths per 1000 members of a population. In themselves, however, crude birth and death rates do not give much information about the composition, or structure, of a population. But the structure of a population directly affects its growth rate.

Crude birth and death rates do not reflect such factors as migration, age distribution, and sex distribution. Migration shifts many people from place to place, but by itself it does not affect the worldwide population growth rate. Sex distribution can have a marked effect on population growth rates, particularly during large-scale wars, which kill disproportionate numbers of young men. World War I killed millions of French and German males, with the result that millions of French and German females of childbearing age never had children. This affected not only the sex distribution of the childbearing generation but also the age distribution of the whole population for decades to come.

Population Profiles and Population Trends

Sex and age distributions are easily and clearly seen in diagrams like those in Figure 8–1. None of the three countries shown lost large numbers of its males in the two world wars. In all three countries the sex distributions are quite symmetric: the numbers of both sexes are about equal in each age group. But the age distribution itself varies greatly among age levels, and the age distribution of each country is quite different. Furthermore—and this is significant in analyzing population trends—population growth is largely determined by the numbers of individuals in various age groups.

In countries such as Mexico where populations are expanding, the distribution of age groups is shaped like a pyramid (Figure 8–1a).

In countries with stable populations, such as Sweden, the age-group structure assumes more rectangular proportions, with a greater percentage of individuals in the older age groups (Figure 8–1b). In countries such as the United States, whose populations are headed toward stability, the age-group structure lies somewhere between the pyramidal and rectangular extremes (Figure 8–1c).

Population profiles like those in Figure 8–1 can tell us something about population *trends* if we know something about the population's birth and death rates. The more we know about those rates, the more the diagrams can tell us. For example, we have said that countries whose populations are growing have population structures shaped like pyramids: they are broad at the base, because of the large proportion of

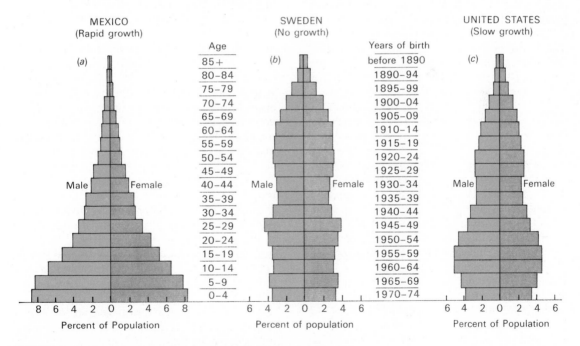

FIGURE 8–1 Age-sex population profiles. (*a*) Mexico (rapid growth). (*b*) Sweden (no growth). (*c*) United States (slow growth). A pyramid with a large base is characteristic of rapidly growing countries such as Mexico. In countries with little or no population growth, the distribution shape is more rectangular. Where slow growth in population occurs such as the United States, a profile somewhere between that of rapid and no growth is representative. (Courtesy of Population Reference Bureau, Inc., Washington, DC.)

younger people, and progressively narrower toward the top.

The population of Mexico, like that of the underdeveloped (or developing) world generally, is growing because the death rates are declining for the population groups from the youngest up through the reproductive period (roughly ages 16 to 45), but fertility (birth) rates have not declined. Infant mortality (death during the first year) in particular has dropped sharply in recent decades. This means that a higher proportion of the children born each year survive into adulthood and add children of their own to the population base. These children in turn grow up and have children. Look again at Figure 8-1a. If most Mexican children survive into their thirties (as they probably will), and if their own fertility rates remain high, what will the population structure look like? It will still be pyramidal, but the pyramid will be much broader. In other words, the population at each level—and therefore the population as a whole—will have grown.

We can assume that the population of any country with a pyramidal population structure is growing. But this assumption is valid only because throughout the world infant mortality has dropped sharply. In the United States, for example, infant mortality has decreased over the past 27 years from about 29 deaths per 1000 live births per year to approximately 16.

Another factor that increases population is an overall decrease in death rates. In the United States, white females now have a life expectancy of about 77 years and white males about 69 years. Because of this trend, the number of elderly persons in the population has more than doubled in the past 35 years. Birth rates also affect population growth, of course. But in most developed (or industrialized) countries they have been declining over the past 100 years or so. By 1930 the birth rate in Europe had fallen to 15 per 1000. In the United States, the birth rate was about 30 per 1000 in the early 1900s; since then it has dropped to about 15 per 1000.

Birth rates in Asia, Latin America, and Africa have remained at about 40 per 1000 (Figure 8-2). But death rates in these countries have declined. A population will obviously continue to increase if the death rate decreases and the birth rate does not, or if the birth rate decreases more slowly than the death rate (Figure 8-3).

The Industrial Revolution and Population Growth

Historically, death rates have been high during infancy, then lower for about 12 years, and then slowly increasing thereafter. The high death rate during infancy greatly reduced the number of people who reached childbearing age. The youngest age group may be large relative to the age groups in their reproductive years, but if mortality is high during infancy and adolescence, the base group has shrunk substantially by the time it becomes a reproductive age group.

This was the situation for our species throughout most of its existence on this planet: the human population was pyramidal in structure and very close to stable in size. And during virtually all of this million years, the death rate was much higher at all age levels than it is today. The so-called "agricultural revolution," which occurred when humans first began to domesticate plants and animals about 10,000 years ago, caused the human population to increase. But the *rate* of increase through the millenia after this great cultural advance was very slight by today's standards (Figure 8-4).

But the Industrial Revolution ended the rough balance between birth and death rates. This revolution did not just involve the production of manufactured goods; it also revolutionized agriculture and medicine. More and better food, combined with medical advances such as the control of communicable diseases, greatly reduced the death rate but left the birth rate more or less unchanged. The result was an increasing world population and an increasing rate of population growth: not just a straight line sloping upward, but a growth curve that turned upward more and more steeply each year.

Until this century, the dramatic drop in death rates—particularly infant mortality—was largely limited to the industrialized nations. In recent decades, however, modern medicine, pesticides, and other "Western" developments

Area	People (millions)	Crude Birth Rate (per 1,000 population per year)	Crude Death Rate (per 1,000 population per year)	Annual Rate of Natural increase (percent)
World	3860	33	13	2.0
Developed Countries	1120	17	9	0.8
Underdeveloped Countries	2740	39	14	2.5
Africa	375	46	19	2.7
Asia (Except Japan)	2100	38	14	2.4
Latin America (Tropical)	265	38	8	3.0
United States	210	15	9	0.6
Japan	108	19	7	1.2
Europe	472	16	11	0.5
USSR	250	18	8	1.0
Others: Canada, Australia, New Zealand, Latin America (Temperate)	80	22	8	1.4

FIGURE 8–2 Status of the human population in 1973. Crude birth and death rates are computed from the estimated population size at midyear. Crude birth and death rates are the annual number of births and deaths per 1000 members of a population. (From "The Human Population" by Ronald Freedman and Bernard Berelson. Copyright © 1974 by Scientific American, Inc. All rights reserved.)

have been responsible for dramatic reductions in the death rates of developing countries. And since the birth rates in these countries have not declined significantly, the growth curve of the world's population is fast approaching the vertical (Figure 8–4).

Population Control: Planned—or Catastrophic?

The steady agricultural, medical, and other advances ushered in by the Industrial Revolution have not, however, made it possible for the human population to keep on growing rapidly forever. These advances have merely postponed the inevitable end to this growth.

As we saw in Chapter 6, every population sooner or later reaches the carrying capacity of its environment. Carrying capacity, which is a measure of the food and shelter available in an environment is an important component of

environmental resistance, also noted in Chapter 6. In that chapter we saw how environmental resistance limited the growth of a bacteria colony (Figure 6–11). In that case environmental resistance involved not only limitation of available food, but also the limitation imposed by toxic wastes produced by the bacteria that were not removed from the colony.

We have not been successful in controlling the toxic wastes produced by the activities of our own species, and this type of environmental resistance is increasing. We cannot remove most types of waste from our own ecosystem because that system includes the land, water, and air of the whole planet. And some toxic wastes have already reached levels that are injuring human health. We shall have more to say about this later in the chapter, when we discuss environmental *pollution*.

But the most critical factor limiting population, now and in the near future, appears to be

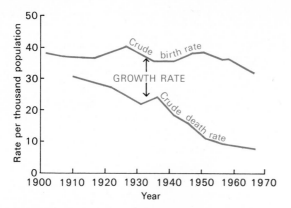

FIGURE 8–3   Birth rate and death rate data from the country of Sri Lanka. The death rate has decreased sharply because of better medical practices and the use of DDT, but the birth rate has dropped only slightly. Under these conditions the population will continue to grow, even though the composition of the age groupings in the total population will change. (Courtesy of Population Reference Bureau, Inc., Washington, DC.)

the environmental carrying capacity—particularly its capacity to produce food and to provide nonrenewable resources.

How many people can the planet support? What is its carrying capacity for our species? No one knows; estimates have ranged from 7.5 billion to several times that number. The higher estimates, however, assume such marvels of technology and such levels of international cooperation that they can be dismissed as unrealistic. In 1971–1974, when there were "only" about 3.7 billion of us, tens of thousands starved in Africa. It is true that there was enough food in the world to feed everybody during this period; the real problem was distribution, not supply. But it is certain that distribution and supply will be serious problems as more billions join us in the next few decades.

Catastrophic Control

It is possible for a population to grow past the carrying capacity of its environment for a brief time. But no population can do so indefinitely. We are no different from bacteria in this respect.

Figure 8–5 shows what happens when a population overshoots the carrying capacity of its environment. A population "crash" follows the peak; during this period the excess population—the portion above the carrying capacity line—dies. The major killer is usually starvation, although diseases encouraged by the stress of overcrowding and malnutrition also take their toll. A population "crash" may be referred to as *catastrophic population control*. When population increase is rapid, such crashes usually occur because of the impact of a large population in a short period of time. Large numbers place a great and immediate stress on the resources of that environment. A population growing at a slower rate would probably not crash so abruptly.

Does Figure 8–5 apply to our own species? It does. We cannot put human population density figures or dates in Figure 8–5 because we do not know what the carrying capacity for our species is now or what it will be later. Nor can we say when our carrying capacity would be reached, particularly since we can increase that capacity by increasing food production. But there is no

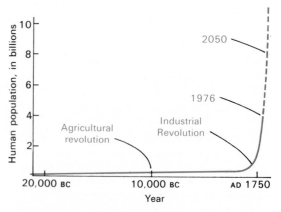

FIGURE 8–4   The growth of the human population was very slow during most of our species' history. The dramatic upsurge began during the Industrial Revolution, when agricultural and medical advances began to make substantial reductions in the death rate. In 1976, world population reached 4 billion. It is predicted that by 2050 there will be approximately 8 billion people on earth.

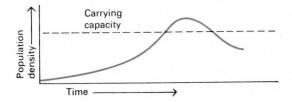

FIGURE 8–5 Generalized curve of a population's growth. When a rapidly increasing population overshoots the carrying capacity of an environment, a rapid decline in population results because of the impact on environmental resources.

doubt that this capacity has an upper limit. If birth rates do not drop sharply very soon, then the carrying-capacity line in Figure 8–5 represents a population size somewhere between 8 and 15 billion; we can thus project that the carrying capacity will be reached during your lifetime.

Catastrophic control of the human population is not just a disturbing possibility. It is a fearsome likelihood unless the world birth rate soon drops rapidly. How many people would die in such a human population crash? There is no way to predict accurately. If the already huge human population exceeded the planet's carrying capacity by just 10 percent, hundreds of millions would probably die—a catastrophic crash indeed.

Controlling Birth Rates: Alternatives to Catastrophe

Most authorities on population agree that the pressing need is to achieve *zero population growth* (ZPG) (Figure 8–6). To accomplish this, the world's population growth rate must be reduced to the *replacement rate* as soon as possible. The replacement rate is the average number of children per couple that will just replace the parental generation. This rate is not an even 2.0 children per couple, because that would assume a zero mortality rate between birth and the end of the reproductive period. Obviously, some children of every generation in every country will die before having children of their own. The replacement rate varies from country to country; for the United States

it is currently calculated as 2.11 children per couple.

Some countries have made encouraging progress toward ZPG. Birth rates in many developed nations have been dropping for years even in the absence of government policies toward this end. In 1973 the combined annual growth rate of the developed countries was 0.8 percent, compared with the world average of 2.0 percent. Japan—a developed country with a population of 108 million in 1973—has officially encouraged contraception for years, and it has legalized abortion to control its population size. Japan's annual population growth rate had dropped to 1.2 percent in 1973. No country has yet attained zero growth, but Japan may reach that goal sometime in this century. Most developing countries have also adopted policies aimed at reducing their population growth.

But for two reasons the picture is not so encouraging as the above discussion might indicate. First, population control policies have not been very successful to date in most devel-

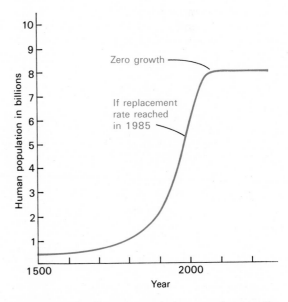

FIGURE 8–6 Human population growth curve if world population could reach "zero population growth" (ZPG). This level, at 8 billion, could be achieved by 2025 if worldwide fertility rates drop to the replacement rate by 1985.

oping countries. With well over half the world's population, these countries had an average growth rate of 2.5 percent in 1973, compared with the world average of 2.0.

India is a case in point: it has encouraged birth control for years but with little success (Figure 8–7). As a result of this failure, India's population stood at 628 million in 1976. And each year it adds 13 million more—"equivalent," as one observer put it, "to absorbing an Australia a year." By 1976 the Indian government had become so concerned about the high birth rate that it took tentative steps toward adopting a compulsory nationwide sterilization program. Initially, this program envisioned requiring one parent to undergo sterilization after a couple had two children. Later, this approach was dropped and less stringent measures were substituted. It remains to be seen if the Indian government can overcome the people's traditional resistance to birth control practices (Figure 8–8).

The second reason why prospects for avoiding a population crash are not encouraging is the lag between the time a reduction in birth rate takes place and the time the population stops increasing. Attaining a replacement birth rate is not the same thing as attaining zero population growth. ZPG is achieved after the replacement birth rate has been effective for many years.

Zero Population Growth: A Distant Goal

Even if the world achieved a replacement birth rate by 1980—and that is hardly possible—world population would exceed 6 billion some years later. If the replacement rate were achieved by the year 2000, the world population would not cease growing until it reached approximately 10 billion around AD 2050 (Population Reference Bureau, Inc., Washington DC).

This time lag can be explained by referring to Figure 8–1. Let us use the United States as our example. Suppose that all the 15 million or so Americans in the 25–29 age group could somehow be persuaded to have just two children and no more (actually, this would be slightly less than the replacement rate). Let us also suppose, for simplicity's sake, that they would have both their allotted children while they were in this age group. Thus the Americans in the 25–29 age group would add just their own number, some 15 million, to the population structure as a new group of 0–4-year-olds.

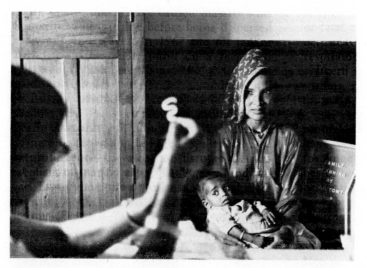

FIGURE 8–7   Family planning in India. The "loop" is explained to an Indian woman. (WHO photo.)

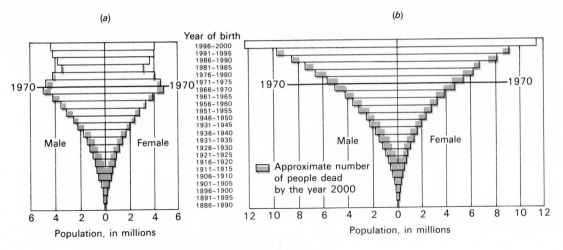

FIGURE 8–8 Predicted population and age distribution of India in the year 2000 under two different sets of circumstances. (a) If birth rate declined to replacement rate by 1985. (b) if present birth and death rates continue. (Courtesy of Population Reference Bureau, Inc., Washington, DC.)

This new youngest group would be considerably smaller than any age group between it and its parental group. And if this group held its own fertility rate at the replacement level when *its* members reached parental age some years later, it too would add only 15 million people to the United States population.

Note, however, that in the meantime the members of the larger prereproductive age groups in Figure 8–1c are also growing up. Most of them will survive into childbearing age. Even if the 10–14 age group, for example, kept its fertility rate at the replacement level, it would add not 15 million but more than 20 million new Americans to the population. And so it would go: If the United States birth rate fell to replacement level tomorrow and remained there, the country's population would continue to grow for several decades after the 0–4 age group in Figure 8–1c finished having just enough children to replace itself. It would be well into the next century before the country attained ZPG. The same dynamics shape the population growth of all countries.

The world population outlook, then, has both gloomy and bright sides. The gloomy side is that world population is almost surely going to double no matter what we do. The really chilling prospect is that we might not do enough, soon enough, to slow the growth rate. In that case the earth's carrying capacity will be exceeded, and many millions will die.

The bright side is that the world probably *can* avoid a catastrophic solution to the population problem. Zero population growth is possible through reduced birth rates. If the world's governments and citizens develop a sufficient sense of urgency, that possibility can become a strong probability. In the meantime the world's population would probably double, but here too there is a bright side. We have good reason to believe that agricultural production—the key factor in the world environment's human carrying capacity—can be increased enough to feed 8 billion people or more.

United States Population Projections

According to the United States Census Bureau, in the year 2000 there will be between 251 and 300 million Americans, depending on what happens to the birth rate between now and then. If the typical family has an average of 2.7

children during this period, then we will reach 300 million by 2000 and keep climbing with each passing year. but if the average is 1.7, slightly below the replacement rate, our population will hit 251 million by 2000. It will continue to grow for a few more years after that, then drop for a few years and finally stabilize.

Figure 8–9 shows what would happen if American families began in 1975 to average 2.7, 2.1, or 1.7 children apiece. This figure clearly shows the considerable time lag between re-

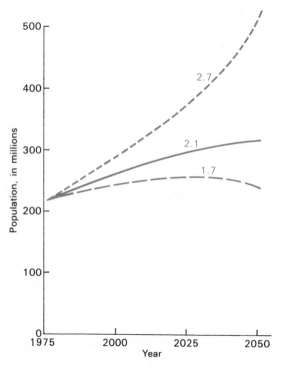

FIGURE 8–9 United States population projections assuming 2.7, 2.1, or 1.7 children per woman. The graph clearly shows the long-range effects of a one-child difference in the average family. An average of 2.1 children per couple is the predicted replacement rate needed to reach ZPG if immigration to the U.S. were eliminated. Under present conditions, 1.7 children per couple is a more realistic birth rate if ZPG is to be achieved in the next 50 to 75 years. (Graph and data based on information from U.S. Bureau of the Census and Population Reference Bureau, Inc.)

placement fertility and zero population growth. In the projection for the U.S. based on a 1.7 child average per family, the time lag between replacement fertility and ZPG is approximately 50 to 75 years.

Recent studies indicate two conflicting and potentially significant population trends in the United States. On the positive side, parts of the United States show a greater decline in unplanned births than in planned births (C. F. Westoff, "The Decline of Unplanned Births in the U.S.," *Science*, vol. 191, January 1976). This trend lowers the country's rate of population increase. On the negative side, however, the decrease in marriage and family rearing during the late 1960s and early 1970s appears to have been merely a postponement of births. People simply put off having children for a while. So the American birth rate could show an upswing (J. Sklar and B. Berkov, "The American Birth Rate: Evidences of a Coming Rise," *Science*, vol. 189, August 1975). Numerous social, political, and technological uncertainties make it impossible to forecast human population trends, especially on a country-by-country basis, with any precision. Figure 8–9 shows a projection of the time lag between attainment of replacement fertility and ZPG for the United States. The graph can also help us see why the *worldwide* birth rate must drop soon if zero growth is to be achieved in the next century and if the world's population is to be kept within manageable limits.

FOOD AND POPULATION

The only long-range solution to the world population problem is a permanent reduction in birth rates. The alternative is grim: widespread famine and a population crash of catastrophic dimensions.

But we have seen that zero growth inevitably lags several decades behind lowered birth rates. The short-range need, then, is for both a reduction in birth rates *and* an increase in the world environment's carrying capacity for our species. Increasing carrying capacity is mainly a matter of increasing food production. What is the outlook for world food production? It is instructive to look first at the gloomy view put forth by an English economist and pioneer in population studies, Thomas Robert Malthus.

Malthus was one of the first to perceive clearly the relationship among population size, birth and death rates, and food supply. In 1798 he published his now-famous *Essay on the Principle of Population* in which he warned that the human population tends to outgrow its food supply. Malthus saw the close relationship between population size and the carrying capacity of its environment. Malthus thought he saw something else as well—that the human race would always produce more children than it could feed. He thought the birth rate would always tend to exceed the death rate, so that population would be kept in check primarily by catastrophic controls: wars, plagues, and especially famines.

Malthus correctly perceived the basic outlines of a very serious problem. The world has certainly suffered many wars, plagues, and famines since his day. But the world's human population has, after all, *quadrupled* since Malthus wrote. Clearly, then, we have managed to increase the planet's carrying capacity greatly; food production has on the whole kept pace with population growth so far.

At present the world's food supply appears to be adequate to sustain its population. But the distribution of that food is unequal. People in affluent (developed) nations consume most of the world's food. In some affluent countries, food is often destroyed for political or economic reasons. At the same time, many people are starving in certain areas of the world; earlier we mentioned the recent six-year drought in Africa that took thousands of lives. Another problem is that much available food is nutritionally inadequate in one or more respects. Two common difficulties are inadequate protein and insufficient vitamins (Figure 8–10).

But the outlook does offer some cause for optimism. Most countries are engaged in research aimed at providing more and better food for their people. There are indications that with new farming practices, India will be able to sustain its population in the foreseeable future. Perhaps the greatest accomplishment in food production has occurred in China, which is now able to feed its 800 million people on

FIGURE 8–10 This young African child suffers from kwashiorkor, the regional name for protein malnutrition. The condition is common where diets are high in starchy foods and low in protein. (FAO photo.)

only a small fraction of its land. By developing high-yield crop varieties, improving irrigation practices, and using more and better fertilizers, many countries have increased their food production significantly.

But there are also more innovative and potentially more important ways to increase food production. We shall consider two which show a sound grasp of the basic ecological concepts discussed in previous chapters.

Matching Crop to Ecosystem

Humans have developed the habit of imposing their cultural preferences on the environment. This can be a bad, even disastrous, habit. In the 1920s, for example, the world market for wheat expanded. Americans in the Great Plains responded by plowing up millions of acres of grassland on which cattle had grazed and planting wheat. Soil erosion had not been a problem in this semiarid region so long as the dirt was protected against the dry wind by a cover of grass with its thickly matted roots. But when the protective grass cover was broken up by plows, the land became vulnerable to wind erosion. And when the already dry soil was further dried by a drought that lasted several years, the wind literally blew away millions of acres of precious topsoil. In a few short years the area became infamous as the Dust Bowl.

Since then, large sections of the Dust Bowl area have been reclaimed for agriculture, partly by modifying the ecosystem to fit the crop. Wheat is still planted on millions of acres. But living windbreaks of trees have been planted at intervals across the prairie. Wind erosion has been further reduced by irrigation, contour plowing, and other improved methods. Nevertheless, serious soil erosion still plagues the Dust Bowl country. In 1976, when a severe drought struck, thousands of acres of newly planted wheat were "blown out" in Kansas, Oklahoma, and Texas.

But why not take the opposite approach? Instead of trying to force inappropriate crops on an ecosystem, why not match the crop to the ecosystem? Food scientists have been studying this alternative for some years. Plants and animals native to an ecosystem are well adapted to it and can use its mineral and energy resources efficiently.

Another promising possibility is to introduce resource-efficient food animals into areas other than their native habitats. We have seen that various parts of the world have different biomes. It has been shown, for instance, that whereas the Kenya Highlands in Africa can support no more than 30,000 pounds of cattle per square mile, they can support 70,000 to 100,000 pounds of wild native hoofed animals of mixed species.

Reducing Food-Chain Lengths: Protein from Plants

Meat and fish are excellent protein sources for the human population. They contain much higher concentrations of protein than grains and other plant crops do. The amino acids from which these animals synthesize protein are produced by the plants they eat. But the amino-acid concentration in plants is low compared with that of meat animals. And no single plant produces all the amino acids essential to the human diet.

Nonetheless, the harvesting of animals is not a very efficient way of obtaining protein. In the process of concentrating proteins for us, animals use up much of the amino acids and other energy-producing materials they obtain in their plant diets. In Chapter 6 we saw that vast amounts of food energy are lost at each step in the food chain or pyramid. We also saw that this loss is especially great from the first level (producers) to the next (first consumers). If we humans (the higher-level consumers) became the first-level consumers of plants and their amino acids, we would have access to far greater protein supplies than we now have. How could this be done? Two approaches seem particularly promising: (1) developing high-protein plant crops for direct human consumption, and (2) developing efficient ways to extract protein from crops with lower protein concentrations.

The first method is already in large-scale use. High-protein crops such as soybeans are being grown in great quantities. (You may be familiar with "meat stretcher" food products available today; they are usually made from high-protein soy flour.) And plant geneticists are working to produce cereal (grain) crops with higher protein yields.

This first method lets the plant itself do much of the protein concentrating. Only the part of the plant in which the protein content is greatest—the seed—is retained for human consumption. There is considerable protein in the rest of the plant too, but it is not concentrated enough to be worth saving. This is why we "separate the wheat from the chaff," even though we lose much protein in the process.

The second method of harvesting protein from plants prevents much of this loss by harvesting most of the green plant, including its protein-producing leaves. The plants are then converted to pulp, and protein is extracted from the pulp. Freshly cut alfalfa, for example, is about one-fifth protein. Recently, experiment-

Bio-Topic: What Can We Do in the Meantime?

The long-range solution to the world's food crisis will involve a combination of lower birth rates and increased agricultural production. Both will take time to achieve. What can we do in the meantime to feed more people with the food that is now available? There are at least two immediate and practical ways to stretch our food supply by changing what we eat.

One approach is to eat more efficient sources of protein. Most Americans rely on beef for a great deal of their protein. A steer must be fed about 21 pounds of plant protein to produce a pound of new beef protein. But it takes only 8.3 lb of plant protein to produce a pound of pig protein, and only 5.5 lb of plant protein to produce a pound of chicken protein. Existing livestock feeds might produce almost four times as much animal protein if we all ate chicken instead of beef.

Another approach is to eat lower on the food chain, by eating plants rather than animals to satisfy our protein needs. The difficulty with a vegetarian diet is that most plant proteins are deficient in one or more essential amino acids. But there is a way to select the plants we eat so as to fulfill our amino acid requirements. Consider the amino acid makeup of rice and legumes (such as soy, mung, or kidney beans):

	Legumes	Rice
Tryptophan	Low	High
Isoleucine	Medium	Medium
Lysine	High	Low
Sulfur-containing	Low	Medium
Other	Adequate	Adequate

Eaten together, rice and a legume provide a "complete" protein. By eating rice together with a legume we can satisfy our amino acid requirements from plant protein alone. For example, one cup of legume and two cups of rice provide the equivalent of about 7.5 ounces of beef protein, both in quality and in quantity. And we can use the food energy that the steer would otherwise have used up. There are many other combinations of plant proteins that can replace beef protein and many vegetarian cookbooks to tell you what they are.

ers at the University of Wisconsin were able to extract 43 percent of the protein in fresh alfalfa and convert it into a green powder that was 35 percent protein. M. A. Stahmann, a biochemist with the Wisconsin group, estimated that nearly 400,000 tons of protein are lost each year in vegetable waste products such as potato vines and beet tops. Much of this loss could be recovered. One unsolved problem is that this plant protein extract has yet to be produced in a really palatable form: people simply don't like the stuff.

Such actual and potential advances in food production are encouraging. But we must not think of them as a substitute for reduction of the worldwide birth rate. Population control is inevitable; the only question is whether we will attain it catastrophically, by a population crash, or humanely by reducing the birth rate. Increased food production is a means of meeting the needs of the billions who will be born despite our best efforts to reduce the world birth rate. If we allow greater food production to become an alternative to reducing the birth rate, then the inevitable population crash will only be so much worse.

ENVIRONMENTAL POLLUTION

More people means the need for more food. But more people need more of *everything*: housing, usable energy, transportation, waste disposal facilities. . . . The list could go on and on. Greater needs, of course, mean greater production—and this in turn means both a greater drain on the world's resources and greater pollution of the world environment. Furthermore, the production of goods to meet today's needs requires materials and methods that not only produce vast amounts of pollution, but also produce new types of pollutants that are extremely dangerous to health and life.

Pollution may be defined as the process of contaminating an environmental medium with a form of energy or matter in quantities sufficient to harm the environment. We shall look at some major forms of environmental pollution, their disruptive side effects, and the prospects for controlling them.

Chlorinated Organics

Among the most damaging pollutants of our modern world are synthetic organic compounds containing chlorine. Their first large-scale appearance was in the form of pesticides, the best-known of which is DDT (Figure 8–11a). Similar compounds, polychlorinated biphenyls or PCBs (Figure 8–11b), were also produced in quantity for use in paints, plastics, caulking compounds, and electric transformers.

Use of chlorinated hydrocarbons such as PCBs has been reduced in recent years as their dangers have become known. But they have

Bio-Topic: What Makes a Pollutant a Pollutant?

News media and textbooks use the term all the time, but no one ever bothers to define it. What is a pollutant? There are two broad categories of pollutants: things we make too much of and things living systems aren't used to.

Carbon monoxide, sulfur dioxide, and fly ash are called pollutants when released by factories but not when produced by volcanoes. The reason is that volcanoes produce relatively small quantities that can be diluted and dispersed by normal atmospheric processes. Concentrations stay below the levels that cause harm to people, crops, or buildings. But when cars, factories, and power plants produce so much of these substances that normal atmospheric processes can't dilute and disperse them, then we call them pollutants.

During the evolution of living systems on our planet heavy metals such as cad-mium, arsenic, lead, mercury, and materials such as asbestos were present only in mineral deposits. Compounds such as PCB's, chlorinated hydrocarbons, vinyl chloride, and benzene did not exist. Our technological civilization has unlocked the mineral deposits and created hundreds of compounds unknown in nature. Living systems that evolved on a planet free of these substances did not evolve ways to cope with them. Heavy metals, asbestos, and industrial chemicals enter body tissues and accumulate because the tissues cannot eliminate them. As these materials accumulate, their concentrations reach harmful levels, and damage to the tissue results. Perhaps in a few million years living systems will have time to evolve ways to cope with these newly-released materials. Until then we will continue to call them pollutants—and rightly so.

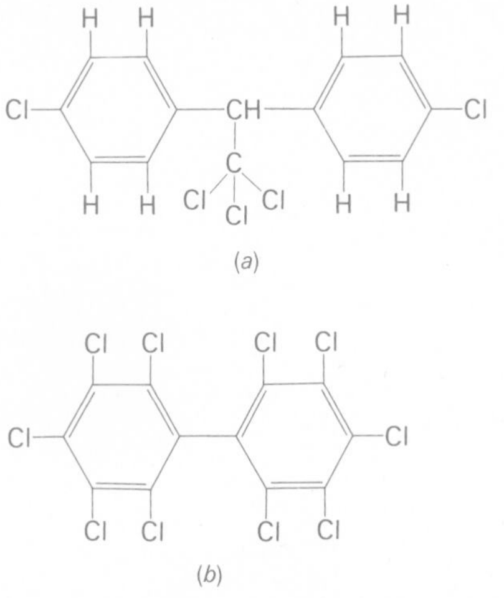

FIGURE 8–11 Chemical formulas of chlorinated hydrocarbons. *a)* DDT. *b)* a PCB.

been accumulating in the environment for approximately 50 years. These PCB compounds went unnoticed as pollutants until about 1968, when they were found to be the cause of illness in Japan. Their harmful effects stem not only from their toxicity but from their persistence in the environment. Chlorinated hydrocarbons are chemically very stable and decompose very slowly. And since they are fat-soluble, they accumulate in the cells of organisms. Because industrial wastes are often dumped into rivers and lakes, and because chlorinated hydrocarbons leach through soil into water, many waterways in the United States now have dangerously high PCB levels. As a result, fish species such as bass may have PCB levels many times higher than those allowed for human consumption.

DDT: Benefits and Problems

Insects endanger our food supplies and transmit deadly diseases. Pesticides are therefore essential for insect control. Chemical pest control has been extremely successful worldwide: formerly disease-ravaged areas are now relatively safe to live in and worldwide agricultural yields have increased. But the massive use of chlorinated hydrocarbon pesticides during the past 35 years has caused serious side effects on other living systems besides the target organisms. The most important and controversial of these pesticides is DDT.

DDT kills by disrupting the functioning of an insect's nervous system. Around 1940, it was introduced as a pesticide. Mosquitoes, flies, tree moths, bark beetles, and a host of other health and agricultural pests became its targets. At first these targets were quite vulnerable. But after a few years of spraying, DDT lost its effectiveness against mosquitoes and many other insects. Through the process of natural selection, increasingly resistant strains evolved. By 1960, more than 65 crop-damaging species had developed this resistance.

What was even worse, experts began to suspect that DDT was producing many disorders in humans, including cancer. The chemical was also linked with the deaths of various birds. In those cases, a series of steps along food chains was involved: leaves of sprayed trees dropped, decayed, and tainted the soil; earthworms ingested DDT in the soil; and birds ate the worms. Fish-eating birds and animals were also affected by DDT. Carried into lakes and oceans, the chemical was ingested by small organisms which in turn were eaten by fish or clams. Since sea birds eat many fish and clams, the DDT became more concentrated in their bodies through the process called *magnification* (Figure 8–12). Stored in fats and oils, DDT is concentrated when these materials are eaten and digested. Clams may show a DDT body concentration of only 0.09 parts per million, for example, whereas a seagull may contain 25 parts per million, principally in its body fat. Even humans may contain as much as 11 parts per million of DDT in their fatty tissues.

In Borneo, DDT was used to kill mosquitoes carrying malaria. Magnification became a serious problem because cockroaches as well as mosquitoes absorbed the chemical. The roaches were eaten by small rodents, which were eaten by cats. DDT was picked up by the cockroaches, concentrated by the rodents, and further concentrated by the cats until the amounts were sufficient to kill them. The result was that the rat population grew as the predator cat population shrank. Soon a new problem emerged—the numerous rats carried

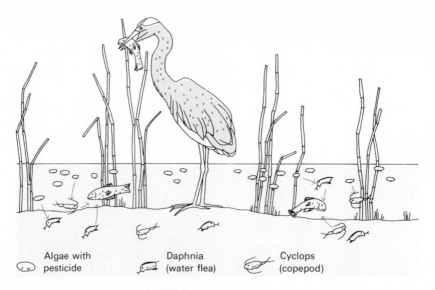

Algae with pesticide

Daphnia (water flea)

Cyclops (copepod)

FIGURE 8–12   Magnification of DDT through a food chain. DDT enters algae cells, which are eaten by *Cyclops* and *Daphnia*. These microcrustaceans are a food source for fish, which are later consumed by Great Blue Herons.

fleas which harbored the bacteria causing another disease, bubonic plague.

DDT has had many such unintended side effects. Most of them have resulted from the chemical stability, which permits it to magnify in food chains. A worldwide problem has thus resulted from what was earlier considered an advantage of DDT as a pesticide—its stability. DDT degrades very slowly; approximately half of a given amount will still be in the environment 15 to 20 years after its application. After another 15 to 20 years, only half of the remaining amount will have broken down.

It is now well documented that many bird populations—especially those birds that eat fish or small mammals—were greatly reduced by DDT. The eggshells of birds that have ingested DDT contain less calcium and are consequently thinner (Figure 8–13). After this discovery was made, biologists began to search for the mechanism of DDT action on bird eggs. D. B. Peakall of Cornell University has studied the effects of DDE (a product of DDT breakdown) on reproduction in ringdoves. His experiments demonstrated that DDE lowers estrogen levels and inhibits the activity of an enzyme essential for the incorporation of calcium into eggshells. The lowered estrogen level affects breeding behavior; if mating is delayed the reproduction cycle may not be completed within a breeding season. Even if it is com-

FIGURE 8–13   Eggs laid by a barn owl who was fed 3 parts per million of DDE. Cracking and crushing of the thin eggshells were common. (Photograph by Dr. Erwin E. Klaas, Patuxent Wildlife Research Center, U.S. Fish and Wildlife Service.)

pleted, the young birds may never hatch. In some parts of the United States today, brown pelicans and bald eagles can crush their eggs merely by sitting on them.

Encouraging recent reports have indicated that residual DDT, DDD, and DDE are declining in certain areas and that some hard-hit bird populations are increasing. For example, brown pelicans are making a comeback along the southwest Pacific coast. And 10 species of migratory songbirds examined in Florida during 1964–1973 showed a gradual decline of DDT in their tissues. This was the period during which DDT usage decreased in the United States.

The use of DDT in the United States is now almost completely banned, but many other countries continue to rely on it. Some of them—those plagued with malaria, for instance—have little choice in the matter: food-chain DDT magnification is bad, but uncontrolled malaria is worse.

Obviously we must continue to control insect pests—but not with DDT in its present form. What are the alternatives?

Alternative Control Methods

Perhaps the molecular structure of DDT can be modified so that it will degrade more quickly; this would insure that it would not move up food chains and be concentrated along the way. Perhaps other, more degradable pesticides can be developed; some of the organic phosphates appear promising in this respect.

But degradable or not, chemical pesticides have two important drawbacks: the target organisms are likely to develop resistance to them, and other organisms are likely to be poisoned by them. For example, DDT and other chemicals kill earthworms, which are beneficial organisms. Chemical pesticides also kill bees, upon which many important plant crops depend for pollination.

A more promising prospect is the development of biological alternatives to chemical pesticides. One such alternative, which is not new, is to fight pests with their own natural enemies. For example, tussock moths, which are a menace to fir trees, might be controlled by viruses to which they are susceptible. Certain wasps feed on the larvae of some beetle pests; import-

ing these wasps into beetle-infested areas has helped keep the beetle population down.

A very promising new development is the use of insect pests against their own kind. This works best in species whose females mate only once in a season or lifetime. The technique calls for raising millions of individuals of the pest species in the laboratory, sterilizing the males, and releasing them in infested areas. Females mating with the sterilized males cannot produce fertile eggs and therefore do not produce offspring. This technique has helped to control screwworm flies, whose larvae are parasites on livestock and other mammals.

In 1976, this method saved the citrus crop of Los Angeles County, California, from the Mediterranean fruit fly, which had infested about 50,000 acres the preceding October. The county pest control department responded by releasing 150 million sterile fruit flies. Several months later, no wild flies could be found in the previously infested area—a sign that they had been virtually wiped out. As one newspaper account put it, the flies had "mated themselves nearly to extinction."

Ideally, these and other nonpolluting alternatives to stable chemical pesticides will someday make DDT obsolete. In the meantime, the use of DDT has become a controversial issue whose resolution could affect all of us.

Heavy Metals

The heavy metals are a group of elements including copper, zinc, cadmium, mercury, lead, and arsenic. Under certain conditions, they can be very harmful to living systems (Figure 8–14). We will focus on mercury and lead in this discussion, because their effects have been studied in detail.

Mercury

Mercury, familiar to most of us as a silvery liquid of great density, is not harmful unless it occurs in an organic form such as ethyl or methyl mercury. These organic mercurials are produced when inorganic mercury compounds are dumped into a body of water and settle on a muddy bottom. There bacteria convert the inorganic mercury into organic mercury, com-

Element	Sources	Health Effects
Mercury	Coal, electrical batteries, other industrial	Kidney damage, nerve damage, and death
Lead	Auto exhaust, paints	Brain, liver, and kidney damage; convulsions, behavioral disorders, death
Cadmium	Coal, zinc mining, water mains and pipes, tobacco smoke, burning plastics	High blood presssure and cardiovascular disease, interferes with zinc and copper metabolism
Nickel	Diesel oil, residual oil, coal, tobacco smoke, chemicals and catalysts, steel and nonferrous alloys	Lung cancer
Arsenic	Coal, petroleum, detergents, pesticides, mine tailings	Hazard disputed, may cause cancer
Germanium	Coal	Little innate toxicity
Vanadium	Petroleum (Venezuela, Iran), chemicals and catalysts, steel and nonferrous alloys	Probably no hazard at current levels
Antimony	Industry	Shortened life span in rats

FIGURE 8–14   Some of the heavy metals, their sources, and their effects on health.

monly the methyl form. The highly toxic methyl mercury then enters the food chain, where it is concentrated in fish; it may be further concentrated in humans who eat much fish. These magnified toxic effects are mainly on the central nervous system; they include impaired muscle function, blurred vision, and brain damage. Mercury poisoning can be fatal.

For years, industrial mercury was dumped into Minimata Bay in Japan. Eventually the bay fishermen and their families, who lived chiefly on the fish they caught, began to show the crippling effects of mercury poisoning. By 1970 the effects of the Minimata dumping had reached epidemic proportions. At least four dozen people died and dozens more were crippled.

Tuna and swordfish concentrate mercury to high levels, and high levels have been found in canned tuna in the United States. These levels seldom exceed those set by the Food and Drug Administration as being safe for human consumption, but nobody really knows what the "safe" level is—or even if there is such a thing.

Mercury also enters our environment in other ways: from the burning of fossil fuels and from the use of methyl mercury as a fungicide used to treat paint, planting seeds, wood, grass, and certain trees. Some of this mercury also ends up in our bodies.

Early in 1976, the Environmental Protection Agency banned the production of most pesticides containing mercury. Citing the cases of mercury poisoning in Japan, the EPA ruled that mercury from pesticides posed an "unreasonable" hazard to human health. According to the EPA, more than 350,000 pounds of this hazardous metal were used in pesticides in 1973.

Lead

Lead is a biological contaminant that has various harmful effects on organisms. Symptoms of lead-poisoning in humans range from fatigue, headache, and nausea to liver, kidney, and brain damage, and ultimately death. Lead has invaded our environment from many directions. It has contaminated living systems from plumbing pipes, paints, pottery glazes, electric

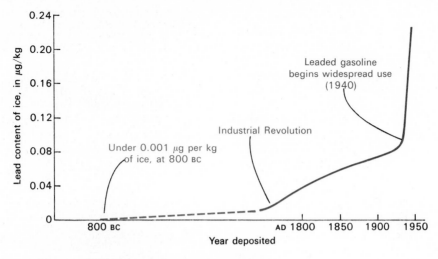

FIGURE 8-15   Influence of human activities on the increase in atmospheric lead as recorded in the layers of Greenland ice.

storage batteries, coal smoke, and leaded gasoline. Many children are poisoned each year by licking or eating paint flakes containing lead.

The chief source of environmental lead contamination is tetraethyl lead, an "antiknock" gasoline additive (Figure 8-15). This lead, spewed into the atmosphere by the thousands of tons each year, is breathed in by humans and other animals. It is also absorbed from the air and soil by plants, which are in turn eaten by animals, including those we eat (Figure 8-16).

Lead, like mercury, accumulates in living tissues. So the more lead we release into the air, water, and soil, the greater the danger to all of us. There is a bright side to the picture, however: all the publicity about lead and its harmfulness is having an effect. Unleaded gasoline is used extensively in autos whose engines have been designed for it. Water pipes are now manufactured from plastic or metals other than lead. Pottery makers are using glazes which do not contain lead, and the use of lead-free paints is growing.

Radioactive Wastes

Probably the gravest pollution threat we face is that posed by radioactive wastes—the deadly, long-lived byproducts of nuclear explosions, atomic power plants, and certain other technological processes.

When a nuclear bomb explodes high in the atmosphere or at the earth's surface, the explosion releases fine radioactive dust particles and gases, which are then spread around the globe by the winds. As these particles settle to earth of their own weight or are brought down in rain or snow, they become "radioactive fallout" that may be breathed or otherwise ingested by living things. Fallout products, including the chief hazard, strontium-90, become magnified

Group	Amount of Lead in Blood (mg/100 g of blood)
Rural residents	.012
City employees	.019
City firemen	.025
City traffic policemen	.031
City parking attendants	.034
City garage mechanics	.038

FIGURE 8-16   Concentrations of lead in the blood of selected groups of males. (Selected from U.S. Dept. of HEW, Public Health Service Publication No. 999-AP-12, 1970.)

as they move through food chains. Cows, for instance, concentrate strontium-90 in their milk, which we drink. Like lead and mercury, strontium-90 is a cumulative poison. Since its chemical properties are very much like those of calcium, it accumulates in bone. There it can cause bone cancer and leukemia.

Radioactive wastes from nuclear plants generating electricity are more of a potential threat today than an actual one, but that potential is staggering. At present, the deadly stuff is being encased in steel and concrete containers. There it should remain, undisturbed, forever—or at least for thousands of years until it has degraded completely into harmless, nonradioactive materials. But these wastes are so deadly that even one leaky waste container or one leaky power-plant core could cause a large-scale human tragedy. And hundreds of tons of radioactive wastes are being produced each year in the United States alone.

In the last few years, however, public concern over the threat of radioactive poisoning has grown. Political opposition to the construction of more atomic power plants is stiffening. Fearing lawsuits by citizens' groups, some power companies have already tabled construction plans for atomic plants and decided to build more coal-fired plants instead.

Air Pollution

Bad as it already is, the pollution of our atmosphere will grow worse until our primary fuels—coal, oil, and gasoline—are replaced by substances that burn more cleanly (such as hydrogen gas) or by noncombustible energy sources (such as solar and wind power). Air pollution—the most common visible form of which we have come to call *smog*—results primarily from the burning of hydrocarbons such as coal and gasoline (Figure 8–17). Smog conditions can be worsened by photochemical effects that are caused by the sun's rays on these airborne particles. Smoke and other airborne pollutants are ordinarily carried away from their point of origin, because air is generally warmer near the surface of the earth, and warm air rises. But sometimes a still warmer layer of air forms above the lowest layer. When

FIGURE 8–17   Aerial photograph of a smog-laden valley showing the condition caused by a thermal inversion. (Courtesy of Statewide Air Pollution Research Center, University of California, Riverside.)

such a *temperature inversion* occurs in an industrialized area, air pollutants cannot rise (Figure 8–18). Instead, a blanket of polluted air—smog—lies close to the ground. It grows thicker and thicker until a change in the weather disrupts the inversion.

The fact that air pollution could result from coal smoke must have been evident as early as the fourteenth century, but little concern was expressed until the 1940s and 1950s. As industrialization increases and automobiles become more abundant, air pollution problems also increase. Waste products from these energy processes are chiefly sulfur, nitrogen, and organic compounds. Sulfur oxides (SO_2 and SO_3) are among the most harmful pollutants; they result when sulfur, which is present in coal and oil, burns and unites with oxygen. Exposure to as little as 0.2 parts per million of sulfur oxides for 24 hours can be a health hazard to humans. Sulfur dioxide (SO_2) can also react with water in the atmosphere to produce sulfuric acid,

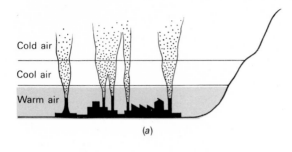

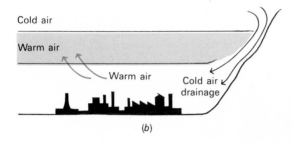

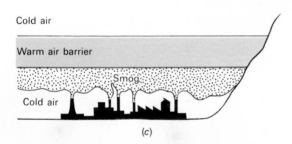

FIGURE 8-18   (a) Dissipation of smog-producing materials under normal atmospheric conditions—warm air rising into cold air. (b) Cooler air moves down mountainside to produce an inversion layer. (c) An inversion layer of warm air forms some distance above the ground and traps polluted air to produce smog.

which falls to earth in "acid rains" that can damage crops and endanger life. Millions of tons of nitrogen oxides (NO and NO_2), produced by incomplete combustion of gasoline, enter the atmosphere each year from automobile tailpipes. Organic compounds—hydrocarbons—are released in great quantities by the incomplete burning of fossil fuels.

Carbon monoxide and carbon dioxide are also released in huge amounts as fossil fuels are burned. Ozone, a powerful oxidizer, and other oxidizing compounds result from reactions between nitrogen oxides and hydrocarbons in sunlight, causing severe problems in sunny, polluted areas. Probably the most harmful effects are produced by irritation to most tissues of plants and animals. We know, however, that in certain areas smog may even be produced by hydrocarbons released from plants. "Natural" smogs can therefore be produced by the effects of sunlight on leaves.

We have much yet to learn about the causes of air pollution. But we know a great deal about its *effects*. It can reduce visibility; it can cause eye and respiratory irritation; it can stunt and kill plants, including agricultural crops; and it can kill animals, including people. Probably the greatest impact of smog on humans is the damage it does to lungs and other respiratory organs. Many of the pollutants found in air are *carcinogens* (cancer-causing agents), and many can poison the enzyme systems of organisms. The dismal facts about the role of smog in respiratory illness were impressed upon the public in the late 1940s by "killer smogs" in Los Angeles, California and Donora, Pennsylvania. The most disastrous, however, was the London smog of 1952, which claimed more than 3000 lives.

For more than a decade now we have had experimental evidence that smoking injures the smoker's health. Some of the injurious substances found in tobacco smoke are tar, cadmium, carbon monoxide, nicotine, nitrogen dioxide, and hydrogen sulfide. Some of these substances have been demonstrated to produce cancer in rats. Only recently, however, have the harmful effects of cigarette smoke to nonsmokers been publicized. In 1976, researchers at the University of Cincinnati measured the carbon monoxide (CO) levels produced by smokers in a poorly ventilated Cincinnati bar. They found that without ever lighting up himself, the bartender inhaled as much CO during an 8-hour shift as he would by smoking 36 cigarettes! Carbon monoxide is harmful because it reduces the amount of oxygen available to an individual. The general effect is a strain on the heart and respiratory system.

Bio-Topic: Exporting Pollution

Concerned over accelerating deterioration of the environment, many industrialized countries have begun to curb pollution by combinations of voluntary and legislative means. Emissions from automobiles and factories are now limited by law in the United States and many European countries. The use of DDT and other persistent pesticides is now restricted in the United States to emergency situations in which no other agent would be effective. In many countries, public funds are invested to monitor known and potential pollutants. Current levels of pollutants are being maintained and in many cases reduced, and new sources of pollution can often be identified before serious environmental effects occur. The United States, for example, now requires that the environmental impacts of all proposed construction projects be considered in advance. Projects that threaten unacceptable risks are delayed until they are redesigned to reduce the risks.

The combined effect of these policies and practices has been a slow but perceptible reduction in the levels of pollution in most industrialized countries. The skies over Pittsburgh and London are clear, the Great Lakes may be recovering from near destruction, and new pollutants are often avoided before damage occurs.

These efforts and effects have been limited largely to North America and western Europe, while pollution is a global problem that does not recognize national boundaries. DDT and other persistent pesticides are still widely used. Factories that are moved from one country to another to avoid stringent antipollution laws simply pollute elsewhere. Indeed, one of the most obvious effects of antipollution legislation has been the exportation of pollution-generating practices to more tolerant countries.

Pollution generated thousands of miles away may be less obvious, but it is still pollution that may threaten the global ecosystem. Until the global community recognizes that the biosphere is a closed system—that there can be no escape for any from the actions of all—pollution will continue to threaten living systems on our planet.

Another possible threat to our already endangered air is the destruction of ozone (O_3) in the stratosphere, the layer of atmosphere extending from about 10 miles to about 30 miles above the earth. This threat has two sources: high-flying supersonic transport planes (SSTs) and aerosol spray cans. SST engines release pollutants such as nitrous oxides, which may react chemically with ozone and deplete the limited supply of it. Aerosol sprays contain fluorocarbons; these rise into the stratosphere and liberate chlorine, which breaks down the ozone layer. By depleting the ozone layer, which filters out most of the ultraviolet radiation from the sun, we may become more susceptible to harmful effects of ultraviolet radiation, such as skin cancer. Perhaps we may eventually find that SSTs, aerosol sprays, or both do *not* pose a serious threat to the ozone layer. Such a finding would not discredit the environmentalist's position that technological advances should not be developed on a large scale until there is strong evidence that their development would not seriously harm the environment.

Water Pollution

A few years ago, most of us took for granted our usually pure and plentiful supplies of drinking water. Even news of heavily polluted rivers did not disturb most Americans—especially if the pollution was in another part of the country or the world. Today fewer of us take our water supplies for granted; the problems are much closer to home for many of us. And we are more conscious of the fact that, although water is a resource that is renewed through a global cycle of evaporation, condensation, and return as rain or snow, the quality of the earth's water is rapidly deteriorating.

Water is an excellent solvent. It dissolves most substances—and therein lies a major problem. When water passes through a polluted environment, it carries many pollutants with it; much of this polluted water ends up in drinking and irrigation supplies. To compound the problem, many highly toxic chemicals are difficult to detect in water because they do not affect its odor, clarity, or taste. Until recently,

water quality problems mainly involved hardness (excessive amounts of dissolved minerals) and sewage pollution. Filtration and chlorination have greatly reduced these problems. But chemical pollutants from industrial wastes and agricultural leaching are not easily controlled. Pesticides, other toxic organic compounds, and heavy metals find their way into drinking and irrigation water. Natural filtration—seepage through soil and gravel beds—removes most natural pollutants. But this natural filtration system is being overloaded with increasing amounts of synthetic materials, many of which it cannot deal with at all.

Striking examples of these problems have occurred in New Orleans and other cities in the United States (Figure 8–19). Petrochemical residues, detergents, and asbestos fibers appear in lakes and wells in alarming quantities. Many

FIGURE 8–19 Water pollution: detergent foam on the Mississippi River. (John H. Gerard; National Audubon Society/Photo Researchers.)

of these substances, particularly organic chemicals and asbestos fibers, are known to be carcinogenic; others are highly suspect. Chlorinated hydrocarbons are sometimes present in drinking water, indicating that chlorine added to kill bacteria can also react with hydrocarbon wastes to form these hazardous chemicals.

About 70 percent of the earth's surface is covered by oceans, and this marine environment supplies much of the food for our species. Until recently, however, use of the oceans as dumping areas aroused little concern. Garbage, raw sewage, industrial wastes, and substances too toxic for safe storage on land have been dumped mindlessly into the sea.

Safe, pure water is not only a basic human need—it is necessary to support most of the organisms in the biosphere. We must seek solutions to these problems in both technology and politics. All peoples of the earth must become aware of the seriousness of polluted water. And the people of industrialized nations must do something about it.

Since the large-scale development of petroleum as an energy source, a disturbing new pollution problem has emerged. Oil spills from huge tankers and from offshore drilling operations have produced thick gooey films ("slicks") of oil that float on the ocean's surface (Figure 8–20). These slicks, which may cover many square miles, have caused massive kills of marine and bird life before being dispersed by winds and waves. In 1967 the oil tanker *Torrey Canyon* ran aground on a reef near Cornwall, England, and poured 117,000 tons of crude oil into the sea. This tremendous spill eventually settled on French and English beaches. Oil spills literally paint tidal areas; nearly all marine life adhering to the beach or living on the bottom is killed. Spilled oil also emulsifies into seawater and disrupts the metabolism of marine algae, plants, eggs, and larvae. Even when the organisms are not killed, the effects of petroleum derivatives can be very serious (Figure 8–21).

Environmental Diseases

Perhaps the most troublesome side effect of technology and industrialization has been the introduction into the natural environment of chemicals that threaten human health. *Environmental diseases* are caused not by infecting organisms or "natural" malfunctions of physiological processes, but by the accumulation of toxic and other substances from air, water, and food.

Environmental diseases have been known for years; they were usually associated with some occupation. Chimneysweeps, coal miners, hatmakers using mercury to process felt, painters of radioactive luminous substances on watch dials, asbestos workers, dentists who use x-rays, and many other workers have had their traditional occupational disease hazards. (The "Mad Hatter" in Lewis Carroll's *Alice in Wonderland* had his counterparts in real life. Hatmakers suffered brain damage from mercury vapors. "Mad as a hatter" was a common nineteenth-century expression whose origin was more tragic than humorous.)

Today we understand more about the diseases associated with these and other occupations. But we also know that these diseases are no longer simply "occupational." The entire world population is increasingly exposed to synthetic chemicals, radioactivity, heavy metals, industrial chemical wastes, and non-degradable mineral substances such as asbestos. These industrial wastes—and often the industrial products themselves—can have crippling or fatal effects. The growing incidence of cancer, heavy metal poisoning, birth defects, and respiratory ailments evokes more and more concern among public health authorities, labor unions, politicians, responsible leaders in the offending industries, and the general public.

But the pressing need is to *prevent* environmental diseases, not to cure them after they have struck. There is, in fact, no known cure for some types of environmental diseases. Asbestos workers who have breathed in tiny asbestos fibers for 20 or 30 years, for example, will probably die from asbestos-induced cancer if it develops.

But in this problem area, as in others discussed earlier, the outlook is not entirely bleak. Now that people are aware of the threat posed by environmental diseases, they are starting to do something about it. Legal and legislative

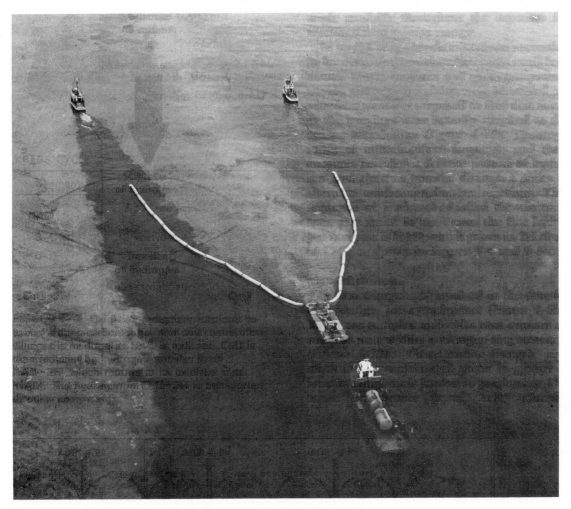

FIGURE 8–20 Two vessels towing a boom and skimmer into an oil slick. The oil is collected by the skimmer and stored in the support vessel towed behind. This system can handle up to 2200 gallons per minute. (Courtesy of Clean Seas Incorporated.)

action and the pressure of public opinion, are beginning to force at least some industrial firms to reduce their emissions of toxic materials into the environment and to step up their search for less toxic substances.

ENERGY

Another environmental problem of massive proportions is the energy crisis. Energy use is increasing at a rapid rate and will continue to do so unless we change our habits. For example, at least 90 percent of all oil and natural gas resources will probably be depleted by the year 2020 (Figure 8–22). This means that we must ultimately find new energy sources. And we must find energy sources that do not pollute.

Solar energy, direct energy from the sun, is one of our best prospects. An intense research effort has been devoted to developing solar

Types of Petroleum or Petroleum Derivative	Organism Observed to Be Affected	Concentration	Observed Sublethal Effect
Oil	Phytoplankton Barnacle larvae Black Sea turbot	0.1 ppm 10–100 ppm 0.01 ppm	Inhibition or delay in cellular division Abnormal development Delay in hatching— deformed, inactive larvae
Kerosene	Phytoplankton Snail Lobster larvae	3 ppm 0.001–0.004 ppm 10 ppm	Depression of growth rate Reduction in chemotactic perception of food Stress behavior, affects chemoreception and feeding times
No. 2 fuel oil	Mussel Clam	Collected after spill Collected after spill	Inhibition in development of gonads Gonadal tumors
Kuwait crude	Phytoplankton	1 ppm	Depression of growth rate
Prudhoe Bay crude	Pink salmon fry	1.6 ppm	Avoidance behavior could affect migration
Iranian crude	Codfish larvae	Aqueous extracts from 10^3 ppm, 10^4 ppm	Adverse effects on behavior leading to death
Venezuelan crude	Lobster larvae	6 ppm	Delay molt to fourth stage
Toluene	Kelp	10 ppm	75 percent reduction in photosynthesis within 96 hours

FIGURE 8–21   Some observed sublethal effects of petroleum products on marine life. (Courtesy of EPA.)

equipment for space heating, water heating, and air conditioning (Figure 8–23). Now we must decide how rapidly to develop solar energy on a large scale.

Another candidate for further development is geothermal energy—steam or hot water produced within the earth. Geothermal energy can be used to heat buildings and water and to generate electricity. Still another alternative is wind power.

But fossil fuel supplies are being depleted, solar energy would have to be supplemented in cloudy regions, geothermal sources appear to be limited, and the wind doesn't always blow. So we must find additional energy sources to meet our ever-growing needs. One promising future source is liquid hydrogen, which might largely replace hydrocarbon fuels. It would have many advantages; in particular, it is pollution-free, burning cleanly to produce H_2O.

Nuclear power is, of course, a proven energy source (Figure 8–24), and it does not present a supply problem. "Breeder" reactors in which nuclear wastes are recycled to produce more energy, actually produce more fuel than they consume. But they also produce great quantities of highly radioactive wastes. We have already noted the dangers of these accumulating wastes. If nuclear reactors become a mainstay of our energy system, we can only hope that technological solutions to the waste storage problem will be found.

One of the most promising long-range energy possibilities is thermonuclear power: power from controlled nuclear fusion processes like those that generate the sun's heat and light. Uncontrolled fusion is the source of the terrible power of the hydrogen bomb; controlled fusion could generate electricity. Fusion power would have two major advantages. First, its fuel

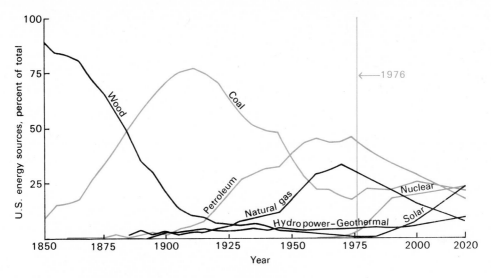

FIGURE 8-22 United States energy sources. Americans can no longer rely on any single resource for the bulk of their energy, as they have periodically throughout their history—first with wood, later with coal, and today with oil. By 2020, six energy sources, none supplying more than 25 percent of the total, may power the nation. (Adapted from a National Geographic Society graph, 1976.)

would be cheap and abundant—nonradioactive hydrogen isotopes found in water. Second, damaging side effects to the environment, such as oil spills, strip mining, and radioactive wastes would be avoided. Both the United States and the Soviet Union have extensive fusion-power research programs underway.

Thermal Pollution

Nuclear and fossil fuel power plants produce great amounts of heat; this heat ends up in the air and water of the environment. This waste heat, called *thermal pollution*, can cause severe problems, especially in aquatic environments. Many aquatic species are very sensitive to changes in temperature and oxygen levels. Since warmer waters contain less oxygen, some species cannot survive in water heated by power plants and factories that use the water to cool their equipment.

In some cases heat from power plants can be used advantageously. It can increase yields in certain aquaculture systems, speed up seed ger-

mination through the use of warmer water, and raise cold water to temperatures suitable for recreational use. But the increasing problems thermal pollution causes will probably continue to outweigh whatever benefits might be derived from it.

Many experts believe that in spite of its deadly radioactive wastes nuclear (fission) power is the only source adequate to meet the world's ever-growing energy needs in the foreseeable future. Other authorities think that nuclear and fossil fuel energy sources would eventually produce intolerable levels of thermal pollution as energy consumption continues to rise. These troubling prospects should spur two lines of attack on the energy problem. First, efforts should be intensified to develop nonpolluting energy sources such as solar power, wind power, and possibly even power from temperature and tidal differentials in the oceans. Second, efforts to conserve energy should be pursued by developing more energy-efficient appliances, and by making do with less energy. Must we heat our homes to 72°F—or could we

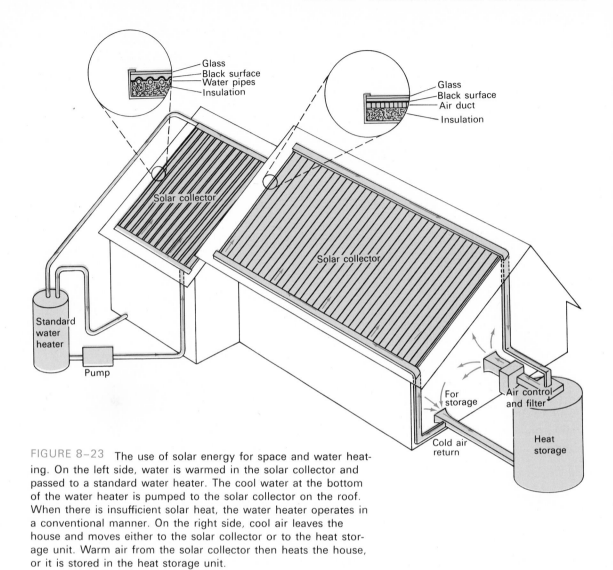

FIGURE 8–23   The use of solar energy for space and water heating. On the left side, water is warmed in the solar collector and passed to a standard water heater. The cool water at the bottom of the water heater is pumped to the solar collector on the roof. When there is insufficient solar heat, the water heater operates in a conventional manner. On the right side, cool air leaves the house and moves either to the solar collector or to the heat storage unit. Warm air from the solar collector then heats the house, or it is stored in the heat storage unit.

live with 68°? Do most of us who live in temperate climates really need air conditioning? Depending on our answers to these and similar questions, we could save tremendous amounts of energy each year.

NATURAL BALANCE, HUMAN DISRUPTION

Most natural ecosystems reach a balance between the living populations and their environment; certain limits provide the pivotal points for this balance. These balances can be upset and shifted by natural forces such as storms and fires. And as this chapter has already made clear, humans can also disrupt them. Even farming methods and, to a certain extent, forest management are based on intentional disturbances of natural conditions: humans clear the land and replant it with a desired crop or use it for grazing or reforestation. Improper farming techniques, overgrazing, or

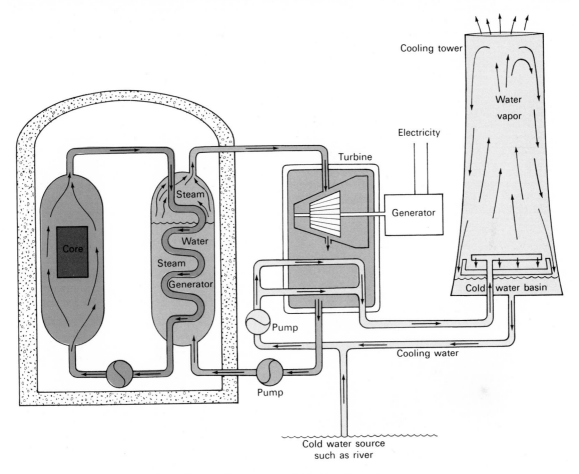

FIGURE 8-24 One type of modern nuclear power plant, a pressurized water reactor (PWR). As the boiler does in fossil-fuel power plants, a nuclear power reactor produces steam to drive a turbine which turns an electric generator. Instead of burning fossil fuels, a reactor fissions nuclear fuel to produce heat to make the steam. The PWR shown here is fueled by uranium oxide pellets held in zirconium alloy tubes in the core. Water is pumped through the core to transfer heat to the steam generator. This steam drives the turbine.

faulty forest management may reduce vegetational cover, which in turn leads to erosion of the soil. A greater and uneven runoff of water usually flows from an eroded area; this increase, along with the added soil and rocks, can affect aquatic ecosystems many miles from the site of erosion.

Another concern is the introduction of new plant and animal species into areas that are in relative balance. For example, the accidental introduction of the chestnut blight fungus from China virtually eliminated the American chestnut. In the early 1900s the Belgian hare was introduced as a commercial enterprise on San Juan Island in Puget Sound. But some rabbits escaped the breeding farms, reproduced rapidly, and soon overran the island. It became practically impossible to raise a home garden, and pea farms suffered severe damage during cyclic peaks of the population. A similar situation has occurred in Europe and parts of Asia, where the American muskrat has been introduced and is spreading. In such cases as these, the absence of natural predators permits the problem to develop. Many serious problems have developed as a result of human interference, either deliberate or accidental, with natural, balanced ecosystems. The environmental balance of an area should be carefully studied and relationships between all members of that area should be understood before species are added or removed.

CONSERVATION AND SOLUTIONS

Some aspects of human interference with natural ecosystems may not seem so important as those just discussed. These concern the preservation of natural areas and of certain species such as the bison, or American buffalo, which are important to our aesthetic and recreational needs.

Our imprudent disruption of ecosystems and as well as our inability to use all natural resources efficiently, have caused many of the massive problems facing the human race. But many people now realize the importance of *conservation*, the wise management of natural resources. In the United States, our first conservational concern was for the forests that were logged heavily and indiscriminately in the 1800s. A relationship between logged land, water runoff, and soil erosion was soon noted. We cannot afford to exhaust resources such as soil which cannot soon be replaced. We are beginning to realize that not all environmental problems are beyond solution. Public awareness and political pressure groups have prompted government agencies and private industry to use technology in both preventing and cleaning up pollution. Another process that holds much hope for the future is *recycling* of such materials as metals and paper.

Earthwatch

An exciting new concept—worldwide environmental monitoring and control—has recently been recognized officially by the United Nations in the form of a promising new program. This program is Earthwatch. It will provide monitoring, research, evaluation, and exchange of information about the world environment. The overall United Nations environmental effort and the Earthwatch program are outlined in Figure 8-25.

Many thousands of years ago our species became the dominant form of animal life on this planet. We permanently reduced our natural predators to levels that did not seriously threaten us. We triumphed over harsh environments by harnessing fire, clothing our bodies, devising effective shelter, and inventing agriculture. Some 250 years ago, we set in motion a revolutionary process—industrialization. This brought about agricultural and medical advances that enabled us to overcome the infectious diseases and food shortages that had so effectively held our population in check. In other words, we were spectacularly successful in expanding the carrying capacity of our environment and reducing environmental resistance against us.

But from its very beginnings, industrialization had its dark side. Industrially caused environmental pollution affected relatively few people at first, but by the 1970s its potentially disastrous impact had become all too clear. By the 1970s our potential for populating the planet beyond its carrying capacity was also unmistakably clear.

But the 1970s also marked the time when we finally began to realize that, ecologically, we are our own worst enemy. Perhaps by the 1980s we will have begun to act, on a worldwide scale, as if we could become our own best friend.

SUMMARY

Environmental problems have developed because of the greatly increasing human population. During most of the history of the human species, growth was slow; but in the past 250 years, achievements in agriculture and medicine have led to a steady and substantial population increase. Today we have more than 4 billion people; this figure will probably be doubled by 2050. Analysis of these population

(a) UNITED NATIONS ENVIRONMENT PROGRAM

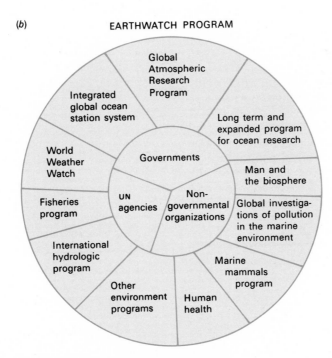

(b) EARTHWATCH PROGRAM

FIGURE 8–25 *(a)* Functional framework for the United Nations environmental program. *(b)* Earthwatch aspect of the United Nations environmental program. (Courtesy C.E. Jensen, D.W. Brown, and J.A. Mirabito, *Science 190*, 423, 1975. Copyright © 1975 by the American Association for the Advancement of Science.)

trends takes into account the birth rate, death rate, and age structure of a population. The most critical factor limiting population seems to be the food-producing capacity of the environment.

In order to prevent a catastrophic form of population control, the human species must achieve zero population growth. Certain problems are involved in achieving ZPG: population control measures have not been very successful in developing countries, and even when replacement birth rate is reached, a lag of many years precedes ZPG. Since population growth is certain to increase for some time, we must increase the carrying capacity of the world's environment for the human species. In producing more food, we must consider quality, particularly adequacy of protein and vitamins.

A larger population with greater needs brings about greater pollution—the contamination of the earth to a quality level that is less desirable. Some of the worst pollutants are chlorinated organic compounds such as DDT and PCBs, heavy metals such as mercury and lead, and radioactive wastes. Pollutants contaminate our air and water to unsafe levels; and some have been demonstrated to cause cancer. Environmental diseases have been caused by the accumulation of toxic substances in air, water, and food. Since energy needs have also increased, we must look for new sources of energy that cause a minimum of thermal pollution.

But it is encouraging that humans are aware of this pollution and of the necessity for a clean environment from which safe food, water, and air can be obtained. We are realizing the importance of natural balances and learning conservation practices that respect those balances. Moreover, we are coming to realize that the entire world is one interconnected ecosystem.

REVIEW QUESTIONS

1. List some of the ways you believe the carrying capacity of the earth for humans can be increased. How can these be accomplished without using more energy or polluting the environment more?

2. What other practices might help prevent

catastrophic population control besides extending carrying capacity and decreasing the birth rate?

3. List five major environmental problems facing humanity today and suggest two solutions for each.

4. What are some of the positive steps people are taking to avoid pollution and make better use of our resources?

5. Name some of the sources of mercury and lead pollution in the modern environment. How do humans pick up harmful levels of these metals?

6. What is the cause of a smog-trapping temperature inversion? What components of smog can be particularly harmful to living things?

7. What new energy sources are being developed to replace our dwindling supplies of fossil fuels?

8. What political and economic restraints must be considered in reducing pollution and practicing conservation?

SUPPLEMENTARY READINGS

Freedman, Ronald and Bernard Berelson, "The Human Population," *Scientific American*, September 1974. This article is one of a series in this issue which is entirely devoted to the human population. This article deals with the rapid growth of the human population and presents possible directions for future growth. Other articles in this series consider other aspects of population dynamics, populations in different countries, and resources in relationship to population.

Jackson, Wes, *Man and the Environment*, Wm. C. Brown, Dubuque, 1973. This is a collection of articles from a variety of sources—popular magazines, government reports, and scientists—on a variety of population and environmental issues—food, resources, pollution, and population growth and control.

Keyfitz, Nathan, "World Resources and the World Middle Class," *Scientific American*, July

1976.   The rate at which people throughout the nations of the world move into middle-class status will determine the stabilizing level of the population, and the amount of resources that can be used to maintain middle-class life will therefore be established. The article touches on population, resources, and energy.

Rose, David J., "Energy Policy in the U.S.," *Scientific American*, January 1974.   The energy crisis and alternatives for the future are discussed. Statistics are used to emphasize the problems we face, and some possible solutions are presented.

Wagner, Richard H., *Environment and Man*, 2nd edition, W. W. Norton, New York, 1974.   The theme of this book is humans' relationship to their environment and the changes this has undergone over the course of human history. Human technology is seen as the cause of environmental disruption.

Unit IV
Metabolism

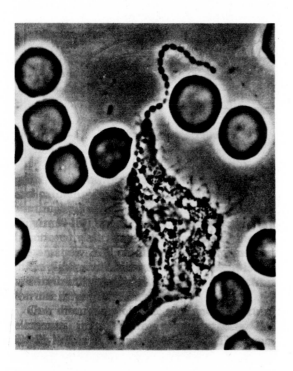

All living systems need energy inputs to drive the chemical reactions that maintain their structures and power their internal processes. We made this fundamental point in Chapter 3. All the chemical reactions that occur in an organism are referred to as its metabolism. These metabolic processes can be charted in a sequential manner much like the listings of arrivals and departures on a train schedule.

Often, however, the term is used in a more restricted sense. In this narrower sense metabolism refers to: (1) the chemical processes that trap, store, and release biologically useful energy; and (2) the supporting processes, such as digestion, circulation, gas exchange, and excretion, that facilitate both the basic energy-processing reactions and the subsequent use of that energy in life functions such as reproduction and behavior. In this unit we shall focus on the chemical re-

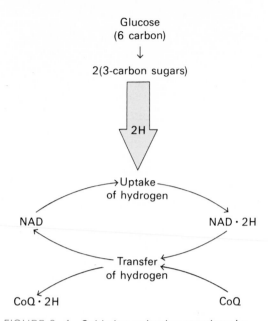

FIGURE 9–4 Oxidation-reduction reactions between a three-carbon sugar and two coenzymes. Glucose is oxidized as NAD is reduced. CoQ is then reduced by hydrogen transfer from NAD · 2H, which returns to its oxidized state (NAD). The hydrogen in CoQ · 2H is transported to other compounds.

made available throughout the organism for reactions that require energy.

In recent years, biochemists have succeeded in breaking the mitochondrion into small fragments. When enzymes and other compounds within the mitochondrion were identified, researchers were not surprised to find that many of the enzymes were actually attached to the cristae membranes (Figure 4–16). Thorough study of mitochondrial fragments and their enzymes revealed a definite pattern of hydrogen and electron transfer through a series of alternate oxidation-reduction reactions. This sequence of reactions is called the *electron-transport series.* In most cases the first hydrogen acceptor is NAD, which passes its 2H along to CoQ, as shown in Figures 9–4 and 9–5a.

Cytochromes

The next compounds involved in the transfer of hydrogen are *cytochromes* (Figure 9–5b). These are complex molecules that contain an atom of iron within a nitrogen ring structure (Figure 3–23). These carbon-nitrogen ring structures (pyrrole rings) occur in groups of four in compounds known as porphyrins. The name *cytochrome* (cyto, "cell," chrome,

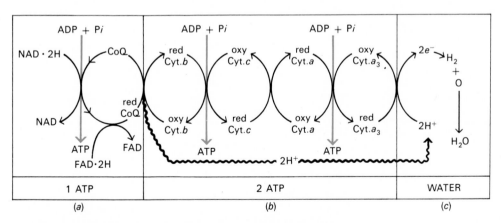

FIGURE 9–5 Electron-transport series. The compounds in (a) are coenzymes; (b) and (c) involve cytochromes *b, c, a,* and a_3. Note that in these coupled reactions one compound is reduced as another is oxidized. For example, NAD · 2H is oxidized to NAD as CoQ is reduced to CoQ · 2H; next, CoQ · 2H is oxidized to CoQ as Cyt *b* (oxy) is reduced to Cyt *b* (red), and so on. Note also that CoQ may be reduced by either NAD · 2H or FAD · 2H.

"color") refers to the fact that the basic pyrrole ring is a colored compound or pigment found within a cell. Porphyrins are essential components of many important substances found throughout the living world. In fact, the porphyrin structures of both chlorophyll, the pigment of green plants, and hemoglobin in blood are similar to cytochromes.

An iron atom (Fe) is bonded to the nitrogens of a cytochrome in such a way that it can pick up or lose electrons. The cytochromes in this sequence, which have been studied primarily in the mitochondria of beef heart muscle, are named b, c, a, and a_3 (Figure 9–5). These cytochrome molecules differ from one another only slightly, and they each transport electrons along the folded inner membrane of a mitochondrion (Figure 9–6).

Electrons are passed along the electron-transport series (from NAD · 2H to cytochrome a_3)

by the action of enzymes known as *reductases*. In this process, enough energy is released at three points to complete the enzymatic phosphorylation of ADP to ATP. Although the mechanism is not fully understood, electron energy is probably used to synthesize energy-rich, phosphorylated intermediate compounds, which then transfer phosphate to ADP to form ATP. For every 2H made available by NAD · 2H to the transport series, three molecules of ATP are synthesized (Figure 9–5).

It is important to note that when CoQ gives up its hydrogens to the cytochromes (Figure 9–5b), protons (2H⁺) are not directly transferred, since the iron accepts only the electrons. As the electrons are transported along the cytochrome series, the protons are released into the mitochondrial fluid. At the very end of the chain, protons and electrons are united with the help of cytochrome a_3 (Figure 9–5c). At this

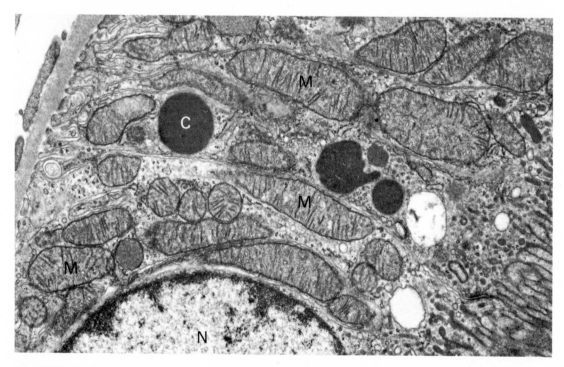

FIGURE 9–6   Electron micrograph of a rat kidney tubule cell showing mitochondria (M) with inner cristae membranes, nucleus (N), and cytoplasmic inclusions containing lipids (C) (× 13,800). (Courtesy of James D. Newstead.)

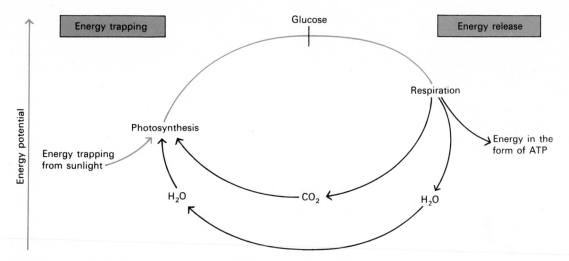

FIGURE 9–7 Summary of the energy concept, showing the relationship between photosynthesis and respiration. Energy is trapped and stored on the left side of the "hill"; it is released or utilized on the right. Note that CO_2 and H_2O move cyclically between these two processes.

point, cytochrome a_3 also catalyzes the addition of oxygen to the two hydrogen atoms to form water. Oxygen thus acts as the final hydrogen acceptor; this is the vital role oxygen plays in respiration.

Harnessing and Releasing Energy

We now have a concept of biological energy, but we must still understand the *phototrophic* process by which solar energy is trapped to produce new organic molecules. Later, hydrogen can be removed from these molecules to release energy for the synthesis of ATP. This process, often called *cellular respiration*, occurs in all living cells.

Energy trapping and energy release can be illustrated as an "energy hill" in which the greatest potential energy lies in the molecules at the summit. The diagram in Figure 9–7 summarizes the energy situation we will discuss— the harnessing or trapping of energy from the sunlight by *photosynthesis* and the subsequent release of this energy through the process of respiration in living cells.

PHOTOSYNTHESIS: MAKING FOOD

The world's green plants (including algae) trap only about one one-thousandth of the light energy our planet receives from the sun. But that energy is enough to produce enormous amounts of food—more than 150 billion tons of dry organic matter per year. And it is enough to enable green plants to release billions of tons of free oxygen (O_2) into the atmosphere each year.

The Concept

Photosynthesis occurs in a very orderly, systematic series of chemical reactions. This sequential process can be compared with the orderly activities of a manufacturing plant. Raw materials are brought into a phototroph and processed, just as they are in a factory. And just as workers assemble parts to make a final product, the "chemical machinery" of a green plant likewise turns out a final product. During the past 250 years many scientists have contributed to our knowledge of what occurs in the photosynthetic factories of green plants. These years of research have produced the following facts about photosynthesis as it occurs in blue-green algae and eucaryotic phototrophs:

1. Light is the energy source.

2. Chlorophyll is necessary to trap the light.

3. The raw materials are carbon dioxide and water.

4. Organic molecules (sugars) are the product.

5. Oxygen is released as a by-product.

The entire relationship that summarizes these findings can be written as an equation:

$$6CO_2 + 6H_2O \xrightarrow[\text{chlorophyll}]{\text{light}} C_6H_{12}O_6 + 6O_2 \uparrow$$

This process represents the production of a high-energy compound (glucose) from low-energy raw materials (carbon dioxide and water).

The important relationship between the gases carbon dioxide and oxygen was discovered by the English scientist Joseph Priestley as early as 1771. In his experiments Priestley discovered that "plants purify the air for animals."

Placing a green plant and a mouse together in a sealed container, he observed that the organisms lived together much longer than either could exist alone (Figure 9–8). Although Priestley did not understand the exact mechanism of "purification" by plants, his experiments led ultimately to the discovery that plants use carbon dioxide as a raw material and release oxygen.

You may have experimented with goldfish or guppies and green aquarium plants in a manner similar to Priestley's experiment to produce a "balanced aquarium" (Figure 9–9). In such a system, closed except for light energy, many factors must be balanced between the plants and animals, including gas exchange and assimilation of waste products. Only when both plant and fish are together can either survive in such a system. Although this coexistence can actually persist for only a short time because such aspects as growth and reproduction rates have not been considered, it does illustrate the interdependence of plants and animals. We must remember that use of oxygen and release of carbon dioxide occur in the plant as well as the animal. The green plant is capable of producing organic food such as glucose, but it must also convert—oxidize—this food to car-

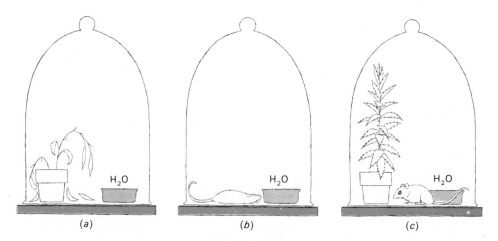

FIGURE 9–8   An experiment designed to show the interdependence of gas exchange between plants and animals. (a) Plant alone dies. (b) Mouse alone dies. (c) Plant and mouse together live.

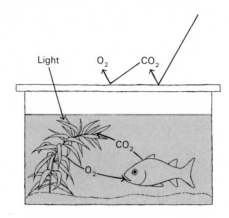

FIGURE 9–9   A balanced aquarium illustrating the relationships of light, oxygen, and carbon dioxide.

bon dioxide, water, and ATP energy to continue its growth and function. Note the use of double arrows in Figure 9–9 to illustrate this respiration requirement.

The Role of Water

In nature, water is always partially dissociated. As we saw in Chapter 3, most of the water on our planet is in the molecular form, but one liter of pure water contains 10^{-7} (1 ten-millionth) gram of hydrogen ion (H^+). The dissociation can be expressed as follows:

$$2H_2O \rightleftharpoons 2H^+ + 2OH^-$$

If water is to contribute to the formation of organic fuel, there must be some mechanism for removing the electrons to be used in photosynthesis. Essentially, this involves the interaction of light and chlorophyll; it is called *photolysis*. The photolytic dissociation may be outlined as follows:

$$2OH^- \rightarrow H_2O + \tfrac{1}{2}O_2 + 2e^-$$

What is the ultimate fate of these particles in the food-making process? The hydrogen is used to reduce carbon dioxide to produce sugars. Discovery of this fact resolved the long controversy over the source of oxygen in photosyn-

thesis: it comes from the dissociated water. Definite proof that the oxygen given off in photosynthesis comes from water molecules was provided by the use of water containing "heavy oxygen," oxygen-18. This isotope contains two more neutrons than the common oxygen-16. Oxygen liberated from plants watered with H_2O^{18} is mainly heavy oxygen, and no oxygen-18 shows up in the sugars produced by such plants.

The Stages of Photosynthesis

After the oxygen-18 experiments, many investigators began research into the chain of events in the photosynthetic process. Notable among them was Melvin Calvin of the University of California at Berkeley. Calvin used carbon-14, a radioactive isotope of carbon, to trace the sequence of carbon compounds in the formation of glucose. He was able to demonstrate the exact steps in this process by introducing $C^{14}O_2$—carbon dioxide containing carbon-14—into green algae. Through this experiment he showed that carbon-14 became part of the intermediate compounds produced during glucose synthesis. Calvin and his co-workers identified not only the carbon compounds involved but also their sequence in the photosynthetic pathway.

In recent years many new explanations have been postulated for the actual mechanism of photosynthesis. Several new compounds in chloroplasts have been discovered and isolated, and their functions in oxidation-reduction reactions have been verified. Scientists now explain the process of photosynthesis in two interrelated stages: (1) the *light reaction*, in which radiant energy is trapped to produce excited electrons from chlorophyll, and (2) the *dark reaction*, in which hydrogen is used to reduce carbon dioxide to simple sugars.

The Light Reaction: Trapping Energy
The physical mechanisms by which electrons are raised to sufficiently high energy levels and transported into carbon compounds are only partially understood. We do know, however, that chlorophyll molecules trap light energy and liberate electrons. These excited electrons

Bio-Topic: Farming the Desert

An inconspicuous plant that grows in Death Valley may help to open the deserts to agriculture. The plant, Tidestromia, has evolved an unusual form of photosynthesis that allows it to thrive at temperatures above 120°F and with practically no water. In evolving this system, Tidestromia has solved a dilemma that all land plants face: how to absorb carbon dioxide without losing water.

All land plants take in CO_2 through specialized pores at the surface of the leaf. These stomata open to let CO_2 in during daylight and close when the light dims. But every minute that the stomata open to admit CO_2, water escapes in the other direction. Most land plants can tolerate the loss of some water; desert plants must conserve every drop. The solution evolved by Tidestromia and plants like it involves a two-stage dark reaction that allows the stomata to stay closed far longer than in other plants.

The heart of the Tidestromia system is a dark reaction that begins with the reaction of carbon dioxide with a compound known as PEP (rather than with RuDP as is usually the case). The carbon atom

that combines with PEP eventually enters the usual Calvin cycle that all green plants use. The secret lies in the properties of PEP and the system of which it is a part.

PEP functions much more efficiently at low concentrations of CO_2 than RuDP does. Tidestromia can keep its stomata closed while the concentration of CO_2 falls to levels at which RuDP works very poorly. With its stomata closed, water is conserved. When the stomata do open, CO_2 diffuses in very rapidly because of the large difference in concentration between the inside and outside of the leaf. The stomata thus stay open only briefly, again conserving water.

This PEP-based system has two other advantages over the RuDP-based system. The PEP system is more efficient at high light intensities, and it is more efficient at high temperatures. Both are adaptive for desert plants.

By hybridizing common crop plants with those that use the PEP-based system, agricultural botanists may be able to breed new, desert-tolerant varieties of major importance.

are transported by carrier molecules and eventually incorporated into sugars. Chlorophyll, then, is a pigment which can absorb light energy. There are several kinds of chlorophyll, but green plants and eucaryotic algae always contain chlorophyll *a*. Plants always contain chlorophyll *a* and *b*; eucaryotic algae contain other kinds in addition to chlorophyll *a*. Besides chlorophyll, other pigments such as carotenes also absorb light and pass this energy to chlorophyll *a*.

Strong evidence suggests that the light reaction consists of two phases called *systems* which work in tandem (Figure 9–10). In Sys-

tem I, chlorophyll *a* is excited by light energy, causing electrons to be raised to a higher energy level. An iron-containing protein called *ferredoxin*, a very strong electron acceptor, next takes up the electrons from chlorophyll *a*, leaving it in an oxidized state. In a subsequent transfer, ferredoxin passes the electrons to NADP (nicotinamide adenine dinucleotide phosphate). In this reduced state NADP has the negative charges necessary to attract two protons (H^+) into its structure from ionized water. The final result of this phase of the light reaction is the formation of reduced coenzyme NADP · 2H. Electrons captured by ferredoxin

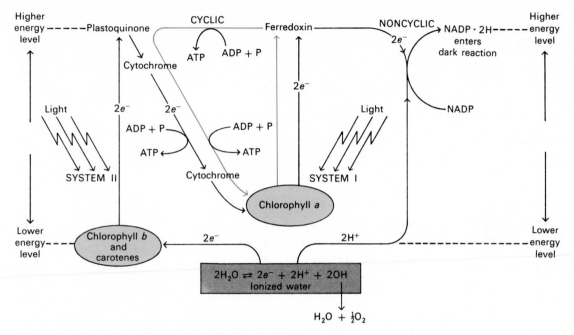

FIGURE 9-10 Two steps (systems) of hydrogen transfer in photolysis. Note that electrons lost in System I are replaced by electrons gained from ionized water in System II. Note also that the electrons from ferredoxin may either be passed to NADP to form hydrogen or cycled back through the cytochromes and chlorophyll *a* to produce ATP.

may also be returned to chlorophyll *a* in a cyclic series of events. These reactions, called *cyclic electron transfer*, yield most of the ATP produced in the light reaction. This ATP can be used in the life activities of a plant just like ATP resulting from respiration.

In the second phase of the light reaction, known as System II, excited electrons are passed from other pigments such as chlorophyll *b* and carotenes to a carbon-ring compound known as *plastoquinone*. The electrons are then passed to cytochromes. Since these electrons are passed to lower energy levels, the energy they release may be used in this downhill reaction to convert ADP to ATP. In other words, the difference in potential energy between plastoquinone and a cytochrome supplies the energy to produce ATP. This is another example of a coupled reaction in which energy is simultaneously released and absorbed.

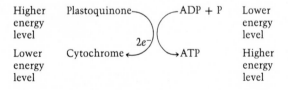

Electrons made available in System II are finally passed to chlorophyll *a* to replace the electrons transferred to ferredoxin. The electrons lost in System II are replaced from ionized water through the action of an unknown carrier substance.

The light reaction ends with the formation of NADP · 2H and the release of oxygen. This process has taken hydrogen from ionized water and converted it to a usable form. It may now be transferred to another compound by the coenzyme NADP · 2H for the formation of carbohydrate.

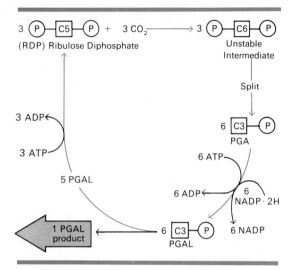

FIGURE 9–11   Major steps in carbon fixation. Six PGAL molecules are produced by the enzymatic splitting of three C_6 compounds. Five PGALs are converted back to RDP; the other one PGAL represents the net gain.

The Dark Reaction: Fixing Carbon Dioxide

Remember that the source of carbon for photosynthesis is atmospheric carbon dioxide. Conversion of energy-poor carbon dioxide into energy-rich carbohydrate is sometimes called "carbon fixation." It occurs through a complicated series of enzymatic steps. This conversion is called the "dark reaction" because it can take place in the dark, unlike the "light reaction" that synthesizes ATP and NADP · 2H.

Since some sequences in the dark reactions are cyclic, we must pick a point to begin our study. If we begin with ribulose diphosphate (RDP), a five-carbon (C5) sugar with two phosphate groups, we can show how this substance is reformed (Figure 9–11).

Three molecules of RDP contain fifteen carbons. The addition of three carbon dioxide molecules brings the total to eighteen carbons. Three six-carbon, double-phosphate molecules are formed:

$$3\underset{}{(P)}-\boxed{C5}-(P) + 3CO_2 \rightarrow 3(P)-\boxed{C6}-(P)$$

This intermediate is very unstable; it is quickly split into six three-carbon acids known as *phosphoglyceric acid*, abbreviated PGA. Calvin and his associates showed that PGA is a very important intermediate in CO_2 fixation. NADP · 2H next reduces PGA to its aldehyde form, *phosphoglyceraldehyde* (PGAL), which contains one less oxygen atom than PGA.

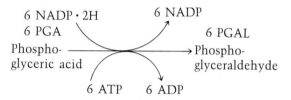

Note that the light reaction and the dark reaction combine to produce the end product of photosynthesis, PGAL. PGAL can be used for energy, and so is the true end product. But it is usually converted to glucose and starch. In our general equations of photosynthesis, glucose is usually shown as the end product.

Of the six PGAL molecules produced, five must be phosphorylated and rearranged to replace the original three RDPs and keep the process going.

Thus the net product is only one PGAL. But if the cycle is repeated, enough PGAL is accumulated to synthesize glucose.

Later in this chapter we will see how a cell can burn PGAL directly for energy. If immediate energy requirements are satisfied, however, two PGALs are synthesized into glucose, and then many glucose molecules are converted into starch, which is stored. The cell also uses PGAL in the synthesis of other compounds such as glycerol, fatty acids, and amino acids.

The Site of Photosynthesis

Most of us think of photosynthesis as occurring in the leaves of green plants, but it is also ac-

Bio-Topic: Photosynthesis without Chlorophyll

The biological world runs on solar energy. Only a few groups of photosynthetic organisms have the enzymatic machinery to trap solar energy and convert it into chemical energy. All other organisms on our planet depend on this ultimate source of energy. At the end of the 1960s, the list of known photosynthetic organisms included the algae and multicellular plants, the blue-green algae, and a few groups of bacteria. All employ chlorophyll or chlorophyll-like pigments as the basis of photosynthesis. Early in the 1970s a new type of photosynthetic organism, quite different from the others, was discovered in natural salt lakes.

The organism, the bacterium Halobacterium halobium, thrives in salt solutions seven times more concentrated than ordinary seawater, and it produces ATP from sunlight. Unlike all previously known photosynthetic organisms, H. halobium contains no chlorophyll or chlorophyll-like pigments. Instead, H. halobium traps solar energy by means of a purple pigment familiar to biochemists in a completely different context. When a cell of H. halobium is illumi-

nated in the absence of oxygen, it makes ATP by a two-step process. In the first step, light is absorbed by a patch of cell membrane containing the purple pigment and a hydrogen ion (H^+) is pumped out of the cell. This sets up a chemical and electrical difference across the membrane. In the second step, an ATP-synthesizing enzyme in another patch of cell membrane brings hydrogen ions into the cell and concurrently forms ATP from ADP. All this happens without chlorophyll.

Studies of this unusual organism may contribute to our understanding of the structure and function of membranes, the mechanisms by which ions are pumped across membranes, and the conversion of light to chemical energy. There has even been speculation that artificial membranes containing the purple pigment may someday help us convert salt water to fresh water.

The purple pigment is rhodopsin, also known as visual purple. It is the pigment that functions in our eyes and makes sight possible. How a single pigment came to be involved in two such different systems is perhaps the biggest mystery of all.

complished in algae and some bacteria. The organisms that make up the green scum of ponds and lakes, for instance, and the minute pigmented phytoplankton of the seas are extremely important in synthesizing nutrients. As we saw earlier, these photosynthetic organisms are the primary producers of organic compounds.

For many years it was believed that the entire leaf was the organ of photosynthesis. But it was shown that suspensions of powdered leaves gave off oxygen when light was shined on them. Experiments on isolated chloroplasts pinpointed them as the major site of photosyn-

thetic activity. A diagram of the relationship of the chloroplast to gross leaf structure is presented in Figure 9–12.

Leaves, Chloroplasts, and Pigments

A cross section of a green leaf shows a functional arrangement of tissues (Figure 9–12). The palisade cells, lying just beneath the upper epidermis, contain functional photosynthetic units called chloroplasts. Other leaf cells such as spongy tissue and guard cells also contain chloroplasts and are capable of photosynthesis. We discussed the structure of chloroplasts in Chapter 4; recall the platelike, membranous

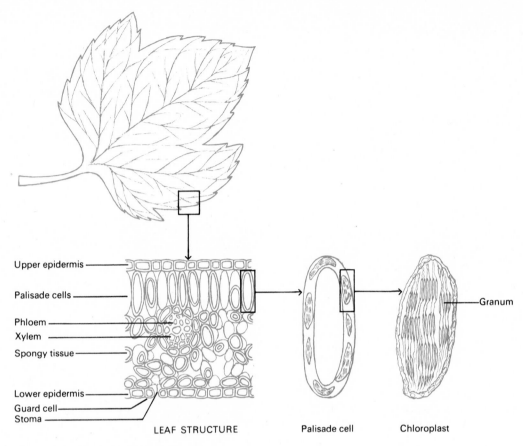

Upper epidermis ——
Palisade cells ——
Phloem ——
Xylem ——
Spongy tissue ——

Lower epidermis ——
Guard cell ——
Stoma ——

LEAF STRUCTURE   Palisade cell   Chloroplast

—Granum

FIGURE 9–12   The site of photosynthesis.

grana. We know that grana contain chlorophyll and carotenoid pigments such as carotene and xanthophyll which are used in photosynthesis (Figure 9–13). Recent research suggests that the functional unit is still smaller, containing approximately 300 chlorophyll molecules and other pigments. This amount of pigment is the minimum that can produce an excited electron for use in photosynthesis.

Our discussion of the site and structural elements involved in photosynthesis has finally led us to the molecular level. The structure of chlorophyll was mentioned earlier in this chapter; a diagram of the molecule is shown in Figure 9–14. Note particularly the similar porphyrin configurations of the main part of the chlorophyll molecule and of the

cytochromes (Figure 3–23). The metallic atom in the structure of chlorophyll, however, is magnesium rather than iron.

The chlorophylls and other pigments located within a leaf trap light for the photosynthetic process. The light providing energy for photosynthesis comes from the visible range of the electromagnetic spectrum. The portions of the visible light spectrum absorbed by the photosynthetic pigments of green plants are shown in Figure 9–15a. Chlorophyll *a* has widely separated absorption peaks in the blue and red wavelengths; chlorophyll *b* has its highest absorbency in the blue-green and, to a lesser degree, red.

The absorption spectra for all three pigments interact to form the characteristic *action spec-*

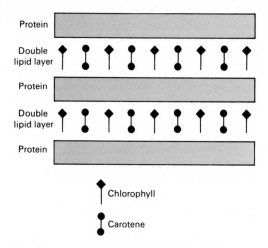

FIGURE 9–13 Hypothetical arrangement of the photosynthetic pigments in the chloroplast membrane. Note that the chlorophyll and carotene lie in the double lipid layer of the granum.

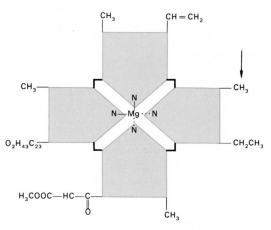

FIGURE 9–14 Molecular structure of chlorophyll *a* and *b*. The broken lines represent the possible valence bonds of magnesium. Note that chlorophyll *b* differs in having a —$\overset{\displaystyle O}{\overset{\|}{C}}$—H group instead of CH_3 at the arrow. For the structure of the shaded areas, see Figure 3-23.

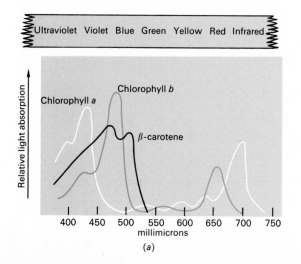

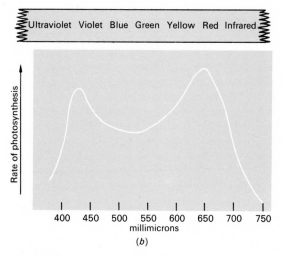

FIGURE 9–15 (*a*) *Absorption spectrum*. The relationship between wavelength and light absorption by chlorophyll *a* and *b* and β-carotene. Note the regions of the visible light spectrum that are most effective in photosynthesis. (*b*) *Action spectrum*. Plotting the rate of photosynthesis against the wavelengths of light effective in photosynthesis shows the combined absorption of all pigments involved in photosynthesis.

trum for photosynthesis. To illustrate this the rate of photosynthesis is plotted against wavelengths of light (Figure 9–15b). Excited electrons released by chlorophyll *b* and *β*-carotene are passed to chlorophyll *a* for production of NADP · 2H as outlined earlier in this chapter.

RESPIRATION: USING FOOD

The story of the breakdown of organic molecules into usable energy is complex. Most cells can use all classes of foods—carbohydrates, fats, and proteins—for energy. For example, the polysaccharide starch may be split into many glucose units by the action of several digestive enzymes. In vertebrates these enzymes are secreted in the mouth, pancreas, and small intestine. After starch is hydrolyzed into glucose, the cells lining the intestine absorb glucose and release it into the blood, which transports it to all cells of the body. Every living cell has the enzymes necessary to convert the potential energy of glucose into usable form, the high-energy bonds in ATP.

The release of energy from glucose can occur in two major processes: *glycolysis* and the *Krebs cycle*. Glycolysis occurs in all living cells, but the Krebs cycle functions only in cells in which oxygen is available. The energy in glucose is converted into ATP bond energy through a series of steps. Each step along the route is catalyzed by a specific enzyme. The process can be generalized as follows:

In the cytoplasm, enzyme action breaks the

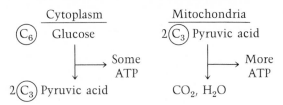

six-carbon glucose molecule into two three-carbon fragments called pyruvic acid. The biochemical term for the series of reactions that break down glucose or glycogen is *glycolysis*. Consult Figure 9–16 as we discuss this sequence.

Glycolysis: Splitting of Glucose

The first step in glycolysis prepares glucose for the process; it is sometimes called a priming reaction. A phosphate group is added to the sixth carbon by the enzymatic transfer of phosphate from ATP. (The 6 in glucose-6-phosphate refers to the carbon on which the phosphate is attached.) In many reactions catalyzed by en-

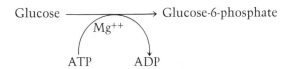

zymes an additional metallic ion is necessary, such as the magnesium ion shown above.

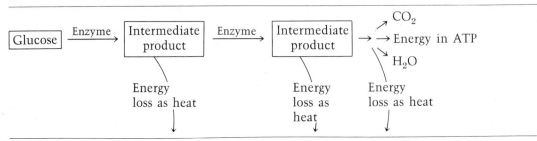

This conversion of glucose into carbon dioxide, water, and energy can be separated into two major phases: (1) the cytoplasmic phase, and (2) the mitochondrial phase.

Both phases produce ATP, but by far the most energy is liberated in the mitochondrial phase.

Glycogen—the polysaccharide storage form of carbohydrates found in liver and muscle—can also enter glycolysis by the addition of a phosphate group to one of its glucose units. However, ATP is *not* required to accomplish this phosphorylation—inorganic phosphate (P_i)

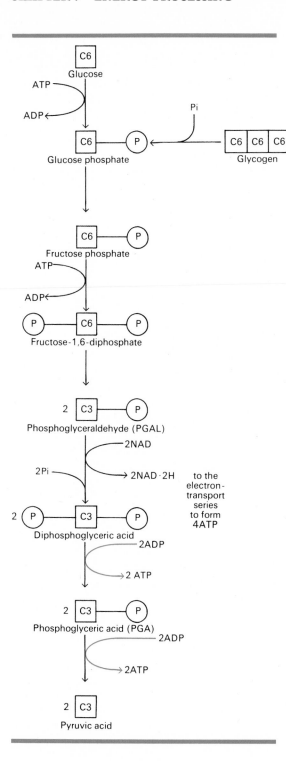

FIGURE 9–16 Summary of the chemical reactions in glycolysis. P_i indicates inorganic phosphate.

can be used instead. This is very economical for the cell because it conserves ATP:

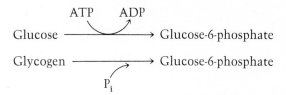

Glucose is now prepared for the second step, which involves a complete rearrangement of its carbon-ring structure. In this step, glucose is changed to another type of sugar, fructose.

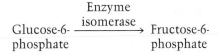

Next this newly formed fructose-6-phosphate is phosphorylated on its first carbon by the expenditure of another ATP:

$$\text{Fructose-6-} \xrightarrow[\text{ATP} \quad \text{ADP}]{} \text{Fructose-1,6-}$$
phosphate   diphosphate

We now have a six-carbon sugar with a phosphate group at each end. At this point, a very significant event occurs—the fructose-1,6-diphosphate is split into two molecules, each with three carbons and a phosphate group on one end. For our purposes, we shall consider these three-carbon compounds to be PGAL. (Remember that PGAL is also the end product of photosynthesis.)

Fructose-1,6-diphosphate → 2PGAL

PGAL now gives off hydrogen to NAD and is transformed into an acid, PGA. But mitochondrial membranes are impermeable to NAD · 2H, so a penetrating carrier molecule is required. This carrier can pass the hydrogen to

FAD inside a mitochondrion. Thus the first synthesis site, NAD, for ATP is bypassed. Therefore, each $NAD \cdot 2H$ generated in glycolysis produces only two ATP molecules. As the hydrogens are lost from PGAL, an additional phosphate group is attached to the number one carbon. This forms a glyceric-acid molecule with phosphorus at the one- and three-carbon positions. The overall reaction is:

$$PGAL \xrightarrow[]{P_i} 1,3\text{-diphosphoglyceric acid}$$
$$NAD \qquad NAD \cdot 2H$$

Note two important things at this point: hydrogen has been given off to the electron-transport series, and the 1,3-diphosphoglyceric acid now contains energy in the form of two high-energy phosphate groups. This compound contains enough energy to allow the direct enzymatic conversion of ADP to ATP in two steps:

1. $P \sim PGA \sim P \xrightarrow[\text{ADP} \quad \text{ATP}]{} PGA \sim P$

1,3 diphospho-   3-phospho-
glyceric acid   glyceric acid

2. $PGA \sim P \xrightarrow[\text{ADP} \quad \text{ATP}]{} $ Pyruvic acid

In these dephosphorylations of diphosphoglyceric acid, two ATPs are formed from each three-carbon molecule. However, since we started with a six-carbon molecule (glucose), ATP production must be doubled to four for each glucose molecule entering glycolysis.

Recall that if we started with glucose, two ATP molecules were needed to prime the glycolysis process—one to phosphorylate glucose and one to produce fructose-1,6-diphosphate (refer to Figure 9–16). Since four ATPs are formed in converting 1,3-diphosphoglyceric acid to pyruvic acid, and since the conversion of PGAL to PGA yields four ATPs through the

electron-transport series, the net gain is $8 - 2$ or six ATP molecules per glucose molecule processed to the level of pyruvic acid. The cell is getting a threefold return for its original investment of two ATP molecules.

Pyruvic Acid

When glycolysis reaches the pyruvic-acid stage, the phosphate bond energy is spent. All that is left is the potential energy of the C—C and C—H bonds; yet, as we will see, this constitutes a tremendous amount of energy. Pyruvic acid, a three-carbon compound, is the end product of glycolysis. The further conversion of pyruvic acid into energy and carbon dioxide in the mitochondrion requires oxygen; it ceases to occur if oxygen is not supplied. The final breakdown of pyruvic acid is accomplished through a cyclic series of reactions discovered by the Englishman Hans Krebs and named for him. We will discuss the *Krebs cycle*, also called the citric-acid cycle, shortly.

Pyruvic acid may be broken down in organisms by three possible routes (Figure 9–17). If oxygen is available in a cell, pyruvic acid can enter the Krebs cycle and the electron-transport series to produce carbon dioxide and energy. If no oxygen is available (anaerobic conditions), as might be the case in strenuously exercised muscle cells, the electron-transport series cannot operate, and lactic acid is formed. Note that it requires 2H to make this conversion from pyruvic acid to lactic acid. Thus the result of this conversion is a loss of four ATP molecules which would have been made if oxygen were present. This occurs because the hydrogen produced during glycolysis in the conversion of PGAL to PGA is now used to convert pyruvic acid to lactic acid. Most lactic acid formed in oxygen-starved cells, is carried by the blood to the liver, where it is converted to glycogen when aerobic conditions return. This process, however, requires additional energy; about 20 percent of the original energy of pyruvic acid is lost. Formation of lactic acid under anaerobic conditions is a very inefficient means of producing energy. The same is true in yeast cells, where alcohol and carbon dioxide are the end products.

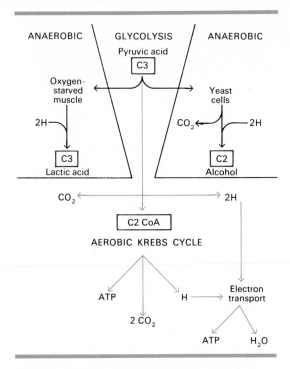

FIGURE 9–17 Three possible fates of pyruvic acid under anaerobic or aerobic conditions. The anaerobic condition in animal cells is shown at the upper left. Yeast cells under anaerobic conditions are shown at the upper right.

The Krebs Cycle: Completing the Breakdown

Under aerobic conditions, pyruvic acid enters the Krebs cycle. We shall only note the names of the intermediate compounds in the Krebs cycle. It is important, however, to keep track of the loss of carbon dioxide as the three-carbon molecule of pyruvic acid is completely converted to carbon dioxide and energy. To get pyruvic acid into the cycle, a sort of "key" compound is added. This compound, called *coenzyme* A (CoA), contains the vitamin pantothenic acid. With the loss of carbon dioxide and the addition of CoA, a molecule of pyruvic acid becomes a two-carbon structure known as acetyl CoA (Figure 9–18).

In the next step, acetyl-CoA (or "active ace-

tate," as it is sometimes called) is condensed with a four-carbon compound, oxaloacetic acid (OAA), to form a six-carbon acid called citric acid. At this point the 2H fragments are transported into the electron-transport series by the coenzymes NAD and CoQ. At another point, between C5 ketoglutaric acid and C4 succinic acid, ADP is converted to ATP without the use of the cytochromes. Since the electron-transport series is not involved, the yield is only two ATPs per glucose molecule.

Another unique reaction is the direct transfer of 2H to FAD between C4 succinic acid and C4 fumaric acid. As a result of this the production of ATP between NAD and CoQ is skipped, so the electron-transport series produces only four ATPs. The important events shown by the lettered segments in Figure 9–18 are summarized in Figure 9–19. The complete oxidative breakdown of one glucose molecule into carbon dioxide, energy, and water yields 36 molecules of ATP. With the compound glycogen an additional ATP occurs as net gain, because inorganic phosphate rather than ATP is used to produce glucose-6-phosphate.

So far we have been discussing only the metabolism of carbohydrates. Can other foodstuffs enter into this scheme? Yes: such energy-rich compounds as glycerol, fatty acids, and amino acids may enter into the carbohydrate pathway at various steps and be oxidized as fuels (Figure 9–20).

At this stage you may wonder just what use can be made of all the ATP produced in cellular respiration. Some ATP is used to "prime" the early stages of glycolysis. In addition to these requirements all biological work—muscle movement, bioluminescence, active transport, and so on—requires energy. In practically every case ATP is the energy supplier. The energy events and relationships discussed in this chapter are summarized in Figure 9–21.

We turn next to the supporting processes by which living forms make possible the production of ATP by cellular respiration. We will examine these supporting processes in Chapters 10 and 11. Then, in Chapters 13 through 18, we will study the further uses to which this biological energy is put: regulation, reproduction, development, and behavior.

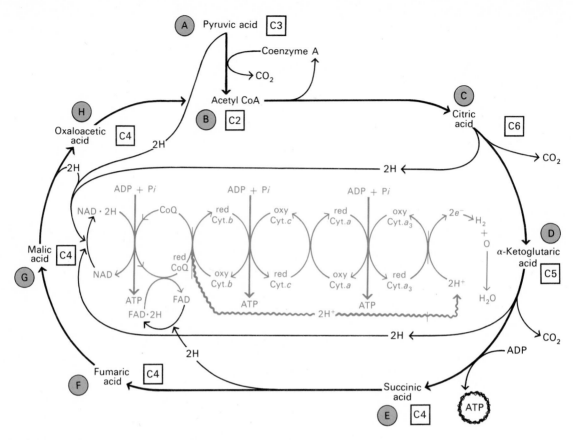

FIGURE 9–18 Summary of the interrelated events of the Krebs cycle and the electron-transport series occurring in the mitochondrion. Water enters the cycle between *D* and *E* and between *F* and *G*.

SUMMARY

A continual supply of energy is necessary for the chemical reactions that sustain life. The ultimate source of energy for living systems on the earth (except for some bacteria) is the sun. Living systems and their environments are open systems with respect to energy. The sun and the products of photosynthesis continually provide energy input for organisms to maintain life, grow, and reproduce.

The most important form of biological energy is the ATP molecule. When the terminal phosphate group of ATP is enzymatically removed, energy is released to drive chemical reactions. ATP is a unique intermediary between higher- and lower-energy compounds.

Energy reactions involve the breaking and formation of chemical bonds. The electrons that participate in bonding are exchanged in oxidation and reduction reactions. Oxidation is the loss of hydrogen or electrons from a compound, whereas reduction is the gain of hydrogen or electrons. Electrons are the basic source of energy in all cells; the energy-making reactions in cells trap the energy of hydrogen electrons to produce ATP.

Photosynthesis occurs in plants with the aid of chlorophyll, light, water, and carbon dioxide. Photosynthesis can be considered as a two-step

GLYCOLYSIS

Segment	Loss	Gain
Glucose → 2 PGAL 2 PGAL → 2 pyruvic acid	2 ATP	8 ATP
Net Gain = 6 ATP's	2 ATP	8 ATP

KREBS CYCLE

Segment			Loss	Gain
A–B	2 pyruvic acid	2 acetyl CoA	2 CO_2, 4H to NAD	6 ATP
B–C	2 acetyl CoA	2 citric acid	2 CoA	
C–D	2 citric acid	2 ketoglutaric acid	2 CO_2, 4H to NAD	6 ATP
D–E	2 ketoglutaric acid	2 succinic acid	2 CO_2, 4H to NAD	6 ATP 2 ATP
E–F	2 succinic acid	2 fumaric acid	4H to FAD	4 ATP
F–G	2 fumaric acid	2 malic acid		
G–H	2 malic acid	2 oxaloacetic acid	4H to NAD	6 ATP
			6 CO_2, 20H	30 ATP's

Net Gain = 30 ATP's

Total Net Gain = 36 ATP's

FIGURE 9–19 ATP energy released from one molecule of glucose oxidized in glycolysis and the Krebs cycle (compare with Figure 9–18). Note that the excess hydrogen and oxygen come from water molecules added during several steps.

process: (1) the light reaction, which produces ATP and makes electrons available in the form of reduced coenzyme NADP (NADP · 2H); and (2) the dark reaction, or carbon fixation, in which a five-carbon sugar, RDP, is combined with carbon dioxide and NADP · 2H to form the usable fuel PGAL. Two molecules of PGAL can be converted into glucose, and many glucose molecules may be made into starch.

The breakdown of food molecules to form energy is called respiration. The hydrogen of such fuel molecules as glucose is removed in two enzymatically catalyzed series of reactions: glycolysis in the cytoplasm and the Krebs cycle

in the mitochondria. Electrons removed in these processes are transferred to the electron-transport series, also in the mitochondria, for synthesis of ATP and the release of water.

REVIEW QUESTIONS

1. How does a cell use high-energy bonds such as those found in ATP? How is the energy content of ATP related to its structure?

2. What makes hydrogen important in energy processes? What is the role of water in respiration and photosynthesis?

	Glycerol	Fatty acids	Amino acids
Other possible fuels	Pyruvic PGAL	Acetyl CoA Ketoglutaric acid	Acetyl CoA Pyruvic acid Ketoglutaric acid Fumaric acid Oxaloacetic acid
Steps of respiration where non-carbohydrate fuels may enter			

3. Where is most of an animal's ATP produced? How do cytochrome molecules interact in this process?

4. What is the function of System I in photolysis? What are the roles of ferredoxin and NADP?

5. What are the differences between cyclic and noncyclic photolysis? In what ways are they related?

6. What are the sites of photosynthesis in a green plant?

7. What is the end product of glycolysis in muscle tissue after strenuous exercise? Why?

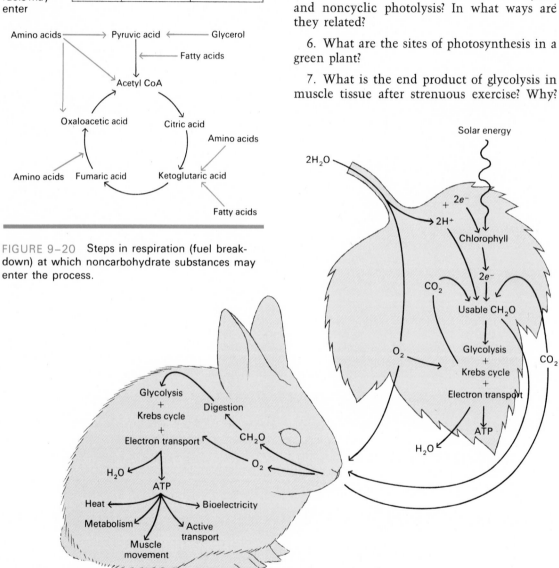

FIGURE 9–20   Steps in respiration (fuel breakdown) at which noncarbohydrate substances may enter the process.

FIGURE 9–21   Summary of nutrient and energy relationships in plants and animals.

8. Compare respiration and photosynthesis in terms of raw materials, site of occurrence, energy relationships in the cell, and end products.

9. Cyanide inhibits the enzyme cytochrome oxidase from transferring electrons in the electron-transport series. What effects would this have on a cell?

10. What are the products of the Krebs cycle? Draw a simple summary sketch of the major events in the Krebs cycle.

SUPPLEMENTARY READINGS

Govindjee and Rajni Govindjee, "The Primary Events of Photosynthesis," *Scientific American*, December 1974. The complex series of chemical events occurring during photolysis are summarized in detail along with two pigment systems that absorb light and transfer electron energy.

Lehninger, Albert L., *Bioenergetics*, W. A. Benjamin, New York, 1965. This small book is designed to provide beginning biology students with an introduction to the chemical and physical aspects of energy transformations in living systems.

Racker, Efraim, "The Membrane of the Mitochondrion," *Scientific American*, February 1968. The inner membrane of mitochondria contains the enzymes necessary for producing most of the energy in plant and animal cells. This article describes how the energy process can be understood better by taking this membrane apart and attempting to put it back together.

Stoeckenius, Walther, "The Purple Membrane of Salt-Loving Bacteria," *Scientific American*, June 1976. The purple pigment in these photosynthetic bacteria is compared to the structure and function of the visual purple pigment of vertebrate eyes.

Stryer, Lubert, *Biochemistry*, W. H. Freeman, San Francisco, 1975. An up-to-date treatment of the molecular basis of life. The common molecular patterns that underlie the diversity of life are stressed throughout.

Chapter 10

Nutrition & Digestion

In the previous chapter, we saw how energy from the sun enters the biosphere through the chemical reactions that take place in the green plant. This energy is used to produce comparatively large molecules which are then available to both plants and animals as food. *Nutrition,* the process by which organisms acquire food material—either by producing it themselves or finding it in their environments—is the first step in the overall chemical process we call metabolism.

Just as there is a wide range of types of food within the general concept of nutrition, there is a wide range in the energy we can extract from different types of food. The energy available in food is measured in calories, and each kind of food has a characteristic energy associated with it. And organisms have characteristic rates of using the energy in food. *The Metabolic Rate* is a standardized measure of the use of food energy by an organism under standardized conditions.

Not all substances in our diets are essential because of the energy they provide. *Vitamins* are essential compounds because of their role in assisting specific chemical processes in the body that are necessary for good health.

Most of this chapter is devoted to the general phases of *Digestion: The Breakdown of Food.* A controlled series of physical and chemical changes in the incoming food materials breaks down large food molecules into smaller ones. They can then be absorbed into the bloodstream for distribution to the body's cells.

The Vertebrate Digestive System, like all body systems, is actually a coordinated series of individual organs. However, it is far more useful for us to study this system in terms of its functional stages. Through the entire process digestive enzymes work on specific classes of food molecules yielding chemically smaller digestive products which are then absorbed at the end of the process.

How is the chemical functioning of the body regulated? How is incoming food energy distributed so that the body can have a constant supply without dangerous starts and stops? *The Liver: An Organ of Many Functions* is the largest and most chemically complex part of the digestive system. We conclude the chapter by studying the variety of its roles.

232

Photosynthesis produces basic food molecules. The cells of all organisms synthesize, or build up, larger food molecules from smaller ones. Respiration is the process of releasing energy from these foods. In this sense, food is a fuel burned to release energy in a cell. In most living systems large food molecules must be broken down into smaller molecules such as glucose before they can enter cells to be used as a fuel. All organisms but phototrophs and some bacteria must acquire food from some source and extract energy from it through the process of *nutrition*. Nutrition, then, is part of metabolism. It is the means by which an organism obtains raw materials from its exterior and changes them to a usable form in its interior. The specific mechanism that breaks down bulk food into usable fuel is *digestion*. This process breaks up large molecules into small ones that can move through cell membranes.

Absorption by cells is an important aspect of nutrition; it is the means by which small digested food molecules actually become available to all cells of an organism. Once food molecules have been absorbed, they can be transported and distributed throughout an organism by a circulatory system. We shall discuss circulation in the next chapter. In many animals food is first transported to an organ called a *liver* for distribution or storage. As we shall see, one of the chief functions of the liver is to distribute food evenly throughout an animal over a period of time. Once food molecules arrive at the cells, they can serve as fuel from which energy can be released. Food molecules thus contain potential energy, which can be released through respiration. And just as the release of energy occurs as an orderly sequence of steps, we will see that digestion proceeds similarly.

NUTRITION: MAKING FOOD AVAILABLE

How much energy does food contain? The energy value of foods can be measured, so we can predict how much energy a specific amount of a given food can release. This energy value, usually stated in *calories*, is important in matters of health. But other aspects of food are also important to health. Vitamins and mineral ions are also factors in the nutrient requirements of any organism.

We shall now relate nutrition and the distribution of nutrients to the overall concept of metabolism. This relationship should make clear why nutrition is so important in supporting energy metabolism.

Food and Calories

The source of raw materials for energy production is food. Organic foodstuffs are composed mainly of carbohydrates, fats, and proteins; we discussed these chemical structures in Chapter 3. Fats contain the greatest potential energy because fatty acids and glycerol contain more hydrogen, per unit of molecular weight, than carbohydrates or proteins. We discussed the important role of hydrogen and its electron in energy production in Chapter 9.

Foods contain varying amounts of food energy, which we measure in *calories*. A *calorie* is defined as the amount of heat necessary to raise 1 milliliter of water 1°C. A special closed container called a calorimeter is used to determine caloric content. The sample to be burned is placed in the inner chamber of a calorimeter. The chamber is then charged with oxygen and sealed, and the contents are ignited with an electric current. The amount of heat produced by the combustion is read directly from the thermometer and converted to calories. One gram molecular weight of glucose (180 grams), for example, yields 686,000 calories when completely oxidized. A calorie is thus a heat equivalent in calculating the potential energy of foods. Calories are usually expressed as kilocalories (units of 1000 calories): in that case the term is capitalized, *Calories*. For example, a slice of white bread typically contains 63,000 calories (or 63 Calories); one fried egg contains 77,000 calories (or 77 Calories).

In Chapter 9 we learned that one gram molecular weight (one mole) of glucose oxidized through glycolysis and the Krebs cycle yields 36 moles of ATP. If we consider that one mole of ATP contains about 7300 calories of energy available to drive biological reactions, one gram molecular weight of glucose biologically oxidized would yield 263,000 calories. With this information we can now calculate the efficiency of the enzymatic energy production (in the form of ATP) from glucose to be about 263,000/686,000, or approximately 38 percent.

Calculation of Metabolic Rate

Any individual's minimum caloric energy requirement may be calculated. This *basal metabolic rate*, or BMR, is a measure of the energy used by an organism that is awake but completely at rest. The word *basal* refers to a "baseline" of activity; below this baseline the organism is unconscious, and above it the organism is in a state of physiological arousal requiring more energy than the resting condition. The amount of oxygen used and carbon dioxide released over a specific time interval are the factors normally measured to determine basal metabolic rate. These amounts vary with the

kinds of foods in an individual's diet. A normal human diet, for example, is a mixture of carbohydrates, proteins, and fats; each of these foodstuffs requires a characteristic amount of oxygen when burned (oxidized). The amount of oxygen necessary to oxidize glucose to carbon dioxide and water is:

$$C_6H_{12}O_6 + 6O_2 \rightarrow 6CO_2 + 6H_2O + \text{energy}$$
$$\text{(input)} \qquad\qquad \text{(output)}$$

Thus the ratio of carbon dioxide output to oxygen input is 6/6 or 1.0. This mathematical relationship is called the *respiratory quotient* (RQ) value. For proteins, the value is about 0.9; for fats, 0.7. As we mentioned earlier, fats contain the highest food-energy value. One gram of fat produces about 9.0 Calories, whereas carbohydrates and protein produce only about 4.0 Calories. The average RQ value for a balanced diet is approximately 0.86.

Bio-Topic: Anatomy and Endurance

Pound for pound, females may be physiologically better suited than males to excel at long-distance running. The reasons have to do with the physiology of long-distance running, the properties of fat, and anatomy.

Male long-distance runners often mention the phenomenon of "hitting the wall," a sense of sudden exhaustion that sets in after running about 20 miles. Female long-distance runners never report this sensation—a difference that may result from differences in the hormonal makeup of males and females.

After about two hours of running, athletes of both sexes are obtaining most of their energy by oxidizing fat rather than from the usual energy source, glycogen. Gram for gram, fats deliver six to seven times as much energy as glycogen, so that fat is a more compact and efficient energy

source than glycogen. A female of a given age and size is usually lighter than a male of the same age and size. Part of this difference comes from the larger deposits of fatty tissues that females carry, and fatty tissues are lighter than muscle.

Other things being equal, females carry larger amounts of this more efficient energy source. Females may thus outperform equal-sized males because of this combination of hormonal and anatomical differences. Why then are there no women competitors in the Olympic and other marathon events? The present rules exclude women from marathons, and no one has made any effort to change the rules.

Will further research verify these early observations? Will women seek to compete in marathons in the future? Time will tell.

A generalized BMR for humans is about one to two Calories per kilogram of body weight per hour. Significant variation from this normal relationship may indicate an organic imbalance in hormone or enzyme production. For example, an individual whose BMR is significantly less than one Calorie per kilogram of body weight may have an abnormally low secretion of the hormone thyroxine. A *hormone* is a substance secreted in one part of an organism that has effects in other parts of the organism. Unlike enzymes, hormones are transported in the extracellular fluids. Thyroxine, for instance, is secreted by the thyroid gland; it helps to regulate carbohydrate metabolism in all body cells.

In addition to weight, factors such as age, sex, and body surface area influence basal metabolic rate. BMR varies widely among individuals. The basal metabolic rate for an 18-year-old male college student is calculated as follows:

Oxygen consumed in 1 hour = 18 liters
Body weight = 185 pounds ÷ 2.2
$$= 84 \text{ kilograms}$$

One liter of oxygen will produce about 4.8 Calories from a mixed diet; 18 liters $O_2 \times 4.8$ Cal = 86.4 Cal.

The BMR relationship is thus:

86.4 Cal/84 kg/1 hr

or approximately 1 Cal/1 kg/1 hr.

Diet and Metabolism

The chemical balance of the foods an organism consumes is just as important as the energy the foods provide. Carbohydrates alone might provide enough caloric energy, and they fulfill some nutritional requirements. But fats, proteins, mineral ions, and vitamins are all essential for growth and repair of cells, enzyme function, molecular synthesis, and support of the energy process. These nutritional requirements lead to the important relationship between a balanced diet and good health.

There are many kinds of diets because various people have various needs. Young organisms, including young humans, generally need more protein than older organisms. The protein needs of people who do hard physical work—athletes, lumberjacks, farmers, and so on—are also higher than average. And many people need special diets to overcome abnormal nutritional deficiencies.

But the most common kind of special diet is the ever-popular weight-reducing diet. Any special diet is best undertaken under the guidance of a physician. Nevertheless we can outline some general principles common to all sensible reducing diets.

The important rule in losing body weight is simply to eat fewer calories than you burn. The fantastic weight reductions attributed to fad diets usually result from loss of tissue fluid. Although this is an important part of weight loss, one must be careful to maintain enough water for proper kidney and circulatory function. The greatest amount of fat that can be metabolized during complete fasting is about one-half pound per day. True weight loss, then, is a slow process once excess body fluids are lost. Dieting should be spread over several months during which water, mineral, and vitamin intake are carefully monitored. In most cases reducing the amount of food eaten—particularly such high-calorie foods as fats and carbohydrates—will produce a significant weight reduction.

The thyroid glands of many people become less active after age 35. If thyroid functioning falls below the normal range (a *hypothyroid* condition), they may have trouble keeping their weight down. In such cases a physician may prescribe thyroxine to supplement the reduced amounts produced by the patient's thyroid gland. Thyroxine promotes the utilization of food molecules and thus prevents their storage which results in weight gain.

Vitamins: Essential in Small Amounts

Vitamins are a large and varied group of organic compounds that are required in small amounts; since animals cannot synthesize these compounds they must obtain them in their diets. (one exception as noted below is Vitamin D.) The study of vitamins began when

Vitamin B$_1$ crystals. (Hoffman-LaRoche & Co., Basle, Switzerland.)

certain foods were found to prevent deficiency diseases such as scurvy and beriberi. Later, as analytical techniques were refined, the active substances were isolated from disease-preventing foods. Approximately 30 compounds have been isolated and classed as vitamins. In some instances we still do not know exactly what a vitamin does in a cell. We do know, however, what happens if the vitamin is not present.

Our knowledge of the cellular functions of vitamins is increasing rapidly, however. For example, vitamin B$_2$ (riboflavin) is known to be the precursor of FAD, a component of the electron-transport system discussed in Chapter 9. In fact, most members of the large B vitamin group seem to be raw materials used to make coenzymes for catalyzing vital functions.

Vitamin D is the only vitamin humans can synthesize; the process occurs in the skin under the stimulation of ultraviolet light. Vitamin D is involved in the distribution of calcium and phosphorus, and a serious lack of this vitamin leads to rickets, a softening of the bones. But the molecular role of vitamin D in regulating calcium and phosphorus metabolism is still unknown. Figure 10–1 lists several vitamins and their functions and sources.

DIGESTION: BREAKDOWN OF FOOD

Autotrophic organisms synthesize most of the nutrients they need and get the rest in the water they absorb. But heterotrophic organisms cannot synthesize all their own nutrients; they need mechanisms to procure and digest food. *Saprophytes*, organisms which live on dead organic matter, and *parasites*, which obtain food from a living host, are highly specialized heterotrophs.

Digestion is the breakdown of large food molecules into smaller molecules that can be absorbed into cells and used in the building (synthesis) of other large molecules, energy processing, maintenance, and repair. Large molecules are split into smaller units by the enzymatic addition of water at certain bonding sites. This splitting process, called *hydrolytic cleavage*, is the reverse of dehydration synthesis, the synthesis of polysaccharides, proteins, and fats through the removal of water. Digestion is an obvious process in heterotrophs, but unicellular organisms and plants must also digest large food molecules to smaller units. This is true even though they have synthesized these large starches and proteins themselves.

Digestion in Protists and Animals

Many types of digestive systems occur among protists and animals. Some of these are diagrammed in Figure 10–2. In many organisms digestion is entirely *intracellular* (within the cell). An *Amoeba* captures its food with a flowing pseudopod; a *Paramecium* takes in food particles carried into a groovelike gullet by beating cilia. In both cases, the cell membrane surrounds the food, pinching off to form a food vacuole within the cell. Intracellular enzymes from lysosomes then begin to digest the food, and usable nutrients diffuse into the cytoplasm.

Sponges are considered to be at the cellular level of development because each cell of the sponge colony is metabolically independent of the others. The sponge has a cavity lined with flagellated collar cells called *choanocytes* (Figure 10–2d). The beating flagella produce a water current that brings food particles within reach. These are caught and engulfed by the cytoplasm in the collar of the cell. This is another example of intracellular digestion.

Even in the coelenterates that contain tissues, such as jellyfish, sea anemones, and

Vitamin	Deficiency Symptoms	Cell Function	Source
Fat soluble			
Vitamin A	Night blindness; dry, scaly epithelial tissue; susceptibility to infection	Forms part of the molecules involved in the visual process	Yellow and green vegetables, fish oil, liver
Vitamin D	Rickets—abnormal bond development	Metabolism of calcium and phosphorus	Fish-liver oil, eggs, butter
Vitamin E	Muscle and nerve disorders: sterility	H transport in oxidation	Plant products, especially wheat-germ oil
Vitamin K	Slowed blood clotting	H transport in oxidation; synthesis of prothrombin	Most green plants
Water soluble			
Vitamin B$_1$ (thiamine)	Beriberi, nerve inflammation; muscle paralysis	Coenzyme to remove CO_2; for example, from pyruvic acid	Wheat germ, yeast, pork, eggs
Vitamin B$_2$ (riboflavin)	Lip lesions and inflamed eyes	Component of FAD, necessary for H transport	Milk products, green vegetables, liver, cereals
Vitamin B$_6$ (pyridoxine)	Dermatitis and reduced growth	Coenzymes for removal of CO_2 and trans-animation	Cereals, eggs, meat
Vitamin B$_{12}$ (cyanocobalamin)	Pernicious anemia—reduced number of red blood cells	Coenzyme necessary for nucleic-acid metabolism	Meat, liver, egg yolk
Nicotinic acid (niacin)	Pellagra—diarrhea, mental disorder, dermatitis	Component of NAD and NADP, necessary for H transport	Meat, liver, milk, yeast
Pantothenic acid	None known in humans	Component of coenzyme A	Most foods
Biotin	Mouth lesions—rarely seen in humans	Part of an enzyme necessary for carboxylation (addition of CO_2)	Vegetables, liver, milk, meat
Folic acid	Anemia—reduced number of red blood cells	Nucleic-acid synthesis	Leafy vegetables and most foods
Vitamin C (ascorbic acid)	Scurvy—inflammation of gums, anemia, and weakness	Aerobic H transport; synthesis of connective tissues	Citrus fruits and tomatoes

FIGURE 10–1   Summary of some of the important vitamins.

hydra, digestion is largely intracellular. Threadlike filaments projecting from the thin layer of gastric cells lining the gastrovascular cavity contact the food. These gastric filaments secrete enzymes that initiate the digestive process outside the digestive cells; the process is completed inside these cells. The one opening to the digestive area (gastrovascular cavity) of these organisms serves as both mouth and anus.

The earthworm has a digestive tract with two openings, a mouth and an anus. This tract contains specialized regions for digestion and absorption of food. These specialized organs include the crop, a thin-walled portion in which food is stored; the gizzard, a muscular

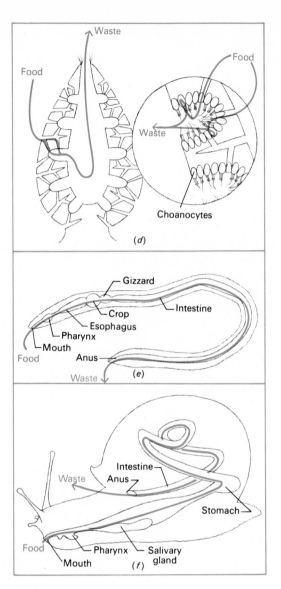

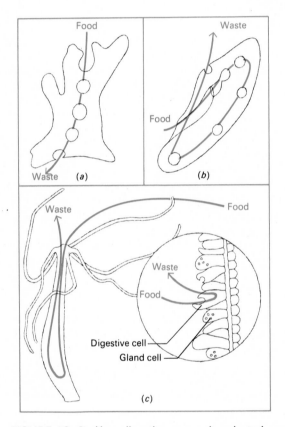

FIGURE 10–2   How digestion occurs in selected protists and animals. (a) Amoeba. (b) Paramecium. (c) Coelenterate (*Hydra*). (d) Sponge. (e) Earthworm. (f) Snail.

region where food is ground up; and the intestine, in which specialized cells secrete digestive enzymes and digestion takes place. Digestion occurring in a cavity outside of cells, as in the digestive tract of an earthworm or a human, is called *extracellular* digestion.

Mollusks exhibit a variety of digestive processes. Some aquatic snails digest most of their food within large digestive gland cells, whereas octopi and squids depend almost entirely on extracellular digestion.

In general, digestive systems become more

complex and extracellular digestion more predominant as the total structure of orgnisms becomes more complex. The fundamental enzymatic mechanisms of hydrolysis, however, remain roughly the same.

The Vertebrate Digestive System

In vertebrates, digestion takes place in the *alimentary canal*. This passage includes the mouth, esophagus, stomach, small intestine, large intestine, rectum, and anus. The digestive system also includes three accessory digestive organs, the liver, gallbladder, and pancreas. Although foodstuffs do not pass through them, these accessory organs produce hormones and enzymes essential for digestion. The structure and function of vertebrate digestive systems vary according to the foods eaten (Figure 10–3). For example, the digestive tracts of cattle and other animals that eat plants are generally long, with one or more pouches for storage. While the food is stored, bacteria break down tough, fibrous cellulose and provide nutrients for the host. Cattle and deer have four-part stomachs; the largest part, the rumen, is the site of extensive bacterial action.

We shall use the human digestive process as an example of vertebrate digestion. Functionally, the digestive process has three phases: salivary, gastric, and intestinal. These phases provide for an orderly breakdown of foodstuffs, to small molecules that can be absorbed.

Salivary Phase of Digestion

The mouth contains the teeth and tongue, which mechanically break down, mix, and transport solid food. The permanent human teeth include four incisors, two canines, four premolars, and six molars on each jaw. Incisors are used in biting, canines are for ripping and tearing, and molars are broadly ridged for chewing. Since human teeth are efficient for masticating (chewing) both flesh and vegetable matter, we are classified as *omnivores* along with such animals as bears and pigs (Figure 10–4). Meat-eaters, or *carnivores*, such as cats and dogs have sharply pointed teeth for tearing and shredding flesh. *Herbivores* such as cattle and beavers eat only vegetable matter; they have flattened tooth surfaces for crushing and grinding.

During mastication saliva enters the mouth from three pairs of salivary glands, the *parotid* located just beneath each ear, the *submaxillary* near the angle of the jaw, and the *sublingual* under the tongue. Saliva is a viscous liquid that contains water, salts, a glycoprotein substance called mucin, and two enzymes. The pH of mouth fluids is normally near 7 (neutral). Saliva breaks down starches and lubricates food for its passage through the alimentary canal. In addition it facilitates speech and makes possible the sensation of taste by liquifying dry foods. Saliva flow may be activated by the presence of food in the mouth, by the smell of food, or simply by the thought of food. Control of salivation rests with the autonomic nervous system, which will be discussed in Chapter 12.

Salivary secretions contain two enzymes, *salivary amylase (ptyalin)* and *maltase.* Salivary amylase hydrolyzes starches into smaller units, the double sugar maltose ($C_{12}H_{22}O_{11}$). In vertebrates, amylases act only on alpha carbohydrate linkages and not on beta-linked cellulose molecules. (These linkages were discussed in Chapter 3). Maltase splits maltose into two glucose units by the catalytic addition of water. Glucose, as you learned in the previous chapter, is immediately available for energy metabolism when absorbed into the bloodstream. But carbohydrate digestion is not usually completed in the mouth. Food is swallowed and passes to the stomach, where the high acidity inhibits the action of amylase. The final stages of starch digestion take place in the small intestine.

Gastric Phase of Digestion

The stomach, a muscular J-shaped organ, lies just below the diaphragm. A tube called the esophagus descends from the mouth and enters the stomach through a constriction called the *cardiac valve.* The stomach is divided into three parts; the upper or *cardiac* portion including the saclike *fundus,* the *body,* and the lower region or *pylorus,* where the small intestine begins. Three layers of muscle make up the stomach wall—an outer longitudinal layer, a middle circular layer, and an internal oblique. The stomach also has a lining made up of

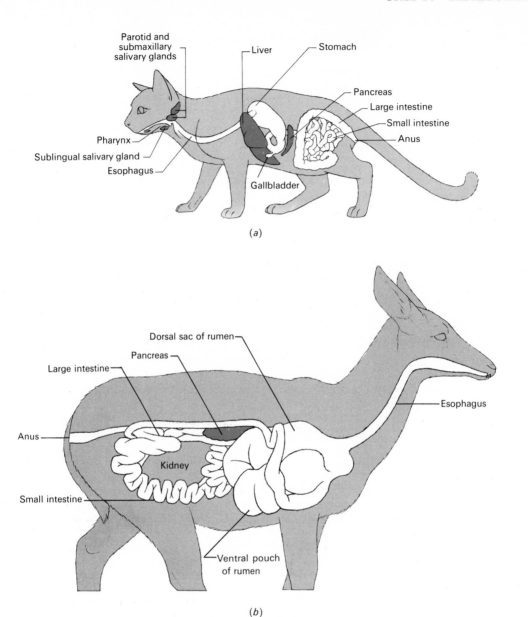

Parotid and submaxillary salivary glands
Liver
Stomach
Pancreas
Large intestine
Small intestine
Anus
Pharynx
Sublingual salivary gland
Esophagus
Gallbladder

(a)

Dorsal sac of rumen
Pancreas
Large intestine
Esophagus
Anus
Kidney
Small intestine
Ventral pouch of rumen

(b)

distinct longitudinal ridges called *rugae* which allow for expansion.

The entrance to the small intestine from the stomach is guarded by a circular muscle, the *pyloric valve*. This valve, also called a *sphincter*, keeps food in the stomach for digestion and protects the relatively thin-walled intestine against the entrance of large, abrasive chunks of food. As food is digested, it is transported through the alimentary canal by means of rhythmic waves of smooth muscle contraction called *peristalsis*. Peristalsis, like salivation, is controlled by the autonomic nervous system.

The vertebrate stomach has a definite role in secretion. *Parietal cells* in the mucous lining secrete hydrochloric acid (HCl), and *chief cells*

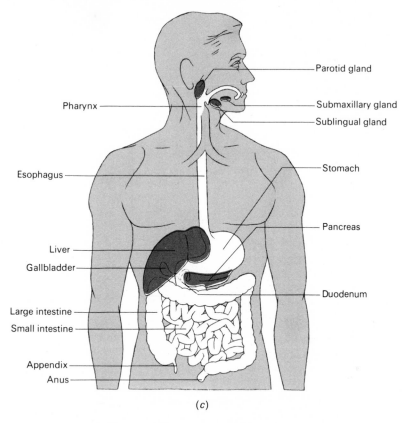

Parotid gland

Pharynx

Submaxillary gland

Sublingual gland

Esophagus

Stomach

Pancreas

Liver

Gallbladder

Duodenum

Large intestine

Small intestine

Appendix

Anus

(*c*)

FIGURE 10–3 Comparison of digestive systems. (*a*) Cat. (*b*) Deer. (*c*) Man. Note the large storage pouches in the deer, a herbivorous ruminant.

secrete an inactive proteolytic (protein-splitting) enzyme, *pepsinogen.* Hydrochloric acid acts on pepsinogen to form *pepsin*, which in turn hydrolyzes protein into polypeptides, dipeptides, and amino acids (Figure 10–5). The hydrochloric acid also kills bacteria and breaks down the intercellular cement of fibrous plant and animal tissues.

When food enters the stomach through the cardiac valve, the stomach lining secretes digestive juices. The presence of food also activates cells in the stomach lining to release the hormone *gastrin* into the bloodstream. Gastrin stimulates secretion of hydrochloric acid and pepsinogen. The hormone *enterogastrone*, produced in the small intestine, inhibits the secretion of gastric juice; this mechanism prevents

overproduction. In young mammals, a special milk-coagulating enzyme, *rennin*, unites the normally soluble casein protein of milk with calcium and fat to form insoluble curds. This curdling of milk causes it to remain longer in the stomach, where gastric enzymes can digest the curds. As an individual matures, rennin production decreases greatly or ceases entirely. Curdling is adequately accomplished, however, by pepsin and hydrochloric acid. The curds are finally digested by enzymes in the stomach and small intestine.

The occurrence of ulcers in about 10 percent of adults in the United States illustrates the fact that gastric secretions are controlled primarily by the autonomic nervous system. An ulcer is an area of the alimentary canal that has been

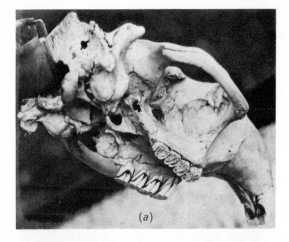

(a)

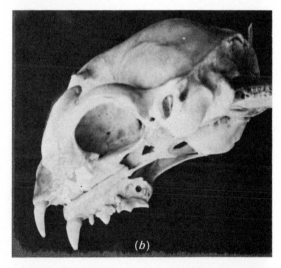

(b)

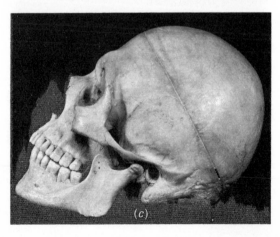

(c)

eroded away by excessive peristalsis or the action of hydrochloric acid and digestive enzymes. One common type of ulcer is the gastric, or stomach, ulcer. The stomach is normally lined with mucin, which protects the cells from autolysis (self-digestion). Anxiety and nervous tension may cause excessive secretion and peristaltic action in the absence of food, removing this protective coating. Ulcers are often painful and may lead to internal bleeding if blood vessels lying below the lining are also eroded. Pain from an ulcer may be felt in the middle of the upper back. The explanation for this *referred pain* lies in the fact that nerves from the stomach and the upper back converge in the same area of the spinal cord. Pain from the stomach is therefore felt as coming from the back.

Intestinal Phase of Digestion

Peristaltic contractions force partially digested food through the pyloric valve from the stomach into the first portion of the small intestine. The first 10 inches of the small intestine, called the *duodenum*, is the site of several digestive and absorptive functions. The duodenum contains numerous fingerlike projections called *villi* (Figure 5–28), which extend into the lumen (inside) of the tube. These villi greatly increase the surface area for absorption. The fluids in the small intestine are generally alkaline, in contrast to the acidic secretions of the stomach. This alkaline condition is necessary because the enzymes acting in this region function best at pH values near 8.

PANCREATIC ENZYMES. The pancreas is a large organ, some of whose glandular tissues secrete digestive enzymes. (Other pancreatic tissues secrete hormones, as we will see in Chapter 12). The presence of partially digested food in the duodenum stimulates cells in the duodenal mucosa to secrete the hormone *secretin;* this substance in turn causes the pancreas to secrete large amounts of sodium bicar-

FIGURE 10–4   Dentition of the upper jaws of three animals. (*a*) Beaver (herbivore). (*b*) Cat (carnivore). (*c*) Human (omnivore). (Courtesy, Field Museum of Natural History, Chicago.)

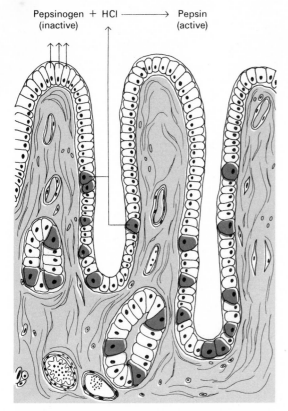

Pepsinogen + HCl ⟶ Pepsin
(inactive)   (active)

FIGURE 10-5 Pepsinogen secreted by the chief cells of the gastric mucosa is activated by HCl, which is secreted by the parietal cells (color).

bonate. This maintains the alkaline condition in the duodenum. Sodium bicarbonate and other secretions of the pancreas are released into the duodenum through the pancreatic duct. A second duodenal hormone, *pancreozymin*, stimulates the pancreas to release its digestive enzymes. Each day the pancreas produces 500 to 800 ml of fluid containing enzymes for hydrolysis of all types of food. The enzymes produced by the pancreas and the types of food molecules they hydrolyze are: (1) *pancreatic amylase*, for starch, (2) *pancreatic lipase*, for fats, (3) *trypsin*, for protein such as albumins and collagen, and (4) *carboxypeptidase*, for the peptide linkages adjacent to a free carboxyl (COOH) group on polypeptides.

The action of pancreatic amylase on starches is very similar to that of salivary amylase. Pancreatic lipase splits fats at the ester bonds to release glycerol and fatty acids. Large globules of fat are emulsified by *bile*, a yellow-green fluid produced in the liver and stored in the gallbladder. Bile enters the small intestine near the pancreatic duct, through the common bile duct from the liver and the gallbladder. Bile is only an aid to fat digestion, not an enzyme. It lowers the surface tension surrounding fat globules and converts them to smaller droplets, exposing more surface area to lipase. The presence of fats in the small intestine stimulates the intestinal mucosa to secrete the hormone *cholecystokinin*, which enters the bloodstream to cause the release of bile from the gallbladder.

Trypsin, an enzyme for breaking protein, is comparable to the gastric enzyme pepsin. Unlike pepsin, it acts in an alkaline medium; it also hydrolyzes complex proteins more slowly than pepsin. Trypsin is secreted by the pancreas in an inactive form called *trypsinogen*. Trypsinogen is converted to trypsin by the action of a nondigestive enzyme called *enterokinase* secreted by the intestinal mucosa. Enterokinase removes a fragment from the trypsinogen molecule and thus causes it to become active. Since enzymes have very specific geometry with important contact areas called "active sites," this conversion process is probably just an unmasking of active sites (Figure 10-6).

Carboxypeptidase serves a very specific function. It hydrolyzes the peptide linkages of polypeptides adjacent to free carboxyl (acid) groups and thus releases individual amino acids.

INTESTINAL ENZYMES. The small intestine, the site of final digestion, secretes a number of enzymes that supplement those secreted by the pancreas. These intestinal enzymes are secreted in two locations: by individual cells lying at the base of the villi and by the compound intestinal glands located in the submucosa layer. The flow of intestinal enzymes is triggered by release of the hormone *enterocrinin* from the intestinal mucosa. All digestive hormones included in this discussion are summarized in Figure 10-7.

Intestinal lipase and amylase have functions similar to pancreatic enzymes already de-

Bio-Topic: Genetic Chauvinism?

Milk is an almost complete food for humans. It contains minerals, vitamins, fats, proteins, and a single carbohydrate, the disaccharide lactose. Physicians were therefore very surprised to find that many people, including infants, become ill after drinking milk.

Lactose is digested in the duodenum of the small intestine. The enzyme lactase hydrolyzes lactose to the monosaccharides glucose and galactose which enter the bloodstream. In most mammals the enzyme begins to form in the fetal intestine late during gestation and reaches a peak about the time of birth. The amount of the enzyme then falls slowly during the first month of life to a low level that seems to be sustained throughout life. This adult level of the enzyme varies from individual to individual, which is why some persons can tolerate lactose and some become ill from it.

Problems start when a person eats more lactose than the amount of lactase in his or her intestine can digest. This can happen either when there is very little enzyme or when a large quantity of lactose is eaten. The undigested lactose passes from the duodenum into the colon where two kinds of intestinal upsets may occur. One is osmotic: a large amount of lactose can remove water from the colon wall by osmosis. The other is biochemical: bacteria in the colon metabolize lactose to carbon dioxide and irritating organic acids.

The symptoms of these processes include dehydration, or cramps and diarrhea, respectively.

By 1970, it became clear that adults from most parts of the world cannot digest lactose. In fact, it appears that populations with large proportions of lactose-tolerant adults occur in only three areas: northern Europe, Nigeria, and the United States (where many persons have either European or African ancestors).

Cross-cultural genetic and nutritional studies suggest an explanation. Lactose-intolerance in adults appears to be the usual condition in humans and most mammals. Rare mutations to lactose-tolerance may have occurred throughout human history. Because a gene for lactose-tolerance was of no advantage, it was lost each time it appeared.

About 10,000 years ago, two human cultures turned to milking other mammals as a source of additional food. Africans milked cows, and northern Europeans milked reindeer. In these cultures, a gene that enabled adults to digest milk without ill effects would be expected to spread until most adults carried the gene.

If this bit of evolutionary detective work is verified, then American programs of supplying powdered milk to underdeveloped countries will need reevaluation. These programs would be in conflict with the genetic heritage of the recipient cultures and clearly inappropriate.

scribed. Intestinal dipeptidases split double amino acids into individual acids to be absorbed and utilized. *Aminopeptidase* acts much like carboxypeptidase, except that it breaks peptide bonds adjacent to free amino groups. By this point in the digestive process, most complex carbohydrates have been broken into six- and twelve-carbon sugars by salivary and pancreatic amylases. The intestine produces not only an amylase but also three enzymes commonly classed as *disaccharases* which split disaccharides (pairs of simple sugars). These three enzymes and the breakdowns they catalyze are: *maltase* (maltose → glucose + glucose); *sucrase* (sucrose → fructose + glucose); and *lactase* (lactose → galac-

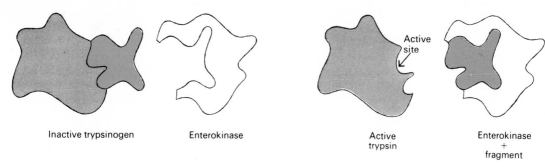

Inactive trypsinogen   Enterokinase   Active trypsin   Enterokinase + fragment

FIGURE 10–6   Model of the unmasking action of enterokinase on a trypsinogen molecule. Removal of a fragment of the molecule frees the active site, and trypsin becomes functional.

tose + glucose). The digestion of foods is thus a step-by-step process in which intermediate products are formed on the way to end products (Figure 10–8).

Absorption of Digestive Products

As we have seen, the first stages of digestion take place in the mouth and stomach. But no digested food is absorbed until after it enters

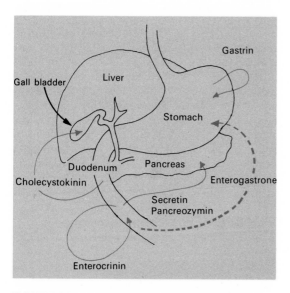

FIGURE 10–7   The hormones involved in the human digestive process. The curved arrows indicate hormones transported by the bloodstream and tissue fluids. The broken arrow indicates inhibition of gastric secretion by enterogastrone.

the small intestine. (Aspirin and alcohol are exceptions; they are absorbed through the stomach.) Peristaltic waves similar to those in the stomach continue along the entire small intestine, moving the food products along (Figure 10–9).

Absorption occurs along the length of most of the small intestine, beginning at the duodenum.

The cells of the intestinal villi can absorb substances against a *concentration gradient*. In our discussion of diffusion (Chapter 3), we noted that particles tend to diffuse away from the area of their greatest concentration. As absorption continues, the concentration of nutrients in the cells of the villi surpasses that found in the intestinal juice. Therefore these substances must be moved into the cells and bloodstream against a gradient by active transport; this requires energy in the form of ATP. (You might benefit by reviewing the section on active transport in Chapter 4 at this point.)

All along the small intestine, absorbed nutrients pass through intestinal cells and enter the bloodstream. Each villus contains an arteriole and a venule connected by a capillary network. These venules converge to form a larger vein called the *hepatic portal vein*. The blood in this vein, highly concentrated with absorbed nutrients, passes directly to capillary beds of the liver. As we shall see later in this chapter, the liver acts on these products of digestion to store some, convert others, and detoxify waste products.

Food	Enzyme Action	Intermediate Products	Enzyme Action	End Products
Carbohydrates	salivary, pancreatic, and intestinal amylase →	Disaccharides →	maltase, sucrase, lactase →	Monosaccharides
Protein	pepsin, trypsin →	Polypeptides and dipeptides →	carboxypeptidase, dipeptidase, aminopeptidase →	Amino acids
Fats (bile added)	→	Emulsified fat →	lipase →	Glycerol and fatty acids

FIGURE 10-8 The intermediate and end products of digestion. Some of the major enzymes that function at each step are noted.

A third type of vessel called a *lacteal* is located in each villus (Figure 10-10). Lacteal vessels are part of an accessory circulation system known as the *lymphatic system*. Lacteals absorb emulsified fats and route them away from the liver and into a larger lymphatic duct, the *thoracic duct*, which passes upward through the diaphragm and empties into the left subclavian vein above the heart. This produces a rapid increase in fats in the blood following a meal.

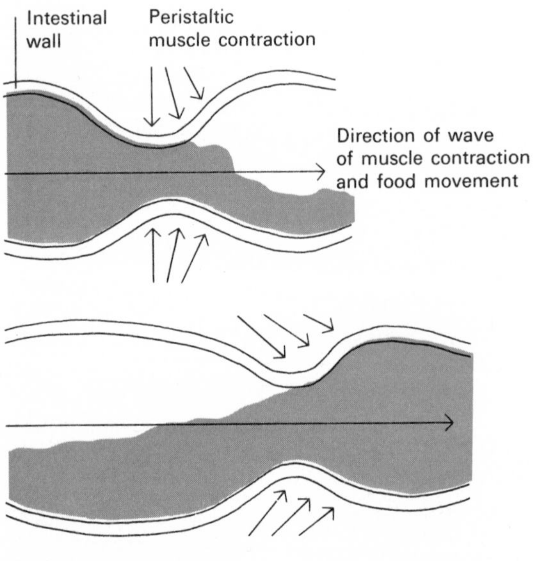

Past the duodenum, the small intestine is divided—although there is no precise dividing line—into the *jejunum* (about 8 feet long) and the *ileum* (about 12 feet). These regions of the small intestine are important for absorption of digested foods. The junction between the ileum and the ascending colon of the large intestine is controlled by the *ileocecal* valve, which keeps unabsorbed wastes from backing up in the system. The *vermiform appendix*, a vestigial organ in humans, extends from the caecum, or blind pouch, of the ascending colon. The appendix apparently no longer serves a vital function. The major organs and enzymes involved in human digestion are summarized in Figure 10-11.

The Role of the Large Intestine

The functions of the large intestine, or colon, relate primarily to water and ion absorption, concentration of feces, and defecation. The small intestine is so efficient in the absorption of foods that little, if any, absorbable matter ever reaches the large intestine. Bacteria are common in the colon, where residual polysaccharides and cellulose may be further broken down by bacterial enzymes. In addition, some

FIGURE 10-9 Peristalsis in the small intestine. The lower drawing shows that the food is moving down the intestine.

Intestinal wall
Peristaltic muscle contraction
Direction of wave of muscle contraction and food movement

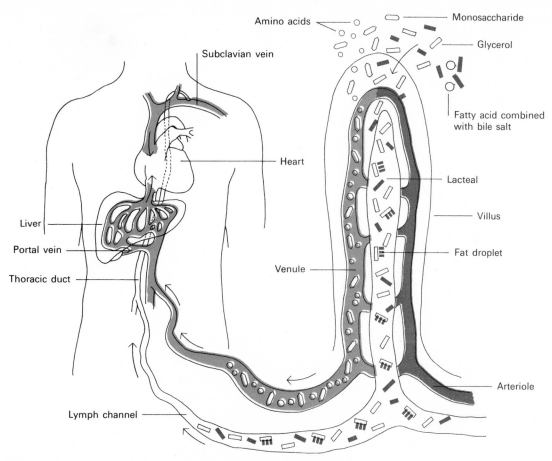

FIGURE 10-10 Absorption of digestive end products into the blood and lymph systems. In a villus, amino acids and monosaccharides move into capillaries, and the end products of fat digestion pass into lacteals. The lacteals merge into a common lymph vessel which enters the thoracic duct.

bacteria produce vitamin K and a few B vitamins. The colon is larger in diameter than the small intestine, and is 5 to 6 feet long. The lower portion of the descending colon, shaped like an S, is often called the sigmoid colon. The last 8 to 10 inches of the alimentary tract consists of the rectum, anal canal, and anus.

If normal water absorption from the large intestine cannot occur because of disease or irritation, *diarrhea* or *constipation* may result. In diarrhea the material in the large intestine is moved along by peristalsis so rapidly that nor-

mal water absorption cannot occur. The feces are therefore very watery. Constipation occurs when movement of contents is slow and too much water is absorbed from the large intestine. Under these conditions, fecal material becomes hard and difficult to pass.

THE LIVER: AN ORGAN OF MANY FUNCTIONS

The largest and one of the most important metabolic organs in vertebrates is the liver. In

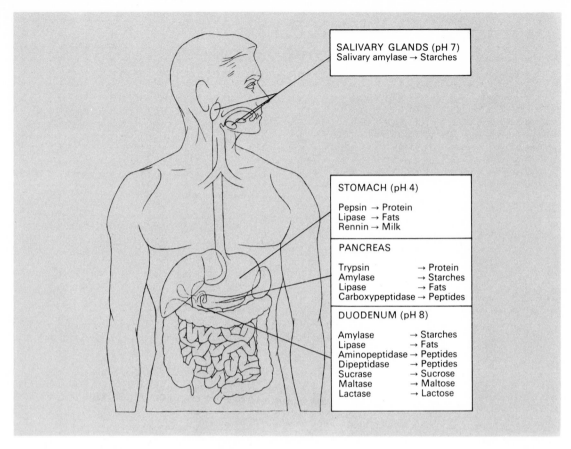

FIGURE 10-11   Summary of human digestion.

humans the liver has four-lobes; it lies just below the diaphragm and above the stomach. Liver cells are all similar, so each cuboidal cell is apparently capable of digestive, circulatory, and metabolic functions. We shall consider the functions of the liver in synthesis, storage, regulation, and detoxification.

Synthesis

The liver is the site of many chemical reactions. Some of the glucose molecules brought from the small intestine by the hepatic portal vein are synthesized in the liver into the polysaccharide glycogen (Figure 10-12). The formation of glycogen from glucose molecules is called *glycogenesis*. Liver cells can also convert

noncarbohydrate molecules such as amino acids and fats into glycogen through a more complex process called *glyconeogenesis*. (Neo-, meaning "new," indicates that glycogen was synthesized from molecules other than carbohydrates.)

Amino acids may be converted into *keto* acids in the liver by *deamination*—enzymatic removal of an amino group. The term *keto*

$$\overset{\text{O}}{\underset{\|}{}}$$

refers to the structural group C—C—C. Most amino acids can be transformed into other amino acids by *transamination*, an enzymatic exchange of an amino group between an amino acid and a keto or fatty acid (Figure 10-13). In this way the liver regulates the amino acid

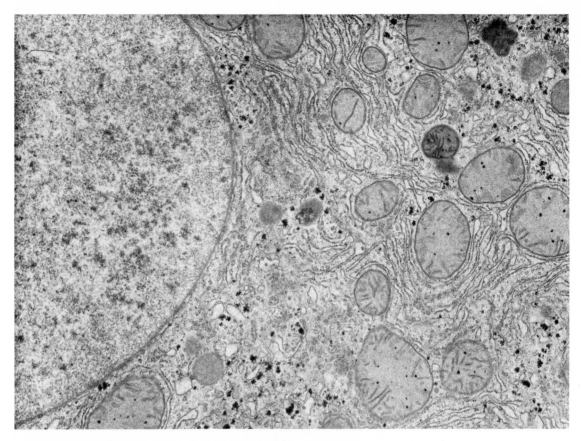

FIGURE 10-12   Electron micrograph of a rat liver cell, showing granules of glycogen synthesized in the cytoplasm. ($\times$ 12,000). The glycogen granules are the small, darkly stained masses throughout the cytoplasm. (Courtesy of Keith R. Porter.)

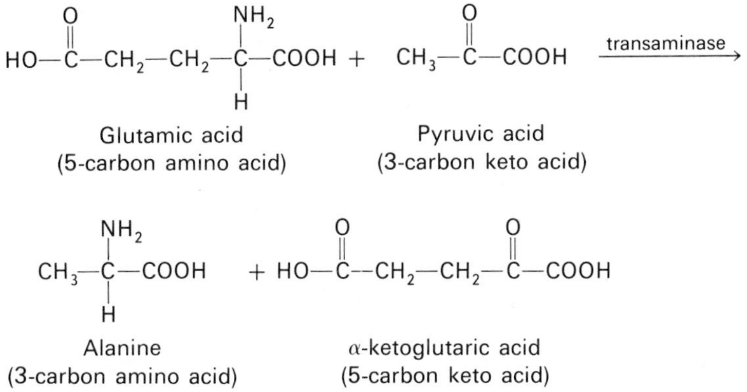

FIGURE 10-13   Transamination between glutamic acid and pyruvic acid. This reaction yields alanine and α-ketoglutaric acid.

balance of the body and supplies required amino acids efficiently. The body does not store amino acids except in the form of protein. Any amino acid that cannot be synthesized at all or that cannot be synthesized fast enough is termed *essential;* that is, it must be obtained from food. In humans 10 amino acids out of approximately 20 have been defined as essential.

Liver cells produce bile continuously. It is collected by bile ducts and transported to the gallbladder for storage. Bile is a complex substance made up chiefly of pigments, salts, cholesterol, and water. The pigments biliverdin (green) and bilirubin (yellow) are derived from the hemoglobin of old red blood cells broken down in the spleen, liver, and bone marrow. Bile is released from the gallbladder into the small intestine, where it emulsifies fats. In some individuals, cholesterol precipitates in the form of crystals and combines with bile salts and pigments to produce gallstones. Large gallstones may block the bile duct, causing poor fat digestion and pain.

Storage and Regulation

Cells and intercellular spaces of the liver provide storage space for glycogen, fats, vitamins, iron, and bile. Vitamins D, E, and B_{12} are stored in limited amounts. But enough vitamin A may be stored to meet normal requirements for nearly a year.

The liver is also important in maintaining the general balance of many chemical activities in the body. Its regulation of carbohydrate metabolism is especially important. Glycogenesis is accelerated by the hormone *insulin* from specific cells in the pancreas. Hormones from the adrenal cortex and the anterior pituitary gland also help regulate glycogenesis. *Glycogenolysis* (meaning "splitting of glycogen"), the breakdown of stored glycogen into blood sugar, is enhanced by a second pancreatic hormone, *glucagon.* Insulin and glucagon provide a good example of the antagonistic action of hormonal control, which will be discussed further in Chapter 12. The interrelationships of carbohydrate, protein, and fat metabolism in the liver are illustrated in Figure 10–14.

Detoxification

Many organic compounds are toxic (poisonous) to an organism if they accumulate in sufficient amounts. Amino groups (NH_2) are released by the process called *deamination* and produce the extremely toxic compound ammonia (NH_3). This toxicity results from the reaction of ammonia with water to produce an alkaline pH. In the next chapter we will see how the liver incorporates ammonia into a less poisonous substance, urea, which is then excreted by the kidneys. About 1500 ml of blood filters through the liver every minute, and large detoxifying cells (macrophages) in liver capillaries engulf and digest small particles such as bacteria and parasitic protozoa. The star-shaped macrophages move somewhat like amoebae in trapping and engulfing foreign material. Figure 10–15 presents a general summary of liver functions and metabolic processes.

One familiar substance metabolized by the liver is ethyl alcohol. Large amounts of alcohol can have a detrimental effect on liver cells. The disease *cirrhosis* occurs when normal liver cells are destroyed and replaced by fibrous connective tissue. Cirrhosis is one cause of death among heavy users of alcohol. Recent studies show that ingestion of large amounts of alcohol damages the endoplasmic reticulum of liver cells in rats and humans. Moreover, alcohol has been found to inhibit the normal metabolism of other drugs.

We have now seen how heterotrophs—and particularly human beings—break their food down into metabolically useful energy and materials by the chemical processes collectively called *digestion.* In Chapter 11 we shall examine the other vital supporting processes: circulation, gas exchange, and excretion.

SUMMARY

Supporting processes include the chemical reactions and physical processes not directly involved in energy production. The combination of all chemical reactions occurring in an organism is called metabolism.

Organic foodstuffs composed of carbohydrates, fats, and proteins are the principal raw

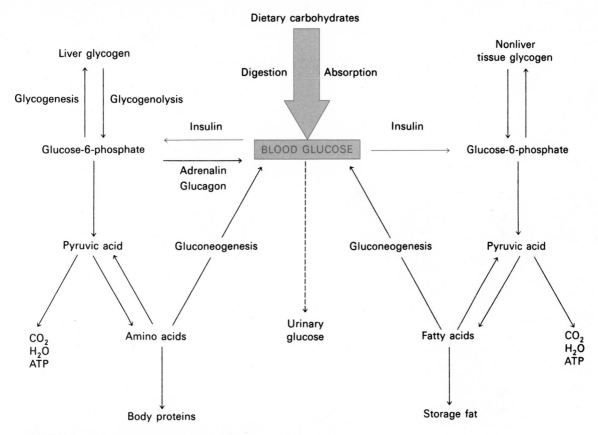

FIGURE 10-14 Various metabolic transformations of glucose.
When blood glucose is high, insulin promotes the phosphorylation
of glucose to produce glycogen. When blood sugar is low, glucagon and adrenalin initiate the conversion of glycogen to glucose.

materials for metabolism in heterotrophs. Food
energy may be expressed in terms of Calories,
and the number of Calories an organism uses
when awake and completely at rest determines
its basal metabolic rate (BMR).

Minerals and vitamins are also important in
nutrition. Vitamins are a large and varied group
of organic compounds required in small
amounts which animals cannot synthesize and
therefore must obtain in diets. They are essential to cellular metabolism. Some vitamins are
important structural parts of coenzymes.

Heterotrophs procure and process food by
various mechanisms, but the basic processes

are intracellular and extracellular. Some organisms combine the two. In general, more complex animals rely more on extracellular digestion. In that process, large food molecules must
be broken into smaller molecules that can be
absorbed into the bloodstream and used by
cells. This process is known as enzymatic digestion.

In humans and other mammals the digestive
process and the enzymes involved can be organized into three phases—salivary, gastric, and
intestinal. The pancreas is an important accessory gland supplying enzymes to the small intestine for all classes of food. The end products

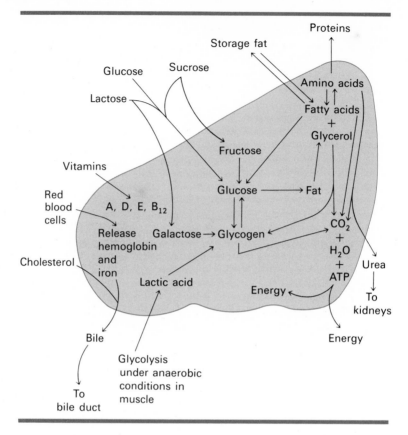

FIGURE 10–15   Some metabolic functions of the liver.

of digestion include simple sugars, fatty acids, glycerol, and amino acids.

Digestive products are absorbed by the epithelial cells lining the small intestine. Most of these products are transported by the blood to the liver. The liver performs many essential functions, including storage and regulation, synthesis of essential compounds, and detoxification.

REVIEW QUESTIONS

1. Why do most fad diets produce a rapid decrease of weight within a week?

2. Why are vitamins considered essential compounds? What is the function of the B vitamins in metabolism?

3. What do you think your BMR should be? How does activity affect caloric requirements?

4. Distinguish between intracellular and extracellular digestion.

5. What effects would bicarbonate of soda have on the digestive action of the stomach?

6. How does alcohol, taken in large quantities over a long period of time, affect the liver?

7. List the hormones that regulate digestion. Where are the most hormones produced?

8. What effect does removing the gallbladder have on an individual's digestion? What effect does it have on diet?

9. The general pattern of food digestion in the mammalian body is:

large, nonabsorbable

$$\text{molecules} + H_2O \rightarrow \text{smaller, absorbable molecules}$$

Give examples of this scheme noting the specific molecules produced by carbohydrate, fat, and protein digestion.

SUPPLEMENTARY READINGS

Fried, John J., *The Vitamin Conspiracy*, E. P. Dutton, New York, 1975. A hard look at the role of vitamins in human diets and a criticism of vitamin therapy for prolonging life and curing diseases.

Kappas, Attallah and A. P. Alvares, "How The Liver Metabolizes Foreign Substances," *Scientific American*, June 1975. Enzyme systems in the liver are capable of breaking down many drugs and environmental pollutants and thus provide an important detoxification system for the body.

Lieber, Charles S., "The Metabolism of Alcohol," *Scientific American*, March 1976. Complications of liver, kidney, and brain function due to excessive alcohol consumption are directly related to alcohol and its breakdown products.

Steincrohn, Peter J., *Low Blood Sugar*, Henry Regnery, Chicago, 1972. The symptoms of hypoglycemia and the treatments available for this often undiagnosed condition are given in nonscientific language.

Stroud, Robert M., "A Family of Protein-Cutting Proteins," *Scientific American*, July 1974. The mechanism of action for a group of enzymes that function in digestion, blood clotting, immune reactions, and fertilization is discussed. There is good evidence that individual members of this family of enzymes may all be related to a common ancestral enzyme.

Verrett, Jacqueline and Jean Carper, *Eating May Be Hazardous to Your Health*, Simon and Schuster, New York, 1974. A critical review of the use of food additives and the role of the Food and Drug Administration in keeping foods free of dangerous chemicals in the United States.

Chapter 11

Circulation, Gas Exchange, & Excretion

We have seen that living systems obtain their energy from the chemical processes that store it and the chemical and physical processes that release it. There is another side to the story of energy in living systems—the distribution of energy within the organism and the removal of the waste products formed by its release in the cell.

The *Circulation and Transportation* of needed materials might not seem a complex problem in a small, single-celled organism. But if you consider more complex systems with millions of cells, the task of getting gases and food molecules from where they are to where they are needed is crucial.

Transportation in Plants relies on a neat trick of nature: water molecules carried in narrow tubes tend to stick together. This partially explains the ability of plants to move dissolved materials through their two-tube systems—the xylem and phloem networks.

Circulation in Animals occurs in two kinds of systems: open and closed. In open systems, the circulating materials are not completely retained within specialized structures. In a closed system, the circulating materials are kept within a network of channels that runs throughout the system. In most higher organisms, a pumping mechanism of some kind forces the circulating material through the body.

The Closed System in Humans is the example we will look at in the most detail. In addition to discussing its normal functioning, we will also review the many serious ailments to which it can fall victim.

As important as circulation in the overall metabolism of a living system is the availability of a fresh supply of certain gases. How is *Gas Exchange* achieved? We will look at the four kinds of breathing systems used by living systems. Despite their overall differences they all achieve the same thing: they bring needed gases to the cellular site where they are used in respiration and they remove the gaseous waste products.

Once energy has been released, waste products would accumulate in living systems if there were no way of removing them. To conclude this chapter, we will see how *Excretion of Metabolic Wastes* is achieved.

As a living system processes food and metabolizes chemical compounds, various materials must be *transported* to and from energy-production, synthesis, and waste-removal sites. Internal circulation is essential to every living system from single-celled organisms to 100-ton whales.

Metabolic processes take place within cells. Therefore materials must enter and leave the cell. In Chapter 4 we examined several mechanisms by which materials cross cell membranes; because of this we have a fairly clear picture of how single cells—including unicellular organisms—solve their transport problems. Some very small multicellular animals do not have transport problems much more complex than those of single cells. Flatworms (Planaria), for example, adapt successfully with no specialized circulatory or respiratory systems.

Larger multicellular organisms face a crucial transport problem: how to get metabolically needed materials to, and waste products from, millions or even billions of cells that are not directly exposed to the outside environment.

Individual cells in multicellular organisms are rather like individual people in a large office or factory building. Most workers (during the eight or so hours they spend in the building each day) do not have direct access to the input materials they need for their work. Nor can they simply dump the waste products of their work (or their own bodily wastes) into the space immediately around them. Specialized transport mechanisms—conveyor belts, elevators, escalators, heating and cooling ducts, plumbing systems, and so on—solve the problem by bringing in materials and taking out finished products, including waste products.

Large office buildings may even need a mechanical "breathing system" for their inhabitants: air ducts and mechanical "lungs" provide for continuous gas exchange by bringing in oxygenated air and carrying out air laden with carbon dioxide. A few years ago, the ventilation system of the Empire State Building broke down. Within minutes the air became stale, and the thousands of occupants had to be evacuated.

Larger buildings require more complex transport systems than smaller buildings do. Larger organisms require the same—and for the same fundamental reason. In general, the larger the structure, be it a building or an organism, the greater its volume compared with its surface area, and the smaller the proportion of cells with direct access to the outside environment. Without specialized supporting processes, the cells of most multicellular organisms would die from lack of food, lack of oxygen, or poisoning by their own waste products.

The building/organism analogy points up some mechanistic aspects of living systems, particularly of their supporting process. Living systems are also *physical* systems, and they are subject to the constraints common to all physical systems. Entropy is one of these constraints, as we saw in earlier chapters. Three-dimensional scale (volume vs. surface area) is another.

Discussing the mechanistic aspects of living systems in no way suggests that an organism is "just a machine." Rather, we can learn a great deal about living systems by approaching them in physical—and even machinelike—terms.

CIRCULATION AND TRANSPORTATION

Because of their high ratio of volume to surface area (Figure 11–1), large multicellular plants and animals need special systems to facilitate nutrition, gas exchange, and excretion. They need such systems because most of their cells are not directly exposed to the environment. In plants, nutrients and raw materials are *transported* from one region of the plant to another—water and minerals are carried upward and manufactured food goes downward. In most animals, materials are generally *circulated* in a cyclical pattern through a circulatory system.

The circulation or transportation systems of multicellular organisms function in two related ways. First, they vastly increase *interior* surface areas available for input and output of material from cells. Second, they provide transport channels to get materials to and from the increased surface area.

Transportation in Plants

In Chapter 5 we saw that vascular plants contain tissues specialized for transport. Xylem

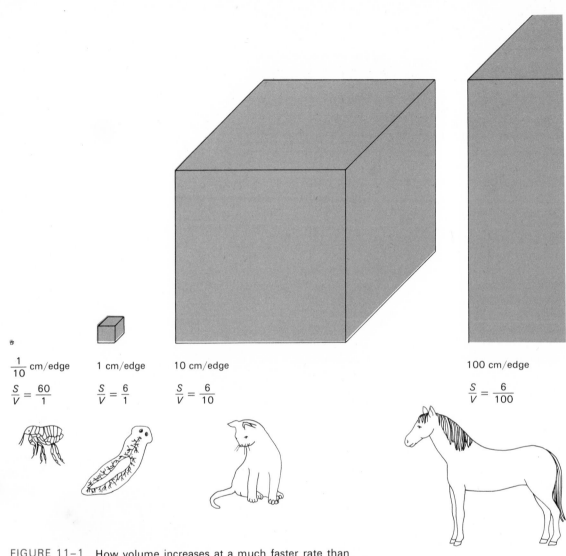

FIGURE 11–1 How volume increases at a much faster rate than surface area. Each cube is 10 times larger on each edge than the previous cube, but the volume increases by 1000 each time. The animals shown below each cube are only approximate examples of variations in surface to volume relationships. These geometric and biological examples show that tiny protists—much smaller than the smallest cube shown—do not have any need for specialized internal transport mechanisms; their supporting processes can all take place directly across their cell membrane. Larger organisms depend on specialized internal transport systems; a major feature of such systems is the great expanse of *internal* membrane surfaces they provide. (The surface-to-volume ratios of organisms are not usually so extreme as those of cubes or spheres because legs, arms, snouts, and fins have proportionately greater surface areas than central body portions.) (Scale: 4.5 mm = 1 cm)

vessels carry water from the roots to all branches and leaves. How a redwood tree can lift water more than 300 feet against gravity is still an intriguing question. The most widely accepted explanation is that presented by an English botanist, H. H. Dixon. Dixon demonstrated that molecules of water standing in slender tubes have very high cohesion—that is, they tend to stick together. As water is lost through *transpiration* (evaporation from pores) or used in photosynthesis, new water molecules diffuse into the xylem tubes at the root level. Roots generally have high osmotic pressure because of the presence of sugar-laden fluids. This high osmotic pressure attracts water into root cells from soil—that is, from a region of greater concentration to a region of lesser concentration. But osmotic pressure alone cannot account for the lifting of the water. Transpiration creates a pull on the unbroken column of water. The high cohesion of water molecules and the pushing effect of osmotic pressure from below combine to make the water column rise rather than break as a result of the pull. These events are summarized in Figure 11–2.

Phloem vessels transport sugars from leaves to other plant organs; the direction of this flow is principally downward toward the roots. Movement of organic nutrients in phloem is called *translocation*. In flowering plants, living companion cells adjacent to the sieve tubes are thought to supply the metabolic drive necessary for this movement. In this process a companion cell absorbs glucose and converts it to sucrose, which is actively secreted into the sieve tubes. As a result of the increased sucrose concentration, water is absorbed by osmosis into the sieve tube and the resulting pressure pushes the sucrose solution into the next sieve tube down the stem.

Circulation in Animals

Many small animals, particularly parasitic forms such as tapeworms and liver flukes, lack specific circulatory and respiratory systems. In general, however, animals have blood circulatory systems that may be of two types, open and closed. In an *open circulatory system*, blood is pumped from a contractile heart into a

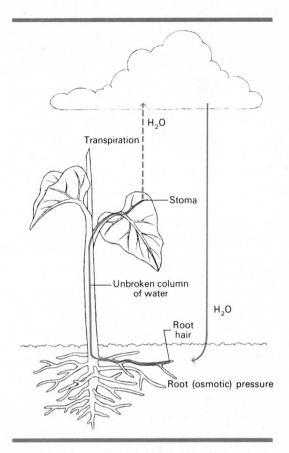

FIGURE 11–2   Movement of water from the roots to the leaves of vascular plants. An unbroken column of water between root pressure and transpirational pull is essential. (Root hairs are greatly enlarged in this drawing.)

main artery that supplies body tissues. Blood is distributed into sinuses (spaces) in the tissues, bathing each cell with nutrients and providing a medium for gas exchange. It is then collected in a large sinus or *hemocoel* before recirculation through the heart. A good example of an open system is found in the crayfish (Figure 11–3).

Closed circulatory systems occur in such animals as earthworms (Annelida) and all vertebrates (Chordata). The structure of a closed system consists of arteries, capillary beds, and veins (Figures 11–4 and 11–5). Body cells ex-

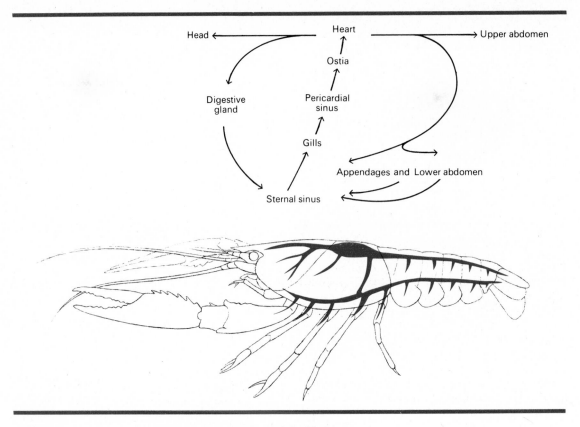

FIGURE 11–3   Open circulatory system of the crayfish. The
blood flows from the arteries into sinuses (spaces) around the organs. After collecting in the hemocoel or sternal sinus, the blood is
returned to the heart.

change gases, take up nutrients, and release
waste materials across capillary membranes.
Arteries and veins serve to carry blood to and
from capillary beds. The pressure in a closed
system greatly aids this process, as we shall see.

The Closed System in Humans

In humans the closed circulatory system separates the respiratory function from the general
circulation. All deoxygenated blood collects in
the right atrium of the heart, passes through
the three-lipped tricuspid valve into the right
ventricle, and is pumped to the lungs through
the pulmonary valve and the pulmonary artery.
This is the only artery that carries deoxygenated blood. After it receives oxygen in the

lungs, the blood returns to the left atrium and
passes through the bicuspid valve into the left
ventricle. Contraction of the heavily muscled
left ventricle forces blood through the aortic
valve into the aorta, a large vessel that distributes oxygenated blood to arteries serving all
parts of the body. After passing through capillaries, the blood returns to the heart through
veins (Figures 11–5 and 11–6). The flow of
blood is maintained by pressure resulting from
the strength and rate of contraction of the left
ventricle and from the size and elasticity of
arteries. The pressure resulting from contraction of the left ventricle is called *systolic* pressure. (Pressures are generally stated in terms of
millimeters of mercury—mm Hg—that is, the

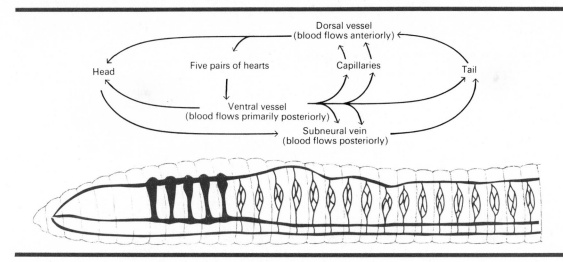

FIGURE 11-4 Closed blood flow in the earthworm. Each segment has a set of arteries that supply blood to the digestive tract, excretory organs, and muscles. All the arteries and veins are connected by capillary vessels. Oxygenation occurs by diffusion through the skin.

pressure required to support a column of mercury one centimeter in diameter at that height.) In the upper left arm, where it is usually measured, it is approximately 120 mm Hg. The pressure remaining when the ventricle relaxes, *diastolic* pressure, is approximately 80 mm Hg. Blood pressures are generally reported as systole/diastole—120/80 mm Hg in this example.

The average human heart contracts (beats) about 72 times per minute. This rate is determined primarily by the pacemaker, also called the sinoatrial (SA) node, a node of specialized muscle tissue in the wall of the right atrium. The SA node sends impulses through the atria to another node, atrioventricular (AV), located in the lower part of the septum between the two atria. After a delay of about $\frac{1}{10}$ second the impulse passes down the ventricular septum and out into the muscle of the ventricles. Heart muscle is fully capable of contraction without any external stimulation, but the specialized muscle tissue that makes up the pacemaker system coordinates this contraction into a concerted beat (Figure 11-7).

Electrodes placed in various positions on the body can pick up electrical events occurring while the heart is beating. In one standard pattern, electrodes placed on the right wrist and the lower left leg trace the electrical events beginning in the SA node and ending in the ventricles. The impulses are recorded on paper to form an *electrocardiogram* or ECG. A typical ECG displays three major segments, denoted P, QRS, and T (Figure 11-8). The P wave indicates an impulse generated from the SA node, which causes atrial contraction. The QRS spike indicates passage of the impulse through the ventricles to cause ventricular contraction. The T wave represents repolarization during ventricular relaxation. ECGs are useful in detecting abnormal heart functioning. A complete heart examination uses 12 different electrode positions.

The heart rate is also influenced by two sets of involuntary nerves—one increases heart rate and the other slows it. In addition, hormones and other chemicals may affect the heart rate. Adrenalin, for example, causes an increase in the rate and strength of contraction.

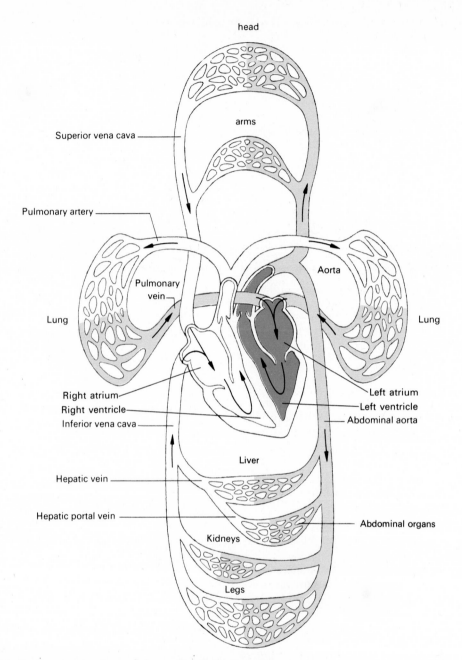

FIGURE 11–5 Human circulatory system. Shaded areas represent oxygenated blood. Note that the liver collects the venous blood from the digestive organs through the hepatic portal vein.

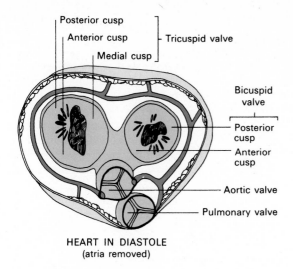

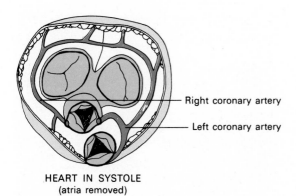

FIGURE 11-6   Heart valves as viewed from the top with atria removed. In diastole (top) the tricuspid and bicuspid valves are open, and the aortic and pulmonic valves are closed. During systole (bottom) the reverse occurs.

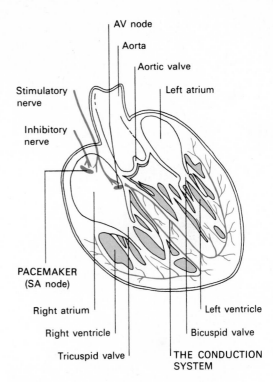

FIGURE 11-7   The human heart, showing the chambers, pacemaker, conduction system, and two sets of involuntary nerves that influence heart rate.

Malfunctioning of the heart's control system can often be corrected by an artificial pacemaker. This is a battery-operated generator that sends regularly spaced impulses to the heart muscle (Figure 11-9). Most pacemakers pace the heart at 80 beats per minute, but some newer models have variable settings to match various levels of activity.

Human Circulatory Problems

When one of the coronary arteries that supply blood to the heart is narrowed by fat deposits—a condition called *atherosclerosis*—the supply of oxygen and nutrients to certain areas of cardiac muscle is reduced. This can produce a heart attack. The coronary artery system has very few interconnections, so narrowing or stoppage of one vessel may affect a fairly large amount of muscle. If this muscle dies, it blocks the passage of pacemaker impulses to other heart areas. Exercise, however, can cause the heart to produce more small arterial branches. Individuals who survive heart attacks are placed on rigid exercise schedules. Moreover, because of the increased cardiovascular circulation, individuals who exercise regularly are less likely to have a heart attack.

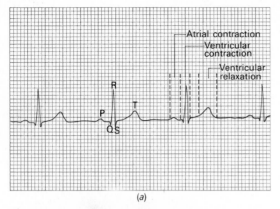

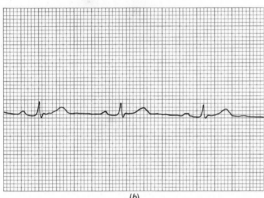

FIGURE 11-8   Electrocardiograms (ECG). (*a*) A normal heart. (*b*) An abnormal heart. The small QRS wave shown in (*b*) indicates reduced electrical conduction through the ventricles because of dead muscle cells.

Another potentially fatal problem associated with the circulatory system is high blood pressure. About one out of five Americans suffers from high blood pressure, although most are not aware of the problem. Blood pressure is easy to measure indirectly, using an apparatus with a pressure gauge and a cuff, called a sphygmomanometer (*sphygmo*, "pulse"). A cuff wrapped around the upper arm is inflated until the brachial artery is compressed enough to stop its flow. As the air pressure is slowly reduced, a surge of blood in the artery near the elbow can be heard with a stethoscope. This is systolic pressure. As the pressure is further reduced, the pulsing sound disappears; the air

pressure in the cuff at this point represents the diastolic pressure.

The normal ranges for blood pressure are 120–140 mm Hg systolic and 60–90 mm Hg diastolic. An increase in the diastolic pressure above 90 mm Hg indicates a circulatory problem. When major arteries become narrowed and inelastic because of atherosclerosis, blood pressures can be as high as 180/120 mm Hg (Figure 11–10). Continued high pressures are almost certain to cause *stroke*, the rupture of thin-walled vessels in the brain. Strokes can produce a range of effects, from dizziness and slurring of speech to complete paralysis and death.

Atherosclerosis is not the only cause of high blood pressure. A complicated disease syn-

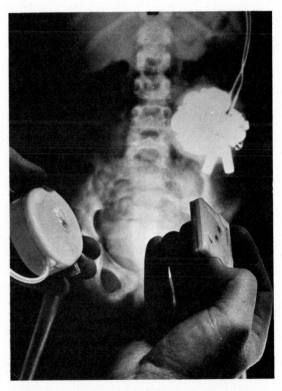

FIGURE 11-9   Artificial pacemaker. A small pacemaker the size of a book of matches is shown on the right. The larger one on the left is the same type implanted in the person whose x-ray is shown in the background. (WHO/NIH photo.)

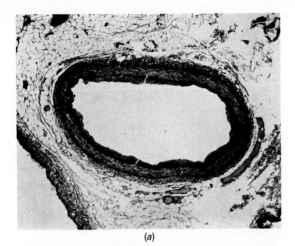

(a)

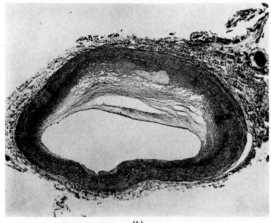

(b)

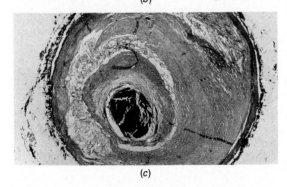

(c)

FIGURE 11–10 Cross section of three arteries showing progressive stages of atherosclerosis. (a) Normal artery. (b) Atherosclerotic artery with deposits formed on its inner lining. (c) A severely blocked artery. (Courtesy of the American Heart Association.)

drome called *hypertension* is known to have a major influence in deaths caused by strokes, kidney failure, and heart attack. Hypertension apparently stems from many factors, including excessive salt intake, obesity, a demanding life style, and smoking. All these factors constitute stresses. *Stress* is a general term for any condition, external or internal, that alters the smooth functioning of an organism. "Psychological stress" is a phrase commonly used, but it also applies to disruptive physiological factors such as injury, infectious disease, malnutrition, and overexposure to sun, cold, or air pollution. When a person undergoes stress, adrenalin is released, stepping up the heart rate and blood pressure. In about 90 percent of hypertension cases, no direct cause is established. We do know, however, that the kidneys are involved in the control of blood pressure. They produce a hormone called *renin* to stimulate the adrenal cortex to secrete another hormone, *aldosterone*. Aldosterone in turn promotes the retention of sodium which causes an increase in blood volume due to water uptake by osmosis.

Clinical blood pressures are taken at the level of the upper arm, but blood pressures vary significantly throughout the body. This results partly from the fact that blood vessels vary in size. An artery carrying blood to capillaries branches into many smaller arterioles. The opposite occurs on the other side of a capillary network: small *venules* unite to form a larger vein. As blood passes progressively from the aorta through the arteries, arterioles, capillaries, venules, and veins, pressure falls from a high of 140 in the aorta to near 0 in the large veins (Figure 11–11). The reason for this drop is that the total cross-sectional area increases as the number of vessels increases. Even though each vessel is smaller, the total space through which the blood flows is larger. Venules and veins have very little muscle; venous flow in portions of the body below the heart depends almost entirely on the contraction of leg and abdominal muscles to help push the blood along. Almost all veins contain one-way valves to keep blood from moving back away from the heart. Blood flow in humans thus results from blood pressure, which in turn depends on the strength and rate of contractions by the left

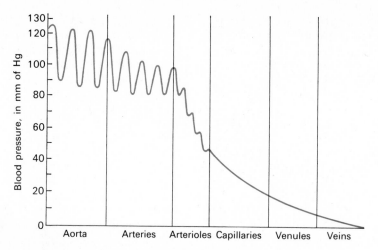

FIGURE 11–11   Blood pressure in different vessels of the circulatory system. Note how the fluctuations between systolic and diastolic pressures in the arteries diminish in arterioles and disappear in capillaries, venules, and veins.

Bio-Topic: Folk Medicines

Hypertension has long been a major public health problem in the Western world, yet one of the most effective anti-hypertensive drugs available came to the West through the folk medicine of India.

Hypertension has long been recognized in India by its obvious symptoms: a flushed complexion, shortness of breath, ringing in the ears, and a predisposition to heart failure and stroke. For centuries, practitioners of Indian folk medicine have prescribed teas and extracts made from the root of a plant in the dogbane family as a cure for the symptoms of hypertension. The extracts were remarkably effective and known throughout India.

So effective was the treatment that it came to the attention of European physicians and pharmacologists. Some years ago, a plant biochemist was induced to try to isolate an active ingredient from the plant. A pure compound was isolated in 1952 and tested on laboratory animals. Promising results led to limited, then extensive, trials with humans. It soon became clear that the drug was quite effective. By 1956 the drug, named reserpine, had been synthesized in large quantities for general use. Reserpine is now known to be effective in dilating blood vessels, which lowers blood pressure, and is also a valuable tranquilizer used in the treatment of certain kinds of mental illness.

Reserpine is not the only drug with such a history. Aspirin, quinine (used to treat malaria), and several vitamins were "discovered" through the careful analysis of folk medicine.

ventricle, the amount of blood pumped per beat, and the friction blood encounters as it flows through the many blood vessels of the body.

GAS EXCHANGE

Small organisms such as bacteria, amoebae, and even the relatively much larger flatworms (Planaria) can exchange gases with their environment by direct diffusion. In these organisms any one cell is close enough to the surface so that simple diffusion meets the needs of all the cells, and no special breathing organs are necessary. This situation does not exist in vertebrates or most of the larger invertebrates (Figure 11–1); these organisms need some mechanism or organ system for breathing. Cellular respiration, discussed in Chapter 9, uses oxygen both in the Krebs cycle and the electron-transport series. Carbon dioxide given off in this process must be carried away from the cell and eventually released into the environment. Keep in mind that although gas exchange (breathing) is related to cellular respiration, it is not the same process.

Four basic breathing systems are found in living systems: (1) direct diffusion (in monerans, protists, plants, and some invertebrate animals such as flatworms); (2) gills (in crustaceans, some mollusks, and fish); (3) lungs (in snails and vertebrates); and (4) tracheal tubes (in insects). These four systems are illustrated in Figure 11–12; we will discuss them individually in the following sections. In most breathing systems a thin, moist membrane is necessary for gas exchange. Moisture is necessary because oxygen and carbon dioxide are more easily exchanged with cells when in a liquid medium.

Direct Diffusion

All aerobic protists (those that require oxygen) exchange gases through diffusion on their body surfaces. Since most of these organisms are aquatic and unicellular, dissolved oxygen in the water can diffuse easily into the cellular fluids. Although they are larger and multicellu-lar, sponges, coelenterates, and flatworms require no special breathing organs or systems. In plants, the exchange of gases occurs principally through small openings in leaves called stomata, described in Chapter 5.

Gills: For Use in Water

Aquatic animals with many tissues have evolved organs known as *gills* to increase surface area available for gas exchange. Very sluggish invertebrates such as tubeworms and snails have gills. Gas exchange takes place as water moves over the large surface area of these gills. Starfish have small projections from the skin which function as a type of gill. In more active animals such as fish, water must be moved across the gills. Fish accomplish this by swimming; crayfish and other crustaceans have special paddlelike appendages to move water past the gills. The moist membranous surfaces of gills are a single layer of epithelial cells with one side exposed to environmental fluids (with their dissolved gases) and the other to the organism's internal fluids.

Lungs: For Use on Land

The great volume of the vertebrate body relative to its surface area requires a highly efficient gas exchange and transport system. These animals possess lungs that open into a mouth cavity through a *trachea* (windpipe). Lungs are simply air chambers with an opening to the outside and a rich blood supply. They vary in structural complexity. Some snails have a simple sac-like lung. In lungfish the lung consists of one chamber; in amphibians and reptiles, it is basically a series of folds. Birds and mammals show the most complex lung development, with the surface area and blood supply both greatly increased.

Lungs are filled with air in one of two ways: (1) air can be forced into the lungs directly, (*positive-pressure breathing*); or (2) air can be drawn into lungs when the pressure around the lungs is decreased (*negative-pressure breathing*).

Amphibians and reptiles have positive-pres-

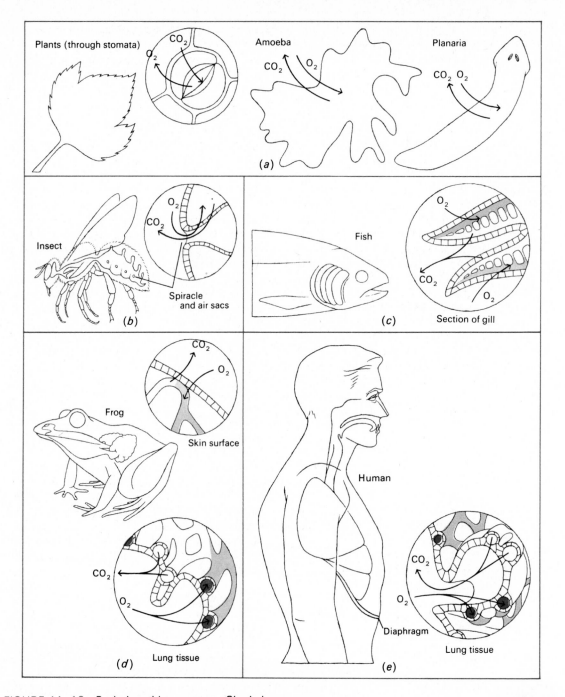

FIGURE 11–12   Basic breathing systems. Shaded areas represent oxygenated blood. (*a*) Diffusion. (*b*) Tracheal tubes. (*c*) Gills. (*d*) Positive-pressure lungs and cutaneous diffusion. (*e*) Negative-pressure lungs.

sure lungs. They inflate their lungs by closing their mouths tightly and compressing the muscular floor of the mouth cavity to force air in. Amphibians that spend much of their time in moist habitats also exchange gases through their thin, moist skin, since they have blood capillaries very close to the skin surface. Some frogs accomplish one-third or more of their total respiration by this *cutaneous diffusion.* This method is especially important during winter hibernation at the bottom of ponds.

Birds and mammals breathe by negative pressure. The tissue of human and other mammalian lungs is a good example of the thin, moist membranes needed for gas exchange. Tiny *alveolar sacs* are composed of extremely thin cells bathed continuously by tissue fluids (Figure 11–13).

An average adult human male inhales about 500 ml of air with each normal breath. The amount of air that can be exhaled forcibly after maximum inhalation is called *vital capacity;* it varies from 4500 to 7000 ml. During inhalation a dome-shaped, muscular structure called the diaphragm contracts and moves downward, away from the lungs, while muscles of the ribs lift the chest cavity upward. These efforts com-

bine to cause a temporary decrease in pressure (negative pressure) in the *thoracic cavity.* Air then rushes in through the nose and mouth to fill the lungs via the trachea.

Birds have lungs but no diaphragm. Birds in flight require a great deal of energy to maintain their very high metabolic rates. Gas exchange is thus a critical problem during flight; to solve it, birds have evolved a unique breathing system. Bird lungs include four pairs of lung sacs that extend from the main lung into practically all parts of the body. Expansion of the muscular chest (inhalation) fills the lungs and air sacs, and the fresh air trapped in the air sacs is forced back into the lungs upon exhalation. Thus the main lung actually receives fresh air at both inhalation and exhalation—from the entering air and then from the air sacs. Although a small amount of gas exchange may occur in the air sacs, most of it takes place in the main lung.

Tracheal Tubes

In insects gas exchange takes place a͟ air is circulated directly to and from body tissues. In grasshoppers and honeybees, for example, air enters the body through small openings called *spiracles.* It then passes through a complex branched system of tiny tubules called *tracheae* and air sacs to all parts of the body. The tracheae are supported by tiny rings of *chitin,* the same hard material found in the insects' exoskeleton. This breathing system resembles an air conditioning system in which ducts deliver fresh air and remove stale air. Air flow may be controlled by the opening and closing of the spiracles.

The Role of Transport Fluids

Once oxygen is taken into an organism, it must be carried to cells. Carbon dioxide waste must be also removed from the organism. Plasma, the fluid portion of blood can transport some oxygen, but this is not sufficient to meet the needs of most blood-containing animals. Consequently, many animals have special molecules capable of transporting oxygen. Since these molecules usually make solutions that appear

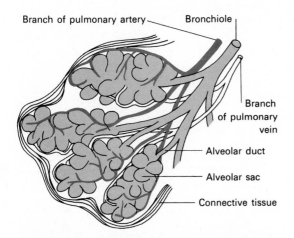

Branch of pulmonary artery — Bronchiole

Branch of pulmonary vein

Alveolar duct

Alveolar sac

Connective tissue

FIGURE 11–13 Portion of a mammalian lung, showing four alveolar sacs with branches of pulmonary arteries and veins. Note the close association of blood vessels with the alveoli.

Bio-Topic: The Philadelphia Killer

The Pennsylvania chapter of the American Legion held its 1976 convention in Philadelphia from 21–24 July. Two thousand members with their families and friends came from all over the state, met for three days, and returned to their homes. Within three weeks, twenty-five legionnaires were dead, as were several persons with only casual connections with the convention. All died from what came to be called the Philadelphia Killer. Symptoms of the disease began with a headache and chest pains, developed into a high fever and congested lungs, and, for many, ended in death.

By the end of August 1976, with the death toll nearing 30 and 150 people hospitalized, the disease faded away as unexpectedly as it had come. In no instance did a victim pass the disease on to a friend or relative; no new cases were reported. Initial fears of a widespread epidemic evaporated, and the nation breathed a collective sigh of relief.

Local authorities had recognized a lethal pattern within a few days. By early September, the massive machinery of state and federal public health agencies was fully mobilized. Nearly 150 medical sleuths—including many from the National Center for Disease Control in Atlanta, Georgia—undertook one of the most intensive microbe hunts in our history. One by one, patients and their contacts were examined, tested, interviewed. One by one, potential disease agents were eliminated. The disease was not swine flu, plague, typhoid fever, ornithosis, tularemia, or even exotic tropical diseases such as Lassa fever or Marburg disease. No known virus, bacterium, fungus or chemical agent could be identified as the cause. When the investigation was ended in September 1976, the cause remained a mystery.

Why did this episode attract so much national attention and so intensive an investigation? More people are killed on our highways during a typical holiday weekend. Less furor is created by natural catastrophes that kill many hundreds more.

Perhaps part of the reason was that the killer was invisible, unpredictable, and impartial. The question, "Am I next?" was in the minds of many. So were memories of the 1918–1919 flu epidemic that killed 500,000 Americans and as many as 20,000,000 people worldwide.

Perhaps part of the answer was the unexpected inability of the public health agencies to contain, cure, or even identify the cause of the disease. We have become so accustomed to the regular success of medical technology that this failure came as an uncomfortable reminder of our mortality.

colored, we refer to them as respiratory pigments.

The earthworm has a rather complex circulatory system which contains plasma and small, colorless blood cells. Earthworm blood is red because of the iron-containing pigment *hemoglobin* dissolved in the plasma. Although this pigment is extracellular, it is very similar to the hemoglobin of human red blood cells, and it does transport oxygen. The blood of arthropods is generally colorless, but in crayfish, crabs, and lobsters, oxygen is carried by a bluish, copper-containing pigment called *hemocyanin* dissolved in the plasma.

Hemoglobin and Oxygen

Hemoglobin is the respiratory pigment of all vertebrates and some invertebrates. The porphyrin structure of hemoglobin (Figure 11–14)

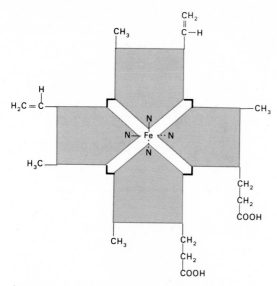

FIGURE 11-14   Structure of heme, the porphyrin part of the hemoglobin molecule. Note its similarity to chlorophyll, shown in Figure 9-14.

is very similar to the basic structure of cytochromes and chlorophyll. This molecule gets its name from its iron-containing porphyrin, called a *heme* group, and the fact that its protein portion is globular in form (Figure 11–15).

The primary function of hemoglobin is to combine with oxygen in the lungs and to transport this oxygen to all tissues of the organism. When hemoglobin picks up oxygen it forms a bright red complex known as oxyhemoglobin (often denoted by the symbol HbO_2). Oxygenated arterial blood is easy to distinguish from bluish venous blood, which contains much less oxygen. The combination of oxygen with hemoglobin is chemically quite loose, since oxygen uptake and release must occur rapidly and easily. Uptake of oxygen in the lungs ("loading") takes place across the thin, moist alveolar membranes.

Since oxygen pressure is higher in alveolar sacs than in the blood, oxygen diffuses into the blood, whereas the high pressure of carbon dioxide in venous blood causes CO_2 to diffuse into the alveolar air. When red blood cells reach tissue capillaries, the reverse occurs. Tissue cells have used up oxygen, so they have a

low oxygen content. Because of the diffusion gradient across capillary membranes, hemoglobin immediately releases its oxygen to the cells. And since carbon dioxide was released to the environment through the lungs, arterial blood has a comparatively low carbon dioxide pressure. This allows carbon dioxide to move from the tissues into the bloodstream (Figure 11–16).

Carbon monoxide (CO), a product of incomplete combustion such as produced in automobile exhaust, combines with hemoglobin about 200 times more readily than does oxygen. When large amounts of carbon monoxide bind to hemoglobin, sufficient oxygen cannot be transported to cells.

Carbonic Anhydrase and Carbon Dioxide

Although a small amount of carbon dioxide combines with hemoglobin to form $HbCO_2$, most of it is transported in another way. An enzyme called *carbonic anhydrase* located

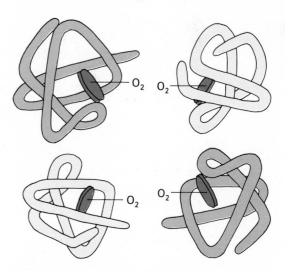

FIGURE 11-15   The hemoglobin molecule, a globular protein made up of two alpha and two beta polypeptide chains, each of which has an iron-containing heme group (colored disks). Each heme binds one oxygen molecule. Although the four polypeptide chains are shown separated here, they are actually held tightly together, intertwined in a quaternary structure.

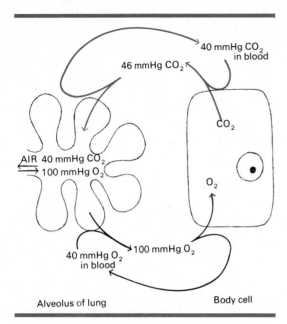

FIGURE 11–16   Gas exchange between lungs and body cells showing the pressures that cause diffusion.

pons and the medulla oblongata (these areas are discussed in Chapter 12). The medulla contains the *expiratory* and *inspiratory* centers. A *pneumotaxic center* located in the pons has nervous connections with the expiratory and inspiratory centers; it relays impulses and coordinates the breathing rhythm, especially during labored breathing. The centers in the medulla control the rate and depth of normal quiet breathing and of breathing during sleep. Nerve

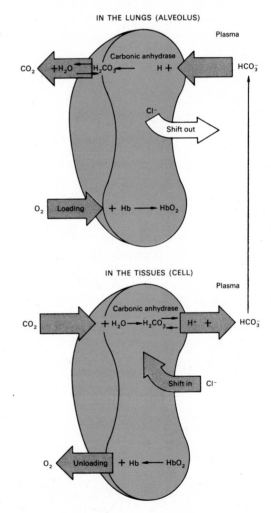

FIGURE 11–17   Major gas exchange events occurring in the lungs and in body tissues. This schematic view depicts a red blood cell in the two locations. Note that carbon dioxide is carried in the plasma as the bicarbonate ion.

within red blood cells catalyzes the combination of carbon dioxide with water to form carbonic acid (H_2CO_3). Carbonic acid dissociates into H^+ and HCO_3^-, and the bicarbonate ion (HCO_3^-) diffuses into the plasma. Carbon dioxide is thus transported to the lungs primarily as bicarbonate ions dissolved in the plasma and red blood cells. In the lungs, the reaction in red blood cells is reversed ($HCO_3^- + H^+ \rightarrow H_2O + CO_2$) to release carbon dioxide.

When bicarbonate ion diffuses from red blood cells in capillaries, an imbalance of charges results. Ionic balance is restored when a chloride ion (Cl^-) moves into each red blood cell. This exchange of negatively charged ions is called the *chloride shift* (Figure 11–17). A reverse exchange takes place in the lungs, when bicarbonate ions enter red blood cells to produce carbon dioxide. At this time chloride ions leave red blood cells to maintain ionic balance.

The Control of Breathing

In humans, coordination centers for breathing are found in two areas of the brain stem—the

pathways enter the breathing centers from the cerebral cortex and the hypothalamus. Because of the cerebral cortex associations, we may consciously regulate our breathing and hold our breath for a short time.

The inspiratory center constantly sends impulses to the rib muscles and diaphragm to cause inspiration. At the same time it sends impulses to the pneumotaxic center, which activates the expiratory center to inhibit inspiratory impulses. As inspiratory impulses cease, a passive expiration occurs. The diaphragm relaxes and returns to its dome shape and the rib muscles relax, allowing the chest to fall. Another regulatory mechanism found in the lungs is provided by tiny nerve endings called *stretch*

receptors, located in the lungs. As the air sacs fill and stretch during inspiration, the stretch receptors send impulses to the expiratory center. These impulses inhibit the inspiratory center enough to permit expiration. This feedback mechanism between the alveoli and the expiratory center is known as the *Hering-Breuer reflex* (Figure 11–18). It works with the pneumotaxic center to insure that expiration will occur.

The inspiratory center is sensitive to the level of carbon dioxide in the blood; in fact, this is the primary stimulation for inspiration. This center can also be stimulated by nerve receptors called *carotid bodies*, sensitive to oxygen and carbon dioxide, located in the carotid

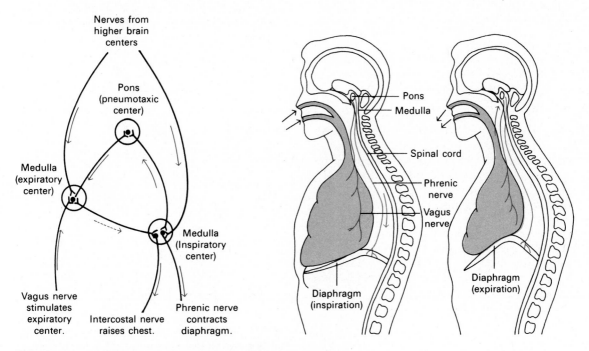

FIGURE 11–18 The nervous control of breathing. (a) The cycle begins when carbon dioxide stimulates the inspiratory center in the medulla of the brain. Impulses travel to the diaphragm and rib muscles, causing the diaphragm to contract and inspiration to occur. At the same time, impulses are also sent to the pneumotaxic center in the pons. This center stimulates the expiratory center to inhibit the inspiratory center (see dashed arrow). As the lungs fill with air, stretch receptors are stimulated; these impulses are sent to the expiratory center via the vagus nerve. (b) A schematic diagram of the events described above.

arteries and in the wall of the aorta. When a decrease in oxygen or increase in carbon dioxide in the blood occurs, these bodies stimulate the inspiratory center by way of nerves and increase the rate and depth of breathing.

EXCRETION OF METABOLIC WASTES AND WATER BALANCE

All organisms must rid themselves of metabolic wastes, some of which are extremely toxic even in small amounts. Many unicellular organisms dispose of these wastes by direct diffusion. Plants, which lack excretory systems, have evolved a variety of mechanisms for disposing of metabolic wastes. Some wastes are given off as diffusible gases; others may be deposited in certain parts of cells or on external surfaces. Synthetic processes in plants can actually perform an excretory function: certain toxic nitrogen compounds can be synthesized into nontoxic compounds. Caffeine and morphine are examples of these synthetic secretions. But as we know, these compounds can be toxic to other organisms.

In animal cells, the metabolism of amino acids and the breakdown of other nitrogen compounds release large amounts of nitrogen into the tissue fluids and blood. This is especially true of vertebrate liver cells. Waste nitrogen combines readily with water to form toxic ammonia. Small organisms living in an aqueous environment quickly discharge ammonia by diffusion. But most terrestrial animals must hold nitrogenous wastes in the body longer. The cells of most animals have enzyme systems to detoxify nitrogen compounds. The most common products of nitrogen detoxification are urea and uric acid. Since animals may excrete their nitrogenous wastes as ammonia, urea, or uric acid, they are sometimes classified by these products—as *ammonotelic* (excreting ammonia), *ureotelic* (urea) or *uricotelic* (uric acid). Ammonia is the most toxic, followed by urea; the almost insoluble uric acid is the least toxic.

Three Types of Excretion

Most aquatic invertebrates are ammonotelic: they are relatively small and can easily diffuse waste compounds into the water. Freshwater bony fish also excrete ammonia through their gills. Earthworms excrete urea into the air and ammonia into water.

Ureotelic organisms—those with urea as the major detoxification product—include amphibians, sharks, and mammals. Urea is synthesized in the liver, released to the bloodstream, and filtered into urine by the kidneys. Urea synthesis has been found to occur in a cycle (Figure 11–19). In this cycle ammonia and carbon dioxide combine with ornithine to produce a series of intermediate compounds, culminating in the production of urea and the regeneration of ornithine. Aspartic acid, an amino acid, is essential to this cycle. Most of the aspartic acid molecule is removed, however, and it can enter the citric-acid cycle to be oxidized (Chapter 9). One nitrogen atom from aspartic acid remains, becoming part of the released urea molecule.

Animals producing uric acid include some insects, birds, reptiles, and land snails. The white portion of bird droppings indicates the presence of uric acid. Uric acid, the least toxic nitrogenous waste compound, is synthesized by animals that must retain body water and by those that lay their eggs on land. Reptile and bird embryos, for example, develop inside eggs in which toxic wastes must be stored with the developing embryo. Formation of uric acid, which is insoluble, is vital to the survival of the embryo. The ability of organisms to produce detoxification products suited to their environment is a good example of adaptation.

Excretion in Invertebrates

Invertebrate excretion mechanisms range from simple diffusion in unicellular organisms to the highly developed systems of arthropods (Figure 11–20). Although unicellular organisms excrete most waste by direct diffusion, entire vacuoles may be expelled by reverse pinocytosis. Specialized organelles called *contractile vacuoles* occur in organisms such as *Paramecium*. In addition to regulating water content by collecting it from the cell and releasing it with rhythmic contractions, these vacuoles eliminate nitrogenous wastes.

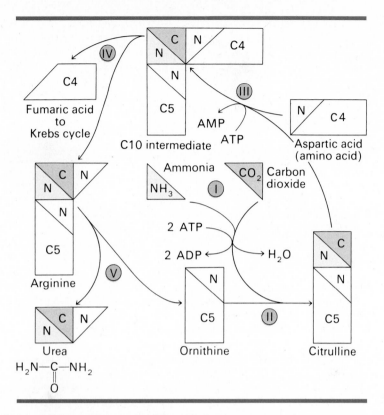

FIGURE 11-19 The urea or ornithine cycle. The cycle begins at 1 and continues counterclockwise. Each numbered segment requires a specific enzyme. The liver removes excess nitrogen and carbon dioxide by forming urea. The urea is removed from the blood and excreted by the kidneys.

In nonparasitic flatworms such as Planaria the excretory system is composed of two longitudinal ducts connected to a network of branching tubules. These ducts open to the outside through excretory pores. The tubules end in large *flame cells* that lie among the body cells. Flame cells are specialized, having a central cavity with a tuft of cilia. When the cilia beat (resembling a flame), excess water and metabolic wastes are carried into the tubules to be excreted.

In earthworms, each segment contains two excretory organs called *nephridia*. Each nephridium has a ciliated funnel that projects through the wall of the preceding segment and filters body fluids from that segment into a collecting duct (Figure 11-20d). A capillary network surrounds the collecting tubules so waste products can be absorbed from the blood into the tubules. Near the end of each nephridium is a bladder from which wastes are discharged to the outside through a pore.

Crayfish, crabs, and lobsters utilize their respiratory gills as efficient organs of excretion in aquatic environments. These invertebrates also possess two organs known as *green glands* (because of their color). The green glands are located in the anterior portion of the blood sinus at the base of the antennae. Each green gland removes metabolic wastes from the blood and passes them through a collecting tubule into a thin-walled bladder. A duct leads from the

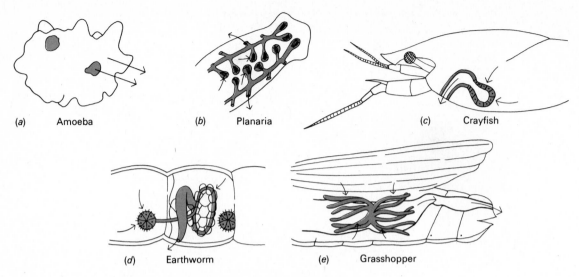

FIGURE 11–20 Mechanisms of nitrogenous waste elimination in invertebrates. (*a*) Diffusion and vacuoles. (*b*) Ciliated flame cells. (*c*) Green gland. (*d*) Nephridium. (*e*) Malpighian tubules.

bladder to an opening at the base of the antenna. The collecting tubule, practically absent in saltwater forms, probably functions to retain salts in freshwater crayfish. These glands, which function somewhat like kidneys, will also be discussed in connection with water balance.

The excretory organs of insects consist of numerous long, thin-walled tubules attached to the digestive tract between the stomach and intestine. These structures, called *Malpighian tubules*, project into the body cavity, where they absorb nitrogenous wastes and salts from the blood; they empty into the intestine.

Excretion in Vertebrates: The Kidney

The major organs of excretion among vertebrates are *kidneys*. These paired, bean-shaped organs lie against the dorsal (back) body wall on either side of the vertebral column. The kidneys receive a large supply of blood from the abdominal aorta and return venous blood to the inferior vena cava (Figure 11–21a). Wastes are filtered from the blood in the *cortex*; in the human kidney, the cortex contains about one million *nephron* units (Figure 11–21c and d).

Blood enters the capillary network of the kidney, known as the *glomerulus*, at a pressure of approximately 75 mm Hg. Since local capillary pressure in other, immediately adjacent tissues is only about 20 mm Hg, filtration in the glomerulus is essentially by diffusion under pressure, sometimes called *ultrafiltration*. The thin membranes of glomeruli allow filtration of glucose, vitamins, fatty acids, and amino acids, but normally they do not permit serum blood proteins to pass through. Persistent or severe infection may cause glomerular membranes to degenerate so much that they allow large amounts of protein to enter the urine. In this condition, called Bright's disease, loss of protein from the blood causes a decreased osmotic concentration in the plasma; the tissues thus collect water, bringing about edema (swelling).

The material filtered through the glomeruli is collected in the *Bowman's capsules* and passed into *proximal convoluted tubules*, where substances required by the body are reabsorbed. For example, all glucose filtered through a glomerulus is normally reabsorbed into surrounding capillaries, the *peritubular capillaries*, by diffusion and active transport. When the glucose level of the blood rises above 180 mg per 100 ml of blood, all the glucose

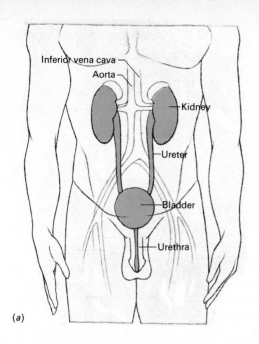

(a)

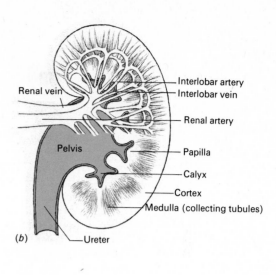

Inferior vena cava
Aorta
Kidney
Ureter
Bladder
Urethra

Interlobar artery
Interlobar vein
Renal artery
Papilla
Calyx
Cortex
Medulla (collecting tubules)

Renal vein
Pelvis

(b)
Ureter

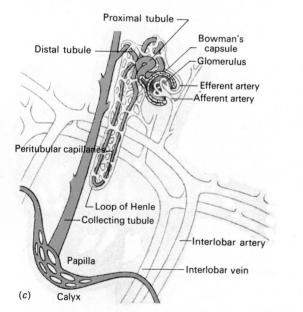

Proximal tubule
Distal tubule
Bowman's capsule
Glomerulus
Efferent artery
Afferent artery

Peritubular capillaries

Loop of Henle
Collecting tubule
Interlobar artery
Papilla
Interlobar vein
Calyx

(c)

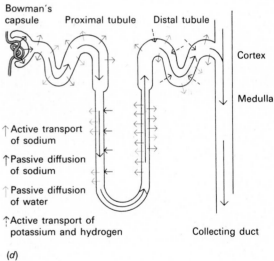

Bowman's capsule   Proximal tubule   Distal tubule

Cortex

Medulla

↑ Active transport of sodium
↑ Passive diffusion of sodium
↑ Passive diffusion of water
↑ Active transport of potassium and hydrogen

Collecting duct

(d)

FIGURE 11–21   (a) Human urinary system. (b) Longitudinal section of the kidney showing the location of major blood vessels. (c)
Structure of the nephron unit of a vertebrate kidney. The principal
functions of the segments are as follows: *Proximal tubule:* reabsorption of glucose, water, Na$^+$, K$^+$, and amino acids. *Loop of
Henle:* reabsorption of Na$^+$, K$^+$, and Cl$^-$; obligatory water reabsorption. *Distal tubule:* reabsorption of Na$^+$ and K$^+$; secretion of
H$^+$ and NH$_3$. *Collecting tubule:* reabsorption of water. (d) An isolated nephron unit, showing the transport and diffusion of various
substances.

cannot be reabsorbed, and some glucose appears in the urine. Proximal convoluted tubules reabsorb Na^+, K^+, Cl^-, glucose, water, amino acids, and some urea and uric acid. To some degree, reabsorption of mineral ions is controlled by a group of hormones called mineralocorticoids, secreted by the cortex of the adrenal glands.

When ions and molecules are transported from the tubules into the surrounding capillaries, they create an osmotic gradient. Water must then move into the capillaries according to the gradient; this situation is *obligatory water reabsorption.* Osmotic reabsorption of water also occurs in the next segment of the nephron, the *loop of Henle.* This long tubule bends back upon itself to form a U-shaped loop. Sodium, potassium, and chlorine ions may also be reabsorbed in this segment.

In the *distal convoluted tubules* and *collecting tubules,* water reabsorption is controlled by *antidiuretic hormone* (ADH), a hormone produced in the posterior lobe of the pituitary gland. ADH increases the permeability of tubule cells to water, thereby increasing water reabsorption. This concentrates the urine and conserves body water. Distal convoluted tubules actively reabsorb ions of sodium, potassium, calcium, and magnesium, and they can also secrete ions from the blood and pass them into urine. They remove large amounts of hydrogen ions (H^+) and ammonia (NH_3) from the blood; this helps to maintain a proper acid-base balance in the body.

Distal tubules reabsorb more selectively than proximal tubules. The high hydrostatic pressure in proximal tubules causes many substances to diffuse into the peritubular capillaries. Urine is composed of water (95 percent), urea, uric acid, ammonia, and creatinine (a product of amino acid metabolism). A number of ions, pigments, hormones, and vitamins may also be found in this waste product.

Human kidney malfunction is quite common; it often reaches the potentially fatal stage at which the kidneys cannot rid the body of nitrogen wastes. Artificial kidneys have been developed to assist or replace normal kidney function (Figure 11–22). These machines shunt a patient's blood through a series of artificial membranes surrounded by a special fluid. The wastes diffuse across the membrane from the blood into the fluid. In this process, called *dialysis,* the blood is routed from the body, cleansed of its nitrogenous wastes, and returned.

Osmoregulation

Kidneys are not simply organs for the elimination of toxic nitrogenous wastes. They are also involved in the balance of water, sugar, and ions within an organism. In fact, throughout the animal kingdom the excretion of nitrogenous wastes is closely related to ion and water balance. The ability of an organism to control its fluid content is called *osmoregulation.*

Terrestrial Animals

Land animals must conserve internal water. Perhaps the most important defense against a dry environment is a thick epidermis. Scales, hair, fur, or feathers add varying degrees of protection against water evaporation. Besides such physical barriers against evaporation, most terrestrial animals also possess well-developed kidneys to provide for water reabsorption. Animals in extremely dry habitats eliminate very dry feces and highly concentrated urine. The small desert kangaroo rat (*Dipodomys*) shows a further adaptation; it has no sweat glands. These tiny rodents live in underground burrows and forage for food only at night; if they came out in the sun they would overheat and die, since they lack the cooling mechanism of sweat glands. Under normal conditions kangaroo rats never require a drink of water, since water from their food is sufficient.

Mammals lose most of their water through breathing and perspiration. Humans, for instance, must maintain a body temperature of about 37°C. When the outside air temperature is higher than that, we maintain our temperature primarily through evaporation of perspiration. Camels are well adapted to desert conditions with their mat of insulating fur; they do not begin to sweat until their body temperature rises to about 41°C.

One of the most interesting adaptations is found in marine birds. All marine birds possess

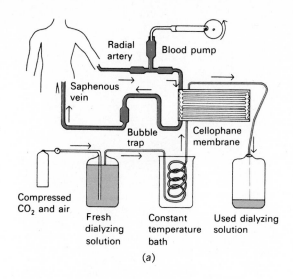

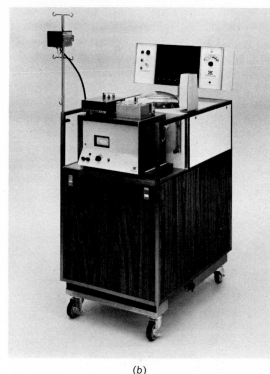

FIGURE 11–22 (a) The flow of blood through a kidney machine to perform the cleansing function (dialysis). (b) A Travenol RSP® artificial kidney machine. (Courtesy Travenol Laboratories, Inc.)

special glands called salt glands above the eyes, which actively excrete sodium chloride when the bird's body fluids acquire excess salt (Figure 11–23).

Aquatic Organisms

In aquatic organisms one of three osmotic conditions may exist (Figure 11–24). (1) The concentration of water and dissolved substances may be the same inside an organism as in the environment, so the organism neither gains nor loses water. This condition is called *isosmotic*. (2) The concentration of water may be lower and the concentration of dissolved substances higher inside an organism than in the environment. This means that water moves into the organism by osmosis. This condition, typical in freshwater organisms, is called *hyposmotic*. (3) The concentration of water may be higher and the concentration of dissolved substances lower inside an organism than in the environment. In this case, water tends to move from

the organism into the environment, a condition called *hyperosmotic*.

Isosmotic conditions are found in many marine invertebrates. A simple example of hyposmotic conditions is found in *Paramecium*. The contractile vacuole of this freshwater protist is a structure that eliminates excessive amounts of water. Freshwater fish eliminate water by producing large amounts of very dilute urine. But salts also tend to be lost in this waste product, so special cells in the gills actively absorb salts from water to maintain internal salt balance.

The hyperosmotic condition of saltwater fish presents the opposite problem from that of freshwater fish. These animals are constantly losing water. They drink large quantities of sea water but produce very little urine. In addition, the gills of these fish secrete excess salt back into the sea. Marine sharks and their relatives have solved the balance problem in yet another way. They maintain urea and other organic

Bio-Topic: Trading Old Problems for New?

The loss of a vital organ is no longer a death sentence. It is now possible to live with artificial or transplanted replacements for organs lost to injury or disease. The advances in medical technology that make these replacements possible bring with them entirely new kinds of medical, emotional, and ethical problems. Experiences with the treatment of kidney failure provide examples.

The first major advance in the treatment of kidney failure involved the use of an "artificial kidney machine" to dialyze a patient's blood. Dialysis is no cure, nor is it without problems. Patients must regulate their lives around the schedule and location of the needed equipment. A recent in-depth psychiatric study suggests that dialysis patients pay a significant emotional cost. Of 18 patients, only 12 were rated as having made a fair or even poor adjustment to treatment. The dependence on the machines caused despondency, guilt, and other emotional problems.

The next advance, and one that offered a cure, was the transplantation of kidneys from healthy donors. The ideal donor would be an identical twin or a close blood relative. Most persons can function normally with a single kidney as long as it remains healthy. But both donor and recipient must cope with the uncertainty of risking the health of the donor. Although many such transplants are successful, physicians end up with two patients, not one.

The most recent advance is the transplantation of kidneys from unrelated donors who die with healthy kidneys. Unfortunately, many transplanted kidneys are rejected by the recipient's body when they are recognized by the immune system as foreign protein. The reason for using close relatives as donors is that their proteins are likely to be similar enough not to be rejected. To avoid rejection, physicians try to match the proteins of the donor to those of the recipient.

But proteins are like fingerprints and are difficult to match. Current research is aimed at improved methods of matching and at ways to suppress the immune response without exposing patients to excessive risk of infection. Even if these goals are reached, hospitals report long lists of dialysis patients waiting for the accidental death of a suitable donor, and the shortage of transplantable kidneys is likely to continue.

Medical technology may eventually solve these problems. In the meantime, we seem to be trading old problems for new ones.

---

compounds normally excreted at high levels in their blood. This raises the concentration of dissolved substances in the animals until it is equal to or greater than that in the sea, producing an almost isosmotic state of equilibrium. The high urea level is unique as an adaptation; shark tissues show an unusually high tolerance to this toxic substance. The conditions described here for fish and sharks are shown in Figure 11–25.

In most marine invertebrates, body fluid salt concentration is equal to that of sea water. If the salt concentration of the water changes, the salt content of the internal fluid changes. These marine forms can survive only short-term variations slightly above or below normal. Organisms that cannot maintain their internal fluid concentration against that of the environment are known as *nonosmoregulators*. The colored line in Figure 11–26 indicates the survival

FIGURE 11-23   Marine birds such as this sea gull possess salt excreting glands. A highly concentrated salt solution flows into the nasal cavity and drips off the beak. (Courtesy of Henry B. Kane.)

range, under varying seawater concentrations, of nonosmoregulating marine invertebrates such as the spider crab.

Many marine animals can move from their normal saltwater environment into more dilute or brackish water, as in estuaries. Studies of estuarine invertebrates have shown that certain species of crabs can regulate their internal fluid and salt concentration actively by taking up salt through their gills. The green glands, discussed earlier with respect to excretion, are also involved in this process; in fact, they function primarily in the regulation of body water. The shore crab, one species capable of such regulation, normally lives in brackish water but can move easily onto shore or even into fresh water in search of food. Shore crabs, however, do not fare well in saltwater concentrations higher than normal. They react much like nonregulating forms under these conditions (Figure 11-26).

Perhaps the most striking example of osmoregulation is the Chinese mitten crab (*Eriocheir*), which migrates up rivers in central Europe. These crabs possess one of the most efficient osmoregulatory mechanisms known; they are equally at home in fresh and salt water. The mitten crab can actively transport salt from its blood into the water.

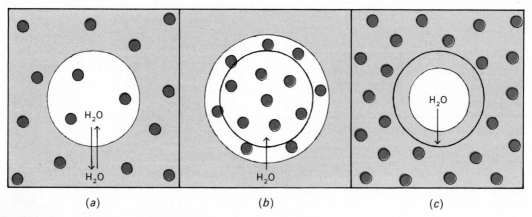

FIGURE 11-24   The three possible osmotic conditions in aquatic organisms. (*a*) Isosmotic environment, in which water moves in equal amounts into and out of the organism, producing no net gain or loss of water. (*b*) Hyposmotic environment, in which the organism gains water. (*c*) Hyperosmotic environment, in which the organism loses water.

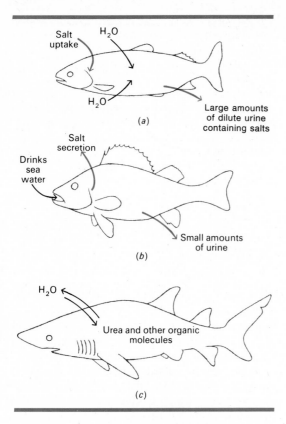

FIGURE 11–25 Mechanisms for the maintenance of osmotic balance. (*a*) Freshwater fish. (*b*) Marine fish. (*c*) Shark (marine).

All the metabolic processes described in the past two chapters support energy production in some way, and all contribute to the maintenance of a balanced state. Although these metabolic supporting processes and their structures are interrelated, they serve different functions, and we have examined each of them separately. But clearly these metabolic processes must work together in a coordinated, or integrated, way. The various metabolic processes must somehow be regulated so that each contributes to a smoothly functioning whole: the organism as a living *system*. In the next unit we shall examine the principal control mechanisms of living systems.

SUMMARY

Nutrients, gases, wastes, and other materials must be circulated and transported from one part of an organism to another. Monerans and protists may accomplish circulation by simple diffusion, but multicellular organisms with tissues and organs must have systems to perform this function. Plants have vascular tissues, xylem and phloem. Large animals have a blood vascular system composed of a heart and conducting vessels. Blood vascular systems may be either open, as in mollusks and insects, or closed, as in annelids and chordates.

Gas exchange, which is intimately associated with circulation, may be accomplished in a variety of ways: direct diffusion (in monerans, protists, plants, and some invertebrate animals); gills (in crustaceans, some mollusks, and fish); tracheal tubes (in insects); and lungs (in amphibians, reptiles, birds, and mammals). Many animals use specific gas-transporting pigments such as hemoglobin to increase gas exchange efficiency.

All organisms must eliminate toxic substances such as nitrogenous wastes. Some specific systems include green glands (in crus-

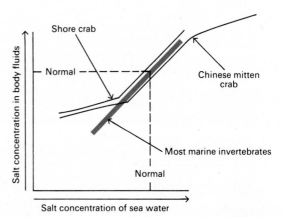

FIGURE 11–26 Relationships of body fluid and salt concentrations to varying concentrations of sea water. The colored line indicates equal (isosmotic) concentrations found in nonosmoregulating invertebrates.

taceans); Malpighian tubules (in insects); nephridia (in annelids); flame cells (in flatworms); and kidneys (in vertebrates). Most invertebrates are ammonotelic, releasing nitrogenous wastes as ammonia; vertebrates may be ureotelic (producing urea) or uricotelic (producing uric acid).

Excretion is closely related to regulation of water and ion balance. Any of three osmotic conditions may exist: isosmotic, hyposmotic, or hyperosmotic. The tubules of the vertebrate kidney are very important in water and electrolyte balance. The kidneys of land vertebrates excrete a concentrated urine in order to conserve body water. Organisms that can control and regulate their internal fluid content are called osmoregulators.

REVIEW QUESTIONS

1. How do plants solve the problems of circulation? How do animal systems differ from plant systems?

2. What are the major differences between an open and a closed circulatory system?

3. What kind of information can an ECG provide about the functioning of the heart?

4. Trace the passage of the bioelectrical impulse through the human heart, beginning at the SA node.

5. What are some causes of high blood pressure? How may the adrenal glands be involved?

6. What is the role of bicarbonate ion (HCO_3^-) in gas exchange?

7. How does the respiratory system of a bird differ from that of a human?

8. Why is carbon monoxide a deadly poison, whereas carbon dioxide is not?

9. Draw a diagram of a nephron unit and describe the functions of each segment.

10. Explain how the following organisms regulate their body fluids: *Paramecium*, freshwater fish, shark, and sea gull.

SUPPLEMENTARY READINGS

Barrington, E. J. W., *The Chemical Basis of Physiological Regulation*, Scott, Foresman, Glenview, Ill., 1968.   The basic concepts of the uptake of oxygen, the uptake of energy, storage and release of energy, water and ions, temperature and water, and temperature and terrestrial life are covered in this booklet.

Friedman, M. and R. H. Rosenman, *Type A Behavior and Your Heart*, Alfred A. Knoff, New York, 1974.   This book poses and defends the theory that certain people have behavior patterns that make them more susceptible to coronary artery and heart disease. In addition there are sections on self-diagnoses and what to do if you find that you are type A.

Likoff, William, B. Segal, and L. Galton, *Your Heart*, J. B. Lippincott, Philadelphia, 1972.   Information about the normal heart plus many abnormal and disease conditions that may cause loss of effective function or heart attack.

Ray, P. M., *The Living Plant*, 2nd edition, Holt, Rinehart, and Winston, New York, 1972.   A brief and well-written introduction to plant physiology that includes excellent treatment of gas exchange, transport, and water balance.

Schmidt-Nielsen, Knut, *Animal Physiology*, 3rd edition, Prentice-Hall, Englewood Cliffs, NJ, 1970.   An interesting, easy-to-read booklet that compares gas exchange, circulation, and water balance among various animals.

Warren, James V., "The Physiology of the Giraffe," *Scientific American*, November 1974.   Direct blood pressures taken in giraffes show that exceptionally high blood pressure is necessary to circulate blood to the head, some seven feet above the heart. Several adaptations of the giraffe's behavior and body structure are necessary to make this possible.

Unit V
Regulation

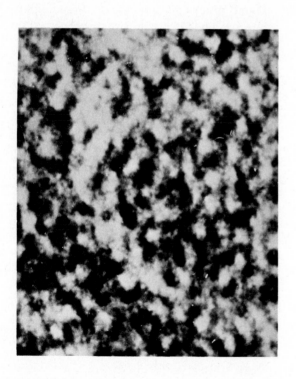

In previous chapters we have discussed many of the chemical reactions that take place in living systems. Thousands of these reactions must occur each second simply to keep a complex organism alive, and they must all be coordinated, both within each cell of the organism and throughout the organism's whole structure. If living systems are to continue their existence on earth, they must grow and reproduce; these processes too require regulation. Thus all organisms must achieve two types of regulation: (1) that which takes place over a relatively short period of time, often from moment to moment, and (2) that which occurs over a longer period, from generation to generation.

In the first type of regulation, enzymes and other chemicals previously discussed are essential. But three additional control mechanisms are also required: immune systems, hormones, *and* nervous systems. *Immune systems protect against foreign materials. Hormones are regulatory chemicals that may function at sites distant from where they were secreted. Nervous systems are involved in control activities ranging from simple reflexes to learning. In this unit we shall examine these three types of regulatory systems.*

Immune systems, hormones, and nervous systems, however, provide regulation only for individual members of a species. When members of a species reproduce, the offspring resemble one another. Yet they also differ from each other in many ways. An information system, functioning through the generations, must regulate hereditary processes—and it must have a great degree of stability yet still permit variation and change. In Chapter 3 we discussed DNA as the key component of this hereditary information

system. In this unit we will see how the hereditary material is transmitted from generation to generation and how it exerts its control. The mechanism of the transmission of genetic information plays an essential role in regulation because it is the means by which the control agent (DNA) is passed from generation to generation. Furthermore, the actual regulatory effects of genes (DNA) are understood better after the fundamentals of heredity are provided through the study of transmission genetics.

Chapter 12

Balance and Control

The life processes are a continual balance between constancy and change. Organisms—from the simplest to the most complex—maintain a consistent internal environment during sometimes drastic environmental changes. But how can organisms balance the two seemingly opposite tasks of maintaining stability while also adapting as the environment around them dictates?

We begin this chapter by studying the chemical and physical equilibria of living systems. Taken together, they lead us to a **Basic Scheme of Control.** Biological control is really chemical in nature. **General Metabolic Regulation** directs the processing of raw materials, the distribution and storage of energy, and the maintenance of a stable internal chemical environment in which the delicate reactions of life can take place.

Have you ever thought about the variety of potentially harmful substances with which you come in contact every day? Yet if you are like most organisms, you are healthy more often than not. The processes of **Protection and Immunity** depend both on physical barriers such as your skin and on numerous circulating chemicals called antibodies that respond to "invasion" by specific foreign substances.

Among the most powerful chemical stabilizers are **Hormones.** In both plants and animals, small amounts of these complex molecules direct the growth, development, and reproduction of living systems. **How Do Hormones Work?** Hormone regulation of life processes is a comparatively slow mechanism. If you had to rely only on hormones, it might take hours, days, or even years to respond.

The essence of **The Nervous System** is speed and flexibility. **The Anatomy of the Nervous System** is composed not only of the separate organs—the spinal cord, the brain—but can also be considered from the viewpoint of function. Different functional parts of nervous systems handle specific kinds of stimuli and responses.

The basic communication process of the nervous system is **The Nerve Impulse,** a flash of information that is actually a complex electrical-chemical unit whose function and control are not yet completely understood. New methods of control, such as **Biofeedback,** might eventually make it possible for us to control completely the workings of our internal environment.

transport them to all parts of an organism, but the hormones exert their effects only at specific sites. Hormones are so potent that only small quantities are required to produce their effects. We discussed several examples of hormonal control under the topic of digestion in Chapter 10. But a broader range of hormones serve regulatory functions in both plants and animals.

Hormones in Plants

Plants produce hormones that control growth, bending movements (*tropisms*), and reproduction. The growth hormones, or *auxins*, are produced in all actively growing regions of plants, but especially in stem and root tips. The most common of these growth hormones is *indole-acetic acid*.

Growth Hormones: Auxins

Studies of plant growth were stimulated by the observation that plants move in response to external stimuli such as light. Charles Darwin and his son Francis performed some of the first studies on plant movement in the 1870s. Their studies on grass seedling coleoptiles—sheath-like structures only a few cells in thickness which cover the emerging grass shoots—showed that when a coleoptile is exposed to light from one side, it bends toward the light. This bending (phototropism) could be prevented either by covering the tip or removing it (Figure 12–9). Since the bending occurred along the stem just below the tip, Darwin suggested that the stimulus for growth passed from the tip to the stem.

Researchers have since confirmed Darwin's hypothesis by performing various experiments. One of the most widely used techniques has been to remove a stem tip, place it on a block of agar (a gelatinlike substance), and permit auxins to diffuse onto the agar. In this manner various concentrations of auxins can be accumulated; the blocks of agar can then be used in experiments to determine the degree of bending (Figure 12–10).

If the uppermost, or apical, bud of many plants is pruned, the lateral buds lower on the stem will grow. This observation led to the theory that the apical bud exerts an inhibiting influence on lower buds through its auxin supply. Some plants show strong apical dominance, growing tall and straight, where other plants branch heavily and are bushy, showing weak apical dominance (see Figure 16–5).

Auxins also seem to affect the developing stem and root. When a seed germinates, the root bends downward into the soil and the stem bends upward. These behaviors are thought to be controlled by the differential effects of auxin concentration on the two structures. When the embryonic parts of a germinating seed emerge, (Figure 12–11), the pull of gravity concentrates more auxin on the lower side of the structures. This apparently stimulates cells of the lower side of the stem, and they enlarge more rapidly than cells on the upper side. This uneven growth causes the stem to bend upward. On the other hand, auxin concentration inhibits the growth of cells in the lower part of the root and permits the upper cells to grow faster; this causes the root to turn downward.

Almost everyone knows that plants bend toward light as they grow. This bending is caused by unequal growth of the stem, which in turn results from uneven auxin distribution. Auxin migrates from the side of the stem closer

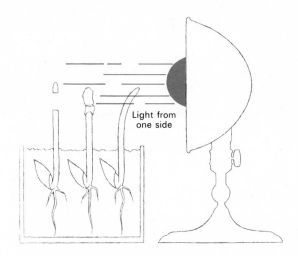

FIGURE 12–9 Phototropism in grass seedlings. The seedling with the covered tip and the one with its tip removed do not bend toward the light.

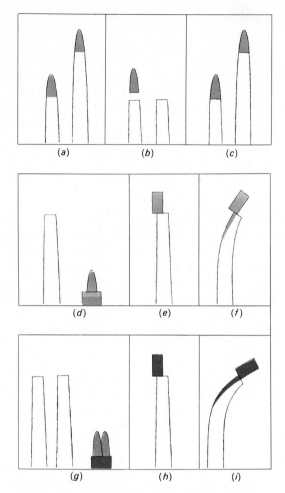

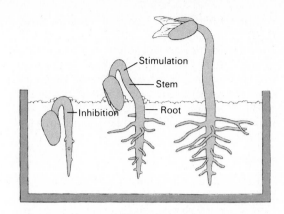

FIGURE 12–11 In the developing root, the pull of gravity concentrates auxin in the lower side. The auxin thus inhibits elongation of the lower cells and permits elongation of the upper cells, causing the root to grow downward. On the stem, however, the concentration of auxin on the lower side stimulates elongation of the lower cells, so the stem turns upward.

ity of cell walls. This permits a cell to take in more water and thus increase its size.

Gibberellins

Another group of growth compounds are the *gibberellins*, discovered by Japanese botanists in 1926. Gibberellins are produced by the fun-

FIGURE 12–10 Experiments on grass coleop-tiles. (*a*) Tip intact: growth. (*b*) Tip removed: no growth. (*c*) Tip replaced: growth. (*d*) Tip removed and placed on block of agar: auxin diffuses into block. (*e*) Section of agar block placed on tipless coleoptile. (*f*) Coleoptile bends in response to auxin. (*g*) Two tips removed: more auxin diffuses into block. (*h*) Section placed on tipless coleoptile. (*i*) Coleoptile bends farther in response to in-creased auxin.

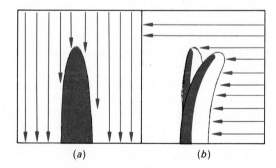

FIGURE 12–12 Effect of light on auxin concen-tration and stem movement. (*a*) When the light strikes the stem from above, the auxin is evenly distributed. (*b*) When the light is principally from one side, the auxin is more concentrated on the dark side. The resulting unequal growth and bending is the phototropic response of plant stems.

to the light to the opposite side, stimulating cells away from the light to grow faster. This causes the bending (Figure 12–12).

What does the auxin actually do to cells to produce growth? The exact details are not clear, but we do know that auxins decrease the rigid-

(a)   *(b)*

FIGURE 12-13 Effect of gibberellic acid on plant growth. (*a*) Plants treated with a 1 percent mixture of the acid. (*b*) Untreated controls. (Courtesy of U.S. Department of Agriculture.)

gus *Gibberella fujikuroi*, which causes the condition in rice known as "foolish seeding disease." The chief symptom of this disease is exceptionally tall stem growth. Botanists have conducted many experiments with gibberellins on other plants; other effects may result, but the primary action of gibberellins in all cases is to produce rapid stem elongation. Gibberellins may prove to have economic value, since they can typically induce biennial plants (those which require two years to complete their life cycle) to complete their growth in only one year. Most plants are thought to produce hormones similar to gibberellins, which may interact with auxins in the control of stem growth and development. Recent studies indicate that the action of gibberellins increases enzyme synthesis and cell division (Figure 12–13).

Synthetic Growth Stimulators

Certain chemical compounds not normally synthesized in plants have growth effects similar to hormones. One of the most familiar is 2,4-dichlorophenoxyacetic acid (commonly known as 2,4-D), a weed killer. At a certain concentration this compound produces abnormally rapid growth in broad-leaved plants such as dandelions and ragweed, thus killing them. At the same concentration 2,4-D has no harmful effect on narrow-leaved grasses; consequently it is an effective weed killer in lawns.

The growth and development of ovaries into fruits normally results from fertilization. In the absence of fertilization, however, some plant ovaries can be forced to grow and develop fruit through the use of synthetic substances similar to hormones. Seedless fruits can thus be induced in such plants as watermelons, tomatoes, oranges, and cucumbers.

Flowering: Photoperiodism

All plants do not flower at the same time of year. Experiments conducted in the early 1900s showed that in some plants, flowering is determined by the relative periods of light and darkness. Some plants, known as "short-day" plants, will not flower unless subjected to periods of short illumination such as normally provided by a period of short days. Others will not flower until exposed to long periods of light; these are called "long-day" plants. A third group of plants, the "day-neutral" species, are reproductively insensitive to light and can bloom under varying light conditions. Asters, strawberries, cockleburs, some chrysanthemums, and poinsettias are short-day plants; corn, clover, lettuce, and beets are long-day plants. Day-neutral species include dandelions, tomatoes, sunflowers, and cucumbers. This effect of varying light periods upon flowering is called *photoperiodism* (Figure 12–14). The critical phase of photoperiodism is the length of the dark period. Flowering plants must therefore be capable of measuring these critical periods. How do they do this?

The explanation lies in the fact that plants contain two forms of a light-sensitive pigment called *phytochrome*. One form, *P-red*, absorbs visible red light, which converts it to *P-far red*. *P-far red* is converted back to *P-red* when it absorbs wavelengths of invisible far red (infrared) energy. *P-far red* is also converted slowly to *P-red* in the darkness (Figure 12–15). *P-far red*

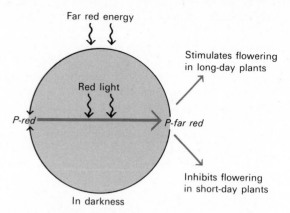

FIGURE 12-15 The phytochrome mechanism.
Under visible light containing red light, *P-red* phytochrome is converted to *P-far red*. Energy of far
red wavelengths converts *P-far red* to *P-red*. Since
visible light contains more red light than far red,
P-far red is generally more abundant. During
darkness *P-far red* is changed back to *P-red*. *P-far
red* actively stimulates flowering in long-day plants
and inhibits flowering in short-day plants. By this
mechanism plants recognize relative periods of
light and dark.

FIGURE 12-14 Photoperiodism in chrysanthemums. (*a*) This control plant, subjected to approximately 14 hours of darkness per day, bloomed.
(*b*) This plant was given one hour of light in the
middle of its dark period; blooming did not occur.
The graphs illustrate the relative lengths of light
and dark. (Photos courtesy of U.S. Department of
Agriculture.)

is the active form which measures light and
assists in stimulating flowering in long-day
plants and inhibiting flowering in short-day
plants. (*P-red* on the other hand produces the
opposite effects.) Thus exposing a plant to red
light produces more of the form of phytochrome *P-far red* and leads to the effects listed
above (Figure 12-15). During daylight hours
the *P-far red* form accumulates; at night, *P-red*
builds up. By this mechanism, then, plants
distinguish light from dark.

Experimentally, a normal dark period may be
interrupted by a flash of visible light containing
a large component of red light. This inhibits
flowering of a short-day plant. But if the flash of
visible light is followed by a similar flash of far
red energy, the inhibition is cancelled. This far
red energy converts the phytochrome from the
P-far red type to the *P-red* type. The phytochrome mechanism apparently works closely
with a plant's internal biorhythm cycle to stimulate the production of a flowering hormone
often referred to as *florigen* but as yet not isolated. However it has been shown on plants
with more than one shoot that illuminating
one shoot only will induce flowering on all of
the shoots indicating that some diffusible substance is involved.

Hormones in Animals

The hormone systems of animals show remarkable examples of growth, metabolic control, and coordination. The importance of these hormonal control systems is dramatized by the many growth anomalies and aberrant patterns that result in humans from malfunctioning hormonal systems. Hormones have been identified in most animal groups and have been studied in some detail in insects, crustaceans, mollusks, worms, and echinoderms. For exam-

ple, the metamorphosis process in insects is under hormonal control.

But we know more about mammalian hormonal systems than about others, so we shall use human hormones as examples of hormonal control. Hormones are produced by cells in *endocrine glands* that have no ducts and secrete their hormones directly into the bloodstream. Although we speak of endocrine glands individually, the glands of the endocrine system often interact. A hormone from one gland may stimulate or inhibit another gland or rein-

Bio-Topic: Hormonal Warfare

Insects may pass through four or more developmental stages: egg, one or more larval (caterpillar) stages, pupa (the cocoon), and adult. In many agricultural pests, the transition from one stage to another is controlled by hormones produced in the brain. For example, the transition from larva to pupa occurs in many species when the brain produces less of a chemical known as juvenile hormone. An insect of this kind, if treated with extra juvenile hormone, will never form a cocoon and will never mature into an adult. Zoecon Corporation in Palo Alto, California is now marketing a synthetic mosquito juvenile hormone. Mosquito larvae sprayed with this material never complete development and die as overgrown larvae. The Department of Agriculture is presently perfecting synthetic insect hormones that prevent other species from molting (shedding the outer skin between larval stages). Treated larvae may grow large enough to split their skins and die.

In learning to control insects by hormonal warfare, humans are once again mimicking evolution. The common garden plant known as mistflower (Ageratum) produces substances that block the pro-

duction of juvenile hormone by larvae that feed on the plant. These antihormones interfere with normal development, causing some larvae to develop into sterile adults; others form cocoons from which they never emerge.

Hormonal control of insect pests offers many advantages over conventional insecticides. Each group of insects produces a chemically distinct kind of hormone. By spraying a field with a particular hormone, it should be possible to control only the pest species, without harming other, potentially beneficial insects in the field. Insect hormones, even synthetic ones, will be biodegradable because they will contain no "unnatural" elements or chemical bonds. For the same reason, they are not likely to be persistent.

But nature often has the last word. Many species of insects have eventually evolved resistance to conventional insecticides, and we can expect that resistance to hormonal insecticides will also evolve sooner or later. It may take longer since the insects will have to reorganize the chemistry of their own development, but then, living systems are extremely versatile.

force the action of another hormone. Most cases of endocrine malfunction involve more than one gland. The locations of the principal endocrine glands in humans are shown in Figure 12–16.

The Pancreas

Perhaps the best-known example of endocrine deficiency is *diabetes mellitus*, a potentially fatal disease in which large amounts of sugar (glucose) are excreted in the urine. About 1890, two physicians experimenting with dogs discovered that a substance produced by the

pancreas alleviates the symptoms of diabetes. When the pancreas was removed surgically, more sugar appeared in the urine. In 1922, two other researchers successfully isolated that substance—the hormone *insulin*—from excised dog pancreases. It is now common knowledge that insulin injections will counteract a diabetic condition. Insulin was the first protein whose amino-acid sequence was determined. This was accomplished in 1954 by Frederick Sanger of Cambridge University.

In Chapter 10 we noted the role of the pancreas in digestion. The pancreas contains two distinct types of tissue (Figure 12–17). The more abundant of these two tissues consists of dark-staining tubule cells which secrete digestive enzymes. Scattered irregularly throughout this tissue are larger, lighter-staining cell groups that secrete hormones. These patches are called *islets of Langerhans*. The islets contain two types of cells (beta and alpha), each producing a different hormone: the beta cells produce insulin, and the alpha cells make glucagon.

We shall now return to the relationship between insulin and sugar in the urine, first discussed in Chapter 10. You should recall from that discussion that digested carbohydrates in the form of glucose (blood sugar) are carried to the liver by the hepatic portal system. In the liver much of the glucose is converted to glycogen and stored. This conversion of glucose to

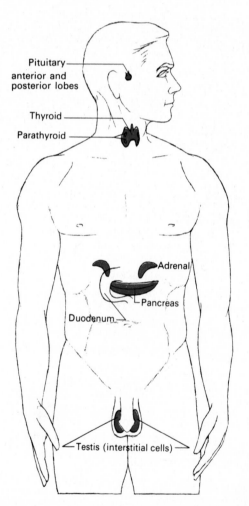

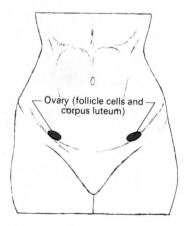

FIGURE 12–16 Location of the principal endocrine glands in humans.

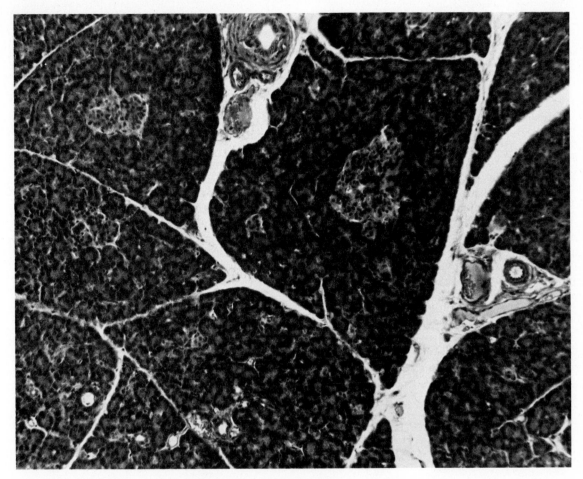

FIGURE 12-17 Microscopic section of the pancreas (×450).
The lighter stained areas in the lobes are the islets of Langerhans.
The more abundant, darkly stained tissue secretes digestive en-
zymes.

glycogen can also take place in the muscles.
Under normal conditions the blood retains
about 70 to 110 mg of glucose per 100 ml of
blood; the remainder is converted to glycogen
by the liver and muscles. Glycogen can also be
converted back to glucose, distributed to the
blood, and carried to tissues for fuel.

When the concentration of glucose in the
blood reaches 180 mg per 100 ml, glucose begins
to be excreted in the urine. This is where insulin enters the picture. Glucose must either
enter cells to be burned as a fuel or be converted to glycogen in liver and muscle cells. We

know that insulin facilitates the conversion of
glucose to glycogen. Insulin is also thought to
increase membrane permeability in liver and
muscle cells to permit glucose to enter these
cells more quickly.

Glucagon has the effect opposite to insulin:
it causes an increase in blood sugar level. Glucagon is also involved in the pathology of diabetes. Whereas insulin is usually deficient in
diabetic individuals, glucagon is usually present in excess. The treatment of diabetes by
insulin has obscured the role of glucagon. Recently another hormone, *somatostatin*, pro-

duced in the hypothalamus of the brain, has been shown to be involved in the regulation of insulin and glucagon production. Somatostatin, which suppresses the release of both insulin and glucagon has helped clarify interrelationships between these two hormones and diabetes. Researchers discovered that somatostatin could depress excessive levels of glucagon and thus decrease blood glucose levels. But insulin is necessary for the movement of glucose into cells.

Several other hormones also control blood sugar. We know, for instance, that *epinephrine* (adrenalin) can increase blood sugar levels; we shall discuss this hormone later. *ACTH*, a hormone secreted by the pituitary gland, stimulates the cortex of the adrenal gland to produce *glucocorticoid hormone*, which can also increase the level of blood sugar. Still another hormone involved in the glucose-glycogen relationship is thyroxine, secreted by the thyroid gland. Thyroxine controls the rate at which glucose is burned in glycolysis and the Krebs cycle. When the thyroxine level in the blood increases, glucose is burned faster; increasing thyroxine in the blood thus tends to decrease the blood-sugar level. The role of these hormones in glucose-glycogen metabolism is summarized in Figure 12–18.

The diabetic individual is not harmed by the sugar in the urine. The damage results when cells must burn fats and proteins for fuel rather than glucose. Oxidation of large amounts of fats releases toxic products the body cannot cope with. These products alter the body pH and can cause death. Patients with diabetes can supplement their faulty metabolism with insulin from other animals and thus live normal lives. But they must be careful, because *insulin shock* can result from an overdose of insulin. An overdose causes the blood sugar level to drop so low that the brain does not receive enough glucose; unconsciousness or convulsions can result.

The Pituitary: "The Master Gland"

Any discussion of the human endocrine system must give considerable attention to the pituitary gland, which lies beneath the midbrain at the base of the skull. The pituitary is the principal initiator of many behavioral patterns; this role will be stressed in Chapter 17.

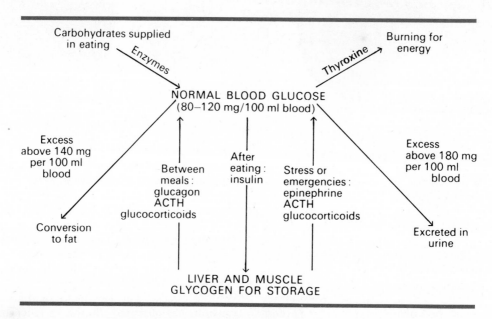

FIGURE 12–18   Factors involved in glucose-glycogen metabolism.

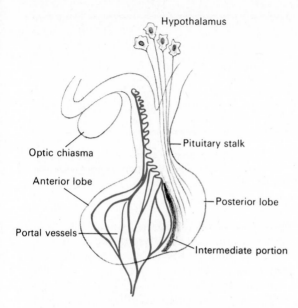

Hypothalamus

Optic chiasma

Anterior lobe

Portal vessels

Pituitary stalk

Posterior lobe

Intermediate portion

FIGURE 12–19 Section of the pituitary gland, showing nerve fibers to the posterior lobe and portal vessels to the anterior lobe.

The gland has two lobes: posterior and anterior (Figure 12–19). It is connected to the *hypothalamus* of the brain by a stalk containing both neural connections portal and blood vessels. This is important because the nervous system also produces hormones. In fact, the hormones secreted from the posterior lobe appear to be produced in the hypothalamus and transported to the posteior lobe. Since vascular (blood) connections exist between the hypothalamus and the anterior pituitary, hormones secreted from the hypothalamus can stimulate the anterior pituitary to release its hormones. At least nine such "releaser" hormones have now been identified; these hormones apparerently regulate the release of most anterior pituitary hormones. Somatostatin, discussed earlier under the topic of diabetes, is also produced in the hypothalamus.

Two more hormones, *oxytocin* and *vasopressin*, are produced in the hypothalamus and stored in the posterior lobe of the pituitary. Oxytocin causes the muscles of the uterus to contract. Vasopressin, often called the "antidiuretic hormone," brings about reabsorption of water in the kidney tubules. Vasopressin also constricts arterioles, especially during hemorrhage, to maintain blood pressure.

The intermediate region of the pituitary secretes the hormone *intermedin*. This substance controls the distribution of pigmentation in the skin of certain amphibians and, to a lesser degree, in humans.

The anterior lobe has often been called the "master gland" of the endocrine system. The reason for this name lies in the fact that it secretes *tropic* hormones that stimulate other glands to secrete. Probably the most familiar anterior lobe hormone is *somatotropin*, the growth hormone which, along with thyroxine, controls growth of the entire body. Excessive amounts of somatotropin during the growing stage can lead to *giantism*, whereas a subnormal level produces *dwarfism*. Later in life, oversecretion of somatotropin stimulates the growth of the few bones that are still capable of growing, including those of the hands and feet and some facial bones. This condition is known as *acromegaly.*

Two important anterior lobe hormones controlling other glands in the endocrine system are *thyrotropic* hormone, which stimulates the thyroid gland, and *adrenocorticotropic hormone (ACTH)*, which controls the adrenal gland. During periods of stress, the anterior lobe is stimulated to produce ACTH by a releasing hormone from the hypothalamus.

Two other anterior pituitary hormones control the development and function of the gonads (ovaries and testes). These are called *gonadotropic hormones* (GTH). They are follicle-stimulating hormone (FSH) and luteinizing hormone (LH). One of the clearest examples of hormonal control takes place in the female, where critical ratios of FSH and LH control ovulation. We will discuss this in more detail in Chapter 15. The secretion of these hormones is also regulated by releaser hormones from the hypothalamus—LH-releasing hormone (LH–RH) and FSH-releasing hormone (FSH–RH). In the male, LH stimulates the interstitial cells of the testis to produce *testosterone*, the principal male hormone. FSH in the male stimulates the germinal epithelium to produce sperm. *Lactotropic hormone* (LTH), also called *prolactin*, stimulates female mammary glands to produce milk after the birth of a baby.

The Thyroid

Thyroxine, the hormone from the thyroid gland, has already been mentioned in connection with the burning of fuel in the body. The relationship is direct—the more thyroxine, the faster the food is oxidized. Thus people with an overactive thyroid tend to be thin, nervous, and irritable. Opposite symptoms in adults, such as overweight and sluggishness, are associated with an underactive thyroid. If the thyroid undersecretes during early childhood, the result may be *cretinism*, a condition in which the child's growth, sexual maturity, and mental development are retarded.

Thyroxine is an amino acid containing four atoms of iodine. *Goiter*, the overdevelopment of the thyroid gland, occurs when thyroid cells lack enough iodine to make fully functional thyroxine. If each molecule has fewer than four atoms of iodine, the hormone exhibits only a fraction of normal activity. This type of goiter, called hypothyroid goiter, is treated by the addition of iodine to the diet to increase the production of thyroxine. The excess thyroid tissue may then be removed surgically. Hypothyroid goiter was once common in inland areas such as Switzerland and the Great Lakes region of the United States, but today iodized salt prevents this type of goiter in most areas. An oversecreting thyroid gland can also produce goiter. This type of goiter, known as hyperthyroid goiter, is more serious and may increase metabolism by 50 percent above normal.

The thyroid gland secretes thyroxine in response to stimulation by the thyrotropic hormone, also known as thyroid-stimulating hormone (TSH), from the anterior lobe of the pituitary. In this case the releaser hormone from the hypothalamus which stimulates the anterior pituitary is thyrotropin-releasing hormone (TRH). A negative feedback mechanism signals the anterior lobe when enough thyroxine has been produced. This feedback system is believed to work as follows: a high concentration of thyroxine inhibits the production of TSH; when the supply of TSH drops off, so does

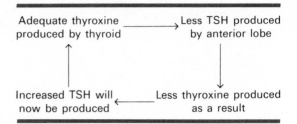

FIGURE 12-20   Control of thyroxine secretion. The feedback principle is evident in this cycle of events.

the amount of thyroxine, since TSH is no longer stimulating the thyroid gland; when the concentration of thyroxine is reduced, TSH can again be secreted to stimulate the thyroid gland to produce thyroxine. This would provide a fairly constant level of thyroxine in the body (Figure 12-20).

Thyroxine stimulates most body functions. It increases the production of many enzymes, speeds up heart rate and circulation, and increases the excitability of the nervous system. Metamorphic development in frogs, for example, is under control of the thyroid gland. If the thyroid gland is removed from a tadpole, it does not develop into an adult frog. Moreover, if thyroxine is added to the water surrounding developing tadpoles, they enter metamorphosis much earlier than those not receiving additional thyroxine.

The thyroid gland produces another hormone, *calcitonin*, which is involved in the regulation of calcium balance. Calcitonin lowers the blood concentration of calcium by inhibiting the release of calcium from bone to blood. This hormone exerts an effect opposite to the parathyroid hormone, which we will consider next.

The Parathyroids

When the four parathyroid glands, located near or in the thyroid (Figure 12-21), are surgically removed from experimental animals, muscle twitching and convulsions occur. The animals die if they do not receive injections of parathyroid hormone, or *parathormone*. The calcium level in the blood drops when parathormone is

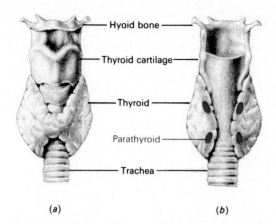

(a)   (b)

FIGURE 12–21 Human thyroid gland. (a) Anterior view. (b) Posterior view, showing the parathyroid glands embedded in the thyroid.

absent and rises when it is added. Essentially, then, the parathyroid glands regulate calcium metabolism and circulation of calcium in the blood. Insufficient secretion of parathormone produces irritability of nerve and muscle tissue, causing cramps and convulsions.

These glands also control phosphate removal from the body by the kidneys. Parathormone decreases the concentration of phosphates in the blood. An undersecretion of the hormone, then, increases the phosphate level in the blood. Bones are composed partly of a calcium phosphate compound, so when calcium is released to the blood the excess phosphate is removed from the body. The antagonistic action of parathyroid hormone and calcitonin from the thyroid controls both of these activities.

The Adrenals and Gonads

The adrenal glands lie on top of the kidneys. They serve a variety of functions, some of which have already been mentioned. Each gland is divided into two distinct parts with distinct functions. An inner mass called the *medulla* is surrounded by an outer layer, the *cortex* (Figure 12–22). The cortex produces three different groups of hormones. The *glucocorticoids* assist in controlling the conversion of glycogen to glucose (their action is opposed

to that of insulin) and regulate aspects of fat and amino-acid metabolism, including conversion of these two groups of compounds to glucose.

The second class of hormones secreted by the cortex are the *mineralocorticoids*. As the name implies, these hormones are involved in salt and water balance. If a malfunction or disease decreases production of these hormones, the concentrations of sodium, chloride, and water in body fluids drop, but potassium concentration increases. The mineralocorticoids tend to increase kidney reabsorption of sodium and excretion of potassium. In Addison's disease, caused by a degeneration of the

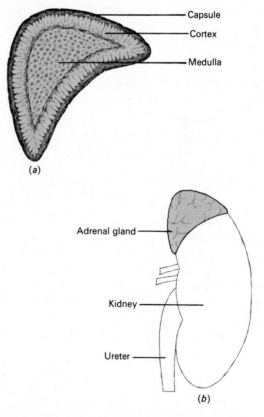

(a)

(b)

FIGURE 12–22 Adrenal gland. (a) Cross section, showing the cortex and the medulla. (b) Position of the adrenal gland on the top surface of the kidney.

cortex, dehydration and changes in skin pigmentation occur. Moreover, the victim has difficulty coping with mild disturbances and illnesses which are usually of minor consequence. An intact, normal cortex seems to be important in dealing successfully with emotional stress.

Sex hormones are the third group of hormones produced by the cortex; these are predominantly male hormones (*androgens*), but female hormones (*estrogens* and *progesterone*) are also secreted. Overactivity of the cortex at an early age can produce early, abnormal sexual maturity.

ACTH from the pituitary stimulates the cortex to produce its hormones. A faulty pituitary can thus cause the cortex to oversecrete or undersecrete. Note also the structure of some of the hormones secreted by the cortex. Most show the basic steroid configuration with varying side chains (Figure 12–23).

The medulla of the adrenal gland produces the hormones *epinephrine*, noted earlier, and *norepinephrine*. These are commonly called *adrenalin* and *noradrenalin*, respectively. Adrenalin has often been called the *emergency hormone* since it increases the blood sugar level (opposite to insulin), increases heart rate and blood pressure, dilates blood vessels in the heart and skeletal muscles, constricts vessels in smooth muscle, and causes erection of skin hairs to produce "goose bumps." You probably recognize most of these characteristics as those that would enhance the responses of an individual faced with an emergency. The body mobilizes its resources in emergencies, and adrenalin seems to be the hormone that does it.

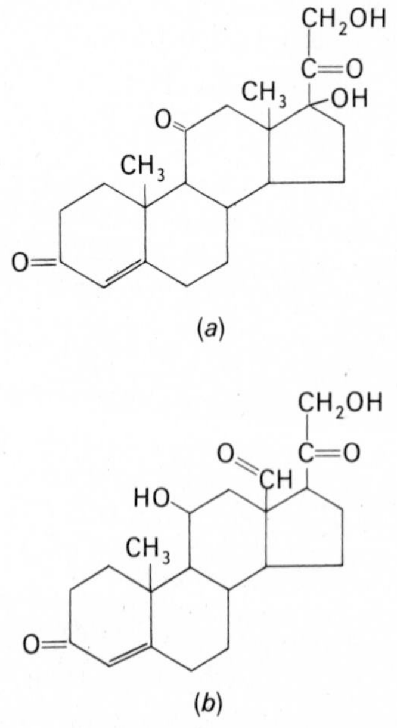

The ovaries in females and the testes in males produce hormones that cause the development of secondary sex characteristics at the onset of puberty (about 10 to 12 years of age in humans). Common secondary sex characteristics in humans include pubic and underarm hair and sweat glands in both sexes, deep voice and beard in males, and enlarged breasts and characteristic distribution of body fat in females. In the male these hormones are called *androgens* (including testosterone), in the female they are *estrogens*. Actually, each sex produces both hormones, and the relative amounts of each determine sex. In males more androgens than estrogens are produced, whereas the opposite is true in females. These glands are also stimulated by tropic hormones from the anterior lobe of the pituitary. A summary of the principal endocrine glands and the major hormones they secrete is shown in Figure 12–24.

Other Hormones

The hormones of the digestive system were discussed in Chapter 10. The thymus gland, besides producing lymphocytes and antibodies, secretes a hormone called *thymosin*. This hormone is thought to be essential for the full development of the antibody-producing ability of lymphocytes. *Histamine*, a substance released from damaged tissues, has questionable status as a hormone at this time. Antigen-antibody reactions such as those which occur in hay fever damage the lining of the nasal passages, permitting histamine to escape. Histamine makes the blood vessels more permeable and increases mucus secretions. Antihistamine

FIGURE 12–23 Two hormones secreted by the adrenal cortex. (*a*) Cortisone, a glucocorticoid. (*b*) Aldosterone, a mineralocorticoid.

drugs are commonly taken to relieve this condition. The bronchioles, small air passages from the lungs to the trachea, are also constricted by histamines, making breathing difficult (the condition known as *asthma*). Antihistamines also counteract this effect.

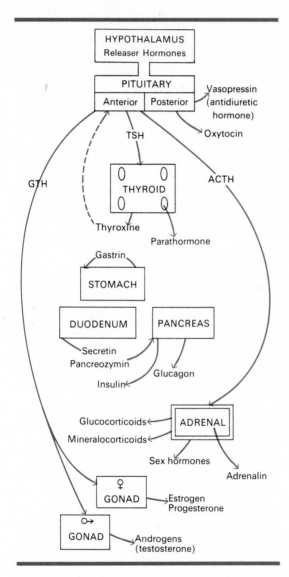

FIGURE 12–24 Principal endocrine glands and their secretions. One feedback flow is indicated by the broken line; other feedback mechanisms exist but are not shown.

Recently, a group of hormonelike compounds known as *prostaglandins* have been found to have a variety of effects, including contraction of the smooth muscle of the uterus and inhibition of gastric secretions. One prostaglandin lowers blood pressure; another one raises it. These compounds may also function to clear the nasal passages and relax the bronchioles. Many cells have minute amounts of prostaglandins in their membranes, but the richest sources are the seminal vesicle secretions of males and female menstrual fluids. Prostaglandins may affect the functioning of cell membranes and, in some cases, regulate hormone action by functioning with the cyclic AMP mechanism described in the next section.

How Do Hormones Work?

Hormones are secreted into the bloodstream, where they flow freely through the circulating fluids of an organism. Thus they bathe many cells besides those of their specific "target" tissues and organs. Why, then, do they affect only their "targets?" Researchers in the 1950s and 1960s attempted to find answers to this problem; they made some progress when they found that estrogen exerts some of its effects by uniting with a specific protein in the uterus. We now know that hormones act by at least two mechanisms that appear to be related to their molecular structure—one mechanism for the steroids and one for other hormones such as those composed of peptides. Some hormones of the peptide type are large molecules, with molecular weights of 10,000 or more; many of them do not dissolve in lipids, which are found in cell membranes. Steroids, on the other hand, are smaller molecules with molecular weights of about 300. These smaller, fat-soluble molecules pass easily through cell membranes, whereas the larger peptides are stopped at the cell surface. This fact may be the basis for the different molecular modes of action of these two groups of hormones. The steroids function inside the cell; the peptide hormones and others exert their effects at the surface of the cell membrane.

The late Earl W. Sutherland, who won the Nobel Prize for Physiology or Medicine in 1971 for his research, studied the reactions through which adrenalin accelerates the breakdown of glycogen to glucose in the liver. The hormone adrenalin functions at the cell membrane. Sutherland and his colleagues discovered the series of steps leading from secretion of the hormone to the final action, the enzymatic breakdown of glycogen by *phosphorylase*. This enzyme must be activated by other enzymes before it can function, and adrenalin must activate these enzymes.

When adrenalin is released from the adrenal gland, it stimulates an enzyme called *adenyl cyclase* in the cell membranes of target cells. Next, activated adenyl cyclase on the inner membrane surface catalyzes the synthesis of cyclic AMP (cAMP) from ATP inside the cell. Cyclic AMP then affects the rates of various cellular processes. In this case, it activates the enzymes that convert inactive phosphorylase to an active state (Figure 12–25). In the active state, phosphorylase catalyzes the breakdown of glycogen to glucose. Adrenalin may thus be called a "first messenger," acting on a receptor

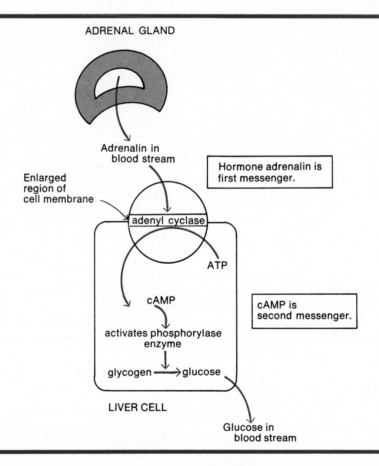

FIGURE 12–25 The action of adrenalin in stimulating the formation of glucose. Adrenalin is the first messenger, and cAMP is the second messenger. Cyclic AMP (cAMP) activates inactive phosphorylase, which then catalyzes the breakdown of glycogen to glucose.

on the outside of the membrane; cAMP, the "second messenger," produces its effect inside the cell. Other hormones are also thought to exert their effects through a "two-messenger" pattern. Among them are glucagon, ACTH, TSH, and parathormone.

Since steroid hormones can penetrate all cells, biologists had to explain how these substances exert their effects only on their target cells. It is now known that *receptor* molecules are present in target cells but not in nontarget cells. Receptor molecules apparently attach to hormone molecules and carry them into the nucleus of a target cell. In 1968, through the use of radioactive tracers, Walter E. Stumpf showed that steroid hormones indeed accumulate in the nucleus of a target cell. Once inside the nucleus, the hormone-receptor complex can interact with DNA in chromosomes to regulate RNA and protein synthesis (Figure 12–26). In fact, a segment of DNA must be "turned on" in

some way to produce a specific protein product in response to the stimulation of the hormone-receptor complex. Bert W. O'Malley and William T. Schrader of Baylor University conducted a series of experiments in which they introduced radioactively labeled progesterone and estrogen to chicks and to parts of chick cells from the oviducts. These experiments show that the hormone receptor unit can bind to DNA and bring about RNA synthesis. After RNA is produced, specific proteins can be synthesized on the ribosomes in the cytoplasm. We will discuss protein synthesis fully in Chapter 14). Many details, such as the means by which a specific section of a DNA molecule is activated and how the process stops, are not yet understood. But a basic model has been established and receptors for steroid hormones have been found in all target cells.

THE NERVOUS SYSTEM

Taken as a whole, the hormonal system is rather slow in responding to change. There are exceptions: distant parts of the human body respond within seconds to the secretion of adrenalin. But many hormonally regulated responses take minutes, hours, even days. This leisurely rate is all right for plants; most of them are rooted in one spot and cannot go anywhere in any case. But it is far too slow to meet all of an animal's needs for behavior control.

In contrast, the nervous system is speed itself: reaction times are measured in fractions of seconds. The nervous system can provide for immediate action, which may save an animal's life. A fly sitting on a table becomes aware of a sudden change in its environment (the rapid approach of a flyswatter) because of *receptors* that can detect the change (a *stimulus*). Nerve impulses are then carried to *modulators* (the central nervous system), which in turn direct an impulse message to the appropriate *effectors* (wing muscles), which permit the animal to fly to safety. Not only does the nervous system respond rapidly, but the message is directed to a specific effector. The hormonal and nervous systems differ in this way as well as in reaction time. Hormones may be thought of as commu-

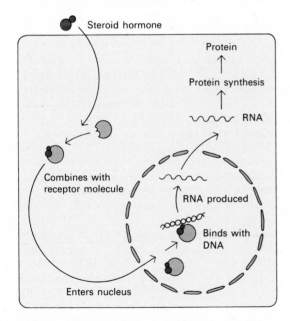

FIGURE 12–26 Proposed mechanism of steroid hormone action. The hormone diffuses into a target cell and unites with receptor molecules. This hormone-receptor complex enters the nucleus, attaches to DNA, and stimulates the production of RNA. The RNA in turn directs the production of a protein.

nications addressed "to whom it may concern," whereas nerve impulses are like letters sent with a specific name and address. Special cells must thus provide for two-way communication, both between an animal and its environment and between parts of an animal. Neurons or nerve cells are irritable: they respond to stimulation. In addition, they show a high degree of conductivity. These neurons provide for the rapid and often complex behavioral activity of animals. Some plants such as the Venus' flytrap respond to touch, but they have no real counterpart to neurons or the nervous system. Plant cells are also irritable, but plants respond to stimuli with reactions such as tropisms, described earlier.

Most multicellular animals have some type of nervous system to provide coordination and communication. In simple animals such as the hydra, this system may consist of nothing more than a group of connected neurons scattered throughout the animal's body to form a *nerve net*. In more complex forms such as earthworms, many neurons may come together to form a *ganglion* (a group or collection of nerve cell bodies), which acts as a coordinating center. In some animals a series of connected ganglia form a nerve cord, from which lateral nerves can emerge to distant parts of the body. Many invertebrates and all vertebrates have groups of ganglia that store information and coordinate neural activity. These structures are called *brains*. Some of the various nervous systems found among animals are shown in Figure 12–27. (You might find it helpful to review the discussion of nerve tissue in Chapter 5 before reading further.)

The Anatomy of the Human Nervous System

Vertebrate animals have the most complex nervous systems of all. We will use the human as our example here, but all vertebrates possess similar structures, differing only in size and number of parts. For example, the cerebrum of the human brain shows considerably more development and complexity than that of any other vertebrate.

The Central and Peripheral Nervous Systems

The vertebrate nervous system consists of two parts: the *central nervous system* (CNS) and the *peripheral nervous system* (PNS). The CNS is composed of the brain and spinal cord; the cranial and spinal nerves form the PNS. Information in the form of nerve impulses (to be discussed later in this chapter) can be carried from the brain and spinal cord to various parts of the body over the peripheral nerves. In the same manner, information from various parts of the body can be transmitted to the CNS. A nerve leading into the CNS is called a *sensory* or *afferent pathway*. A nerve leading from the CNS is referred to as a *motor* or *efferent pathway*. Of the 12 pairs of cranial nerves that emanate from the lower surface of the brain, some are motor, some are sensory, and some are mixed—they contain both sensory and motor nerves. The 31 pairs of spinal nerves attached to the spinal cord are all mixed nerves. The cranial nerves serve mainly the head and neck regions. The spinal nerves serve the rest of the body, supplying the skeletal muscles, skin, sweat glands, and blood vessels. In addition, some spinal and cranial nerves give rise to lateral ganglia, which send nerve fibers to visceral organs. This part of the nervous system is not normally under voluntary control; it is often referred to as the *autonomic nervous system* (ANS). The peripheral nervous system thus consists of two parts: the *voluntary*, serving skeletal muscles and so on, and the *involuntary* (ANS), serving internal organs. Figure 12–28 outlines the anatomy of the human nervous system.

Each spinal nerve is connected to the spinal cord by two roots, one dorsal and one ventral. All the nerves leading to the spinal cord (sensory nerves) enter the dorsal root, and those leaving the cord (motor nerves) travel over the ventral root. These are shown more clearly in Figure 12–29, which illustrates reflex action.

Reflexes

A discussion of reflexes may clarify some aspects of the structure and function of the nervous system. In Chapter 17 we will examine the

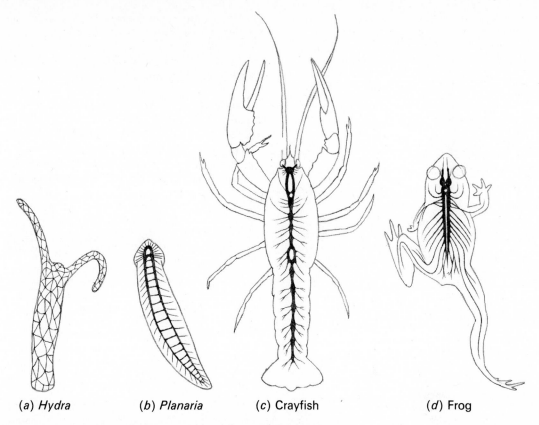

(a) *Hydra*   (b) *Planaria*   (c) Crayfish   (d) Frog

FIGURE 12–27   Nervous systems found in the animal kingdom.
(a) Nerve net. (b) Ladder type of nerve system. (c) Ventral nerve
cord. (d) Dorsal nerve cord.

relationship of reflexes to behavior. A *reflex* is a simple form of behavior in which a stimulus evokes a specific response. One of the most familiar reflexes is the extension of the lower leg upon stimulation (tapping) of the patellar (knee cap) tendon. The immediate withdrawal of the foot or hand upon touching a hot object is another familiar reflex. These actions occur instantaneously and involuntarily. A natural reflex can, however, be modified by experience. The modifying process is often referred to as *conditioning*, and the modified reflex pattern is called a *conditioned reflex*. In such a modification, the original sensory pathway of the reflex is over-ridden by a different sensory element. The response, or motor pathway, however, remains the same. We will discuss Pavlov's fa-

mous experiments on conditioning in Chapter 18.

A reflex results when a nerve impulse travels over a *reflex arc*. The spinal cord (but not necessarily the brain) is part of this reflex arc. The arc may consist of only two neurons, or it may involve three or more. The neuron that picks up the stimulus and brings the information to the spinal cord is called the sensory or afferent pathway. The information, in the form of a nerve impulse, then passes to a second neuron that carries the impulse out over a motor, or efferent, pathway to an effector, which produces a response. Many reflexes also involve connecting neurons called *interneurons*. These neurons are located in the spinal cord between the two pathways (Figure 12–29).

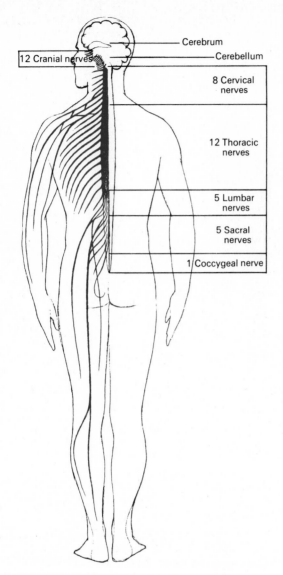

FIGURE 12-28   The human nervous system, showing location of the 12 pairs of cranial nerves and the 31 pairs of spinal nerves.

Note that where two neurons meet, the axon of one is closely associated with the dendrite of the other. As we saw in Chapter 5, this association is called a synapse, and the nerve impulse passes across this narrow gap by a chemical process (Figures 5–26 and 5–27).

Note how well the reflex arc illustrates the processes of control and regulation we de-

scribed earlier in Figures 12–2 and 12–3. A reflex results from a change that requires action from a living system; the regulating mechanism here is the nervous system, including sensory and motor neurons and the spinal cord.

The Brain

The CNS is the controller of nervous activity, since it receives and sends messages to all parts of the body through the PNS. The brain is the chief organ in this integration; it receives messages transmitted upward through the spinal

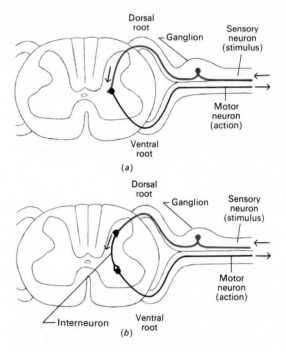

FIGURE 12–29   Reflex arcs. In these cross sections of the spinal cord, note that the cell body of the sensory neuron is in the ganglion of the dorsal root, but the cell body of the motor neuron lies inside the spinal cord. The direction of the nerve impulse is indicated by the arrows. The H-shaped area of the spinal cord is the so-called gray region in which the cell bodies lie; the white region of the cord is composed only of nerve fibers carrying impulses to and from the brain. (a) Reflex arc involving two neurons. The knee-jerk reflex is of this type. (b) Reflex arc involving three neurons. Removing your hand from a hot stove is a reflex of this type.

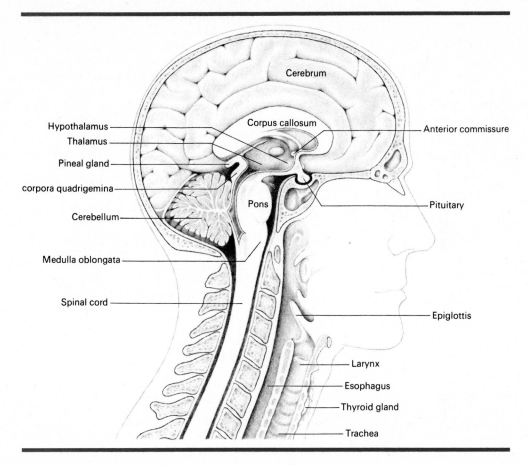

FIGURE 12-30 Median longitudinal view of the human brain.

cord, sorts them out, and relays this information to the appropriate parts of the CNS for action. Reflexes may be modified as a result of brain action. Practically all learning and intelligent behavior involves the brain, so certain parts of this organ warrant examination (Figures 12-30 and 12-31).

The *cerebrum* contains the nerve centers that govern and integrate motor and sensory functions. It is also the site of reasoning, intelligence, and memory. The cerebrum, composed of two hemispheres, is by far the largest part of the human brain. The *corpus callosum* is a band of nerve tracts connecting the two hemispheres of the cerebrum. The *thalamus* relays sensory impulses to the cerebrum and it is an

important region in determining the sleep-wakefulness arousal state of a person.

The small area known as the *hypothalamus* regulates involuntary or autonomic functions such as appetite, sleep and waking states, water balance, and body temperature. It also regulates the pituitary gland through releaser hormones. In fact, the hypothalamus is the most important regulatory center for most visceral activities. Since we know that body temperature is controlled by the hypothalamus, we can now understand the entire cycle of events occurring in this regulatory pattern (Figure 12-32). Sensory receptors and the bloodstream transmit the sensation of cold to the brain. Through its releaser hormones, the hypothalamus stimu-

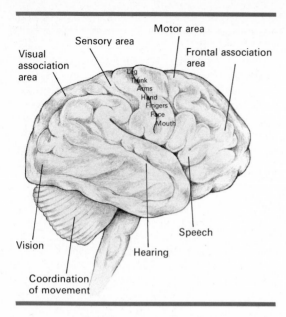

FIGURE 12-31   Some functional areas of the cortex in the human brain.

lates the pituitary, which in turn secretes TSH (thyroid-stimulating hormone). This causes more thyroxine to be produced by the thyroid gland. Thyroxine, as we saw earlier, increases the metabolic rate and thus produces more body heat. The feedback mechanism to govern the amount of thyroxine released was described earlier (Figure 12–20). Other glands such as the adrenals may also be involved in this series of events, especially in extreme cold.

The *cerebellum* helps coordinate muscular movements and control posture. The *medulla* contains reflex centers for such functions as coughing, sneezing, and swallowing. More important, however, the medulla contains the vital centers for the control of breathing and heart action.

The Autonomic Nervous System

Earlier, we mentioned a division of the nervous system that is not under willful control: the *autonomic nervous system* (ANS). Although this part of the nervous system is "self-controlled," it is connected to the rest of the nervous system through the spinal and cranial

nerves (Figure 12–33). The ANS is classified as two divisions on the basis of function and structure (Figure 12–34). The *sympathetic* division arises from all the spinal nerves in the thoracic region and from the first three lumbar nerves. The *parasympathetic* division consists of branches of the third, seventh, ninth, and tenth cranial nerves and the second, third, and fourth sacral spinal nerves.

These two divisions come from different regions of the CNS and also function differently. In fact, they act antagonistically. The sympathetic system accelerates the heartbeat, whereas the parasympathetic slows it down. The sympathetic system produces dilation of the pupils of the eyes, and the parasympathetic brings about their constriction. The sympathetic system mobilizes body resources for emergencies, whereas the parasympathetic returns the body to a more normal state after an

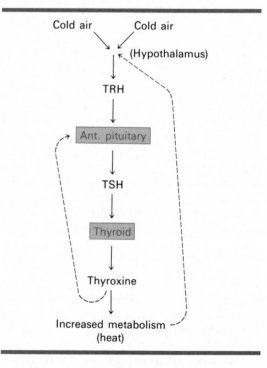

FIGURE 12-32   How the stress of cold air can stimulate a series of events to alleviate the stress. Dotted lines indicate feedback loops.

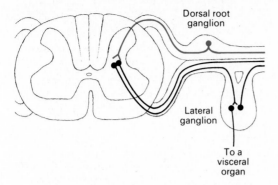

Dorsal root
ganglion

Lateral
ganglion

To a
visceral
organ

FIGURE 12–33 Relationship between the autonomic and peripheral nervous systems. A lateral
autonomic ganglion (sympathetic) is shown arising
from a spinal nerve.

emergency passes. Through their accelerating
and decelerating effects, the two divisions work
together to provide a normal range of operation
for the body. Figure 12–34 illustrates some of
the effects of each system upon the body.

The Nerve Impulse

Earlier we mentioned a nerve "message" traveling along a nerve. This message, more accurately called a *nerve impulse*, travels along an
axon when a nerve is stimulated. Biologists
have studied the process of nerve conduction
for many years. In 1902 Julius Bernstein, a
German biologist, proposed a theory for the
transmission of the nerve impulse; experimental evidence obtained in the 1930s and 1940s,
especially by Alan L. Hodgkin and Andrew F.
Huxley, extended and confirmed his theory.
With slight modifications, Bernstein's model is
still used today to explain nerve impulse transmission. The theory is based on the fact that
certain ions have different concentrations inside the neurons from their concentrations
outside. The concentrations of some of these
ions change very rapidly—almost instantaneously—with the passage of the nerve impulse.
Therefore the process must be due to changes
in ionic concentrations along the cell membrane.

In a nerve that is not conducting an impulse,
more negative ions (mostly proteins carrying

negative charges on their carboxyl groups) are
inside the cell than are outside. This means
that the inside of the cell is negatively charged
in comparison to the outside. This uneven
distribution of ions produces an electrical potential (a difference in potential electrical energy, or an electrical imbalance) of 50 to 70
millivolts across the membrane of the nerve
cell. This *resting potential* establishes a measurable charge difference (negative versus positive) between the inside and the outside of the
membrane. The concentration of sodium ions
(Na^+) is much greater outside the cell than
inside, and more potassium ions (K^+) are
found inside the cell (Figure 12–35a).

When a nerve is stimulated the membrane
becomes more permeable to sodium ions,
which rush into the cell across the membrane
(Figure 12–35b). This reverses the previous po-

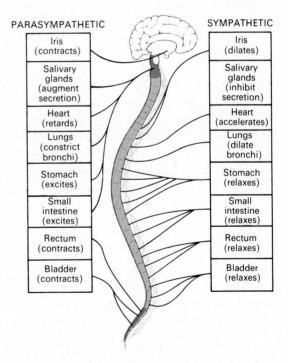

PARASYMPATHETIC   SYMPATHETIC

Iris (contracts)	Iris (dilates)
Salivary glands (augment secretion)	Salivary glands (inhibit secretion)
Heart (retards)	Heart (accelerates)
Lungs (constrict bronchi)	Lungs (dilate bronchi)
Stomach (excites)	Stomach (relaxes)
Small intestine (excites)	Small intestine (relaxes)
Rectum (contracts)	Rectum (relaxes)
Bladder (contracts)	Bladder (relaxes)

FIGURE 12–34 The two components of the autonomic nervous system and their action on various organs. Darker shades denote the parasympathetic system; lighter shades indicate the
sympathetic system. Note the opposing effects of
the two divisions.

Bio-Topic: Right or Left?

The human brain is an extraordinary organ that seems more fascinating as we learn more about it. It now appears that the functional asymmetry of the brain may explain our abilities to excel at some tasks and not others.

Anatomically, the human brain is quite symmetrical. The left half is a mirror image of the right. Functionally, however, each half of the brain is more efficient at perceiving certain kinds of stimuli and at controlling certain kinds of motor responses. The left half of the brain is almost twice as efficient as the right in perceiving spoken words; the right half is more efficient at tasks involving stereoscopic depth perception. Our understanding of these functional asymmetries comes from many sources. Physicians, for example, have long noticed that damage to the left half of the brain impairs the motor control of the right side of the body and that damage to the right half impairs control of the left side.

The separation is not complete, either anatomically or functionally. The two halves of the brain are connected by several bundles of nerves that cross from each half to the other. These cross-connections evidently help to integrate the functions of the sides of the brain and body. Occasionally these cross-connections are broken, either by injury or during surgical treatment of certain mental disorders. Studies of "split brain" individuals have been very informative, especially when young persons are compared with adults. These studies reveal that many functional asymmetries are learned, not built in.

It now seems probable that each of us carries in our brain two independent modes of consciousness. The left side usually performs orderly, linear thought; what we generally call analytical or rational thinking. The right side usually performs intuitive, synthetic thought; what we generally call creative or artistic thinking. We seem to move from one mode of consciousness to the other, but often with difficulty. Will we someday learn to move back and forth at will? The ability to do so might enhance our lives immensely.

larity, producing a temporary positive charge on the inside of the cell relative to the outside. When this *depolarization* occurs, we say that an *action potential* has developed. Immediately following the influx of sodium ions, the membrane becomes highly permeable to potassium ions, which flow through the membrane to the outside (Figure 12–35c). But the nerve cell must be restored to its state before stimulation, with a greater concentration of sodium ions outside the cell and a greater concentration of potassium ions inside. This recovery is normally almost instantaneous, due to the movement of potassium ions out of the cell, and within a few thousandths of a second the

neuron is ready to conduct once more (Figure 12–35d). After the passage of many impulses (perhaps 50,000), the sodium and potassium gradients are greatly reduced.

For sodium ions to move outside the cell again and for potassium ions to move inside requires movement of these ions against a concentration gradient. This can only be done by an active transport mechanism such as that described in Chapter 4. Sodium is actively transported to the outside, and potassium is moved back inside the cell. The model proposed to account for these activities has been called the "sodium pump" or, more recently, the "sodium-potassium exchange pump." The

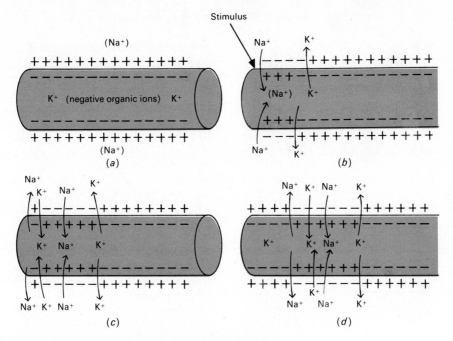

FIGURE 12–35 Events during stimulation of a nerve and the subsequent conduction of the impulse. (*a*) Segment of inactive nerve fiber. (*b*) Stimulus applied and inflow of sodium ions; very shortly thereafter, potassium ions move out. (*c*) The adjacent region becomes depolarized and the impulse is conducted along the nerve; note the region of the original stimulus is beginning to recover. Sodium ions are being transported out and potassium ions back in. (*d*) Conduction continues along the nerve to the right as recovery (return to resting potential) occurs at the left end of the fiber.

latter formulation postulates that the same system which transports sodium out of the cell also moves potassium back into the cell.

If the events we have described account for the transmission of an impulse at one spot on the nerve, we can assume this same process accounts for transmission along the entire length of the nerve. But how are the events set off in the region adjacent to the stimulated area and in succeeding regions? Bernstein proposed that the disturbance in membrane permeability responsible for starting the impulse upset the normal membrane permeability in the adjacent area. The impulse would then move to neighboring regions of the nerve until it had traveled the length of the nerve. Thus a wave of depolarization moving along a nerve is self-propagat-

ing and is "powered" at each step along the way. This movement of the impulse along the nerve has been likened to a burning dynamite fuse, which propagates itself by lowering the kindling temperature in the adjacent regions as the fuse burns. The series of events just described is summarized in Figure 12–35.

All nerve impulses are the same, whether the stimulus is touch, light, or sound waves. The impulse does not differ, but various receptors lead to different parts of the brain for interpretation. For example, both light and pressure can trigger nerve impulses in the receptor cells of the retina in the eye: a punch in the eye can make the victim "see stars." But a stimulus must be of sufficient strength in order to initiate an impulse. This intensity is often called a *threshold;* once this threshold is reached, the impulse will be propagated the entire length of the nerve cell.

The basic nerve impulse is electrochemical—that is, the ionic changes which occur along the membrane produce electrical events. These events can be visualized and studied by the use of electronic instruments such as the *oscilloscope.* This device provides visual images of electrical events on a fluorescent screen. A nerve impulse monitored by electrodes leading to an oscilloscope produces a pattern, called a "spike," on the screen. This is the visual representation of the action potential (Figure 12–36). We often refer to these electrochemical changes as *bioelectricity,* but the concept is entirely different from the conventional electricity that travels through copper wiring. Common electricity results from electron movement along a wire, but bioelectricity is caused by a separation of charged particles (ions) by a membrane, a process requiring active transport by the membrane. Electricity travels at the rate of 186,000 miles per second, much faster than the nerve impulse, whose speed may vary from 1 to 300 meters per second.

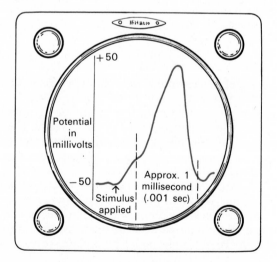

FIGURE 12–36 Visualization of a nerve impulse (the "spike") as it would appear on an oscilloscope.

Biofeedback

Earlier in this chapter we noted that the autonomic nervous system (ANS) was involuntary, or not under willful control. We further indicated that skeletal muscles (such as those used in walking) could be controlled, but that visceral functions could not. But it has been known for some time that visceral, or "involuntary," factors such as blood pressure can indeed be controlled to some extent. People and animals can be trained to exert varying degrees of conscious control over their visceral functions. The study and application of this phenomenon has come to be called *biofeedback.* (This is an unfortunate term because it is so similar to "biological feedback," which, as we have seen, encompasses far more than conscious control of the ANS. But we are stuck with the term.)

Biofeedback, presently a fascinating area of research in the Western world, has long been practiced in Eastern cultures. Yogis, for example, can control their heart rate, blood pressure, and even body temperature. Some early experiments in biofeedback by Americans used rats as subjects; the rats were trained to alter their heart rates (Figure 12–37). We cannot strictly say that rats that alter their autonomic processes are doing it "consciously" or "willfully." They are rewarded (given food, for example) if their heart rates speed up or slow down, depending on the experiment. The rat is probably not "conscious," in the sense that a person would be, that it is being rewarded for changing its heart rate. The point, though, is that an animal—human or otherwise—can *learn* to regulate ANS functions. The learning process used in biofeedback is a kind of conditioning known as *operant conditioning;* we will discuss it further in Chapter 18. Although biofeedback is a relatively new concept to us and is undergoing considerable experimentation, we should at least understand its basis.

Electrical potentials (nerve impulses) called *brain waves* are produced by cells of the cerebral cortex. These waves can be recorded on an instrument known as an electroencephalograph when electrodes are placed at appropriate locations on the head of a subject. The brain wave recording is called an *electroencephalogram* (*EEG*). Various EEG patterns are registered during activities such as sleeping, reading, and so forth; four basic kinds of brain waves result (Figure 12–38). Of these four, *alpha* waves are associated with a comfortable, relaxed, often creative, and restful state; they are generally the predominant type of waves. Since alpha waves reflect a relaxed and contented state, it would be advantageous to be able to train oneself to produce "alpha activity." This can be done by monitoring a person's brain waves and signaling (by a noise or a flashing light) when alpha waves are produced. When one can discriminate alpha from nonalpha states, one can train oneself to maintain alpha activity. In recent biofeedback experiments, humans have been able to switch alpha waves on and off at will. Humans have also been able, through feedback mechanisms, to control heart rate, blood pressure, and even migraine headaches.

Biofeedback, then, is the return of an individual's biological information to that person. It permits self-awareness of internal state and

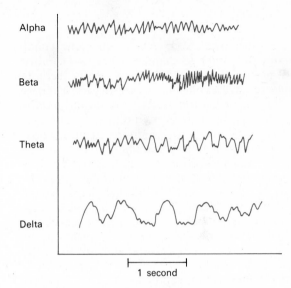

FIGURE 12–38   Electroencephalogram of four kinds of brain waves in a normal individual. Alpha waves are characteristic of a relaxed or resting state; beta waves occur during nervous activity; theta waves are often associated with stress; and delta waves occur during deep sleep. Since deviations from these wave patterns occur in some brain disorders, EEGs can be used to diagnose brain damage.

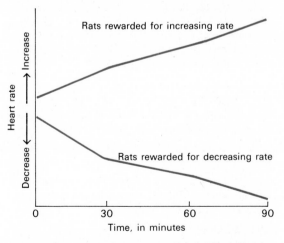

FIGURE 12–37   Rats can be trained to increase or decrease their heart rates when they are rewarded with electrical brain stimulation for doing so. (From *A Primer of Psychobiology: Brain and Behavior* by Timothy J. Teyler. W. H. Freeman and Company. Copyright © 1975.)

brings with it the opportunity to control or regulate internal conditions.

In this chapter we have discussed one important type of regulation: the maintenance of an organism's internal steady state in the face of continuous, potentially disruptive environmental change. But living systems not only maintain their internal stability, they also perpetuate themselves by reproducing. This vital process also involves regulation—the regulation of hereditary processes. It is to these processes that we now turn in Chapters 13 and 14.

When we have explored hereditary mechanisms, we shall find that we have a better understanding of homeostatic regulation too. This is because the basic unit of heredity, the *gene*, regulates the production of enzymes and hormones. The gene is the ultimate control agent of homeostatic mechanisms, and indeed of *all* mechanisms and processes in living systems.

SUMMARY

All organisms must react to changing conditions in order to maintain internal stability. Internal conditions are never static, because materials are continually entering and leaving a living system; and external conditions continually change as well. Maintenance of a steady state or dynamic equilibrium within an organism is accomplished through active coordination and regulation of chemical and physical processes. All control activities follow a similar pattern: an external or internal change undergoes a regulation process within the organism before action occurs; feedback is necessary to prevent overreaction; receptors pick up the stimulus caused by a change and effectors carry out the action.

One important part of an organism's homeostatic control system is a defense against foreign substances. Immunity against foreign substances, or antigens, is provided by white blood cells through the production of antibodies. Antigen-antibody reactions cause allergies and often make organ transplants difficult.

Hormones are secreted by tissues or specialized organs into extracellular fluids of an organism. They are then transported throughout the organism, where they exert their effects at specific sites. Hormones produced by plants control growth, bending movements, and flowering. Animal hormones, usually secreted from endocrine glands, produce widespread effects. Some examples of animal hormone action are regulation of growth, development, metabolism, reproduction, digestion, and water and ion balance. Hormones may function in at least two different ways: those of smaller molecular size (steroids) penetrate the cell membrane and function inside the cell; larger hormones (such as polypeptides) exert their effects at the cell membrane surface.

The nervous system is composed of neurons and nerve tracts; whereas hormonal control is often slow and generalized, the nervous system provides for fast, specific action. The human nervous system may be considered in three functional divisions: central (CNS), peripheral (PNS), and autonomic (ANS). A reflex arc is a nerve pathway involving sensory, motor, and sometimes interneurons. Reflex arcs travel across the spinal cord from dorsal root to ventral root before the brain can modulate the sensory input. Some reflexes can be conditioned through training.

Nerve cells have the ability to pass a nerve impulse (wave of excitation) along their full length and to transfer this excitation to other nerve cells. Electrochemical events involving ions, especially sodium and potassium, account for this wave of excitation.

We now know that animals can learn to regulate some ANS functions, such as blood pressure, through biofeedback mechanisms.

REVIEW QUESTIONS

1. Give several examples showing how changes in an organism's external environment can affect its internal environment. Then state briefly what steady-state processes would occur to counteract these changes.

2. Can you explain the value of having both nervous and hormonal systems in animals? What are the advantages of each?

3. Describe the control or regulatory actions that would occur in the following situation: You are hiking in the woods; as you round a bend in the trail you see a bear in the middle of the trail about 50 feet ahead.

4. If a potato tuber is grown in a jar, the apical bud develops into a large, vigorous shoot and the lateral buds ("eyes") produce small shoots, if any. However, if the tuber is cut into five or six pieces, all "eyes" will develop sprouts of about the same size. Explain.

5. What changes would you expect in a young rabbit that has been given periodic injections of pituitary extract?

6. What are some of the effects of an excessive growth of adrenal cortex tissue (a tumor)? Consider the changes that might occur in a 5-year-old male and in a 35-year-old male.

7. How are hormones believed to function at the molecular level?

8. Why would a physician test several spe-

cific reflexes on a patient after an accident that leaves the individual unconscious?

9. Explain why it is possible to start a nerve impulse along a nerve by applying electrical stimulation, pressure, or certain chemicals.

SUPPLEMENTARY READINGS

Brown, Barbara B., *New Mind, New Body— Bio-feedback: New Directions for the Mind*, Harper & Row, New York, 1974. Bio-feedback is the process by which humans can learn to control their own biological and mental functioning. Dr. Brown presents evidence of how this is done and why this process is therapeutically important to medical and behavioral problems.

Cooper, Max D. and A. R. Lawton III, "The Development of the Immune System," *Scientific American*, November 1974. The origins and functions of cell mediated and humoral immune responses are discussed in detail. The two cell types that perform these functions come from a single cell type but differentiate according to the environment in which they mature.

Llinàs, Rudolfo R., "The Cortex of the Cerebellum," *Scientific American*, January 1975. A well-illustrated description of the structure and functions of the cerebellar cortex. Interconnections of the various cell types are clearly shown and related to the control of body movement.

McEwen, Bruce S., "Interactions between Hormones and Nerve Tissue," *Scientific American*, July 1976. Steroid hormones secreted by the adrenal cortex and gonads have been traced to target cells in several regions of the brain. These hormones appear to influence the development of neuron patterns and behavior through interaction with the genetic material.

O'Malley, Bert W. and William T. Schrader, "The Receptors of Steroid Hormones," *Scientific American*, February 1976. Steroid hormones produced by endocrine glands are small molecules that easily diffuse into cells. Only target cells contain specific protein molecules called receptors. A hormone-receptor complex is formed that combines with specific chromosome segments to promote protein synthesis.

Raff, Martin C., "Cell-Surface Immunology," *Scientific American*, May 1976. Antibodies that combine with specific cell surface antigens are excellent tools for studying the structure of cell membranes as well as diagnosing bacterial and viral infections.

Chapter 13

Heredity: Transmission of Genetic Traits

We have seen the extraordinary range of things organisms do to stay alive. But how is the information to coordinate these activities conveyed to each generation? The process of heredity, the transmission of traits between generations, is not foolproof, nor does it provide exact copies of the parent generation. But it consistently conveys the basic information that guarantees the continued identity of the species.

The first step for us in this chapter is tracking down *The Physical Basis of Heredity.* What component carries information between generations? Recall the process of mitosis in Unit II, which simply duplicates the existing hereditary information of a cell and distributes it to the next generation of two cells. But mitosis doesn't explain how genetic information is mixed from two parents. *Meiosis: The Genetic Basis of Sexuality* explains sexual reproduction at the cellular level: the subdivision and then combination of genetic information from two parent forms.

The *Basic Mendelian Principles* that began the systematic study of heredity are noteworthy more for their simplicity than for anything else. In the mid-nineteenth century Gregor Mendel isolated traits and tracked their frequency in test crosses of parent generations. He found ratios of traits, that is, relationships between the number of times specific traits appeared in successive generations. From these data, he theorized that traits moved between generations as discrete units.

Although Mendel was fundamentally correct in his theories, he had no idea of the form of these traits at the cellular level. By going *Beyond Mendel's Work,* twentieth-century scientists turned heredity into a cellular science called genetics. One of their most important discoveries is the mechanism of *Sex Determination,* how specific factors in the parent cell nucleus determine the sex of the offspring. Continued work in genetics has demonstrated that heredity is not as simple as Mendel had suggested. The independent assortment of traits is actually modified by *Linkage and Crossing Over.*

Genes do not tell the whole story of traits in succeeding generations. The relationship between *Environment and Heredity* is of great interest today. These two factors interact to influence many characteristics, traits which are only partially outlined in the organism's genetic background.

Historical records show that ancient civilizations conducted breeding experiments to improve stocks of plants and animals. These practices have been continued down through the ages in attempts to obtain better domesticated organisms. Of course the early experimenters did not understand the cellular mechanisms involved. As we saw in Chapter 4, the cell itself was not discovered until the seventeenth century and its central role in living systems was not recognized until the *cell theory* was put forward around 1840. And as we shall see, several more decades passed before scientists gained any real understanding of the physical (cellular) mechanisms of heredity.

Some early breeders attributed their results to a process in which the characteristics of each parent blended together to produce the effects observed in the offspring. For example, they believed that a camel and a sparrow could cross and that their characteristics would blend to produce an ostrich. Others believed that all heredity was carried in either a sperm or an egg; two schools of thought arose from this controversy, the spermists and the ovists. Still others believed that heredity was carried by blood. The *pangenesis* theory had a long history of acceptance; it was held by some Greeks and later by Charles Darwin. This theory proposed that each structure in the body contained tiny "pangenes" (*pan*, "everywhere"), which moved into eggs and sperms prior to fertilization. Each structure was represented by a pangene; if the structure changed, so would the pangene. Such a mechanism "explained" the theory that acquired characteristics could be inherited, a misconception we will discuss in Chapter 19.

A few early scientists attempted experimental studies of inheritance, as distinguished from practical efforts by breeders. But most of those studies were too ambitious, involving many genetic and environmental factors that could not be controlled, and accurate records were rarely kept.

THE PHYSICAL BASIS
OF HEREDITY

The first notable experiments dealing with inheritance were conducted by an Austrian monk, Gregor Mendel, and reported in 1866 in an obscure local journal. Mendel's work went unnoticed by the scientific community during his lifetime. In the 1890s, working independently on different organisms, Karl Correns of Germany, Hugo DeVries of Holland, Erich von Tschermak of Austria, and William Spillman of the United States obtained results similar to Mendel's. These studies provided a logical explanation for the transmission of traits from generation to generation and stimulated intense interest in heredity.

Important cellular studies undertaken in the 1880s and 1890s provided information later used to support these explanations of hereditary mechanisms. German cytologists discovered chromosomes and worked out the details of chromosome division and sex cell production. So while explanations were being sought in breeding and heredity experiments, cytological studies were advancing far enough to supply some of the answers.

It was inevitable that sooner or later investigators would see relationships between these two fields. About 1902, two notable publications discussed the relationship between the fields of heredity and cytology. Working independently, Walter Sutton in the United States and Theodor Boveri in Germany correlated the results of inheritance experiments by Mendel and others with the behavior of chromosomes in cells. This splendid synthesis gave birth to the field of *genetics* and "the chromosome theory of heredity."

At first, not all biologists accepted the chromosome theory of heredity; many sought more definite proof. Such proof would involve associating a specific trait with a visible chromosome makeup in the cells of an organism. In other words, a definite chromosome change must be demonstrated when a physical change occurs in an individual. This demonstration became possible in the early 1900s as a result of improved microscopy and pioneering experiments with the fruit fly (*Drosophila*). Thomas Hunt Morgan (1866–1945), an American geneticist, realized the possibilities for genetic studies offered by this small fly. Populations can be kept in small bottles and fed on a nutrient medium, and a new generation can be pro-

Bio-Topic: Of Sex and Death

The evolution of sexual reproduction ranks among the most significant events in the history of living systems. The essence of sex, at least in genetic terms, is recombination. Each sexual event produces new combinations of genes (through crossing-over) and new combinations of chromosomes (through independent assortment and fertilization). Recombination vastly increases the genetic variability of a population, which in turn increases the rate at which a population can adapt to its environment. The evolution of sexual reproduction made possible a tremendous increase in the pace of organic evolution, and led to the evolution of multicellularity.

Reproduction among unicellular organisms involves individuals that are, in the absence of accidents, immortal. When a unicellular organism reproduces asexually, it divides to form two new unicells that will live to divide again. When a unicell reproduces sexually, it contributes all its substance to its offspring, and this is repeated at each sexual generation. In either case, each unicell contributes all of its substance to its descendants.

The situation is quite different in the case of multicellular organisms. The es-sence of multicellularity is the division of labor among specialized cells. And almost universally, among the first specialized cells to evolve were reproductive cells. When a multicellular organism reproduces sexually, it contributes only the substance of its reproductive cells to its descendants. The remainder of the multicellular organism may continue to live and may even reproduce again. But its genetic task is finished, it has produced recombinant offspring to be tested by natural selection.

A multicellular organism that outlives its ability to reproduce does little more than compete with its offspring for energy, nutrients, and other limited resources, thereby reducing the offspring's chance for survival. Natural selection favored genes that program the elimination of postreproductive individuals. Such genes decreased competition between generations and enhanced the success of new generations. Selection for such genes programmed the elimination of postreproductive individuals into the life histories of most multicellular organisms. The evolution of sexual reproduction, which led to the evolution of multicellularity, also led to the evolution of death.

duced in approximately ten days. Fruit flies have four pairs of chromosomes that can readily be studied under a microscope (Figure 13–1). Furthermore, fruit flies show considerable variation in body structure, and genetic crosses among flies with these variations can be made. Studies of *Drosophila* provided crucial evidence for the chromosome theory of heredity about 1914. We will discuss this evidence later in this chapter, after the basic laws of heredity have been presented. For now, we may simply say that specific traits can be correlated with changes in chromosome composition, not only in fruit flies but also in other organisms, including humans.

An important feature of the chromosome theory of heredity is the concept that each chromosome is composed of many *genes*. It is known that each gene determines the structure of one protein. In turn, a specific protein may produce or influence several traits, and most traits are probably influenced by many genes. In most organisms chromosomes occur in pairs. Genes, therefore, must also occur in pairs, so a specific trait may be affected by a specific pair of genes. In *Drosophila*, the larvae contain

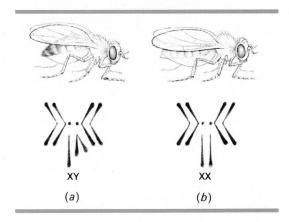

FIGURE 13–1 Male and female fruit flies (Drosophila) and their chromosomes. (*a*) The male sex chromosomes, XY. (*b*) The female sex chromosomes, XX.

giant chromosomes that are easily studied. It has been possible in these larvae to correlate specific characteristics with specific bands or regions on a chromosome. It will be shown later that it is likely that these bands correspond to genes or groups of genes. If we assume that these bands are genes, we can show that a specific characteristic is produced by genes that are distributed in the same pattern as chromosomes are distributed to offspring. But since chromosomes are the carriers of heredity, we must understand how chromosome distribution relates to the transmission of genetic traits. This occurs in the process of *meiosis*.

Meiosis: The Genetic Basis of Sexuality

Most organisms are capable of sexual reproduction. In this process, they produce gametes (sex cells) that come together in pairs to form new single-celled *zygotes* (individuals). The zygote then develops by means of a series of cell divisions to form a new multicellular organism (see Chapter 16). But we saw in Chapter 4 that gametes are *haploid*; that is, they contain one-half the chromosome number of a species. In humans, for example, the haploid chromosome number (*n*) is 23; the *diploid* number is therefore 2*n* or 46. Chromosomes of diploid organisms occur in pairs. We use the term *homologous chromosomes* to describe two members of a pair that are similar in size and shape and carry similar hereditary information. Each chromosome has a *centromere*, the region at which spindle fibers attach during cell division.

At fertilization, then, the gamete of each parent contributes one-half the number of chromosomes characteristic of the species. (One can easily see what would happen to chromosome numbers in succeeding generations if the chromosome number in gametes were not reduced by one-half.) The process by which this chromosome reduction occurs, producing gametes capable of carrying hereditary characteristics from generation to generation with a stable number of chromosomes, is called *meiosis*. The same phases we observed in mitosis in Chapter 4 occur in meiosis: *interphase, prophase, metaphase, anaphase,* and *telophase.*

Meiosis essentially involves two cell divisions but only one duplication of chromosomes (Figure 13–2). In the first division (meiosis I), the duplicated chromosomes are separated into two cells. One member of each duplicated homologous pair moves to each daughter cell. At this stage these cells are considered to be hap-

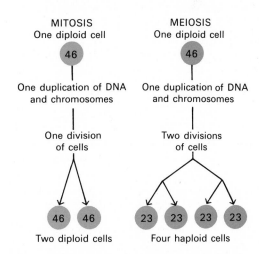

FIGURE 13–2 A general comparison of mitosis and meiosis. Mitosis produces two identical cells; meiosis results in four haploid cells, each containing half the number of chromosomes of the original diploid cell from which they came.

loid, because the nucleus contains only one member of each duplicated pair of chromosomes from the original nucleus, although it also contains a duplicate of that member. In the second division (meiosis II) each chromosome separates from its duplicate, and four haploid cells result (Figure 13–3).

About midway through a prolonged prophase of the first division, the chromosomes are observed to be doubled. Each strand is called a *chromatid*. Homologous chromosomes also become paired at this stage: each chromosome attracts its homologous partner, and the two become closely associated along their full length. This process, called *synapsis*, forms the basis for all subsequent meiotic events. Because one member of each chromosome pair comes from the individual's mother and the other from its father, we speak of the pairing of maternal and paternal chromosomes. The synapsed, duplicated chromosomes are called *tetrads* (tetra, "four") because the four chromatids are together, side by side (Figure 13–4). The centromeres apparently have not duplicated at this point, so each pair of chromatids shares only one centromere.

During synapsis, certain segments of the chromatids may *cross over*. That is, the chromatids may break and recombine with parts of other homologous chromatids. This causes an exchange of genetic information. The results of one crossover in one pair of gametic chromosomes are shown in Figure 13–5. In this diagram, letters represent *genes* (units of heredity). A comparison of crossover and noncrossover chromosomes shows how new combinations of genes may form in gametic chromosomes. The genetic significance of this process will be discussed later in this chapter. Here we shall make only two points: (1) crossover of chromosomes allows for the recombination of an offspring's grandparental genes, and (2) the ability of an organism to adapt to its environment depends in part on this recombination of genes.

At metaphase I, chromosomes are aligned on the equatorial plane. They then segregate at random. Each centromere-linked half of each tetrad has an equal chance of going to either daughter cell. The segregation possibilities for

the chromosomes at anaphase I can easily be visualized. If two pairs of chromosomes are involved, four possible chromosomal combinations can result (Figure 13–6a). When three pairs of chromosomes are present, eight different combinations are possible (Figure 13–6b). In humans, with 23 pairs of chromosomes, there are 8,388,608 possible combinations. To compute the segregation possibilities for an organism, we raise the base number 2 (the number of chromosomes in a pair) to an exponential power equal to the number of chromosome pairs in the species:

$$2^2 = 4, 2^3 = 8, \ldots, 2^{23} = 8{,}388{,}608$$

It is strictly a matter of chance which half of each tetrad goes to each daughter cell. We must assume, therefore, that each combination has an equal probability (chance) of moving to either daughter cell. This random segregation of chromosomes is a key factor in the fundamental principles of heredity.

In anaphase I, the tetrad separates between synapsed chromosomes (Figures 13–3 and 13–6), so an original chromosome and its duplicate move to each pole. The chromosome number is halved at this point, since a maternal chromosome and its duplicate go to one daughter cell, and a paternal chromosome and its duplicate go to the other daughter cell. Remember, however, that because of crossovers some parts of some chromosomes may have been exchanged.

Prophase II and metaphase II are usually very brief. During anaphase II, the centromere of each double-stranded chromosome divides, and the original chromosome and its duplicate are finally separated. Each chromatid moves to a separate cell. Each gamete receives a chromosome from each original homologous pair. Thus each homologous pair in a fertilized egg contains one chromosome from each parent— one from the egg and one from the sperm.

The meiotic events that occur in males to produce sperm are called *spermatogenesis;* the production of eggs in females is known as *oögenesis* (Figure 13–7). Figure 13–7 uses the chromosome number for humans, but the 2n and n may represent other numbers for other

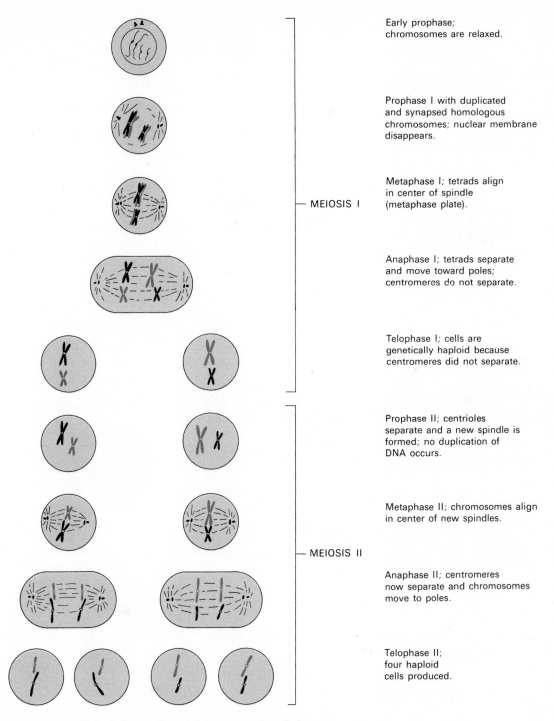

Early prophase;
chromosomes are relaxed.

Prophase I with duplicated
and synapsed homologous
chromosomes; nuclear membrane
disappears.

Metaphase I; tetrads align
in center of spindle
(metaphase plate).

MEIOSIS I

Anaphase I; tetrads separate
and move toward poles;
centromeres do not separate.

Telophase I; cells are
genetically haploid because
centromeres did not separate.

Prophase II; centrioles
separate and a new spindle is
formed; no duplication of
DNA occurs.

Metaphase II; chromosomes align
in center of new spindles.

MEIOSIS II

Anaphase II; centromeres
now separate and chromosomes
move to poles.

Telophase II;
four haploid
cells produced.

FIGURE 13–3   Meiosis in a cell containing two pairs of chromosomes. Duplication of chromosomes is shown in color.

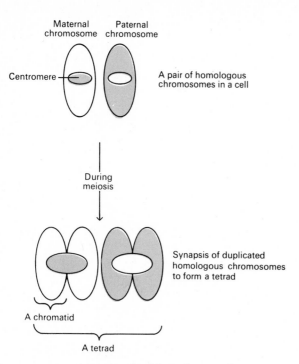

Maternal chromosome Paternal chromosome

Centromere —

A pair of homologous chromosomes in a cell

During meiosis

Synapsis of duplicated homologous chromosomes to form a tetrad

A chromatid

A tetrad

FIGURE 13-4 A pair of homologous chromosomes during the early stages of meiosis.

species. (We humans are complex organisms—in some ways we are the most complex known. You might therefore guess that we have the highest chromosome number among living species. But you would be wrong. Many organisms do have fewer; the diploid, or $2n$, number in some roundworms is 2, and in fruit flies it is 8. But in the lowly potato the diploid number is 48, two more than our 46, and in a few organisms such as crayfish, the number reaches 200.)

The major difference between spermatogenesis and oögenesis is that *polocytes* (polar bodies) are produced in oögenesis. In oögenesis one gamete is a full-sized egg, the other three are polar bodies that contain the haploid chromosome complement but only a small amount of cytoplasm. Although these polar bodies cannot be fertilized, this process conserves the egg cytoplasm and its protein-synthesizing ribosomes, which will be essential to a developing embryo.

Now that we have seen how the chromosomes are distributed in gametes, we shall re-

turn to the role that chromosomes (and genes) play in heredity. The details of meiosis just studied are a necessary background for understanding the processes by which genetic material is transmitted from one generation to the next.

BASIC MENDELIAN PRINCIPLES

Our discussion of genetic transmission begins with the work of Gregor Mendel. Mendel, whose experiments extended over an eight-year period, selected the garden pea as his experimental subject. This selection was fortunate because this organism has many characteristics produced by single pairs of genes. Also, because of the structure of the pea flower, self-fertilization usually occurs; this process had produced many pure strains of plants. An experimenter, however, can introduce pollen from another plant to produce cross-fertilization. Mendel (whose original paper is still worth reading) realized that simple experiments contrasting only one characteristic at a time were necessary to shed light on the principles of inheritance. He also realized the importance of keeping accurate records. Mendel selected seven pairs of contrasting characteristics on which he experimented individually. Two of these characteristics were the shape of the seeds—either round or wrinkled—and the color of the embryonic seed leaves (the cotyledons), which was either yellow or green.

Monohybrid Cross

A *hybrid* is an offspring organism that results when two genetically different parents are *crossed* (bred). A *monohybrid cross* is a genetic cross involving only one characteristic, such as smoothness in pea seeds.

Mendel started his work with pea plants that had round seeds and that produced only round seeds when they were self-pollinated—that is, they *bred true*. The offspring of this self-cross are called the F_1, or first filial generation. Mendel also had plants with wrinkled seeds that always bred true for wrinkled seeds when self-pollinated. When a variety producing round seeds was crossed with a variety producing

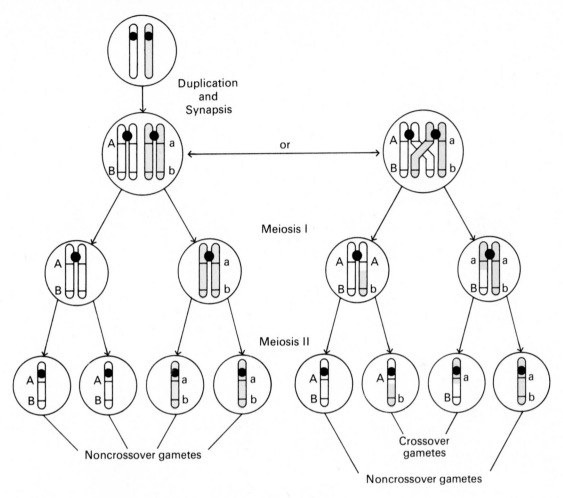

FIGURE 13-5 Comparison of the chromosomal changes that occur in noncrossover and crossover during synapsis of homologous chromosomes. Crossover occurs in almost all chromosomes.

wrinkled seeds, all the resulting hybrid seeds were round. The plants resulting from this cross (the F_1) were self-pollinated (crossed with themselves) to produce the generation called the F_2 or second filial. Some of the plants in this generation had round seeds, whereas others had wrinkled seeds. The ratio was approximately three round to one wrinkled (Figure 13-8). In this particular experiment, out of 7324 seeds obtained from 253 self-pollinated plants, 5474 were round and 1850 were wrinkled. Thus the wrinkled characteristic was not lost in the original cross.

Mendel's explanation of this cross is summarized in Figure 13-9. Each parent plant has two "units" for a given characteristic. When gametes are produced, each gamete gets one unit. Therefore, individuals produced from a cross between a round-seed plant and a wrinkled-seed plant would contain one unit of each characteristic. These plants in turn can form two kinds of gametes, and when they are crossed four fertilization combinations are possible. Approximately three-fourths of the resulting offspring would possess at least one unit for round seed, and three-fourths would also

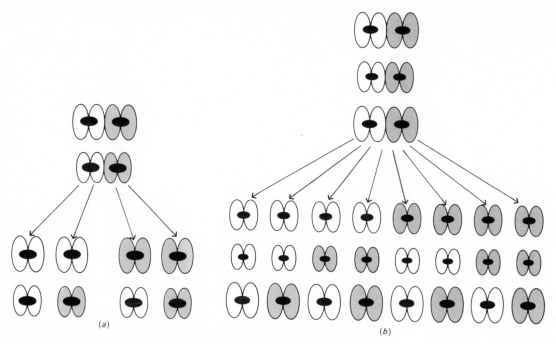

FIGURE 13–6 The possibilities of chromosomal combinations that can result at anaphase I. (a) Organism with two pairs of chromosomes. (b) Organism with three pairs of chromosomes.

have at least a unit for wrinkled seed. But since round seed is a *dominant* character, and wrinkled seed is *recessive*, individuals receiving a unit for round seed always produce round seeds, even if they also contain a unit for wrinkled seeds.

Mendel knew nothing about the process of meiosis. But his explanation of the cross was remarkably similar to the details of meiosis as we now understand them. The similarity between Mendel's "units" and the genes, we mentioned earlier is quite obvious. In fact, if we placed chromosomes in the scheme in Figure 13–9 and showed the units or genes on the chromosomes, we would have an illustration of the modern explanation of the inheritance of this trait. Thus in this example, the gene producing round seed is known as a *dominant gene* because it always produces its characteristic when it is present. Mendel pointed out that the units carrying simple traits act as discrete factors. This is known as *Mendel's Law of*

Segregation, and we have seen its basis in the process of meiosis.

Chromosomes occur as homologous pairs, and genes are located on chromosomes, so there are two genes for each trait. We call these genes *alleles*, by which we mean alternative or contrasting forms of genes that affect the same trait and that are located at the same position on homologous chromosomes. Alleles always line up beside one another when chromosomes undergo meiosis. Individuals of the pure round-seed variety have the makeup *RR*; since both genes are the same, we say that with respect to the round/wrinkled seed condition they are *homozygous* ("same in the zygote"). Individuals of the pure wrinkled-seed variety, with makeup *rr*, are also homozygous.

Each gamete, however, carries only one-half of the chromosome complement—either *R* or *r*. When a gamete carrying *R* unites with a gamete carrying *r*, a *hybrid*, *Rr*, is formed. We say that this hybrid is *heterozygous* ("different in

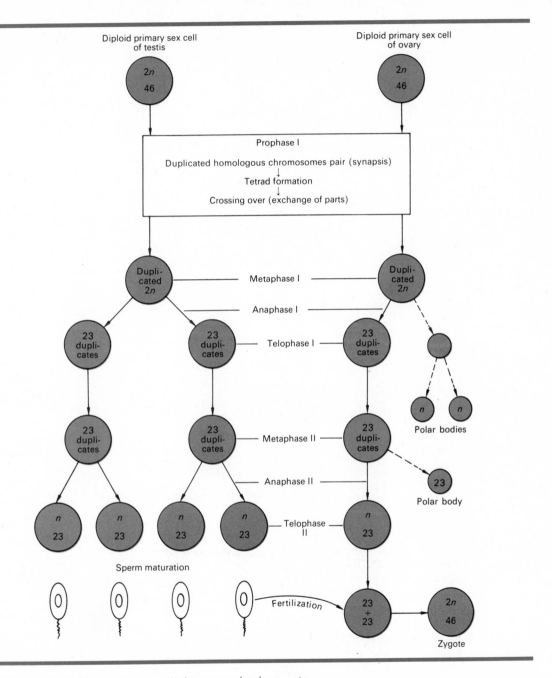

FIGURE 13-7 Meiosis as it occurs in human males (spermato-genesis) and in females (oögenesis). Fertilization of an egg by a sperm to form a zygote is also indicated.

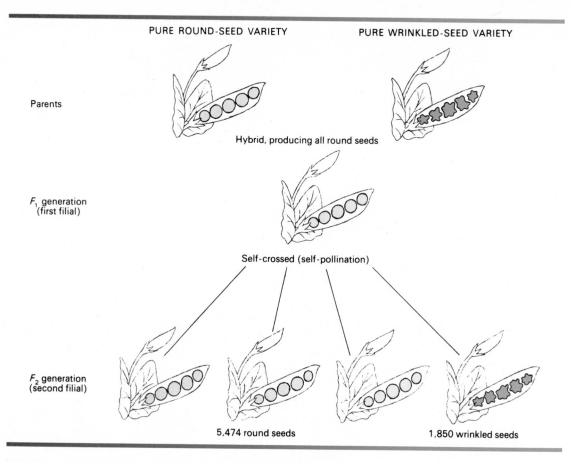

FIGURE 13-8 Mendel's experimental cross of round-seed pea plants with wrinkled-seed pea plants. The exact ratio obtained here was 2.96 : 1.

the zygote") with respect to the alleles for seed shape. The hybrid appears round, however, because of the presence of the dominant gene R. (Dominant genes are usually symbolized by capital letters and recessive genes by lower-case letters—here, R and r respectively.)

The observable characteristics of an individual are referred to as the *phenotype*, and its genetic makeup is called the *genotype*. Thus genotypes RR and Rr have the same phenotype, round seed. Although an Rr individual is round, the wrinkled gene r has not changed and will probably show up in the next generation if two hybrids are crossed. You may have noted already that it has a one in four, or 25

percent, chance of showing up when two hybrids are crossed.

When the heterozygous or hybrid individual, Rr, undergoes meiosis, two kinds of gametes are produced, R and r. If two hybrids are crossed, as in Figure 13–9, four fertilization combinations are possible:

<table>
<tr><td></td><td></td><td colspan="2">♂ gametes</td></tr>
<tr><td></td><td></td><td>R</td><td>r</td></tr>
<tr><td rowspan="2">♀ gametes</td><td>R</td><td>RR</td><td>Rr</td></tr>
<tr><td>r</td><td>rR</td><td>rr</td></tr>
</table>

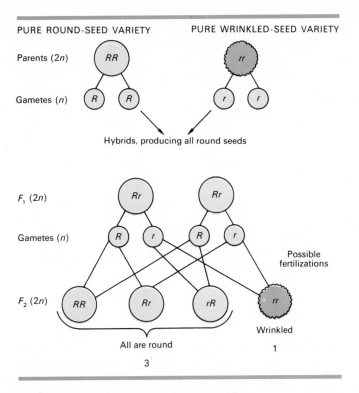

PURE ROUND-SEED VARIETY   PURE WRINKLED-SEED VARIETY

Parents (2n)

Gametes (n)

Hybrids, producing all round seeds

F_1 (2n)

Gametes (n)

Possible
fertilizations

F_2 (2n)

Wrinkled

All are round   1

3

FIGURE 13–9   Mendel's explanation of the cross of round-seed
pea plants with wrinkled-seed plants. R = a unit (gene) for round
seed; r = a unit (gene) for wrinkled seed. This explains the approximate 3 : 1 ratio obtained in his experiment (Figure 13–8).
Dominant genes are usually represented by capital letters and recessive genes by lower-case letters.

Note that the ratio of phenotypes (actual ap-
pearances) would be three round to one wrinkled, whereas the ratio of genotypes would be
one RR to two Rr to one rr.

Test Cross
In the cross between round (R) and wrinkled
(r) seeds, genotypes RR and Rr produced the
same phenotype. In breeding experiments it is
often important to know the exact genotype for
a particular trait—that is, to know whether an
individual is homozygous or heterozygous for
that trait. This can be accomplished by a *test
cross* (sometimes called a *back cross*). The organism under question is crossed with a pure
recessive, since the genotype of a pure recessive

is known. The genotype of the organism under
question can be determined by examining the
resulting ratios. When RR is crossed with rr, all
offspring will be Rr and will show the dominant characteristic. In a cross between Rr and
rr, however, one-half of the progeny will show
the recessive trait, rr (Figure 13–10). Therefore,
if all offspring are round, the plant being tested
is RR; if half the offspring are round and half
are wrinkled, the plant is Rr.

Incomplete Dominance
So far we have considered only genes that are
dominant or recessive; the fundamental laws of
heredity are most easily explained in these
terms. However, in many pairs of genes (al-

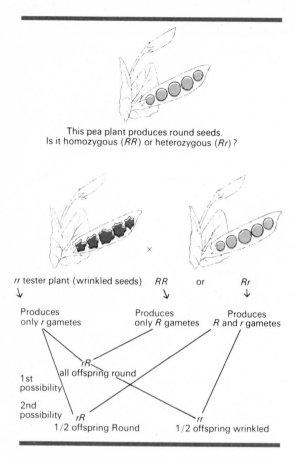

This pea plant produces round seeds. Is it homozygous (*RR*) or heterozygous (*Rr*)?

rr tester plant (wrinkled seeds)   *RR*   or   *Rr*

↓   ↓   ↓

Produces only *r* gametes   Produces only *R* gametes   Produces *R* and *r* gametes

rR
1st possibility — all offspring round

2nd possibility
rR   *rr*
1/2 offspring Round   1/2 offspring wrinkled

FIGURE 13–10 The process of making a test cross and examining the results.

leles), dominance does not occur. In these situations neither gene is dominant, and hybrids show an intermediate effect. This effect is *not* produced by a "blending of the genes," since further crosses of these intermediate hybrids will produce offspring showing the original parental types. The principle of inheritance involved here, called *incomplete dominance*, has been demonstrated by several classic experiments on flower color in a plant family commonly called the four-o'clock family. In one experiment, a white-flowering plant crossed with a red-flowering plant produces plants with pink flowers. When two pink-flowered plants are crossed, the resulting plants have a ratio of

one red, two pink, and one white (1:2:1) (Figure 13–11).

Later in this chapter we will note the importance of nondominant genes in determining human traits such as height and skin color.

Dihybrid Cross

Mendel also made dihybrid crosses—crosses involving two different traits. For example, he crossed round-seed, yellow seed coat plants with wrinkled-seed, green seed coat plants (hereafter referred to as "round, yellow" and "wrinkled, green"). Figure 13–12 shows the results of this cross, and the results are explained in Figure 13–13. The phenotype ratio resulting from this cross is:

9	3
round, yellow	round, green
3	1
wrinkled, yellow	wrinkled, green

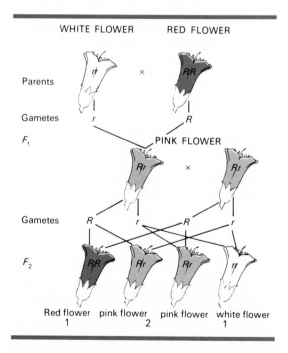

FIGURE 13–11 Inheritance of flower color in the four-o'clock family. This experiment demonstrates the principle of incomplete dominance of genes.

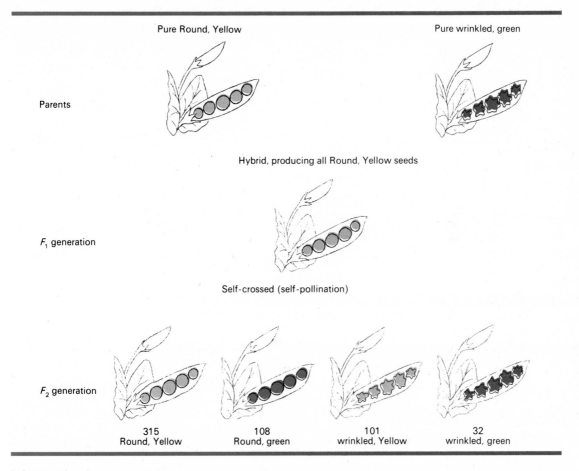

FIGURE 13–12 One of Mendel's experimental crosses involving two characteristics. Actual outcomes are very close to the theoretically expected ratio of 9 : 3 : 3 : 1.

Thus $\frac{9}{16}$ of the offspring show both dominant characteristics, $\frac{3}{16}$ show one dominant trait, $\frac{3}{16}$ show the other dominant trait, and only $\frac{1}{16}$ show both recessive traits.

We can explain these results by assuming that the two traits are controlled by different genes on separate chromosomes. Members of each pair of genes segregate independently, since they are on separate chromosomes. This principle is often called *Mendel's Law of Independent Assortment*. Note that when we are dealing with two pairs of genes on separate chromosomes, four kinds of gametes are possible. The principles of meiosis show why this is true. Members of a pair of homologous chromosomes normally never go to the same gamete (an unusual exception will be considered later). Whether the chromosome carrying R or the chromosome carrying r will segregate with the chromosome carrying Y or with the chromosome y is purely a matter of chance. If a large number of gametes are produced, we would expect a 1 : 1 : 1 : 1 ratio of RY, Ry, rY, and ry gametes (Figure 13–13).

Modified Dihybrid Cross: Gene Interaction

In some cases one pair of genes may interact with another pair to modify the phenotypic

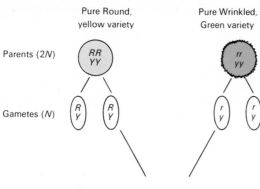

Pure Round,
yellow variety

Pure Wrinkled,
Green variety

Parents (2N)

Gametes (N)

Hybrids, producing all Round, yellow seeds

F_1 (2N)

Gametes (N)

gametes

gametes

F_2 (2N)

FIGURE 13–13   Explanation of Mendel's dihybrid cross.

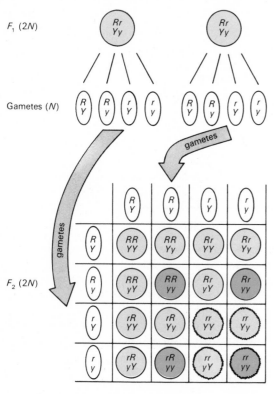

ratios in the F_2 generation. The suppression of a gene at one position on a chromosome by the action of a gene at another position is called *epistasis* ("standing above"). Coat color in mice illustrates this principle. Gray color (agouti) in mice is caused by a dominant gene (*B*). The

homozygous recessive condition (*bb*) produces a black coat. However, another gene (*A*) is necessary for any pigment to be produced. In the homozygous recessive condition (*aa*) no pigment is present, an albino results. This is true whether the mouse is *BB* or *Bb* or *bb*. Since two genes are involved here, we might expect a cross of two F_1 hybrids to yield a typical dihybrid ratio. But because of the epistatic action of one gene pair on another, the ratio is 9:3:4 (Figure 13–14). This is an example of gene interaction.

An example of epistasis in humans is the albino condition in blacks. Dark pigmentation genes are present, but they cannot express themselves in a phenotype because of the lack of a dominant gene that permits their expression.

Probability in Genetics

Mathematical *probability* is defined as *the ratio of the number of ways a particular event might occur to the total number of events possible.* Thus the probability P of an event X occurring is

$$P(X) = \frac{f}{n}$$

where f equals the number of events in which X is found, and n equals the total number of events that can occur.

In Mendel's dihybrid cross, it is a matter of chance whether a male gamete carrying the RY constitution will unite at fertilization with a female gamete carrying RY, Ry, rY, or ry. Chance also determines whether one of the other three types of male gametes will unite with a gamete carrying RY, Ry, rY, or ry. When we consider all the fertilization possibilities shown in Figure 13–13, we note that a $\frac{9}{16}$ probability exists for getting a round, yellow offspring from this cross. The probability is $\frac{3}{16}$ for a round, green offspring, $\frac{3}{16}$ for a wrinkled, yellow, and $\frac{1}{16}$ for a wrinkled, green. In certain genetic crosses, then, we can state a specific theoretical probability for obtaining a particular phenotype.

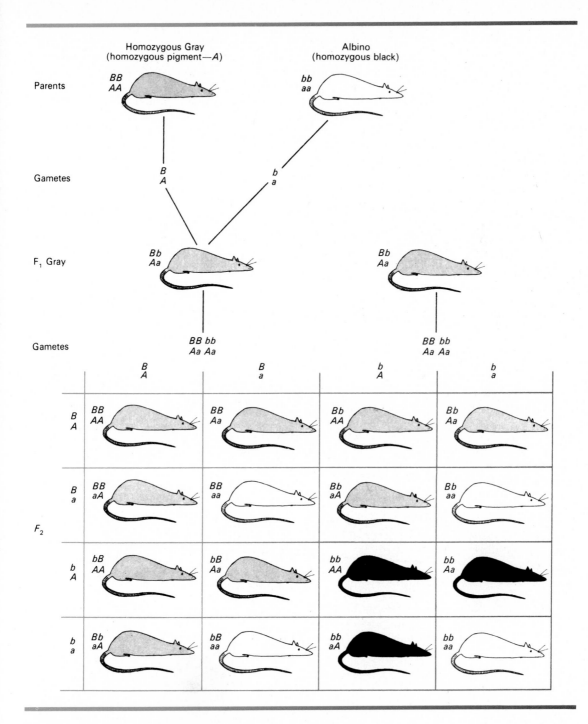

FIGURE 13-14   Gene interaction (epistasis) in mouse coat color.
The ratio produced is 9 gray : 3 black : 4 albino.

We stressed the role of chance in the independent distribution of chromosomes to produce various classes of gametes and in the union of gametes in fertilization. Since these events are matters of chance, they follow the laws of probability. Many other natural phenomena involving chance occurrence may also be stated in terms of probability. Examples are electron positions in the atom and weather conditions (weather forecasters speak of "precipitation probabilities").

In Mendel's cross between round-seed and wrinkled-seed plants, we note that the offspring would all have round seeds but would be heterozygous (Rr). When we cross these F_1 hybrids (or allow them to self-cross), what is the probability of obtaining a round-seeded offspring? From Figure 13–9 we see that the gametes could have united at fertilization as follows:

$\male$ gametes

	R	r
R	RR	Rr
r	rR	rr

$\female$ gametes

The probability of an offspring with round seeds can then be computed as:

$$P \text{ (round seed)} = \frac{f}{n} = \frac{3}{4} = 75\%$$

where f represents the number of events that will produce round seeds (RR, Rr, Rr) and n is the total number of events that can occur (RR, Rr, Rr, rr).

In humans, *albinism* (a condition in which the hair and skin lack pigment) is produced by a recessive gene. If two normal parents have an albino child, the series of events can be outlined as follows:

Parents Aa × Aa

Gametes A a A a Fertilization possibilities

F_1 AA Aa aA aa

In this case, A represents a normal pigmentation gene and a represents an albino gene. These parents may be concerned about the pigmentation of future offspring. Someone without much knowledge of either genetics or probability could compute for them the probability of having an albino child:

$$P \text{ (albino child)} = \frac{f}{n} = \frac{1}{4} = 25\%$$

The probability that these parents can have a normal child is:

$$P(\text{normally pigmented child}) = \frac{f}{n} = \frac{3}{4} = 75\%$$

Note that *all* the probabilities for any event always add up to 100 percent, or one: 75 percent plus 25 percent equals 100 percent.

The parents might also wish to know the probability of having two albino children in a row. This could be calculated by applying the principle of probability governing two events occurring at the same time or directly after one another. This principle states that *the probability of two independent events occurring jointly is the product of the individual probabilities.* Thus the probability of their having two albino children in a row would be:

$$P \text{ (two albino children)} = \frac{f}{n} \times$$

$$\frac{f}{n} = \frac{1}{4} \times \frac{1}{4} = \frac{1}{16}$$

Again, if we consider all the combinations possible if this family had two children, these must add up to one.

$$P \text{ (albino and normal)} = \tfrac{1}{4} \times \tfrac{3}{4} = \tfrac{3}{16}$$
$$P \text{ (normal and albino)} = \tfrac{3}{4} \times \tfrac{1}{4} = \tfrac{3}{16}$$
$$P \text{ (normal and normal)} = \tfrac{3}{4} \times \tfrac{3}{4} = \tfrac{9}{16}$$
$$P \text{ (albino and albino)} = \tfrac{1}{4} \times \tfrac{1}{4} = \tfrac{1}{16}$$
$$\tfrac{16}{16} = 1$$

Note that for each occurrence the probability of a child being albino is still $\tfrac{1}{4}$. However, if we are asked what the probability of having two albinos in a row is, before any children are born, the answer is $\frac{1}{16}$. This is like attempting to roll two sevens in a row in a dice game. Since there are six ways of making a seven with dice, the chance on a single roll is $\frac{6}{36}$ or $\frac{1}{6}$. The chance of rolling two sevens in a row, however is $\frac{1}{6} \times \frac{1}{6}$, or only $\frac{1}{36}$.

The probabilities involved follow the same law as those encountered in flipping a coin. The probability of flipping heads twice in a row is $\frac{1}{2} \times \frac{1}{2}$, or $\frac{1}{4}$. The probability of getting heads three times in a row is only $\frac{1}{2} \times \frac{1}{2} \times \frac{1}{2}$, or $\frac{1}{8}$. But of course the probability of getting heads is always $\frac{1}{2}$ for each individual flip, no matter what the outcome of earlier flips.

The principles of probability are important to plant and animal breeders. They often decide whether or not to conduct a particular breeding program by computing the probability of obtaining desired offspring.

BEYOND MENDEL'S WORK

Mendel provided the fundamental principles for our understanding of heredity. The study of genetics developed from his basic concepts of the way traits are passed from generation to generation. But since Mendel's time, biologists have found more relationships and come to new understandings of genetic mechanisms. Although these are extensions of Mendel's ideas, they often show more complexity because they involve interaction and position of genes or chromosomes.

Sex Determination

In the males of many species, the members of one pair of chromosomes are visibly different from the corresponding pair in females. In fruit flies, for example, the two homologous chromosomes labeled X are similar in females, but the corresponding chromosomes in males consist of only one X and a shorter homologue labeled Y (Figure 13–1). These chromosomes are called *sex chromosomes*, whereas other chromosomes are referred to as *autosomes*. All the traits we have discussed so far in this chapter have been carried by genes on autosomes. Genes on almost all parts of sex chromosomes

may exhibit a different pattern of inheritance than those on autosomes, because X and Y chromosomes are generally not homologous, and an individual receiving only one X chromosome will receive only one allele of the X chromosome genes. This changes the pattern of inheritance, as we shall see.

In many organisms, the differences between the sexes are ultimately caused by chromosomal differences. In some species the chromosome difference between the sexes is quite apparent; fruit flies are a good example. In the early 1900s it was noted that the females of many insect species had one more chromosome than males; for a while some thought that this was the universal difference between sexes.

Soon, however, the smaller Y chromosome was detected in the cells of fruit flies and in many other organisms, including humans. At first the X chromosome was thought to carry genes for determining femaleness and the Y chromosome genes for maleness. But this generalization was found to be untrue. In the fruit fly and many other organisms, the Y chromosome has very little to do with sex determination. Sex in fruit flies is determined by the *ratio* of autosomes to sex chromosomes; this seems to be the situation in most organisms. In humans (and presumably all mammals), however, a Y chromosome is necessary to produce male characteristics.

The correlation between visible differences and chromosomal differences in organisms certainly provides proof for the "chromosome theory of heredity." In one example, all individuals of a particular species with 22 chromosomes are females and all individuals with 21 chromosomes are males; the difference in sex is obviously caused by the chromosome composition. Various mechanisms of sex determination have evolved among organisms; some of them are listed in Figure 13–15.

Sex-Linked Heredity

In the late 1700s two examples were recorded of what we now know to be sex-linked heredity in humans—red-green color blindness and hemophilia, a disorder in which the blood clotting mechanism functions improperly. In each case

Organism	Male	Female
Human	44 autosomes + *XY*	44 autosomes + *XX*
Fruit fly	6 autosomes + *XY*	6 autosomes + *XX*
Grasshopper	20 autosomes + *X*	20 autosomes + *XX*
Fowl	16 autosomes + *ZZ*	16 autosomes + *ZW*
Honeybee	16 chromosomes (*N*)	32 chromosomes (*2N*)

FIGURE 13–15 Various mechanisms of sex determination. In fowl, sex determination is opposite to that of humans: females are heterozygous rather than males. To avoid confusion, the male is designated *ZZ* and the female *ZW*. Honeybees have no sex chromosomes; fertilized eggs develop into females and unfertilized eggs become males.

the trait is produced by a recessive gene carried on an *X* chromosome. Recall that human males have one *X* chromosome and one *Y* chromosome. The smaller *Y* chromosome generally does not contain the genes found on the *X* chromosome. Since females have two *X* chromosomes and males have only one, we would expect these traits to occur more often in males because in them a single recessive gene will produce the disorder. For example, a homozygous normal female (X^c,X^c) and her color-blind husband (X^c,Y) will produce sons with normal vision and carrier daughters (X^c,X^c). When a carrier daughter has children by a male with normal color vision, one-half of the daughters may be carriers (Figure 13–16). This pattern is often called "crisscross" inheritance, because an affected father can pass the gene to his daughters, who can then transmit it to their sons.

Experiments with *Drosophila* have provided many examples of genetic transfer mechanisms, and we can turn to this organism again for another example of sex-linked heredity. The case of red/white eye color is shown in Figure 13–17. Note that red-eyed daughters of the F_1 generation were produced by a red-eyed father and that in the F_2 generation red-eyed females transmit the trait to one-half of their sons.

Nondisjunction

The pattern of inheritance for red/white eye color in fruit flies had been worked out early in the 1900s by T. H. Morgan and his students. However, one of Morgan's students, Calvin Bridges, noted some exceptions to the F_1 pattern shown in Figure 13–17. On very rare occasions, a cross between a white-eyed female and a red-eyed male produced white-eyed females and red-eyed males. Such a cross normally produces only red-eyed females and white-eyed males. In order to explain these rare exceptions, Bridges postulated a phenomenon known as *nondisjunction* of chromosomes. Normally, homologous chromosomes separate at meiosis, with one member of each pair going to a gamete:

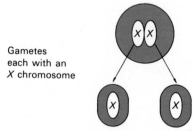

Gametes
each with an
X chromosome

If the chromsomes failed to separate—if nondisjunction occurred—then the gametes would appear as below:

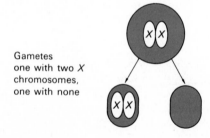

Gametes
one with two *X*
chromosomes,
one with none

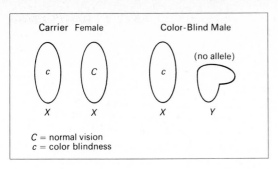

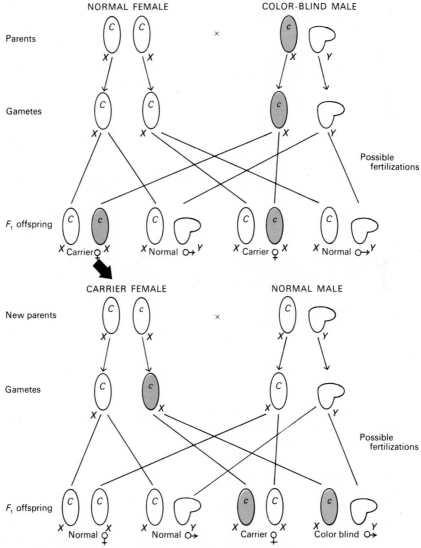

FIGURE 13–16 Sex-linked heredity in humans: the inheritance of red-green color blindness. Note that the daughter of a color-blind man can be a carrier and can pass color blindness to her sons. Color blindness in females, though not impossible, is less common because both recessives are required.

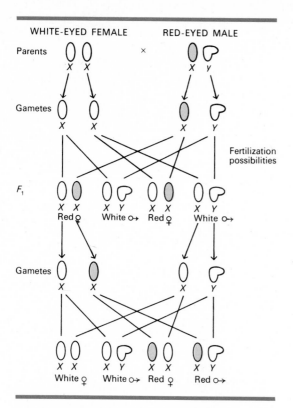

FIGURE 13–17   Sex-linked heredity in *Drosophila*: the inheritance of red/white eye color. Shaded *X* chromosomes indicate presence of the gene for red eyes; clear X chromosomes show the gene for white eyes.

A cross between a white-eyed female in which nondisjunction occurred and a red-eyed male is shown in Figure 13–18. By looking at cells of the offspring from this cross under a microscope, Bridges verified the chromosome compositions he had predicted in these offspring. This was the proof needed for the chromosome theory of heredity.

Nondisjunction has also been observed in human chromosomes, and several developmental phenomena such as *Turner's syndrome* and *Klinefelter's syndrome* have been traced to nondisjunction of the *X* chromosomes. Turner's syndrome results from union of an *O* egg (one without an *X* chromosome) with an *X*-carrying sperm to form *XO*. This individual is a sterile female with many male characteristics such as heavy neck muscles and narrow hips. In Klinefelter's syndrome, a nondisjunct *XX* egg unites with a *Y*-carrying sperm to produce *XXY*, a fundamentally male individual because of the presence of a *Y* chromosome. But this male possesses female characteristics, and sex organs do not reach maturity. Another anomaly, *Down's syndrome*, resulting in mongoloid individuals, is caused by the presence of an extra chromosome (number 21). An extra chromosome 21 may appear in human cells by three different mechanisms.

The most common genetic abnormality in Down's syndrome is *trisomy* (Figure 13–19a) in which the child has three number 21 chromosomes instead of the normal two. This occurs when chromosome pair 21 fails to separate during gametogenesis in the mother; the offspring thus has a total chromosome count of 47 instead of the normal 46.

Translocation, a process by which part of one chromosome breaks off and fuses with another chromosome, is a second mechanism that leads to Down's syndrome (Figure 13–19b). In this case, the total chromosome count is the normal 46, but, as in trisomy, the individual has an extra amount of chromosome 21. This originates from a carrier parent with 45 chromosomes resulting from translocation between chromosomes 15 and 21. In other words, one chromosome 15 of the carrier parent also has chromosome 21 material attached to it.

Mosaicism (Figure 13–19c), the third mechanism causing Down's syndrome, occurs when cells with different chromosome counts coexist in one individual. Skin cells, for example, may have 46 chromosomes, whereas blood cells may have 47 (an extra number 21 chromosome). This abnormality results from an error in division of an early embryonic cell; it is not passed to the individual from a parent.

Linkage and Crossing Over

Each species has thousands of genes that control the myriad chemical processes and structures necessary for life. But organisms do not have thousands of chromosomes, so each chromosome must contain many genes. We can further state that the genes on a particular

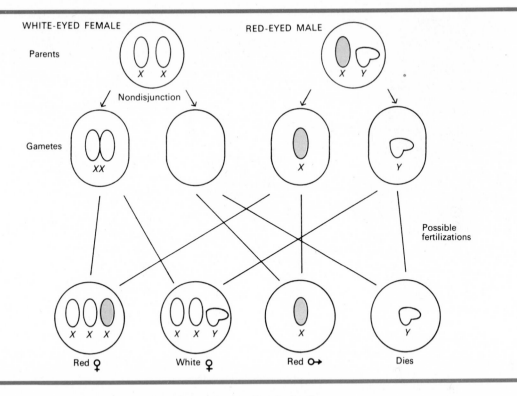

FIGURE 13–18 Bridges' explanation of the rare results obtained in this cross-nondisjunction.

chromosome are linked together in a group. For example, all the known genes in the fruit fly fall into four *linkage groups*, a fact that Morgan and his students recognized early in their studies. If Mendel had chosen traits other than the seven he experimented with, he might have noted linkage in peas. Figure 13–20 shows the locations of some of the genes on the number 2 chromosome of the fruit fly. The numbers on the left side of the diagram refer to the relative distances of genes from one end of the chromosome. This type of diagram is called a *chromosome map*. Fairly complete maps have now been made for all four chromosomes of fruit flies as well as for chromosomes of corn, some bacteria, and some viruses. A few chromosomes of mice and humans have also been partially mapped. Let us see how these maps are constructed.

In Figure 13–20, arrows point to two recessive genes—*b* for black body and *vg* for vestigial wings, a condition in which the wings are greatly reduced in size (Figure 13–21). The allele for normal gray body is usually indicated by *B*, and the allele for normal long wing is represented by *Vg*. Thus gray body and long wings are dominant over black body and vestigial wings. If we crossed flies homozygous for gray bodies and normal wings with black-bodied, vestigial-winged flies, the F_1 generation would all have gray bodies and long wings but would be heterozygous (Figure 13–22).

If these genes were on separate chromosomes, they would assort independently according to Mendel's law of independent assortment. (Recall that in his dihybrid cross, the two traits under consideration were carried on separate chromosomes.) But since the genes are linked, they should not assort independently at meiosis. Let us look at the results of an experi-

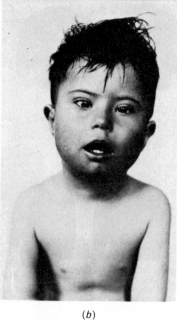
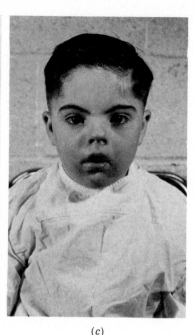

(a)   (b)   (c)

FIGURE 13–19   The three types of Down's syndrome. (a) Standard trisomy, 1 : 600 births, rarely familial. (b) Translocation, rare, familial. (c) Mosaicism, very rare, not familial. (From *Chromosome 21*; courtesy of The National Foundation—March of Dimes.)

mental cross between parents heterozygous for both of these traits (the F_1 of Figure 13–22). We can test cross individuals from our new F_1 generation with individuals homozygous for black body and vestigial wings (double recessive individuals). These double recessive "tester" flies can produce only one type of gamete, *b vg*, whether or not the genes for these traits are linked on one chromosome. If the genes are inseparably linked, our F_1 individuals would produce two types of gametes, *B Vg* and *b vg*; offspring from the test cross would be produced in a 1:1 ratio (Figure 13–23a). If the genes are not linked but are on separate chromosomes, however, four classes of gametes would be formed with equal frequencies: *B Vg*, *B vg*, *b Vg*, and *b vg*. Four kinds of offspring would therefore be produced in a 1:1:1:1 ratio (Figure 13–23b).

As it turns out, neither possibility provides the true answer. The results of the actual experiment are:

Gray body, long wings	965
Black body, vestigial wings	944
Gray body, vestigial wings	185
Black body, long wings	206
	2,300

All four types of offspring postulated in Figure 13–23b are present, but *not* in a 1:1:1:1 ratio. The two parental types—gray body, long wings and black body, vestigial wings—are present in almost a 1:1 ratio, but how can we account for the small numbers of the other two types of offspring? The answer lies in the fact that although the genes are linked, crossing over occurred, exchanging these genes on the homologous chromosomes. We considered the details of this process from a cytological viewpoint earlier in this chapter. An experimental cross, showing crossover, is diagrammed in Figure 13–24.

We further note that a total of 391 crossovers occurred (185 + 206); this is about 17 percent

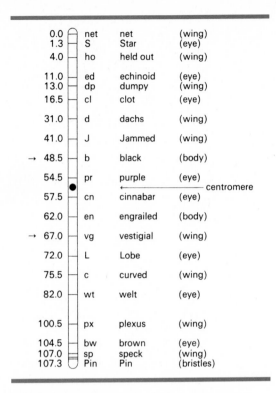

0.0	net	net	(wing)
1.3	S	Star	(eye)
4.0	ho	held out	(wing)
11.0	ed	echinoid	(eye)
13.0	dp	dumpy	(wing)
16.5	cl	clot	(eye)
31.0	d	dachs	(wing)
41.0	J	Jammed	(wing)
→ 48.5	b	black	(body)
54.5	pr	purple	(eye)
57.5	cn	cinnabar	(eye)
62.0	en	engrailed	(body)
→ 67.0	vg	vestigial	(wing)
72.0	L	Lobe	(eye)
75.5	c	curved	(wing)
82.0	wt	welt	(eye)
100.5	px	plexus	(wing)
104.5	bw	brown	(eye)
107.0	sp	speck	(wing)
107.3	Pin	Pin	(bristles)

←———————— centromere

FIGURE 13–20 **Map for the second chromosome of *Drosophila*.**

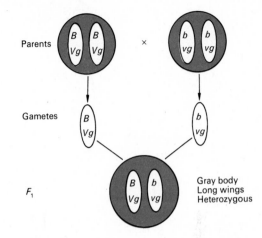

FIGURE 13–22 **Cross in *Drosophila* between gray-body, long-wing flies and black-body, vestigial-wing flies.**

of all the offspring produced (391 ÷ 2,300). If this cross were conducted again and again (and it has been), approximately the same percentage of crossovers would occur each time. The crossover frequency is directly related to the distance between these two genes on the chromosome. The closer two genes are, the lower the percentage of crossovers; the farther apart they are, the greater the percentage. This principle will be more evident if you examine the chromosome map in Figure 13–20 again. The units to the left of the chromosome map represent percent of crossovers.

In Figure 13–20, note also that the distance between the black-body gene and the vestigial-wing gene is 18.5 units, so we would expect a crossover rate of 18.5 percent. We have stated that the crossover frequency here is only 17 percent, and the discrepancy should be explained. Crossing over occurs all along the chromosome, and a *double crossover* between these two genes would return them to the original chromosome. This would obscure the actual percentage of crossing over between the two genes. In comparing the crossover rates of these two genes with other genes between them, we note that the true distance is closer to 18.5 than 17; the difference results from the double crossovers (Figure 13–25). Because multiple crossovers occur, crossover frequencies between widely separated genes may total more than 100 percent.

The mechanical processes that occur during crossing over are not completely understood. We can observe crossovers between chromatids under the microscope, and we can observe the offspring that are products of the gametes. Re-

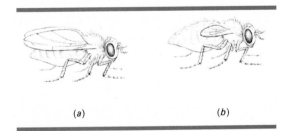

FIGURE 13–21 **Comparison of wings in *Drosophila*. (a) Normal. (b) Vestigial.**

(a)   (b)

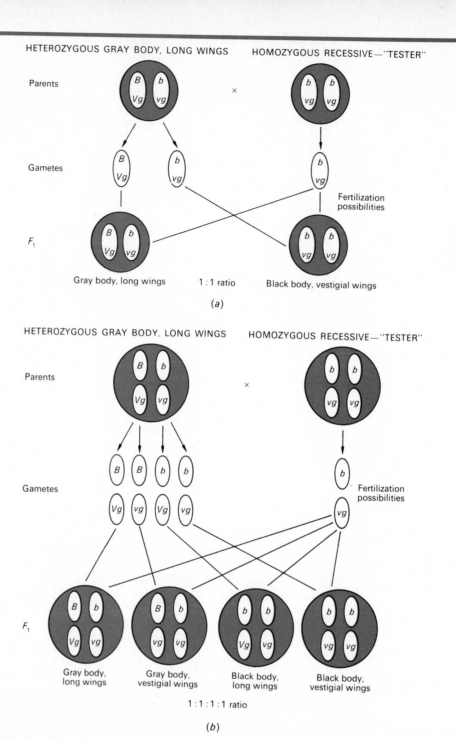

FIGURE 13–23 Test crosses of the F_1 produced in the cross shown in Figure 13–22. (a) Results if the genes are linked on the same chromosome. (b) Results if the genes are on separate chromosomes.

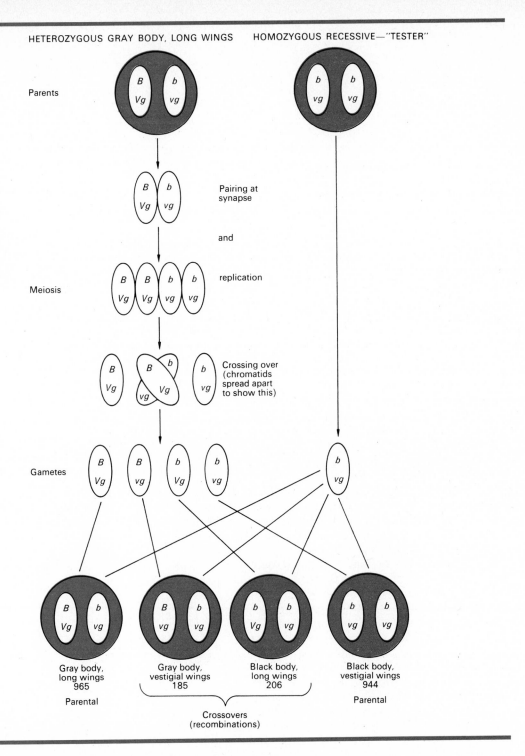

FIGURE 13–24 Explanation of the results of a test cross in *Drosophila* to determine whether the black and vestigial genes are linked and, if so, the amount of crossing over that occurs.

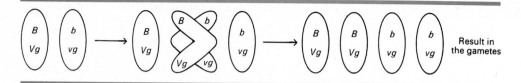

FIGURE 13–25   How double crossovers can return two genes to the same chromosome. The fact that crossing over occurred between these two genes could then be missed.

combination probably involves actual breaking and exchange of parts of homologous chromosomes during meiosis.

Abnormal Rearrangements in Chromosomes

Other structural rearrangements besides crossing over may occur in chromosomes. These alterations, known as *deletions, translocations,* and *inversions,* involve segments of one or more chromosomes (Figure 13–26).

Deletion occurs when some part of a chromosome breaks away during division and is lost in the cytoplasm. Deletion usually results in the production of zygotes that do not develop, because they lack crucial genetic information. A deletion may occur because of a single break at the end of a chromatid or as a result of two breaks in the middle of the arm. In the second case, the broken ends may fuse to save the remainder of the chromosome.

Translocation means that a segment of a chromosome has shifted from its normal position and fused with its homologue or even with a nonhomologue.

Inversion is the reversal of a section of a chromosome. It may happen as a result of a single break in a terminal segment or two simultaneous breaks in another portion. When a chromosome with an inversion pairs with its homologue in prophase of meiosis, it forms a loop called an inversion loop to facilitate gene-to-gene pairing (Figure 13–26c). If a crossover occurs within the loop during meiosis, certain regions can be repeated or deleted on one chromosome. When this occurs, chromosomes with either two centromeres (dicentric) or none

(acentric) may be produced. The dicentric chromosome is broken during division, and the acentric chromosome is lost completely. Cells do not usually survive such structural changes.

Multiple Alleles

So far we have treated a gene as though it could exist in only two forms—that is, as two alleles.

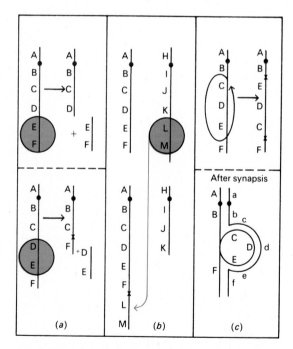

FIGURE 13–26   Three common types of chromosome aberrations. (*a*) Deletion (two types). (*b*) Nonhomologous translocation. (*c*) Inversion. Note the formation of the inversion loop during synapsis.

Thus we spoke of the gene for body color on the second chromosome of the fruit fly as producing either a gray body color (*B*) or a black body color (*b*). The vestigial-wing gene, however, may have five different forms, although we noted only two alleles, normal wings and vestigial. Three other intermediate alleles seem to exist—those which produce wings with a small nick at the tip (nicked), larger nicks (notched), and band-shaped, (strap)—but any individual fruit fly can have only two of these alleles.

There is no particular reason why a gene must have only two varieties or forms. If we assume that a normal gene changed once, it is natural to assume that it could change again. If the altered gene were successful in the environment, then it would be present in a definite frequency in the population. Some inheritance patterns can be explained only on the basis of *multiple alleles*—several forms of a specific gene.

Coat color in rabbits results from various combinations of any two of four different alleles at one locus (position) on the chromosome. Wild gray color (*C*) is dominant to all

others; chinchilla (*c^{ch}*) is dominant over the other two; Himalayan (*c^h*) is dominant to albino; and albino (*c^a*) is recessive to all the other alleles. Any individual rabbit has only two of these alleles, and its coat color is determined according to the hierarchical scheme listed.

A, B, AB, and O Blood Types

Blood types in humans also result from multiple alleles (in this case, three). Humans are placed in one of the four blood groups, A, B, AB, or O, on the basis of tests of *agglutination* (clumping of red corpuscles). This clumping occurs when *antigens* on the corpuscles react with *antibodies* in the plasma. Two different antigens, *A* and *B*, and two different antibodies, *a* and *b*, are known (Figure 13–27). A person with type A blood carries antibody *b*, capable of agglutinating the red blood corpuscles of type B blood. In transfusions, therefore, care must be taken not to administer blood that can be agglutinated by the antibodies of the recipient. Compatible and incompatible types are evident from Figure 13–27.

The three alleles listed below account for the

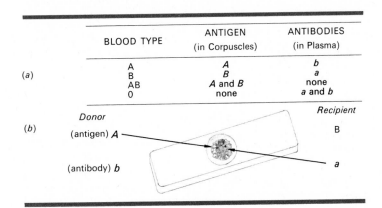

BLOOD TYPE	ANTIGEN (in Corpuscles)	ANTIBODIES (in Plasma)
A	*A*	*b*
B	*B*	*a*
AB	*A* and *B*	none
O	none	*a* and *b*

(*a*)

(*b*) Donor — (antigen) *A* — (antibody) *b*   Recipient — B — *a*

FIGURE 13–27   (*a*) Human blood types, showing distributions of antigens and antibodies. (*b*) The result of transfusing incompatible blood types. The antigen *A* in blood type A reacts with the antibody *a* in blood type B to produce clumping of the red blood corpuscles. Clumping also occurs if blood from a B donor is transfused into an A individual. From (*a*) we can see that type O blood can be given to all blood types, but O individuals can receive only type O blood. What other possible donor-recipient combinations are safe?

inheritance of blood type. (Since there are more than two alleles, the symbol I is commonly used to indicate the gene.)

I^O no antigen produced
I^A antigen *A* produced
I^B antigen *B* produced

The following genotypes then explain the various blood groups:

I^AI^A or I^AI^O type A
I^BI^B or I^BI^O type B
I^AI^B type AB
I^OI^O type O

This information is useful but not always conclusive in cases of disputed parenthood. On the basis of blood types it is possible to state only that a man could not possibly be the father of a specific baby, or that he could be the father. Blood type can also help to establish possible motherhood in disputes over parentage.

Rh Blood Factors

Other antigens also occur in human blood. One medically important antigen is designated as the Rh factor, since it was originally discovered in rhesus monkeys. When red blood cells from a rhesus monkey are injected into a rabbit, the rabbit makes antibodies against an antigen contained in these red blood cells. The antibodies thus formed cause a clumping reaction when added to rhesus monkey blood. Almost all members of the Mongoloid and Negroid races have this antigen and are classified as Rh-positive (Rh^+). About 85 percent of the Caucasian individuals in the world are RH^+. The remaining 15 percent of the Caucasian population have no antigen and are therefore termed Rh-negative (Rh^-). Individuals who are Rh^- also do not normally carry Rh antibodies.

Two theories have been proposed to explain the inheritance of Rh antigens: (1) a series of three closely linked genes on a single chromosome; and (2) one gene with at least eight alleles. Whichever theory is correct, we can deal with the situation by assuming that Rh^+ is

dominant to Rh^-. In this simplified explanation, then, Rh^+ Rh^+ = Rh^+; Rh^+ Rh^- = Rh^+; and Rh^- Rh^- = Rh^-.

The most common problems encountered with Rh factor occur in blood transfusions and in childbirth. An Rh^- person may be transfused once with Rh^+ blood with no adverse effects. When that occurs, however, the blood becomes sensitized and antibodies are produced. A second transfusion of Rh^+ blood may be fatal because of extensive agglutination. If an Rh^- mother bears an Rh^- child, no blood complications arise. Furthermore, no problems are usually encountered with an Rh^- mother bearing her first Rh^+ child. Seepage of blood across the placenta, however, may allow some Rh^+ red blood cells from the fetus to enter the mother's blood and sensitize her. A subsequent Rh^+ child is in serious danger of having its blood clumped by antibodies produced in this manner. This condition, known as *erythroblastosis fetalis*, may be fatal to the infant. No problem arises, however, if both the mother and father are Rh^- or if the mother is Rh^+.

Today Rh factor complications may be detected before birth and the infant may be given a complete blood transfusion. An Rh factor serum has also been developed which can be given to an Rh^- mother immediately after each childbirth to protect the next child. This serum contains Rh antibodies that destroy fetal Rh antigens before they can cause the mother to produce Rh antibodies.

Quantitative Inheritance

In previous examples we have spoken of traits in a qualitative sense—simply whether or not a given trait was present. Moreover, we have attributed most traits to a single gene. Mendel's peas, for example, had either round seeds or wrinkled seeds, and the trait was due to two alleles. Two groups were therefore present in the population, round-seed and wrinkled-seed varieties. Some characteristics of organisms, however, do not fit into discrete, contrasting groups. These characteristics show a continuous distribution in the population and are usually represented by the well-known *normal distribution curve* (Figure 13–28). Such traits

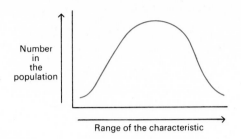

FIGURE 13–28 Normal distribution curve in the human population for traits such as intelligence and body stature.

are examples of *quantitative inheritance*. Characteristics such as these can be explained only on the basis of several nondominant genes that sort independently but exert a cumulative, or additive, effect on the particular trait. We have already considered the effect of one pair of nondominant alleles on a characteristic such as flower color (Figure 13–11). When two pink hybrids were crossed, the resulting ratio of phenotypes was 1:2:1 (1 red:2 pink:1 white).

What if a trait such as height in an organism is controlled by two pairs of alleles, each of which lack dominance but which together have a cumulative determining effect on that trait? The phenotypic ratio under these conditions would be 1:4:6:4:1 (Figure 13–29). In a trait produced by three pairs of nondominant alleles, the ratio would be 1:6:15:20:15:6:1. Such a ratio would produce a much smoother curve than one for only two alleles. Skin color in humans is thought to be produced by four to seven pairs of alleles.

ENVIRONMENT AND HEREDITY

We inherit genes, not traits. When we say that a boy got his brown eyes from his father, we really mean that he got the genes for brown eyes from his father. Every gene must develop in an environment, and the environment influences how that gene will develop. In the case of fruit flies, the vestigial-wing characteristic (Figure 13–21) will develop if the flies are raised at room temperature. If the flies are reared at about 92°F (33°C), however, the wings will be almost normal.

In the final analysis, the question, "Which is more important, heredity or environment?" has no meaning. There can be no "heredity *versus* environment" situation: both factors, heredity *and* environment, must interact for an organism to develop.

Still, we can get some idea of the *relative contributions* of heredity and environment to certain traits. To do this, we must determine the genetic mechanism for a particular trait. We must also determine how much effect the environment can have on the trait. Neither of these determinations is easy, but for a few traits they have both been made.

In the case of Down's syndrome, for example, we know that the presence of an extra number 21 chromosome sets limits on the development of the intelligence and largely determines certain other abnormal characteristics of the victim. Unfortunately, no amount of environmental manipulation can cause the victim's intelligence to exceed a certain "subnormal" level. Thus we can say that in the development of the phenotype of a person with Down's syndrome, heredity makes a relatively great contribution—by imposing severe limits.

But in most situations one can study, the role of the environment is very much in evidence. Identical human twins (twins with exactly the same genotypes) who have been reared apart show quite noticeable phenotypic differences, in personality and even in some physical characteristics.

The problem of assessing the relative contributions of heredity and environment to human intelligence is notoriously difficult—and controversial. On the one hand, many studies have shown high correlations between the intelligence of individuals and their degree of "relatedness" (genetic similarity). On the other hand, the many variables encountered in studies of this type make interpretation very difficult. But some studies have found correlations suggesting environmental factors influence intelligence more than genetic factors do. So the question of intelligence and inheritance is still very much up in the air. The problems and the controversy should not, however, obscure one basic fact: Intelligence, like any other trait, depends on the interaction of *both* genetic and environmental factors.

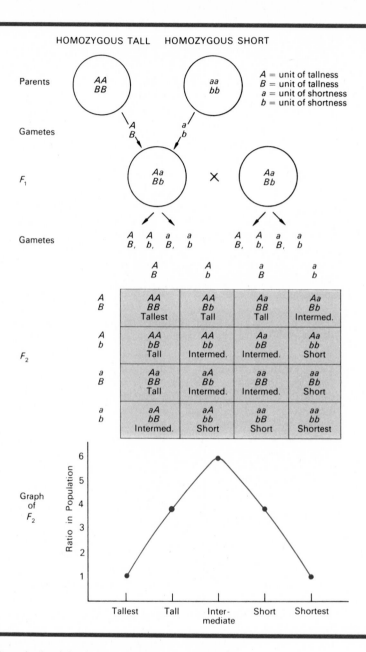

FIGURE 13-29 Quantitative inheritance of height in an organism assuming that the trait is produced by two pairs of cumulative, nondominant alleles. The graph of the F_2 generation shows a normal curve.

Bio-Topic: Genetic Conservation

Each time an endangered species goes out of existence, the genetic diversity of our planet is diminished. The loss of a few species each year may seem unimportant, but over time such losses amount to a global game of Russian roulette.

A species may be thought of as a gene pool—the sum of all the genes of all the individuals of the species. The alleles in a modern gene pool evolved and survived over many thousands of generations. Operating singly and in combination, these alleles direct the development and functioning of individuals that are adapted to a particular life style in a particular range of environments. Sudden, drastic changes may exceed the limits in which the gene pool can continue to survive. A gene pool subjected to such changes may go out of existence and be lost forever.

Our ability to cause sudden, drastic, and widespread environmental changes subjects more and more species to stresses they are unable to cope with. We first speak of these as endangered species, then as extinct species. The Eastern cougar and Oregon bison are extinct; the blue whales and grizzly bear are on the way out.

The loss of a species should concern us

for several reasons. An obvious reason is that the extinction of a species empties a link in a formerly balanced community. Our understanding of ecological interactions is not yet sufficient to enable us to predict all the consequences of disrupting the balance of natural communities. Ripple effects caused by an extinction often show up in unexpected ways.

Another reason is that contemporary species are the raw materials from which plant and animal breeders develop improved crops and livestock. The Green Revolution of the late 1960s is based on highly productive varieties of corn, rice, and other crops. These varieties were developed, in part, by introducing genes from wild varieties into domesticated varieties. Ranchers are now breeding beef cattle with buffalo. The goal is beefalo, cattle that will survive on the harsh, open range and still produce quality beef.

In other words, contemporary gene pools are a genetic resource. By "rescuing" endangered species from extinction—through zoos, game preserves, sperm banks—we can conserve a genetic resource that may later enhance or at least maintain the quality of our lives.

In this chapter we have discussed the mechanisms of hereditary transmission. Although we have said that these mechanisms involve genes located on chromosomes, we have not yet seen how genes produce their effects. The next chapter will discuss gene action.

SUMMARY

Chromosomes are the physical carriers of heredity. This was confirmed when it was shown that the results of inheritance experiments could be correlated with the behavior of chromosomes in cells. Chromosomes are distrib-

uted through meiosis, the process by which the chromosome number is reduced to one-half the normal, diploid number in the production of gametes. In meiosis, two cell divisions occur with only one duplication of chromosomes. Genes on chromosomes are sometimes redistributed, when crossovers occur between homologous chromosomes or when various combinations of chromosomes result from segregation.

The passing of genetic traits from generation to generation occurs with the transfer and recombination of the DNA in the chromosomes. Heredity follows Mendel's Law of Segregation and Law of Independent Assortment in mono-hybrid and dihybrid crosses and Mendel's concepts of dominance and recessiveness. The chance of occurrence of a genetic event can be predicted by using the laws of probability.

Further aspects of transmission genetics are: sex-linked heredity, linkage, crossing over, multiple alleles, and quantitative inheritance. Sex determination in most organisms can be correlated with a specific pair of chromosomes, the sex chromosomes. Since every gene must develop in an environment, variations in environmental factors can affect the expression of a gene.

REVIEW QUESTIONS

It is helpful to use a systematic approach in solving genetic problems. A dominant trait is usually indicated by a capital letter and the corresponding recessive trait by the corresponding lower-case letter. For example, R is used to indicate round seeds in peas, the dominant trait, and r is used for the recessive condition, wrinkled seeds.

Use this notation to list the genotypes of the parents in the problems that follow. Next, note the types of gametes produced by each parent. Then match the gametes of each parent against the gametes of the other parent in a checkerboard pattern like the ones used in this chapter to explain Mendel's work. You can then analyze the genotypes resulting from a cross to determine the possible phenotypes produced. Finally, tally similar phenotypes and express the result as a ratio. Some problems request the probability of a specific genotype or phenotype, which can be computed by using the approach just described. In each problem, determine exactly what the problem asks you to do. Then modify the above procedure according to the specific problem.

1. In tomatoes, red fruit color (R) is dominant over yellow (r). List the genotypes and phenotypes that could result from the following crosses: (a) $RR \times rr$ (b) $Rr \times RR$ (c) $rr \times RR$ (d) $Rr \times Rr$

2. Some species of plants have flowers that are red, pink, or white. Flower color in these species is determined by a single pair of genes. In one experiment pink was crossed with pink and the following ratio was obtained: 25 percent red, 49 percent pink, and 26 percent white. How can you explain this ratio?

3. In broccoli glossy leaves result from a recessive mutation and are susceptible to insects. Normally, broccoli has dull leaves. A farmer wants to eliminate the glossy trait from his crops. In this process he needs to determine which plants are heterozygous and which are homozygous. How should he proceed?

4. In humans, free earlobe (F) is dominant over attached earlobe (f), and the ability to taste phenylthiocarbamide (PTC) (T) is dominant over the inability to taste PTC (t). A woman with free earlobes who cannot taste PTC, whose mother had attached lobes, marries a man with attached lobes who can taste PTC but whose mother could not. What are the possible phenotypes of their children?

5. The polled or hornless (P) variety of cattle is dominant over horned (p). The heterozygous condition between red coat (R) and white coat (r) is roan. A polled, roan cow is mated to a horned, red bull. A horned, red offspring results. Show the genotypes of the parents and the offspring of this cross.

6. In fruit flies, long wings (V) are dominant over vestigial wings (v) and gray body color (B) is dominant over black body (b). A fly homozygous for both dominant traits is crossed with a fly showing both recessive traits. Diagram this cross, the F_1, and show the resulting genotypes. Now cross two of these and show all the genotypes and phenotypes of the F_2 generation.

7. A color-blind man marries a woman who has normal vision but whose father was color-blind. Describe the possible genotypes and phenotypes of their children.

8. Nondisjunction in human chromosomes causes developmental problems such as Turner's and Klinefelter's syndrome. Draw a diagram that shows how XO, XXY, and XYY can be produced.

9. If a man who is blood type O marries a woman who is blood type AB, can they have a

child with type O? With type B? With type AB? Explain.

SUPPLEMENTARY READINGS

Brown, Donald D., "The Isolation of Genes," *Scientific American*, August 1973. Two DNA regions containing the genes that code for ribosomal RNA in two species of African clawed toads were isolated. The process for accomplishing this is described in this article.

Goodenough, U. and R. P. Levine, *Genetics*, Holt, Rinehart, and Winston, New York, 1974. An up-to-date reference for all aspects of the field of genetics.

McKusick, Victor A., "The Mapping of Human Chromosomes," *Scientific American*, April 1971. Many genes are identified by their products. Most genes also have alternate forms or alleles, and it is possible to follow the distribution of these alleles through many successive generations. The position of certain genes on specific chromosomes can therefore be established.

Mendel, Gregor, *Experiments in Plant Hybridization*, Harvard University Press, Cambridge, 1948. This is a description of Mendel's original work, translated from his paper of 1866—an interesting, firsthand account of his now famous research.

Smith, Anthony, *The Human Pedigree*, J. B. Lippincott, Philadelphia, 1975. Although the theme is human genetics, new facts and new problems in the areas of reproduction, abortion, eugenics, artificial pregnancy, and future ethics are presented.

Winchester, A. M., *Human Genetics*, Charles E. Merrill, Columbus, OH, 1971. The transmission and genetic causes of many human abnormalities and diseases are discussed in simplified language.

Chapter 14

Heredity: Gene Action

The material in genes is the only physiological and chemical link between generations. If the gene is indeed the blueprint, what is the machinery it directs? Given the complexity of living systems, how can something as small as a gene contain all the information that living systems require to function? In short, how do genes work?

We have seen how important proteins are in the regulation of an organism's chemistry. It should not be surprising therefore that we begin this chapter by exploring *Gene and Protein Relationships.* In Chapter 13 we saw how geneticists have learned a great deal about the alignment of genes within chromosomes by tracking abnormal genetic situations and measuring their effects. So too have they been able to learn about the gene-protein relationship by researching abnormal examples of that relationship, particularly *Inborn Errors of Metabolism,* the basis of many diseases.

As we will see in this chapter, genes operate by controlling the protein-construction mechanism of the cell and directing the formation of specific proteins. The term "construction" might surprise you, but as you will see, *Protein Synthesis* is literally a building process

in which constituent amino acids are linked together according to the "plans" carried by the gene. The process begins with *DNA and the Genetic Code.* The key to the DNA molecule's ability to carry information in a code is the sequence of the nucleic acids (described in Chapter 3) that form the cross-links of the double helix.

As we move *Toward Defining a Gene,* we will look at the abnormal side of genetic functioning, *Mutations.* These alterations in the genes of an organism are the raw material of evolution, because they provide a comparison of traits which will be selected for or against by the environment.

The cumulative adjustments in our answer to the question, *What Is a Gene?* lead us to an interesting discovery. The best way to think of a gene is not as a specific cellular structure, but as a functional unit, identified more by what it does than by what it is.

Not all genes operate in the cells that carry them; nor do specific genes work all the time. The *Mechanisms of Gene Regulation* are composed of both proteins and gene components that turn genes on and off and regulate protein synthesis.

Some of the most active ongoing efforts in modern biology are attempts to learn how a gene, at the molecular level, produces a visible phenotype. Researchers are attempting to discover, trace, and explain the process of *gene action*, or *gene expression* as it is sometimes called. Up to this point we have been concerned with mendelian or classical genetics, the study of the transmission of genes from one generation to the next. But modern genetics focuses more on how the gene functions in a cell, the field of molecular genetics.

During the last three decades we have learned that this process is complex—but we have also unraveled many of its complexities. We now have a good, although incomplete, picture of the molecular mechanisms by which genes express themselves in phenotypes.

Experiments on peas, fruit flies, bacteria, and other organisms have shown that the distribution of hereditary characteristics follows specific patterns. But just how does the fundamental hereditary substance, DNA, function to produce these characteristics? In explaining how a gene produces its effect, we will follow the principle that DNA directs the synthesis of specific proteins in cells. This synthesis involves the intermediate functioning of RNA, and so our discussion of gene action will be based on the basic scheme mentioned in Chapter 4.

DNA → RNA → Protein

As we proceed with our discussion of gene action we will note several important studies that substantiate this concept. Our examination of hereditary processes will conclude with a look at some important recent work on gene-control mechanisms.

GENE AND PROTEIN RELATIONSHIPS

Research has definitely shown relationships between genes (segments of a DNA molecule) and proteins. Early observations and studies indicated that a gene might be responsible for production of a specific enzyme (protein) which could bring about a change in phenotype. Later, blood proteins were found to be produced under the direction of genes. Each gene was therefore assumed to produce one enzyme or one protein; the *one gene–one enzyme* theory was the first model used to explain gene action. This theory, correlating genes and proteins, provided the basic foundation for our understanding of how genes work. As research progressed, however, biologists learned that more than one gene is necessary to produce many proteins. One gene usually directs the synthesis of only one part of a protein molecule, a *polypeptide*. Thus the original concept of gene function has now been modified to *one gene–one polypeptide*. This new, more specific, relationship became possible as our knowledge of the structure of genes progressed.

The development of the concept of gene action is one of the most exciting episodes in the history of biology. Moreover, the mechanism of gene action has proved to be invaluable in advancing our knowledge in medicine and agriculture. We shall now follow the series of studies that led up to our modern theory of gene action.

Inborn Errors of Metabolism

The first notable discussion of gene action was published in 1908 by an English physician, Sir Archibald Garrod. In a book titled *Inborn Errors of Metabolism*, he dealt with a group of inherited metabolic disorders. As he traced the inheritance patterns of these diseases, Garrod noted that they seemed to be produced by the action of a single gene. One of the "inborn errors" he studied was *alcaptonuria*, a disease whose phenotypic manifestations (symptoms) include blackening of urine upon exposure to air and darkening of certain cartilages. The substance responsible for these symptoms is homogentisic acid, a carbon-ring compound that is split in the metabolism of normal individuals.

Garrod believed that alcaptonuria was caused by the inability of afflicted individuals to split this ring compound because of the absence or inactivity of an enzyme. He further hypothesized that the lack of an effective enzyme resulted from the absence of the normal

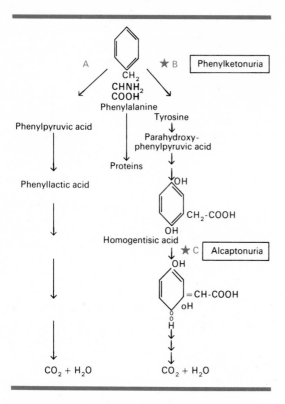

FIGURE 14–1 Partial metabolism of phenylalanine. This amino acid can be incorporated into proteins in the cell or converted to tyrosine or phenylpyruvic acid. If the enzyme at B is lacking, then most of the phenylalanine converts to phenylpyruvic acid, producing the disease phenylketonuria. If the enzyme at C is lacking (or defective), alcaptonuria results. Note that normally the ultimate products enter the Krebs cycle to produce $CO_2 + H_2O$. Several arrows in series indicate that intermediate products have been omitted.

form of a particular gene. Garrod was, then, suggesting that a gene is responsible for producing a specific enzyme—an idea that led to the *one gene–one enzyme* theory. During the 1930s researchers discovered that individuals afflicted with alcaptonuria lack the liver enzyme homogentisate oxidase, which is essential for catalyzing the reaction that splits the ring of homogentisic acid (Figure 14–1).

A more serious "inborn error" is the disease *phenylketonuria* (PKU), which produces extreme mental retardation in children. This disorder occurs when phenylalanine cannot be converted to tyrosine because an enzyme is missing (Figure 14–1). When this malfunction occurs, phenylpyruvic acid accumulates, affecting brain development. PKU has been shown to occur in individuals who are homozygous for a recessive gene. This is a fairly rare occurrence: only about one child in 25,000 in the United States is born with PKU. Urine tests can determine at birth whether an infant is phenylketonuric; such tests are mandatory in some states. If affected individuals are placed on low phenylalanine diets in the early years of their lives, most of the damage can be prevented.

A Suitable Experimental Organism: *Neurospora*

If we want to know what a gene is doing in an organism, it is better to study haploid organisms (those with one set of chromosomes) than diploid organisms (those with two sets). The reason is that in a diploid form, a recessive gene can be masked by a dominant allele, whereas in a haploid organism the single gene must express itself. George Beadle and Edward Tatum (who, with Joshua Lederberg, were later awarded the Nobel Prize in Physiology or Medicine for their work in genetics) took advantage of this fact and used the red mold *Neurospora* to study gene action. This mold is in the haploid state throughout most of its life cycle (Figure 14–2).

Neurospora is well suited to genetic experiments for the following reasons:

1. It can easily be grown in the laboratory on a *minimal medium* (sugar, inorganic salts, and biotin, a B vitamin).

2. The spores produced by meiosis are in a linear order (Figure 14–3) in a spore case, so they can be analyzed readily. (Spores are tiny cells each capable of germinating into a new organism.)

3. It can reproduce asexually as well as sexually, so various types can be propagated without genetic change.

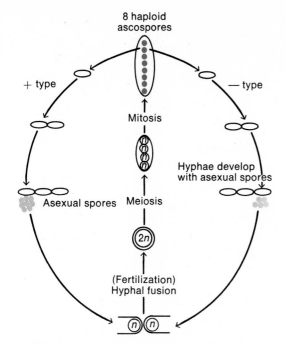

FIGURE 14–2 Life cycle of the red mold *Neurospora*. The events in the cycle start at the hyphal fusion stage (a hypha is a filamentous strand). The combining forms are represented as + and − types. Note that *Neurospora* can also produce asexual spores.

4. It is haploid throughout most of its life cycle, so recessive genes cannot be masked by dominant alleles.

Beadle and Tatum knew that it would be difficult to determine what a gene was doing if only the normal gene was available to study. If a gene could be changed so it no longer peformed normally, however, they would be able to study its action more closely. Figure 14–4 describes an analogous situation in an assembly line. Their objective, then, was to produce *mutations* (relatively stable changes) in genes and determine what related chemical changes occurred in the organism. By noting specific chemical differences between the mutants and the normal molds, they thought they could associate a normal chemical function with a normal gene.

The procedure used by Beadle and Tatum can be outlined as follows:

1. Asexually produced spores were x-rayed to produce mutations.

2. These x-rayed spores were crossed with another strain to produce eight haploid spores (ascospores).

3. The ascospores were then transferred to a complete medium that included minimal medium plus all the vitamins and amino acids; here they grew and produced colonies.

4. Portions of these colonies were next transferred to minimal medium; some could not grow there. Since all normal *Neurospora* can grow on minimal medium, those that could not were evidently mutated.

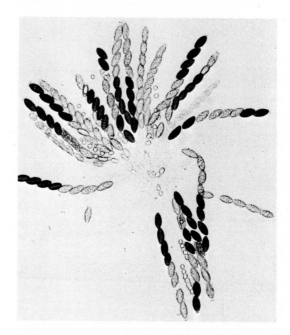

FIGURE 14–3 The spore-containing structures (asci) produced when a wild strain of *Neurospora* is crossed with a mutant that exhibits delayed maturation. The dark spores are the wild type; the lighter ones are mutant. Eight spores are produced in each ascus. When the spores are aligned with four dark and four light in an ascus, crossing over did not occur at meiosis. Other combinations indicate crossing over at meiosis. (Courtesy of Dr. David R. Stadler.)

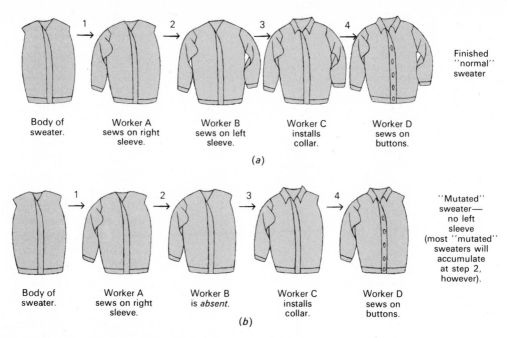

Body of sweater. Worker A sews on right sleeve. Worker B sews on left sleeve. Worker C installs collar. Worker D sews on buttons. Finished "normal" sweater

(a)

Body of sweater. Worker A sews on right sleeve. Worker B is *absent*. Worker C installs collar. Worker D sews on buttons. "Mutated" sweater— no left sleeve (most "mutated" sweaters will accumulate at step 2, however).

(b)

FIGURE 14–4   Hypothetical sweater factory, an analogue of the biochemical pathways in synthesis. (a) Normal assembly-line procedure, corresponding to normal functioning of a biochemical pathway. (b) Changed or interrupted assembly-line procedure, corresponding to mutated (abnormal) functioning of a biochemical pathway. When the normal sequence is changed or interrupted, the finished product is changed. If worker B is absent, for example, the factory piles up sweaters with no left sleeve, no collar, and no buttons. If worker C is absent, sweaters accumulate with no collar and no buttons. Thus, by observing the factory on a day when B is missing and on another day when C is missing, we can deduce that B puts on left sleeves, that C puts on either collars or buttons, and that B handles the sweaters before C does.

5. Beadle and Tatum hypothesized that these mutated forms had lost the ability to synthesize necessary vitamins or amino acids. Their next step was to transfer portions of colonies unable to grow on minimal medium to each of two different kinds of media—minimal plus vitamins and minimal plus amino acids. In this way they could determine whether the mutation had produced the inability to synthesize a necessary vitamin or a necessary amino acid. Those spores that grew on minimal-plus-vitamin medium and died on minimal-plus-amino-acid medium had evidently lost the ability to produce a particular vitamin; those

that displayed opposite results could not make certain amino acids.

6. The next step was to determine which vitamin or amino acid the mold was unable to synthesize. Beadle and Tatum accomplished this by placing portions of the mutant colony that could not synthesize necessary vitamins on individual cultures that each contained minimal medium plus one vitamin. If, for example, the mutants would grow only on minimal medium plus vitamin B_1, the mutants had evidently lost the ability to produce vitamin B_1. These steps are summarized in Figure 14–5.

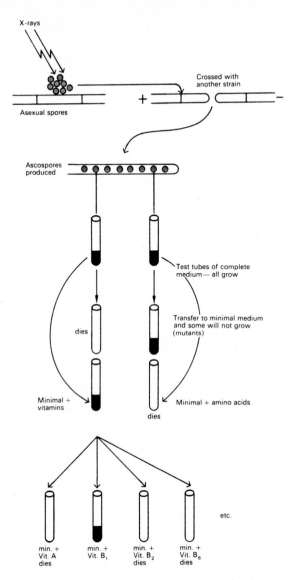

FIGURE 14-5 *Neurospora* experiment of Beadle and Tatum. Note that the mutant ultimately grows on minimal medium plus vitamin B_1 only.

Beadle and Tatum found that one of their mutants was unable to make vitamin B_1 because it could not produce a specific enzyme necessary for B_1 synthesis. They further hypothesized that this inability resulted from a mutated gene. Through genetic crosses of the mutant strain with a normal strain, Beadle and Tatum were able to show that inheritance of the mutant trait followed the pattern of Mendel's monohybrid cross. Their work thus strengthened the one gene–one enzyme theory of gene action held at that time.

Studies on *Neurospora* have been extremely helpful in tracing the biochemical pathways in the synthesis of vitamins and other products. Through the method of deductive reasoning shown in Figure 14-4, specific intermediate steps can be determined. These studies have made it possible to correlate steps in biochemical pathways with particular genes. Through these correlations we arrive at a better understanding of the way genes act. For example, several steps in the synthesis of niacin (another B vitamin) from anthranilic acid in *Neurospora* are known, as well as the enzymes that control these steps (Figure 14-6). We also know, on the basis of genetic crosses, that specific genes are responsible for the production of specific enzymes in this sequence of events.

Hemoglobin Studies: Mutuated Proteins

Another approach to understanding gene action was taken by Vernon Ingram at the University of Cambridge. Ingram reasoned that if genes determine the synthesis of specific proteins, an examination of two different proteins—one produced by a normal gene and one produced by a mutant gene—should reveal how the genes produced these different proteins. Of the several known deviant forms of human hemoglobin, perhaps the most familiar is the sickle-cell type. This deviation produces sickle-cell anemia, a hereditary disease transmitted by a single gene.

Ingram and his coworkers chose these two closely related proteins—normal hemoglobin and sickle-cell hemoglobin—for analysis and comparison. They degraded and separated each type into 28 peptide groups and searched for differences between the supposedly same peptides of each type of hemoglobin. The peptides in the two proteins were alike except for one peptide unit in which normal hemoglobin has a glutamic acid molecule that is replaced by a

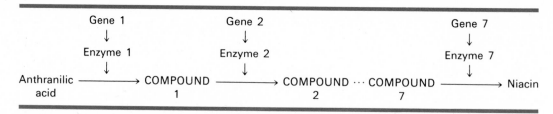

FIGURE 14-6 General scheme for the synthesis of niacin from anthranilic acid, showing the relationship among genes, enzymes, and intermediate compounds.

valine in sickle-cell hemoglobin. Thus the two proteins differ in only one amino acid out of 300. This difference may seem insignificant. But the shape of red blood cells containing sickle-cell hemoglobin can be radically changed and the circulation to tissues greatly reduced by that single amino acid variation. In much the same way, one loose electrical connection out of 300 in a TV set might also seem "insignificant." But it can, and usually does, make the set malfunction.

In looking for the mechanism that produced these structural changes, Ingram used the concept, noted in Chapter 3, that DNA provides a code for the construction of specific proteins. The gene would therefore be a segment of the DNA molecule whose nucleotide sequence would instruct the cell which protein to make

(Figure 14–7). We shall now look at the process by which DNA directs the synthesis of proteins.

PROTEIN SYNTHESIS

There is present in plants and in animals a substance which . . . is without doubt the most important of all the known substances in living matter, and, without it, life would be impossible on our planet. This material has been named protein.

These lines were written in 1838 by G. J.

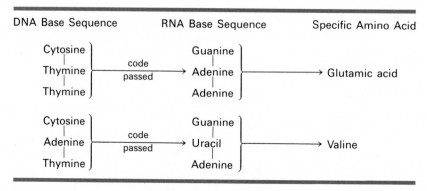

FIGURE 14–7 The coding of glutamic acid and valine. A change of only one nitrogen base (adenine for thymine) in the DNA base sequence changes the code in the RNA so that a different amino acid is incorporated into the protein.

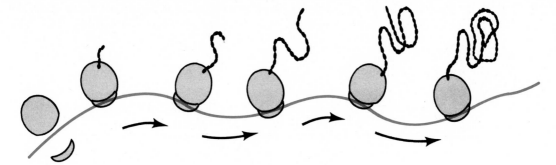

FIGURE 14–8   Simplified diagram of protein synthesis. The poly-peptide chain (protein) is formed as the ribosome moves along the mRNA molecule (colored line). Each dark unit of the polypepticle represents an amino acid.

Mulder, a Dutch chemist who was the first to use the word *protein* in print. The word was derived from the Greek *proteios*, meaning "primary" or "of first importance."

Our evaluation of protein's importance today is the same as the one Mulder made in 1838. But we know much more than he did about what proteins are and how they are made. One of the great biological discoveries of all time, the deciphering of the genetic code during the 1950s and 1960s, has enabled us to trace the synthesis of proteins from the "blueprint" stage to the "finished products" in muscle, skeleton, skin, enzyme, hormone, and so on.

Protein synthesis involves the DNA in chromosomes and three types of RNA: messenger (mRNA), ribosomal (rRNA), and transfer (tRNA). A DNA code is first transferred to mRNA, then the mRNA interacts with ribosomes and tRNA to produce a polypeptide chain. The ribosomes move along the mRNA as a polypeptide is synthesized. When the ribosome reaches the end of the mRNA strand, the completed polypeptide is released to become a functional protein (Figure 14–8).

The production of a specific polypeptide begins with chromosomal DNA, which contains the "blueprint," or code, for that polypeptide. (At this point it would probably be a good idea to review the structure and the self-duplicating process of DNA, outlined in Chapter 3, Figures 3–21 and 3–22.)

DNA and the Genetic Code

As we saw in Chapter 3, DNA is a long, double-stranded molecule. It consists of repeating pairs of nucleotides with nitrogen base pairs arranged in a meaningful pattern called a *code.* This code provides the information that governs protein synthesis. But how many nucleotides are involved in each information "unit"?

Since proteins are made up of various combinations of about 20 different amino acids, the DNA code must be capable of "recognizing" each of these amino acids. If the code were "one nucleotide–one amino acid" only four amino acids could be coded, because there are only four different DNA nucleotides. If a sequence of two nucleotides were used, 16 amino acids could be recognized ($4 \times 4 = 16$). Sequences of three nucleotides, or *triplet nucleotides,* could handle the operation ($4 \times 4 \times 4 = 64$) with plenty to spare. If the code were analogous to a language of letters and words, it would be reasonable that some of these triplet nucleotides would be synonyms for others, and some might serve as punctuation.

In fact the code does employ just such a "triplet" system. Each coded unit of genetic information, composed of three nucleotides, specifies the arrangement of nucleotides along a messenger RNA molecule. The code is therefore passed to mRNA. This three-nucleotide segment is known as a *codon.*

Messenger RNA and Ribosomes: Transcribing The Code

Because of the pioneering work of Severo Ochoa and Marshall Nirenberg in the early 1960s, we now know all of the triplet codons for the 20 amino acids (Figure 14–9). Note that most amino acids can be represented by more than one codon. Threonine, for example, may be represented by any of four different codons.

As messenger RNA is synthesized along a segment of chromosomal DNA, its nucleotides form a base sequence complementary to that portion of the DNA molecule (Figure 14–10). This phase of protein production is known as *transcription*. The coded mRNA then leaves the nucleus through a nuclear pore and combines with one or more ribosomes in the cytoplasm. Ribosomes consist of two parts of unequal size; each part, in turn, is composed of RNA and protein. The larger particle is called the 50s and the smaller one the 30s; the -s

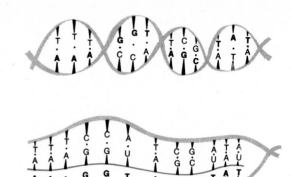

FIGURE 14–10   The transcription phase of protein synthesis. A segment of DNA opens by breaking the hydrogen bonds between nitrogen bases, and mRNA with complementary nitrogen bases, is synthesized along one strand. Note that the base uracil is found in RNA, whereas thymine is present in DNA.

designations refer to their respective rates of separation in an ultracentrifuge (Figure 14–11). Ribosomal RNA is synthesized by DNA in the nucleolus and may be stored there for some time before it is incorporated into ribosomes (Figure 14–12). In order to function, the two parts of a ribosome come together, clamping the coded mRNA molecule between them. When several ribosomes attach to mRNA, the resulting complex is a *polyribosome* (Figure 14–13).

Role of Transfer RNA

At this point another form of RNA—transfer RNA—becomes involved. Although tRNA is synthesized in the nucleus by the chromosomes, it has a very different structure than either rRNA or mRNA. The tRNA is a folded chain containing several areas of paired bases as well as at least three areas of unpaired bases.

Most models of the structure of tRNA are based on the "cloverleaf" design proposed by R. W. Holley in 1965. A chain of approximately 80 nucleotides is folded into a series of three major loops with one open end (Figure 14–14). Helical spiraling of the entire molecule has also been reported.

Amino Acid	RNA Codon	Amino Acid	RNA Codon
Phenylalanine	UUU	Aspartic Acid	GAU
			GAC
Threonine	ACU	Alanine	GCU
	ACC		GCC
	ACA		GCA
	AGA		GCG
Serine	UCU	Methionine	AUG
	UCC		GUG
	UCA		
	UCG	Glycine	GGU
Leucine	CUU		GGC
	CUC		GGA
	CUA		GGG
	CUG	Start	AUG
Tryptophan	UAU	Stop	UAA
	UAC		UAG
			UGA

U	uracil	C	cytosine
A	adenine	G	guanine

FIGURE 14–9   Messenger RNA triplet codons for some selected amino acids. Note that triplet AUG codes for methionine, but it is also the codon that initiates a coding sequence.

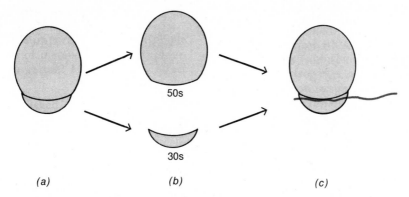

FIGURE 14–11 The three phases of ribosomes. (*a*) Nonfunctional. (*b*) Separate 50s and 30s particles. (*c*) Functional, when attached to messenger RNA (colored line).

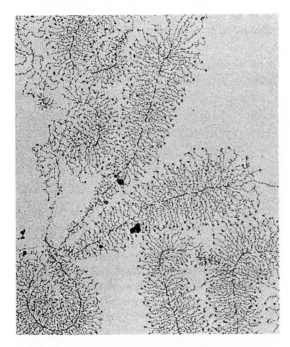

FIGURE 14–12 Electron micrograph of nucleolar DNA from a salamander egg synthesizing precursor molecules of ribosomal RNA ($\times$ 25,000). The long axial filaments are DNA, and the lateral fibrils are RNA molecules coated with protein. This is apparently the first photograph of DNA-directed synthesis of RNA and protein. (Courtesy of O. L. Miller, Jr., and Barbara R. Beatty, Biology Division, Oak Ridge National Laboratory.)

When tRNA begins its function in protein synthesis, an amino acid becomes attached by an ester linkage to one strand at the open, "acceptor" end, which terminates in the unpaired bases C—C—A. Specific enzymes and

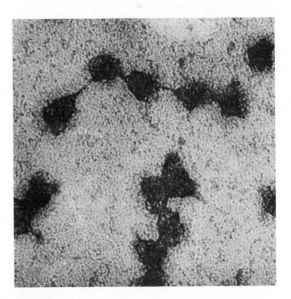

FIGURE 14–13 Electron micrograph of polyribosomes (the dark bodies), each consisting of several ribosomes ($\times$ 400,000). The strand connecting the polyribosomes is probably messenger RNA. (Courtesy of Alexander Rich, Massachusetts Institute of Technology.)

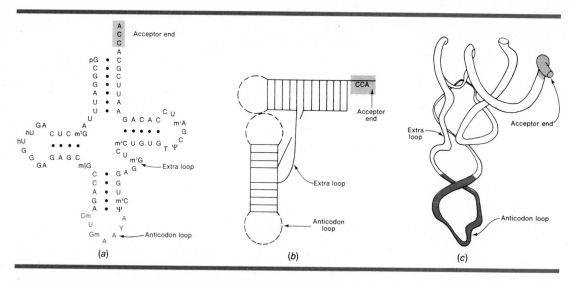

FIGURE 14–14   Three representations of tRNA structure. (*a*) Cloverleaf model of yeast phenylalanine tRNA. (*b*) Diagram of cloverleaf twisted into L shape. (*c*) Perspective diagram showing the helical loops of the L-shaped model. The unfamiliar letter symbols represent nitrogen bases of slightly different structure. (Redrawn from "Three-Dimensional Structure of Yeast Phenylalanine Transfer RNA: Folding of the Polynucleotide Chain" by Sung-Hou Kim *et al., Science,* Vol. 179, pp. 285–288, January, 1973. Copyright ⓒ 1973 by the American Association for the Advancement of Science.)

ATP are required to attach amino acids to tRNA molecules. Opposite to this amino acid end is the *anticodon* loop of tRNA, containing three unpaired bases that complement a specific mRNA triplet codon. These two counterparts, codon and anticodon, provide the "recognition" necessary to bring a particular amino acid into a prescribed polypeptide (Figure 14–15a). There are one or more tRNA molecules for each of the 20 amino acids. Each type of tRNA must be linked to the particular amino acid specified by the anticodon so that a specific amino acid can be brought into sequential order along the mRNA (Figure 14–15b and c). In this manner tRNA molecules "read" the message contained in the mRNA and construct a polypeptide as dictated by the code, which came originally from the DNA molecule.

The Process in Action

In order for protein synthesis to get started, then, several components must come together. A complex must be formed between mRNA, tRNA, and the ribosomes. This process requires a high-energy nucleotide similar to ATP, called guanosine triphosphate or GTP. Moreover, a specific nucleotide triplet is required to initiate the process of linking amino acids together to form a polypeptide. AUG, a code for methionine (an amino acid containing sulfur), has also been found to signal "start" (see Figure 14–9).

The 30s portion of the ribosome appears to have specific attachment sites for messenger RNA. The 50s subunit is thought to contain two functional areas, one for an incoming tRNA molecule and its specific amino acid,

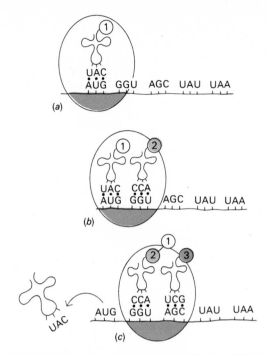

FIGURE 14–15 Translation of mRNA by tRNA in the ribosome. (*a*) The 50s and 30s ribosomal particles clamp onto one end of mRNA, and a tRNA anticodon pairs with the first codon of mRNA. (*b*) The ribosome complex shifts to the next codon, and a second tRNA comes into position. (*c*) A peptide linkage forms between the first two amino acids, and the ribosome shifts to the next codon as a third amino acid is brought in. The first tRNA is now released to the cytoplasm, where it can combine with another amino acid.

and another for the synthesis of peptide bonds. The entire ribosome moves along the messenger RNA chain as tRNAs bring in their amino acids and peptide bonds are formed. Several proteins, which probably function as enzymes, have been found to be necessary for the formation of these bonds. After donating an amino acid to the growing polypeptide chain, each tRNA is released to the cytoplasm, where it may pick up another amino acid. When the end of the mRNA molecule is reached, the completed polypeptide chain is released and the ribosome splits into its original subunits. Three different nucleotide triplets—UAA,

UAG, and UGA—have been found to signal termination of a "message" and trigger the release of the completed polypeptide. In the language analogy, these triplets may be thought of as "periods." And since none of them carries a code for an amino acid, all three convey just one message: "stop."

As the peptide comes off the ribosome (even while more remains to be synthesized), hydrogen and disulfide bonds (discussed in Chapter 3) form between certain amino acid components of the peptide chain to complete the secondary and tertiary protein structure. The messenger RNA molecule may either be read again or it may dissociate into unreadable fragments and return to the cytoplasmic pool of nucleotides. The following summary of the step-by-step process of protein synthesis is correlated with the numbered segments in Figure 14–16.

1 Double-stranded DNA with hydrogen-bonded nitrogen base pairs contains the information for the synthesis of a specific protein.

2 Strands of DNA separate, and messenger RNA (mRNA) is synthesized along one strand of DNA by complementary base pairing. Note that uracil is present in RNA but not in DNA and that thymine is absent in RNA.

3 The strand of messenger RNA, containing triplet nucleotide code sequences (codons), leaves the nucleus and enters the cytoplasm, where one or more ribosomes attach to the mRNA molecule. The RNA making up the ribosomes is produced in the nucleolus and may be stored there before becoming a ribosome.

4 Transfer RNA (tRNA) molecules, synthesized by DNA in the nucleus, leave the nucleus and pick up a specific amino acid (represented by circled letters) in the cytoplasm. ATP energy is required to form this linkage.

5 The three unpaired bases of the tRNA molecule's anticodon loop "recognize" the corresponding mRNA codon, so the appropriate amino acid is brought into correct position in

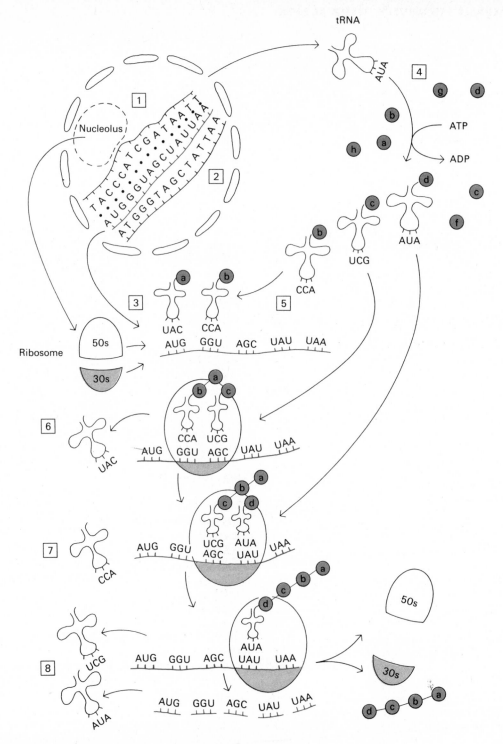

FIGURE 14–16 Summary of protein synthesis. The numbers
within squares correspond to the numbered steps in the text.

the mRNA-ribosome complex. Energy is provided by GTP.

6 The ribosome now moves to the next codon, and the next specified amino acid is brought into position by another tRNA. With energy from GTP, a peptide linkage is formed between the first and second amino acids. The first tRNA is released and may pick up a new amino acid from the cytoplasm.

7 The ribosome continues its movement along the mRNA molecule until all the amino acids necessary for the protein being synthesized are brought into position and peptide linkages are formed between the amino-acid molecules.

8 When the ribosome reaches the end of the mRNA, it separates into its 50s and 30s components. The mRNA may be "read" by another ribosome, or it may break up. The specifically ordered polypeptide is released and assumes its final secondary and tertiary structure.

TOWARD DEFINING A GENE

The word *gene* was first used in 1909 to indicate a single unit of heredity that occupied a specific position on a chromosome. Today, more than half a century of intensive research has left that original definition woefully inadequate. What, then, should replace it? We shall see that several lines of research have led to new ideas about the gene itself as well as to new data about its role.

Mutations

Since DNA directs protein synthesis, changes in the DNA code should cause changes in the proteins produced. We call such changes *gene mutations;* they apparently involve only one or a few nucleotides in a chromosome (Figure 14–7). Hugo DeVries, whose Mendelian experiments were mentioned in Chapter 13, proposed the mutation concept in 1901 to account for some sudden changes he observed during his experiments on the evening primrose. Such

spontaneous mutations occur at random, for unknown reasons; their rates vary considerably among organisms and among specific genes. *Induced mutations,* on the other hand, may be caused by exposure to radiation or to certain chemicals. The frequency of spontaneous gene mutations is given roughly as one per 100,000 to one per 1,000,000 cells. The mutation rate for the gene that produces hemophilia is rather high (one in approximately every 40,000 gametes, whereas the gene producing aniridia (absence of an iris, the colored portion, in the eye) mutates in humans with a frequency of about one in every 200,000 gametes.

Chromosomal and gene mutations are crucial in the evolutionary process because they are the only source of new "raw material" on which natural selection can work. In Chapter 13 chromosomal changes (mutations) such as deletions, translocations, and inversions were discussed. Some of these changes can result in phenotypic changes and can therefore be considered as mutations. In some cases the reshuffling has an effect because of a gene's new position on a chromosome. In other words, a gene's function may be altered by its association with its new neighbors. In addition, new *combinations* of chromosomes and genes can be produced through meiosis, crossing over, and random fertilizations, but these processes simply reshuffle already existing material.

Most mutations are usually harmful. Since a long selection process has resulted in well-adapted organisms, any change in evolutionary development is more likely to be harmful to organisms than helpful. We should therefore expect useful mutations to a well-adapted organism to be quite rare. There is an important distinction, however, between what is harmful or helpful to *individual organisms* and to *populations* or *whole species.* A nonfatal mutation might be marginally harmful, or merely useless, to the individual in which it occurs. But over a long period of time, during which climatic or other environmental conditions might change, that harmful mutation could become a useful mutation to the organisms in which it survived. We shall have more to say about this when we discuss evolution in Unit VIII.

If a mutation is to be passed on to the off-

spring of an organism, it must occur in gametes. Mutations in body cells, which often
reveal themselves as patches of abnormal tissue,
are not transmitted to the next generation.

Mutations that are harmful to a particular
species may be selected by humans for their
own benefit. A seedless condition in oranges
(Figure 14–17) can obviously be harmful to the

particular plant whose ability to reproduce by
seeds has been lost, but to humans it represents
a fruit that can be eaten conveniently. The
Ancon breed of sheep, characterized by extremely short legs, arose from variant individuals first described in Massachusetts in 1791. We
now know that this short-legged condition is
caused by a single gene mutation. For the sheep

Bio-Topic: Microbes, Mutations, and Medicine

*The first antibiotics, sulfa drugs and peni-
cillin, became widely available during the
early years of World War II. Since then,
antibiotic therapy has become an essential part of modern medical practice. New
antibiotics are developed each year to replace old ones that have become less effective. And we must continue to develop
new antibiotics in order to keep pace
with the evolution of pathogenic bacteria.*

*Alexander Fleming's discovery of antibi-
otics dates back to 1928. Fleming was preparing to discard several cultures of the
mold Penicillium that had become contaminated with bacteria. He noticed that
bacteria nearer the mold had grown less
than those further away. He speculated
that the mold produced a substance,
which he called an antibiotic, that inhibited the growth of the bacteria. Fleming
was able to prove his guess correct, and
thus began the age of antibiotics. The antibiotic made by Penicillium is now
known as penicillin.*

*The production of antibiotics is a way
of life among microbes that live in soil
and compete fiercely for limited nutrients.
Any microbe able to inhibit its competitors will have more nutrients available
for itself. Hundreds of antibiotics have
been isolated from hundreds of different
microbes. Relatively few have the combination of properties that make them suitable for medical use: the antibiotic inhibits disease-producing bacteria, is nontoxic*

*to humans, and can be purified and pro-
duced economically.*

*In general, antibiotics inhibit pathogens
by interfering with some essential cellular
process. Penicillin, for example, interferes
with the synthesis of bacterial cell walls.
A penicillin-sensitive bacterium exposed
to penicillin continues to make cytoplasm but cannot make new cell wall.
The bacterium eventually outgrows and
splits its old cell wall and is killed. Other
antibiotics affect other essential cellular
processes such as the synthesis of DNA,
RNA, or proteins.*

*Antibiotics are not universally or per-
manently effective. One reason is that
sensitive bacteria become resistant as a
result of rare, spontaneous mutations. A
mutation in an operator gene, a repressor
gene, or in any codon, may make a bacterium and all its descendants resistant to a
formerly inhibitory antibiotic. The longer
an antibiotic is in use, the more common
are mutant strains that have become resistant to the antibiotic. "Hospital staph"
and super-resistant gonorrhea strains are
common examples of such mutant
strains.*

*Each time a new antibiotic is intro-
duced for general use, the cycle is repeated as the target bacteria inevitably
evolve resistance. The antibiotic industry
is rather like the White Rabbit in Alice
in Wonderland—it must run faster and
faster just to stay in the same place.*

FIGURE 14–17   Seedless navel oranges. The seedless condition is the result of a natural mutation. (Grant Heilman.)

this condition is definitely detrimental, since it restricts their movement. But for their human owners it is advantageous because lower fences are sufficient to contain the sheep.

Some of the first induced-mutation experiments were those performed with x-rays on *Drosophila* in 1927 by Herman J. Muller, who later won the Nobel Prize in Physiology or Medicine for his contributions to genetics. Since that time, numerous experiments have shown many chemicals and radiations to be mutagenic (to cause mutations). The list of chemicals includes formaldehyde, peroxide, caffeine, nicotine, nitrous oxide, 5-bromouracil, 2-aminopurine, and mustard gas. Heat, ultraviolet light, and high-energy radiation such as x-rays, gamma rays, alpha and beta particles, and cosmic rays can also be mutagenic.

How these many agents act to bring about mutations is still a puzzle to biologists. The mutations must somehow change the DNA molecule by changing one or more base pairs in the normal sequence of its nucleotides. A group of compounds known as base analogues, represented in our list of mutagens by 5-bromouracil and 2-aminopurine, are similar in structure to the normal purine and pyrimidine bases in

DNA. The fact that these base analogues are highly mutagenic suggests that one of them could replace a normal base in a certain position and then pair with a different normal base. This would bring about a change in the original nucleotide sequence. Such a process could, for example, change the base pair thymine-adenine to cytosine-guanine. When such a change occurs, T—A to C—G (or A—T to C—G, or T—A to G—C, etc.), the message coded in DNA has been changed (Figure 14–18). This kind of change would produce a difference in only one amino acid out of hundreds—the difference between proteins such as normal and sickle-cell hemoglobins. Modern medicine uses base analogues, as well as x-rays and other radiation, to interfere with the mechanism of abnormal cell growth in cancer.

Bacterial and Viral Genetics

For an experimental study to be successful, it is extremely important to select organisms that

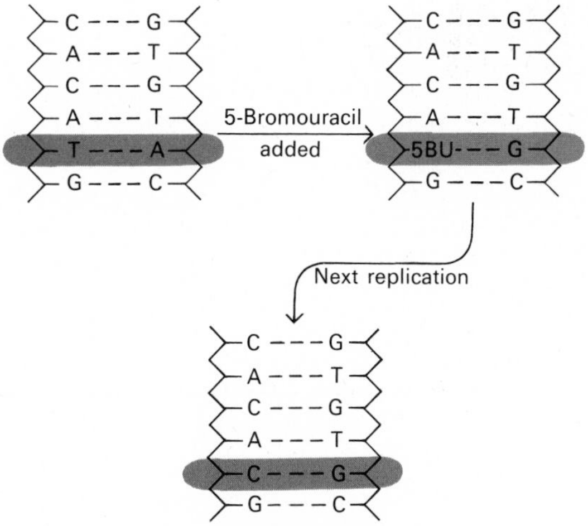

FIGURE 14–18   Hypothetical events that might produce a change in the code of the DNA molecule. First, 5-Bromouracil (5-BU) replaces thymine; then, during replication, 5-BU pairs with guanine (G). In the next replication, cytosine (C) replaces 5-BU and combines with guanine. The ultimate effect is a change from a T-A base pair to C-G.

are well suited for the investigation of the particular problem. The fruit fly, for example, has been of immense value in the study of transmission genetics, and *Neurospora* has distinct advantages for studies of gene action. In studies on the fundamental hereditary material, viruses and bacteria, which have all their genes in one chromosome, have been helpful. In bacteria and some viruses, the chromosome is circular and consists only of DNA (Figure 2–8). Other viruses, however, have a chromosome made up of RNA. Genetic studies of bacteria and viruses have suggested that genes are far more complex than we originally thought. For example, it is now evident that crossing over and mutation can occur within genes as well as between genes.

In 1946 *conjugation* (or sexuality) in bacteria was discovered. In this process a bridge is formed between two bacteria of compatible strains, and genetic material is passed from donor to recipient (Figure 14–19a). The amount of genetic material transferred varies with the length of the conjugation period.

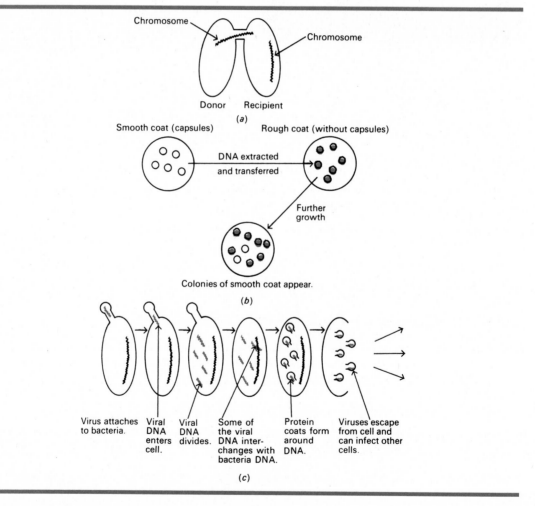

FIGURE 14–19   Types of genetic transfer in bacteria. (*a*) Conjugation. (*b*) Transformation. (*c*) Transduction.

Another means by which genetic transfer may be accomplished in bacteria is *transformation*, a process in which DNA extracted from one strain of bacteria is taken up by another strain. This process, performed in the laboratory, gave some of the first strong indications that DNA is the chief substance of heredity. For example, pneumococcus bacteria (producers of bacterial pneumonia) are typically enclosed in smooth capsules. But a mutation may produce bacteria that appear irregular and rough because they cannot make a capsule.

Bio-Topic: Carrots, Frogs, . . . , and People

The DNA of a fertilized egg contains the genetic instructions for the assembly of a complete organism. When an egg divides mitotically, each resulting cell receives a complete copy of the egg's DNA. Repeated mitotic divisions lead to the formation of an embryo and eventually an adult, made up of millions of cells. Barring rare mutations and errors in mitosis, each of these millions of cells contains a faithful copy of an egg's DNA. Any nucleus of an adult organism should thus contain all the genetic instructions for the assembly of a complete and identical individual.

F. C. Stewart of Cornell University was the first person to produce an organism from cells that were not eggs. Stewart began with cells isolated from a carrot. The cells were first grown in a nutrient solution, then transferred to a solid medium that contained nutrients and hormones. The cells became organized into distinct tissues that eventually developed into a normal carrot that produced flowers and seeds.

R. Briggs and T. King of the Institute for Cancer Research in Philadelphia pioneered similar work with animals. Briggs and King stimulated an unfertilized frog egg to develop by puncturing it with a fine glass needle. They then removed the egg's haploid nucleus and replaced it with a diploid nucleus from a cell of a frog embryo. In many but not all cases, eggs with transplanted nuclei developed into

normal embryos, suggesting that the donor nucleus contained all the genetic information needed for the assembly of a complete individual.

These elegant experiments were later extended by J. B. Gurdon of Oxford University. Gurdon began with eggs of the African clawed toad, the nuclei of which were killed by ultraviolet irradiation. Gurdon then transplanted a donor nucleus from an intestinal cell of a tadpole. The unfertilized egg containing the donor nucleus developed normally. In fact, Gurdon produced dozens of genetically identical frogs by transplanting many donor nuclei from one tadpole into many irradiated eggs. The technique, called cloning, demonstrates that the DNA in a single nucleus contains the genetic instructions for assembling a complete individual.

It has been suggested that humans could be cloned. The nucleus of an unfertilized human egg would be removed or inactivated, then replaced by a donor nucleus from an outstanding philosopher, artist, or scientist. Or a parent could choose to fertilize an egg with one of his or her own nuclei. The egg carrying the donor nucleus would be implanted into a willing "incubator mother" and allowed to develop. In this way, we could produce genetic copies of ourselves or other desirable persons at will.

Are we ready for such a world? And is it only the DNA that makes the difference?

DNA can be extracted from a colony of smooth, encapsulated bacteria and introduced into a culture medium containing rough-coated bacteria. When this is done, a small proportion (but higher than the mutation rate) of smooth colonies appear among the rough colonies (Figure 14–19b). The DNA from the smooth bacteria is thought to become incorporated into the DNA of the rough strains. If the protein but not the DNA from encapsulated bacteria is placed in the culture medium containing rough-coated bacteria, transformation does not occur. The fact that DNA is required to bring about transformation gives support to the role of DNA as the carrier of heredity.

Recently, we have learned that transformation can involve transfer of particles of DNA smaller than the bacterial chromosome. Tiny extrachromosomal bits of DNA called *plasmids* can pick up pieces of DNA from the chromosome of one bacterial cell and transfer them to another cell. In 1973, Stanley and Cohen and his coworkers at Stanford University produced functional DNA molecules in a test tube by combining segments of plasmids from *Escherichia coli* (*E. coli* for short), a species of bacteria found in the human colon. Later, they transferred plasmid genes from a staphylococcus bacterium (*S. aureus*) into *E. coli*. Carrying these experiments in plasmid engineering further, Cohen and others transferred genes from a single toad's cell into bacteria! Their experiments involved splitting DNA molecules and splicing them back together through the use of enzymes. This type of genetic manipulation presents interesting possibilities—and potential problems—as we shall see in Chapter 21.

A third type of genetic transfer in bacteria is *transduction* (Figure 14–19c). In this process *bacteriophages* (often shortened to *phages*), which are viruses that infect bacteria, transport DNA from one bacterium to another. Originally it was thought that these viruses were eating the bacteria and the term phage (from the Greek *phagein* meaning to eat) has since been used. After a virus enters a bacterial cell, the DNA of the virus can combine with the DNA of the host under certain conditions. The viral DNA then uses the protein synthesis mechanism of the bacterium to reproduce itself. After the reproduced viruses leave a bacterium, they can transfer part of that bacterium's DNA to another bacterium. Evidence from several studies indicates that only the DNA enters the bacterium cell; the protein jacket stays outside. This is one more bit of evidence that DNA is the genetic substance.

Some viruses contain DNA as their chromosomal material but others have RNA; genetic studies have been conducted on both types. We will consider the DNA-containing T2 and T4 viruses that infect *E. coli* (Figure 14–20). These viruses consist of a head, a tail base or end plate bearing spikes, and tail fibers. The effects of phages can be studied rather easily since they leave *plaque* (a clear area) in a bacterial culture where they have destroyed the bacterial cells. Mutant forms of phages can be studied, and often identified, by the type of plaque that develops when they infect their hosts.

A T4 virus attaches itself to the surface of an *E. coli* cell by the tail fibers and spikes of the end plate. The tail then penetrates the cell wall, permitting DNA to pass into the cell from the head of the virus (Figure 14–21). Upon entering the cell, the viral DNA takes over the protein synthesis machinery of the bacterial cell, causing it to make viral DNA and protein. About one-half hour after infection, approximately 200 new viruses have been produced; they destroy the cell, leaving it as the cell membrane ruptures. (This process is called *lysis*; plaques form where it occurs.) To be infective, a normal virus must be complete: the head, tail, end plate, and other structures must be put together in an orderly manner. More than 40 genes are known to control the normal development of a T4 phage, and more than 75 mutations have been identified that can interfere with normal development.

William B. Wood and R. S. Edgar from the California Institute of Technology have studied the steps involved in normal assemblage of a T4 virus. They infected bacteria with various mutants, determined which parts of the virus had been constructed, and analyzed electron micrographs of the viral structures at various stages. Through these experiments, they constructed a partial genetic map of the T4 virus chromosome (Figure 14–22).

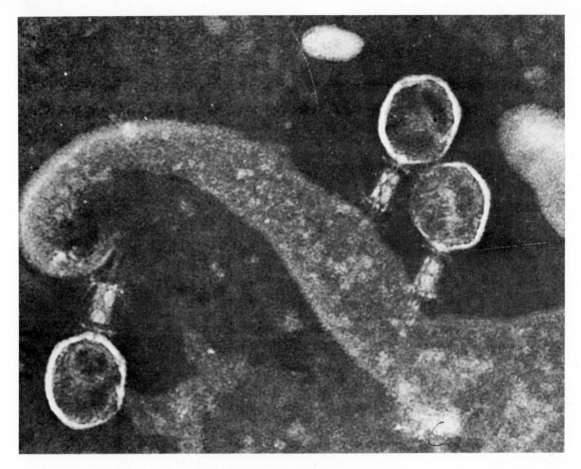

FIGURE 14-20   Electron micrograph of T2 bacteriophages attached to a fragment of a bacterial cell wall (× 200,000). (Courtesy of Dr. R. W. Horne.)

What Is a Gene?

Experiments on *Drosophila* gave us an understanding of the gene in terms of recombinational (crossing over) and mutational units. *Neurospora* studies shed light on the gene as a functional unit—on what it actually does in the cell. Microbial genetics (studies of bacteria and viruses) made a twofold contribution: first, transformation and transduction experiments confirmed the fact that DNA is the hereditary substance and showed that a gene is a segment of DNA; second, studies on these simple forms which contain less complex genetic material have provided new concepts in the recombina-

tional and mutational aspects of the genes. For example, we once thought that crossing over and mutation involved an entire gene, but we now know that these processes can occur within a gene.

In 1953, while geneticists working with bacteria and *Neurospora* were making significant contributions, a model of the DNA molecule that could account for its duplication, coding, and mutational features was proposed. The Watson-Crick model, discussed in Chapter 3, suggested that the hereditary substance was composed of pairs of nucleotide bases and that these bases spelled out the code to the cell's machinery. Since the one gene–one enzyme

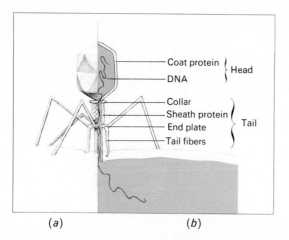

FIGURE 14–21   (a) External view of a
bacteriophage particle, showing the six-sided
"head" containing the strands of DNA and the
"tail" with its central core, "tail" plate, and
fibers. (b) The same bacteriophage particle, showing the movement of DNA into the bacterial cell.
The central core has penetrated the wall of the
bacterium, and the DNA is passing down into
the cell.

theory was strongly held at that time, the code
was thought to direct the cell to manufacture
specific enzymes or proteins. Studies of the
protein hemoglobin showed that the normal
form differed from a mutant form by only a
single amino acid. A change in the code, perhaps involving only one nucleotide, could account for the substitution of the wrong amino
acid. A mutation could then be defined as a
change in the coded message of the DNA molecule.

So our concept of a gene has been modified
considerably from the "factors" of Mendel to
the nucleotides of the modern geneticist. The
modern concept visualizes a gene as a segment
of DNA coding for a complete polypeptide,
which may be an enzyme, a structural protein,
or a subunit of an enzyme or structural protein.

It is useful, however, to consider a gene in
other ways besides its primary functional role;
a gene can also be thought of as a unit of recombination (crossing over) or as a unit of
mutation. In all three roles it is still considered
as a series of nucleotides along the DNA molecule. Microbial genetics, however, have shown
that these three activities can occur within
sites formerly thought of as genes. Thus the
"gene" may have different boundaries depending on how we conceive of it. The term *cistron*
is now used to describe the gene as a unit of
function, composed of many mutable and
recombinable nucleotides. Most geneticists accept the general definition of a gene as a sequence of nucleotides forming a code for a
specific polypeptide. We have followed this one
gene–one polypeptide principle throughout our
discussion of gene action.

Finally, we must remember that each gene is
part of a functioning system. A gene producing
an enzyme to catalyze one step in the production of the vitamin thiamine could not really
do its job if it were not for other genes producing the other enzymes necessary for the complete synthetic pathway. In fact, experimental
evidence suggests that even the position of a
gene on a chromosome is vital to its function.

In Chapter 2, we discussed the work of H. G.
Khorana in synthesizing a functional gene in
E. coli bacteria. Although he constructed a gene
that codes for transfer RNA of a specific amino
acid, it was necessary to add regulatory portions
to this gene in order for it to be fully functional
in a bacterial cell. Portions had to be added at
each end of the gene that provides the code for
tyrosine transfer RNA. At one end, nucleotides
were added to instruct the gene to "start" action (called the promoter) while at the other
end, nucleotides were added for signaling
"stop" (called the terminator). Of the 199 pairs
of nucleotides in this tyrosine transfer RNA
gene, the first 52 are the promoter and the last
21 comprise the terminator. Khorana's technique, assembling genes artificially from stock
chemicals, differs from the work of other investigators who produce new hereditary units
by rearranging or transferring existing genes or
parts of genes (discussed in Chapters 16 and
21). Now we should consider more specific
schemes that help in our understanding of gene
regulation.

Mechanisms of Gene Regulation

Studies on bacteria and viruses have shown
that control of gene activities depends not only

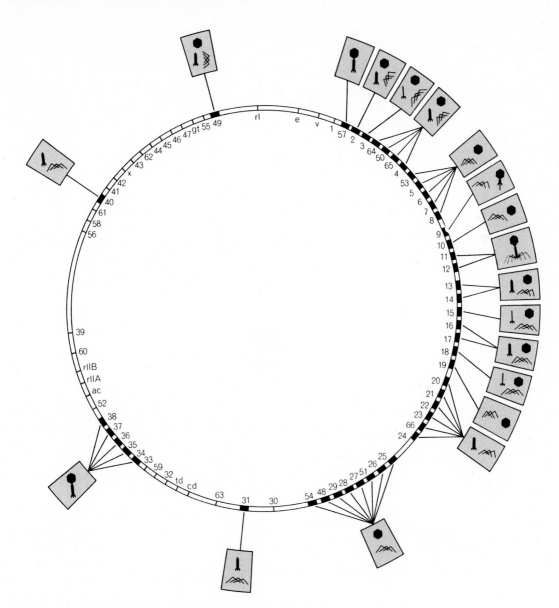

FIGURE 14–22 Genetic map of the T4 virus. The circle represents the chromosome of the virus. The numbers represent genes identified so far on the basis of mutations. The small diagrams radiating from each blackened gene area show the effect of a mutation in that area. A mutation in gene 19, for example, produces a virus without a collar and most of the tail. (From "Building a Bacterial Virus" by William B. Wood and R. S. Edgar. Copyright © 1967 by Scientific American, Inc. All rights reserved.)

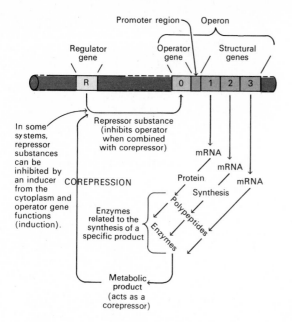

FIGURE 14–23 Functional relationships among structural, promoter, operator, and regulator genes. The metabolic product apparently combines with a repressor substance produced by the regulator gene to inhibit action of the operator gene. Note the feedback mechanism (corepression).

on many genes functioning together but also on the interaction of protein molecules known as *repressors*, which "turn on" or "turn off" genes. In 1961 two French microbiologists, F. Jacob and J. Monod, proposed that a series of genes called an *operon* influence the synthesis of enzymes in *E. coli*. In their model, an operon consists of *promoter genes*, *operator genes*, and *structural genes*. *Regulator* genes control the activity of a specific operon. The regulator apparently produces a protein that acts as a *repressor* by binding to the operator gene to prevent transcription of RNA and thus preventing protein synthesis. Recently, this model of genes functioning under the influence of protein molecules has been confirmed experimentally. The general mechanism, shown in Figure 14–23, can be summarized as follows:

1. *Structural genes.* These genes code messenger RNA for the synthesis of a specific poly-

peptide on the ribosomes. This is the gene we discussed earlier in this chapter with respect to protein synthesis.

2. *Operator gene.* This gene controls the functioning of a specific series of structural genes by turning them on and off. It is always located adjacent to the genes it controls. The operator gene, promoter gene, and related structural genes are termed an operon.

3. *Promoter genes.* The sites at which transcription of mRNA begins.

4. *Regulator genes.* In combination with chemical compounds from the cytoplasm, these genes control the operator genes. A regulator gene, which may be located some distance from the operator gene it controls, produces a protein *repressor* substance that can combine with the operator gene to repress its action. The repressor must apparently combine with a cytoplasmic substance called a corepressor; in some systems, this may be the metabolic end product catalyzed by the last structural gene of that operon. The repressor and corepressor act together to "shut off" the operator gene. In other cases, *inducers* from the cytoplasm may unite with repressor molecules and thus prevent the repressor from inactivating the operator gene. Inducer substances may be the substrate on which the enzymes produced by that operon will act.

The process by which the synthesis of enzymes is initiated is called *enzyme induction.* Some insight into enzyme induction came from the discovery that certain enzymes are produced only in the presence of the substrate they act upon. For example, the presence of lactose in a culture of *E. coli* can induce the production of enzymes that hydrolyze lactose. In different situations, then, repressor substances may be inactive when combined with inducers or active when associated with corepressors. When a repressor is inactive, an operon functions; when a repressor is activated, the operon is shut off.

The details of such a DNA operator-repressor system in a virus have been worked out by Tom Maniatis and Mark Ptashne at Harvard. Using a bacteriophage called lambda (the

Greek letter "L") phage, which infects *E. coli*, they have correlated many interactions of repressor molecules with specific regions of the phage's DNA. When lambda phage infects an *E. coli* bacterium, the phage may rapidly produce protein molecules through the action of an RNA polymerase enzyme on the operator and structural genes of its own DNA (Figure 14–24). Under some conditions, however, repressor molecules are produced which bind to

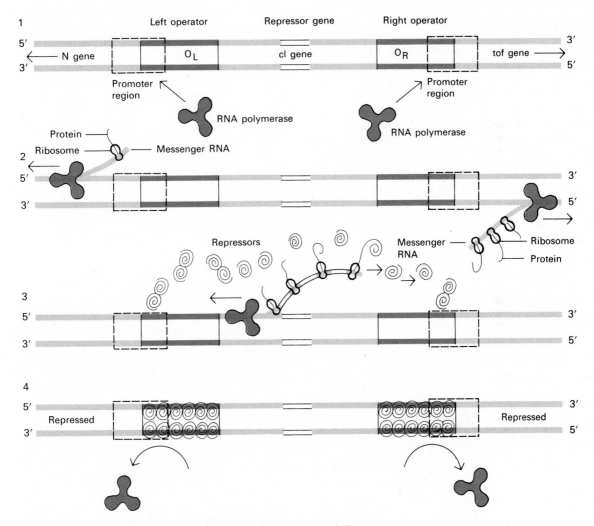

FIGURE 14–24 Expression and repression of genes in lambda bacteriophage, a virus that infects *E. coli*. Lines 1 and 2 show transcription of lambda DNA into mRNA and protein, catalyzed by the enzyme RNA polymerase. Lines 3 and 4 show how, under other conditions, repressor molecules can be produced that are capable of blocking RNA polymerase from the operator gene. (From "A DNA Operator-Repressor System" by Tom Maniatis and Mark Ptashne, Copyright © 1976 by Scientific American, Inc. All rights reserved.)

operator genes, and thus interfere with the access of RNA polymerase to this region of the chromosome. These operator genes can be made functional again by inactivating the repressor. Maniatis and Ptashne discovered that operator genes may be repressed at any of several different binding sites. For example, one operator gene, composed of more than 70 base pairs, has three binding sites of 17 base pairs each. Why several binding sites exist is not fully understood. Experimental studies such as this indicate the complexity of gene action and suggest that complex relationships exist between protein repressors and genes.

The gene regulation system we have described is a repressor-type mechanism. Genes can also exert their effects through positive regulatory means. Such regulation was described with respect to hormone action in Chapter 12, where we discussed receptor molecules. It was proposed that hormones united with these receptors to form a complex that activated the DNA. The repressor mechanism of gene action has been studied and confirmed in the procaryotic cells of bacteria and viruses. Positive gene regulation, on the other hand, was discovered in eucaryotic organisms. It is possible that genes may act through different mechanisms in procaryotes than in higher organisms.

As you recall from Chapter 4, two types of proteins, histones and nonhistones are associated with DNA in chromosomes. The histones are actually bound to the DNA molecule. Studies now indicate that these proteins may be involved in gene regulation. Gary Stein, Janet Stein, and Lewis Kleinsmith have suggested a model showing the relationship of these proteins to gene action. This model assumes that histone-bound DNA is repressed from making proteins. Nonhistone proteins can cancel the repressor effect of the histones by combining with a segment of DNA bound by histones. When this occurs, the segment of the DNA molecule freed of its histone becomes available for RNA transcription and protein synthesis.

The mechanisms that "turn on" and "turn off" genes are closely related to the developmental stages of all organisms. Why do certain genes function in some cells and not in others? Why do certain genes function at one time and not at another? We do not yet know, but these mechanisms clearly play key roles in developmental processes.

Our discussion of gene action—the aspects we do not understand as well as those we do—will be pertinent to our examination of reproduction, growth, and development in the following two chapters. Our growing knowledge of gene regulation and techniques for transferring DNA from one individual to another also presents thorny ethical problems for the future.

SUMMARY

Early observations and studies indicated that genes might be responsible for the production of enzymes, and more recent research has demonstrated that genes direct the synthesis of proteins. Important information came from an understanding of "inborn errors of metabolism," studies on *Neurospora*, and studies of various types of hemoglobin.

A segment of DNA (a gene) transfers its code to messenger RNA (mRNA), which interacts with ribosomal or rRNA and transfer or tRNA to produce a polypeptide chain. This occurs on the ribosomes. Thus DNA, carrying the "master blueprint," transfers this code to RNA for the production of specific proteins. Changes in a DNA molecule would change the code to produce different proteins. We call such a change in a DNA molecule a gene mutation.

Viruses and bacteria, which have all their genes in one chromosome, have been useful in studying the basic hereditary material and in defining a gene. A gene is now considered to be a sequence of nucleotides carrying the code for a specific polypeptide. One functional concept of gene action is the operon, which consists of several types of interacting genes: promoter, operator, and structural. Regulator genes control the activity of operons.

Besides this repressor functioning, we know that genes can also exert action in a positive way. Learning more about how genes function as the ultimate regulators in cells will help us to understand development and other processes.

REVIEW QUESTIONS

1. What was the importance of the principle of "inborn errors of metabolism" to an understanding of gene action? How did this affect further research?

2. If you were asked, "How do you know that DNA is the primary hereditary material?" how would you answer in support of this concept?

3. What was the significance of Beadle and Tatum's research on *Neurospora* for the field of genetics?

4. How does the modern concept of a gene correspond to the earlier notion that a gene was a structure on the chromosome?

5. Summarize the process of protein synthesis. What would happen if the DNA with which you start your summary had its nucleotide sequence changed?

6. How can mutations be associated with certain types of diseases? With certain types of inherited disorders?

7. How does the Jacob-Monod model suggest that most genes function in concert with other genes?

SUPPLEMENTARY READINGS

Jacob, Francois, *The Logic of Life: A History of Heredity*, Pantheon Books, New York, 1973. A challenging work that follows the workings of science to the molecular action of genes while touching on fundamental questions such as, can humans control their own evolution.

Lane, Charles, "Rabbit Hemoglobin from Frog Eggs," *Scientific American*, August 1976. Messenger RNA from specialized cells of one species (mouse or rabbit or bee) can be injected into frog eggs, and the frog egg manufactures the protein specified by this RNA. The protein-making response of a cell is therefore determined by the type of mRNA it receives.

Maniatis, Tom and Mark Ptashne, "A DNA Operator-Repressor System," *Scientific American*, January 1976. The functions of the operator, promoter, and repressor segments of DNA in gene regulation are described for a bacteriophage virus. Complex patterns of gene regulation appear to be accomplished through specific interactions between protein and DNA.

Ruddle, Frank H. and R. S. Kucherlapati, "Hybrid Cells and Human Genes," *Scientific American*, July 1974. Human genes can be mapped by fusing human and mouse cells and analyzing the resulting genetic functions. This technique is important to the treatment of genetic diseases and the understanding of malignancies.

Sobell, Henry M., "How Actinomycin Binds to DNA," *Scientific American*, August 1974. Actinomycin, an antibiotic, blocks protein synthesis by binding to DNA and preventing formation of mRNA, tRNA, and ribosomal RNA.

Stein, Gary S., J. S. Stein, and L. J. Kleinsmith, "Chromosomal Proteins and Gene Regulation," *Scientific American*, February 1975. The regulation of genes in higher organisms is probably related to the action of histone and nonhistone proteins associated with the DNA; nonhistones turn genes on and histones turn them off.

Unit VI
Reproduction and Development

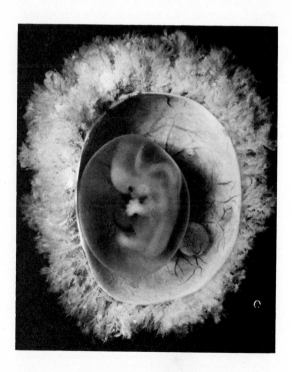

No living system lives forever. Individual organisms of certain species do live a relatively long time—we may doubt the 969 years of the biblical Methuselah, but some humans live 130 years or more. Among at least a few marine animal species, some hardy (and lucky) individuals live for hundreds of years. Many individuals of some tree species survive for thousands of years; certain bristlecone pine trees in California's White Mountains are nearly 5000 years old.

But no organism is immortal. Why?

This question has philosophical and religious overtones. In this book, however, we are interested only in scientific questions and answers. We can restate the question on a scientific level, and cell biologists are asking it in this form: How do cells *die*? We do not yet have certain, detailed answers, but entropy and the second law of thermodynamics provide answers in a very general sense. Indeed, we have already given an answer in Chapter 3: all processes and systems in the universe are moving toward a state of complete disorder. For living systems, aging and death are steps along this route to complete disorder. As we will note in this unit, aging is an important part of the life cycle of most organisms.

All living systems grow. Growth may be defined as an increase in the amount of living matter—an increase in size and mass. This may seem obvious, but it is helpful because it leads to a meaningful and useful distinction between growth and development.

What, then, is development? The growth of every living thing involves a kind of development that filling a balloon with air does not. When a unicellular organism such as a bacterium reproduces (divides), the cellular machinery of each new bacterium proceeds to synthesize various kinds of materials: nucleic acids, carbohydrates, proteins, and so on.

But in biology the word development is usually reserved for growth processes in multicellular organisms that involve cell differentiation, or development of various kinds of cells. By this we mean, of course, specialized cells.

So we see that growth is a characteristic of all living systems, but development—in the sense that biologists usually use the term—is a characteristic only of multicellular living systems. All organisms grow, but only multicellular organisms develop.

As we shall see in this unit, a great deal has been learned about the processes of growth and development. But the knowledge we have gained has made us realize that we are still a long way from a full understanding of how living systems develop.

Chapter 15

Reproduction

Throughout this book, we have seen the wide range of ways different species carry out the basic functions of life. If an organism could not perform these functions, it would die. In this chapter, however, we are going to look at reproduction—the one process with no significance for the continued existence of a single individual within a species. But reproduction is the basis for the continued existence of a species.

We move from the simple to the complex, first by comparing asexuality and sexuality. In asexual reproduction, one set of genetic information is simply duplicated and passed on to the next generation by a single parent. In sexual reproduction, new combinations of genetic material are made possible by the reproductive role of two parents.

We will see that all reproduction in the living world fits into three *General Reproductive Patterns*. *The Protist Pattern: Haplontic* covers the boundary line bewteen the asexual and the sexual. *The Plant Pattern: Diplohaplontic* includes both asexual and sexual phases, which are frequently alternated in a process called alternation of generations. *The Animal Pattern: Diplontic* can be generally summed up as follows: two haploid units, an egg and a sperm, are formed by the process of meiosis. They combine and form a new diploid individual.

We then study *Reproduction in Mammals* using *The Human Example.* Human reproduction is quite complex and is regulated by a group of hormones in both males and females. In human females, these hormones regulate not only the production of egg cells, but also the prebirth development of the new individual.

Human reproduction is significant not only in terms of its importance to each of us as individuals, but also because of the population explosion of recent decades. Because human reproduction is a multi-stage process, it can be controlled in numerous ways by *Preventing Fertilization: Contraception.* Various methods can be used to prevent the egg and the sperm from coming in contact with each other.

Cycles and Reproduction are often closely related activities. Why? Cycles and other rhythmic activities help to coordinate the time of reproduction for all members of a species and thereby insure fertilization.

We have seen that organisms process energy to do the work of self-synthesis and maintenance. During much of its life cycle, a living system is able to increase its structural order and decrease its entropy. Eventually, however, its structural order decreases and its entropy increases. This can happen suddenly (as when an organism is eaten or suffers a fatal heart attack), or more slowly (as it passes through the decline known in our species as "old age"). Sudden or slow, the ultimate outcome is always the same: death, followed eventually by complete structural disorder. Individual living systems are just as subject to eventual entropic disorganization as any other kind of system.

But living systems, alone among all known systems in the universe, have developed a sort of "group immortality" as an alternative to individual permanence: they continue by *reproduction*. The individual dies, but the species maintains itself over time and manages to survive for many thousands and even millions of years before dying out or diverging into other life forms through the process of *speciation*. To be sure, no mortal individual of the near-immortal species group is exactly like its ancestors of the same species. This, as it happens, is a good thing for the species. But this matter must be deferred until we discuss evolution and adaptation in Unit VIII. In earlier chapters we examined the hereditary mechanisms underlying reproduction. In this chapter we are concerned with the processes of reproduction themselves and with their immediate rather than their long-range outcomes.

GENERAL REPRODUCTIVE PATTERNS

There are two main categories of reproduction: sexual and asexual. Asexual reproduction requires only a single parent; the offspring often has the same hereditary makeup as that parent. Although the products of asexual reproduction are generally similar to the parent stock, mutations do occur affording opportunity for change. This is especially evident in single-celled, rapidly dividing organisms such as bacteria, where a mutation in one cell can be incorporated into a new colony within a very short time. Sexual reproduction, on the other hand, produces offspring with new combinations of genetic material. The many variations in a species that are produced through sexual reproduction provide the basis for adaptation.

Sexual and asexual reproductive processes are found among both procaryotes (bacteria and blue-green algae) and eucaryotes (protists, plants, and animals). But the asexual mechanism in procaryotes differs markedly from that of eucaryotes. Procaryotes reproduce asexually by means of *binary fission* or simply "splitting in two," which does not involve mitosis. In this process, a portion of the cell wall grows between the duplicated DNA strands to form two new cells. Some unicellular protists also reproduce by binary fission, but the cellular reproduction here is by mitosis. In most algae, filaments simply add more cells at their ends until a cell or group of cells detaches. This process is effective because filaments are often fragmented by rough water and animals feeding upon them. Many eucaryotic organisms, such as yeasts and *Hydra*, reproduce by *budding* (Figure 15–1). In budding, cells reproduce by mitosis to form a small organism resembling the parent on the surface of the parent organism.

It is not surprising that sexual reproduction is so widespread, since the sexual process provides for recombination of genetic information. Organisms use various means to transfer genetic material (DNA) from one individual to another. Binary fission in bacteria and protists is often preceded by *conjugation*, a form of sexuality in which two cells exchange hereditary material. Conjugation is a simple type of sexual process occurring in bacteria and some protists. Since organisms produced through a sexual process always differ somewhat from either of their parents, they may be even better suited to their environment. These variations come about by means of: (1) gene recombination during meiosis and (2) mutations—mechanisms which were discussed in the two previous chapters.

383

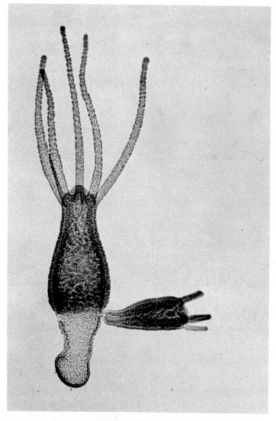

FIGURE 15–1 *Hydra* with a bud. Budding is a type of reproduction in which a new individual develops directly from the parent's body. (Courtesy Carolina Biological Supply Company.)

A Protist Pattern: Haplontic

Spirogyra, a haploid (n) filamentous green alga, reproduces both asexually and sexually (Figure 15–2). Asexually a filament simply adds more cells at its ends by mitosis. Sexual reproduction involves conjugation and occurs when two filaments come to lie side by side and hollow tubes grow out from adjacent cells. When these tubes meet, the end walls dissolve, and the nuclei of the cells of one filament (the donor) flow through the tubes and fuse with nuclei of the other filament (the recipient). The zygote thus formed is diploid; in order to return to the haploid chromosome number, the first division of the zygote is meiotic. Of four haploid cells

produced, three distintegrate and one continues to divide by mitosis to produce a new filament. This type of reproductive pattern, in which the dominant form of the organism is haploid, is called a *haplontic* life cycle (Figure 15–3).

The Plant Pattern: Diplohaplontic

Both asexual and sexual reproduction occur in the plant kingdom. Plants propagate in many asexual ways; new individuals may arise from bulbs, runners, cuttings, and in some cases even leaves. In some species, stems erupt through the soil from underground runners to produce new leaf-bearing individuals. In others, such as strawberries, surface runners growing away from the main plant take root and become new plants. One interesting asexual pattern occurs in the maternity plant, in which tiny buds produced at the edges of the leaves fall from the parent and root in the soil. Plants with characteristics that will not breed true from seeds, such as specially developed hybrid varieties of roses and fruit trees, can be propagated by grafting and by the rooting of cuttings. This "forced" asexual reproduction ensures that the offspring will have the same characteristics as the parent.

Sexual reproduction in plants is part of a general life cycle that can be observed in all members of the plant kingdom. The plant pattern includes an asexual stage that produces haploid spores by meiosis and a sexual stage that gives rise to gametes by mitosis. In this pattern, known as *alternation of generations,* the plant is called a *sporophyte* in its spore-producing stage and a *gametophyte* in its gamete-forming stage. Because the life history of a plant follows an alternating cycle, it is often referred to as *diplohaplontic* (Figure 15–4).

Alternation of generations can also be observed in some protists, including algae. In green algae the gametophyte generation dominates; in brown algae the sporophyte is dominant.

In mosses the green, leafy gametophytes are haploid, producing gametes, whereas the stalked sporophytes are diploid and produce spores. In ferns and seed plants, gametophytes

Bio-Topic: Biological Pest Control

Sexual reproduction is one of the few biological functions that multicellular organisms cannot give up. To forgo sex is to become extinct. It should be no surprise that the search for safe insecticides has led to controls that interfere with sexual reproduction.

One of the earliest sexual controls was used against the screw-worm fly that was devastating the Florida livestock industry. The female lays her eggs under the skin of domesticated cattle. Larvae hatch and burrow into the muscle of the cattle, causing pain, infection, and economic loss. When conventional insecticides proved ineffective against the screw-worm fly, biologists attempted a biological control by taking advantage of the fact that the female mates only once in her life.

Biologists raised millions of screw-worm flies to the cocoon stage. The female cocoons were destroyed. The male cocoons were exposed to doses of x-rays that sterilized the testes but did not affect other tissues. The irradiated cocoons were allowed to hatch into adult male flies that were released from airplanes during the normal breeding season. Because the sterile males vastly outnumbered the normal males, most females mated with sterile males and produced nonfertile eggs.

By using this technique for several consecutive seasons, the screw-worm fly was virtually eradicated and the Florida livestock industry was rescued. This kind of biological control can be applied to any insect pest with the following characteristics: the female mates only once; the species can be reared in large numbers; male and female cocoons are different enough to sort; and a sterilizing agent can be found that does not inhibit mating behavior. To be effective, the size of the normal population must be significantly reduced before the sterile males are released. When these characteristics are all present, the technique is highly effective.

It is not likely that an insect species will evolve a defense against this kind of biological control: sexual reproduction is too fundamental. On the other hand, eradication of any species disrupts a stable ecosystem. We understand too little about natural ecosystems to be able to predict the long-term effects of such disruptions. Could the cure turn out to be worse than the disease?

---

are reduced in size and haploid, while the sporophytes are larger and diploid. Examples of specific plant life cycles are given in Chapter 23.

The Animal Pattern: Diplontic

Animals do not show an alternation of generations such as that found in plants. All animals can undergo sexual reproduction, however, and throughout the animal kingdom a single pattern dominates: a sperm and an egg produced by meiosis unite to form a diploid zygote that develops into a new individual. Since most animals have diploid body cells, the reproductive pattern is termed diplontic (Figure 15–5).

This pattern does have exceptions, however. In honeybees, for example, males are haploid. The life cycle of jellyfish shows an alternation of asexual and sexual stages. In both stages, however, the body cells are diploid. Free-swimming *medusas* represent the sexual stage of an alternation, producing gametes by meiosis. After the gametes are fertilized in the water, the zygote develops into a flat, ciliated larva called a *planula*. The planula swims about for a time and finally attaches itself to a surface and produces small buds asexually (see Chapter 24).

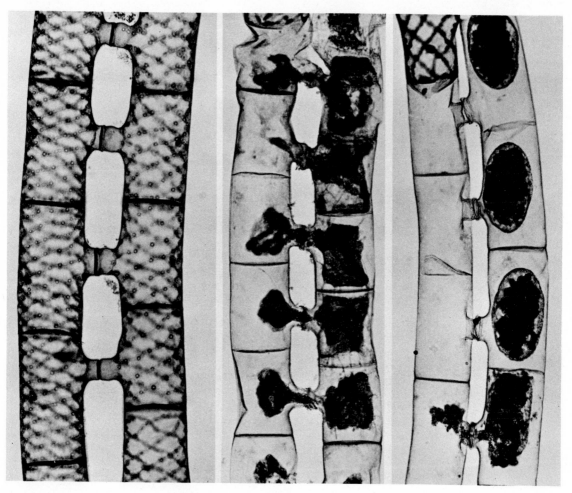

FIGURE 15–2   Conjugation in *Spirogyra*. At left, two filaments come together and produce conjugation tubes. In the center, contents of donor cells flow into recipient cells. At right, diploid zygotes form. (Carolina Biological Supply Company.)

Sea anemones, which rely primarily on sexual reproduction, also reproduce prolifically by budding. Some species form matlike colonies on intertidal rocks and on the ocean bottom.

In most aquatic invertebrates, fertilization occurs outside the body. This process requires release of tremendous numbers of gametes into the water, so that enough sperms encounter eggs to ensure the perpetuation of the species. In ocean tidepools, release of gametes into the water by one sea urchin will "trigger" all the other urchins in the tidepool to release gametes. This stimulation to discharge gametes simultaneously is caused by chemical messengers in the gamete fluid. The gelatinous egg coat contains a chemical that reacts with sperms, causing them to gather in masses around the egg (Figure 15–6). Here, then, are two mechanisms that aid in the success of external fertilization: synchronous release of gametes and production of chemicals to increase the probability of fertilization.

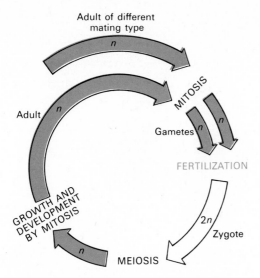

FIGURE 15–3 Generalized haplontic reproductive pattern of many protists such as *Neurospora* and *Spirogyra*. Gametes are produced by mitosis; the haploid condition is restored by zygotic meiosis.

A few invertebrates and all land vertebrates except amphibians use methods of direct internal fertilization. For example, each planarian (a flatworm) has both a penis and a vagina. The

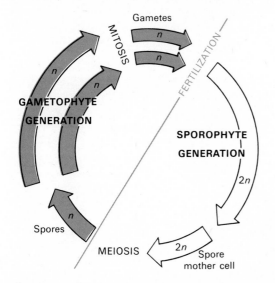

FIGURE 15–4 Generalized diplohaplontic reproductive pattern of plants. Gametophyte phase is shown in color.

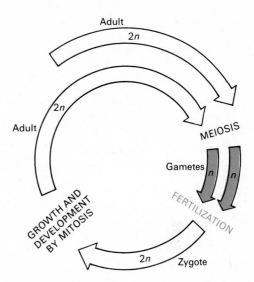

FIGURE 15–5 Generalized diplontic reproductive pattern of animals. Haploid stages are shown in color. Adults may be male, female, or in some cases, monoecious (having both ovary and testis in the same organism).

sperms of one planarian are transferred to the vagina of another (Figure 15–7). This organism is *monoecious* or hermaphroditic: each worm possesses both male and female organs. (*Dioecious* organisms, on the other hand, are those with separate sexes.) Although both male and female organs are present in planaria, self-fertilization does not occur.

In amphibians such as frogs and salamanders, the male sits astride the back of the female during mating and deposits sperms as the eggs are released. Since these animals usually mate in water, the urinary, intestinal, and reproductive tracts all come together to form a common canal called the *cloaca*, from which the sperms and eggs are released (Figure 15–8). Birds and lizards also have a cloaca, but since mating always occurs on land rather than in water, fertilization must be accomplished by direct apposition of the cloacal openings of the male and the female. In mammals and most reptiles, sperms are introduced through a penis.

Some asexual reproduction does occur in animals, however; sponges, for example, have a great ability for asexual reproduction. If a sponge is cut into very small pieces, each piece

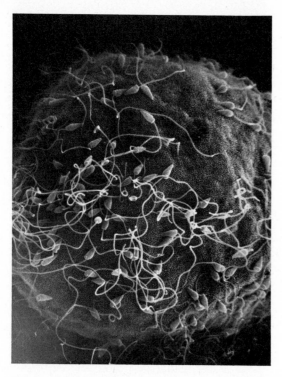

FIGURE 15–6   Scanning electron micrograph of a sea urchin egg surrounded by sperm (×1500). (Courtesy of Mia Tegner, from *Science,* vol. 179, pp. 685–688, 16 February 1973. Copyright © 1973 by the American Association for the Advancement of Science.)

develops into a new individual. Generally, however, as animals become more complex, their ability to reproduce asexually decreases. A crab may replace a lost pincer and a lizard may grow a new tail through a process called *regeneration,* but they cannot match the regenerative powers of the common planarian flatworm or of a starfish. If a planarian is cut in half, the head produces a new tail and the hind portion forms a new head. In a more limited example, a starfish can regenerate lost arms, one arm can produce a complete individual if it includes a portion of the central disc (Figure 15–9).

Reproduction in Mammals: The Human Example

We will discuss the reproductive structures and physiology of our own species as an example of

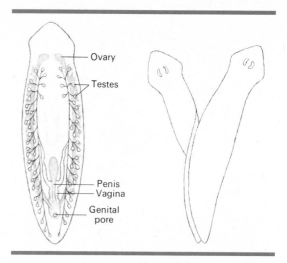

FIGURE 15–7   Internal fertilization process of Planaria. Since each animal contains both male and female reproductive structures, reciprocal fertilization occurs at each mating.

mammalian reproduction. In males (Figure 15–10) the sperm-producing tubules of each testis unite to form an *epididymis.* This coiled tube, which serves as a reservoir for sperm, emerges from the testis as the vas deferens. Each vas deferens enters the abdominal cavity, where it unites with the urethra, a common tube for the genital and urinary systems. Three

FIGURE 15–8   Frogs in copulation. The male mounts the female and grasps her around the abdomen. The male sheds sperm as eggs are released into the water. (Richard Gross.)

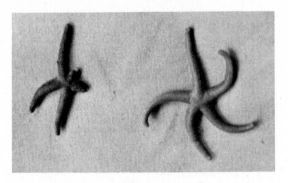

FIGURE 15–9   Regeneration of arms in starfish. The starfish on the left has lost two arms and is in the process of regenerating them. At the right is a normal starfish.

pairs of accessory glands—seminal vesicles, prostate glands, and Cowper's glands—enter the system to add lubricating and nutritional fluids to the seminal fluids. The seminal vesicles empty into each vas deferens, but secretions from the prostate and Cowper's glands enter the urethra.

One of the paired ovaries of females (Figure 15–11) discharges an ovum (egg) into the fallopian tubes. At the junction of the fallopian tubes is a muscular organ, the uterus, with a cellular lining called the *endometrium.* After fertilization the embryo embeds in this lining, which develops many blood vessels to provide nutrients for the growing embryo. Females of most mammalian species undergo *estrus,* cyclic periods of egg production and sexual receptivity to males. Mammals vary in their number of estrus cycles. The English fox, for example, is monestrus—that is, it breeds only once each year. Guinea pigs, rats, and rabbits are polyestrus; estrus occurs every four to five days until conception takes place.

In human females the sexual cycle is called the *menstrual cycle.* It differs from estrus in two ways: (1) there is no distinct period of receptivity to the male; and (2) at the end of the monthly cycle the cellular lining of the uterus is shed and bleeding occurs. If fertilization takes place, the lining and embryo are maintained for approximately nine months. The normal menstrual cycle, which requires approximately 28 days, is summarized in the

following paragraphs, along with the events that accompany fertilization and interrupt the menstrual cycle (see Figure 15–12).

1. A hormone from the hypothalamus of the brain triggers the release of gonadotropic hormone, follicle-stimulating hormone (FSH), from the anterior pituitary lobe. The ovary, stimulated by FSH, produces a follicle which in turn releases an ovum.

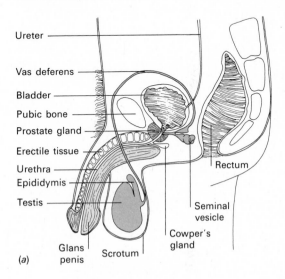

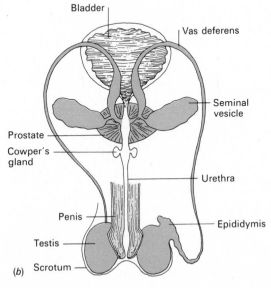

FIGURE 15–10   Reproductive system in the human male. (*a*) Side view. (*b*) Front view.

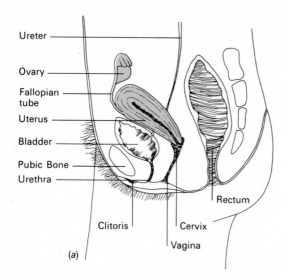

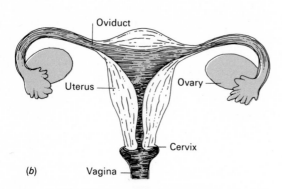

FIGURE 15–11   Reproductive system in the human female. (a) Side view. (b) Front view.

This event, called *ovulation*, occurs as the concentrations of FSH and LH are at their peaks.

5. The anterior pituitary continues to secrete LH, which acts to change the follicle into a yellow body known as the *corpus luteum*. The corpus luteum secretes estrogen, but in smaller amounts than those secreted by the follicle. However, the corpus luteum also secretes another hormone, *progesterone*, that continues the development of the uterine lining and maintains it throughout pregnancy. Progesterone is also necessary for proper implantation of a fertilized ovum in the uterus. Progesterone inhibits the production of FSH, which would otherwise trigger a new cycle. In the absence of fertilization, high levels of progesterone also inhibit LH production.

6. If fertilization does not occur and the LH level declines, the corpus luteum degenerates and stops secreting progesterone. The uterine lining is then shed in a process known as *menstruation*. This phase of the cycle requires about four to five days.

7. Lowered levels of progesterone and estrogen permit the stimulating centers in the hypothalamus to stimulate the pituitary to produce FSH again, thus initiating a new cycle.

8. If fertilization occurs and the fertilized egg implants in the uterine lining, the corpus luteum continues to secrete progesterone, which maintains the uterine lining, inhibits ovulation, and prevents the uterine muscles from contracting.

The menstrual cycle of the human female is controlled by an orderly, successive relationship among FSH, estrogen, LH, and progesterone. FSH and estrogen function together at the beginning of the cycle, whereas LH and progesterone take over later. This is an excellent example of a hormonal control system with both positive and negative feedback features (Figure 15–13).

Although this is the normal process that occurs in human females of reproductive age and leads to conception and birth of new individuals, it is important to be able to control whether fertilization takes place. This birth

2. This follicle secretes the female hormone estrogen into the bloodstream; estrogen inhibits FSH and stimulates the hypothalamus to release a hormone that in turn stimulates the production of luteinizing hormone (LH) in the pituitary.

3. Estrogen also stimulates the lining of the uterus to grow and vascularize (produce additional blood vessels) in preparation for implantation of a fertilized ovum.

4. After about 14 days a mature ovum is ejected from the follicle into the fallopian tube.

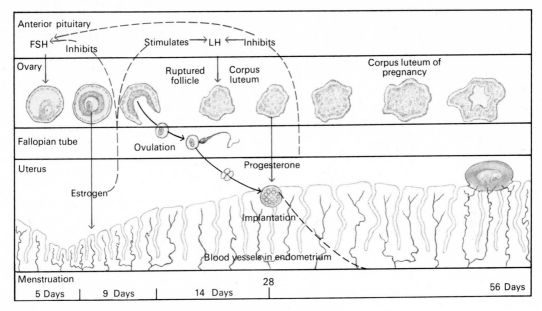

FIGURE 15-12 Menstrual cycle of human females. The activities of four major body areas are correlated: anterior pituitary, ovary, fallopian tube, and uterus. If implantation does not occur, the corpus luteum degenerates and the uterine lining is shed after about 28 days, as indicated by the black broken line. If fertilization and implantation do occur, the lining is maintained to nourish the embryo until birth.

control is necessary in order to control the number of children born and the size of families. *Contraception*, preventing a sperm from reaching an egg, is the means of achieving birth control.

Preventing Fertilization: Contraception

The explosive growth of the world's population (discussed in Chapter 8) has brought about increased interest in efficient ways to prevent fertilization. A variety of techniques are now used to prevent conception. Two of the most common are birth control pills and sterilization. Probably the most widely used and reliable nonsterilization method is "the pill." Our understanding of the menstrual cycle and its relationship to hormones has enabled us to control the ovulation phase of the cycle. Birth control pills inhibit the secretion of FSH and LH that would be necessary for ovulation through daily doses of synthetic estrogen and

progesterone. These hormones block ovulation and maintain the uterine lining. In general, the pills are taken from the fifth through the twenty-fourth day of the cycle. When they are discontinued, the uterine lining is shed as part of the menstrual phase. Many women have reported undesirable side effects of the pill. Because the pill is so effective in preventing conception, however, researchers have developed numerous variations on the concept which might reduce the side effects while preserving the method's advantages.

The side effects occur because synthetic estrogen and progesterone affect other body systems in addition to the ovary and uterus. These hormones may affect the functions of kidneys, adrenal glands, and the pituitary gland. If the kidneys are stimulated to reabsorb mineral ions, excessive weight gain may occur from water retention. In some women birth control pills affect the blood clotting mechanism, in-

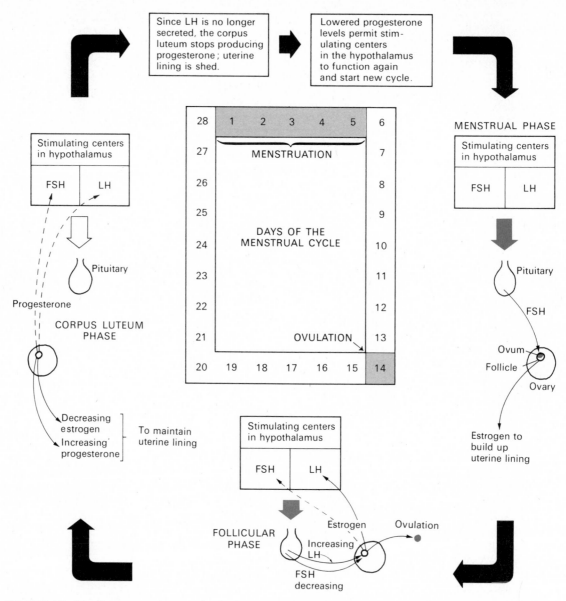

FIGURE 15–13 Sequence of events in the human menstrual
cycle. Solid arrows indicate stimulation; broken arrows represent
inhibition.

creasing the danger of internal clotting. Birth
control pills are also suspected of causing headaches, nausea, breast tenderness, and other
symptoms in some users. There is also some
evidence that they may cause breast cancer.
Hormone contraceptives should be selected

and used initially under the supervision of a
physician.

Before the days of the pill and the IUD, the
more common contraceptive techniques were
the "rhythm method," rubber condoms, and
diaphragms—the latter two often used with a

vaginal spermicide. The rhythm method is simply abstinence from intercourse during the time when ovulation is expected to occur. This method is only about 70 percent reliable, however, since it is based on prediction of the time of ovulation. Ovulation time is not perfectly constant, even in women whose menstrual cycles are regular. It generally occurs on about the fourteenth day of the menstrual cycle, but it can take place at any time. In contrast to the rhythm method, the "pill" has proved to be almost 100 percent effective in women who use it properly.

Sterilization techniques have been developed that involve very little discomfort. For men the most common method is *vasectomy*, in which the sperm-carrying vas deferens of each testis is cut and tied. A small vertical incision is made on each side of the scrotum and a short segment of the vas deferens on each side is removed. The remaining ends are ligated (tied tightly with surgical thread) (Figure 15–14). This operation is simple, and any swelling or discomfort it may cause lasts for only a few days. Since almost all fluid ejaculated by the male is produced by the seminal vesicles, Cowper's glands, and the prostate glands, no noticeable changes in sexual physiology or behavior result—except, of course, that fertilization cannot occur. The sperms produced in the testes are most probably reabsorbed in the blocked tubules.

Women can also be sterilized by minor surgery in which the fallopian tubes are cut and ligated. Recently, the development of a telescopic instrument called a laparoscope has enabled surgeons to locate the fallopian tubes by inserting the scope through a tiny incision near the navel. Through a second incision, the tubes are cut and cauterized with a hot needle to prevent bleeding. Most patients complain only of temporary tenderness in the areas of the two incisions. These surgical techniques are currently the most effective methods of achieving contraception. Reversal of surgical sterilization is theoretically possible, but it is not yet a practical reality.

A non-contraceptive method of preventing pregnancy involves inserting an intrauterine device (IUD), usually a plastic coil or loop, into

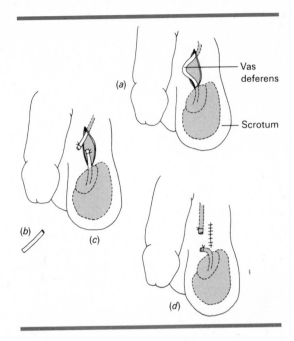

FIGURE 15–14   Steps involved in a vasectomy. (*a*) An incision is made in both sides of the scrotum and the vas deferens located. (*b*) A section is cut out of the vas deferens. (*c*) The remaining ends are tied. (*d*) The incision is closed and sutured.

the uterus. It is not known how IUDs work, but they are believed to act as a stimulus to the uterine lining which prevents implantation.

CYCLES AND REPRODUCTION

The year-round reproductive behavior of our own species is exceptional. In most animals and plants, reproduction occurs in a cyclic pattern—it takes place only during a definite breeding season each year. Moreover, cyclic internal changes associated with the reproduction process occur in each member of a species. These internal changes can often be correlated with changes in the external environment.

Lunar cycles—periodicity related to the phases of the moon—are involved in the reproduction of several animals. The grunion, a small fish of the southern California coast, swims onto beaches during high tides of the spring and summer months to lay eggs in the sand (Figure 15–15). Females, which are 5 to 8 inches long, bury their tails in the wet sand to deposit their eggs, while male grunion lying nearby release sperms that fertilize the eggs. The fish are then carried back to sea by the next waves.

The most intriguing aspect of this reproductive behavior is the grunion's unerring sense of the tidal cycle. The tides that bring the fish onto the beach are called *spring tides*—those produced at the new moon and full moon. Tides are influenced by the gravitational pull of the moon and the sun. At new moon the moon is between the sun and the earth, and at full moon the earth is between the sun and the moon. High tides are higher at these two times,

when the sun and moon are "lined up" with the earth, because then the pulls of sun and moon reinforce each other. But in addition to sensing the exact time of the spring tides, grunion must also deposit their eggs at a level somewhat below the highest water. This insures that the high water of the next tidal cycle will release the young from the sand and carry them back into the sea. Predictably, grunion accomplish this by swimming onto the sand on the night *following* the peak of the spring tides.

Another animal whose reproduction is linked to lunar phases is the segmented Palolo worm of Samoa and Bermuda (Figure 15–16). These segmented worms, which live in burrows in coral reefs, consist of two parts: an asexual

FIGURE 15–15 Grunion spawning on a California beach. (Moody Institute of Science; California Academy of Sciences.)

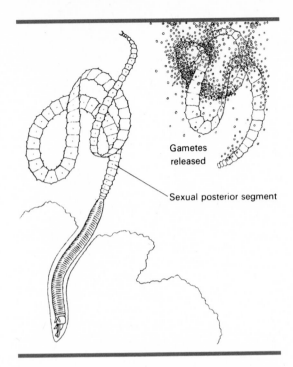

Gametes released

Sexual posterior segment

FIGURE 15-16   Palolo worm releasing gametes.

anterior segment and a sexual posterior portion. In the Samoan species, the posterior sexual segments break away and swim to the surface in the early morning on the first and second days of the last quarter of the October-November moon. After swimming for several hours on the surface, these sexual segments finally burst, releasing gametes into the sea; soon the surface of the water is soupy with gametes and spent segments. The asexual segments remain in the burrow and produce new sexual segments.

In Bermuda the pattern is similar except that the worms release their gametes in May or June. The monthly reproductive cycles of these two species are similar, then, yet the yearly time is different. Most investigators believe that the phase of the moon is only one aspect of reproductive regulation in Palolo worms. Their cycles may also be correlated to ocean turbidity and wave action.

Many birds and mammals breed either in the spring or the fall. Deer and elk, for example, breed in late fall, whereas mating in the varying hare occurs in March or April. Charles Lyman of Harvard University has shown that the increasing length of the days during spring is responsible for estrus in female hares and for development of the testes in males. In certain breeds of sheep the shorter days of fall produce estrus in females and increase sperm production in males. Day length triggers internal changes in these hares and sheep to determine that reproduction will occur at a specific time each year. These internal clocks apparently recognize the duration of individual photoperiods (days), leading ultimately to an accumulative effect—the breeding time.

Why are rhythmic and cyclic activities important to organisms, especially in reproduction? Certainly the probability of fertilization increases greatly when all members of a species are under the control of similar biological clocks and hence are capable of breeding at the same time. For a particular plant species, for example, pollen and eggs would reach maturation at the same time. Worms or starfish living in the vast expanses of the ocean must all produce gametes at exactly the same time or the chance of fertilization is greatly reduced. Organisms that produce their gametes at exactly the same time have a greater chance of successful fertilization. For most vertebrates the cycle includes preparatory events leading up to the vital final event of fertilization. Courtship—specialized and sometimes elaborate behavior to attract a mate by male, female, or both—may be a part of the reproductive cycle (Chapter 17). Reproductive, or breeding, cycles are therefore activities that insure a greater probability of survival. The synchronization of internal mechanisms with rhythmic environmental phenomena such as light and temperature provides a common synchronization for all members of a particular species.

After conception, a complex series of mitotic divisions produces a remarkable sequence of embryonic events, leading to the development first of a fetus and, ultimately, of an adult. We will examine this process of growth and development, known as *embryology,* in the next chapter.

Bio-Topic: A Convenient Mutant

A large part of the California citrus industry is based on a mutation that occurred in Brazil more than 150 years ago. The mutation results in the formation of succulent oranges without seeds. Although convenient for the eater, seedless plants are a dead end unless propagated asexually—and this is what happened.

An American missionary working in Brazil in the early 1800s learned about a local orchard that produced tasty, seedless oranges. The seedless oranges had first appeared on a single limb of an otherwise ordinary tree. The Brazilian orchardist who noticed the unusual fruit propagated the mutation by a technique known as bud grafting. A bud from the mutant branch was placed under the bark of a normal orange tree and fastened into place. After some time, the tissues of the graft grew connections to the tissues of the tree. The graft grew into a complete branch which was entirely mutant because it was derived mitotically from the cells of the mutant graft. The mutant branch then provided buds for additional rounds of bud grafting. By grafting mutant buds to stumps of normal orange trees from which all the branches had been removed, the orchardist produced mutant trees.

The missionary, impressed with the tasty and convenient fruit, brought the mutation to the attention of an acquaintance employed by the United States Department of Agriculture in Washington, DC. The acquaintance obtained several trees from Brazil and added them to the collection in the USDA propagation greenhouses in Washington. The greenhouses were visited in the early 1870s by a woman who was about to migrate to California to stake out a homestead. She too was impressed. At her request, the USDA sent her two trees when her homestead in Riverside, California was established. She in turn passed out buds to her neighbors who were starting the citrus groves for which southern California became famous. The mutant orange flourished in the mild climate and became popular with growers and consumers.

The more than 15,000,000 trees propagated asexually from the two originally sent to California now cover well over 100,000 acres and are the basis of a major industry. We call the fruit of this mutant line the navel orange.

SUMMARY

There are two main types of reproduction, sexual and asexual. Examples of both of these are found throughout the living world, in both procaryotes and eucaryotes. Offspring resulting from asexual reproduction are almost always like their parent; offspring from sexual reproduction always differ somewhat from either parent.

Reproduction in protists includes the asexual processes of fragmentation, budding, fission, and spore production. Conjugation in *Spirogyra* involves formation and fusion of gametes in a sexual process that insures an exchange of genetic material.

In plants, sexual reproduction is part of a life cycle that includes two separate phases, a gametophyte (haploid) and a sporophyte (diploid). In general, both stages are necessary to complete a reproductive cycle.

As adults, most animals have diploid cells. Since the adult produces haploid sperm and egg, which unite to form a new diploid individual, the pattern is called diplontic. Some animals can replace body parts by cell division—an asexual process called regeneration.

Fertilization in mammals is internal; in humans the fertilized egg embeds itself in the lining of the uterus. The endometrium, or uterine lining, is built up and shed each month as a female undergoes menstrual cycles. Each menstrual cycle involves a complex interaction of hormones produced in the pituitary gland (FSH and LH) and the ovary (estrogen and progesterone). The menstrual cycle is controlled by both positive and negative feedback. Contraception, however, can prevent fertilization and can be used for birth control.

Birth control pills containing doses of estrogen and progesterone inhibit the formation and ovulation of mature eggs. These pills are a popular and effective form of contraception. Sterilization by vasectomy or tubal ligation is becoming more popular.

In many organisms reproductive cycles appear to be triggered by specific environmental conditions such as periods of light and dark, changes in temperature, seasons of the year, and phases of the moon. The reproductive success of a species may depend on the synchronization of gametes among its members.

REVIEW QUESTIONS

1. What advantages does sexual reproduction have for the survival of a species? Why do you think asexual reproduction still occurs in many organisms?

2. Explain why conjugation in *Spirogyra* is called a sexual process.

3. What are the structural and functional differences between the two phases of diplo-haplontic life cycles of plants?

4. What are two differences between estrus and a menstrual cycle? Give some examples.

5. Trace the development of human sperm and its passage from the testis through the urethra.

6. Outline the interaction among FSH, estrogen, LH, and progesterone in the menstrual cycle. How do birth control pills prevent conception?

7. What are the most effective means of contraception? What are the most widely used?

8. How are rhythmic and cyclic reproductive activities important to organisms? Do you think humans show rhythmic biological behavior?

SUPPLEMENTARY READINGS

Cronquist, Arthur, *Introductory Botany*, 2nd edition, Harper & Row, New York, 1971. Many chapters in this textbook deal with reproduction in the various plant groups, in the algae, and in fungi; a good reference for the details of reproduction in these groups of organisms. Other general botany books could be used if this one isn't available.

Goss, Richard J., *Principles of Regeneration*, Academic Press, New York, 1969. The basic principles of regeneration are examined through selected examples and experimental design.

McCary, James L., *Human Sexuality*, Van Nostrand Reinhold, New York, 1973. A contemporary treatment of the physiological, sociological, and psychological aspects of human sexuality is related to today's changes in attitudes and behavior about these topics.

Michelmore, Susan, *Sexual Reproduction*, The Natural History Press, Garden City, NY, 1964. The biological role of sex in reproduction and evolution is outlined in this short, popularly written booklet.

Vander, Arthur J., J. H. Sherman, and D. L. Luciano, *Human Physiology*, 2nd edition, McGraw-Hill, New York, 1975. The physiology of human reproduction including the role of hormones is thoroughly described in one chapter. Pregnancy, development, differentiation, puberty, and menopause are also covered. If this physiology text isn't available, other physiology textbooks usually cover most of this material.

Chapter 16

Growth & Development

This chapter poses a fascinating string of questions. In fact, you will find more unanswered questions in this chapter than anywhere else. For example, how does a single fertilized cell turn into a multicellular organism with millions or billions of cells that carry out a variety of functions? A nerve cell is very different from a muscle cell, yet the organism that contains both kinds of cells began as a single cell with only one set of genetic information.

As we begin by looking at the *Pattern of Development in Seed Plants,* we approach another intriguing question: how does nature provide for the maintenance and support of the developing individual that cannot yet nourish and protect itself? In plants, the seed is one possible answer. The processes of *Seed Germination* (the beginning of plant growth) and *Bud Development* (the start of differentiation into specialized tissues) cover the early stages of plant development.

The *Pattern of Development in Animals* offers most of the intriguing unanswered questions. The development of starfish, frogs, and then humans gives us some insight into the cumulative complexity of the process. All higher animals begin development by some kind of differentiation into layers of cells which then give rise to specific organ systems. Up to a certain time, this is a reversible process, but as development continues, each cell becomes more and more "committed" to becoming a specific type of cell.

This leads to the problem of the *Control of Development.* What determines the timing and pace of differentiation? Biologists who study development often do research by *Disrupting the Pattern to Understand It. The Classical Experiments in Development,* performed over the past 70 years, were based on interfering with the "normal" development processes to see how—and more important, *when*—the process could be put off the track. Three factors: genetics, hormones and nerves, and the environment appear to be involved in different kinds of development.

The counterpart of normal cell development is abnormal development. The *Loss of Developmental Control: Cancer* is one of the most serious health problems in the United States. Another important health aspect of the developmental process is *Maturation and Aging.* Our cells—and by extension, our bodies—do not stay young forever. What happens when we age? Research is now going on to understand it and perhaps control it.

Before we begin a detailed consideration of growth and development, it might be useful to pose a few basic questions.

The first question we might ask is, "Why grow?" Perhaps the most basic answer is that *it makes reproduction a workable strategy for survival.* We can see this more readily if we turn the question around and ask, "What would be the consequences of *not* growing?" If individual organisms did not increase in mass, the individuals in each successive generation would necessarily be smaller than those before them, until . . . . Clearly this would be a losing strategy with a single outcome: extinction.

We might next ask, "Why is growth always accompanied by cell division?" We appreciate the importance of cell division to the reproductive process, but why does growth itself always entail cell division? Why doesn't a single bacterium, paramecium, or muscle cell just get bigger and bigger? We have already discussed one basic reason in Chapter 11. There we saw that in general as any object, living or nonliving, gets bigger, its volume increases at a faster rate than its surface area. For cells of living systems, this situation is a limiting factor. Once a typical individual cell grows beyond a certain size, it no longer has enough surface area for diffusion of materials in and out to sustain its metabolism.

Finally, we might ask: "Why cellular differentiation (specialization)?" Here again, an important part of the answer comes from the limitations imposed by the faster rate of increase in volume than in surface area. Metabolism takes place within cells. We have seen that simple diffusion can provide effective metabolic inputs and outputs only over relatively short distances. Therefore cells that are relatively deep within an organism (that is, relatively far from the external environment) need specialized *supporting processes.* We discussed some of these processes in Chapters 10 and 11.

These processes, in turn, require specialized transport and processing systems. Thus the need arises for digestive, circulatory, breathing, and excretory systems. And this brings about the need for specialized (differentiated) cells—epithelial, connective, muscle, nerve, and other types. As a result of these specialized tissues, a division of labor is made possible and a greater efficiency is possible.

During the development of any organism, a precise and orderly sequence of events gives rise to cells, tissues, organs, and organ systems. The results of this developmental process are amazing in their diversity, both in form and function. But equally remarkable is how predictable these results are. In animals, for example, liver cells aggregate into an organ with specific functions and with predictable size, shape, and location. Moreover, ducts, blood vessels, and nerves interconnecting organs develop in a fashion that assures proper circulation and regulation.

Many of us have seen examples of developmental dysfunction—two-headed calves, one-eyed pigs, or perhaps Siamese twins (Figure 16–1). Abnormalities of this type, however, occur in only a small proportion of births. Small variations of little consequence are often detected by physicians as they perform x-rays or surgery for other reasons. Some of us may ourselves contain the outcome of a minor developmental dysfunction, such as two fused vertebrae. Medical students often find that the cadaver they are dissecting possesses a "new" artery or vein. Patterns of development, then,

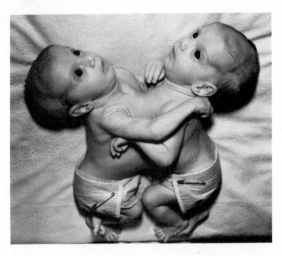

FIGURE 16–1 Siamese twins, an example of abnormal development. (Courtesy of the National Foundation—March of Dimes.)

although generally precise and predictable, allow a limited amount of variation and adaptability. In this chapter we will first examine some general development patterns in plants and animals and then discuss the mechanisms that produce these patterns.

PATTERN OF DEVELOPMENT IN SEED PLANTS

Seed germination and growth is often taken for granted. If we plant and water a seed, an embryonic plant soon pops to the soil surface (Figure 16–2). With light, water, and occasional fertilizer if the soil is not naturally rich enough,

this plant will thrive. And, unlike an animal, it will continue to grow throughout its life.

A seed consists of a multicellular embryo, food-storage tissue, and a protective seed coat (Figure 16–3). During the first phases of development, the embryo differentiates into three structures—one or two embryonic seed leaves (cotyledons), an embryonic shoot (plumule and epicotyl), and an embryonic root (hypocotyl with radicle).

Seed Germination

A seed placed in warm, moist soil absorbs water and swells. When this occurs the embryo,

FIGURE 16–2   A developing plant emerging through the soil.
(John H. Gerard, National Audubon Society/Photo Researchers.)

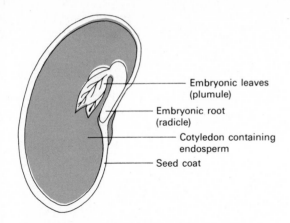

FIGURE 16-3 The contents of a mature bean seed.

which was in a dormant state (low metabolism and no growth), increases its rate of metabolism and begins to grow. First the hypocotyl emerges from the seed and grows downward in the soil. In the early stages growth is principally by swelling, but mitosis and elongation begin later near the tip of the growing root, producing an apical meristem. (*Apical* means "at the tip"; a *meristem* is a group of rapidly dividing embryonic cells. See Figure 5-5). In seeds such as peas, the cotyledons remain below the surface; the epicotyl grows upward and the hypocotyl downward. In beans, on the other hand, the hypocotyl develops in the form of an arch. As the structure elongates and straightens out, the cotyledons and the epicotyl are pulled out of the soil (Figure 16-4). In either case the epicotyl begins a series of cell divisions at its tip. This growth forms an apical meristem usually called a *bud*, consisting of a group of rapidly dividing cells. The plumule develops rapidly into primary leaves, and photosynthesis becomes available as a source of energy for growth.

Bud Development

Buds are the primary areas of plant growth and development. New branches and leaves are produced along a growing stem at the lateral or axillary buds, which are sites of increased cell division. Each lateral bud has the potential to

become the terminal bud of a new shoot and to grow and branch according to the pattern of its species. We know very little about how a plant's genetic pattern is transformed into its actual structure, but each species of plant definitely follows a specific pattern in the shapes and arrangements of stems and leaves (Figure 16-5).

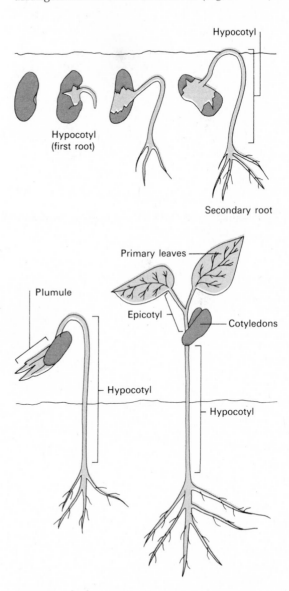

FIGURE 16-4 Germination and development of a bean. The stages shown require about one week in warm, moist soil.

(a)

(b)

FIGURE 16–5 Various patterns of plant stem growth. (a) Columnar, with no branches growing from lateral buds. (b) Cone-shaped (excurrent branching), growth dominated by terminal bud. (c) Spreading type (deliquescent branching), with weak or no terminal bud dominance. (Courtesy U.S. Forest Service and Japan National Tourist Organization.)

(c)

Developing apical buds and shoots produce hormones called *auxins*, noted in Chapter 12, which promote the growth of apical meristems but inhibit development of lateral buds. A gardener can thus produce bushier plants by clipping the tips of upper shoots.

Some cells in bud tissue divide to produce fundamental tissues (parenchyma, collenchyma, and sclerenchyma, discussed in Chapter 5), and others give rise to vascular tissues (xylem and phloem). The process by which immature plant or animal cells change into specific cell types to form various tissues is called *differentiation*. In stems of woody flowering plants, the apical meristem may form distinctive terminal and lateral buds (Figure 16–6). In a dormant bud, the conical central cell mass (body) is surrounded by a sheath consisting of several hardened leaves (bud scales). Following dormancy, the scales spread

FIGURE 16-6   Young twig of a woody dicot, showing a terminal (apical) bud and several lateral buds. (New York Botanical Garden).

open and fall away, leaving a ring-shaped scar on the stem.

Besides dividing rapidly, meristematic cells also remain relatively unspecialized through several cell divisions. These new cells have the potential to develop into the specialized plant tissues. Directly beneath an apical meristem,

then, the new cells begin to differentiate into epidermal, vascular, and fundamental tissues.

PATTERNS OF DEVELOPMENT IN ANIMALS

Embryology, the study of embryonic development, has two major areas, *descriptive* and *experimental*. Descriptive studies deal with the visible changes that take place during the development of an organism. Experimental embryology investigates the cellular mechanisms that cause or control these visible changes. For example, what determines the future of a particular cell? Why does one cell become a muscle cell while a nearby cell develops into a connective-tissue cell? Why are a specific number of cells produced in one region of an organism? Why does development of one structure begin only after another structure is developed? Many experiments have been performed in attempts to answer these and other questions of development. Before discussing these questions, we will first briefly outline the descriptive embryology of the starfish, frog, and human—organisms representing three distinct patterns of development. These will introduce most of the basic principles of animal embryological development.

Development in Starfish

Starfish offer a relatively simple example of development from a fertilized egg into a multicellular organism. Early cleavages of a starfish zygote are said to be equal, because cells of equal size form from each division. The first stage of development is characterized by a series of rapid mitotic divisions (occurring every 25 to 50 minutes) in which 2, 4, 8, 16, and 32 cells are produced (Figure 16–7). After several hours a solid ball of cells called the *morula* is formed. After many more divisions, this ball of cells develops a central cavity, the *blastocoel*, and becomes the "hollow ball" or *blastula* stage (Figure 16–8). During this initial period of cleavage (approximately 7 to 8 hours) the cells become progressively smaller; the overall mass of the blastula is about the same as the egg.

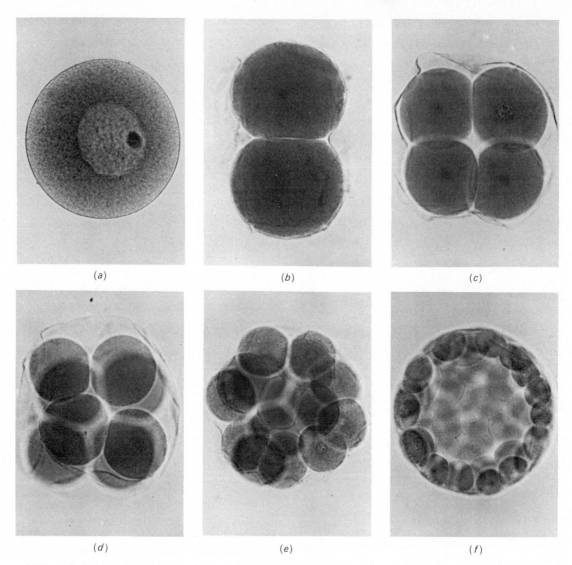

FIGURE 16–7   Starfish development: early cleavage stages.
(a) Unfertilized egg. (b) Two-cell stage. (c) Four-cell stage.
(d) Eight-cell stage. (e) Sixteen-cell stage. (f) Sixty-four-cell stage.
(Courtesy of Carolina Biological Supply Company.)

Shortly after the blastula forms, an area of the blastula wall begins to push into the blastocoel. The effect is similar to that produced by sticking one's finger into a balloon or tennis ball. This invagination of cells is the beginning of the *gastrula* stage. The process of gastrulation produces a new cavity called the *archen-* *teron*, or primitive gut, and leaves an opening the *blastopore*, in the wall. The old blastocoel, pushed ahead of this advancing invagination, gradually disappears. Gastrulation produces two cellular layers, the *ectoderm* (outer layer) and *endoderm* (inner layer). A middle layer, the *mesoderm*, is next produced by a prolifera-

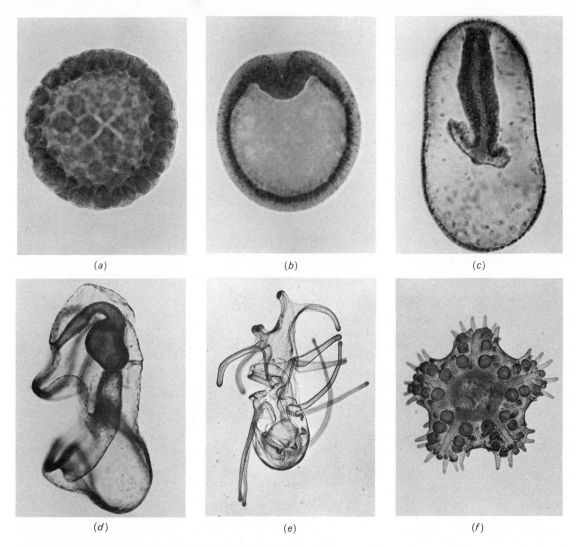

FIGURE 16–8   Starfish development: blastula through young starfish. (a) Blastula. (b) Early gastrula. (c) Late gastrula. (d) Late bipinnaria. (e) Brachiolaria. (f) Young starfish. (Courtesy of Carolina Biological Supply Company.)

tion of cells from endoderm or the ectoderm and endoderm, depending on the species.

Animals that show this type of early embryonic development are termed *triploblastic.* All tissues and organs of the adult animal arise from these three primary layers, ectoderm, endoderm, and mesoderm. In vertebrates, for example, the ectoderm gives rise to the epidermis and nervous system. Mesodermal structures include the skeleton, the dermis layer of the skin, blood, muscles, connective tissues, and most of the excretory and reproductive systems. Endodermal tissues include the lining of the digestive and respiratory tracts and the urinary bladder.

Following gastrulation in starfish, the primitive gut develops a mouth, stomach, and anus; the anus is formed in the region of the blastopore. At this point ciliated bands form on three pairs of lateral lobes, transforming the embryo into a free-moving, feeding larva called a *bipinnaria*. A *larva* is an immature form of an animal that undergoes a series of changes before assuming the adult form. This bilateral bipinnaria larva later develops long ciliated lobes and becomes a *brachiolaria* larva. Brachiolaria finally develop into very small, radially symmetric starfish (Figure 16–8).

Development in Frogs

Frogs are *oviparous*, which means that fertilized eggs develop outside the parent's body. One half of a fertilized frog egg is highly pigmented. This dark hemisphere is called the *animal pole* because the embryo will develop in this area. The white hemisphere, or *vegetal pole*, contains a heavy concentration of yolk nutrients. About one hour after fertilization, the egg undergoes a mitotic cell division called the first cleavage. A second cleavage, perpendicular to the first, occurs after about 30–45 minutes (Figure 16–9). Subsequent cleavages occur more rapidly than the first two, and cells in the animal hemisphere divide more frequently than yolk cells. This cleavage process has not increased the mass of the original egg.

The frog blastula is similar to that of a starfish, but the blastocoel is relatively smaller and displaced toward the animal pole because of the unequal cleavage. The process of gastrulation, however, is different in the frog. At a point 180 degrees from the entrance of the sperm and in the region where the cells of animal and vegetal portions merge, cells of the animal pole turn inward and move into the blastocoel. In this process, animal cells actually overgrow yolk cells and turn inward, forming a blastopore. Yolk cells fill the hole produced by gastrulation and form a yolk plug (Figure 16–9g). The position of the blastopore and its yolk plug marks the eventual orientation of the animal, since the blastopore is finally replaced by the anus. The head develops approximately 180 degrees from this spot.

After gastrulation, the three primary germ

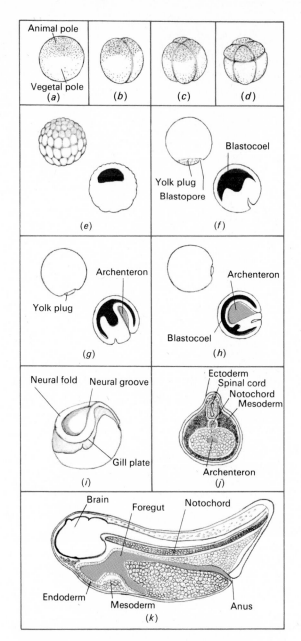

FIGURE 16–9   Early embryology of the frog. (*a*) Egg. (*b*) Two-cell stage. (*c*) Four-cell stage. (*d*) Eight-cell stage. (*e*) Blastula stage. (*f*), (*g*), (*h*) Developing gastrula stages (cross sections are through the yolk plug). (*i*) Neurula stage. (*j*) Cross section of late neurula. (*k*) Longitudinal section of early embryo.

layers begin to differentiate into various organs. The first of these is the neural tube. The dorsal ectoderm sinks to form a groove, which then closes at the top to form a single hollow tube. The anterior portion of this tube develops into the brain; the remainder forms the spinal cord (Figure 16–9i). This stage of development is called the *neurula*.

In frogs and other chordates a unique structure called the *notochord* develops at this time. The notochord, formed primarily of mesodermal cells, is an elastic rod running along the middorsal region (the middle of the back). Later, the notochord is replaced by vertebrae of the spinal column. In frogs, the coelom (body cavity) is formed by the splitting of two mesodermal sheets that have developed from endodermal cells roofing the archenteron. Half of each mesodermal sheet is attached to the external wall as a body lining, and the other half surrounds the visceral organs (Figure 16–9j).

By this time the embryo has elongated. A segmental series of paired mesodermal blocks called *somites* have formed along the length of the organism. Each somite consists of three regions: an outer part that will form the dermis of the skin, a middle region from which most skeletal muscles will develop, and the initially inner part that will give rise to the vertebrae. Internal organs and external gills develop next. In 10 to 12 days, depending on the particular species, a tadpole can be recognized. Limb buds and internal lungs then develop, and the tail is gradually reabsorbed. Development of a young frog takes approximately 90 days after fertilization.

Development in Humans

In mammals both fertilization (Figure 16–13, on color plate following p. 416) and development are internal, and a female gives birth to well-developed young. This system of development is called *viviparous* development. In humans, cleavage produces cells of equal size with each division because the amount of yolk material is small. Once the formation of a solid ball of cells (morula stage) occurs, a distinction can be made between the outer layer of cells (the *trophectoderm*) and the inner cell mass

(Figure 16–10a). Trophectoderm cells flatten and enlarge to produce a blastocoel along one edge of the morula. As trophectoderm cells divide, the blastocoel becomes larger; an inner cell mass remains at the animal pole (Figure 16–10b). The layers of the inner cell mass soon separate to form a cavity that will become the *amnion*, a fluid-filled sac enveloping the embryo. Cells from the lower edges of the inner cell mass proliferate and move along the inner wall of the blastocoel to form a yolk sac (Figure 16–10c and d). The layer of the inner cell mass between these two cavities, the embryonic disc, will develop into the embryo.

At this point, mesoderm begins to form in several areas. This corresponds to gastrulation in other animals. Ectoderm lines the amniotic cavity and forms the upper layers of the embryonic disc; endoderm lines the yolk sac and forms the lower layers of the disc; mesoderm occurs in the center of the embryonic disc and forms sheets of cells covering the outside of the amnion and the yolk sac, as well as the inside of the trophectoderm (Figure 16–10e and f). An outer membrane, the *chorion*, composed of trophectoderm and mesoderm completely envelops the developing embryo (Figure 16–11).

Another sac, the *allantois*, next pouches out from the gut of the embryo near the yolk sac and pushes close to the chorion. The mesoderm in the allantois is rich in blood vessels; the area of its contact with the chorion is called the chorio-allantoic membrane. Small fingerlike villi from the chorion mesh with the endometrium of the uterus, forming a *placenta* for exchange of gases and uptake of nutrients from the mother's blood (Figure 16–12 and Figure 16–16, on color plate following p. 416). The allantoic sac with its blood vessels—two arteries and a vein—and the yolk sac form the umbilical cord. Normally the mother's blood never mixes with the baby's blood; exchange of products occurs across the thin membranes of the placental villi.

Development proceeds in an orderly, sequential manner; after about a month the heart is functional, limb buds are showing, eyes are forming, and remnants of pharyngeal gill slits may be seen (Figure 16–14, on color plate following p. 416).

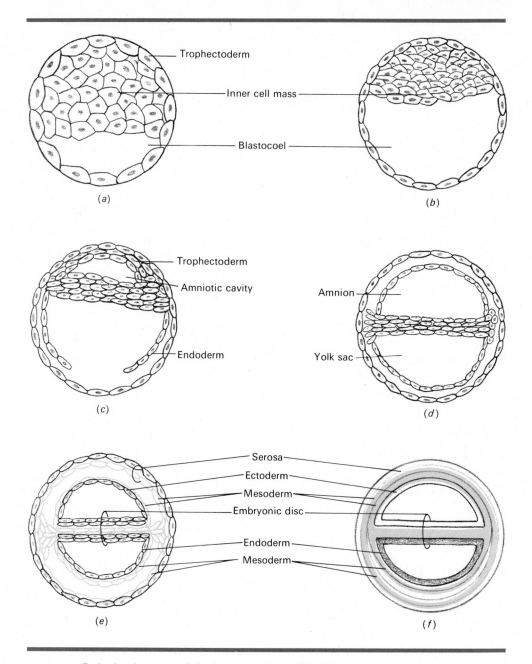

FIGURE 16–10   Early development of the human embryo. (*a*), (*b*) Development of the inner cell mass. (*c*), (*d*) Formation of the amnion and yolk sac. (*e*), (*f*) Embryonic disc stage, showing position of the primary germ layers.

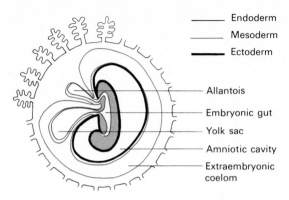

Endoderm
Mesoderm
Ectoderm

Allantois
Embryonic gut
Yolk sac
Amniotic cavity
Extraembryonic coelom

FIGURE 16–11 Early human embryo, showing distribution of germ layers (endoderm, mesoderm, and ectoderm) and formation of extraembryonic membranes.

After about two months the developing embryo looks definitely human (Figure 16–15, on color plate following p. 416). By the twelfth week (Figure 16–16 on color plate following p. 416) the *fetus* is about three inches long, weighs nearly an ounce, and has some hair. Note that during the first three months (12 weeks) of development we speak of an embryo. From three months to birth the developing human is called a fetus. By this time all organ systems have begun to develop. During the next six months (Figures 16–17 and 16–18, on color plate following p. 416) the fetus will continue to grow, with further development of organs in all systems (Figure 16–19). In the fetus, blood is shunted away from the lungs, which are not functional. This is accomplished

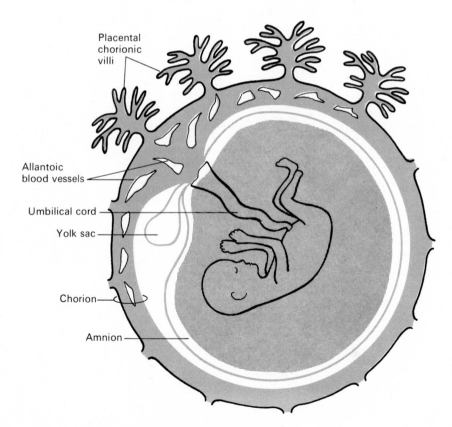

Placental chorionic villi

Allantoic blood vessels

Umbilical cord

Yolk sac

Chorion

Amnion

FIGURE 16–12 Diagram of the structures shown in Figure 16–14.

Month	Approximate Size	General Developmental Events
1	1/8 inch	Implantation by 12th day after fertilization; nervous system begins development and eyes, ears, nose begin to form; 32 pairs of somites (blocks of mesoderm which form muscles); pharyngeal arches and clefts; heart becomes functional; small tail-like growth; primitive type of kidneys form (pronephros); major systems start to develop; limb buds show.
2	1 inch	Gill clefts incorporated into developing face and neck; vestigial tail-like structure resorbed; skeleton begins to form; ovaries or testes form; arms and legs assume characteristic shape; all major skeletal muscles developed; brain equals about one-half total length of embryo; completely bathed by amniotic fluid which can be taken into the gut and lungs.
3	3 inches 3/4 ounce	Facial hair produced; further skeletal development; brain equals less than one-third total length.
4	7 inches 5 ounces	Fingerprints develop; complex development of brain surface; eyes and ears assume characteristic shapes; reflexes develop; hair appears on head and body.
5	10 inches 1/2 pound	Fingernails and toenails form; fetal movements (kicking); loss and replacement of cells of tissues such as the skin; digestive system well developed; blood being formed in bone marrow.
6	12 inches 1½ lb	Increased skeletal formation (ossification); development of many sweat and oil glands in skin; fetus now looks like small human.
7	15 inches 2½ lb	Fetus could live outside of uterus but would require hospital care; respiratory system functional; testes descend into scrotal sac.
8	16 inches 4 lb	Fat tissues accumulate and body fills out; roots of teeth begin to grow; intensive calcium deposition.
9	20 inches 6–8 lb	Most of hair coat has disappeared; brain equals one-fourth total length; growth and development slow down; kidneys reach full development; maturation of nervous system and reflex patterns.

FIGURE 16–19   Developmental events in the human embryo.

through an opening between the right and left atria and by a duct between the pulmonary artery and the aorta. At birth these openings close to provide full pulmonary circulation. In some newborns, one or both of these openings fail to close completely. The blood is therefore poorly oxygenated, since it continues to be directed away from the lungs. This condition, known as "blue baby," can usually be corrected surgically. Generally, birth can be expected to occur about 280 days from the mother's last menstruation, although this period may vary by several days or weeks.

Birth of a Baby

About two weeks before birth (or parturition) the fetus normally settles head downward into the pelvic cavity. At this time the opening of the uterus at the cervix (the lowermost region of the uterus which projects into the vagina) dilates slightly and a mucous plug may be discharged. Many women undergo "false labor" several weeks before actual delivery. False labor is characterized by irregular uterine cramps of short duration. True labor, on the other hand, consists of strong, regular contractions. The onset of true labor may be signaled by sharp uterine pains and the release of amniotic fluid ("breaking of the water"). Rhythmic uterine contractions increase in duration and intensity until they last for about 1 minute and occur every 2 or 3 minutes. By this time the cervix is well dilated and the infant's head may be visible (Figure 16–20). The time required to com-

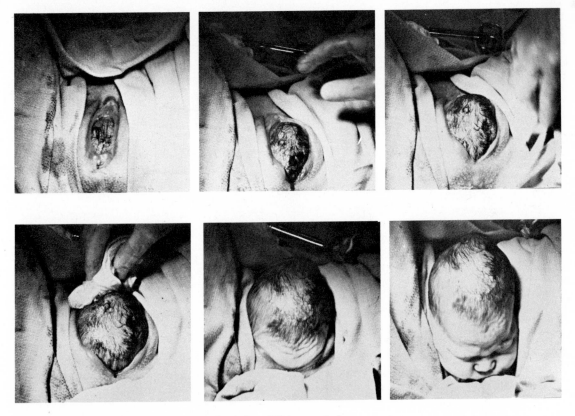

FIGURE 16–20   Stages in the birth of a baby. (With permission from Dr. Roberts Rugh, from Rugh and Shettles, *From Conception to Birth,* Harper & Row, 1971.)

plete parturition varies, usually between 6 and 20 hours. Women generally experience a longer labor having their first child than with subsequent births.

The uterine muscle is thought to contract in response to decreased progesterone and increased levels of oxytocin. In cases of prolonged pregnancy or cessation of labor, oxytocin may be given intravenously in a solution similar in concentration to body fluids. As the oxytocin level builds up, uterine contractions begin or recommence and birth is induced. As the mother bears down with helpful abdominal compressions, the baby is forced through the birth canal. Mucus is then cleared from the baby's mouth and nose, and the umbilical cord is tied and cut. The final stage of delivery is expulsion of the placenta (called the afterbirth)

about 3 to 10 minutes after birth. Further contractions occur in the uterus which close the cervix and prevent excessive bleeding.

CONTROL OF DEVELOPMENT

But how is the development of an individual animal controlled? We know that all of the cells of an individual contain the same genes, and we also learned in Chapter 14 that genes control development. As we will see, certain genes function at specific times in some cells and not in others. But how does gene action relate to patterns of development? Embryonic patterns have been recognized and observed since the early 1600s, but the control mechanisms were completely unknown until the late nineteenth century. We have looked at several different

Bio-Topic: Genetic Screening

More than 2000 genetic diseases of humans have now been identified. In the past, the discovery that a child carried a genetic disease occurred only at or after the child's birth. Recent developments in genetics and biochemistry now enable physicians to detect many genetic diseases prior to birth. But these developments raise thorny moral and ethical issues that are yet to be resolved.

Many genetic diseases result either from gene mutations or from chromosomal abnormalities inherited from a parent who also carried the mutation. Prospective parents can be examined to determine if either carries a mutation that might be passed on to their child. Chromosomal abnormalities can be identified by examining a stained tissue sample taken from each prospective parent. Gene mutations can often be detected through biochemical tests of parental blood that reveal the products of mutant genes or the absence of the products of normal genes. If either prospective parent is found to carry an abnormal gene or chromosome, the couple can be advised of the risk of having a child with a genetic disease.

Other genetic diseases result from mutations in the ovaries or testes of a parent and could not have been detected before conception. These mutations include chromosomal abnormalities that stem from errors during meiosis, as well as gene mutations. There are now at least two ways to detect such genetic diseases after conception but prior to birth. In one, a sample of maternal urine is analyzed for unusual chemicals that are produced by a mutant fetus and pass, via the placenta, into the mother's circulatory system. The other, amniocentesis, involves removing a sample of the amniotic fluid that surrounds the fetus and usually contains a few suspended fetal cells. The amniotic fluid is removed through a needle inserted through the mother's abdominal wall, the fetal cells are cultured, then stained and scanned for abnormal chromosomes.

Our present ability to diagnose many genetic diseases before birth has led to the suggestion that prospective parents—especially those with histories of genetic diseases in their families—be required to undergo tests to determine if they might produce a fetus with a genetic disease. The birth of a child with a genetic disease places a burden on society and adds to the gene pool mutant genes that may be passed on to later generations, thus increasing the burden. The argument is that society must protect itself against such economic and genetic burdens.

Many couples now voluntarily avail themselves of these kinds of genetic screening. The issue to be resolved is whether genetic screening should become mandatory. Who shall conduct the screening? Who will be screened and who will not? Who will receive the results? How will the results be used? Will we issue licenses for birth, or require that mutant fetuses be aborted? A balance must be maintained between protecting the personal freedom of the prospective parents and protecting the interests of the society of which they are members.

Again, research has advanced more rapidly than our capacity to deal with the emotional, ethical, and social issues raised.

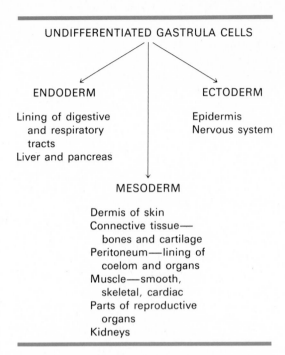

UNDIFFERENTIATED GASTRULA CELLS

ENDODERM

Lining of digestive
and respiratory
tracts
Liver and pancreas

ECTODERM

Epidermis
Nervous system

MESODERM

Dermis of skin
Connective tissue—
bones and cartilage
Peritoneum—lining of
coelom and organs
Muscle—smooth,
skeletal, cardiac
Parts of reproductive
organs
Kidneys

FIGURE 16–21 Some of the structures formed from the three germ layers.

developmental patterns, each giving rise to obviously different organisms: starfish, frogs, and humans. The details of each pattern differ significantly, but some processes are common to all. For example, all three organisms go through a gastrulation stage, producing three germ layers—ectoderm, mesoderm, and endoderm. Each of these primary germ layers is destined to give rise to specific tissue types as development proceeds (Figure 16–21).

As with plants, unspecialized animal cells become specialized through a process known as *differentiation*, which causes permanent changes in cells during the course of development. We now know that these changes can result from interactions with other cells, from chemicals produced by cells or, sometimes, from external influences.

C. H. Waddington of England has used a "landscape" model to compare cell differentiation to a ball rolling down an inclined surface toward a series of valleys. As the ball rolls, it commits itself to a particular region; the further it continues, the fewer opportunities are available. At certain stages there may be alternative valleys, but these become fewer and fewer, until the ball ends up at the bottom of one valley. A dividing embryonic cell also becomes committed along its course of development, gradually losing the ability to form various cell types.

Embryonic cells—all contain the same genetic information. But they pass through phases that are determined not only by their genetic information but also by *association with other cells*. The descendants of these cells finally occupy positions in the mature organism where they perform specific functions. The sequential changes through which developing cells lose their equal potentials are termed *restrictive phases*. Each restrictive phase may be followed by an *expressive phase* in which final, fully functional tissues are produced such as pancreas cells that are able to secrete all of their different enzymes.

Many theories have attempted to explain how such a wide variety of cell types, tissues, and organ systems are formed with such precision and accuracy. It has not been possible to understand development completely just by observing normal patterns; progress has been made only through extensive experimentation. Although we have learned a great deal during the past 50 years, much remains to be learned about the complex mechanisms that control development.

Disrupting the Pattern to Understand It

In Chapter 14 we saw that geneticists have made progress in understanding normal gene activity by *disrupting* that activity. For example, they induce mutations and study the resulting abnormal effects. Embryologists have also used "disruptive" techniques with considerable success.

When normal development is interrupted, embryonic cells often survive but change into different types of cells; in other words, they take on different developmental potentials. Embryologists have used a wide variety of techniques to alter or block normal patterns. Exper-

Bio-Topic: More Than Two Parents

Developmental biology is one of the great frontiers of contemporary biology. The goal is to understand how a single cell, the fertilized egg, develops into the tissues and organs of a multicellular individual. In their search for understanding, biologists have explored many odd and unusual developmental systems. Along the way, they have produced individuals with more than two parents.

In one series of experiments with mice, a recently fertilized egg was removed from the lining of its mother's uterus. The egg was transplanted to the uterus of a second female that had been treated with hormones to simulate the conditions of pregnancy. The egg developed normally and a normal mouse was born. The mouse had three "parents"—a mother and a father that contributed genes and an "incubator mother." The incubator mother technique has found a practical application in the breeding of horses and cattle. A fertilized egg is removed from the uterus of a genotypically valuable fe-

male and transplanted into the uterus of an ordinary female. After a few weeks, the valuable female can be mated again and a second fertilized egg transplanted into another incubator. In this way, breeders can breed a single female several times a year instead of only once.

In another series of experiments, very early embryos were removed from two pregnant mice. The embryos were placed in a nutrient fluid and gently squeezed together until the cells of the two embryos stuck to one another. The fused embryo was then implanted in an incubator mother who eventually gave birth to a single infant mouse. This mouse carried genes from two mothers and two fathers, and its fifth "parent" was its incubator mother. Studies of these "multiparental" mice are providing new insights into the ways in which the cells of an embryo interact as tissues and organs are formed. These unlikely organisms may eventually help biologists to solve the puzzle of development.

iments of this kind can yield valuable information about the expression of genetic potentials and the intricate timing of development. Interpretation of results is extremely difficult, however, because numerous unknown factors could also influence a particular stage of development.

Classical Experiments in Development

In 1891 it was demonstrated that if cells resulting from the first or second cleavages of sea urchin eggs were separated, each would develop into a complete miniature embryo. In cells derived after the third cleavage, however, complete development was impossible. These cells had evidently differentiated, or lost their equal potential for development, after two divisions.

This conclusion gave rise to the idea that each cell in a developing embryo contained the information necessary to become a specific part of the organism, and that as development proceeded each cell became more and more specialized.

In the 1920s Hans Spemann, a German embryologist, performed a significant series of experiments with frog embryos. Working with embryos in the late gastrula stage, Spemann transplanted a small piece of dorsal ectoderm (from the area that would become the neural tube) in place of a piece of potentially belly ectoderm, and vice versa. The transplanted neural tube ectoderm differentiated into belly skin, and the graft from the belly region became part of the neural tube. Spemann then

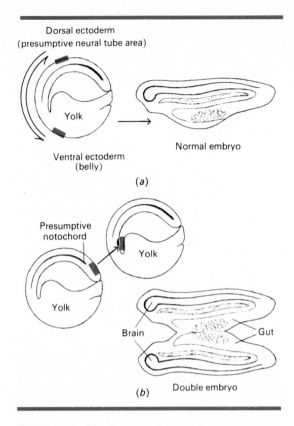

Dorsal ectoderm
(presumptive neural tube area)

Yolk

Normal embryo

Ventral ectoderm
(belly)

(a)

Presumptive
notochord

Yolk

Yolk

Brain

Gut

(b)   Double embryo

FIGURE 16–22 Spemann's germ-layer transplants. (*a*) Interchange of tissue between dorsal
ectoderm and ventral (belly) ectoderm at the gastrula stage results in a normal tadpole. (*b*) Transplant of section of notochord to the belly region
results in a double embryo.

transplanted a piece of the underlying notochord (beneath the neural tube) into the belly
region. The result was a double embryo attached belly to belly (Figure 16–22). Obviously,
the notochordal cells had produced something
that altered normal development of the embryonic tissues in the belly region.

The results of Spemann's work gave support
to the theory of *induction,* which states that
certain cells in an embryo can induce or control the development of other cells. The fate of
a developing cell thus depends on the influence
of neighboring cells, or simply on its position in
the embryo. The exact molecular mechanisms
of induction, including the formation of "orga-

nizer areas" in the embryo, are not completely
understood, but many experiments have
been performed in attempts to understand the
process.

Most of these experiments involve moving
tissues from one region of an embryonic organism to another. In the formation of the vertebrate eye, for example, the optic vesicle growing
from the midbrain induces the ectoderm in the
head region to form a lens (Figure 16–23).
Other eye tissues are then formed. If the optic
vesicle is removed, a lens is not formed in the
region of the ectoderm where it normally develops. The optic vesicle can thus be considered an inducer for the development of a lens
from the ectoderm.

Since we know that enucleate cells (those
without nuclei) soon die, nuclei must perform
an essential role in development. This role
certainly includes the protein synthesis process
described in Chapter 14. Several experiments
using innovative techniques have shed light on
the role of the nucleus in differentiating embryos. For example, it is possible to pierce an
egg with a micropipette and suck out the nucleus. In 1952 Thomas King and Robert Briggs
succeeded in transplanting nuclei from the
early gastrula stage of grass-frog endoderm (destined to form intestine) into enucleate eggs.
Some of the eggs developed into normal or
nearly normal tadpoles. But endoderm nuclei
transferred at the late gastrula stage or later
produced very few tadpoles. King and Briggs
proposed that by the late gastrula stage, many
cells had become differentiated (restricted) so
that their nuclei could no longer initiate normal development. King and Briggs repeated this
pattern of transplants for several generations—
that is, they removed nuclei from the gastrula
stages that did develop and injected them into
other enucleate eggs. In these transplants development continued to stop at the same stage of
incomplete tadpole development as it did in
the original transplant.

In 1963 Joachim Hammerling of the Max
Planck Institute performed a number of simple
experiments with the single-celled green alga
Acetabularia. This organism consists of a base
containing the nucleus, a two-inch erect stalk,
and a flaring umbrellalike cap (Figure 16–24).

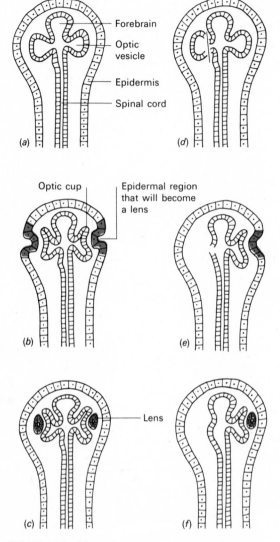

FIGURE 16–23   Development of the lens of the frog eye from the ectoderm. In normal development (*a, b, c*), each optic vesicle induces the region of the epidermis adjacent to it to form a pocket of cells that sinks inward to become the lens. If one optic vesicle is cut away, no lens will develop on that side (*d, e, f*).

By cutting sections of stalk out of two algae with different caps and transplanting them onto bases of the opposite type, Hammerling observed that the regenerated caps always resembled the type of the base to which it was transplanted. Although the cytoplasm was essential to regeneration, the process appeared to be controlled by the base, which contained the nucleus.

The Developmental Role of DNA

We are already familiar with the controlling influence of nuclear DNA in the cytoplasmic synthesis of cellular protein. It seems likely that at certain times during development, the nucleus could produce specific enzymes which in turn could synthesize "organizer substances."

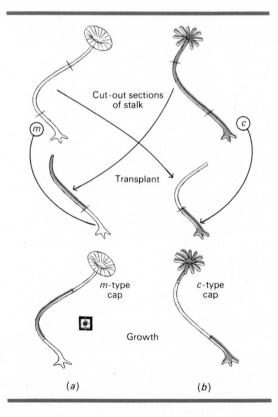

FIGURE 16–24   Nuclear control of cap development in the unicellular alga *Acetabularia*. (*a*) *A. mediterrania* (smooth cap). (*b*) *A. crenulata* (lobed cap).

Hammerling noted that these algae have great regenerative powers: if the cap is clipped off near the tip, a new cap quickly forms.

Several closely related species of *Acetabularia* have characteristically different caps.

PLATE IX

FIGURE 16–13 Human egg being fertilized.
(Dr. Roberts Rugh.)

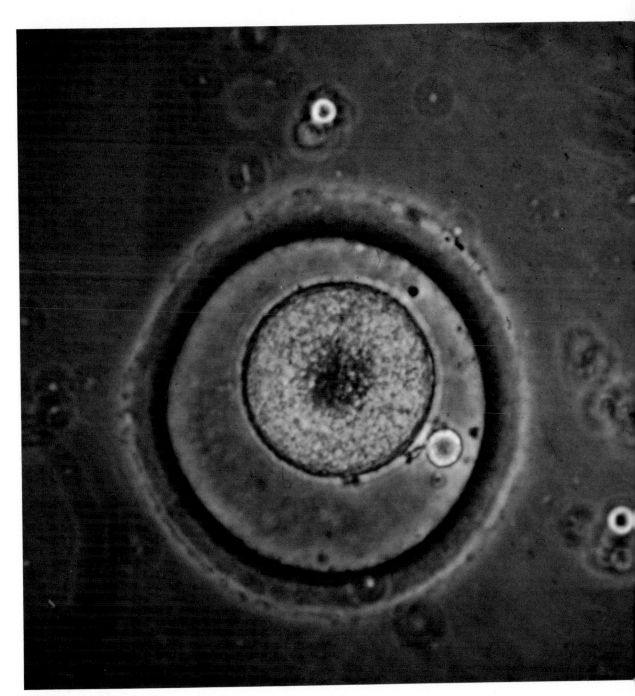

FIGURE 16–13

PLATE X

FIGURE 16-14 Human embryo at 38 days. The eyes and limb buds are developing, and the heart is functional. (Dr. Roberts Rugh.)

FIGURE 16-15 Human embryo at 2 months, in the amnion. (Dr. Roberts Rugh.)

FIGURE 16-16 Human fetus at 3 months. Extraembryonic membranes and part of the placenta are visible. (Dr. Roberts Rugh.)

FIGURE 16-17 Fraternal twin fetuses at 4 months (18 weeks). (Dr. Roberts Rugh.)

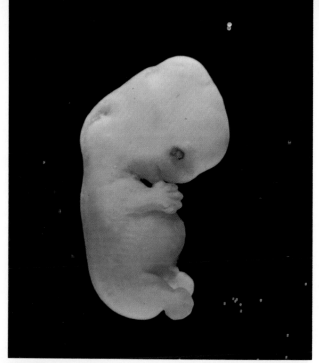

FIGURE 16-14

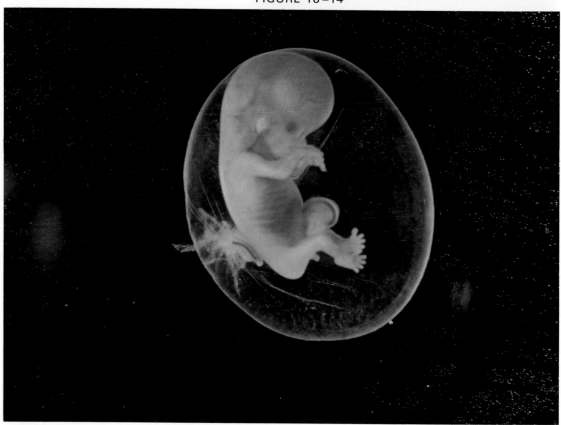

FIGURE 16-15

PLATE XI

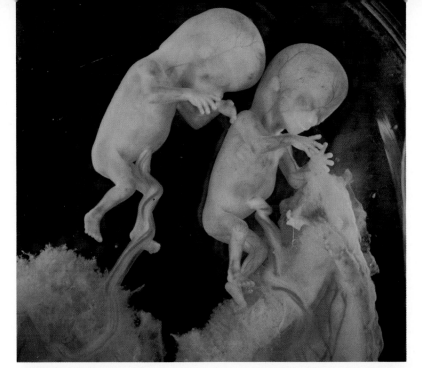

FIGURE 16-17

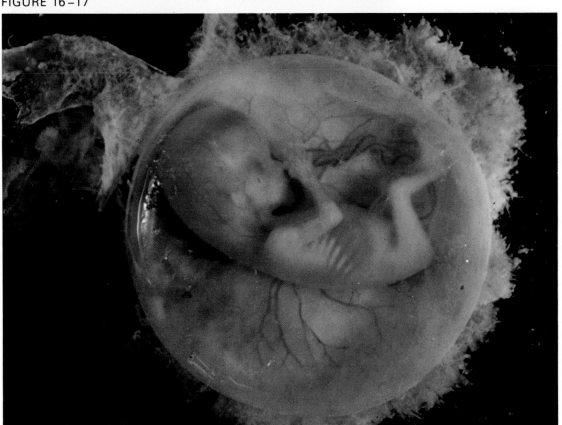

FIGURE 16-16

PLATE XII

FIGURE 16–18   Human fetus at 5 months
(20 weeks). (Dr. Roberts Rugh.)

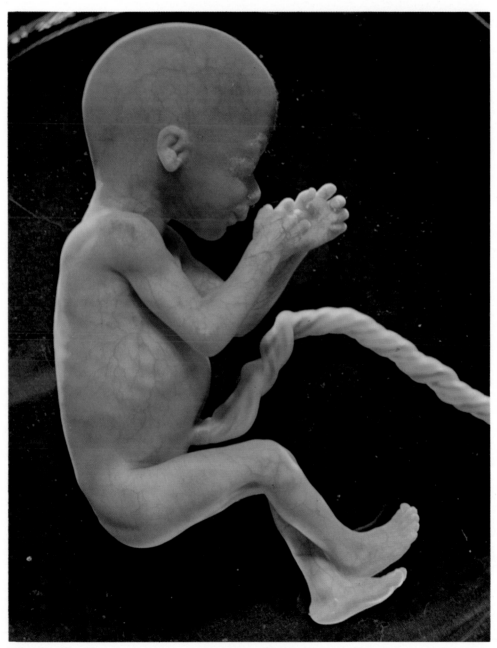

FIGURE 16–18

Support for this hypothesis came in 1959 when Wolfgang Beermann reported the activities of giant chromosomes in differentiating larval cells of chironomid fly (small flies related to the fruit fly, *Drosophila*). These chromosomes are more than 10,000 times the size of normal chromosomes, because the DNA has duplicated many times without chromosome division (Figure 16–25). These chromosomes are much thicker and thus more visible than normal chromosomes. Beermann discovered that the giant chromosomes produce large puffs of threadlike DNA material, facilitating the synthesis of messenger RNA. Beermann cut out several of these puffs and analyzed the associated messenger RNA. By studying the puffing patterns in several different embryonic tissues, Beermann discovered that puffs form at specific locations and seem to be related to develop-

mental changes in these tissues. This evidence suggests that genetic action in the chromosomes is directly related to protein synthesis and cellular differentiation.

In 1968, J. B. Gurdon of the University of Oxford took the experiment of King and Briggs one step further. Gurdon removed nuclei from intestinal cells of frog tadpoles and transplanted them into eggs whose nuclei had been destroyed by ultraviolet light (Figure 16–26). Only a few tadpoles developed at each transplant stage, but the results support the theory that genes are not lost or permanently inactivated during differentiation. Genes are now thought to be "turned on" during development in a reversible manner.

A completely different approach to the regulation of development was made in 1973 by F. H. Ruddle and R. S. Kucherlapati at Yale University. Using tissue-culture techniques, they produced living hybrid cells containing both human and mouse genes. These hybrid cells are certainly abnormal, but they provide a method for studying the expression of genes. For example, both human and mouse liver cells can make albumin, but human white blood cells cannot synthesize this protein. When mouse liver cells are fused with human white blood cells to form a single cell, some of the resulting hybrid cells produce both human and mouse albumin (Figure 16–27). Genes from the mouse liver cells apparently activated genes in the human white blood cells to produce albumin. The white blood cells, then, still had the genes for synthesizing albumin but required some agent to "turn on these genes."

The Developmental Role of Hormones and Nerves

Control of development does not rest entirely with individual cells. We know, for example, that well differentiated tissues also help to direct the process. As an animal develops, its circulatory system carries hormones throughout its body. For example, the cornea (outer transparent portion) of the eye will clear up only if exposed to thyroxine. This demonstrates that interaction among tissues is essential and that developmental processes are af-

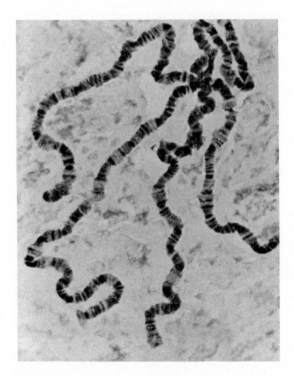

FIGURE 16–25   Giant chromosomes from the salivary gland of fruit fly larva ($\times$1000). The bands represent sites of specific gene action. (Courtesy of Dr. B. P. Kaufmann.)

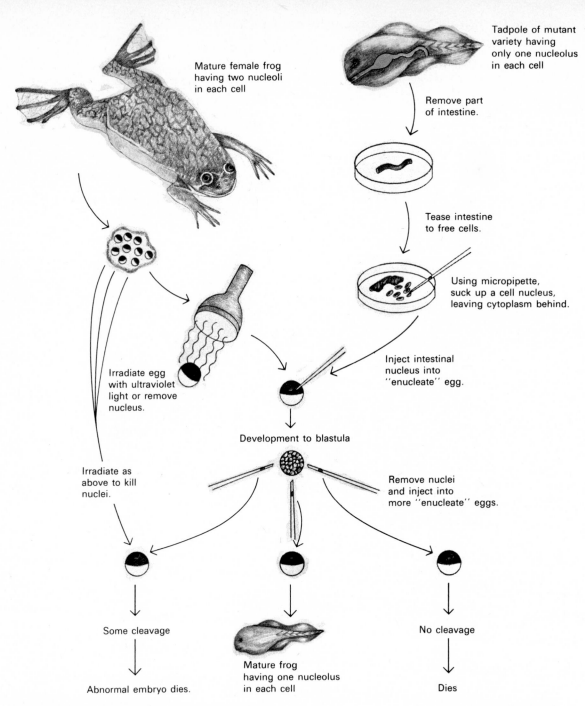

Mature female frog having two nucleoli in each cell

Tadpole of mutant variety having only one nucleolus in each cell

Remove part of intestine.

Tease intestine to free cells.

Using micropipette, suck up a cell nucleus, leaving cytoplasm behind.

Irradiate egg with ultraviolet light or remove nucleus.

Inject intestinal nucleus into "enucleate" egg.

Development to blastula

Irradiate as above to kill nuclei.

Remove nuclei and inject into more "enucleate" eggs.

Some cleavage

No cleavage

Abnormal embryo dies.

Mature frog having one nucleolus in each cell

Dies

FIGURE 16–26 Frog eggs may be exposed to ultraviolet light to destroy their nuclei, producing "enucleate" eggs. When nuclei from the intestinal cells of a mutant tadpole (with only one nucleolus per nucleus) are injected into irradiated eggs (which normally have two nucleoli per nucleus), three results are possible: (1) no cleavage, producing no embryo; (2) some cleavage, producing an abnormal embryo; or (3) a normal tadpole and mature adult with one nucleolus in each cell nucleus. Development of a normal adult frog from a single intestinal nucleus taken from a tadpole would indicate all genes for growth and development are present in intestinal cells.

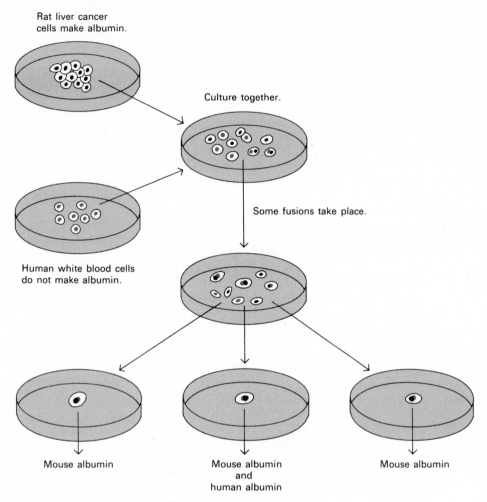

Rat liver cancer
cells make albumin.

Culture together.

Human white blood cells
do not make albumin.

Some fusions take place.

Mouse albumin

Mouse albumin
and
human albumin

Mouse albumin

FIGURE 16–27   Rat liver cancer cells in culture can produce albumin, whereas human white blood cells cannot. When these cells
are cultured together, a few cells of different types fuse together
to form hybrids. Some of these hybrids can produce both mouse
and human albumin. Thus some factor in the mouse genome must
"turn on" normally repressed human genes.

fected by the development of a circulatory
system.

Nerve tissue also appears to function in
growth and development. Nerves can apparently stimulate cell division in a nonspecific
way. Kidney tubules, for example, develop
more rapidly in the presence of nerve tissue,
although normal tubules can be produced

without nerve interaction. Salamanders can
regenerate amputated limbs, but regeneration
has been found to depend on the presence of
nerves. If the nerve tracts leading to the stump
of a lost limb are removed, regeneration does
not occur. This leads us again to the assumption that nerve tissues produce some nonspecific substance that stimulates cell division.

The Role of Environment in Development

For many years biologists have suspected that environment plays a role in development. Experiments such as those on wing development in fruit flies (Chapter 13) have supported this idea. Experiments on the eyes of newborn kittens have contributed further evidence. Kittens are born with their eyes closed, so they do not see their environment for several days. In one experiment, one eye of a newborn kitten was sewn shut for several months and then opened. A substantial number of cortical nerve cells in the brain of this kitten, normally responsive to light, did not react when the "blind" eye was exposed to light. These cells did, however, respond when the normal eye was exposed to light.

Two plausible hypotheses have been proposed to explain these effects of environment: (1) genes code only for a basic outline of possible neural connections, but the ultimate connections occur in response to environmental stimuli at critical periods of the animal's life; and (2) genetically ordered (innate) patterns deteriorate when normal environmental stimuli are removed. Experiments with monkeys, which can see at birth, support the second hypothesis as a major part of the answer. Deprivation of sight during the first three weeks after birth causes deterioration of nerve pathways set up during embryonic development. It is likely that both of these hypotheses have merit; further research may generate a broader hypothesis that will unify them.

LOSS OF DEVELOPMENTAL CONTROL: CANCER

Uncontrolled cellular growth—cells dividing so rapidly that normal functions cannot be established, producing large growths that crowd out or destroy normal cells—is characteristic of a feared and often deadly disease, cancer. Not all cancers are lethal, and many potentially dangerous growths may be eliminated by surgical, radiation, or chemical treatment. But cancer in all its forms is the second ranking human killer in the United States. During the past few years more than 250,000 Americans annually have died from it.

Common Types of Cancer

Many different types of cancer have been recognized and treated (Figure 16–28). Cancers may arise in all kinds of tissues; each tissue type produces cancer with a distinct pattern of development and symptoms. Tumors, abnormal nonfunctional growths of cells, may be classed as *benign* (not spreading or dangerous) or *malignant* (injurious and potentially fatal). Surgery is usually an effective treatment for

Name	Description
Adenoma	Tumors of gland-like structure formed in epithelial tissue
Myeloma	Tumors of bone marrow type cells often found in other parts of the body. A particularly deadly cancer.
Lymphoma	Excessive numbers of lymphocytes produced in the lymph nodes and spleen
Sarcoma	Solid tumors arising from tissues of mesodermal origin such as connective tissues, bone, and muscle
Carcinoma	Solid tumors that arise from tissues of ectodermal origin such as epidermis, glands, nerves, breasts, lungs, digestive tract, genital organs, and urinary system.
Leukemia	Large numbers of white blood cells are produced and enter the circulation
Myeloid	Leukemia centered in the bone marrow characterized by excessive neutrophils, basophils, or eosinophils
Lymphoid	Leukemia centered in the lymph nodes producing large numbers of lymphocytes (lymphoma)

FIGURE 16–28   Some types of cancer.

benign tumors, because they do not spread from their site of origin.

Benign means "wholesome" or "favorable." Benign tumors, however, are neither. Normally they may not threaten life, but they cannot be taken lightly. If they arise in regions inaccessible by surgical means, such as the interior of the brain, benign tumors may lead to impairment of function or to death. The only "favorable" thing about them is that their treatment may have a favorable outcome—if undertaken in time. Benign tumors should receive prompt medical treatment because they can turn into malignant growths.

Malignant tumors spread rapidly and can start new tumors throughout the body; they are particularly dangerous in the liver and the brain (Figure 16–29). Surgery, radiation, and chemical treatment are the principal means of treating malignancies.

Some Causes of Cancer

Warts, which do not usually threaten health, are localized areas of cell division caused by a virus infection. Some investigators feel that most types of cancers are viral diseases. This has not been proved in humans, although certain cancers in chickens, mice, and frogs have definitely been shown to result from viruses. Since cancers are cells that are out of control, more than one mechanism may cause them. Skin cancer, for example, may be triggered by exposure to ultraviolet light, and many types of cancer have been traced to x-ray damage or carcinogenic chemicals. Most researchers hold that these types of cancer result from abnormal cell division in response to gene mutations caused by the action of these agents on chromosomal DNA. For this reason, several types of cancers may be considered as *environmental diseases* (Chapter 8).

FIGURE 16–29 Scanning electron micrograph of a malignant cancer cell, magnified more than 3000 times. Note the spreading growth. (Wide World Photos.)

Lung cancer and cancer of the lips, mouth, and respiratory tract have been linked to cigarette and pipe smoking. Incidence of cancer has also been related statistically to increasing age, but we do not yet know whether these data indicate increased susceptibility to cancer with age or simply that more people are living long enough to develop cancer.

Medical records also show that particular cancers affect human males and females differently (Figure 16–30). But we know little about the reasons for most of these variations. Cancer of the breast has been linked to excessive estrogen production, but just how this causes cancer is not yet known.

In 1976 the United States Council on Environmental Quality estimated that 60 to 90 percent of all cancer was caused by increased exposure to carcinogenic chemicals in our deteriorating environment. Some cancers are now thought to be caused by certain viruses called *proviruses.* These simple viruses enter a host cell and become part of its chromosomes, where they replicate with the host's DNA. Proviruses also have the ability to produce messenger RNA and proteins.

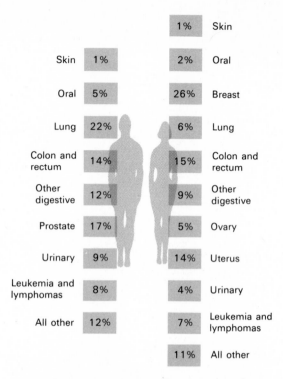

FIGURE 16–30   Incidence of some types of cancer in human males and females. (Courtesy of American Cancer Society, Inc.)

Treatment of Cancer

Extreme methods are necessary to treat cancer, because cell division must be stopped. Since very few specific differences are known between normal cells and cancer cells, treatment cannot be completely selective against the cancer cells. Thus when a cancer patient receives radiation or drug treatment, both normal and malignant cells are affected. Currently the most effective drugs in treating most cancers, especially those which cannot be surgically removed, are chemical mutagens. These drugs either inhibit DNA synthesis or crosslink DNA molecules so tightly that cell division cannot occur. Chemotherapy (drug treatment) of certain types of tumors gives an 80 percent chance of complete remission and cure.

Chemotherapy can effectively lengthen the productive life of leukemia patients. Children with acute leukemia can be given combinations of drugs that cause complete remission of the disease, a return to normal, for several

months. Unfortunately, the disease usually returns; when it does, a new combination of drugs must be administered. With this method, leukemia patients who would live for perhaps two months without treatment may survive for three years or more.

One form of bone marrow treatment for leukemia has produced some complete, permanent remissions—evidently total cures. When leukemia occurs in one of a set of identical twins, the twin with leukemia is treated with cytoxan (a drug that kills dividing cells) and given a total body exposure of x-rays. The x-ray treatment kills all dividing cells that the drug treatment may have missed. Next, bone marrow cells taken from the healthy twin are injected into the patient; these cells migrate to the bone marrow and begin producing normal blood cells. One big problem in such transplant treatment between nonidentical persons is immune rejection; because drugs must be used to

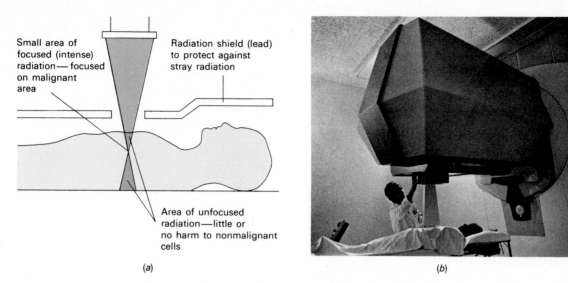

Small area of
focused (intense)
radiation— focused
on malignant
area

Radiation shield (lead)
to protect against
stray radiation

Area of unfocused
radiation—little or
no harm to nonmalignant
cells

(a)

(b)

FIGURE 16–31 (a) How the radiation beam focuses on the malignant cells. (b) Patient receiving radiation treatment. (Courtesy of American Cancer Society.)

suppress immune responses, the patient is dangerously susceptible to other diseases and infection.

The idea behind most cancer chemotherapy is that it will kill more cancer cells than normal cells because the cancerous ones are dividing faster. Treatment with nonlethal levels of drugs may thus kill all the cancer cells. In radiation therapy, the high-energy beam is focused on the tumor, while shields protect the rest of the patient's body (Figure 16–31). If detected early, nearly all cancers can be treated to extend life or permit complete recovery. Unfortunately, most cases are detected too late, and most cancer victims die of their affliction.

Cancer may someday be treated by immunotherapy. Most cancer cells possess specific antigens, and immunity to cancerous cells has been produced experimentally in rats (Figure 16–32). It might be possible, then, to stimulate an individual's own immune reaction to cancer cells or to use a passive immunization developed in another animal. Experimental treatments are currently taking place with humans, and limited success has been reported. Immunotherapy may prove most valuable when used in combination with conventional therapy techniques.

MATURATION AND AGING

So far we have discussed normally developing cells and the abnormal development called cancer. Under normal conditions all organisms develop, grow, and enter a stage of maturity. In humans, generally speaking, maturity is thought to peak at about 30 years of age; thereafter the body shows evidence of senescence (deterioration and loss of normal function) and a slow decline toward death. Some biologists think senescence is programmed into the genetic message of all body cells; others believe that aging results principally from accumulated mutations. Perhaps the most meaningful research on aging was carried out by Leonard Hayflick in 1962 while at the Wistar Institute in Philadelphia. Observing human cells in tissue culture, Hayflick and his colleagues found that these cells would double only a limited number of times before ceasing to divide and die. Significantly, the number of doublings was found to be related to the age of the donor. Human cells taken from embryos, for example, divided about 50 times, whereas those taken after birth divided only 20 to 30 times. Hayflick thinks that senescence may result from the loss

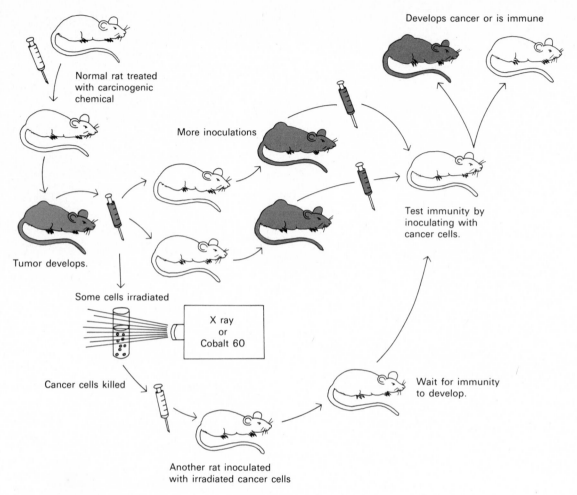

Develops cancer or is immune

Normal rat treated
with carcinogenic
chemical

More inoculations

Test immunity by
inoculating with
cancer cells.

Tumor develops.

Some cells irradiated

X ray
or
Cobalt 60

Cancer cells killed

Wait for immunity
to develop.

Another rat inoculated
with irradiated cancer cells

FIGURE 16–32　Diagram showing development of immunity to
viral cancer in rats. Rats with tumors are shown in color.

of certain cellular functions before cells lose
the ability to divide. Thus entire organs and
organ systems may deteriorate, leading to the
death of the whole organism.

Currently, there are almost as many theories
of aging as there are groups doing research in
this area. Aging may well be caused by interrelated mechanisms that occur in various cell
types and at various times in the life of an
individual. Programmed genetic senescence
and accumulation of sublethal mutations are
not mutually exclusive; both may be part of the
process.

SUMMARY

All organisms undergo growth at some stage of
their lives. In multicellular plants and animals,
new generations usually arise through the
union of egg and sperm. After fertilization, a
complex series of mitotic cell divisions produce
a new individual according to an inherited
genetic pattern. Thus growth and development
are ultimately controlled by genes through the
interaction of DNA and protein synthesis.

Seeds, produced by gymnosperms and angiosperms, contain an embryo, food storage tissue,
and a protective seed coat. Given warm, moist

soil, a seed absorbs water and swells. This triggers the dormant embryo to grow and develop into roots, stems, and leaves. The process by which immature cells develop into specific cell types and tissues is called differentiation. Rapidly dividing cells in the buds, called apical meristem, differentiate into epidermal, vascular, and fundamental tissues of plant structure.

Patterns of development among various animals are strikingly similar during early stages, from fertilized egg through gastrulation. Development in starfish, frogs, and humans involves specific embryonic stages and primary differentiation of germ tissue into ectoderm, endoderm, and mesoderm. These three germ layers eventually give rise to the various organs and structures of the adult. In humans and most other mammals, fertilization is internal and development occurs in the uterus. Embryonic membranes form around the developing embryo, and exchange of gas and nutrients occurs through the placenta.

As an animal develops, many cells divide and differentiate. Control of cell differentiation by neighboring cells or tissues is called induction. Protein synthesis (directed by DNA), induction, hormones, and nerves all play essential roles in animal development.

Cancer cells divide so rapidly and in such an uncontrolled manner that normal functions may not develop. In some cases, large masses of cancer tumor cells crowd out and block the functions of normal tissues. Cancer may often be treated successfully by surgery, radiotherapy, and drugs, but incidence of the disease is increasing. Various cancers are known to be caused by viruses, ultraviolet light, radioactivity, and many chemicals.

After growth and development, all organisms go through stages of maturity, senescence, and finally death. Many theories have been advanced to explain these natural processes, but thus far no completely satisfactory mechanism has been found.

REVIEW QUESTIONS

1. What developmental events take place in a seed as it germinates and produces a new plant?

2. Why is cell division necessary for growth?

3. What are some developmental differences between the gastrulation of starfish and of frogs? What are some similarities?

4. What are the four embryonic membranes or sacs formed in reptiles, birds, and mammals? What are the functions of each?

5. Distinguish between restrictive and expressive phases of embryonic differentiation.

6. What experimental evidence supports the theory of embryonic induction?

7. Why has *Acetabularia* been a valuable experimental organism? How has it been useful in developmental studies?

8. Describe some successful treatments for cancer. What is the basic mechanism for all of these treatments?

SUPPLEMENTARY READINGS

Bonner, John T., *On Development*, Harvard University Press, Cambridge, 1974. Written for biology students at all levels, this discussion of development ties together the great progress made in this century in all areas that bear on the development of animals.

Cairns, John, "The Cancer Problem," *Scientific American*, November 1975. The nature of cancer in man and the prospects for its prevention and cure are presented in simple terms. Exposure to carcinogens in our polluted environment is believed to be the cause of most cancers.

Cohen, Jack, *Living Embryos: An Introduction to the Study of Animal Development*, Pergamon Press, New York, 1967. A series of concise descriptions of development in both invertebrates and vertebrates.

Waddington, C. H., *How Animals Develop*, Harper Torchbooks, Harper & Row, New York, 1962. A classic, short account of the science of embryology. It presents, in an elementary way, an outline of how animals develop and some of the causes of embryonic differentiation.

Unit VII
Behavior

Salm

A mathematician slouches behind a desk, silent and still, lost in thought. A deer flees from a pack of pursuing dogs. A child blushes. A lizard moves out of the direct sunlight into the shade. A bacterium moves in a drop of water. A peach tree flowers. A fir tree bends its branches toward the light in the forest.

Each of these organisms is doing something; they are all engaging in behavior. Can we, then, simply say that behavior is what organisms do? This is a good start toward a working definition of behavior, but organisms "do" a great many other things besides those we would be likely to call "behavior." For example, they all respire and synthesize proteins. Some digest food; some photosynthesize; some think. Are these and all other life processes forms of behavior? If they were, then the meaning of the word behavior would be too broad to be of much use in the study of living systems.

Perhaps it is most useful to define behavior as any externally observable action or activity of a living system. The restriction to externally observable actions or activities enables us to make a distinction between basic physiological processes and behavior. By this definition, then, we would not consider digestion and photosynthesis as behavior.

The deer's flight, the dogs' pursuit, the child's blush, the bacterium's motion, the peach tree's flowering—all these activities are observable from the outside, so they may be considered as behavior. What about the mathematician who sits quietly, thinking? Sitting is behavior because it is observable activity (of an inactive sort). But what about the thinking of mathematical thoughts? By our definition, we would not call thinking behavior because we cannot observe it, although we can infer that it is taking place from observable actions: writing equations, reading a mathematical trea-tise, or talking about angles and tangents.

Although we usually associate behavior with animals, plants (and protists and monerans) clearly exhibit behavioral responses. Some of these were discussed in Chapter 12, where we saw that hormonal regulation produced observable, external effects in plants. Plants react to touch. A familiar example of plant behavior is "insect catching" plants such as the Venus' flytrap. These plants, which generally live in environments lacking in nitrates, trap and digest insects to secure nitrogen from amino acids.

Behavior helps to fulfill an organism's need to maintain a stable environment, both internal and external. In other words, behavior helps an organism to survive and adapt to its environment. In this unit we shall bring together principles and ideas derived from the study of behavior, show the adaptive importance of behavior to organisms, and explain how some behavioral patterns occur.

Chapter 17

Behavior: Basic Patterns

Much of the precision of good scientific research depends on care in defining what we want to study. Our approach to the broad subject of behavior is no exception. **Studying Behavior,** one of the most fascinating subjects of interest to biologists, requires concentrating on those aspects of organismic function that are external and observable.

We begin with **Simple Types of Behavior.** These include all of the basic turning and bending movements of plants and many animals. These simple forms of behavior are extremely efficient in helping the organism adapt to and exploit environmental conditions. As we move toward **Complex Species Behavior,** we find patterns of behavior that cannot be explained solely in terms of "simple" components. **Sequential Behavior Patterns,** particularly those related to reproductive behavior, seem to combine both innate (hereditary) aspects and learned behavior.

The question of inherited vs. acquired behavior is particularly well dramatized in current research on **Behavior and Biological Clocks.** Think how much of your daily and indeed seasonal behavior is related to the time of day. Research into **Circadian and Cir-** **cannual Rhythms**—patterns of a day's or year's duration, respectively—has shown that external cues are only part of the answer. We do have some kind of clocks within our bodies that keeps us "on schedule."

Another complex behavior pattern that appears dependent on a mixture of internal and environmental cues is the annual **Migration** of birds, fish, and some other species. How do they know where they are going? How do they coordinate the mass movement of thousands of individuals into a united expedition?

A primary behavior factor in organizing a group of individuals into an interacting species is **Communication.** From colorful arrays of feathers to spoken language, species have developed ways of transmitting information.

One of the most widespread kinds of behavior is **Territorial Behavior.** Many species have means of marking the boundaries of their "turf" and defending it against invaders. This behavior is frequently related to patterns of population control that involve regulating the mix and number of sexes during mating season.

We close this chapter by summarizing what is now known about the **Development of Behavior.**

In the study of living systems it is useful to distinguish between behavior and physiology. But we must not forget that "physiology" and "behavior" are human constructs. Just as there is no sharp dividing line in nature between "life" and "nonlife," there is no clear-cut natural division between "physiology" and "behavior." For example, behavior is crucial in the maintenance of homeostasis, either directly or indirectly. A deer flees a predator that would fatally disrupt its homeostasis. A lizard crawls under a rock out of the hot sun to keep its internal temperature within tolerable limits. You too seek shade, or take off your sweater, on a hot day.

Where, then, does physiology leave off and behavior begin? In nature there is no such point: an organism and its processes form an integral whole. But as we study nature, our working definition of behavior—any externally observable action or activity of an organism—enables us to make a convenient division for our purposes. For example, consider panting in dogs. In discussing metabolism and its supporting processes, we may find it useful to consider panting as a physiological process that involves cellular respiration, muscle contraction and relaxation, and so on. But when we focus on an animal's behavior we can also consider panting, as a behavioral process, because it is an externally observable activity.

Most behavior is complex, and it is often difficult to determine how or why a particular organism acts as it does. For example, how do certain birds migrate in such predictable pathways each year? Behavior is central to our own daily lives, and we frequently ask ourselves, "Why did he do that?" or, "Why did I act as I did?" To study and understand behavior, however, demands the most highly developed scientific tools and methods from biology, psychology, and other fields. In fact, the study of behavior has become so interdisciplinary that one needs a background in chemistry and neurophysiology to understand many facets of behavior. Since most research on behavior has been conducted with animals, we will emphasize examples of animal behavior.

Some studies of animal behavior have been unproductive, either because scientific procedures were not followed, or because all variable factors were not considered, or because researchers used an overly simple theory to cover a broad area. Another obstacle to understanding behavior has been the tendency to explain animal behavior with models of human behavior, a process called *anthropomorphism*. This is often difficult to avoid, as any pet owner knows. For example, we often say that an animal is happy or sad. But these are descriptions of human feelings, and they are not necessarily appropriate explanations of an animal's observed response to a stimulus.

STUDYING BEHAVIOR

Animal behavior studies often require a great deal of time and patience. A good example of patient, successful effort is Jane van Lawick-Goodall's study of wild chimpanzees near Lake Tanganyika in Tanzania, Africa (Figure 17–1). Goodall invested nearly a year of effort before she could get close enough to the animals to study them; during this time, they avoided and even threatened her. Only after she gained acceptance from the chimpanzees by giving them bananas did they permit her to follow them through the bush and observe their social structure. She was then able to study and record many aspects of their daily lives and habits.

Goodall's work, which began in 1960, was the first comprehensive study of the social behavior of chimpanzees. Previously the social structure of all primates, including the ancestors of our own species, had been envisioned as rigid, like the society formed by baboon colonies in captivity. But field studies have shown an enormous variation in the life styles of various primates. Chimpanzees interact in a very loose social structure that allows a great deal of individual freedom. They do not have a strict, hierarchial social structure. Social bands are nomadic, traveling to find food. Consequently, a chimpanzee seldom sleeps two nights in the same tree. Not much aggressive behavior is shown among members of a band; arguments are usually short, without physical violence. Mothers devote a great deal of time and patience to their young, and the mother-child bond is very strong. Nursing ceases after four or

FIGURE 17–1   Wild chimpanzees in Africa's Gombe Stream Game Reserve may charge and bristle with excitement, but at times they can be as gentle and affectionate as this one is with Jan van Lawick-Goodall. (Baron Hugo van Lawick; © National Geographic Society.)

five years, but the young may remain with their mother for as long as eight years.

One surprising observation about chimpanzees was the extent to which they make and use tools. Chimpanzees learn from one another how to fashion thin probes from vines or grass and how to use these probes to extract termites from underground nests and logs. On rare occasions chimpanzees were observed hunting and killing smaller primates—red colobus monkeys and young baboons. The animal making the kill sometimes shares the meat with others. Chimpanzees are one of the few nonhuman primate groups known to share kills with others besides mate and offspring.

Chimpanzees are gregarious, often relating to one another through exaggerated displays of expressive behavior, including dancing, hugging, and shrieking. This behavior occurs especially when a band finds a source of food or when two bands meet. Greeting ceremonies, accompanied by much noise and movement, often take place when two unfamiliar groups meet.

Analysis and Interpretation

Since most behavior is complex, especially in "higher" animals, researchers must be exceptionally careful when they analyze and interpret their experiments. For example, a series of experiments was conducted at the Western Electric Company's Hawthorne Works in Chicago during the 1920s and 1930s. Better lighting and frequent rest periods were found to improve the morale and increase the production of one group of employees. In an attempt to show that the enhanced productivity and morale resulted from these changes, the working conditions were returned to their previous levels. But morale and production remained high. The experiments apparently made the employees feel that the company cared for them and considered them special; therefore they produced more and were more secure in their work. The term *Hawthorne effect* is now used to describe positive results obtained merely because an experiment is conducted.

SIMPLE TYPES OF BEHAVIOR

In all organisms, some behavioral responses to stimuli appear to be automatic. An organism's orientation to its environment often fits this description. Almost all protists and most animals respond automatically to such environmental stimuli as light, chemicals, gravity, and temperature. *Euglena*, a photosynthetic, flagellated protist, moves toward moderate light; *Paramecium*, a ciliated protist, avoids strong acids; and *Amoeba*, moving with its pseudopods, follows the chemical stimulus of food (Figure 17–2). When a paramecium bumps into an object, it backs away by reversing the beat of its cilia, turns approximately 30°, and moves forward again. If it again encounters an object, it again reverses direction, turns another 30°,

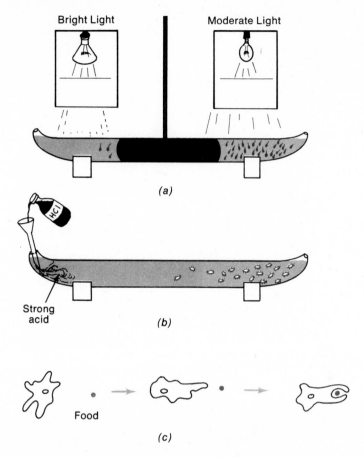

FIGURE 17–2 Simple orientation responses to environmental stimuli by some protists. (a) *Euglena* moving toward moderate light. (b) *Paramecium* avoiding strong acid. (c) *Amoeba* moving toward food.

and goes forward again. This activity continues until the object is cleared and the paramecium can swim past it freely (Figure 17–3).

Tropisms

A type of movement known as *tropism* is common in sedentary organisms such as vascular plants. We discussed instances of this behavior in Chapter 12. For example, we saw that when grass seedlings are exposed to light from one side, the stems bend toward the light. (Recall the explanation given for this movement: an unequal distribution of plant hormones in the stem.) This tropism is a relatively simple type of behavior—a single, directed response to a stimulus.

Another interesting tropism occurs in *Mimosa*, the "sensitive plant" (Figure 17–4). The leaves of this plant are composed of many pairs of leaflets. When the tip of a leaf is touched, the leaflets fold upward and the entire leaf droops. These changes result from loss of water from large cells at the base of the leaflets and leaves. Water pressure in these cells normally holds the leaflets and leaves in position.

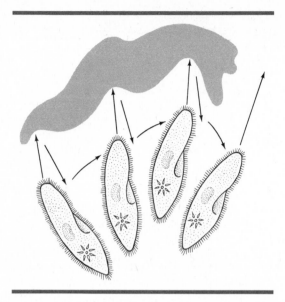

FIGURE 17-3   Trial-and-error behavior of a paramecium. As it bumps into an object, the paramecium backs off, turns about 30°, and moves forward again. This behavior continues until the obstacle has been cleared.

Taxes

A *taxis* is an orienting movement of an entire motile organism. One type of taxis occurs when an animal orients itself so that the intensity of a stimulus is equal on both sides. For example, the dronefly (*Eristalis*) reacts positively to light after a period in darkness by flying or walking directly to a light. To find its way, the fly turns until each eye receives an equal amount of light stimulation. Grayling butterflies escape from predators by flying toward the sun. They orient themselves by moving in a direction in which the eyes are stimulated equally. This taxic behavior has adaptive value because it provides an escape from enemies, which are blinded by the sun. Such individuals which escape increase their fitness or reproductive potential.

Reflexes

We introduced reflexes in Chapter 12 when we discussed the anatomical relationships of a reflex arc, noting that reflexes are automatic

(a)

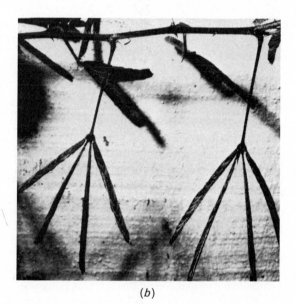
(b)

FIGURE 17-4   The response to touch by the sensitive *Mimosa*. (a) Leaflets in normal position. (b) Leaflets in response to touch. (Edward S. Ross: California Academy of Sciences.)

actions involving two or more neurons. A single reflex usually involves only part of an animal whereas a taxis is movement of the total organism. In this chapter we are concerned with the function of reflexes—what they do for an organism. One example of the adaptive value of a reflex is the stinging apparatus of a bee. The stinger is activated by touch stimulation, and the reflex operates even if the abdomen is severed from the rest of the body. Our eyes blink in response to an object thrust before them. In each of these examples the reflex produces a prompt response to an emergency.

In organized behavior, one reflex often follows another. These *chain reflexes* can be observed in a feeding frog. First the frog's tongue extends to catch an insect. The presence of an insect on the tongue then stimulates the mouth to close and finally provides a stimulus for swallowing reflexes. Reflexes may also occur in coordinated groups. The stimulus of stepping on a tack, for example, brings about the response of lifting the foot. Other reflexes, perhaps not so apparent to the person who steps on the tack, occur in other parts of the body; for example, the opposite leg stiffens in an effort to maintain balance (Figure 17–5). Since the message is also transmitted to the brain, nonreflex behavior may accompany the initial reflex action. A cry of pain might be uttered, or the injured foot might be lifted for inspection and removal of the tack.

Broadly speaking, we might explain all behavior as a series of complicated interactions among reflexes in which one stimulus may set off more than one response. If we confined our studies strictly to reflex patterns, however, we would not advance very far in our understanding of more complex behavior. We shall see in our study of more complex behavior that reflexes are one of several types of behavior organization that we must consider.

COMPLEX SPECIES BEHAVIOR

Animals appear to inherit behavior patterns much more complicated than taxes and tropisms, because many patterns or responses pass without change from one generation to the next. Certain behavior patterns appear to occur as chains of reflexes in some animals, although in others these events may be modified by learning. This inherited, stereotyped behavior is often called *instinct* (or *innate* behavior), although "instinct" is now considered to be an oversimplification. It is not possible to fully separate inherited and environmental factors.

The importance of the genetic contribution to behavior has been stressed in many studies by European zoologists. Three leaders in natural behavioral studies are Konrad Lorenz, Karl von Frisch, and Niko Tinbergen, recipients of the Nobel Prize in Physiology or Medicine in 1973. Today we apply the term *ethology* to the study of animal behavior, regardless of the degree to which that behavior is learned or innate. Ethologists frequently stress the role of animal behavior in adaptation by emphasizing that behavior, like any other characteristic, evolves according to the laws of natural selection.

As we shall see in the examples that follow, it is difficult, and sometimes impossible, to distinguish in a specific behavior pattern between what is learned and what occurs as a result of heredity. Moreover, ethologists disagree over the concept of instinct and the exact neurophysiological basis of such behavior. In a complex animal, behavior is the result of an organized response in a given environment; this output depends on both heredity (evolutionary relationships) and past experiences (learning). Some behavior seems to involve a larger component of inherited patterns, whereas other behavior results more from learning. Most animal behavior results from a mixture of both learned and innate responses. We shall first consider examples of behavior that have been attributed mainly to instinct and attempt to understand some of the conditions under which such behavior occurs.

Sequential Behavior Patterns

The reproductive behavior of solitary, or digger, wasps is a good example of an innate sequence of activities that apparently involves no previous learning or training. The sequence begins when a female wasp digs a hole for a nest. Then she seeks out her prey, usually a caterpillar, and

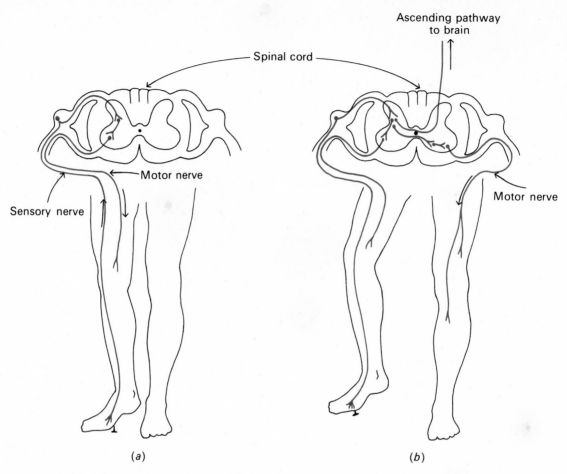

FIGURE 17–5   Reflex behavior. When a person steps on a tack
(a), the foot is immediately lifted (b). (a) The simple reflex from the
receptors in the foot, through the spinal cord, and to the upper
leg muscles. (b) Impulses are shown going to the brain through an
ascending pathway in the spinal cord, where the sensation of pain
is registered. In addition, impulses are sent across the spinal cord
to muscles of the opposite leg which maintains balance.

paralyzes it with a sting. Next she drags it to the
nest and pushes it in; she may add several more
caterpillars in a similar manner. The female
then lays an egg on the caterpillars and seals the
nest (Figure 17–6). When the egg hatches, then,
it has a source of food. The larva matures, spins
a cocoon, and remains in the sealed cell until it
emerges as an adult. An adult female can perform this reproductive behavior even though
she has never observed the process. Each re-

sponse in the series apparently acts as a stimulus to produce the next response. If the process
is disrupted experimentally by removing the
caterpillars before the egg is laid, the wasp will
lay an egg and seal the nest anyway. Each step
follows the previous step in an automatic manner, and interference may or may not alter the
behavioral sequence. In nature, of course, the
caterpillars are not normally removed; thus the
fixed behavior pattern has adaptive value for

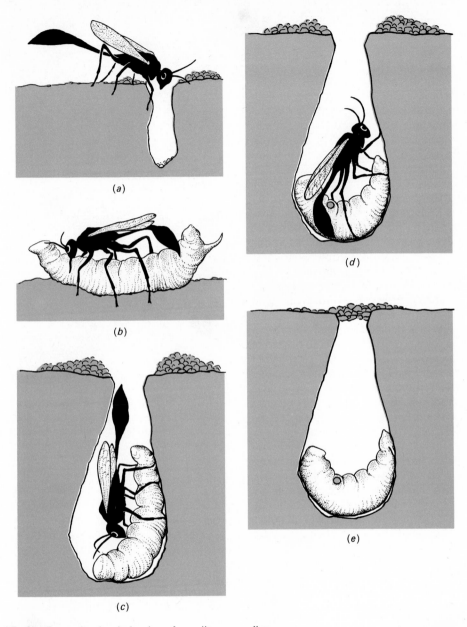

FIGURE 17–6   Reproductive behavior of a solitary, or digger,
wasp. (*a*) She digs a nest. (*b*) She captures and stings a caterpillar. (*c*) She drags the prey into the nest. (*d*) She lays an egg on
the caterpillar and crawls out of the nest. (*e*) The nest is finally
sealed.

the wasp, since this precision helps to insure continuation of the species.

Sticklebacks and Mating

The three-spined stickleback, a fish approximately 3 inches long, occurs commonly in both Europe and North America in a variety of habitats, including salt water, freshwater streams and ponds, and brackish water. In the spring, sticklebacks migrate into shallow fresh water where they perform a very precise sequence of mating behavior. A male stickleback first establishes a territory and defends it from other males. Next he builds a nest by scooping out a pit from the sandy bottom. Then he brings in weeds to form a mound, held together by sticky kidney secretions. Then he completes the nest by making a hole through the mound.

During this time the male changes color, from a drab gray or brown to a bluish back and a bright red spot on his underside. He is now ready to court any female that enters his territory bulging with eggs. He is also ready to drive off any males that move into his established domain. He will attack any red object near his territory, even though it may not otherwise resemble another male stickleback (Figure 17–7). The important stimulus appears to be the red color rather than the shape.

If a shiny female, swollen with 50 to 100 eggs, enters a male's territory, he responds immediately with a zigzag movement toward her. He continues this motion until she responds by raising the head end of her body. The male then swims to the nest and makes several pokes toward it with his head; the female follows and enters. Once the female is inside the tiny nest, with her head and tail protruding, the male jabs her several times near the base of the tail with his snout; she responds by laying eggs. When this is done, she slithers out of the nest, and the male quickly moves in to fertilize the eggs (Figure 17–8). Soon after mating, the male must care for the eggs. With his pectoral fins he fans the water near the nest opening to increase the supply of oxygen to the developing eggs. This fanning activity gradually increases until the eggs hatch. The details of this mating cycle have been described by many biologists, but the

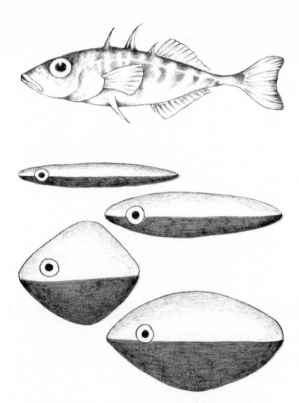

FIGURE 17–7 Models of three-spined stickleback fish used in experiments with male sticklebacks. The four models with red bellies were attacked much more frequently than the more realistic model, which lacked the red underside.

most eloquent report is that by Tinbergen in his book *The Study of Instinct.*

The reproductive behavior of the stickleback shows how a series of stimulus-response activities can create a complex behavior pattern with adaptive value not only to the individual but also to the species. The response to one stimulus becomes the stimulus for the next response in the sequence. In complicated behavioral activity each stimulus may not "take," so a sequence may not go through to completion. Other factors in the environment may influence the reactions of the fish: the female may not respond to the initial courtship; a male intruder may interrupt; or one member of the mating pair may not follow through with one

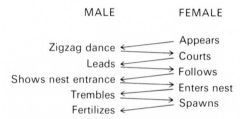

MALE		FEMALE
Zigzag dance	⇄	Appears
Leads	⇄	Courts
Shows nest entrance	⇄	Follows
Trembles	⇄	Enters nest
Fertilizes	⇄	Spawns

FIGURE 17–8   The usual sequence of events in the mating behavior of the three-spined stickleback. Activity starts as a female enters a male's nesting territory. After this initial stimulus, the reaction sequence proceeds as indicated.

of the specific responses. This behavior, then, can be described in terms of probability. The sequence of events described here is the most probable one after the behavior is initiated.

Releasers

Let us take a closer look at some of the stimuli that contribute to stickleback mating behavior.

A male stickleback will attack almost any object with a red underside that enters his territory. The critical stimulus that causes the response is therefore the red color of the object and not its shape (Figure 17–7). The characteristic that produces the behavior is called a *releaser*, a term originated by Konrad Lorenz. "Releaser" is now used to describe any stereotyped object, structure, behavior, or sound that can initiate a fixed sequence of responses. A hen, for example, reacts more strongly to a call from her chick than to the chick's actions. In other words, if a chick is in trouble, the releaser that triggers a response from the mother is a sound rather than a visible activity. The releaser for the female stickleback to lay eggs is the poking of its posterior end by the snout of the male. At this stage of the cycle, egg laying can be released by poking the female's posterior end with a rod.

Releasers are important in animal behavior because every animal is confronted with many stimuli. There is definite survival value in reacting to a relevant stimulus with a satisfactory response. The steps of reproductive behavior vary among the species of sticklebacks. Two members of different species cannot mate because they break off the mating behavior when one of them produces an ineffective releaser. Thus releaser behavior not only helps to synchronize mating but also protects against mismatches.

How does a behavioral sequence begin? What initiates the sequence of steps that follow? Many behavior patterns are triggered internally by variations in hormone production. In sticklebacks, for example, the thyroid gland releases an increased amount of hormone in springtime, and the fish respond by moving from salt water into fresh water to begin breeding. Migratory behavior is also quite specific in some birds. In the white-crowned sparrow, migratory behavior occurs when the length of day increases in the spring. At this time the pituitary gland releases gonadotropic hormones, and the testes develop. Apparently environmental changes (such as day length) trigger these behavioral responses. We will discuss this further later in the chapter.

BEHAVIOR AND BIOLOGICAL CLOCKS

A variety of rhythmic environmental changes occur because of the relationships between the earth and other bodies in our solar system and because of the tilt of the earth's rotational axis with respect to the sun. We recognize these changes as a regular day-night cycle, an orderly progression through the seasons of a year, and the recurring phases of the moon (*lunar cycles*). As a result, the earth is subject to rhythmic changes in light, temperature, and in the tides of the ocean. These physical cycles have specific, measurable effects upon reproduction and other activities of living systems. We discussed the photoperiodic response of plants in reproduction in Chapter 12; examples of rhythmic reproductive activity in animals were presented in Chapter 15.

Circadian Rhythms

Some behavior takes place in response to internal timing mechanisms, often called *biological clocks*, which continue to operate independent of environmental conditions (Figure 17–9). Behavioral patterns that occur approximately every 24 hours are called *circadian rhythms* (*circa dies* is Latin for "about a day"). The effect on rats of a specific dosage of amphetamines, for example, depends on the time of day the drugs are administered. If given early in the daily cycle a given dose kills only 6 percent of the rats, but the same dosage kills 77 percent when given during their nighttime period of greatest activity.

Crabs found in tidal flats are excellent subjects for biological clock experiments, since they show rhythmic behavior in molting, feeding activities, and color changes. Fiddler crabs that scurry around the shore with changes in the tide are darker in color during the daytime, but as night falls they become lighter. These animals undergo this daily color variation even when kept under constant light in a laboratory.

Another species, the green crab, shows a similar color change cycle and an activity cycle as well. Green crabs are more active during high tides, but their activity is greatest when high

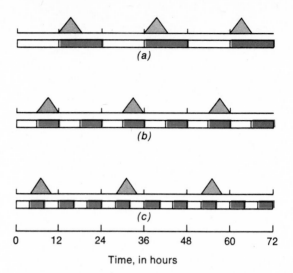

FIGURE 17–9 Effects of various photoperiods on activity rhythms of an insect. (*a*) Photoperiod is 12 hours light, 12 hours darkness. Activity rhythm (shaded triangles) is on 24-hour cycle, with the peak of activity shortly after dark. (*b*) Photoperiod is 6 hours light, 6 hours darkness. Thus two photoperiods occur every 24 hours, but the insect shows only one activity period during each 24-hour period. (*c*) Photoperiod is 4 hours light, 4 hours darkness. Activity rhythm still on 24-hour cycle. (From *Animal Photoperiodism* by S. D. Beck. Copyright © 1963 by Holt, Rinehart and Winston, Inc. Redrawn by permission of the publishers, Holt, Rinehart and Winston, Inc.)

tides occur at night (Figure 17–10). Like the color changes in fiddler crabs, these cyclic characteristics persist under constant conditions in the laboratory for about a week. Researchers are interested in the causes of these changes; in other words, what is the underlying mechanism controlling this behavior?

Secretions from neuroendocrine glands in crab eyestalks are known to inhibit molting. If the eyestalks are surgically removed, molting will soon begin. B. L. Powell of Trinity College, Dublin, has shown that these eyestalk glands also control the color change rhythms in green crabs. In Powell's experiments, stalkless crabs could not change color. When eyestalks from normal crabs were implanted, however, this

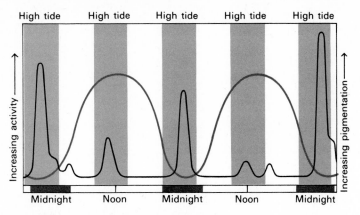

FIGURE 17-10 Two circadian rhythms of the green crab. Black curve: activity increases during high tide and is greatest when the high tide is at night. Colored curve: color changes occur on a daily cycle. During daylight hours the crab turns dark; at night body color is much lighter.

ability was restored. Other experimenters have learned that the activity rhythm of green crabs is also governed largely by eyestalk glands. Green crabs raised from eggs in the laboratory were induced into a tidal rhythm of movement simply by one immersion in a 15-hour cold bath. Crabs with their eyestalks removed could not be similarly induced, however. Since none of these crabs had ever been exposed to tidal cycles, their tidal-rhythm clock is probably innate, requiring only an environmental stimulus, such as a cold bath, to activate it. Neuroendocrine secretions control these cyclic activities in the green crab, but they may not be the control mechanism in all crabs.

A circadian rhythm is also evident in the movement of bean seedling leaves that are elevated during the day and lowered at night. Many plants continue these "sleep movements" even under constant light and temperature.

Travelers who ordinarily awaken at 7:00 AM each day on the West Coast may fly to the East Coast and find that it is quite easy to sleep until 10:00 AM. After several days on the East Coast, their sleeping behavior will have adjusted to the change in time zones, even though their internal clocks for other functions, such as secretion of certain hormones, may not reset so easily. The fact that normal sleeping behavior persists for several days in a new environment suggests that an individual is not merely responding to the environment but also has some internal timing. Similarly, sheep that are fall breeders in the northern hemisphere continue to breed at the same time of year when transported to the southern hemisphere, where it is spring. Biological clocks thus show a certain amount of stability, supporting the theory that internal timing mechanisms are well established in a wide variety of organisms.

But biological clocks can be reset, even though they are largely internally controlled. After the second year, the breeding behavior of the sheep just mentioned will switch over and conform to the seasonal conditions of the southern hemisphere. If fiddler crabs are moved from their home beach to one where the tides occur at different times, their activity cycles soon change to match the new tidal cycles. The fact that internal clocks can be reset after some period of time also indicates that these mechanisms must be adaptable to assist organisms to adjust to new environments. The mechanisms that determine the timing of biological clocks appear to be complex internal sequences of metabolic events that can closely parallel and be affected by cyclic environmental events.

We have already given one example of circadian activity in humans. Studies on shift workers and travelers and isolation experiments in which environmental conditions were held constant, have provided much information about human circadian rhythms. When they are experimentally kept in a dark environment, humans gradually lose track of time. However, certain body functions, such as pulse and temperature, may continue to exhibit an approximate 24-hour cycle. Metabolic cycles, secretions of hormones, reactions to medications, sensory sharpness, and even susceptibility to infection seem to occur in cyclic patterns.

Circannual Rhythms

Scientists have also investigated biological clocks based on yearly cycles—*circannual rhythms.* Hibernation behavior is one example. A circannual cycle in a species of ground squirrel has been reported by Eric T. Pengelley and Sally J. Asmundson of the University of California at Riverside. These ground squirrels typically lose weight during hibernation. In a series of experiments, one group of squirrels was kept at room temperature and another group at near freezing temperatures. Both groups showed similar hibernation time and weight loss (Figure 17–11). The squirrels apparently have an internal control over hibernation that is largely independent of temperature. The important point here is that nature has "set" the hibernation clock, and it continues to function even under artificial conditions.

Another example of a yearly cycle is the urinary excretion in human males of ketosteroid hormones, many of which are secreted by the adrenal cortex. This follows an annual rhythm with high secretory peaks in September and November and a low in May. It has been suggested that these cycles are correlated with varying emotional states such as moods and aggression. The best examples of yearly behavior, however, are bird migrations.

MIGRATION

Annual migrations of many species of birds have intrigued us for centuries. Each spring and fall, birds fill the air over North and South

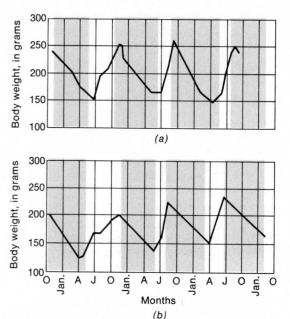

FIGURE 17–11 Records during four years provide evidence that the circannual rhythm of ground squirrel hibernation is not influenced by temperature. The shaded bands indicate hibernation. (*a*) The room temperature is 12°C (53.6°F). (*b*) The room temperature is just above the freezing point. (Redrawn from "Annual Biological Clocks" by Eric T. Pengelley and Sally J. Asmundson. Copyright © 1971 by Scientific American, Inc. All rights reserved.)

America in four major flyways: the Atlantic, Mississippi, Central, and Pacific.

Arctic terns migrate each year from the north pole region to Antarctica and back again, nearly 25,000 miles. Golden plovers travel the Atlantic flyway from the Arctic to Argentina and back each year (Figure 17–12). One group of northern cliff swallows has gained worldwide attention by returning consistently to the mission in San Juan Capistrano, California about March 20 of every year. At the mission, these swallows build vase-shaped mud nests, mate, and rear their young. About the middle of September they leave their nesting territories and fly southward to winter in Brazil.

Not all bird migrations are so extensive. Some birds, such as jays, juncos, and grosbeaks,

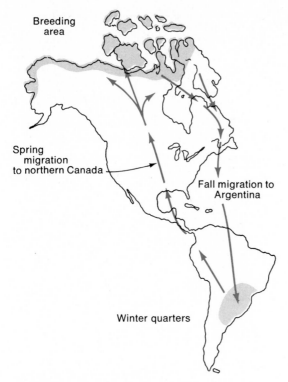

FIGURE 17–12 The migratory route of the eastern golden plover.

simply move to higher altitudes in summer. Western evening grosbeaks, for example, breed in mountains from Canada to Arizona and winter in adjacent lowlands.

Observation and experimental studies have shown that several stimuli control these seasonal movements. The fact that not all birds migrate and that not all migratory birds go in the same direction or at the same time indicates that several variables are involved. In some species migration can be correlated with changes in temperature, food supply, or rainfall, but these correlations do not always hold true even among closely related species. Biologists have thus turned to physiological explanations. The most plausible hypothesis offered today involves responses to varying periods of light and dark. Perception of relative day length enables some birds to set their internal clocks for breeding and migration. Thus daily cycles

can be involved in the control of circannual or yearly cycles.

White-crowned sparrows that breed and spend the winter in temperate latitudes begin to develop gonads in March under stimulation of hormones from the pituitary gland. This development coincides with their annual migration northward to Alaska (Figure 17–13). By the end of May the sparrows are ready to breed and rear their young. About the middle of July the gonads begin to regress, the old feathers molt, and a large amount of body fat begins to be stored. Southward migration begins in mid-September, and the birds reach their winter territory in Mexico or the southeastern United States by November.

Donald Farner of the University of Washington has shown that gonad development, prenuptial molting, and pre-northward-migratory fattening all depend on the long days of spring. Photoreceptors (the eyes, or perhaps direct brain stimulation via the pineal gland) induce the hypothalamus to release neurohormones which in turn stimulate the pituitary gland to secrete gonadotropins. These cause the secondary sex characteristics to develop (Figure 17–14). Regression of the gonads in mid-July does not seem to be controlled by day length. Farner believes that the birds become insensitive to day length during this time. This insensitivity is finally broken during the short days of late fall, and the preparation for the southward journey is completed.

The migratory activities of birds that winter near the equator, where day length is constant all year, are not as easy to explain. How do these birds know when to return north? It has been suggested that these birds can physiologically accumulate the effects of increments of light. This ability to "add up" light periods may be responsible for triggering northward migration.

Orientation

Even more astonishing than the timing of migrations is the ability of many organisms to orient themselves in time and space. After years at sea, green sea turtles return to their native beaches to lay their eggs (Figure 17–15).

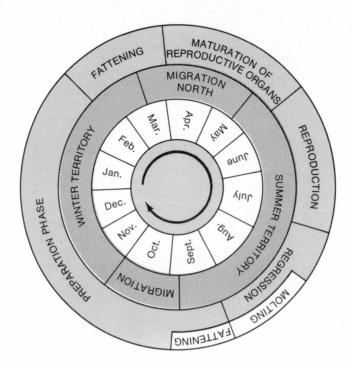

FIGURE 17–13 Generalized breeding and migratory cycle of temperate zone birds. (From *Animal Photoperiodism* by S. D. Beck. Copyright © 1963 by Holt, Rinehart and Winston, Inc. Redrawn by permission of the publishers, Holt, Rinehart and Winston, Inc.)

Gray whales swim annually from the Arctic to Scammon's Lagoon in Baja California; salmon return from the sea to spawn on the gravel-bedded creeks of their birth; and many birds navigate accurately over thousands of miles of earth and sea (Figure 17–16).

Each migrating species needs not only an internal clock to stimulate migration but also a sense of the direction and distance to be traveled. Green turtles that feed for years at sea must hit a tiny target, the Galapagos Islands, nearly 650 miles off the coast of Ecuador. Even a small miscalculation could mean a late arrival at the hatching site and nonviable eggs.

Bird Orientation

Problems of orientation and navigation in birds have been under intense study for the past few years. The factors subjected to experimentation include visual orientation, sensitivity to infra-red radiation (invisible heat radiation), the rotational force of the turning earth, the sun, the stars, and magnetic cues.

There is no doubt that diurnal birds flying over land make use of visual landmarks, but navigation cannot be explained on this basis for birds that fly over vast areas of ocean or for young birds that fly their first course alone. Sensitivity to increased infrared radiation at the equator and orientation to the forces produced by the earth's rotation are difficult to study; evidence that they are factors in navigation is meager.

Scientists do know that orientation through a sense of the sun's position is a significant factor. Experiments have shown that birds of some species have an ability to determine a northward direction from the position of the sun. These birds can orient themselves at any time of day, a procedure requiring an internal

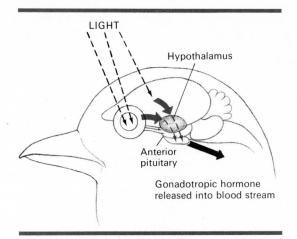

FIGURE 17–14 Proposed mechanism for photoperiodic stimulation of testes in birds. Photoreceptors in the eyes and brain are stimulated by light. Nerve impulses (colored arrows) cause neurosecretory cells in the hypothalamus to secrete neurohormones into a portal blood system linking the hypothalamus and pituitary gland (broken arrows). The anterior pituitary in turn secretes gonadotropic hormones into the bloodstream (black arrow).

calculation with the biological clock. To test the ability of homing pigeons to interpret direction by the position of the sun, a comparison of homing can be made between birds acclimated to regular "sun time" and birds whose internal clocks have been "reset" 6 hours under artificial illumination. The reset birds fly away about 90° to the right of the homeward direction—a phenomenon that shows a definite correlation among the internal clock mechanism, the position of the sun, and the bird's sense of direction.

If certain birds can sense direction according to a sun compass, what about night-flying species? Some researchers believe that nocturnal flyers may set their courses by the setting sun, but recent studies by Stephen Emlen at Cornell University have shown that orientation may be based on the position of the stars. When indigo buntings were placed in a planetarium simulating a night sky in fall, they oriented in a southerly direction—the normal direction of fall migration. When the planetarium sky was ro-

tated so that "south" was not really south, the buntings adjusted themselves to the new position of the artificial stars. In most cases, birds lose their orientation when sun, moon, or stars are not visible to them. Under such conditions, the birds fly restlessly in all directions in their cages. When the sky is again visible, however, the birds quickly reorient.

As scientific interest in continental drift and the changing of the earth's magnetic fields has increased, more experimentation has taken place with magnetic orientation in birds. Magnets glued to the backs of homing pigeons caused serious disorientation, but only when the birds were released under heavy overcast conditions. This suggests that the pigeons use the sun compass as a primary system but may also have the ability to orient to the earth's magnetic fields.

Birds may possess several orientation mechanisms. This could help explain how ducks and geese navigate on overcast nights or how daylight flyers can leave the land and cross great expanses of ocean without serious disorientation. We must admit that we know little about the mechanisms that tell the organism in which direction to orient, when to begin flight, or how far to travel.

Fish Orientation

Another mystery, orientation and migration of salmon, is gradually being solved. Many studies involving tagging, release, and recovery of Pacific salmon have been made under the direction of Lauren Donaldson at the University of Washington. We know that tagged male and female salmon go to sea for as long as four years and then return to the site of their birth—the same creek bed—to spawn. There females lay their eggs and males fertilize them; then both males and females die. Among European and Atlantic species, adults may survive and return to spawn several times.

How do salmon recognize their native river, tributary, and finally their own shallow creek bed? Experiments conducted in several laboratories have demonstrated that returning salmon rely on an exceptionally sensitive sense of smell to detect their home waters. A salmon will choose to swim into a stream containing as

FIGURE 17-15   Female green sea turtle returning to land, Wilson Island, Great Barrier Reef, Australia. (Courtesy of Keith Gillett.)

little as 1 part per billion of its home water. When the nostrils, which allow water to circulate into the olfactory sacs, are plugged, or when the olfactory lobes of the brain are destroyed, the fish cannot recognize its home water. Orientation is thus determined through acute chemoperception. We know little about the factors that sent the fish back to fresh water, but they may be related to the release of pituitary hormones and subsequent reproductive maturity.

COMMUNICATION

Most animals have the ability to send, receive, and interpret meaningful signals. Communication among members of a species has adaptive value in attracting mates, determining territory, securing food, and mutually defending against enemies. It is often convenient to interpret animal communication on the basis of human experience, but we must remember that this practice may introduce bias and inaccuracy.

Animal communication may involve several classes of signals: visual displays, chemical signals, sounds, tactile (touch) systems, and language. An animal may use several of these signals or some combination to communicate specific messages. For example, a rhesus monkey may scream and pound the ground with its hands when threatening another.

FIGURE 17–16   Migrating Canada geese. (Grant Heilman.)

Visual Displays

A male magnificent frigate bird makes effective use of its visual sexual display to attract a mate (Figure 17–17). Approximately 3 to 4 weeks before the mating season, a drab pink strip on the bird's breast suddenly becomes bright scarlet. When the male magnificent frigate spots a female, he pumps air into his lungs, forming a huge inflated pouch that makes the scarlet area larger and much more visible. The male magnificent frigate bird courts only females of his own species, however; he ignores females of a closely related species, the great frigate bird.

Displays also occur in territorial behavior. The red-mouthed lava gull of the Galapagos Islands squawks and gapes repeatedly, showing its bright red mouth, when another bird or a human approaches. The green heron threatens by showing a more subtle series of visual displays: first it raises its crown feathers; next it twitches its tail feathers up and down; and finally it opens its beak and ruffs its back feathers. This series of displays shows increased intensity in the threat message as an intruder nears.

Blue-footed boobies of the Galapagos Islands make full use of their bright blue feet both in proclaiming territory and in courtship. The male blue-foot gains the attention of his intended mate by performing an exaggerated, high-stepping dance (Figure 17–18). He displays the same behavior as he moves about the boundaries of his territory.

Chemical Messengers: Pheromones

A familiar example of chemical communication occurs when ants follow a "trail" to and from their den to obtain food (Figure 17–19). Ants release a chemical onto the ground that others of the species recognize and follow. Chemicals released into the environment to cause a certain behavior are called *pheromones*. The marking ant drags the tip of its abdomen along the ground, releasing small quantities of a pheromone produced in the hindgut or in certain associated glands near the tip. The phero-

FIGURE 17–17   Male magnificent frigate bird displaying inflated throat pouch. (California Academy of Sciences.)

mone dissipates quite rapidly, however, so the trail must be continually renewed by ants returning with food. When the food supply is exhausted returning ants do not excrete the marker, and the trail is quickly obliterated. Extracts made from whole ants or from hindguts have been used to make artificial trails. When experimenters lay a circular trail, the ants will follow it instead of taking a shorter route.

F. E. Regnier of Purdue University and E. O. Wilson of Harvard University have studied the habits of slave-maker ants, *Formica subintegra*. These ants seek out and attack nests of other ant species, subdue or kill the defenders, and carry away worker pupae. They use hindgut secretions to mark the trail to the raid. A pheromone from a gland called Dufour's gland has a unique purpose: When the slave-makers attack they spray the chemical onto the defending ants, causing them to scatter and leave the nest area.

Bert Hölldobler of Harvard University studied one instance of communication between ants and a European beetle. The rove beetle is a parasite found in nests of the wood ant *Formica polyctena*. Host ants feed and groom beetle larvae as well as or better than their own larvae, and they accept the adult beetles as equals. How does this happen? How can the defenseless larvae induce the host ants to perform this behavior? The answer lies in the abil-

FIGURE 17–18 Male blue-footed booby "parading" in front of a prospective mate.

ity of the beetle larvae and adults to mimic the ants' communication signals, both pheromonal and mechanical. Beetle larvae are carried into the ants' nest in response to a chemical they secreted; nourishment is provided when a larva rears its head and touches the host ant's mouth parts with its own. According to Hölldobler, the beetle larvae perform this "begging" behavior so well and so often that they get more food than the ant larvae (Figure 17–20).

The potent chemical bombycol, liberated by female *bombyx* moths, attracts male moths from several miles downwind. Among humans, perfume may have an analogous effect. Chemical messengers have a great variety of uses in activities such as feeding, mating, and complex social behavior.

Sounds

Animals produce many kinds of sounds in a variety of ways, and among certain species this type of communication is very effective. Many examples could be given, but we will mention only birds and insects here.

The familiar songs of birds are useful in establishing and defending territories. A bird sings in certain parts of its territory in order to announce ownership to other males of its species. Alarm calls are also used when an intruder comes too near its nest.

Crickets and grasshoppers use sounds for species recognition or for attracting mates. The cricket sound is produced when a male rubs its wing covers together. The chirping made by

Bio-Topic: Heredity, Learning, and Behavior

A hybrid lovebird provided an interesting example of the interplay of heredity and learning in shaping the behavior of vertebrates. The hybrid was obtained by mating two related species of lovebirds, one from the west coast of Africa, the other from the Lake Victoria region of east Africa. The mating took place in W. C. Dilger's laboratory at Cornell University, where the hybrid was reared and studied for three years. Dilger and his coworkers studied many aspects of the hybrid's behavior, but the most interesting aspect was the nest-building behavior.

Female west African lovebirds use their parrotlike beaks to cut long strips of bark and leaves from which they construct their nests. As each strip is cut, the female tucks it into the feathers on her back. When six to eight strips have been tucked away, the female flies to the nesting site and adds them to her nest.

The nest-building behavior of east African lovebirds is different in two ways. First, the female gathers and uses twigs as well as strips of bark and leaves. Second, the female gathers materials one piece at a time and immediately carries each piece to the nesting site, in her beak.

The nest-building of the hybrid female is at first completely confused. She cuts strips of building materials quite normally, only to drop or ignore many of them. Cutting is often interrupted by premature tucking motions, or by entirely irrelevant activities. Strips she does tuck into her feathers are placed so poorly that all are lost in the flight to the nesting site. The hybrid female does carry a few strips in her beak, but even then fluffs her feathers for tucking and makes tucking motions. Dilger concluded that the hybrid displayed both the tucking behavior of her west African parent and the bill-carrying behavior of her east African parent—but intermixed in a very inefficient way. As the months passed, the hybrid displayed fewer tucking behaviors and more bill-carrying behaviors. But even after two years, when bill-carrying had become the dominant behavior, many movements associated with tucking persisted.

These observations suggest that among vertebrates, innate behavior patterns may be modified by experience, and that the interplay between heredity and learning may be quite complex.

one species of cricket is distinct in pitch and frequency from that made by other cricket species.

Tactile Systems

Touch, or tactile communication, is possible among most animals. When a sender of signals is in contact with a receiver, a great variety of messages may be transmitted by varying the frequency, pressure, and time of contact. Earlier we noted that tactile communication between the wood ant and the rove beetle larva elicits feeding behavior. Tactile communica-

tion is frequent in courtship and mating behavior. Bees use touch as a means of conveying information in the dark hive. The location of a food source, for example, is communicated by feeling the pattern of a scout bee's dance. Alarm reactions can also be spread through tactile communication.

Communication in Bees

Communication among honeybees has been studied extensively. In the late 1940s, the Austrian biologist Karl von Frisch reported the results of his thorough observations of bees. Von

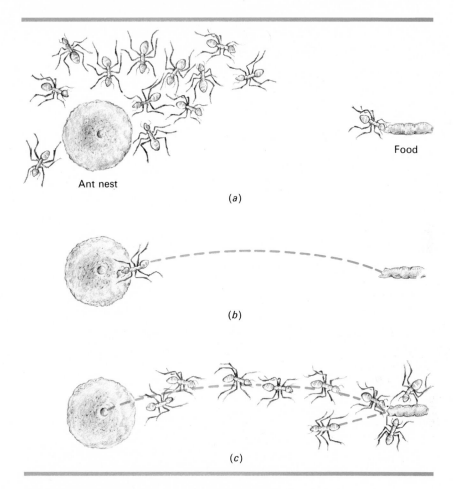

FIGURE 17–19   Foraging behavior in ants. (*a*) An ant finds a source of food. (*b*) The ant brings a piece back to the nest, laying a pheromone trail between the food and the nest. (*c*) Other ants recognize the trail and make their way to the food. As the food supply dwindles, fewer ants make the return trip and less pheromone is laid down; consequently, the trail disappears.

Frisch showed that a bee returning to its hive could communicate the quality, direction, and distance of a food supply. Bees leaving the hive after receiving the message were able to fly directly to the food. Through careful observations, von Frisch learned that the messenger bee transmitted its information by doing a precise dance on the vertical face of a honeycomb (Figure 17–21). One dance is done by tracing a circular path and then crossing its diameter in

only one direction to form two semicircular paths. As the bee crosses the diameter in a straight line, it wiggles its abdomen (represented by the wavy line in Figure 17–21). If the food source is on a line directly between the hive and the position of the sun, the dancing bee makes its straight cross-runs directly up (↑). If the food is on a line directly away from the sun, the cross-runs are straight down (↓). To communicate the location of food that is not

Bio-Topic: Adoption by Deceit

The behavior of social insects is regulated by elaborate systems of visual, chemical, and mechanical cues. These cues integrate the behaviors of several castes and thousands of individuals so that the stability of the nest or hive is maintained.

Among the social ants, many aspects of behavior are controlled by pheromones secreted by specialized glands. Certain pheromones signal alarm, others mark a trail to food, still others are used to mark nestmates. Not all aspects of ant behavior are controlled by pheromones. For example, larvae "beg" for food by tapping the adults' antennae in specific patterns.

Together, pheromones, tactile stimuli, and auditory signals form a "language" that enables the members of a nest to communicate among themselves and to maintain their social organization. The elements of these ant languages, which differ from species to species, are probably "releasers," signals that trigger innate behavior patterns in the individual that senses the signal.

Many insects have evolved behaviors that allow them to parasitize the social systems of ant species. Highwayman beetles, for example, can sense the trail pheromone secreted by wood ants. The beetle waits by an ant trail until a food-laden ant approaches. The beetle stimulates the ant's mouthparts, causing the

ant to give up its food. Dinardid beetles also steal food by stimulating the mouthparts of its host ant. The ant gives up its food, but quickly attacks the thief. The beetle defends itself by secreting from glands in its abdomen an "appeasement" pheromone that calms the ant while the beetle escapes.

Perhaps the most interesting parasites of ants are the rove beetles. When a female rove beetle meets an ant of its host species, it secretes an appeasement pheromone that calms the ant. The beetle then secretes an "adoption" pheromone that induces the ant to treat the beetle as a misplaced ant larva. The ant carries the beetle to the brood chamber of the ant colony where the beetle lays eggs. The beetle larvae produce a pheromone that cause the nurse ants to accept them as ant larvae. The beetle larvae can also induce the nurse ants to feed them until they develop into mature rove beetles.

All of these parasitic beetles have "broken the code" by which the ants communicate and turned it to their advantage. By evolving behaviors and pheromones that deceive their hosts, the beetles can obtain food and can even be adopted as foster ants. Because the parasitism is based on mimicry of the ant's releasers, the ants can do nothing but respond in ways normally beneficial to their species.

on a direct line between the hive and the sun, a dancer angles its cross-runs to correspond to the direction and angle from the hive (Figure 17–21c). For instance, a cross-run angle of 60 degrees to the left of the upward vertical axis means that the food is on a path toward the sun but 60 degrees to the left.

The "bee dance" has since been studied extensively with the aid of instrumentation.

Harold Esch of the University of Notre Dame discovered that bees also emit sounds during their dance. He learned that "voiceless" bees could not stimulate others to leave the hive even after they repeated the dance several times. The exact role of the bee sounds is not yet clear, but they may be essential for interpretation by bees inside a dark hive. In other experiments, Esch proved that the abdominal

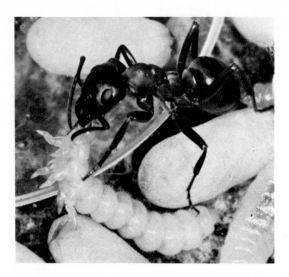

FIGURE 17-20   A beetle larva receiving a droplet of liquid food from an ant in the brood chamber of an ant nest. (Courtesy of Bert Hölldobler, Museum of Comparative Zoology, Harvard University.)

waggling period conveys the distance to the food; the longer the waggling time, the farther away the food.

In 1967, A. M. Wenner proposed that the primary mode of communication among bees about food supplies is odor. Wenner and his co-workers demonstrated that the odors of a food and of the food location are important when a forager returns to the hive to recruit other members to find the food. Von Frisch had also studied the importance of odor in the communication process, but he believed the bee dances to be more important. Both the odors and the dancing may be important. If an abundant food source is readily available, for example, odors alone may be sufficient to recruit other members from the hive. But if food is scarce or farther away, both odor and dance "language" may be necessary.

The bee dance borders on the establishment of a language. A returning bee is conveying the direction and distance to a food source that none of the bees can see. Bee dances, however, appear to be stereotyped and genetically fixed. The bees cannot apparently create new variations to the dance to convey other meanings.

Learning a Language

Language is an important component of almost all human behavior, and we know a great deal about how humans learn language. But we don't know as much about the learning of language in lower primates. Can a chimpanzee learn a language? Several serious attempts have been made to teach chimpanzees to speak, but they have been able to master only a few simple words. We now know that these early experiments had disappointing results because they used *speech* as the mode of communication. The vocal apparatus of a chimpanzee is different from ours, and it is poorly suited to oral linguistic communication.

More recent attempts at teaching chimpanzees to use language in other, nonvocal modes have been more successful. And these attempts have shown that the ability to learn word concepts and to convey these ideas to others is not dependent on the ability to speak. For example, Ann and David Premack at the University of California at Santa Barbara had remarkable success with a three-year-old chimpanzee named Sarah (Figure 17–22). Sarah not only learned 130 words in the form of colored plastic symbols, but she also learned how to place these words into proper grammatical sequences. She further learned to construct questions and mastered the conditional (if-then) concept. The Premacks believe that Sarah's language ability approximates that of a two-year-old human child. One must keep in mind, however, that Sarah must be taught any new words she learns; she probably could not learn them on her own.

TERRITORIAL BEHAVIOR

The fact that birds, wolves, rabbits, mice, sea lions, and other animals exhibit territorial behavior demonstrates that most wild populations regulate their numbers in a given area. This behavior serves a variety of functions. For some species territorial behavior may insure an adequate food supply, while in others it may provide a mating and nesting area. And since territoriality differs with the needs of a species, various patterns have evolved. Territories may

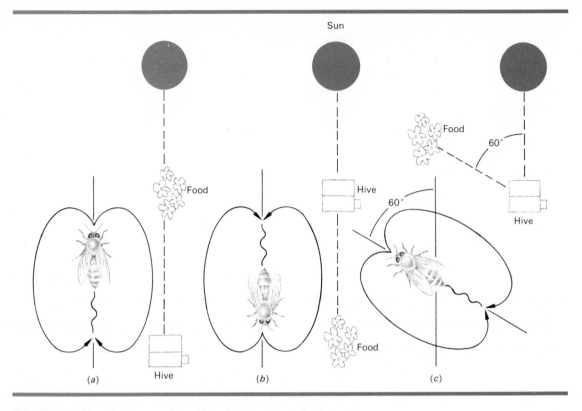

FIGURE 17–21 Three examples of bee-dance communication. (a) The source of food is in a straight path between the hive and the sun. (b) The food is directly away from the sun. (c) The food is toward the sun, but 60° to the left.

be marked off and defended on a permanent or on a seasonal basis.

Rabbits, for example, construct a permanent burrow-filled warren and establish trails and warning signs around it. In this territory they feed, mate, and rear their young. Many of the mechanisms rabbits use to mark and protect their territory are known. Roman Mykytowycz, in working with wild Australian rabbits, has found that two glands produce marking secretions—an anal gland and a chin gland. The anal gland coats fecal pellets with a secretion easily recognized by other rabbits. When a warren is established, male rabbits excrete pellets in mounds and urinate around the periphery, thus warning intruding rabbits that the area is occupied. Secretions from the chin gland serve

to mark twigs and grass, perhaps for the same purpose (Figure 17–23). Development and secretion of these glands appear to be controlled by sex hormones.

Song birds, on the other hand, establish temporary territories early in the spring for breeding and nesting purposes. The male flies from tree to tree around his area singing, repulsing males, and attempting to attract a mate. The bird that sings the loudest most often occupies the largest territory; confrontations over territory seldom involve serious fighting or lead to the death of a combatant. In general, intruders respect the line drawn by the occupant. If an intruder is larger and stronger than a defender, the defender usually retreats and gives up part of the territory. The defense of a territory by an

FIGURE 17-22 Language learning in a chimpanzee. The symbols in the background represent the message given to Sarah, the chimpanzee. Reading from the top, the symbols stand for *Sarah, insert, apple, pail, banana,* and *dish.* In order to make the correct interpretation—that she should put the apple in the pail and the banana in the dish—Sarah had to understand sentence structure and not just word order. (From "Teaching Language to an Ape" by Ann James Premack and David Premack. Copyright © 1972 by Scientific American, Inc. All rights reserved.)

individual, pair, or group of animals is thought to limit the population density of an area and to conserve food and shelter. An invader who crosses into a territory that is too large for an individual or group to defend may be successful in settling. If, however, the population density is already high, the invader will be repulsed and forced to try another area.

Social Hierarchy

In many animals territoriality and *social hierarchy* are closely related. In his study of rabbit territoriality, Mykytowycz also showed that a direct correlation exists between the amount of a rabbit's marker gland secretion and its position in the social structure of the warren.

Social structure or ranking can be found in nearly all animal groups; it is very evident among fish, birds, and domestic animals. Some bird species exhibit rather complex social behavior under caged conditions. If the cage is large enough each bird settles into a specific territory, although eating and drinking facilities may be shared. The addition of more birds eventually upsets this balance, and a rigorous *peck order* will result. Each bird assumes its place in the order between those it can peck and those that peck it. Usually the largest, most aggressive bird becomes dominant and is not pecked by any other bird. This social ranking, especially important with respect to feeding and roosting preferences, provides a stable and efficient society.

DEVELOPMENT OF BEHAVIOR

How does behavior develop in an individual organism? How does an organism come to behave as it does—what causal factors are involved? We have already seen that some behaviors are largely or wholly innate, independent of experience. But we also know that much behavior results at least in part from learning. For example, studies of young sea gulls suggest that learning is necessary before feeding behavior can fully develop. In the laughing gull, a hungry young chick pecks at the parent's bill, grasps it, and strokes downward; this is called a begging peck. This repeated behavior prompts the parent to regurgitate food, which the chick pecks at and eats (a feeding peck) (Figure 17-24).

In order to study how this behavior—which involves interaction of inherited and learned components—develops, J. P. Hailman of the University of Wisconsin studied newly hatched chicks until they were one week old, when feeding behavior is well established. Newborn chicks are quite inaccurate with their initial begging pecks, but their accuracy improves greatly during the first week. Moreover, chicks often do not see food when it is dropped by the parent. When the parent picks up the food and the chick strikes it during another begging peck, the chick *learns* to recognize food. The reward of food also helps a chick to recognize its parent; this recognition is appar-

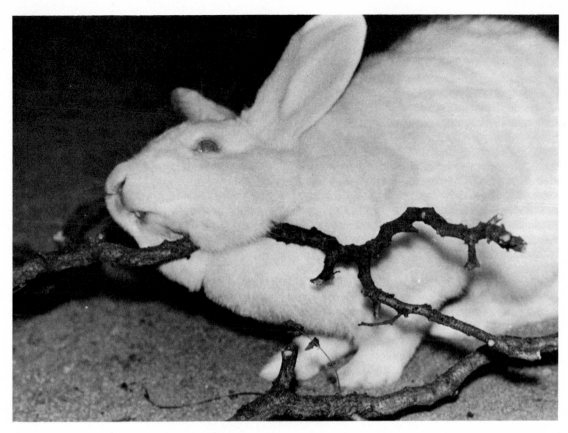

FIGURE 17–23   Wild rabbit rubbing chin-gland secretions on twig to mark its territory. (Courtesy of Roman Mykytowycz.)

ently necessary for accuracy in the begging peck and for full development of the total feeding behavior. Experiments with models have shown that a chick will peck more vigorously at models that resemble the parent's head and that make vertical movements similar to those of the parent. When a chick receives food from the parent, the behavior of pecking is *reinforced,* and we say that the chick learns to peck at its parent's bill because it obtains food through this behavior.

It should not be surprising that the feeding pattern of the gull chick includes a combination of behavioral activities. Most animals use a variety of modes of behavior (taxes, reflexes, instincts, and learning). But whereas invertebrate animals use mostly simple behaviors, such as taxes and reflexes, vertebrates rely heavily on complex behavior (Figure 17–25). Thus a gradation of behavior from simpler to more complex forms exists among animals. In primates and humans, learning and reasoning dominate behavior. In the next chapter we consider learning and how it takes place.

SUMMARY

Behavior can be defined as any externally observable action or activity of a living system; most behavior has adaptive value. Behavior can be studied using a variety of techniques for observation. A good example of a social behavioral study in the field is that done by Jane van Lawick-Goodall on chimpanzees in Africa.

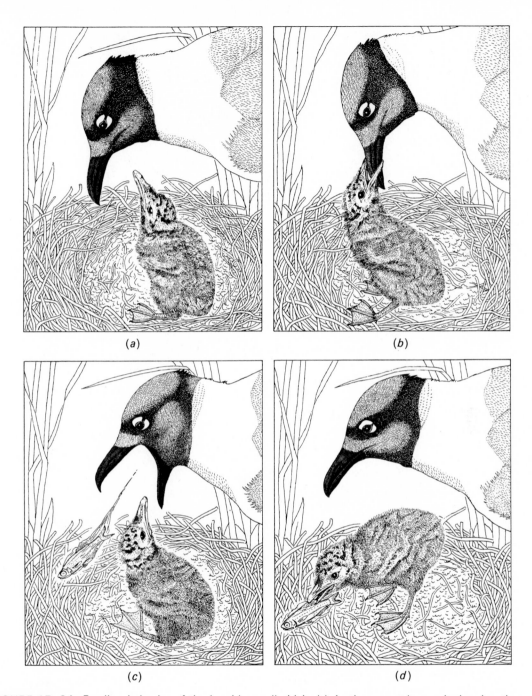

FIGURE 17-24 Feeding behavior of the laughing gull chick. (*a*) As the parent lowers its head, a three-day-old chick directs a begging peck at the parent's beak. (*b*) The chick grasps and strokes the parent's beak. (*c*) The parent then regurgitates partly digested food. (*d*) The chick begins to eat the food, using a pecking action called a ''feeding peck.'' (From ''How an Instinct Is Learned'' by Jack P. Hailman. Copyright ⓒ 1969 by Scientific American, Inc. All rights reserved.)

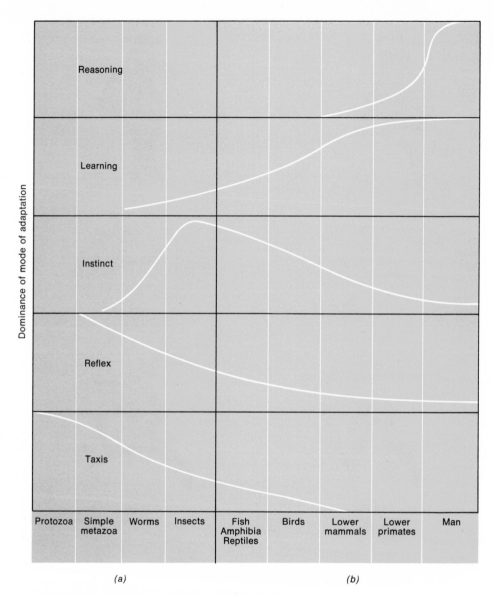

FIGURE 17–25   Relative use of various modes of behavior in animals. (a) Invertebrates rely heavily on taxes, reflexes, and instinctive behavior. (b) Vertebrates show more learning and reasoning in
their behavior. (Redrawn from V. G. Dethier and Eliot Stellar, *Animal Behavior: Its Evolutionary and Neurological Basis,* Second
Edition, © 1964. By permission of Prentice-Hall, Inc., Englewood
Cliffs, New Jersey.)

Some of the simplest types of behavior are tropisms, taxes, and reflexes, which are generally automatic orientations to the environment. Reflexes are principally responses to a stimulus, involve a nervous system, and many serve protective functions. They often occur in chains, in which the response to one reflex is the stimulus for the next, or in coordinated groups.

The behavior of any complex species shows evidence of inheritance and learning. Whereas some behavior sequences appear to be instinctive or innate and other behavior patterns seem to be learned, most behavior is the result of both genetic and environmental contributions. Ethology is the study of species-characteristic behavior. Any object, structure, behavior, or sound that can initiate a fixed sequence of responses is known as a releaser.

Certain biological activities are controlled by internal timing mechanisms called biological clocks, which are often affected by environmental conditions such as day length and the phases of the moon. Behavioral patterns called circadian rhythms occur on a 24-hour cycle; the year is the basis for other cycles.

Seasonal migrations in birds are apparently triggered by photoperiodism, a response made to varying periods of light and dark. In some species, photoperiodism stimulates the pituitary by way of the hypothalamus to produce responses related to migration. Migration involves orientation; some animals may make use of the position of the sun and stars, and perhaps the earth's magnetic field, to orient themselves.

Methods of animal communication include visual displays, chemical signals, sounds, tactile systems, and language. Visual displays are used by many animals for showing aggression, attracting a mate, or defending a territory. Ants release chemicals called pheromones onto the ground to mark trails. Bees bump against each other for communication in a hive; they also communicate the distance and direction of food by dance movements and odors.

Many animals claim and maintain territories for the purpose of breeding and feeding, and territoriality limits population density in an area. Peck order is one type of social hierarchy in birds in which the individuals are in a ranked social order. Behavior patterns probably develop in most organisms through the interaction of inheritance and learning.

REVIEW QUESTIONS

1. Give examples of tropistic and taxic behavior. State the adaptive value of such movements to the organisms involved.

2. Why is it difficult to distinguish in a behavioral pattern between what is learned and what is inherited?

3. Young herring gulls beg for food by pecking at the parent's bill. When models were presented to a group of young gulls, the bill model with a red spot received the most pecks, whereas models with spots of other colors had fewer responses, and models with no spot received fewest pecks. What can you conclude from these experiments about the feeding behavior in young herring gulls?

4. In some birds the color of certain body parts, such as a robin's red breast, may act as a releaser to provoke attack by another bird of the same species. List some examples of other releasers in nature.

5. Organisms can have their biological clocks reset when exposed to new conditions. This resetting generally requires some period of time. Why?

6. Discuss several factors that may influence the annual migrations of birds such as the northern cliff swallows and white-crowned sparrows.

7. Most animals show some territoriality in their natural habitats. What are the advantages of this behavior?

8. Why does a barnyard rooster crow from several different perches early in the morning? Why do wolves and dogs urinate on objects all around a general area?

SUPPLEMENTARY READINGS

Emlen, Stephen T., "The Stellar-Orientation System of a Migratory Bird," *Scientific Ameri-*

can, August 1975. Although it has been shown that indigo buntings can orient themselves by the position of the stars, it is also apparent that other mechanisms of navigation are used to maintain a migratory direction.

Luce, Gay Gaer, *Body Time*, Pantheon Books, New York, 1971. Explores the meanings of human physiological rhythms to behavior, health, stress, productivity, emotions, and learning.

Palmer, John D., "Biological Clocks of the Tidal Zone," *Scientific American*, February 1975. Many marine organisms living in the tidal zone possess both solar day and lunar day biological clocks that are important in feeding, coloration, and reproduction.

Saunders, D. S., "The Biological Clock of Insects," *Scientific American*, February 1976. Diapause, a period of dormancy, occurs in most insects when days become shorter. This behavior may be controlled by an internal photoperiod-measuring clock having two components capable of summating both short and long days.

Wehner, Rüdiger, "Polarized-Light Navigation by Insects," *Scientific American*, July 1976. Many insect species navigate by using the polarized light of the daytime sky. This article deals with the complex receptor system and the insect's ability to continuously integrate all the angles and distances it has traveled.

Wilson, Edward O., "Slavery in Ants," *Scientific American*, June 1975. Although very efficient at fighting and carrying off captive ants to serve as slaves, some raiding species have become so specialized that they cannot feed themselves.

Wurtman, Richard J., "The Effects of Light on the Human Body," *Scientific American*, July 1975. Light has many effects on human beings including synthesis of vitamin D, treatment of disease, and the setting of biological rhythms. The potential effects of artificial lighting are examined.

Chapter 18

Behavior: Learning and Modification

The "simple" forms of behavior we saw in Chapter 17 are only a fraction of the wide range of behaviors most advanced organisms carry out. If innate and "simple" types of behavior were the only kinds possible, most organisms would be helpless to adapt to changing environmental conditions and to transmit these adaptations to their offspring.

We will look at five **Types of Learning** in this chapter. Two of them—**Habituation** and **Imprinting**—might appear so basic as to be inherited, not learned. However, research has shown that these are acquired behaviors. The complex forms—**Classical Conditioning, Operant Conditioning,** and **Reasoning**—are more readily identified as learned behaviors.

What form does a memory take? How is it stored? What happens when we forget something? Perhaps few things could be less substantial than an idea or a recollection, but scientists are finding chemical and physiological aspects of thought and memory. The relationship between **Memory and Chemistry** has been dentified by the chemical changes in the brain as we learn something. The relationship is only barely understood, but perhaps someday it will be possible to transfer memory from one orga-

nism to another by chemical means. Or learning could be chemically stimulated and made more efficient.

As they move ahead in research on behavior, scientists are even finding out a great deal about **Love and Learning.** Five kinds of affection and love are described in this chapter.

Few areas of biological research have been as hampered in development as **Human Sexual Behavior.** Only since World War II has the sociological and biological study of human sexual response, attitudes, and problems been openly possible.

We have seen the wide range of chemical and physiological aspects of behavior. It should not be surprising, therefore, to find that there are many ways in which behavior can be changed. The **Modification of Behavior** is part of our daily lives. You can be influenced, threatened, or encouraged to carry out certain kinds of behavior by a variety of means. **Psychotherapy,** for example, is the medical alteration of behavior to assist the patient in dealing with personal problems or behavior. One possible approach in psychotherapy involves the use of **Chemical Therapy and Drugs.**

Behavior becomes adapted to environmental conditions through two major processes. One is evolution through natural selection. Adaptation by natural selection is a slow process; the evolution of a new behavioral trait may take many generations. This type of adaptation is essential to the long-range survival of species. An individual organism benefits from previous evolutionary change, but it cannot itself develop adaptive behaviors by this process. Yet during its lifetime an organism faces an endless series of environmental changes, some of them quite sudden. If it cannot adapt to these changes, it dies. But as we know, individual organisms can and do make many behavioral adaptations in the face of change.

The process by which an individual makes behavioral adaptations in response to its own individual experiences is called *learning*. Learning may be defined as *a relatively permanent change in behavior that occurs as the result of experience*. Learning is a much faster means of behavioral adaptation than evolution. Learning can take place very rapidly—sometimes in seconds or less, as when a child burns its hand in a flame and "instantly" learns to keep a safe distance from flames.

Learning begins very early in the life of an organism. But this fact creates certain difficulties in studying it, especially in studying the development of learning. We saw in the preceding chapter that pecking accuracy in young laughing gulls increases with practice and maturation (reaching full development). The more a young chick practices in the first week of its life, the more accurate it becomes in its begging pecks. But would this skill improve with age alone? It would certainly improve somewhat as a result of increased neuromuscular development. Thus experience and maturation work together to "fix" the skill in a young animal. Learning a skill such as skiing requires considerable effort and much practice, but once learned it is not easily forgotten, even though a skier may stay off skis for several years. Maturation plays a role in learning this skill, since some children learn to ski much more quickly after they reach a certain age. Thus it is not usually possible to determine whether im-

proved performance results from practice or increased maturity.

Another important principle in learning is *reinforcement*. A performance that is *positively reinforced*, or rewarded, with food or with removal of an unpleasant sensation is likely to be learned; in some cases it is learned very rapidly. Praise, as we all know, can be a very positive reinforcer in teaching children. *Negative reinforcement*—punishment or an unpleasant situation—can also affect learning. Generally, behavior that leads to positive reinforcement is likely to recur. By providing reinforcement, we actually *motivate* an animal to repeat the same behavioral pattern; in other words, we can motivate an animal to learn. A skier must be able to turn the skis in order to ski down slopes. Once simple turning skills are learned, the skier can attempt gentle slopes; skiing down steeper hills becomes possible as the skier masters more difficult turns. Skiing more exciting terrain is thus a reward or reinforcement for perfecting more difficult turns.

TYPES OF LEARNING

Learning can take place in different ways. Some learning processes are complete and as such they are difficult to study. In order to gain an understanding of the foundations of learning, researchers have isolated and studied some simple, relatively clear forms of learning. These include habituation, imprinting, classical conditioning, and operant conditioning.

Habituation

If they are not reinforced, responses to many stimuli gradually decrease. All organisms receive a variety of stimuli as they develop; some of these have more meaning or greater survival value than others. The tendency to disregard stimuli that are not reinforced, called *habituation*, is one of the commonest examples of learning. For example, we all ignore a variety of noises that are capable of provoking a response but that have little meaning to us. By monitoring the brain waves of a cat it can be shown that a repeated tone of a certain frequency soon ceases to arouse the animal, whereas changing the frequency brings about a response. An animal must learn which stimuli are significant and which are not.

Imprinting

Newly hatched goslings or ducklings respond to the first moving object they see by following it. In nature the object is usually their mother; the young birds become *imprinted* on her. When eggs are hatched in an incubator, the young may follow a moving ball, a dog, or a human (Figure 18-1). Konrad Lorenz proposed this concept of *imprinting* in his work with graylag geese. He showed that the process is relatively permanent and that it can occur only during a "critical period" of time soon after hatching. If no visual stimulus of a moving object is pre-sented to the young during the critical period (usually a matter of hours, depending on the species), normal imprinting may not occur. Imprinting, then, is partly innate and partly learned, since the tendency to follow is apparently inherited but the object to be followed is learned. Since Lorenz's observations further research on imprinting has shown that: (1) time of the critical period may vary; (2) imprinting may not be permanent; and (3) the strength of the imprinting depends on the time of exposure to the object. Experiments further indicate that imprinting can occur in adults as well as in young.

Classical Conditioning

One of the most basic types of learning is called *classical conditioning*. You know what hap-

FIGURE 18-1 Konrad Lorenz, recipient of the Nobel Prize for Physiology or Medicine in 1973, and a gaggle of geese that imprinted on him. (Courtesy of Dr. Lorenz.)

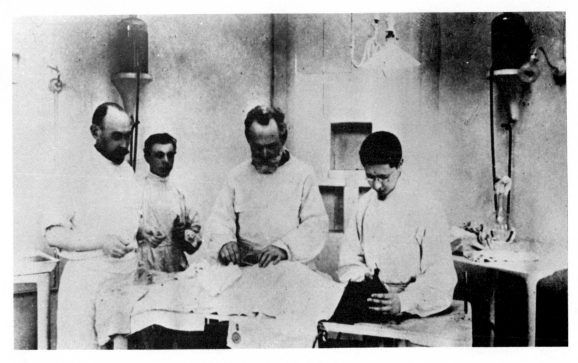

FIGURE 18-2   Ivan Pavlov (1849–1936), Russian physiologist
and Nobel Prize winner in 1904, with colleagues. (WHO photo.)

pens when you are presented with a bite of steak, or perhaps just the sight and aroma—saliva flows, or as we commonly say, "your mouth waters." Ivan Pavlov, a great Russian physiologist during the early 1900s, observed that a dog might salivate before its food arrived, simply upon hearing the footsteps of its master bringing food. Through experimentation, Pavlov showed that a dog which ordinarily responded to food by salivating could be conditioned to salivate in response to a neutral stimulus such as a ringing buzzer. He accomplished this by sounding the buzzer at the moment of feeding or shortly before (Figure 18-2). After food and buzzer were presented together a number of times, the buzzer alone could elicit the salivation response. Pavlov called this a *conditioned reflex*, since it depended on previous training. Much human training of animals is based on this principle: responses that would ordinarily be made to natural stimuli are made to stimuli such as a spoken command or a whistle.

Operant Conditioning

Learning sometimes occurs as a result of *trial and error*, a type of random and often erratic activity. If an act obtains positive reinforcement (reward), it may be tried again. If the behavior meets with negative reinforcement (perhaps punishment), it may be dropped after several trials. In each case a type of learning has occurred. An example of trial-and-error learning in rats or other animals is the running of a maze (Figure 18-3). After the animal runs the maze successfully and is rewarded with food, it is more likely to repeat the same route in the next trial.

The psychologist B. F. Skinner of Harvard University has extended such experiments into an area he has named *operant conditioning*. In classical conditioning an animal does not control the stimulus that leads to reinforcement. In operant conditioning, however, the stimulus that produces a reward is activated or influenced by the animal's own behavior: the ani-

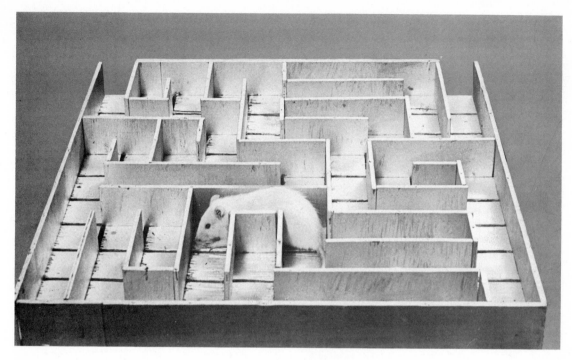

FIGURE 18-3   A maze used in learning experiments with rats.
The rat is rewarded with food when it successfully runs a specific
pattern. (Robert J. Smith, from Black Star.)

mal "operates" on its environment. Thus under classical conditioning an animal has no control over its response or behavior, whereas in operant conditioning the animal's behavior determines whether the reward will occur.

Let us see how this works. A pigeon is placed in a box called a "skinner box," with a plastic key that may be pecked and a small food tray that can open briefly and present food. The key is connected to an instrument that records any pecks during a given period of time. The apparatus can be rigged so that a peck on the key opens the food tray, and the pigeon receives a reward such as a kernel of corn (Figure 18-4). If the pigeon receives food at each peck, it will continue to peck the key at an increasing rate. Such operant conditioning occurs when the pigeon's activity is reinforced at once; in this case, the reinforcer is food. A variety of experiments can be conducted with pigeons or rats in Skinner boxes with more elaborate mechanisms, such as combinations of keys, levers, or other targets to peck or move. For example, a pigeon may be presented with a dozen patterns; if it pecks a matching pair, it is rewarded with grain. The bird thus learns through experience the combinations that produce the prize. Various reinforcement schedules have been tried in order to determine the most effective "pay" period. Greater response rates generally occur when reinforcement occurs more frequently.

An interesting aspect of operant conditioning occurs when a pigeon conditioned to peck at a high frequency is no longer given reinforcement. Essentially, the conditioning is undone. The pecking rate returns to, or drops below, the original level before reinforcement. This process is known as *extinction*. A certain amount of behavior that resembles frustration may be associated with extinction. This condition is commonly seen in deprived animals, including humans, who have learned to expect a reward for certain behavior.

FIGURE 18–4   Pigeon performing in a "Skinner box" during an operant conditioning experiment. When the pigeon pecks the key, food is presented in the food box below. (Will Rapport; courtesy of B. F. Skinner.)

Although we used a laboratory example to illustrate operant conditioning, it is by no means restricted to laboratories. Such behavior ocurs daily in the lives of most animals, including ourselves. Some birds, for example, learn that if they perch in a particular place, an observing human will "reward" them with food. Certainly the "bonus" system used in many businesses is a type of operant conditioning: the company provides an incentive for the employee and, in so doing, makes more money for itself.

Reasoning: Insight Learning

Many forms of learning and learned behavior are very complex and much more difficult to study than the instances we have cited. Complicated behavior patterns can be developed through the use of reinforcement schedules and the combination of various types of learning. Some animals, including humans, often use shortcuts in learning rather than trial and error when placed in new situations. The animal is able to do this because it is able to apply previous learning. In solving a new problem, *insight* occurs when knowledge gained from a former situation is used in a different way to solve the immediate problem. Some psychologists refer to this process as *reasoning* or insight learning. Memory is certainly involved as well.

MEMORY AND CHEMISTRY

What actually occurs inside an animal during learning? In previous chapters we have noted the importance of chemistry to an understanding of many functions in living systems. Perhaps we should now seek an explanation of learning in terms of chemistry. Again, relationships between nucleic acids (DNA and RNA) and proteins may provide some answers to our questions.

Memory, which is a vital part of learning, involves storage of information somewhere in a nervous system, usually the brain. Storage in turn requires that the learner be aware while the information to be learned is received. Two types of memory are apparently possible: *short-term memory* (STM) and *long-term memory* (LTM). In STM the learning may persist (be remembered) for periods of less than a minute to several hours. LTM involves the transfer of information to more permanent storage, a process that usually requires repetition. The amount of LTM possible in humans is tremendous—virtually everything we know about our world is stored in LTM. At any given moment a few things are in STM, but they are soon lost unless transferred to LTM. The learning (and subsequent forgetting) of a telephone number is an everyday example of STM. If, however, we remember the number for days or weeks, LTM is also involved in the learning and storage process.

Many studies on a variety of animals support the view that the process of learning involves

Bio-Topic: Experience and the Brain

The idea that changes in the anatomy of the brain can be caused by experience is an old one. Nearly 200 years ago an obscure Italian anatomist, M. G. Malacarne, performed what may be the first experiments designed to test this idea. Malacarne worked with pairs of animals that were littermates: two dogs, two parrots, and so on. He trained one member of each pair intensively for many months while the other member of each pair was left untrained. All the animals were then killed and their brains examined. According to Malacarne's published observations, the cerebellum of each trained animal showed more folds than the cerebellum of its untrained littermate.

Similar experiments have been performed from time to time since Malacarne's time, but progress has been slow and erratic. The main limitation was that the analytical techniques available to researchers were crude, largely subjective, and thus unreliable. Recent improvements in biochemical analysis and the availability of highly inbred strains of laboratory animals have led to new interest in the original question: does the brain change as a result of experience?

Mark H. Rosenzweig and his colleagues at the University of California at Berkeley investigated the effects of environmental richness on the brains of laboratory mice. Weaned mice were placed
either in an "improverished environment" (a solitary mouse in a small cage) or in an "enriched environment" (12 mice in a larger cage with many playthings that were changed each day). Eighty days later, the mice were killed and their brains compared. Small but statistically significant differences were detected between the two sets of mice with respect to the weight and protein content of the brains, thickness of the cortex, microscopic anatomy, amounts of enzymes involved in brain function, and nearly every other measure that was used. In each case, the brains of the mice from the enriched environment exceeded those of the mice from the impoverished environment. Elaborate control experiments eliminated the possibility that the differences were caused by the amount of handling, stress, developmental differences, or other factors. It seems clear that the anatomy and chemistry of the brain can be changed by experience.

The significance of these observations for humans is not clear. Obviously, it is dangerous to apply these results directly —we are very different from mice. Similar experiments with primates are essential before any generalizations can be supported. The tantalizing implication remains that a human infant may achieve more of its intellectual genetic potential if it is raised in an enriched environment.

synthesis of new RNA and proteins. In one study, imprinted chicks were found to have more RNA and proteins accumulated in their brain tissue than a control group of chicks that were not imprinted. In another study a group of rats learned to reach for food with a certain paw. The side of the brain controlling this motor function was later shown to contain about 40 percent more RNA than the other side. The learning apparently stimulated production of new RNA.

If synthesis of RNA and protein is necessary for learning, interfering with protein synthesis should interfere with the learning process. Indeed, evidence indicates that interfering with protein synthesis in goldfish and mice very soon after a training period reduces the performance of the learned behavior. In experi-

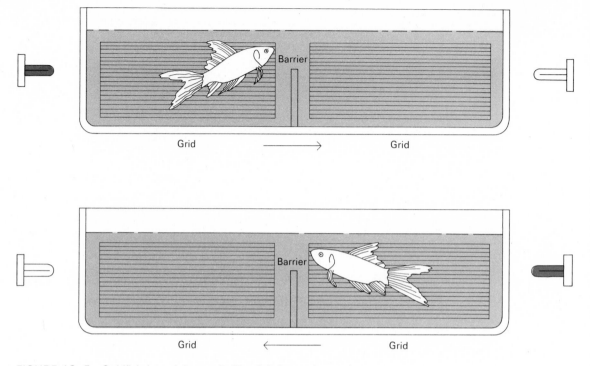

FIGURE 18-5   Goldfish in training tank. The fish learned to swim from the lighted end to the darkened end by being given mild electric shocks when a light was turned on.

ments performed by B. W. Agranoff at the University of Michigan, goldfish were taught to swim from the lighted end of a tank, where they received electrical shocks, to the darkened end (Figure 18-5). The fish learned the task readily. When a solution of an antibiotic, puromycin, was injected into the skull and over the brain of the fish immediately after the training period, their performance deteriorated. Injecting the same solution an hour later, however, had no effect on the learned task.

Clues to what was happening at the molecular level during learning came from an understanding of the effect of puromycin. Part of the puromycin molecule resembles part of a transfer RNA molecule. Puromycin can thus "mimic" the RNA in protein synthesis by entering the polypeptide chain at a certain point. This action prematurely terminates the growth of the forming protein. But how can a defective protein interfere with learning or memory? Pro-

teins are enzymes or structural components of cells, and their normal role along the neuron or at the synapse of neurons is probably essential to the memory process. This hypothesis is currently being explored. Many attempts have been made to link RNA and learning, but the evidence has not been established. RNA is probably important in the process of learning, but its exact role has not been determined. Further, recent studies have seriously questioned the findings of past RNA studies, and much work will have to be done before this important question is resolved. Other chemicals can affect the learning process also; some of these will be discussed later in this chapter.

LOVE AND LEARNING

Love is a concept of great interest; most of us have many questions and feelings about it. One of the most important questions about love may be, "How does it develop?" Because of the ethical and other limitations in working with human subjects, scienists have turned to studies with monkeys for an answer to this fundamental problem in primate behavior. We must recognize that *love* is a term describing human feelings and values, and that its application to monkeys is anthropomorphic. In this discussion, however, we shall use the term *love* for a very diverse group of behavior patterns and mechanisms.

Harry F. Harlow and his associates at the University of Wisconsin summarized and defined five different kinds of love, or *affectional systems*, based on numerous studies of primates during the past forty years. These are: infant, peer, heterosexual, maternal, and paternal. In an individual, these love patterns apparently develop in this sequential order. It is important that each pattern should develop successfully, because each sets the stage for the next. For example, if peer (age-mate) affection does not occur, heterosexual love may be abnormal. Let us briefly examine each of these types of love.

In order to study *infant love* in isolation from maternal love and to determine the extent to which learning is involved, Harlow used surrogate (imitation) monkey mothers. Two types of surrogate mothers were constructed. One was composed of a wire mesh with a wooden head; the other was made of terry cloth with a similar head (Figure 18–6). In some experiments, provision was made for these "mothers" to feed the young. When infant monkeys were placed in cages with both terry-cloth and wire mothers, they showed a much greater preference for the terry-cloth model (Figure 18–7). An infant monkey would spend more time with the terry-cloth mother even though the wire mother provided food— an indication of the security derived from comfortable contact. These findings led Harlow to conclude that contact is a most important aspect of the infant-mother relationship.

When young monkeys were frightened, they invariably ran to the terry-cloth mother. After a period with this artificial mother, they displayed curiosity and investigated the object that had produced the fright (Figure 18–8).

FIGURE 18–6   A young monkey and two types of surrogate mothers. Greater preference was shown for the terry-cloth mother (right), even though food came from the wire mother. (Harry F. Harlow, University of Wisconsin Primate Laboratory.)

During this exploration, the young monkeys returned periodically to the security of the "mother." In other experiments, infants were separated from their mothers before maturation. After a period in which they uttered vocal

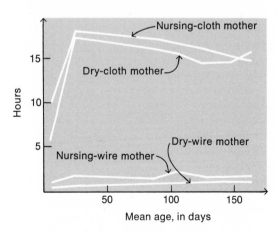

FIGURE 18–7   Time spent by a baby monkey on four different artificial mothers: nursing-cloth, dry-cloth, dry-wire, and nursing-wire. (Redrawn after Harry F. Harlow, *Learning to Love,* 1971. By permission of Albion Publishing Company, San Francisco.)

FIGURE 18–8   When frightened by a toy drummer, the young monkey ran to the terry-cloth mother rather than to the wire mother. (Harry F. Harlow, University of Wisconsin Primate Laboratory.)

protests, they soon went into depression. Normal infant behavior could be restored, however, by returning an infant to its mother.

Age-mate or peer love follows normal separation from the mother. The close motherly contact of infant love is now transferred to another individual, a peer. Various types of play are typical of peer love. In a test of the importance of this stage, monkeys were kept from their peers and raised entirely by their mothers. As adults, these monkeys showed abnormal social and sexual behavior. On the other hand, babies who were raised with terry-cloth mothers but allowed periods of play with other babies developed into normal adults. Thus peer love is probably the most important stage for the future social and sexual development of an individual—a concept contrary to the popular belief that motherly love is the most essential

stage. Close social relationships occur in peer love, preparing the individual for the third stage, heterosexual love. This affectional system, which begins at puberty and continues into adulthood, is affected by the same hormones that control secondary sex characteristics and the development of eggs and sperm. The next types of love, maternal and paternal, are shown by adult females and males toward infants.

Maternal love, the care of a mother for her child, can recur with the arrival of each new infant. This behavior is expressed in several stages, from meeting the child's basic needs to final separation from the child. The basis of motherly love is not entirely clear, but much of this behavior may be learned as stimulus-response mechanisms during the development of the child. Adult female monkeys raised in the absence of a mother show a lack of maternal love. Since these monkeys were not themselves "mothered" and did not observe any other mother, learning deficiencies occurred, causing abnormal reproductive behavior. These females have difficulty mating. If they do mate and have offspring, these "motherless" females are often indifferent or abusive toward the baby.

Paternal love, the relationship between adult males and infants, is expressed in protective and playful ways. Experiments with special cages that house several monkey families in separate units have shed some light on paternal love. Only the infants in these cages were allowed to move among the units and associate with other families. Under these conditions the fathers accepted all infants, showed a playful attitude, and tolerated more abusive treatment in play than did adult females.

Finally we might note how rearing baby monkeys in isolation influences the development of affectional systems. As we have seen, maternal behavior develops abnormally in females raised without a mother. A baby monkey raised in isolation for 6 months does not learn to relate normally to its mother or to its peers. It may later experience sexual difficulties. The basic causes of difficulty involve social relationships and the ability to interact with others.

HUMAN SEXUAL BEHAVIOR

Love and affection in primates result from a developmental process which involves learning. Furthermore, in primates (including humans) certain phases of the expression of the sexual drive are learned. The triggering stimuli leading to sexual behavior are varied, involving sight, sound, smell, and touch—and they are present in most aspects of our everyday lives. Because of this exposure most humans learn readily about sexuality and sexual behavior. This is not to say that all information on this topic is beneficial; many of the available materials are detrimental to some individuals.

In humans and other primates, experience (which includes learning) plays an important role in mating behavior. Remember that monkeys raised in isolation experienced great difficulty in mating. In humans the learned component of sexual behavior is even more crucial for the attainment of normal, satisfactory expression of the sexual process. Family relationships and parental influence during early childhood seem to be very important in the development of heterosexuality in humans. Interference with this heterosexual development may produce susceptibility to homosexuality.

The relationship between love and human sexual behavior has received an increasing amount of attention during the past few decades. Perhaps the best-known studies of human sexuality are those of Alfred Kinsey, published in the early 1950s, and Masters and Johnson, released in 1966. Many other basic human needs have long been studied in great detail, but until quite recently human sexual behavior was rarely investigated because of the social taboos surrounding the subject. The now-famous Kinsey reports, based on more than 10,000 interviews, caused a furor when first published. But they prepared the way for further study of human sexuality, incuding other scientific approaches such as those employed by Masters and Johnson. Kinsey's studies relied on interviews, whereas Masters and Johnson observed human subjects and often monitored them with physiological apparatus. These studies discredited many of the sexual myths common in the nineteenth and early twentieth centuries.

One of the greatest deterrents to understanding the role of sex in human behavior lay in the confusion of the reproductive process with nonreproductive sexual expression. The term *sexuality* has taken on a broader meaning than reproduction. It has come to embrace the sexual components of the development, life, and personality of an individual. This concept of sexuality goes beyond mere consideration of the genital organs, mating behavior, and the fulfillment of the sexual drive; it includes an awareness of the feelings of other people. Furthermore, sexuality or sexual development does not arise suddenly at puberty just for the reproduction of the species. Rather, it develops gradually from birth to adulthood and extends into later life. The natural, normal development of healthy sexual behavior is of utmost importance in the human life cycle. Besides requiring careful guidance in early childhood and understanding in puberty and adolescence, healthy sexuality must undergo further development through all stages of adulthood. Fortunately, the past decade has brought more concern for this viewpoint in educational circles and by groups such as the Sex Information and Education Council of the United States. We now realize that certain aspects of sexuality, such as genital play in early childhood, masturbation, and petting, are behaviors that merit a fuller understanding on everyone's part.

In their studies of human sexual behavior, Masters and Johnson determined the physical reactions that occur as a result of male and female responses to sexual stimulation. Their research, involving 382 women and 312 men, is described and reported in their book *Human Sexual Response*. Masters and Johnson separate the human cycles of sexual response into four phases: the excitement phase, the plateau phase, the orgasmic phase, and the resolution phase (Figure 18–9). The excitement phase is initiated by stimulation, which determines the length of this phase and helps to determine whether the rest of the cycle will be successfully completed. If stimulation is not great enough, if it ceases, or if individual drive is not sufficient, the orgasmic phase may never be

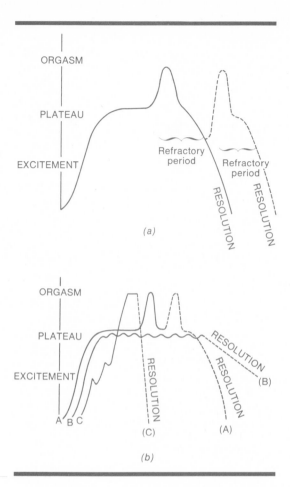

FIGURE 18–9   Sexual response pattern in humans. (*a*) Variations of this pattern for the male occur, but they are more closely related to duration than to intensity of response. (*b*) Three patterns for the female. These are the most frequently observed patterns, but other variations occur. Intensity as well as duration of response may vary. (Redrawn from W. H. Masters and V. E. Johnson, *Human Sexual Response,* 1966. By permission of Little, Brown and Company.)

reached. Females show greater variation in total sexual response during the orgasmic portion of the cycle; this variation is particularly evident in the intensity and duration of female orgasm. Although the resolution phase normally returns both males and females to the prestimulation state, females can, with sufficient stimulation, readily enter into another orgasmic phase. Males, on the other hand, cannot respond as quickly to restimulation; they must undergo a refractory period, during which response cannot occur.

Many physiological and anatomical changes specific to each phase of the cycle were recorded in this study. Several general physiological responses for both sexes were observed: a "sex flush"; an increase in muscle tension; increases in breathing, heart rate, and blood pressure; and perspiration. The sex flush, a red rash primarily over the upper part of the body, results from changes in the blood capillaries. Muscle tension is generally widespread; involuntary contractions occur regularly, often in spasms that produce cramps in the extremities.

Objective studies such as these have made psychiatrists, physicians, and psychologists better able to diagnose and treat such problems as impotence and lack of orgasm. Moreover, as people become more knowledgeable about their basic drives, they become willing to seek treatment, if necessary, for sexual malfunctions. This attitude has also helped society to develop more rational views about atypical sexual behavior.

MODIFICATION OF BEHAVIOR

That behavior can be modified or changed is well known. Advertisers using the mass media have developed sophisticated ways to influence us to buy their products. The media also shape our reactions to our environment in general. In addition to the basic learning processes described earlier, some chemicals—especially alcohol and tranquilizers—affect behavior.

Peter N. Witt of the North Carolina Department of Mental Health used the web-spinning ability of a certain kind of spider to test the effects of various drugs on behavior. A spider of a given species always constructs its web in a characteristic pattern. When various drugs are administered, webs with different patterns will be spun because of the different effect of each drug on the spider's nervous system (Figure 18–10). In fact, we know that almost any chemical, in amounts varying from those an organism is normally accustomed to, will pro-

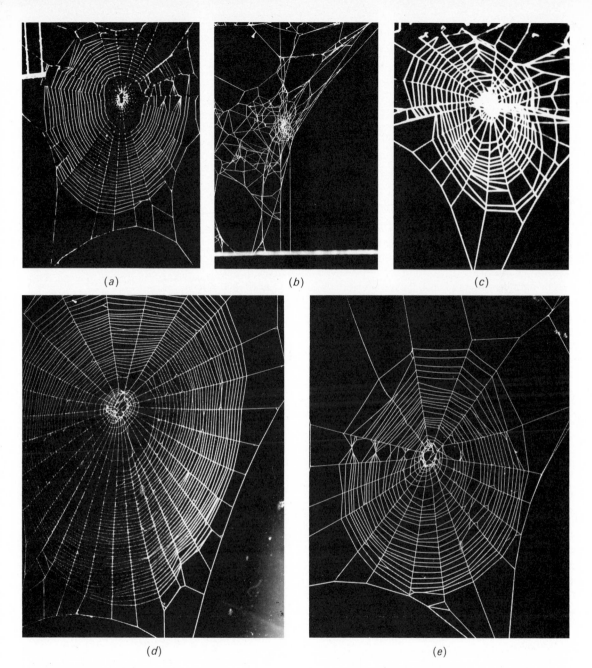

FIGURE 18–10 The influence of drugs on the web-spinning behavior of cross spiders. The upper three photos (a,b,c) show the effects of dextro-amphetamine (''speed''). The lower photos (d,e) illustrate the effects of phenobarbital, a sedative. (a) The control web, built on the first day of observation. (b) Web constructed by the same spider 12 hours later, after drinking about 0.1 ml of a drop of sugar water which contained 1 mg of dextro-amphetamine. The web shows remnants of a hub and erratic radii and strands. (c) Web built 24 hours later, showing signs of recovery. (d) This control web exhibits the normal pattern. (e) Web built one and one-half days after a high dose of the drug (100 mg/kg). It is smaller and less regular. (Courtesy of Peter N. Witt, North Carolina Department of Mental Health, Division of Research, Raleigh, NC.)

duce behavioral changes. For example, the effects of changes in carbon dioxide concentration on breathing and heart rate in humans are well understood. But behavior can be modified by using methods other than chemicals. Some of these methods, such as in psychotherapy, employ the spoken word and utilize the processes of learning.

Psychotherapy

Trained specialists can draw upon a wide variety of techniques to influence behavior. In psychoanalysis, a type of psychotherapy, the psychiatrist attempts to influence the patient's present behavior by analyzing past experiences. The working hypothesis is that uncovering some event or experience in the past will bring about a better understanding of present behavior. This may lead to a change in behavior. The primary causes for current behavior are therefore sought in past experiences.

Psychotherapists may also seek to bring about new behavior patterns in other ways. These behavioral changes may be considered to result from "free will" or choice, but in most cases they involve reconditioning based on reinforcement.

Chemical Therapy and Drugs

The possibilities of chemical therapy for modifying behavior have been widely explored and used since the 1950s, and the use of drugs has become important in the treatment of a variety of mental illnesses (Figure 18–11). Most people today are well aware of the usefulness of tranquilizers in lowering anxiety and tension; they also know that another group of drugs, the antidepressants, act as mood elevators. Fewer people know that a third group of drugs, such as chlorpromazine and reserpine, are used to treat serious mental disorders. These and other chemicals have been useful in treating *schizophrenia*, a serious mental disorder. The hypothesis that schizophrenia results from a chemical imbalance has been pursued vigorously, and researchers have gained some insights into the chemical pathways involved and the chemical therapy needed.

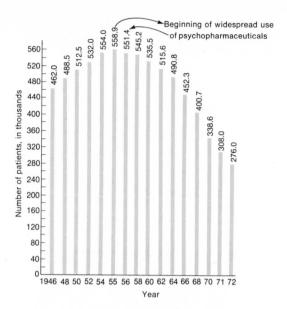

FIGURE 18–11   The use of drugs in the treatment of mental illness has brought about a drastic reduction in the number of resident patients in government hospitals in the United States. (Courtesy of Nathan S. Kline, MD, Director, Research Center, Rockland State Hospital, Orangeburg, NY.)

When people use these drugs without medical supervision, they may induce symptoms similar to the mental disorders the drugs are used to control. Indiscriminate use of drugs can lead to serious behavioral problems. Various schemes for classifying drugs are used; we shall classify them into four groups: Stimulants, sedatives, hallucinogens, and opiates (Figure 18–12).

Stimulants

Stimulants include the *amphetamines* (commonly referred to as "pep pills" or "speed"), which stimulate the central nervous system. The amphetamines are a group of drugs including benzedrine, methedrine, and dexedrine. Their basic chemical structure resembles that of epinephrine and norepinephrine, and in general they produce effects similar to these hormones (Figure 18–13). The amphetamines have been prescribed to increase alertness and vigor, but their medical use is now under careful scrutiny, both because of the possibility of addiction and because more efficient drugs can now be used to achieve the same purposes. It is interesting to note that amphetamines are also used in the treatment of hyperactive children; in that case their effects are reversed, and they have a calming effect. Cocaine, which is legally classified as a narcotic, produces responses similar to those of amphetamines.

One of the most common stimulants to the central nervous system is caffeine, a component of coffee, tea, and cola. Moderate doses of caffeine produce increased alertness and counteract some effects of fatigue, but large amounts can bring about nervousness and increase heart rate, blood pressure, and gastric secretion (a serious effect for ulcer patients). Caffeine also constricts blood vessels in the brain, so it is often used in headache remedies. Caffeine, which has a purine structure, has been shown to produce mutations in bacteria by inhibiting some of the enzymes necessary for nucleic-acid synthesis. Although drinks containing caffeine do not cause physical addiction and generally have no markedly harmful effects, a psychological dependence on them can develop.

The body of knowledge now available on the effects of nicotine, and particularly of cigarette smoking, is tremendous. There is no doubt that smoking tobacco is injurious to health and that it may lead to lung cancer, one of the most difficult cancers to treat effectively. Smoking also increases susceptibility to emphysema, and many smokers die of this disease. Tobacco smoke contains a mixture of gases, resin tars, and nicotine; of these, nicotine and the tars appear to have the greatest carcinogenic effect.

Nicotine also has many other effects on the body. It increases the heart rate, raises blood pressure, and constricts the coronary arterioles. In moderate amounts, nicotine has a slight stimulating effect on the central nervous system. It mimics the action of acetylcholine, a normal synaptic transmitter substance. Over a number of years, however, its use may lead to greatly impaired health and vitality.

Sedatives
The most common sedatives are *barbiturates* (often called "downers"), which depress the central nervous system and lead to a generally relaxed state. Barbiturates may be prescribed for high blood pressure and in some cases for other anxiety symptoms. As with amphetamines, the danger potential of barbiturates is great, and users often become dependent on them. Accidental overdose or use with other drugs takes many lives each year.

Alcoholism is believed to afflict more than 5 percent of the population of the United States, and many physicians consider this addiction to be our most serious and widespread drug problem. Increasing numbers of deaths result from alcohol-induced cirrhosis of the liver, automobile accidents caused by drunken driving, and complex synergistic effects of alcohol with other common drugs such as barbiturates. (A synergistic effect occurs when two substances together produce a much greater or different effect than would be expected from their separate activities.) One side effect of alcohol addiction results from the "empty calories" it contains: many alcoholics suffer serious protein and vitamin deficiencies simply because they have no interest in food. A recent study of alcoholism reported by Emanuel Rubin and Charles Lieber of the Mount Sinai School of Medicine, New York, shows that alcohol damages the endoplasmic reticulum of liver cells in rats and humans. Moreover, ingestion of alcohol has been found to inhibit the normal metabolism of other drugs; this may account for at least part of the synergistic mechanism.

Hallucinogens
Many drugs can produce hallucinations (visions or imaginary perceptions) but the best-known are LSD (lysergic acid diethylamide), mescaline (peyote), and psilocybin. Drugs of this type have been used by humans throughout history, often in religious rituals. The user of a drug such as LSD may have an experience involving altered or expanded awareness, distorted senses, bright flashing colors, and often loss of touch with reality (for example, believing one can fly). Dizziness and nausea usually occur before perceptual alterations. "Trips" may be either pleasant or horrifying. The danger of uncontrolled behavior during an hallucinogenic state is always present. Another dan-

Name	Slang Name	Classification	Medical Use
Hallucinogenic Drugs			
Marijuana	Pot, Grass, Hashish, Tea, Gage, Reefers, Mary Jane	Relaxant, mood elevator; in high doses, hallucinogen	None in U.S.
LSD	Acid, Big D, Cubes, Trips, Sugar	Hallucinogen	Experimental study of mental function, alcoholism
Mescaline	Mesc., Cactus	Hallucinogen	None
Psilocybin		Hallucinogen	None
Stimulant Drugs			
Amphetamines	Bennies, Dexies, Speed, Wake-Ups, Lid Proppers, Hearts, Pep Pills	Stimulant	Relieve mild depression, control appetite, promote wakefulness
Cocaine	Corrine, Gold Dust, Coke, Bernice, Flake, Star Dust, Snow	Stimulant	Local (surface) anesthesia
Tobacco	Fag, Coffin Nail, etc.	Sedative-stimulant	
Sedative Drugs			
Barbiturates	Barbs, Blue Devils, Candy, Yellow Jackets, Phennies, Peanuts, Blue Heavens	Sedative	Sedation, relieve high blood pressure, epilepsy, hyperthyroidism
Alcohol	Booze, Juice, etc.	Sedative	Solvent, antiseptic
Narcotic Drugs			
Heroin	H, Horse, Scat, Junk, Smack, Scag, Stuff, Harry	Narcotic	Pain relief (not legally available in U.S.)
Morphine	White Stuff, M	Narcotic	Pain relief
Codeine	Schoolboy	Narcotic	Ease pain and coughing
Methadone	Dolly	Narcotic	Pain relief, management of heroin dependence

FIGURE 18–12 Summary of some common drugs. The question mark indicates conflict of opinion. (Modified from *To Parents/About Drugs.* Courtesy of the Metropolitan Life Insurance Company. Based on chart in *Resource Book for Drug Abuse Education,* National Institute of Mental Health, Chevy Chase, MD.)

How Taken	Long-Term Symptoms	Physical Dependence Potential	Psychological Dependence Potential	Organic Damage Potential
Smoked or swallowed	May lead to decline of energy and motivation	No	Yes	?
Swallowed	May intensify existing psychosis, panic reactions, decrease anti-body production	No	Yes	?
Swallowed	?	No	Yes	?
Swallowed	?	No	Yes	?
Swallowed or injected	Loss of appetite, delusions, hallucinations, toxic psychosis	?	Yes	?
Sniffed, injected, or swallowed	Depression, delusions, hallucinations, toxic psychosis	No	Yes	?
Smoked, sniffed, or chewed	Emphysema, lung cancer, mouth and throat cancer, cardiovascular damage, loss of appetite	No	Yes	Yes
Swallowed or injected	Addiction with severe withdrawal symptoms, possible convulsions, toxic psychosis	Yes	Yes	Yes
Swallowed	Cirrhosis, toxic psychosis, neurologic damage, addiction	Yes	Yes	Yes
Injected or sniffed	Addiction, constipation, loss of appetite	Yes	Yes	No
Swallowed or injected	Addiction, constipation, loss of appetite	Yes	Yes	No
Swallowed	Addiction, constipation, loss of appetite	Yes, low	Yes	No
Swallowed or injected	Addiction, constipation, loss of appetite	Yes	Yes	No

ger involved with any drug is the possibility of an overdose. A user may intend to be taking only a small amount of a drug but may actually take a harmful or even a fatal dose. Impurities in illicitly obtained drugs pose yet another potential danger.

In small doses marijuana has effects like those of alcohol, acting as a mild intoxicant. In large doses marijuana acts like the other hallucinogenic drugs such as LSD. A mild state of euphoria and some stimulation of the central nervous system may occur initially with small

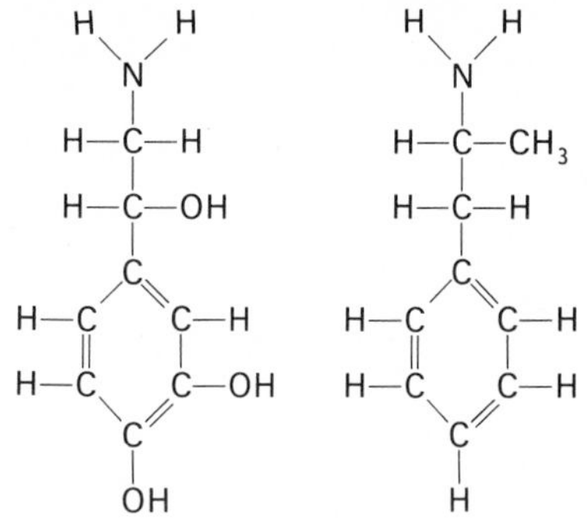

Norepinephrine   Amphetamine

FIGURE 18–13 Comparison of the molecular structures of norepinephrine and amphetamine. Amphetamines produce effects similar to norepinephrine and epinephrine (adrenalin).

doses. Other behavioral changes include sedation, loss of time sense, and alterations in sensory perception. Some studies show that performance on skill tests is slowed in beginning smokers, whereas chronic marijuana users may show no loss or even a slight gain in certain skill tests.

Marijuana, which is usually smoked, is the crude preparation from the flowers, stems, and leaves of *Cannabis sativa,* a hemp plant (Figure 18–14). When the plant's resin is obtained by scraping it from the plant or through chemical refining, the substance is called *hashish.* Hashish, which may be smoked or eaten, contains the most active ingredient in marijuana, the tetrahydrocannabinols (THC). Hashish is about eight times as strong as most of the marijuana available.

Should use of marijuana be legalized? Will the use of marijuana produce harmful personality and physiological effects over a long period of time? Would such effects be more harmful than those of nicotine and alcohol? Many studies have been made on marijuana, but more research must be done to provide society with a sound basis for making objective judgments about its use.

Opiates

Usually classified as narcotics, opiates include the "hard" drugs: heroin, opium, methadone, codeine, and morphine. Opiates relieve pain, tension, and anxiety and often produce a general sense of well-being. But opiates are addictive, and addiction can lead to serious social and physiological problems. If intake of the drug is discontinued, extreme withdrawal symptoms occur, including vomiting, cold sweating and chills, muscle cramps, and diarrhea. Treatment of heroin addiction is difficult, but some progress has been made recently by substituting methadone, another narcotic, for heroin. Individuals on methadone can slowly reduce their usage and break the habit.

The use of drugs—both medical and illicit—is common today. Under medical supervision, drugs relieve pain and provide better lives for many people. But drug abuse causes misery among its victims and their friends and relatives. It is also responsible for a great loss of human productivity and potential. Today we have but little knowledge of drugs and the mechanisms by which they act. But the search for new drugs that alter human behavior continues, and there is little doubt that their potential for service—and abuse—will increase with time.

BEHAVIOR, ADAPTATION, AND EVOLUTION

A behavioral trait is usually either adaptive or maladaptive. If it is adaptive—that is, if it has survival value—it is likely to be perpetuated from one generation to the next. If it is maladaptive it is not likely to persist, because organisms having it will be hampered in surviving to reproductive age, or they will be less likely to succeed in courtship or mating. A rabbit that does not "freeze" when it detects a predator, for example, may end up in the predator's stomach before it can reproduce and pass along this maladaptive trait (if it is heritable). Similarly, an especially docile male primate (or, for that matter, an overly aggressive male primate) may not succeed in mating. In that case the trait of docility or overaggressiveness will not be passed along. Behavior thus plays an important role in natural selection. We will discuss the evolution of new species through the process of natural selection in the next Unit.

FIGURE 18–14   Marijuana and its derivatives. (*a*) Branch of a marijuana plant. (*b*) Hashish. (*c*) Pressed marijuana pollen. (*d*) Manicured marijuana. (*e*) Marijuana seeds. (*f*) Rough marijuana. (Courtesy of Carolina Biological Supply Company.)

SUMMARY

Learning may be defined as a relatively permanent change in behavior that occurs as the result of experience. An activity that is positively reinforced, or rewarded, is likely to be learned and may be learned rapidly. Motivation is also important in learning; reinforcement can provide motivation.

Learning can occur in various ways, including habituation, imprinting, classical conditioning, operant conditioning, and reasoning (insight). Memory is important in the learning process. Nucleic acids and proteins are thought to be involved in memory because in some animals, interfering with protein synthesis soon after a training period can reduce performance of the learned behavior.

The development of love involves learning. In some primates, love develops through a series of stages: Infant, peer, heterosexual, maternal, and paternal. Certain phases of the expression of the sexual drive are also learned in primates, including humans. Studies such as those conducted by Kinsey and by Masters and Johnson have led to a better understanding of human sexual behavior. This information has assisted in the diagnosis and treatment of many sex-related problems.

Behavior can be modified by psychotherapy

Bio-Topic: A Mold That Changed History

Behavior-altering drugs such as cannabinol, LSD, and psilocybin have been used for centuries in religious ceremonies. More recently, such drugs have been introduced into contemporary American culture. At least one of these drugs has altered the course of history.

In 1722, Czar Peter the Great massed his Russian armies to expel the Ottoman Turks from Europe. The campaign failed at least partly because the Russian troops were demoralized by an outbreak of hallucinations, erratic behaviors, muscular convulsions, and unexplained deaths. The outbreak, which caused as many as 20,000 deaths, began when the troops ate rye bread made from flour infected by a mold known as Claviceps purpureum.

The mold attacks the ovaries of rye plants during the spring flowering season. As the rye crop matures, the mold destroys the ovaries, which then dry into hard, pink or purplish masses about the size of rye seeds. These masses, called ergot, have been used medicinally for centuries. The ergot masses are separated from the rye seeds and made into a tea or powder used in the treatment of high blood pressure or to induce contractions during childbirth. The medicinal dose of ergot is very small. Larger doses, which might occur by eating rye flour from which ergot masses had not been re-moved, can cause hallucinations, convulsions, and even death. The first reported instance of ergotism, death from eating ergot-contaminated rye or wheat flour, dates back to AD 857. The devastation of Peter the Great's army is perhaps the most notorious example of recurrent episodes of ergotism throughout history.

Linda R. Caporael of the University of California at Santa Barbara has recently suggested that the Salem witch hunts of 1692 may have been the result of overdoses of ergot. During the witch hunts 20 persons were executed for being witches or for being bewitched. The evidence is circumstantial but provocative. The Salem colonists raised rye in damp fields where the ergot mold would have flourished. Cattle fed on this rye were reported to behave erratically, sicken, and die. Several villagers involved in the trials lived near or owned rye fields and may have made bread from infected flour. A villager who ate ergot along with his or her daily bread would be subject to hallucinations and might display behaviors that were interpreted as signs of being bewitched.

Ergot is now known to contain an organic molecule that, when heated, releases lysergic acid diethyl amine—LSD. In fact, LSD was first isolated from ergot. Peter's army and the Salem villagers may all have been tripping on LSD.

and chemical therapy. Many drugs are clinically used to change behavior patterns. Some of these drugs are also used outside the field of medicine; this use has produced some problems in our society.

REVIEW QUESTIONS

1. Why is positive reinforcement so important in learning? Give an example of negative reinforcement in the learning process, using any species you choose.

2. How does imprinting differ from classical conditioning?

3. What are common examples of conditioned reflexes in humans?

4. Design a simple experiment using a pigeon and a Skinner box to illustrate positive reinforcement in learning.

5. Recently, much attention has been given to the role of RNA in learning. Why?

6. Why do adult female monkeys that were raised in the absence of a mother show a lack of maternal love themselves?

7. Certain drugs are effective in alleviating the symptoms of epilepsy and schizophrenia. Why can these and other drugs be harmful when used by normal individuals under uncontrolled conditions?

SUPPLEMENTARY READINGS

Dethier, Vincent G. (consultant), *Topics in Animal Behavior*, Harper & Row, New York, 1971. This booklet is a good collection of articles by specialists on a variety of topics such as innate behavior, learning and behavior, imprinting, motivation, communication, aggression, and social behavior.

Harlow, Harry F., *Learning to Love*, Albion, San Francisco, 1971. This short booklet presents studies and ideas on five forms of love: maternal, infant, peer, heterosexual, and paternal. It concludes with ideas about aggression, fear and anger, and social behavior.

Hess, Eckhard, H., "Imprinting in a Natural Laboratory," *Scientific American*, August 1972. Imprinting in baby mallard ducks forms a permanent bond between the ducklings and their mother. Exchanges of vocal sounds between the mother and unhatched ducklings begins about two days before hatching and is believed to be involved in imprinting and the synchronous hatching of the eggs.

Hinde, R. A., *Animal Behavior: A Synthesis of Ethology and Comparative Psychology*, 2nd edition, McGraw-Hill, New York, 1970. Modification of behavior is stressed in this highly respected reference work. This is considered one of the best references on current behavioral studies as it attempts to relate studies from various fields bearing on behavior.

Julien, Robert M., *A Primer of Drug Action*, W. H. Freeman, San Francisco, 1975. A medically accurate discussion of the major psychoactive drugs is presented in this paperback. Written in a very readable and objective style, it is a valuable reference on drugs.

Lorenz, Konrad, *On Aggression*, Bantam Books, New York, 1967. An extremely interesting and easy to read classic on aggression that lays the foundation for many of the concepts on the development of aggression in humans. Several recent books take issue with the ideas on aggression presented here.

Teyler, Timothy J., *A Primer of Psychobiology: Brain and Behavior*, W. H. Freeman, San Francisco, 1975. Requiring no specialized training in biology, this primer introduces basic information on the structure and function of the brain and nervous system and their relationship to behavior. It lends itself well to supplementary reading for a biology course.

Unit VIII
Evolution

In Chapter 2 we were concerned with origins: the origin of our solar system, the origin of life, and the origin of species. In each case we used the concept of evolution—step-by-step or gradual development—to account for these origins. In this three-chapter Unit we discuss organic evolution—the evolution of living systems. Our earlier study of genetic processes will help us here, for the essence of the evolutionary process is the selection of certain genotypes by an environment.

In Chapter 19 we shall recount the historical development of ideas about evolution, culminating in the discovery of its mechanism, natural selection, by Charles Darwin and Alfred Wallace. We will review the evidence in support of an evolutionary concept, based on studies of the structure, development, behavior, and chemical composition of living systems. Next, in Chapter 20, we will discuss the current view of organic evolution, which demonstrates the genetic basis of natural selection, largely in terms of population genetics. We will see that adaptations, which increase individual reproductive and survival fitness, are important to the perpetuation of a population. Since adaptations depend ultimately on the genetic makeup of a total population, they provide the basis for speciation; the formation of new species. Finally, in Chapter 21, we trace the evolutionary development of our own species, including our recently developed ability to alter the course of organic evolution. This ability is a product of human culture, which itself is undergoing a rapid evolution. The development of human culture and technology makes a sense of responsibility or a code of ethics essential. We will explore the need for a new ethic—bioethics—that can help us adapt our new technology to our moral, legal, and possibly our religious traditions.

But what is the overall significance of a concept of evolution? Perhaps most important is that it provides a central theme for understanding our natural world. Once we realized that change, which is central to evolutionary thought, is universal, it became possible to integrate physical, biological, and cultural events and processes. The concept of evolution provided by Darwin and Wallace has become the unifying framework for all modern biological study. Furthermore, evolutionary thought can lead to a better understanding of other aspects of life, for as the late Theodosius Dobzhansky has stated, "Evolution is the method whereby Creation is accomplished."

Chapter 19

Evolution: Evidence & Historical Background

As we have seen in the first seven units, life on this planet is marked by change and differences. Each species represents one particular set of answers to the challenge of survival. The differences and variety of living systems are not as random as it might appear. In this chapter we will look in depth at one of the most powerful and useful concepts in modern biology, the theory of evolution of species.

In Chapter 2 we introduced some of the clues that biologists and geologists have relied on in working with the theory of evolution. Here we continue with **More Evidence of Evolution.** Unlike the fossil record discussed earlier, much of this evidence is carried within living organisms today and is reflected in their development, anatomy, and biochemistry. For example, **Embryology** provides us with extraordinary similarities in the early developing forms of many vertebrates. These similarities imply a single common ancestor of related species. Also, there are **Biochemical Similarities** in key substances occurring in different species. Again, these similarities permit us to see relationships that lead us to theorize the existence of one species in the past from which

these chemically linked species descended.

The massive evidence of evolution would be extremely confusing without coordinating theories to explain a large number of phenomena in the briefest possible manner. The process of **Explaining the Evidence** of change in species actually pre-dates the theory of evolution by centuries. The **Early Concepts** probably came from the Greeks, who observed the simple-to-complex array of organisms. As geological and taxonomic evidence accumulated through the eighteenth and nineteenth centuries, the stage was set for the formulation of the theory of evolution by natural selection. Perhaps the solidity of the factual foundation for the theory was best demonstrated by the fact that Charles Darwin and Alfred Wallace formally reported the theory at almost the same time.

The Darwin-Wallace Theory explains the wide variety of species and adaptations within species in terms of (1) natural variation within species, which presents several different possible adaptations to the environment, followed by (2) the natural selection by the environment of those adaptations that help assure survival and reproduction.

C hange is one of the most enduring characteristics of the universe. Planet Earth has been changing continually since it came into existence some 5 billion years ago, and our environment continues to change. Living systems are no exception to this universal rule of change, as we have noted many times in our study of life processes. In Chapter 2, we saw that change played a major role in the origins of living systems. We stressed change again in our discussion of energy, entropy, and living systems in Chapter 3. Later, as we examined homeostatic mechanisms and behavior, we saw that every living system must be capable of change in order to cope with changing environmental conditions.

But living systems must also be capable of structural and behavioral change over time spans far exceeding the life span of any individual organism. We have clear evidence that living systems have changed through the ages, that organisms living today are modified descendants of organisms long extinct. We refer to these changes as *evolution;* today we know that these changes that occur in living organisms as a result of slight variations from generation to generation come about through changes in genes and gene frequencies. From this we can see that *populations* of organisms evolve, not individual organisms.

At this stage of our knowledge, then, we can define evolution as *a change in the genes of or in the gene frequencies of a population.* We shall develop this concept further in Chapter 20. As you read this chapter, however, you may find it helpful to keep this definition in mind.

MORE EVIDENCE OF EVOLUTION

In Chapter 2 we examined some of the evidence of organic evolution: the fossil record and similarities in vertebrate forelimbs. We shall now survey various other kinds of evidence that involve the biological principles studied in preceding chapters.

Embryology

If we become more than casual students of nature, we feel compelled to go beyond individual observations and inquire about relationships. If we look closely at the natural environment, we cannot ignore some of the relationships and developmental patterns. If we look at the developing embryos of several different vertebrate organisms, for example, it is hard not to notice a remarkable similarity during the early stages (Figure 19–1). A closer examination shows *pharyngeal gill clefts* in the throat region of all early vertebrate embryos. These clefts are similar in structure and appearance from one species to another. As development progresses in the various vertebrates, however, these clefts assume different functions. In fish and fishlike animals, some of the gill clefts develop into gill slits associated with respiratory organs. Birds and mammals occupy a habitat in which gills are unnecessary, but they face other problems. For example, sound is much more difficult to produce and to detect in air than in water. So, in birds and mammals, portions of the original gill cleft and arch ar-

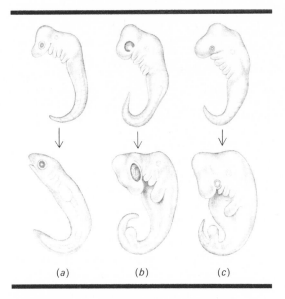

(a)   (b)   (c)

FIGURE 19–1 Sketches of the developing embryos of three vertebrates. (*a*) Fish. (*b*) Chick. (*c*) Human. Note that the embryos are quite similar in the early stage but become more different as development proceeds. Note also the gill arches and clefts in all three embryos.

rangement have been modified into parts of the sound-producing and sound-detecting mechanisms. In humans the auditory canal and the eustachian tube connecting the middle ear with the throat are remnants of gill clefts. This is an example of the opportunistic nature of the evolutionary process: it can take existing structures and modify them for a new environment. Modifications of some of the gill clefts and arches in various vertebrates are shown in Figure 19–2.

Intermediate Forms and "Living Fossils"

Classification systems are simply attempts to group organisms according to similar characteristics. As such, they reflect our interpretation of nature. Classification schemes thus vary, and biologists do not all agree on a single plan of classification. Intermediate forms of life that do not fit in our classification schemes represent "missing links" between classification groups. A famous example of a missing

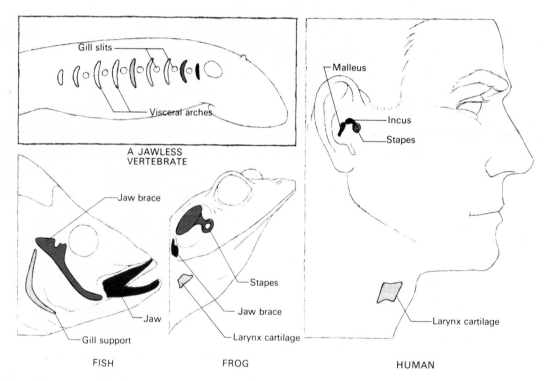

FIGURE 19–2 Modification of pharyngeal slits and arches in selected vertebrates. (a) Fish. (b) Frog. (c) Human. Note that the first visceral arch forms the jaws in adult fish, a jaw brace in frogs, and two bones that conduct sound in the middle ear—the incus and the malleus—in humans. The second arch serves as the jaw brace in fish; in frogs and humans, it forms the stapes, another bone that conducts sound. The fifth arch, which functions as support for the gills in fish, develops into part of the cartilage support for the larynx in frogs and humans. Jaw braces are supporting bones in fish and frogs that are not present in humans and other mammals.

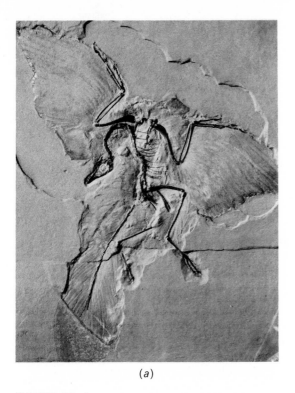

(a)   (b)

FIGURE 19-3   *Archaeopteryx.* (*a*) Cast of the fossil. (*b*) Photo of a restoration. (American Museum of Natural History.)

link is *Archaeopteryx*, a fossil considered to be an intermediate between reptiles and birds (Figure 19-3). It has so many reptilian characteristics that it could have been a member of the flying reptiles except that feathers can clearly be seen in some of the fossils. *Archaeopteryx*, then, is probably an intermediate form between reptiles and birds although all three probably had a common early ancestor.

Peripatus, an interesting little animal resembling a caterpillar, occurs in Africa, New Zealand, Australia, and Central America (Figure 19-4). It is approximately 2 inches long and lives in damp places under bark and leaves. Its present sparse, fragmented range may indicate that it was more widespread in earlier times but is now nearing extinction. This group of animals (about 70 species) has many characteristics of the Annelida (segmented worms) and the Arthropoda (insects, crustaceans, etc.).

These animal groups are discussed in Chapter 24. Its respiratory system, circulation, and mouth parts are distinctly insectlike, whereas its excretory system, reproductive ducts, and body wall resemble the earthworm group. How should we classify this organism—as an annelid or an arthropod? We have avoided the problem by placing this organism species in a separate phylum, Onychophora, even though it has

FIGURE 19-4   *Peripatus,* an intermediate form showing characteristics of two phyla, the Annelida and the Arthropoda. (Courtesy of Carolina Biological Supply Company.)

characteristics of two well-defined phyla. Missing links such as *Archaeopteryx* and *Peripatus* strongly suggest that organisms developed in a continuous fashion rather than being created in discrete, immutable groups.

Occasionally organisms thought to be extinct, and known only from the fossil record, are found alive. An example is *Metasequoia* (Figure 19–5), a deciduous, cone-bearing tree, commonly known as the *dawn redwood* and closely related to the familiar redwood of the genus *Sequoia*. In 1941 a Japanese botanist proposed the genus name *Metasequoia* for fossil specimens of this tree that had been studied for some time. Later that same year, living examples of *Metasequoia* were found in China. After World War II, botanists from the United States studied the plants in their natural habitat and shipped seeds all over the world. Today the tree has been moved back into areas such as the West Coast of the United States where fossils show that it once thrived.

A particularly exciting discovery of a "living fossil" came in 1938, when a prehistoric-looking fish with lobed fins was caught by commercial fishermen in deep water off the coast of South Africa. This fish, which was about 5 feet long, proved to be a coelacanth of the genus *Latimeria*. Coelacanths have been found widely in the fossil record from the Devonian period (about 400,000,000 years ago) through the Cretaceous (about 75,000,000 years ago), but they were thought to have been extinct since the Cretaceous period. Since 1952 more coelacanths have been taken off the coast of Madagascar, near the Comoro Islands; studies of their anatomy have provided important information about animal evolutionary development. This animal is a close relative of the group of fishes that gave rise to the amphibians.

(a)

(b)

FIGURE 19–5 *Metasequoia,* the dawn redwood. (a) Full view. (Lola B. Graham; National Audubon Society/Photo Researchers.) (b) Close-up of a branch. (Courtesy of Eliott Weier.)

Bio-Topic: Evolution Observed—Painfully

In 1956, geneticist W. E. Kerr imported 35 African queen bees to São Paulo, Brazil. Colonies of the African bees were extremely aggressive but produced large amounts of honey. Kerr's plan was to hybridize the African bees with local, domesticated bees that were gentler but produced less honey. It was expected that a gentle but productive hybrid could be developed through selective breeding.

The plan was perfectly reasonable. Selective breeding has been used to develop hundreds of varieties of cattle, poultry, and crops. Unfortunately, 26 of the African queens were accidentally released in 1957. A reasonable selective breeding program was instantly converted into still another instance of natural selection—with painful results.

The African queens invaded the hives of local bees, displaced the resident queens, and produced hybrids. Although less fierce than the African bees, the hybrids are easily provoked and attack persistently in huge numbers. The deaths of at least 150 persons and countless horses, cattle and smaller animals have earned these hybrids the name "killer bees."

The hybrids are spreading outward from the São Paulo area, establishing hybrid hives and also breeding with local bees as they spread. Hybrids are expected to reach Panama by the early 1980s, and the southwestern United States by the 1990s. Is this invasion inevitable, and with it the disturbances experienced in Brazil? What, if anything, will retard or stop them?

Insecticides are not the answer unless we are willing to eliminate domesticated bees along with the hybrids. The hybrids cannot tolerate cold weather, so the climate will establish a natural northern limit (barring mutations that confer cold tolerance). Unexpected predators or parasites might exert a biological control, but this seems unlikely (none has appeared in Brazil).

Genetics offers some hope. As the hybrid bees in Brazil have continued to cross with the local domestic bees, successive generations have become less aggressive. It has been suggested that a genetic barrier be created by releasing hordes of gentle bees over the narrow Isthmus of Panama. Can a second genetic intervention reverse the first one? Or might it make matters worse? What of the ecological impact on Panama that could result from the release of hordes of bees? Given our present limited understanding of ecological interactions, natural selection might be the best problem-solver, although there is no guarantee that we will enjoy the solution.

Thus the coelacanth is closely related to a group of organisms lying in the direct line of descent of the animals who made the transition from water to land.

For years biologists argued about whether coelacanth females are *oviparous* (laying eggs) or *viviparous* (giving birth to living young). The question was finally settled in 1975 when investigators dissected a specimen at the American Museum of Natural History. The dissection revealed a type of reproduction known as *ovoviviparous*, which is common in insects, snails, snakes, lizards, and sharks. In this method of reproduction, the young develop inside the mother but are nourished by a yolk sac (Figure 19–6).

Vestigial Structures

Many plants and animals contain structures that have no apparent function but are homologous to structures of closely related organisms.

FIGURE 19–6   One of five young removed from a female coelacanth at the American Museum of Natural History. Note the attached yolk sac from which the embryo receives food while developing. (Courtesy of the American Museum of Natural History.)

Such apparently useless parts are called *vestig-ial structures.* They provide visible evidence of relationships among groups of organisms. Some snakes, for example, have bones resembling a pelvic girdle (hip bones), indicating a relation-ship to four-legged vertebrates. The small splint bones on the foreleg of the horse are thought to be reduced toes homologous to the two outer toes of some of its three-toed fossil relatives. Humans possess a number of vestigial organs, such as the appendix, the coccyx (the last sev-eral vertebrae), ear muscles, and "wisdom" teeth, which are on their way to becoming completely vestigial (Figure 19–7).

Biochemical Similarities

Important information on relationships among species can often be obtained by comparing the organic compounds found in living systems. For example, all organisms with eucaryotic cells contain cytochrome c_i as we saw in Chapter 9, they use it in energy processing. The sequence of amino acids in this molecule has been worked out for more than 40 species ranging from molds to humans. The most important functional aspect of a cytochrome c molecule is its folded pattern; differences in amino acid sequence are not so important to its function in electron transport. The molecules are remarka-bly similar among species in folded structure and in a large portion of their amino acid mol-ecules (35 out of 104), but differences do exist in the amino acid sequence along certain parts of the molecule.

The greatest difference is found between *Neurospora* (red bread mold) and humans: 44 amino acids differ out of 104. Human cyto-

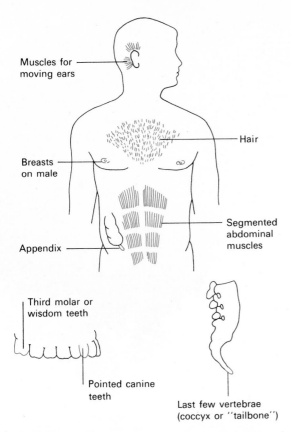

Muscles for
moving ears

Hair

Breasts
on male

Segmented
abdominal
muscles

Appendix

Third molar or
wisdom teeth

Pointed canine
teeth

Last few vertebrae
(coccyx or "tailbone")

FIGURE 19–7   Vestigial structures in humans.
These inherited characteristics have no apparent
function in humans; they were probably useful to
some of our ancestors.

chrome *c* differs from that of the fruit fly,
Drosophila, in 29 amino acids out of the 104.
The difference between human and horse cytochrome *c* is 12 amino acids out of 104; between humans and rhesus monkeys it is just 1
out of 104. And human and chimpanzee cytochrome *c* molecules are exactly alike. Thus the
evolutionary relationships suggested by cytochrome *c* structures throughout eucaryotic
forms closely parallel the classical evolutionary
tree. The greater the difference between two
organisms in the amino acid sequence of their
cytochrome *c*, the more distant their evolutionary relationship.

The biochemical similarity of humans and
chimpanzees extends far beyond cytochrome *c*.

Biochemically, the two species are almost identical as demonstrated by their blood proteins
(Figure 21–4a and c). Moreover, even their
chromosomes appear very similar. So are many
behavioral traits; were it not for the similarities, people would not find the antics of chimpanzees particularly funny or endearing. "Why,
they act just like we do!" is a common remark
by *Homo sapiens* watching the behavior of *Pan
troglodytes*. For example, young chimpanzees
respond to human mothering very much like
human babies; they even learn to imitate
human activities.

Yet in external appearance and many behavioral traits we are radically different from
chimpanzees. Some differences in genes (or
differences in the positions of genes on chromosomes, or both) must account for these dissimilarities.

Behavioral Evidence

Since organisms inherit behavioral traits, we
can use behavior as supporting evidence in
determining evolutionary relationships among
animals. Studies have shown that basic inherited motor patterns are quite resistant to environmental change, so they may be good indica-
tors of evolutionary kinship. But we must use
this information with caution and correlate it
with other knowledge, such as chromosome
studies, chemical analyses, and anatomy. For
instance, social behavior alone might lead one
to believe that ants and termites are closely
related. But comparative studies of other characteristics such as wing structure and reproductive anatomy indicate that termites are
more closely related to cockroaches. Apparently, the social structures of termites and of
ants evolved independently.

Behavioral patterns have been especially useful in establishing species and family relationships in insects, fish, and birds. For example,
observation of the behavior of spawning fish
may provide clues to their evolutionary relationships. When fish of several species were
observed mating in a similar way, such as the
male wrapping around the female, questions
about their kinship arose. Further studies of
bone structure and development have estab-

lished firm evolutionary relationships among some species exhibiting this behavior.

EXPLAINING THE EVIDENCE

So far we have defined *evolution* and presented evidence that it does occur. In the rest of this chapter we shall examine the historical developments that culminated in the Darwin-Wallace theory of evolution—the forerunner of modern, or "neo-Darwinist," evolutionary theory. In Chapter 20 we shall use modern evolutionary theory to discuss the nature of the mechanism of evolution.

Early Concepts

As soon as early societies could provide for their immediate needs they probably began to ponder their relationship to the natural world, their own origins, and the "why" of human existence. People have been pondering these problems ever since those times (Figure 19–8). We do not know when people began this search or how the first cultures answered these questions, but we do know something of Greek thought concerning evolution. Anaximander, a Greek philosopher who lived around 600 BC, believed that life had sprung from mud which once covered the earth. He thought that plants, animals, and human beings arose in that order, with the land-dwelling animals living first in water and then moving onto land.

Aristotle noted a consistent pattern in the living world. He organized the known living organisms into a *scala naturae* ("ladder of life"), beginning with simple forms and ending in more complex forms (see Figure 1–14). Two of his statements describe his evolutionary thought: "Nature proceeds little by little from things lifeless to animal life," and "Nature passes from lifeless objects to animals in such unbroken sequences, interposing between them beings which live and yet are not animals." Anaximander and Aristotle, then, recognized the evolutionary process, although they made little effort to explain the mechanism responsible for it. Aristotle proposed that a "perfecting principle" inherent in the organism could produce change.

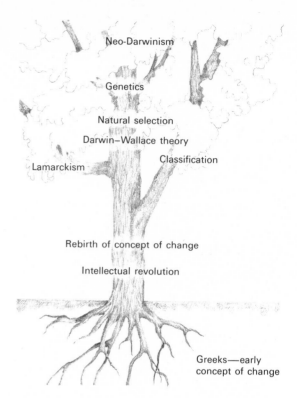

FIGURE 19–8   The development of ideas about evolution can be shown in a treelike structure in which Greek thoughts and contributions represent the "roots." Newer knowledge within a modern concept of evolution forms the trunk and branches. Some branches, such as classification, continue as helpful accessory parts, whereas others, such as Lamarckism, lead to dead ends.

After Aristotle, change and development of organisms were rarely discussed. The predominant viewpoint saw the world as static, without change in living forms or inanimate material. Several factors have been proposed to account for this intellectual climate including the rise of Christianity and the indifference of the Romans to pure scientific work. All of nature was considered to be inert; the mountains would never change, climates were always the same, and living forms were immutable.

This was the prevailing attitude as we entered the seventeenth century, often designated as the "Intellectual Revolution" or the "Age of Enlightenment." The 1600s and 1700s saw widespread social and political change. Individual rights became important and the infallibility of the Church was questioned. Along with changes in social structures came conceptual changes in the physical sciences, resulting from the work of such pioneers as Galileo and Sir Isaac Newton. This background established the groundwork for changes in the geological and biological sciences.

The classification system developed by the Swedish biologist Linnaeus in the 1700s established a static concept of species. Although classification is essential in the biological sciences, this particular system tended to reinforce the position of the Church that the world was unchanging. The immutability of species was challenged, however, by the French natural historian Buffon (1707–1788). Buffon believed that animals did change, contrary to theological doctrine. He was impressed with similarities in structure among some organisms and realized that a "basic plan" often occurred in such structures as the vertebrate forelimb. Buffon concluded that "nature" had produced many organisms over a very long period of time and that some forms had become extinct.

Geologists and the Concept of Change

The very concept of change implies the passage of time; change occurs *over time*. As they pursued their study of rock configurations and landforms, eighteenth-century geologists developed considerable evidence that geologic change had indeed taken place. This led to two closely interrelated problems: what caused these changes, and how fast did they occur?

Changes in the landscape of the earth were long thought to result from catastrophes—that is, sudden disturbances. But in 1788 the Scottish geologist James Hutton, in his *Theory of the Earth*, proposed that the continuous processes of erosion, mountain building, and vulcanism (volcanic activity) have changed the earth's features, and that these same forces are active today. He was the first to recognize that time is an important factor in the development of the earth. Hutton understood the role of cyclical events such as mountain formation

and erosion in the history of the earth; he concluded the first chapter of his treatise with the words, "we find no vestige of a beginning—no prospect of an end."

Around 1790 an English geologist named William Smith, used a bit of deductive reasoning to arrive at the simple conclusion that in beds of rock the oldest strata (layers) were at the bottom and the overlying strata were younger. Pursuing this line of reasoning, Smith argued persuasively that the fossils found in lower strata must be older than those found in strata above. He concluded that a comparison of these fossils would indicate the developmental pattern of life on our planet. Since each particular stratum had its own characteristic fossils, any two layers bearing the same fossils must be of the same relative age. Certain fossils, then, could be used to determine the ages of various strata. Smith thus proposed that the fossil record gives a timetable of the development of life on earth. Somewhat later the English geologist Charles Lyell published a revolutionary textbook, *Principles of Geology* (1830), in which he clearly presented the dynamic effects of physical forces, working through time, in shaping our planet. Lyell paved the way for Charles Darwin's great work, exerting perhaps more influence on Darwin than any other person. Lyell mentioned the appearance of new species in his book and came very close to stating Darwin's theory. He actually recognized natural selection but failed to see how it could be a creative force.

Lamarckism

One of the first evolutionists was the Frenchman Jean Baptiste Lamarck (1744–1829). Lamarck, who first used the term *biology*, made important contributions to biological classification and the study of invertebrates. But he is most famous as a pioneer in evolutionary theory. Lamarck recognized an evolutionary process in nature, but his explanation of the mechanisms that produced this development is incompatible with modern biological knowledge. Lamarck's theory is often called *the theory of the inheritance of acquired characteristics*. It shows that although he recognized the importance of the environment in evolution, he did not completely understand its role. Lamarck proposed that organisms moving to a new environment would require certain structural modifications. In response to this need, changes in structure would occur; and the more a structure was used, the more highly it would be developed. As a result of such modifications, other structures might not be used and would tend to disappear. This part of Lamarck's theory is often called "the use and disuse of parts." Thus one who accepts Lamarck's theory of evolution would explain the reduction of the lateral (side) toes on the horse's foreleg by stating that only the middle toe was used for running.

Lamarck further believed that a change produced by the environment in one generation would be passed on through inheritance to the next generation. Today we know that a weight lifter cannot transmit his bulging biceps to his son, and that the deep suntan a white person acquires during years of exposure to the tropical sun cannot be inherited. Only changes in the sex cells caused by mutations (discussed in Chapter 14) can be transmitted to the next generation.

Darwin and Natural Selection

The most important figure in the development of the modern theory of evolution was Charles Darwin (Figure 19–9). Darwin added to the concept of an evolutionary process and proposed a mechanism to account for it; his proposed mechanism eventually gained almost universal acceptance. Born in 1809 in England, Darwin was the son of a physician and the grandson of a famous natural philosopher, Erasmus Darwin. His grandfather, concerned with changes in living organisms, had accepted Lamarck's theory of the inheritance of acquired characteristics to explain these changes. Young Darwin first pursued a medical program at Edinburgh but soon dropped it and turned to theology at Cambridge. His real interests, however, lay in geology and natural history; he was strongly influenced by the geologist Lyell. Another influence on Darwin was the *Essay on Population* by Malthus, which we discussed in

FIGURE 19–9   Charles Darwin (1809–1882). (Courtesy of Fisher Scientific Company.)

Chapter 8. As we noted, Malthus believed that populations must be held in check or they will soon run out of resources. This suggested to Darwin that populations experience competition and a struggle for existence.

That species could—and did—change was a certainty to Darwin. The production of new varieties of domestic animals seemed to illustrate this point very well, and Darwin became extremely interested in animal breeding. Besides becoming familiar with many animal breeding programs, Darwin conducted breeding experiments himself with various kinds of pigeons. He was acutely aware of the possibilities of obtaining desired traits in offspring by selecting characteristics in the parents. If people could produce new varieties through controlled breeding experiments, Darwin wondered, why cannot nature modify species through a selection process?

Darwin's "Living Laboratory": The Galápagos Islands

Perhaps the greatest aid to Darwin in developing his theory was his voyage on H. M. S. Beagle

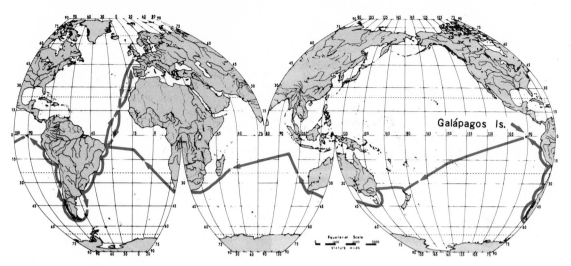

FIGURE 19–10   The voyage of H.M.S. *Beagle.*

during the years 1831 to 1836 (Figure 19–10). The purposes of the expedition were mainly mapping and charting, but the value of including a naturalist in the party was recognized. Darwin was selected for this job. This enabled him to spend considerable time in the southern hemisphere, especially in South America and the Galápagos Islands. Here Darwin observed native tribes and wild animals in an almost undisturbed state; and he described this trip in his widely read book *The Voyage of the Beagle.* Darwin later acknowledged this voyage as his most important preparation for the formulation of his theory of evolution.

The Galápagos Islands (Figure 19–11), located 650 miles west of Ecuador, consist of volcanic peaks. Since some of the peaks are high enough to produce local climatic differences, the islands contain a variety of habitats, ranging from lava cliffs to cactus forests to moist, lush forests (Figure 19–12). Although very near the equator, the islands are washed by cool antarctic currents as well as tropical currents. The individual islands are separated from each other by as much as 60 miles of deep water.

These factors all add up to a unique place. It is no wonder that the Galápagos have been called "one of the most marvelous evolutionary laboratories on the planet." Geologically the

islands are rather young; the oldest islands arose about 10,000,000 years ago, while some are only 100,000 to 300,000 years old. The animal and plant life is American—that is, the inhabiting species probably came from the coast of South America. Seeds, spores, and possibly insects could have blown in with the wind. Other plants and animals could have arrived on "rafts"—floating driftwood and other buoyant materials—from the mainland, while some birds could have flown the distance. But these organisms had to find a suita-

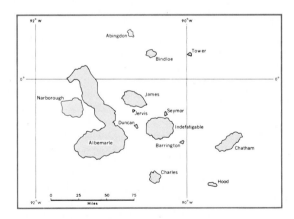

FIGURE 19–11   The Galápagos Islands.

FIGURE 19–12   Sullivan Bay in the Galápagos Islands, showing James Island in the distance. (Courtesy of James Murray.)

ble habitat if they were to survive in this new environment. On these islands a unique fauna developed: giant 400-pound tortoises; iguanas, which are lizards suggestive of small dinosaurs; flightless cormorants, a species of small penguins; boobies; and a variety of finches (Figures 19–13 and 19–14). Darwin studied all these animals; he noted that the iguanas differed from island to island. But with respect to the development of new species the animals he was most interested in were the finches. Through a detailed study of the 14 species of finches in the Galápagos Islands, Darwin arrived at a theory to explain the evolution of new species.

Darwin reasoned that a single finch species came from the mainland long ago and found a variety of habitats available to it. Since individual members of the species varied (and Darwin did not understand the cause of this variability), it was possible for the species to exploit all

FIGURE 19–13   Land iguana from the Galápagos Islands. (Los Angeles County Museum of Natural History.)

FIGURE 19–14   Flightless cormorant. (Courtesy of California Academy of Sciences.)

Both in space and time, we seem to be brought somewhat near to the great fact—that mystery of mysteries—the first appearance of new beings on this earth. Reviewing the facts here given, one is astonished at the amount of creative force, if such an expression may be used, displayed on these small, barren, and rocky islands; and still more so, at its diverse yet analogous action on points so near each other. I have said that the Galápagos Archipelago might be called a satellite attached to America, but it should rather be called a group of satellites, physically similar, organically distinct, yet intimately related to each other, and all related in a marked, though much lesser, degree to the great American continent.

available habitats, including barren ground, grasslands, shrubs, and trees. The 14 species show a great variation in bill structure: this anatomical feature more than any other may have permitted the finches to inhabit various niches (ecological roles). In Darwin's words, this is "a most singular group of finches, related to each other in the structure of their beaks, short tails, form of body, and plumage." He further stated, "Seeing this gradation and diversity of structure in one small, intimately related group of birds, one might really fancy that from an original paucity of birds in this archipelago, one species had been taken and modified for different ends." Actually, this group of finches had filled the niches of birds not found in this environment—warblers, grosbeaks, blackbirds, woodpeckers, nuthatches, and others.

We can sense the value of these islands to our understanding of the evolutionary process when we read Darwin's thoughts on this environment, recorded in *The Voyage of the Beagle:*

THE DARWIN-WALLACE THEORY

In 1859, after he had pondered the material from the voyage of the *Beagle* and other studies, Darwin proposed his theory of evolution in the now famous book called *On the Origin of Species by Means of Natural Selection.* Its first printing was sold out almost immediately, and its contents threw the world into a controversy. The Church and many biologists violently opposed Darwin, while many other biologists and some laymen applauded him. Another biologist, Alfred Wallace, had arrived at conclusions identical to Darwin's and had in fact sent Darwin a copy of his theory in 1858. Wallace had arrived at his concept independently of Darwin by studying the plant and animal life of Malaya. They decided to publish their works simultaneously. Thus most biologists speak of the *Darwin-Wallace theory.* But since Darwin's thesis was much better documented, the theory is often called Darwinism. The Darwin-Wallace theory of the evolution of life to its present diversity can be briefly summarized as follows:

1. Variation exists among members of a particular species. (Look about you at your fellow human beings.)

2. Overproduction usually occurs in a population: more individuals are produced than can be supported in a particular environment.

3. Competition results from population pressure on the environmental resources (a struggle for existence).

4. Individuals with characteristics favored by their particular environment survive (*natural selection*).

5. The characteristics of favored individuals are passed on to their offspring (survival of the fittest).

Bio-Topic: Darwin and Wallace— A Study in Contrasts

The two men who independently conceived of the theory of evolution by natural selection could not have been more different. They both grew up in Victorian England, but came from very different parts of their common culture. Both arrived at the same conclusion after similar experiences, but their reactions to their discoveries were dramatically opposite.

Darwin was born in 1809, the son of a wealthy physician. Raised in comfortable circumstances, he was an indifferent student. After studying medicine for two years, his father insisted that he transfer to Cambridge University to study for a clerical career. The opportunity to sail on the Beagle must have been a relief.

Wallace was born to working class parents in 1823. An apt student, he had to leave school at the age of 14 to earn a living. In 1837, the year after Darwin had returned from the voyage of the Beagle, Wallace became a surveyor for the railroad industry, a life that kept him out of doors and kindled his interest in biology.

Darwin returned to England in 1836 convinced that species diverge over time, but uncertain as to how or why. In 1838, Malthus' essay on populations gave him the needed clue. But it took Darwin until 1842 to write up a 35-page draft of his theory. Another two years passed before

he completed, in 1844, a 230-page version. This draft he sealed and entrusted to his wife with instructions that it be published only after his death. Although he continued to accumulate evidence, Darwin shared his thoughts on evolution only with a few close firiends out of fear of the reactions his theory might provoke.

In 1848 Wallace gave in to his increasing interest in biology and embarked on a career as a professional collector of exotic animals. A decade later, after many financial disappointments, he conceived of natural selection during a feverish illness. Immediately upon his recovery, Wallace summarized his thoughts and mailed them to Darwin whom he knew to be interested in evolution. The fateful letter reached Darwin on June 18, 1858—a full 20 years after Darwin himself had conceived of natural selection.

Darwin was forced to choose between two unattractive alternatives: relinquish his priority to the concept and allow Wallace to take credit; or make public as his own and Wallace's a set of views that he knew would shock his culture. At the urging of friends, Darwin allowed his and Wallace's views to be made public simultaneously. In 1859, Darwin published his famous Origin of Species. The Western world hasn't been the same since.

Darwin failed to recognize the source of variation in organisms, and he looked to a modification of Lamarckism for the answer. This theory, called *pangenesis*, proposed that tiny units called "pangenes" (*pan*, "everywhere") pass from each part of the body into the gametes to determine what the offspring will inherit in the next generation. This was clearly a form of inheritance of acquired characteristics. But the essence of the Darwin-Wallace theory was the concept of *natural selection*—the selective forces of the environment.

The current view of evolution is much the same as that proposed in the Darwin-Wallace theory. But the modern, or neo-Darwinist, theory stresses the source of the variations natural selection operates on. In the next chapter we shall examine this and other modern concepts of evolution.

SUMMARY

Evolution can be defined as a change in the gene frequencies of a population. Evolution, then, is the concept that changes in organisms result from slight genetic variations transmitted through successive generations. Much evidence is available to support this concept. In addition to that presented in Chapter 2, more evidence comes from the development and structure of species living today. For example, many similarities exist in the embryology of closely related species. Also, several known forms have characteristics intermediate between classification categories; this indicates gradual change. Vestigial structures, lacking apparent function but homologous to structures of close relatives, are present in many organisms. Comparison of organic compounds found in living systems also reveal important evolutionary information. Behavioral patterns often support the concept of evolution.

The concept of organic evolution followed the realization that geological changes have occurred over periods of time. Important ideas (many of them erroneous in some detail) were supplied by Anaximander, Aristotle, Linnaeus, Buffon, Hutton, Smith, Lamarck, Lyell, and Malthus. But the statement of the theory of evolution and its probable mechanism, natural selection, was made by Darwin and Wallace in 1859. Although Darwin accepted the Lamarckian theory of the inheritance of acquired characteristics, we now understand the source of variation that natural selection operates on. The essence of the Darwin-Wallace theory was the concept of natural selection and its role in evolution.

REVIEW QUESTIONS

1. Common ancestors or "missing links" are rare in the fossil record. Why?

2. How does study of the molecular structure of cytochrome *c* assist in the understanding of evolutionary relationships?

3. What effects did geological studies have on the study of evolution?

4. Summarize the contribution of the Galápagos finches to Darwin's theory of natural selection.

5. A naturalist studied a species of field mice living both in a wooded hillside and a field. Those in the forest had dark coats, whereas those living in the field had light coats. What is the probable explanation for this?

6. How has the concept of evolution influenced our thought in areas other than the biological sciences, such as political science, sociology, economics, and theology?

7. Outline the major points of the Darwin-Wallace theory of evolution.

8. Define natural selection.

SUPPLEMENTARY READINGS

Dickerson, Richard E., "The Structure and History of an Ancient Protein," *Scientific American*, April 1972. All eucaryotic organisms utilize cytochrome *c* in the process of obtaining energy from food molecules. Cytochrome *c* varies from species to species but is more similar in amino acid content and folded structure in closely related organisms. The differences in cytochrome *c* structure, then, provide a good example of molecular evolution.

Huxley, Thomas H., *On a Piece of Chalk*, Charles Scribner's Sons, New York, 1967. (Edited and with an Introduction and Notes by Loren Eiseley.) A delightful and easily understood essay by one of the greatest biologists of all time on how the story of chalk reveals the evolutionary continuity of the stream of life.

Livingston, John and L. Sinclair, *Darwin and the Galápagos*, Canadian Broadcasting Corp., Toronto, 1966. A popular, well-illustrated version of the work of Charles Darwin. The evolutionary significance of the Galápagos Islands is presented in this small book.

Moody, Paul A., *Introduction to Evolution*, 3rd edition, Harper & Row, New York, 1970. This textbook presents the basic facts about evolution for readers who have little background in the sciences. It is comprehensive in coverage and is an excellent source book on evidences and mechanisms of evolution.

Romer, Alfred S., *The Vertebrate Story*, 4th edition, University of Chicago Press, Chicago, 1959. A classic presentation of the origins, fossil record, and adaptations of vertebrates.

Chapter 20

Evolution: The Modern Concept

The Darwin-Wallace theory of evolution assumes a variety of possible hereditary traits within a species. However, the theory was developed over 40 years *before* Mendel's findings in genetics were dusted off and revealed to the general scientific community. So Darwin had a (basically correct) idea about inherited traits, but he had no mechanism to explain the form of these traits and how they were distributed to the next generation.

The field of **Population Genetics** has given us the basis for the modern concept of evolution. A good case in point is the example of **Sickle Cells and Survival.** Sickle-cell anemia, a debilitating disease characterized by deformed red blood cells, would appear to have little benefit to its victims. But the sickle-cell trait actually aids its carriers by making them resistant to malaria—an adaptive advantage.

The addition of genetics to the existing nineteenth-century concept of evolution has led to an up-dated statement of the theory called **Neo-Darwinism.** The various processes by which new **Adaptations** can enter the gene pool of a species lead us directly to one of the basic questions about evolution.

How do new species develop? If evolution is a selective process, it can only eliminate unsuccessful traits. How does it explain the formation of new species? **Speciation: Unlike from Like** is the process by which the **Splitting of Gene Pools** through natural means leads to the formation of distinct species. Generally the **Isolating Mechanisms** are physical barriers, which separate two groups, followed by biological barriers, which make mating impossible.

Following the formation of a species, that species does not necessarily stay the same. **Divergence and Adaptive Radiation** are the two successive processes by which speciation continues, as members of a single species occupy new habitats and eventually form other new species. Two other processes are **Convergence and Parallelism,** which do not lead to the formation of new species, but rather shape the development of existing species.

The bottom line of evolution is **Extinction: The Eventual Fate of Species.** A variety of environmental or biological pressures can obliterate a species. It is particularly important that humans understand the harmful impact they can have on species whose environment they share.

Since the statement of the Darwin-Wallace theory, discoveries in biology have contributed greatly to our knowledge of the process of evolution. Since studies in sexuality, chromosomes, mutations, and Mendelian genetics have added to this basic theory, we cannot credit the modern concept of evolution to any one person. As in most modern scientific theories, the labors and research of many investigators have gone into formulation of a workable, probable concept to explain the development of life.

One field that has made important contributions to our understanding of evolution is *population genetics*, the area of study that deals with the total *gene pool* (all the genes) of a *population*. The genes of an individual are only part of the gene pool of a population, which may be defined as *a group of organisms of the same species*. The evolutionary process involves changes in the total population. Recall from Chapter 19 that our definition of *evolution* itself is *a change in gene frequencies*. Population genetics, which links genetics and evolution, is essential to our discussion of the modern concept of evolution.

POPULATION GENETICS

In 1908 G. H. Hardy, an English mathematician, and Wilhelm Weinberg, a German physician, formulated a principle (the *Hardy-Weinberg principle*) concerning the frequencies of genes in a population. This principle states that the genotype frequencies in a population will remain in a state of equilibrium (will not change) from generation to generation under the following conditions: (1) the population is large; (2) mutations do not occur; (3) migration in and out of the population is minimal; and (4) mating is random. In a population in which these rules hold, the gene frequencies will remain the same from generation to generation. Evolution will not occur.

Note that the Hardy-Weinberg principle is a theoretical concept; the conditions it proposes never really occur in a natural breeding population. Breeding populations are often small; mutations do occur; migration takes place; and mating is never really random. But the Hardy-Weinberg principle provides an important theoretical baseline condition against which we can compare the actual processes that occur in nature.

Sickle Cells and Survival

We can use a specific example, *sickle cells*, to show how the Hardy-Weinberg principle can be applied.

Sickle-Cell Anemia

Sickle-cell anemia is a hereditary disease caused by a defective type of hemoglobin. It is characterized by sickle-shaped (crescent-shaped) red blood cells produced under low oxygen conditions (Figure 20–1). A rigid crystalline structure is known to form in some cells containing hemoglobin S (sickle-cell hemoglobin). Because of this inflexibility in structure, the affected red blood cells cannot easily pass through small capillaries. The defective cells thus obstruct blood flow to tissues, deprive them of oxygen, and cause a variety of symptoms, including pain, fever, swelling, jaundice, susceptibility to infection, and kidney trouble.

Sickle-cell anemia is mainly a disease of people of African extraction, although Caucasians have it in some parts of the world. It occurs at a rate of approximately 1 in 400 members of the black population in the United States. Sickle-cell hemoglobin occurs in individuals who carry a gene different from the gene that produces normal hemoglobin (hemoglobin A). Sickle-cell anemia results when both an individual's alleles are those for sickle-cell hemoglobin (HbS, HbS).

Sickle-Cell Trait

Sickle-cell trait is the condition that results when an individual has one gene for sickle cell and one gene for normal hemoglobin (HbS, HbA). Sickle-cell anemia kills many victims by age 20 and most others by age 40, but individuals with sickle-cell trait can survive provided they avoid certain unusual conditions, such as unpressurized aircraft or very severe physical strain at altitudes above 4000 feet.

Approximately 1 in 10 blacks in the United States carries sickle-cell trait, but in Africa the

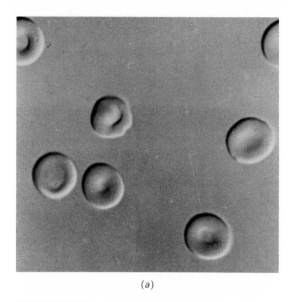
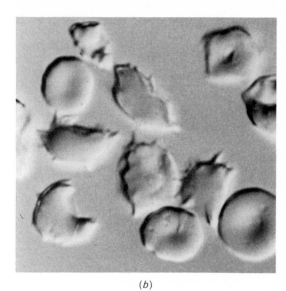

(a)   (b)

FIGURE 20–1   Human red blood cells. (a) Normal (oxygenated). (b) Sickle- or crescent-shaped (deoxygenated). (Courtesy of The National Foundation—March of Dimes.)

incidence is much higher—one in two. Why is the sickle-cell gene more prevalent in Africa than in the United States? The Hardy-Weinberg principle helps explain the answer.

Sickle-Cell Trait and Malaria

The incidence of sickle-cell trait is highest in Africa, where malaria is most common. Apparently the organism that causes malaria, a disease of red blood cells, does not grow and develop as well in red blood cells containing sickle-cell hemoglobin as in those with normal hemoglobin. Malaria is explained in detail in Chapter 22. Thus individuals with sickle-cell hemoglobin have a greater resistance to malaria. The selective pressure of malaria serves to increase the frequency of the HbS gene in the population. The situation in Africa and in parts of India and Greece, where the sickle-cell gene shows a greater frequency in the population, can be explained as follows. Because of selection against the homozygous sickle-cell condition (HbS, HbS) through death by sickle-cell anemia and against the homozygous normal condition (HbA, HbA) through death by malaria, the heterozygous condition (HbS, HbA)—which is resistant to malaria and shows anemia only under great physical stress—is selected. Thus the heterozygote genotype (HbS, HbA) increases in the population. But the selective pressure against sickle-cell anemia is much greater than that against malaria; in other words, more individuals die from sickle-cell anemia than from malaria. This means that the HbA gene has a greater selective advantage than HbS; therefore the frequency of the HbA gene in the population is higher than the frequency of the HbS gene.

In parts of Africa where the frequency of the HbS gene reaches approximately 30 percent, an equilibrium is established. The genotypes in the population are about 49 percent normal (HbA, HbA), 42 percent heterozygous (HbA, HbS), and 9 percent sickle-cell (HbS, HbS) (Figure 20–2).

In the United States, however, malaria is less prevalent and the gene frequencies are much different. The HbA gene is more frequent in the black population in the United States than in Africa. Because of the lower incidence of malaria, the HbS gene has no selective advantage in the heterozygote, and its frequency is

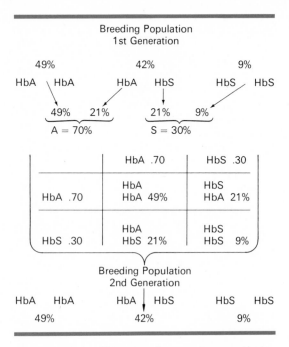

FIGURE 20–2   How gene frequencies remain the same under constant selection pressure. This is the situation in Africa, where malaria selects for the HbS gene. The genotype (HbA, HbA) has a 49 percent frequency in the population, the genotype (HbA, HbS) has a 42 percent frequency, and the genotype HbS, HbS has a 9 percent frequency. This means that the frequency of the HbA gene is 70 percent: (HbA, HbA) = 49 percent, and one-half of the (HbA, HbS) genotype (42 percent) is HbA; 49 percent plus 21 percent equals 70 percent. Calculating in a similar manner, we see that the frequency of the HbS gene is 30 percent. This gene frequency will remain the same in future generations as long as malaria continues to exert the same selection pressure.

less than in Africa—about 10 percent. The sickle-cell story, not only illustrates the effects of selection pressure on a gene but also shows how a gene can be disadvantageous in one environment but advantageous under different conditions.

Gene Frequencies and Evolution

As we have just seen, gene frequencies in a population can change; this is known as evolu-

tion. In this process, the gradual replacement of one genotype by another occurs as natural selection operates on the gene pool of a population. In discussing evolution of the horse in Chapter 2, we spoke of "the gradual replacement of some types of horses by others." We can now state the situation in genetic terms, using the guidelines of population genetics. Recall that in Chapter 2 we did not propose a straight lineage from *Eohippus* to *Miohippus* and *Merychippus* and finally to the modern horse, *Equus*. What probably occurred was that the frequency of the genotype producing *Eohippus* decreased in the population as the genotype that produced *Miohippus* increased. Thus several types of horses with different genotypes could have lived at the same time, but with changing frequencies in the population. As the environment changed (as it always does, however slowly), genotypes that were becoming less well suited to these successive changes gradually gave way to more successful genotypes. In the end only *Equus*, the most successful in our present-day environment, remained. That the species *Equus* itself has genetic variability (varying genotypes) is evidenced by the results of cross-breeding among the various modern breeds.

NEO-DARWINISM

We can now turn to the contemporary concept of evolution. Modern biology attributes variation in living organisms to inheritable chromosomal units called *genes*. Since genes are on chromosomes, variations are produced during the events of meiosis (crossovers and recombination) and through mutation; they are transmitted through fertilization. The environment, then, does not *produce* variations but *selects* them. A particular environment acts as a screen or filter, permitting certain genotypes to continue inhabiting it and eliminating others. The term "natural selection," as used by Darwin and most modern biologists, refers to the selecting function of the environment upon genotypes living in it. We say that those organisms selected by a particular environment are *adapted* to that habitat, and we call those characteristics that are of value in that environment *adaptations.* Because heritable adaptations increase the probable success of a species, adaptive changes are beneficial. Many changes can occur in a species; all of these are evolutionary, but all are not necessarily adaptive.

Better adapted organisms in a particular environment reproduce at a higher rate than those that are less well adapted, simply because more of them live long enough to reproduce. Biologists currently use the term *differential reproduction* rather than the term "survival of the fittest" to denote the success of some forms and the decline of others. As a result of differential reproduction, the frequency of certain genotypes in the population increases while the frequency of others decreases. If the environment changes, the overall frequency of genotypes changes, and organisms of different appearance and function may result. It is quite correct, then, to treat evolution as a change in gene frequencies. Returning again to the horse, we see that horses with the characteristics of *Equus* could better escape their predators, reproduce, and increase their frequency in the horse population. A comparison of Lamarckian, Darwinian, and neo-Darwinian concepts of evolution is shown in Figure 20-3.

The view of evolution prevailing in contemporary biology, then, combines the basic foundation provided by the Darwin-Wallace Theory with the genetic mechanism and stresses differential reproduction rather than differential "survival." This viewpoint is often called *neo-Darwinism.*

Adaptations

We have described adaptations as those traits of an organism (or a species) that enhance its chances for survival and reproduction in a particular environment. Although the most obvious adaptations are variations in body structure, adaptive characteristics may also be physiological or behavioral. The value of some adaptations (such as claws, large muscles, and teeth) for offensive and defensive purposes is clear—sometimes painfully or fatally so. Other adaptations, such as camouflage and mimicry, also provide effective means of protection (Figure 20-4). One of the best-known examples of

protection through mimicry is provided by the monarch and viceroy butterflies (Figure 20-5). Birds avoid monarch butterflies because they are unpalatable. Since viceroys resemble monarchs, most birds avoid them too, although they could be a satisfactory food source. (Birds will eat viceroys if they have never encountered monarch butterflies.)

Many of us are familiar with the adaptive coloration provided by the spots on fawns, and many recognize the "broken wing" behavior of a female grouse as she limps through brush, diverting an intruder's attention from her brood hidden nearby. The pungent odor released by a skunk to deter enemies is also familiar. The whitish uric acid excreted by birds and reptiles is a physiological adaptation for the release of nitrogenous wastes with little loss of water. Examples of adaptation are endless, for they are the essential story of biology—how organisms live, reproduce, and survive in their environments. But to help us understand the basic *process* of adaptation we will consider a single example of an adaptation in a species over a known period of time.

Evolution Observed:
The Peppered Moth

Most species of butterflies and moths display some variation in their coloration. Many light-colored moth species in the British Isles have naturally occurring black mutants. About 1850, in the area of Manchester, England (Figure 20-6), the black form of the peppered moth, *Biston betularia,* represented only about 1 percent of the population (Figure 20-7). This rural area was characterized by a clear atmosphere and white, lichen-covered tree trunks. Thus the white variety of the moth blended into the environment and was camouflaged. The dark variety, however, was under heavy selective pressure from birds which could easily spot them on the trees and pick them off. As the Manchester area became industrialized, however, the environment changed: the air became polluted, and tree trunks were darkened by soot and the death of the lichens. It is estimated that by 1900 the black variety of the moth made up more than 99 percent of the Manchester population.

Birds, such as ducks, that have webs between their toes can swim better and faster than those without webbing. Swimming fast assists them in escaping enemies and obtaining food.

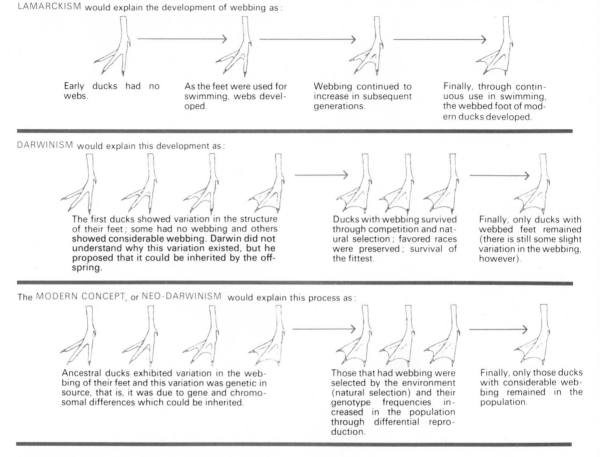

LAMARCKISM would explain the development of webbing as:

Early ducks had no webs.

As the feet were used for swimming, webs developed.

Webbing continued to increase in subsequent generations.

Finally, through continuous use in swimming, the webbed foot of modern ducks developed.

DARWINISM would explain this development as:

The first ducks showed variation in the structure of their feet; some had no webbing and others showed considerable webbing. Darwin did not understand why this variation existed, but he proposed that it could be inherited by the offspring.

Ducks with webbing survived through competition and natural selection; favored races were preserved; survival of the fittest.

Finally, only ducks with webbed feet remained (there is still some slight variation in the webbing, however).

The MODERN CONCEPT, or NEO-DARWINISM would explain this process as:

Ancestral ducks exhibited variation in the webbing of their feet and this variation was genetic in source, that is, it was due to gene and chromosomal differences which could be inherited.

Those that had webbing were selected by the environment (natural selection) and their genotype frequencies increased in the population through differential reproduction.

Finally, only those ducks with considerable webbing remained in the population.

FIGURE 20–3 Comparison of Lamarckism, Darwinism, and neo-Darwinism in interpreting how ducks' feet became webbed. Note that Darwin's concept is very similar to the modern interpretation, or neo-Darwinism, but the modern explanation stresses the genetic source of variation.

In addition to making field observations, H. B. D. Kettlewell of the University of Oxford performed an experiment in 1955 and 1956 to test the hypothesis that predation accounted for the change in gene frequencies in the population of *Biston betularia*. He released equal numbers of black and light forms in a polluted area and in an unpolluted area. He recovered approximately twice as many black forms as light in the industrialized, polluted environment; in the unpolluted area, on the other hand, many more lighter forms survived than black. Note that the environmental changes did not produce the black mutant; it was always present in the population, and its frequency would have remained fairly constant had certain environmental changes not occurred. (Remember the Hardy-Weinberg principle.) When the environmental conditions which favored the light form changed, the black mutant was

FIGURE 20-4 Example of camouflage, in which one type of organism imitates another for protection. This insect resembles the leaf on which it is resting. (Courtesy of Dr. Asa C. Thoresen.)

permits a species to inhabit different environments, and this polymorphism can be extremely useful to a species (Figure 20-8). Balanced polymorphism may be found in environments in which selective pressures are unchanging. The sickle-cell condition in Africa is a good example: the selection pressure of malaria maintains the various genotypes at approximately constant frequencies, favoring the heterozygous condition. Human blood groups offer another example of polymorphism; in the United States as a whole, the four blood groups are balanced. Bear in mind, however, that when we speak of "unchanging" traits and environments, we simply mean that change is taking place too slowly for us to perceive it. Environmental change never stops; neither does evolution.

SPECIATION: UNLIKE FROM LIKE

Some biologists criticized Darwin's theory of natural selection because they could not understand how the process could produce any-

merely selected by the new environment. In other words, light moths adapted to one environment and black moths to another. Variation has definite survival value for a species because, as we have just noted, if the environment changes too much for the predominant variety—the one that was best adapted to the old conditions—certain variant members of the species may continue to exist under the new conditions because they are better adapted to them.

With the enforcement of antipollution laws during the past two decades, tree trunks are becoming lighter again—and recent studies indicate an increase of the lighter form in the peppered moth population. Thus the ratio of light to dark forms is again changing because of natural selection.

Polymorphism

The two different forms of the peppered moth discussed above provide an example of *polymorphism*—two or more distinguishable phenotypes within a species. Polymorphism and evolution are closely intertwined. Variability

FIGURE 20-5 Mimicry in butterflies. The viceroy butterfly mimics the monarch (top), which is not usually eaten by birds because it is unpalatable to them.

Bio-Topic: Cows, Milkweeds, Butterflies, and Birds

Birds avoid eating monarch butterflies because they are unpalatable, and they avoid viceroy butterflies because they resemble monarch butterflies. The evolutionary explanation for this situation is fairly straightforward. A bird that finds monarch butterflies unpalatable soon learns to ignore monarchs. Any viceroy carrying a spontaneous mutation that increases its resemblance to monarchs is also ignored, while normal viceroys are eaten and do not reproduce. After many generations, the viceroy gene pool will contain a high proportion of genes that confer resemblance to monarchs. The protection that viceroys derive from their resemblance to monarchs depends entirely on the intelligence of birds. If birds were not sufficiently intelligent to recognize monarchs, viceroys resembling monarchs wouldn't benefit from the resemblance.

But why are monarchs unpalatable to birds? The answer involves cows and milkweeds, another learned behavior, and the evolution of an innate behavior. The research that provided the answer was conducted by Lincoln P. Brower and his co-workers at Amherst University and illustrates the subtlety of natural selection.

Monarchs are unpalatable because they contain substances that cause irregular heartbeat and nausea in any vertebrate that eats them. The substances, called cardiac glycosides, are not produced by the monarchs, but come from the milkweed plants on which monarch caterpillars feed. The caterpillars are not affected by the glycosides that accumulate in their tissues and persist as the caterpillar develops into an adult. Natural selection has enriched the monarch gene pool for mutations that direct two innate behaviors: that of females laying their eggs on glycoside-producing milkweed and that of the caterpillars eating those plants.

And why do milkweeds produce glycosides? Again, because of natural selection. Milkweeds grow in open pastures in which vertebrate herbivores graze. The herbivores learn to avoid eating plants that cause irregular heartbeat and nausea. This differential grazing enriched the milkweed gene pool for glycoside-producing genes.

The milkweed, monarch, and viceroy can be said to have co-evolved under selective pressures exerted by birds and cows capable of learning. The unpredictable subtlety of these co-evolutionary interrelationships illustrates the complexity of natural associations and the dangers of disrupting such associations. The elimination of milkweeds for some reasonable purpose might well result in the inadvertent elimination of both the monarch and its viceroy mimic.

thing new. They saw that it would bring about the extinction of varieties but, like Darwin himself, they could not understand its creative possibilities. The following discussion will emphasize the creative aspects of natural selection.

What might happen if some members of a species were isolated from the others for a long period of time? Could the two populations change enough to produce two separate species?

Splitting Gene Pools

A large breeding population usually contains smaller breeding groups known as *demes.* Demes are simply local breeding groups whose members are more likely to mate with each other than with individuals outside the group, because they are closer together. The field mice in a certain field may form one deme and those

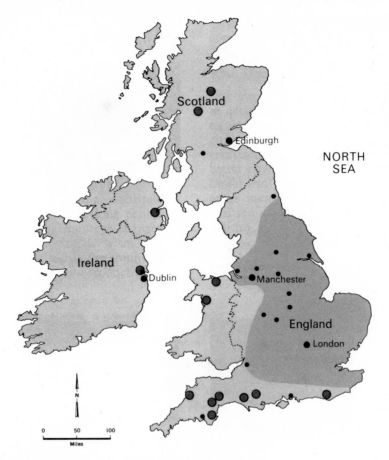

FIGURE 20-6   Relative distribution of the light and dark forms of *Biston betularia* in the British Isles. Industrial areas are designated by black dots. Large colored circles represent moth populations composed largely of light forms, whereas the shaded area represents the population of predominantly dark forms.

half a mile away another. Figure 20–9 shows the breeding pattern among the demes of a population; heavy arrows indicate that a free flow of genes is possible in the complete population (the total gene pool). This figure also shows what happens to the mating pattern if the population is split—that is, if individuals in demes A and B can still mate and exchange hereditary material with each other, but they cannot mate with individuals in demes C and D. This "splitting" of the population, then, is simply an interruption of the gene flow. Essentially, two new populations result.

We must answer two questions at this point: (1) What will happen to each of the new populations under this new mating pattern? (2) What kinds of barriers can bring about situations such as this? In answer to the first question, gene and chromosomal mutations will continue on each side of the barrier—perhaps at the same rate and of the same kind, or perhaps not. The environments on either side of the barrier may be different, or they may change because of the barrier. Through natural selection or through chance, certain hereditary features may be incorporated into one popula-

(a)   (b)

FIGURE 20–7   The peppered moth and its black variety, *carbon-aria*. (a) On a soot-covered oak trunk near Birmingham, England. (b) On a lichen-covered tree trunk in unpolluted countryside, Dean-end Wood, Dorset, England. (From the experiments of Dr. B. D. Kettlewell, University of Oxford.)

tion and not in the other. If the two populations remain separated long enough, selection may cause different gene and chromosome mutations to be incorporated into the separate populations. If, after an extended period of time, organisms from the two populations come together again, they may no longer be able to produce fertile offspring. When this happens, two species exist where only one was present before; we say that *speciation* has taken place. The general time required for this to occur has been estimated as between 10,000 and 1,000,000 years. This large variation in time results from variations in rates of mutation, natural selection, and the time required to produce new generations. The effects of a barrier on a population and the eventual results are summarized in Figure 20–10.

Isolating Mechanisms

The first barriers in the splitting of a population are usually geographic features such as mountain ranges, rivers, or deserts. Such a barrier could be produced when a river cuts through land or when an earthquake dams up a river, changing its course or forming a lake. Mountain-building forces or landslides caused by earthquakes could separate a population with a land mass. Any extensive, unsuitable habitat within the territory of a population will tend to isolate parts of that population. Thus geographic barriers can be preexisting entities such as large expanses of water or high mountain ranges that act as selective "sieves" in the speciation process.

But the formation of new species also re-

FIGURE 20-8 Polymorphism in the land snail, *Helicella virgata.* Note the banded and unbanded forms. Which blend in better on this plant? (M. W. F. Tweedie, National Audubon Society/ Photo Researchers.)

quires the presence of a *biological barrier,* some reproductive isolating mechanism, that prevents the two groups from producing fertile offspring should they come together again. Such biological barriers may include incompatibility of gametes, differences in behavior, or differences in breeding season. One type of biological isolation occurs between two closely related species of pine trees in California. Interbreeding is not possible because the pollen of one species is mature in February, and the pollen of the other is not ready until April. Differences in behavior may isolate two closely related fish species that occupy the same stream. The male of one species of stickleback, for example, may construct its nest slightly

differently from the male of another species, and the females of each species can recognize the difference. Several species of fiddler crabs may occupy the same shore, but the courtship dance performed by the male of each species differs so that only the female of his own species is attracted to him. The donkey and the horse came from similar ancestral stock; they can be mated to produce a sterile mule. The isolating mechanism here, called "hybrid inviability," results from incompatible chromosomes that cannot undergo synapsis at meiosis. The mule cannot produce viable gametes and is therefore a sterile organism.

Both geographical and biological isolating mechanisms are important in speciation. Most biologists believe that usually geographical or spatial isolation must occur first; after that, some type of biological barrier develops to cause reproductive isolation of the two groups of the original population. Speciation thus requires that two important conditions be fulfilled: (1) genetic variability must exist in the population; and (2) the population must be split by isolating mechanisms known as barriers. If these conditions are in effect long enough, speciation will certainly occur.

In Chapter 2 we discussed the Grand Canyon and its geologic timetable. The Grand Canyon also provides a notable example of speciation. The Grand Canyon could certainly have acted as a geographical barrier to divide any population that once occupied the entire area. (It would be a geographic barrier even to birds: it is wide enough to minimize mating between individuals on opposite sides.) Speciation by this means is believed to have occurred in the case of the Kaibab squirrel on the north rim and the Abert squirrel of the south rim (Figure 20-11). These two squirrels are very similar in appearance, with tufted ears and bushy tails, yet they are generally considered to be two distinct species because they cannot interbreed.The canyon is thought to be the barrier that caused their genetic divergence. Several other species in this area have apparently undergone similar isolation and speciation, including the pocket mouse and the antelope squirrel.

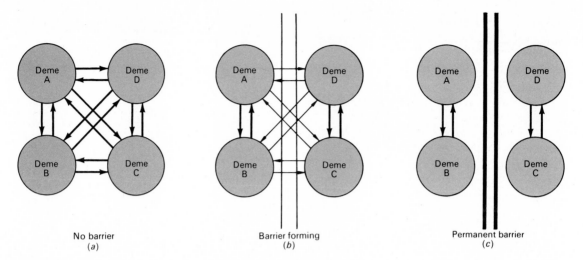

FIGURE 20-9   The splitting of a population by a barrier. (*a*) Initially, free mating among all demes occurs. (*b*) A barrier is forming. (*c*) The barrier has become permanent, restricting mating to form two separate breeding groups. The word *barrier* has two senses here: *Biological* barriers, or genetic isolating mechanisms, usually arise from the isolating effect of *geological* barriers such as mountain ranges.

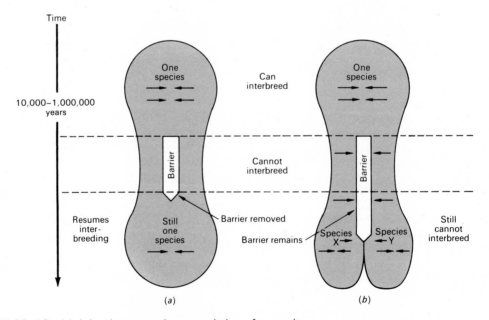

FIGURE 20-10   (*a*) A barrier occurs in a population of a species, but it does not persist long enough for speciation to occur. (*b*) The barrier lasts longer, and two species result.

(a)   (b)

FIGURE 20–11   Closely related squirrels of the Grand Canyon.
(a) The Kaibab, from the north rim, has a distinctly larger and
whiter tail. (Courtesy of Grand Canyon National Park, U.S. Department of the Interior.) (b) The Abert, from the south side, has a
white underside. (Courtesy of National Park Service, U.S. Department of the Interior.)

Polyploidy: "Instant Speciation"

Another mechanism, involving the doubling of
complete chromosome sets, can also produce
new species, especially among plants. In Chapter 4 we discussed diploid ($2n$) and haploid (n)
cells. Most diploid organisms that reproduce
sexually have haploid gametes. But occasionally, because of nondisjunction, diploid ($2n$)
gametes may form. Fertilization between two
diploid gametes results in a new organism with
a $4n$ (tetraploid) chromosome composition.
Tetraploid forms cannot mate with diploid
forms, but they can interbreed. This is a case of
"instantaneous speciation," because these new
polyploid forms can interbreed, and are reproductively isolated from their parents. Polyploidy thus serves as an isolating mechanism.

Polyploid hybrids can be produced by combining diploid gametes of two species. A well-
known example is the tetraploid hybrid of rad-
ish (*Raphanus*) and cabbage (*Brassica*), both of
which have a $2n$ chromosome number of 18.
The tetraploid, *Raphanobrassica*, received two
sets of chromosomes from each parent for a
total of 36. These hybrids cannot breed with
either parent type but are themselves fertile, so
they constitute a new species.

Species of grains with desirable characteristics have been developed by polyploid hybridization. For example, the normal $2n$ chromosome number of wheat is 14, but through
various hybrid combinations species with $4n$
(28) and $6n$ (42) have been produced for use as
food (Figure 20–12). Crosses have recently been
made between wheat (*Triticum*) and rye
(*Secale*) to produce a new genus, *Triticale*. This
hybrid, which is proving to be an important
food source in many countries, combines the
hardiness of rye with the high protein yield of
wheat (Figure 20–13).

Polyploidy has apparently been very important in plant evolution. It is estimated that well
over half of the existing species of seed plants
were formed in this manner. On the other
hand, polyploidy is quite rare as a speciation
mechanism among animals because of the XY
sex determination mechanism. Polyploidy ap-

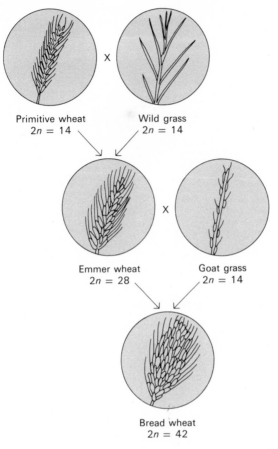

FIGURE 20–12   Development of modern bread wheat through a series of hybridizations that occurred naturally in the Mediterranean region. The complex story involved the natural crossing of a wild wheat with two different grasses. Apparently these events, taking place in the last 10,000 years, produced a wheat with 42 chromosomes.

parently occurs only in a few hermaphroditic species of animals.

DIVERGENCE AND ADAPTIVE RADIATION

The speciation process explains how species can be created. Moreover, each new species may itself undergo speciation at a later time. This further *divergence* leads to *adaptive radiation*, the process in which individuals of a particular species move into different habitats where speciation may continue. Eventually, a variety of species result. This process accounts for the diversity of the millions of different species of living systems on the earth today. Classification systems reflect this divergence; the members of a classification category are simply the subgroups that have diverged from a common ancestral group (Figure 20–14).

Important radiations have occurred in some of the large familiar groups of animals such as placental mammals, (Figure 20–15), marsupial mammals, and the phylum Mollusca. But for our example we will return to a group already discussed—Darwin's finches (Figure 20–16). An ancestral finch species arriving in the Galápagos Islands could have radiated into all avail-

FIGURE 20–13   Speciation by polyploidy. Wheat, *Triticum* (a), is crossed with rye, *Secale* (b), to produce a hybrid genus, *Triticale* (c). (Courtesy of E. N. Larter, University of Manitoba.)

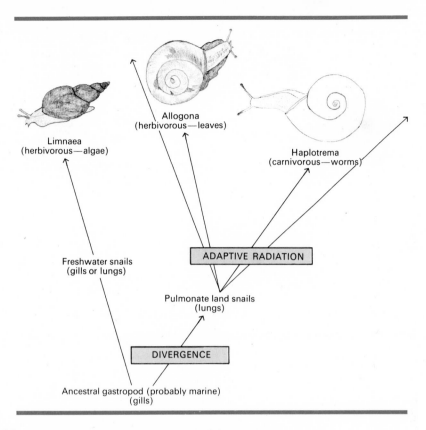

Limnaea
(herbivorous—algae)

Allogona
(herbivorous—leaves)

Haplotrema
(carnivorous—worms)

Freshwater snails
(gills or lungs)

ADAPTIVE RADIATION

Pulmonate land snails
(lungs)

DIVERGENCE

Ancestral gastropod (probably marine)
(gills)

FIGURE 20–14   Evolutionary divergence in snails. Gills developed in the freshwater snails, whereas lungs evolved in the land snails. Note that adaptive radiation occurred in the two closely related pulmonates.

able habitats and ecological niches. Finches could even fill niches usually filled by woodpeckers and warblers, because there was no competition. Some of the finches eat seeds; others feed on insects. Some of the seed eaters eat only cactus seeds, whereas others have adapted to the seeds of various other plants. This speciation and subsequent adaptive radiation was possible because the original species was dispersed throughout the widely separated islands. Because of this isolation, hereditary dissimilarities developed to a point where speciation could occur. The great expanse of water (650 miles) acted as an effective barrier, because finches do not normally fly great distances.

Darwin's finches can be divided into four categories, based on their habitats and food-gathering characteristics:

1. *Ground finches:* six species that feed on seeds of varying sizes. The size of the seed each species eats is related to the size of the bill. Competition for food is therefore avoided.

2. *Tree finches:* six species that live in moist forests and feed on insects in the trees. One tree finch, *C. pallidus*, uses a cactus spine to probe insects from crevices. It occupies a typical woodpecker niche. The use of tools by animals other than humans is quite rare, and the spine-using finch is unique among birds.

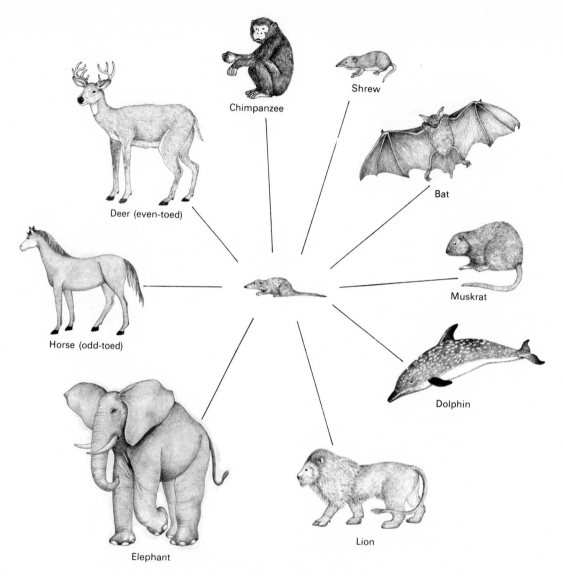

FIGURE 20–15   Adaptive radiation in placental mammals. An unspecialized ancestor (center) is believed to have given rise to the
various types of placental mammals we see today.

3. *Warblerlike finch:* a single species that has found a habitat in the low bushes, feeding on insects.

4. *Cocos Island finch:* a single species that lives in a moist forest and feeds on insects. This bird is isolated from all the others, since Cocos Island is several hundred miles to the northeast of the main group. The Cocos Island species is thought to have come directly from the mainland and thus to be only indirectly related to the others.

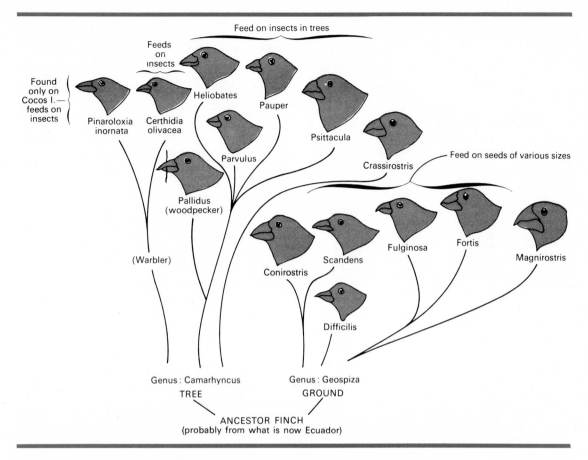

FIGURE 20-16 Adaptive radiation as shown by Darwin's finches. The initial radiation involved habitat—ground and trees. Subsequent radiations were primarily on the basis of food, although they too involved habitat.

CONVERGENCE AND PARALLELISM

Another evolutionary pattern occurs when two groups of organisms with different ancestry develop similar characteristics such as locomotion, food habits, and habitation. Moreover, the physical characteristics of such animals tend to be similar with regard to teeth, limbs, eyes, ears, and other features. This process, known as *convergence*, has occurred in marsupial and placental mammals (Figure 20–17). In placental mammals the embryo develops inside a mother's uterus, attached by a placenta; marsupial embryos undergo an immature birth and then complete their development in an abdominal pouch on the mother. Placental mammals live extensively in all parts of the world. Although marsupial mammals are found in various parts of the world, their main development has been in Australia. There they have radiated into almost every available niche. The principal reason for their extensive evolution in Australia was probably the absence of competition from placental mammals.

Convergence among fairly closely related organisms such as these is often called *parallelism*. It is interesting that no marsupial has

PLACENTAL MAMMALS   MARSUPIAL MAMMALS

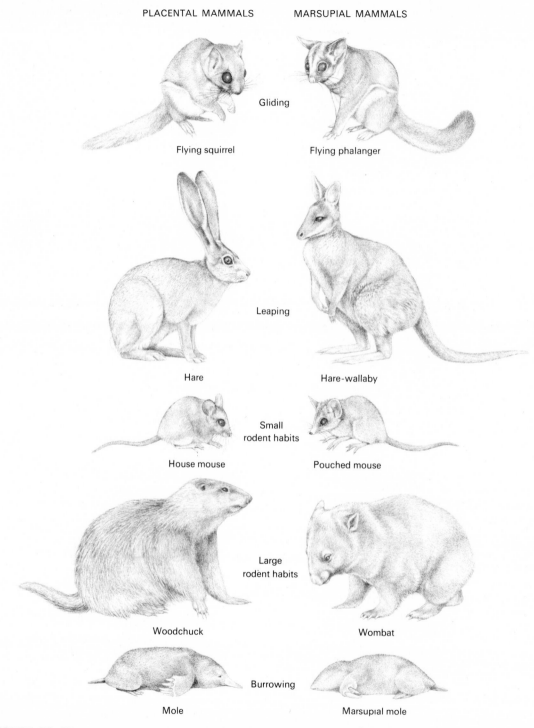

Gliding

Flying squirrel   Flying phalanger

Leaping

Hare   Hare-wallaby

Small
rodent habits

House mouse   Pouched mouse

Large
rodent habits

Woodchuck   Wombat

Burrowing

Mole   Marsupial mole

FIGURE 20–17   Convergent evolution in placental and marsupial mammals.

adapted to the flying niche represented in placentals by bats. Some ecologists have proposed that this flying niche in Australia may have been filled by bats from Asia, so that marsupials could not compete successfully.

EXTINCTION: THE EVENTUAL FATE OF SPECIES

Extinction is also a part of the evolutionary process. Only a small proportion of all the species that ever lived are still alive today. As we emphasized at the beginning of this Unit, change is a universal characteristic of nature. Species change and eventually become extinct—but before they do, other species may evolve from them. The dinosaurs offer perhaps the most striking example of the extinction of a large group. The year 1914 marked the extinction of the passenger pigeon. The intense selection pressure of hunters so reduced the population of this species that the few remaining individuals had too little variation to survive as a species. Selection pressure, of course, is always responsible for the extinction of a species. Some change in the environment—a change in climate, the arrival of a new predator, the rise of a more efficient competitor for the same habitat, or some other factor—reduces the population until the species finally disappears.

What will happen to the human species? Will *Homo sapiens* become extinct? Will it give rise to new species capable of meeting the challenge of a changing environment? It seems only fitting to conclude this Unit on evolution with a discussion of the evolution of our own species and where we may be heading. This we shall do in Chapter 21.

Bio-Topic: Endangered Species: The Living Dead?

One of the keys to evolutionary success is a proper balance between fitness and flexibility. Each generation must be fit enough to survive in the prevailing conditions. Yet the species must retain the flexibility to respond to unpredictable changes in the environment. The "proper" balance between fitness and flexibility depends on the life style and circumstances of each species.

Fitness and flexibility both derive from the gene pool of each species. A gene pool that includes a high proportion of adaptive alleles and few alternative alleles defines a fit, but inflexible, species. A gene pool that includes fewer adaptive alleles and more alternative alleles defines a less fit, but more flexible, species. Alternative alleles are a hedge against an unpredictable future—but a species must be able to afford flexibility.

A species that consists of a very large number of individuals can accommodate a large number of alternative alleles spread over the large number of individuals. A species that consists of a very small number of individuals does not have this capacity. A species with a few individuals and many alternative alleles would produce a high proportion of less fit individuals each generation—a costly strategy for a small population.

Species that consist of a very few individuals are today called "endangered species." The term reflects our perception that the species may soon become extinct unless the forces that reduced its population are eliminated. But from the evolutionary perspective, an endangered species has already lost much of its fitness (it cannot survive) and much of its flexibility (its gene pool cannot accommodate many alternative alleles). A species that is neither fit nor flexible may, for all practical purposes, already be an extinct species.

SUMMARY

Population genetics, which deals with the total gene pool of a population, has contributed to our understanding of evolution. This is true because evolution is the result of changing gene frequencies in populations. Genotype frequencies in natural populations do not always remain the same from one generation to another because mutations, selection, and migration occur. The Hardy-Weinberg principle, which predicts stable gene frequencies, provides a theoretical base against which to compare the actual process in nature. The trait of sickle-cell hemoglobin can be studied as an illustration of the Hardy-Weinberg principle.

The modern concept of evolution, Neo-Darwinism, attributes variation in living systems to genes. It recognizes that changes in species and subsequent natural selection result from genetic changes along with environmental selection for characteristics of adaptive value. Differential reproduction occurs within a population as a result of natural selection. Adaptations are traits that enhance an organism's chance for survival and reproduction in an environment. Polymorphism, which permits species to inhabit various environments, may be very useful in adapting as conditions change.

It is generally accepted that in order for new species to develop, an isolating mechanism must separate two parts of a population long enough for genotypes to become incompatible. In time, further selection upon these two gene pools may give rise to other new species. Polyploidy can also produce new species, especially in plants.

Divergence and adaptive radiation help to explain how a variety of related species can evolve to inhabit many environments. Convergence and parallelism are patterns of evolution in which groups of organisms with different ancestry develop similar characteristics.

REVIEW QUESTIONS

1. What conditions can change gene frequencies in a population? Why is the Hardy-Weinberg principle important in the study of evolution and gene frequencies?

2. How can the proportion of a recessive gene increase in a population?

3. How does the modern concept of evolution (Neo-Darwinism) differ from the Darwin-Wallace theory? What is meant by differential reproduction?

4. What sources of genetic variation are necessary for the evolutionary process to occur?

5. Compare the explanations Lamarck, Darwin, and modern biologists would give for the development of long necks in giraffes.

6. Two marine organisms, the lampshell and the horseshoe crab, appear relatively unchanged from their fossil ancestors dating back more than 300,000,000 years, whereas the horse has changed radically in only 60,000,000 years. How can you account for this difference in rates of evolution?

7. Bacteria exposed to penicillin through a number of generations have been found to develop an immunity to this antibiotic. What is the probable explanation for this?

8. Using mammals, give an example of adaptive radiation and an example of convergent evolution.

9. Show the relationship between the Hardy-Weinberg principle and the concept of natural selection.

10. If you were a researcher who desired a race of rats smaller than normal, how would you set up a breeding program to accomplish this? What problems might you encounter?

SUPPLEMENTARY READINGS

Bishop, J. A. and Laurence M. Cook, "Moths, Melanism, and Clean Air," *Scientific American*, January 1975. Dark-colored moths have had an advantage in recent times in the industrially polluted air of England. Now, as the air quality improves, the light-colored forms are being favored.

Cerami, Anthony and C. M. Peterson, "Cyanate and Sickle-Cell Disease," *Scientific American*, April 1975. Sodium cyanate can be used to inhibit the sickling of red blood cells in persons suffering sickle-cell anemia. Since the cyanate reacts with the terminal amino acid of hemoglobin, it is the first drug used to modify a product of an abnormal gene to restore normal function.

Clarke, Bryan, "The Causes of Biological Diversity," *Scientific American*, August 1975. Diversity among organisms occurs at many levels including the chemical composition of their proteins. Evolution of diversity is not an orderly progression in which one type replaces another, but rather a shifting of dynamic equilibriums maintained by natural selection.

Hulse, Joseph H. and David Spurgeon, "Triticale," *Scientific American*, August 1974. A hybrid of wheat and rye, triticale combines the high yield of wheat with the hardiness of rye. It can be used for animal feed as well as a substitute for wheat products.

Stebbins, G. L., *Processes of Organic Evolution*, 2nd edition, Prentice-Hall, Englewood Cliffs, NJ, 1971. A good short reference on evolution in general, this book provides an excellent presentation on speciation and population genetics.

Chapter 21

Human Evolution

The study of the evolution of our own species is one of the most interesting—and ultimately most important—subjects we will cover in this book. It is interesting because we are curious about our own biological backgrounds and re-lationships. It is an important subject because it can tell us where we are going as a species.

The story starts with the *Early Primates,* the small tree-living creatures from which we, monkeys, apes, and some other mammals de-scended. The move from the trees *Back to the Ground* was thought to be the start of the development of higher primates.

The Rise of the Human Species was not a sudden process. Over millions of years, a series of species evolved, each somewhat less apelike and somewhat more humanlike. Super-imposed on this trail of physical changes was the process of *Cultural Evolution,* through which these developing humans acquired skills that have contributed to that extraordinary characteristic of our species: culture. As we shall see, physical development and cultural development occurred together.

If we have changed in the past, are we still evolving today? How will the human culture develop? We take *A Look to the Future* and venture a few predictions.

Our influence on our environment and the other species within it would not be particu-larly significant if it were not for *The Human Impact on Evolution,* which is altering not only this generation, but future generations. Biological and medical discoveries are now af-fecting our own gene pool and setting the stage for the evolution of our own species.

In past decades, biological research has al-most always been considered a blessing—cur-ing disease, improving agriculture, contributing to a better quality of life. But as we move toward more dramatic methods of biological control, we are running into conflicts with our cultural, moral, and religious values. *Bio-ethics: Science and Human Responsibil-ity* is one of the most serious public issues of our time. And it is not simply a problem for scientists—it affects all of us.

Probably the biggest question in controlling these new techniques and skills is that of con-trol. *To Risk or Not to Risk: Who Shall Decide?* sums up the dilemma. Think of the many times you have disagreed with public policy-makers—in government, in the military, in education. They, like all of us, make mis-takes. Who should control the evolution of our own species?

How did we come to be what we are? What may we yet become? These two questions embrace the past, present, and future evolution of our own species, *Homo sapiens.* We shall probably never know the full story of our evolutionary past, and we cannot see the future. But fossil, biochemical, anatomical, and behavioral evidence, together with our understanding of evolution, has revealed a great deal about where we came from. And this same information, together with a knowledge of current trends in the biological sciences, can help us gain some idea of where we are going.

Of the many factors that have shaped the history of our species, two in particular stand out: our biological heritage as primates and our cultural heritage. As primates, we humans are much less structurally specialized than most other animals. We lack the speed of the deer, the brute strength of the horse, the flying ability of birds, the formidable teeth and claws of many carnivores, the resistance to cold of many furred and feathered animals, the phenomenally sharp vision of the hawk—and the list could go on and on.

But in fact our lack of highly specialized structures is our greatest strength as a species. Precisely because we have remained unspecialized in most respects, we have been able to adapt successfully to innumerable environmental changes during the million or so years of our evolutionary history. Extreme morphological adaptations are fine so long as the environment does not change. But when it does—and it always does, eventually—extreme specialization becomes overspecialization, and it leads to extinction. Perhaps the most specialized human structure is the brain, with its highly developed cerebral hemispheres. Although specialized in structure, this organ is functionally very generalized.

But our physical evolution alone has not made us what we are. The emergence and evolution of human *culture* has also played an indispensable role. For culture was not only created by human beings, in a very real sense it helped make them. During a large part of our past, our physical and cultural evolution proceeded together, each shaping the other. They still evolve together and shape each other, as we shall see.

Culture is the least specialized human attribute of all. Many of its specific manifestations—concepts, objects, jobs, and so forth—are very specialized indeed. The philosopher Bertrand Russell once remarked, a specialist is one "who knows more and more about less and less until he knows everything about nothing." But the *potential* of culture is unlimited—in other words, it is totally generalized. Culture thus makes the adaptive potential of our species almost limitless. Other organisms adapt to the demands of their surroundings by changing their genes. Only human beings can also adapt by changing their environments to fit their genes.

But our continually evolving culture is now giving us the power to *change* our genes by *artificial selection.* Later in this chapter we shall have more to say about cultural evolution, including genetic engineering and its bioethical implications. First, however, we shall look at our primate heritage.

EARLY PRIMATES

The first primates, apparently evolved in the early Cenozoic era, more than 60 million years ago. They were small rodentlike creatures that first lived on the ground and then moved into trees to avoid competitors and predators (Figure 21-1). Some of the primate characteristics shown by these early forms are: five digits (fingers or toes) on each limb, grasping hands or feet (an important characteristic made possible by the thumb or big toe opposing, or moving against, the other digits), eyes that face front, head capable of rotating on the spine, and a brain with highly developed cerebral hemispheres.

Living in trees opened a new niche for primates, and as time passed adaptations for this type of life, such as hands and feet with opposable digits for grasping, became "fixed" in the populations of tree dwellers. Binocular vision—vision in which both eyes focus on a single object—provided superior depth perception. The depth perception is created by com-

FIGURE 21–1   Tree shrew. Some characteristics of early primates can be seen in this species: five fingers or toes, grasping hands or feet, and front-facing eyes. The long snout was reduced in later primates. (Ron Garrison; San Diego Zoo.)

parison in the brain of the two separate, slightly different images. This development too helped tree dwellers in swinging from limb to limb; to misjudge distance could be (and probably often was) a fatal mistake. Eyes that faced forward probably contributed to the evolution of a larger and more complex brain to process and interpret this visual input.

At the same time, the snout was shrinking. The advantages of a long probing snout for ground dwellers that use all four limbs for walking are obvious. But when limbs become available for manipulation, a snout is no longer necessary for grasping and tearing food. A shorter snout also improves vision. Moreover, the keen sense of smell made possible by a longer snout is less advantageous for arboreal life than for life on the ground, where smell is essential for tracking food and evading predators. Tree dwellers depend more on sight than on smell.

Back to the Ground

But many present-day primates, including gorillas, baboons, and chimpanzees, spend much of their time on the ground. Some environmental change must have brought certain primates back down out of the trees. This return to the ground is thought to have occurred when the great forests of the Tertiary period disappeared more than 30 million years ago, as climatic changes caused grasslands to replace forest lands. At about this time the primate group that gave rise to the anthropoids (monkeys, apes, and humans) is believed to have separated from the prosimian line that gave rise to modern tree shrews, lemurs, and tarsiers. Some primate forms stayed in the trees, however; their descendents are found today in some areas where forests have not been replaced by grasslands or other biomes. Lemurs, for example, now live on the island of Madagascar off the east coast of Africa (and nowhere else), and various types of monkeys live in tropical forests of Central and South America (Figure 21–2).

In the preceding chapter we noted that during the evolution of the horse, various forms existed at the same time; one form did not replace another in a nonoverlapping, straight-line sequence. The primates underwent a similar nonlinear evolutionary change. To explain it, we again turn to changes in gene frequencies for our explanation. The gradual change from life in trees to ground life that occurred in several primate groups over a long period of time was associated with genotype changes in populations. Some individuals with certain genotypes spent more time on the ground than others. Through differential reproduction, gen-

otypes associated with ground dwelling increased in the various populations.

The Upright Condition

One more extremely important adaptation had to occur before the primates completed their transition to living on the ground: They had to attain an upright posture. Standing upright increases chances for survival by permitting a better view of enemies, aiding in the search for food, and facilitating communication with other members of one's species. An upright position also frees two limbs for securing food, fighting, and grasping and carrying objects (some of which would, in time, become tools). Development of an upright posture required certain structural modifications of the skeletal

(a)

(b)

FIGURE 21–2 (a) White-fronted lemurs: male at left, female at right. (b) Mindanao tarsier. (Ron Garrison; San Diego Zoo.)

and muscular systems. The vertebral column developed a moderate S-shaped curve; muscle attachments changed or developed differently, as in the muscles of the buttocks; and modifications occurred in the attachment of the head to the top of the vertebral column. In addition, the tail tended to disappear. A tail is of little assistance to upright ground dwellers, and humans have only vestigial vertebrae as tail remnants. In this rearrangement, the body's center of gravity shifted from a point in front of the pelvis to a position directly over it (Figure 21–3).

As these modifications gradually took place, our precursors became able to hunt and travel as never before. An upright posture with an upright gait enabled these prehumans to exploit new niches and ways of life. These anatomical developments—along with a larger brain with increased capacity for visual perception and memory—opened many new modes of life to our still apelike yet increasingly humanoid ancestors.

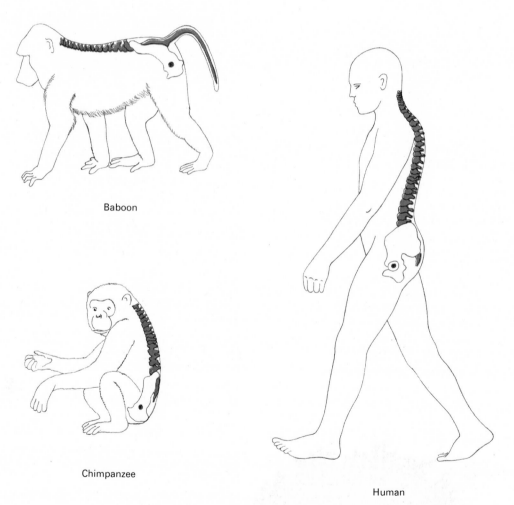

Baboon

Chimpanzee

Human

FIGURE 21–3 Three different postures of primates. A baboon walks on all fours most of the time, chimpanzees have a more bipedal locomotion, and humans are completely upright.

THE RISE OF THE HUMAN SPECIES

The evolutionary events in the primate line that led ultimately to the appearance of our own species make an intriguing story which is not yet fully known. Researchers who have attempted to shed light on this story have done so mainly by studying fossils. More recently, behavioral studies of subhuman primate societies and molecular studies, particularly blood protein analyses (Figure 21-4), have contributed to our understanding of primate evolution. For example, the currently accepted general scheme of primate evolution shows that humans are more closely related to chimpanzees and gorillas, than to Old World monkeys and gibbons (Figure 21-5).

Human Forerunners

Recent discoveries in East Africa and Asia have led most paleontologists to conclude that chimpanzees, gorillas, orangutans, and humans descended from different species of small apes of the now extinct genus *Dryopithecus* (Figure 21-6) which lived during the Miocene epoch. A few teeth and jaw fragments of a somewhat later form named *Ramapithecus* have been found in India and Africa. This genus, considered to have arisen about 14 million years ago, is generally agreed to be an intermediate between *Dryopithecus* and *Australopithecus*, the humanoid ape. We have very little evidence about the pre-Pleistocene ancestors of the gibbon and orangutan of Asia, but they are thought to have split off the stem group during the Miocene or somewhat earlier. We now have somewhat more information on the development of hominids (the family *Hominidae*) in the Pleistocene era, which began some 2 million years ago. Some of the evolutionary gaps in the fossil record have been filled by the discovery of *Australopithecus* (Figure 21-7) in South Africa by Raymond Dart in 1924, and *Zinjanthropus* in East Africa by the late L. S. B. Leakey in 1959. *Zinjanthropus*, now considered as a species of *Australopithecus*, has been estimated to be nearly 2 million years old by radioactive dating.

In general, these humanoid apes (or, perhaps more appropriately, "near-humans") had large faces but small brains not much larger than 600 cubic centimeters. (The modern human brain averages about 1400 cubic centimeters.) The skeletal structure of *Australopithecus* indicates that they were about four feet tall, walked upright, and had stereoscopic vision. Their teeth show human characteristics. Moreover, *Australopithecus* had the ability to use tools; both Dart and Leakey found stone tools with skeletal remains of *Australopithecus* in their excavations.

A study of the fossil remains of African near-humans has led many scientists to conclude that one species of *Australopithecus*, now renamed *Homo transvaalensis*, began to manufacture chip-edged tools about 1½ million years ago. *Homo transvaalensis*, who appears to have been omnivorous, was gradually replaced about 700,000 years ago by another omnivore, *Homo erectus*, who was a more highly skilled tool maker. *Homo erectus* possessed a larger brain (about 1300 cubic centimeters), and apparently had a societal mode of life. Remains of this species have been located in Java, China, and Central and South Africa. Java and Peking man (formerly called *Pithecanthropus*) and Leakey's *Homo habilis* from Kenya are now all classified as *Homo erectus* (Figure 21-8). A 1972 find by Richard Leakey has been dated at 2½ million years. Two later discoveries, one in 1974 by Mary Leakey (wife of L. S. B. Leakey) and one in 1975 by Carl Johanson of Case Western Reserve University, suggest that true specimens of the genus *Homo* existed well over 3 million years ago. This new evidence, indicating that a larger-brained, truly upright hominid lived at the same time as *Australopithecus*, casts serious doubt on the hypothesis that modern humans evolved directly from *Australopithecus*.

Homo Sapiens

The transition from *Homo erectus* to the forerunners of modern *Homo sapiens* is still not entirely clear. We can, however, cite the Neanderthal form as a representative who lived

FIGURE 21–4   Comparison of blood proteins, showing evolutionary relationships. (*a*) Human. (*b*) Gorilla. (*c*) Chimpanzee. (*d*) Gibbon. These patterns are produced when blood serum samples are exposed to an electrical field while on a carrier substance such as filter paper or starch gel. Since proteins vary in size and electrical charge, they move along the carrier at different rates. The patterns of humans, gorillas, and chimpanzees are similar; the pattern of gibbons is considerably different. This evidence supports the theory that the African chimpanzee and gorilla are more closely related to humans than is the Asian gibbon. (Redrawn from Sherwood L. Washburn, editor, *Classification and Human Evolution,* Chicago: Aldine Publishing Company, 1963; copyright © 1963 by Wenner-Gren Foundation for Anthropological Research, Inc. by permission of the author and Aldine Publishing Company.)

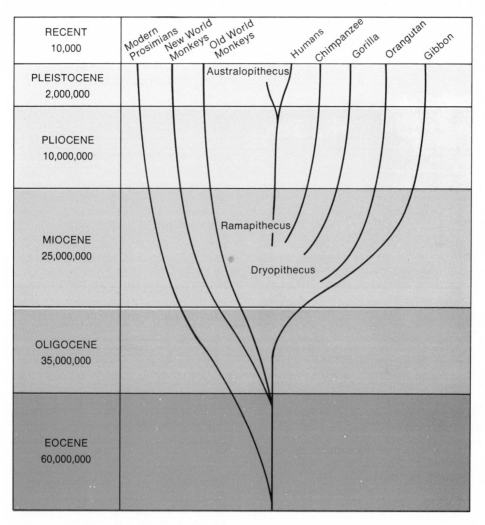

FIGURE 21-5   Generalized family tree of the primates. Times
shown at left are approximate times in years from the beginning
of each geologic epoch.

70,000 to 100,000 years ago. *Homo sapiens neanderthalensis* lived in Europe and Asia and had a brain volume of 1500 cubic centimeters, larger than that of the average modern human. The skeletal bones were thick and heavy, especially those of the limbs. The neanderthal had a low, sloping forehead and heavy brow ridges (Figure 21–9).

The fossil record leads finally to the European form known as Cro-Magnon, first discovered in caves in southern France in 1868. In this type we see a well-developed chin, moderate brow ridges, and a high, full forehead very similar to modern Europeans (Figure 21–10). In addition, Cro-Magnon possessed longer, thinner shin bones than did Neanderthal. It is suspected that Neanderthal became extinct about 30,000 to 35,000 years ago and was superseded by Cro-Magnon, who gave rise to the modern races of humans. Cro-Magnon and Neanderthal

FIGURE 21–6   Drawing of the probable appearance of *Dryopithecus*. (Trustees of the British Museum [Natural History].)

populations were most probably parallel lines of development existing at the same time. Several hypotheses have been advanced for the disappearance of the Neanderthal form. Extermination by rival humans and gradual incorporation by interbreeding have been proposed, but the fossil record has not yet supplied an answer. The answer probably lies in a factor that which cannot be supplied by fossils, such as the ability to communicate by speech. It has been suggested that Neanderthals could not speak, at least not like modern humans. Such an inability might have placed them at a disadvantage in competing with forms that could speak and led to the Neanderthals' decline.

The exact shape of the evolutionary tree leading to modern higher primates is obscured by the simultaneous occurrence, at various times past, of many diverse primate types. But the general picture as currently understood is as follows. Some 30 million years ago a small, short-armed ape, *Dryopithecus*, provided the basic stock for the various lines of apes and hominids. *Ramapithecus* evolved from this line and produced the genera *Australopithecus* and *Homo*. Members of the genus *Homo* developed from a beginning probably more than 3.5 million years ago and culminated in modern humans of the species *Homo sapiens*. Humans probably originated in Africa, where fossils of *Australopithecus* and *Homo* have been found. Tool use was an important early (pre-*Homo*) development as hominids moved from Africa to other areas of the earth. Speech and brain development permitted the further evolution of culture as humans became settled in various parts of the world (Figure 21–11).

Cultural Evolution

Human evolution differs from that of all other species because of *culture*. It is not quite true that our species is the sole possessor of culture. But we certainly possess it to a degree unrivaled by any other species, and we would not be truly human without it. What, then, is culture?

Anthropologists and sociologists—scientists whose fields of study are human evolution, development, and societies—have formulated many definitions of culture. The anthropologist E. A. Hoebel has defined it as "the integrated system of learned behavior patterns which are characteristic of the members of a society and which are not the result of biological inheritance." And the sociologist Robert Bierstedt has written that "Culture is the complex whole that consists of all the ways we think and do and everything we have as members of society."

These two definitions of *culture* stress somewhat different, but nonetheless important, aspects of the concept. The following characteristics of culture are important to us here:

1. Every human social group and every individual has culture. In the scientific sense, *cul-*

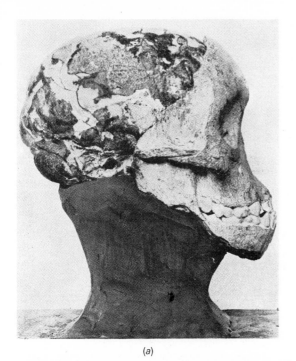

(a)   (b)

FIGURE 21–7   (a) *Australopithecus* skull. (b) *Australopithecus*
restoration. (Courtesy of the American Museum of Natural
History.)

FIGURE 21–8   *Homo erectus* (formerly *Pithecanthropus*) restoration. (Courtesy of the American Museum of Natural History.)

FIGURE 21–9   Reconstruction of a Neanderthal family group. (Field Museum of Natural History, Chicago.)

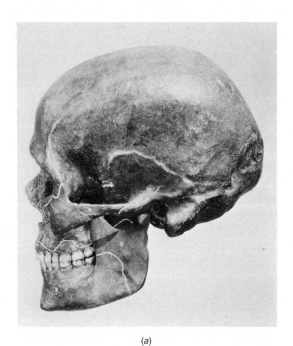

(a)   *(b)*

FIGURE 21–10   Cro-Magnon. *(a)* Skull. *(b)* Restoration. (Courtesy of the American Museum of Natural History.)

Bio-Topic: Hybrids and Humans

The evolution of Australopithecus to Homo sapiens occupied about two million years, a remarkably short time for such a transformation. The earliest Homo sapiens were hunter-gatherers who lived a nomadic life. By 20,000 years ago, some tribes had learned to follow and exploit herds of wild, migratory animals. A mere 10,000 years later, our ancestors had already begun to cultivate plants, domesticate animals, and settle in villages.

The change from a nomadic life to village agriculture was perhaps the largest single step in our cultural evolution. The change began about 10,000 BC, at the end of the last Ice Age, and was based on three genetic accidents in the grasses our ancestors foraged for.

Seeds had long been an important part of the hominid diet. It has even been suggested that the human hand is an adaptation for gathering and handling small seeds and grains. It was quite natural for early humans to gather the small grains of the wild wheats that flourished at the end of the last Ice Age.

The first genetic accident was the natural hybridization of a wild wheat and a goat grass. Each parent had 14 chromosomes, the fertile hybrid we know as Emmer, 28. The larger, more nutritious grains of Emmer formed in loose heads. Winds shook the grains loose and dispersed them widely. Natural populations of Emmer were large and common.

The second genetic accident involved another natural hybridization—this time between Emmer and another goat grass. The new hybrid had 42 chromosomes and would have been sterile except for a crucial mutation that conferred fertility—the third genetic accident. The new hybrid, the first bread wheat, formed very large, nutritious grains. The grains, however, were formed in heads that were so tight that dispersal by the wind was inefficient. Humans must soon have realized that this new, attractive grain did not form large, natural populations as Emmer did. To exploit this improved grain it would be necessary to plant seeds, await the harvest, and do so each year. So began the agricultural revolution.

Agriculture was reinvented many times in many places. A similar series of genetic accidents in the New World, for example, led to an agricultural civilization based on corn. The agricultural revolution was the first triumph of our species over nature. We learned then that we could control some facets of our environment. And we have been doing so ever since.

ture does not mean personal refinement or the "higher" achievements of a society, such as its paintings, poems, symphonies, or scientific theories. The concept of culture does include such things, however, as Bierstedt's definition makes clear.

2. Culture is *learned* rather than instinctive or otherwise genetically determined. Language, for instance, is a cultural (and therefore a human) "universal": all peoples everywhere have one, and there are many hundreds of languages around the world. But a normal infant born into any culture can eventually learn any language as easily and thoroughly as any other.

3. Culture includes *things* as well as ideas and behavioral characteristics. Spears, tennis balls, books, skyscrapers, orchestras, museums, religious relics, and bumper stickers are both products and material components of culture.

4. Culture is *cumulative* and *transmissible.* The experiences and accomplishments of individuals and groups can be passed from individ-

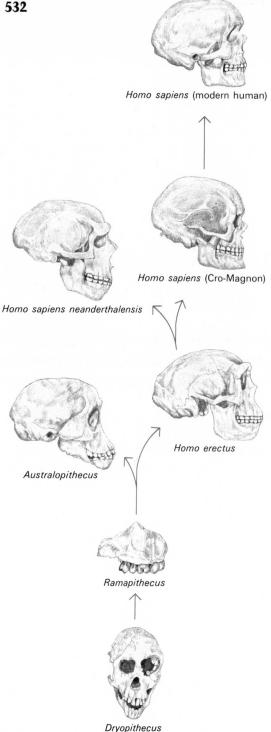

Homo sapiens (modern human)

Homo sapiens (Cro-Magnon)

Homo sapiens neanderthalensis

Homo erectus

Australopithecus

Ramapithecus

Dryopithecus

FIGURE 21–11 Proposed lineage from *Dryopithecus* to modern humans.

ual to individual and from generation to generation, providing the social group with an immensely larger stock of knowledge, behaviors, and objects than any individual could possibly acquire first-hand.

5. The accumulation and transmission of human culture are greatly facilitated by culture's greatest innovation, language. To appreciate the immense value of this capacity, just think how very little you would know and be able to do were it not for language. Many motor skills as well as cognitive abilities depend heavily on it. You could probably learn to ride a bicycle and perhaps to drive a car after a fashion, and you might even learn a rudimentary form of tennis without language. But without language there would be no tennis to learn to play and no bicycles or autos to learn to use. Language gives our species a means of communicating, creating, and storing vast amounts of information that could not be created, communicated, or stored without it.

6. Culture is not limited to humans. Certain other species also show some degree of socially learned behavior—behavior learned from other members of the same species and passed from generation to generation. Some biologists and social scientists prefer to use the term *tradition* instead of *culture* when referring to socially learned "ways of doing" and the products of such activities.

7. Even though it is learned and not instinctive or otherwise genetically determined, culture is in a very real sense a *biological* phenomenon. This follows from the fact that behavior itself is a biological phenomenon, as we saw in Chapters 17 and 18. Items of material culture—shoes, shovels, ships, and so on—are not "biological" in the sense of being alive or even made of once-living material. But they are the products of behavior and thus of biological processes.

8. Culture *evolves*. This should be obvious, given its cumulative and transmissible quality, and given the truism that the culture of today is not the culture of Julius Caesar's, George Washington's, or even Warren G. Harding's

Bio-Topic: Did Human Nature Evolve?

We are a social species. The sociability of our primate relatives and the earliest archaeological traces of our ancestors suggest that we have been social for most of our history. And, along with the other species on our planet, we are products of natural selection. It therefore seems natural to ask to what extent our social behavior is learned and to what extent it is genetically determined and the product of natural selection.

There is no question that many behaviors are genetically determined and have evolved. We call these "innate behaviors" and marvel at their precision and evolutionary utility. On the other hand, most innate behaviors are of a relatively simple sort that might well be based on genetically patterned neural connections. Neural patterning can hardly provide an explanation for complex human social behavior. When we survey the variety of human social systems—from Eskimos to New Yorkers to Bushmen—few universal patterns that might be genetically determined stand out. And the evidence for genetically determined social behavior in primates is equivocal.

E. O. Wilson of Harvard University suggests that the time is approaching when this fascinating question may be answered. He suggests that answers will come, not from philosophers or psychologists, but from neurophysiologists and evolutionary biologists. Wilson proposes the establishment of a new branch of biology, sociobiology, which he defines as "the systematic study of the biological basis of all social behavior." His argument is simple. Our understanding of the physiological basis of animal behavior is substantial and growing rapidly. Our understanding of population genetics, including the population genetics that led to the evolution of social animals is also strong. This knowledge, Wilson asserts, provides a framework within which we may begin to explore the evolution of human behavior, both past and future.

If Wilson's predictions are correct, sociobiology may, within a century or so, reveal how much of our social behavior is inherited. This knowledge and the techniques of sociobiology may enable us to control the future evolution of our behavior. We might choose to select against genes that determine aggression or to select for genes that enhance cooperation. Will we have matured enough to make such decisions?

day. Cultural evolution is much more rapid than organic evolution. Organic evidence (skeletal and dental fragments, etc.) and cultural (architectural, sculptural, and written records, etc.) evidence give us no reason to think that humans of 5000 years ago were noticeably different from ourselves anatomically or physiologically. The only exception is that they seem, on the average, to have been somewhat shorter. But 5000 years ago human culture was quite different from what it was 500 or even 50 years ago.

For the last several thousand years, the evolution of human culture has been quite independent of human organic evolution. This is obvious enough, since our culture has evolved considerably and our bodies have not. But it has not always been the case. The physical and cultural evolution of our early Homo sapiens ancestors, as well as the earlier species of Homo and the near-humans before Homo, proceeded together, each shaping the other. How, then, did cultural change become free of physical evolution?

The brain more than any other characteristic has provided humans with the capacity for culture. Thus the human brain and human culture have evolved together. Speech—the only mode of language during the millennia before writing was invented—has been a primary factor in culturation. This vocal ability developed only as anatomical changes permitted it. An erect posture, the movement of the larynx to a lower position in the throat region, more complex brain centers, and keener hearing all aided in the production and recognition of sounds. Culture could evolve more quickly once the rudiments of linguistic communication developed. Moreover, abstract ideas could not be developed or communicated until speech was available. Perhaps the phrase, "I kill deer" could be communicated by gestures and later by written symbols (Figure 21–12). But to communicate "I kill deer tomorrow" is significantly easier using speech, because *tomorrow* is an abstract concept.

A Look to the Future

As we have outlined, the human species has developed and changed significantly both physically and culturally over the past million years. The accelerated rate of cultural growth which paralleled physical development has permitted humans to exploit and control their environment. Because of this utilization of environmental resources, our cultural evolution may be outstripping our natural physical evolution. Human development has reached a stage at which our very survival depends on our culture. It appears, then, that the future cultural evolution of human beings will determine the fate of our own species as well as that of all other species in our biosphere.

Students of evolution have even speculated on the physical appearance of future human beings. These speculations vary widely, from beings showing very little change to much different forms. Proponents of the "great change"

FIGURE 21–12   Drawings from caves in France. Were these drawings, made about 10,000 years ago, designed to decorate the cave wall or to communicate an idea? (Archives Photographiques—Paris.)

hypothesis believe that because humans have changed so rapidly in their evolutionary history thus far, we can look for continued change in the future. One projected change is in the direction of a larger cranium (to accommodate a larger brain) and finer facial features. Along with this would probably come a wider female pelvic region to provide the wider birth canal required by larger-headed human infants. Another prediction is that 5000 years from now humans will be slightly taller, have a more globular skull with the sensory organs more developed, have a more refined face with fewer and smaller teeth (the wisdom teeth, already vestigial, will disappear), have less hair on the body, and have a smaller appendix. We can be almost certain that some changes will occur, since we know that all species are mutable. The human species may also change as a result of changes humans produce in the environment or through genetic hybridization between human cells and other cells.

THE HUMAN IMPACT ON EVOLUTION

With greater brain development, humans gained the ability to formulate ethical, moral, religious, and biological concepts about the place of the human species in nature. These concepts, in their modern version, underlie today's growing concern about ecological matters. And the ability to use tools, along with imagination and creativity, have provided a technology that seems capable of almost limitless accomplishments. Humans have become evolutionary agents who can modify, create, and destroy species through interference with the natural environment. Practically every domestic plant or animal we use for our subsistence has been selected and bred by humans for that role. Human beings can also bring a species to extinction or near-extinction, as in the cases of the passenger pigeon and the American bison. In fact, extinction of large mammals such as wooly mammoths in northern Eurasia, saber-toothed tigers in what is now California, and giant ground sloths in Central America followed migrations of primitive humans as early as 50,000 years ago.

Humans can regulate populations of wild animals such as deer through game management policies. In other words, nature is not the same since humans evolved. Humans can, if they choose, control the evolutionary development of other species.

But can we control our own evolution? It would appear that we can, since we understand the selective process and are learning more and more about the hereditary mechanism. Our chief problem lies in finding answers to two questions: "How can we establish the principles to be used in selecting human characteristics?" "Which characteristics will be selected?" At the present time, many people would agree that certain traits are harmful to the human species, but the legal procedures required to bring about selection against these traits might be too difficult to achieve.

Medical technology has advanced so far that many individuals with maladaptive genes reproduce, so their genes are retained in the gene pool of the human population. This certainly affects human biological evolution, since under natural conditions most of these genes would be "selected out." Through the use of surgery, artificial aids (such as eyeglasses), and the addition or withholding of chemical substances (insulin, gamma globulin, proteins), both genetic and nongenetic diseases can be controlled, but they cannot be eliminated at the genetic level. From a purely biological viewpoint, then, our gene pool is being cluttered with many genes that are disadvantageous to human evolution. Perhaps technology and other aspects of our culture can take care of the problems created by this accumulation of maladaptive genes. But, on the other hand, we must ask whether our culture can ultimately survive the effects of so many disadvantageous genes.

Many people fear legal control of human heredity, since its use obviously depends on who is in power. There are others, though, who believe that we will be forced to apply our knowledge of genetics and evolution to our own species if we are to survive and develop to our fullest capacities. It becomes evident, then, that the future course of human evolution may be shaped more by ethics, technology, and politics, than by natural forces.

BIOETHICS: SCIENCE AND HUMAN RESPONSIBILITY

Since the future of humanity will inevitably be shaped by human attitudes toward life—especially toward human life—it is extremely important that people be aware of what is being done in the biological sciences today and what may be done in the future. The term *bioethics* refers to the moral, or ethical, aspects of anything done in biology which could affect the human species. Bioethics has many facets, including the impacts of biological science on the individual, the family, the community, society, and the human species as a whole.

Consider for a moment the use of placebos in medicine. Placebos are therapies that have no direct effect on the illness for which they are prescribed. Many types of placebos, are used today, including antibiotics, vitamins, and x-rays, but the most common is a pill made simply of milk sugar. Placebos are sometimes effective simply because the patient feels that some medical treatment is being provided. But in some experiments placebos have been used in such a way that the well-being of the subject is of secondary concern—or, in a few notorious cases, of no real concern at all. In such experiments, placebos are used in the "control" phase. For example, a new medication in pill form may be administered to one group of humans (the "experimental group"), while another group (the "control group," used for comparison in the experiment) is given sugar pills. In an experiment to determine the side effects of birth control pills that was actually done with a group of women, some received birth control pills while others were unknowingly given placebos. Some in the second group became pregnant.

Even less morally defensible was the now notorious experiment in which members of a control group thought they were receiving medication for syphilis. This experiment was conducted by the United States Public Health Service on several hundred black male patients between 1932 and 1972, to study the nature of syphilis and the effects of its treatment. One astonishing aspect of this experiment was that it was continued after the discovery that peni-

cillin was extremely effective against syphilis. Approximately 100 survivors who were not treated (members of the control group) were later awarded a cash settlement in compensation for the outrage perpetrated on them; relatives of untreated patients who had died received a lesser amount. The suffering of the subjects and their relatives makes clear the need for stricter regulation of human experimentation and greater concern for human rights.

Experiments with human subjects are indispensable to the scientific study and treatment of human diseases. Animals such as rats, pigs, and monkeys can be used in the preliminary phases of medical experiments, but tests must ultimately be made on humans. Decisions about such tests involve several questions of bioethics. How do we reconcile the human requirement that the subjects should know what is happening to them with the scientific requirement that the subjects (at least in the control group) *not* know, because such knowledge can affect the outcome of the experiment? And *who* should be experimented on? Many experiments are done on the poor, convicts, the aged, and even on children.

There are other bioethical problems as well. For example, individuals may be told that a new drug is being used for their treatment; patients often interpret "new" to mean "better," when the correct meaning is sometimes "experimental." Still another bioethical aspect of human research concerns the benefit of an experiment as compared with the risks involved. Recently Bernard Barber, a researcher at Barnard College and Columbia University, reported a study in which medical researchers evaluated hypothetical experiments. The researchers were asked to evaluate certain experiments with respect to the benefits to be derived as opposed to the risks involved. Barber found that many respondents approved some experiments even though the benefit-to-risk ratio was low. Barber also noted that only a very small proportion (13 percent) of medically trained respondents had been exposed, while in medical school, to courses or lectures on the ethical considerations in experiments involving humans. Many medical and biological practices have serious bioethical consequences. More-over, advances in biomedical knowledge and techniques are raising new bioethical problems.

Current Bioethical Problems

The explosion of knowledge in science and technology during the last 50 years has enabled humans to control their lives in unprecedented ways. Some of these advances, such as effective birth control, the prevention and cure of deadly diseases, and organ transplants, have brought about ethical problems. How, for example, can abortion be justified in the face of moral opposition by various religious groups? Under what circumstances is it ethically proper to take tissues or organs from living donors? Until appropriate uniform laws are passed, each situation must be considered on its own merits or under local laws where they exist.

Birth Control and Population

Controversies over birth control center not so much on the need to regulate human population as on the methods used to do so. There is little doubt that wherever it occurs, overpopu-lation reduces the quality of human life. In some countries, ignorance or religious restric-tions have contributed to serious overpopula-tion problems even though safe and effective contraceptive methods are available. In many cases resistance to birth control involves the right of individuals to bear as many children as they wish. Another complication involves the right of individuals to choose any method of contraception they prefer. Clearly, population control through sterilization or abortion raises a major bioethical issue. Who has the right to decide how large families should be or which individuals should be allowed to produce chil-dren?

Conventional Treatment of Genetic Diseases

Advances in surgery, genetics, and biochem-istry have now made possible medical treatment of many genetic diseases (Figure 21–13). Only 25 years ago most genetic diseases could not be treated because they were poorly understood. Babies born with genetic disorders either died or lived with a serious disability. Today, physicians are able to detect some hor-

Treatment Approach	Examples
1. Add missing substance (product)	Thyroid hormone, cortisol, insulin, antihemophilic globulin, gamma globulin, blood cells, vitamin B_{12}
2. Prevent accumulation of toxic precursor (substrate)	Phenylalanine in PKU; galactose-1-phosphate in galactosemia
3. Replace the defective enzyme	Plasma pseudocholinesterase deficiency
4. Use drug therapy (inhibit enzymes)	Allopurinol to prevent gout
5. Induce enzyme by drug	Phenobarbital for jaundice in newborn
6. Remove toxic substances	Metal-removing drugs for copper (Wilson's disease) or iron (hemo-chromatosis)
7. Surgically remove organ	Congenital polyp growths in colon; enlarged spleen; lens with cataracts
8. Transplant	Defective kidneys; congenital bone marrow anemia; opaque cornea
9. Use artificial aids	Eyeglasses; hearing aids; kidney machine
10. Block physiological (im-mune) response	Rhogam treatment of Rh-negative mothers who deliver Rh-positive babies

FIGURE 21–13 Current methods of treatment for genetic dis-eases. (From Robert H. Williams, *To Live and to Die: When, Why, and How,* New York: Springer-Verlag, 1973, p. 56.)

mone and enzyme deficiencies and administer appropriate amounts of the deficient substances. Moreover, laboratory synthesis of many such substances has made treatment readily available. In some cases drugs are used to stimulate the natural production of an enzyme or hormone; in others, drugs are given to inhibit the action of a specific enzyme system, as occurs in the painful condition called gout, caused by excessive uric acid.

Genetic diseases such as galactosemia and phenylketonuria (PKU), which produce severe mental retardation if left untreated, can now be controlled by diet. In these diseases the buildup of galactose-1-phosphate or the amino acid phenylalanine has toxic effects on brain cells. When babies with these disorders are put on special diets that contain no galactose or phenylalanine, their brains develop normally.

Selective Abortion

The willful early termination of a pregnancy, commonly called abortion, is still a very controversial subject in the United States. In 1975 the Supreme Court ruled that it was illegal to limit the right of a woman to have an abortion in the first three months of pregnancy. The religious, ethical, psychological, and moral implications of abortion are many; probably no legal solution would satisfy all people. The principal issue involved in the abortion controversy is at what developmental stage an embryo becomes a "living human being" with the same rights as all other humans. New medical techniques make possible early diagnosis of many birth defects and genetic disorders. Defective fetuses may then be aborted. The ethical and legal aspects of abortion are complex, but many people also question the morality of bringing seriously defective children into the world.

Amniocentesis

One medical technique that provides information about the sex and condition of an embryo is called *amniocentesis*. It involves passing a hollow needle through the abdomen and uterus of a pregnant woman and into the amniotic cavity of the embryo (Figure 21–14). A small amount of amniotic fluid is then removed through the needle and tested for the presence of certain substances. Protein analysis provides information on the fluid's enzyme content; about 30 different inborn errors of metabolism can now be detected by this means.

In one developmental defect, *spina bifida*, the neural canal is open to the outside and a certain protein leaks from the opening. Abnormal amounts of it are therefore present in the amniotic fluid. This defect can be detected in about 9 out of 10 cases by protein analysis of amniotic fluid; this information enables the parents to arrange for treatment after birth or to decide on abortion. Embryonic skin cells are always sloughed off into the amniotic fluid, and study of the chromosomes in these cells permits detection of Down's syndrome or of chromosomal damage caused by x-rays or drugs. The sex of the unborn child may be determined by checking the nucleus of one of its cells for the presence of a dark-staining chromosome called sex chromatin or *Barr body*, which is located at the periphery of the nucleus. In females only one of the X chromosomes (females are XX) is genetically active while the other is condensed into a small, compact mass, the Barr body. Barr bodies can be easily observed under the microscope and provide a simple means of determining the sex of a fetus or any other individual.

Amniocentesis is not recommended for routine analysis because a slight miscalculation can seriously injure the unborn baby. But in cases of a family history of genetic disease or suspected damage by radiation or drugs, amniocentesis can provide valuable diagnostic information.

Eugenics

Years ago, when genetics was a young science, the idea of manipulating the genes of organisms to produce desirable characteristics was attractive to many scientists. Since then, selective breeding programs and the alteration of chromosomes by radiation and chemicals such as colchicine have made many of these ideas realities. But *eugenics*—the application of genetic concepts to produce better adapted ("superior") human beings—has seldom been attempted. We know enough about genetics to attempt such a program in certain very limited

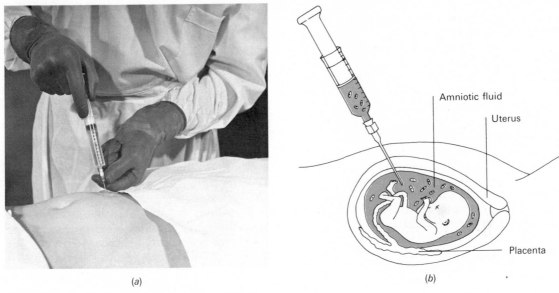

(a)

(b)

FIGURE 21–14 Amniocentesis, a procedure for removing a sample of amniotic fluid for laboratory tests. (a) Photo showing how the process is done. (b) Diagram showing removal of amniotic fluid and cells. (Photo courtesy of The National Foundation— March of Dimes.)

situations. In the future, more general manipulation might be possible, but the impact on the social, religious and ethical fabric of our society might be disastrous. Furthermore, it would be difficult if not impossible to decide which characteristics are desirable. Although we use all our genetic and biochemical knowledge to counteract the forces that produce genetic abnormalities, ethical considerations have prevented any serious attempts to improve intelligence, anatomy, or other human characteristics by selective breeding or by inducing mutations.

One application of eugenics, however, is becoming increasingly popular. Many individuals or couples—particularly those whose family history includes one or more persons with a genetic abnormality—now seek professional genetic counseling and testing. If they find that it is statistically probable that they will produce seriously abnormal offspring, they may decide against having children. In this way the incidence of undesirable genotypes can be reduced.

Transplants and Bionics

Perhaps the most exciting medical news in recent years has been the increasing success of organ transplants. Temporary skin and bone transplants have been routine procedures for many years, but successful transplants of vital organs such as the heart and kidneys are recent developments. The dream of replacing parts lost by aging, disease, or accident is becoming a reality. Many more human lives will be prolonged as our ability to transplant organs improves. Cornea and kidney transplants are now very successful, and new developments in regulating immune reactions should increase the proportion of successful heart, liver, lung, pancreas, and bone marrow transplants in the future.

But organs from human donors may not be the only transplant source. When techniques for overcoming tissue rejection are perfected, organs from other animals, particularly primates, may be used. Furthermore, artificial parts made from plastics and stainless steel have been successfully implanted in many persons. Artificial pacemakers, heart valves, hip and ankle joints, skull plates, teeth, and blood vessels have all been successfully implanted. During the past several years motor-driven prostheses (artificial limbs) for amputees have been produced and fitted experimentally. The motors of these artificial arms and hands are controlled by a system of skin electrodes and implanted microtransmitters. Such devices are cumbersome and their use requires extensive training.

Since artificial limbs are devices produced by engineering, a knowledge of the ways biological systems function can be used in their construction. This relatively new field is called *bionics*. Using this principle, research groups at Northwestern University, the University of Southern California, and the General Atomic Corporation have developed a remarkable new type of myoelectric arm and hand (Figure 21–15). This new bionic limb includes a self-contained battery pack and implanted electrodes that connect directly to nerves in the stump of a severed arm. The patient selectively activates

motors controlling the arm and hand by flexing various muscles in the stump. A feedback circuit has been built into the hand so that the wearer can "feel" how much pressure is needed to perform a certain task. This artificial limb design is clearly a breakthrough, and in the next 5 to 10 years we should see the development of even more sophisticated prostheses.

Completely artificial hearts may someday be available. An implantable plastic pump is now being developed at Baylor Medical School in Houston, Texas. It is designed to take over the function of the left ventricle if a patient's heart cannot be restarted after open heart surgery. Although this pump is designed to sustain life only until the patient's own heart recovers, such experimental models may eventually provide the information necessary to create a completely artificial heart.

Artificial Insemination

It may seem incredible that in a world teeming with people who are in need of food, shelter, and medical attention, time and effort are spent on developing techniques to improve fertility. However, many childless couples want to have children. Adoption and foster-home care have provided many such couples with children, but many want to have children bearing their own heredity. The causes of infertility vary, and in some cases the cause cannot be determined. In males, causes of infertility include insufficient numbers of sperm, weak or premature ejaculation, nonmotile sperm, or inability to experience erection and enter the vagina (impotence). Some women cannot produce eggs, whereas in others, the fallopian tubes may be blocked by a tumor or adhesion.

In many cases, however, a physician can determine the cause of infertility and administer corrective treatment. Or the physician may provide an alternative to natural conception. A husband's sperm may be collected, concentrated, and introduced artificially into the female tract; this method is called AIH (artificial insemination—husband). If the husband's sperm is inactive or otherwise genetically faulty, sperm from an anonymous donor may be used (AID: artificial insemination—donor). Both of these methods are legal in most coun-

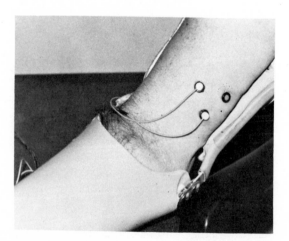

FIGURE 21–15 A bionic arm, showing implanted electrodes to nerves. Through these electrodes the amputee controls the motorized movements of the limb. (Courtesy of Rehabilitation Engineering Center at Rancho Los Amigos Hospital, Downey, California.)

tries, but the AID method has posed thorny moral and legal questions. AID children can be declared illegitimate by courts of law and their rights of inheritance nullified. Or a husband may refuse to support children conceived without his knowledge. In England an AID child could conceivably sue his "real" (biological) father for support if the father could be identified. Most of these problems have not come to trial, but the increasing numbers of AID children are certain to cause some complicated legal problems in the future.

For domestic animals, artificial insemination has been perfected, and quantities of frozen sperm can be kept almost indefinitely. Frozen human semen has been used in limited human trials with remarkable success. Sperm banks for humans are now a reality, but the demand for frozen sperm is presently minimal. The eugenic potential of sperm banks is obvious: women can study the background and traits of men who have sperm on deposit and choose the sperm they desire.

New Biological Frontiers—And New Bioethical Problems

Biological research will doubtless continue and our knowledge about ourselves will increase.

Twenty years ago, most students of biology would never have imagined many of the accomplishments we have discussed. It is a safe bet that we cannot today anticipate all the biomedical accomplishments of the next 20 years. Still, we can make some informed predictions.

Artificial Reproduction

The next step after artificial insemination is the fertilization of eggs by sperm in a test tube! Reports indicate that this has been accomplished, but the subsequent step—successfully implanting the developing blastocyst (blastula) into the uterus—has not been verified. The technology for doing so is available, however. Eggs can be removed from an ovary through a tiny abdominal incision and placed in a nutrient medium with sperm from the husband. The next step after fertilization would be to implant the blastocyst in the uterus. When feasible, this process, often referred to as ETW (egg transfer using wife's egg) will offer one type of artificial reproduction. It will certainly be followed by ETD (egg transfer using donor's egg) and ETDD (egg transfer using donor's egg and donor's sperm) (Figure 21–16). Of course, these methods of reproduction will have bioethical ramifications and will need to be re-

Method of impregnation		Mother's genes	Mother's uterus	Father's genes
Normal conception		Yes	Yes	Yes
Adoption		No	No	No
AIH	Artificial insemination with husband's sperm	Yes	Yes	Yes
AID	Artificial insemination with donor's sperm	Yes	Yes	No
ETW	Egg transfer using wife's own eggs	Yes	Yes	Yes
ETD	Egg transfer using a donor's eggs	No	Yes	Yes
ETDD	Egg transfer using a donor's eggs fertilized with a donor's sperm	No	Yes	No

FIGURE 21–16 Various methods of impregnation and the gene makeup of the offspring. The first four methods are used; the last three should be possible. (From *The Human Pedigree* by Anthony Smith. Copyright © 1975 by George Allen and Unwin Ltd. Reproduced by permission of J. B. Lippincott Company.)

solved. Perhaps babies will some day be developed in artificial wombs or in a mechanism similar to that proposed more than 40 years ago by Aldous Huxley in his classic work of fiction, *Brave New World.*

Cloning

In Chapter 16 we discussed the reproduction of genetically identical frogs. Such identical individuals, produced by a single parent are called *clones.* Cloning is very common among plants and in some animals that reproduce asexually. We also saw in Chapter 16 that cloning may be accomplished artificially by destroying the nuclei of certain amphibian eggs and then inserting a different nucleus into each egg. These nuclei can come from intestinal cells of a developing embryo of the same species. By this process a group of genetically identical animals can be produced. Clones have been produced in amphibians, but this type of reproduction has not been achieved in mammals. But here too, we have the technology to do it, and mammalian—even human—clones could become a reality in the near future.

But do we want human clones? Human cloning would bring up legal problems involving citizenship, voting rights, and inheritance. But a more fundamental issue is also involved. Perhaps the greatest adaptive value of sexual reproduction to a species is the variety of individuals it makes possible. Why would we want a group of exactly identical people when our strength as a species is in diversity? It has been argued that it would be good to have more Einsteins and Newtons. But would we want more Napoleons . . . or more Hitlers? Perhaps in certain experiments we are looking not so much for the fruits of the experiments themselves as for an answer to the question, "Can it be done?" But we never know what knowledge gained by experimentation may lead to. An authoritarian government, for example, could use biomedical technology to produce clones of warriors or workers—or even duplicates of its "superior" leaders.

Genetic Engineering

When biologists discovered the transfer of genes from one bacterium to another by vi-

ruses, an entirely new field opened before them. And when they took the next step, transferring bacterial genes to amphibians and mammals, they envisioned still greater possibilities. This new field, in which genes are actually manipulated by humans, has come to be known as *genetic engineering.* The consequence of new genetic combinations is biological evolution; it is the same whether it occurs naturally or through manipulation by humans. As we noted in Chapter 14, Stanley Cohen and his colleagues have recently inserted genes from toads into the bacterium *E. coli.* More recently, West German scientists reported the transfer of a gene from *E. coli* to cultured human cells through an intermediate virus (by a process of transduction). These researchers used cells from a human who could not produce B-galactosidase, the enzyme needed to digest lactose, the sugar found in milk. Since *E. coli* has a gene that can order the production of B-galactosidase, researchers were able to determine when this bacterial gene was introduced into the enzyme-deficient human cells. Such experiments show that it might be possible to transmit other genes from one organism to another by using viruses as transmitters. We may someday be able to correct genetic deficiencies by replacing defective genes with functional ones.

Such genetic hybridizations may hold great promise for correcting genetic deficiencies or for adding genes to improve certain species, but there are problems associated with the process. Some of these problems, such as concern over excessive hybridizing and over the ability to control humans through the addition of genes, are ethical ones. As we shall note later, other ethical concerns stem from the potential hazards in handling the genetic material and the possible toxicity of such crosses, especially those involving the intestinal bacteria *E. coli.*

Death and Bioethics

All metazoan organisms eventually die. But humans have devised many techniques, including the use of drugs, biochemical supplements, transplants, and artificial devices, for extending life. The possibility of freezing individuals at the moment of death has been proposed as a means of preserving their tissues until cures are found for the diseases that killed them. And the effectiveness of modern medical techniques to postpone what we commonly call death, creates problems of its own. It often burdens relatives with enormous debts, protracted suffering, and false hopes. Many people have proposed that we should reexamine our definition of death. Moreover, it has been proposed that individuals suffering from incurable ailments should, if they choose, be allowed to die naturally without prolonging their life, or even to be put to death painlessly. Such practices are termed *euthanasia.*

The point at which life support mechanisms should be withdrawn from the hopelessly ill remains a much-debated issue. When we arrive at a more widely accepted definition of death, the issue will become easier to resolve. It is important that we develop a standard legal definition of death. But when we attempt to define death, we encounter many of the same problems we faced in attempting to define life (Chapter 1). In fact, some traditional definitions of death were couched in such terms as "the absence of life" or "the absence of vital signs of life." For many years, the cessation of breathing and circulation were used as the legal criteria of death. But the brain can die in stages—first the cerebrum, then the midbrain, and finally the brain stem (medulla), where the control centers for vital functions lie. The lack of brain waves originating in the higher brain centers is now used to define death in some states. When a patient's EEG (electroencephalogram) is flat, indicating that no brain waves are being produced, the patient can be declared dead.

In 1968, a Harvard University committee composed of physicians, lawyers, theologians, and philosophers proposed a new set of guidelines for determining death: lack of responsiveness, absence of breathing and reflexes, and a flat EEG. The committee also proposed that after these conditions are met for at least 24 hours, and when the brain is considered dead by two physicians (one a neurospecialist), the physicians should inform the family that life support mechanisms would be removed.

Many states are now considering "death with dignity," or euthanasia, legislation. Such laws would provide a legal way for an individual to express the desire not to be kept alive when the brain has ceased to function because of an incurable disease or injury. Although this expression of intent has no legal basis at present, the American Euthanasia Society has available a "living will" which may exert some moral force in the matter (Figure 21–17).

To Risk or Not to Risk: Who Shall Decide?

Scientists are becoming acutely aware of their bioethical responsibilities in research and its applications. In July 1974, the Committee on Recombinant DNA Molecules of the National Academy of Sciences called for a voluntary moratorium on a type of genetic manipulation that can produce hybrid molecules of DNA. This action, the first of its kind, was undertaken to guard against possible unknown hazards to the human species. This committee of 11 scientists was concerned that genetic material introduced into bacteria could produce new, more toxic bacterial forms. The committee members were especially concerned about the modification of *E. coli* DNA itself, since this bacterium inhabits the large intestine of humans. In such experiments it is difficult to determine hazards until an experiment is completed. Since this call for a moratorium, several conferences have been held to discuss the issue. The most influential of these was the Asilomar Conference held in Pacific Grove, California, early in 1975. At this historic conference, 140 scientists representing 16 nations voted to lift the 1974 moratorium, although they strongly recommended stringent safety practices. The consensus was that genetic research on the hybridizing of DNA molecules (genetic engineering) should be cautiously resumed. The conferees further specified certain experiments that are too hazardous to be done at the present time. Although the conference's guidelines were not legally binding, they provided the framework for a set of guidelines issued by the National Institutes of Health (NIH) in 1976.

TO MY FAMILY, MY PHYSICIAN,
MY CLERGYMAN, MY LAWYER

If the time comes when I can no longer take part in decisions for my own future, let this statement stand as the testament of my wishes:
I, _____ request that I be allowed to die and not be kept alive by artificial means or heroic measures. Death is as much a reality as birth, growth, maturity and old age--it is the one certainty. I do not fear death as much as I fear the indignity of deterioration, dependence and hopeless pain. I ask that drugs be mercifully administered to me for terminal suffering even if they hasten the moment of death.

This request is made after careful consideration. Although this document is not legally binding, you who care for me will, I hope, feel morally bound to follow its mandate. I recognize that it places a heavy burden of responsibility upon you, and it is with the intention of sharing that responsibility and of mitigating any feelings of guilt that this statement is made.

FIGURE 21-17 An example of a "living will," distributed by the Euthanasia Council.

The NIH guidelines essentially provide for: (1) safe laboratory procedures that will insure containment of possible new types of organisms which may result; (2) the use of a variety of *E. coli* (K12) that is not a major inhabitant of the human large intestine; and (3) the control of the kinds of experiments that can be performed, especially when using recombinant DNAs that are potentially harmful to humans, animals, or plants. Athough the NIH guidelines are only binding on research projects funded by NIH, it is highly probable that these guidelines will be followed by other scientists.

Credit for the Asilomar Conference must be attributed to those relatively few concerned scientists who are now involved in work of a biologically hazardous nature. Ultimately, representatives of other professions, of governments, and of citizens' groups must be involved in the regulation of biologically hazardous research. It may be possible to agree that certain types of research should not be continued. For example, it might be decided that no more "test tube babies" should be brought into our already overcrowded world. However, interference in research in certain hazardous areas might entail risks greater than those involved in continuing the research. Medical research, for example, involves unavoidable risks, but few would argue that medical research should be halted. The same may be said of agricultural research. Genetic engineering may be a key to greater food production for a hungry world. The transfer of nitrogen-fixing genes from legumes (alfalfa, peas, beans, etc.) to nonleguminous vegetables and grains, for example, would have tremendous food-production potential. But perhaps the most important issues involve changing human heredity, which would affect future innocent generations. Do the potential hazards of such research outweigh the potential benefits? How do we decide? *Who* should decide?

Someone once wisely remarked, "War is too important to be left to the generals." We would be less than wise if we did not resolve that bioethics is too important to be left to biologists and other scientists. So far, the scientific community seems to have acted cautiously and responsibly in dealing with the bioethical problems posed by genetic engineering and other developments in biological science. But abuses are possible; recall the syphilis experiment. Besides, potentially disastrous decisions can result from well-intended actions as well as from abuses. We must all demand a voice in the political decisions that will determine the fate of all living systems.

SUMMARY

The first primates were small rodentlike, ground-dwelling animals that moved first into trees and later back to the ground. Many habitats became available to primates as they developed grasping, five-digit hands or feet, front-facing eyes, and complex brains. The upright posture also contributed to successful ground living. The anthropoids (monkeys, apes, and humans) diverged from prosimian stock (tree shrews, lemurs, and tarsiers) about 30 million years ago. Chimpanzees, gorillas, orangutans, and humans descended from several species of a small ape, *Dryopithecus*. *Ramapithecus*, which evolved from this line, was the forerunner to *Australopithecus* and *Homo*. More than 3 million years ago the genus *Homo* evolved, possessing a larger brain and a societal mode of life.

Human culture evolves along with physical evolution: each shaping the other. Human culture is learned, cumulative, and transmissable; it involves language and objects and is the product of behavior—and is thus biological.

Humans have become evolutionary agents who can create, modify, and destroy species by interfering with the environment. We can even control the destiny of our own species. Through medical technology many maladaptive genes are retained in the human gene pool. Because of technology our future may be governed more by bioethics than by natural forces.

Bioethics refers to the moral, or ethical, aspects of the workings of biology. Many biomedical practices today have serious bioethical consequences, and this will be even more true in the future. Currently, bioethical questions are arising in birth control, treatment of genetic diseases, abortion, amniocentesis, eugenics, transplants, bionics, and artificial insemination. New problems are likely to emerge in artificial reproduction, cloning, and genetic engineering.

Advances in medicine have made it possible to prolong the lives of fatally ill individuals. New definitions of death have been used and euthanasia has been proposed. As biological research continues and moves into new areas, we must decide who is going to be involved in these bioethical decisions.

REVIEW QUESTIONS

1. How can highly specialized characteristics be disadvantageous to a species?

2. List some adaptations that made possible the evolutionary development from the early tree-dwelling primates to primitive humans.

3. From what you now understand about genetics and evolution, describe events that could have led from *Dryopithecus* to modern humans.

4. How can cultural evolution be of adaptive value to a species?

5. How have humans modified evolution in the dog, cat, and horse?

6. "Should individuals with genes harmful to the total human population be restricted from reproducing?" Take both sides of the issue and list reasons for each viewpoint.

7. Should we humans be concerned with our evolution even though it occurs in a more artificial environment than the evolution of other species?

SUPPLEMENTARY READINGS

Barber, Bernard, "The Ethics of Experimentation with Human Subjects," *Scientific American*, February 1976. The results found by a research group on human experimentation indicate inadequate ethical concern among biomedical investigators. More and better controls appear to be essential in this area of research.

Leakey, L. S. B., *By the Evidence*, Harcourt Brace Jovanovich, New York, 1974. This outstanding anthropologist tells us about his life and his work from 1932 to 1951. He not only describes much of his anthropological work but he also discusses his experiences in Africa.

Williams, Robert H., *To Live and to Die: When, Why, and How*, Springer-Verlag, New York, 1973. Written in response to the many new ethical issues and new attitudes facing modern humans, this book deals with such topics as abortion, genetic engineering, population control, homosexuality, euthanasia, drugs, and contraception.

Unit IX
The Diversity of Life

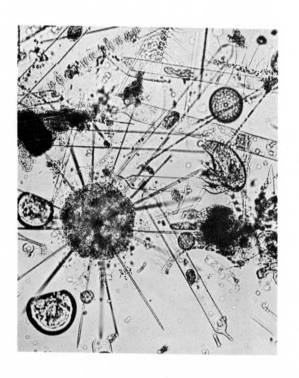

It is fitting to follow our discussion of evolution with a survey of the diversity of living systems, because this diversity is the consequence of 3 billion years or more of organic evolution. And it is appropriate that we conclude our study of living systems with a survey of the various kinds of living systems. Up until now we have been concerned with the individual functions of living systems. We have examined physical structure, metabolism, genetics, reproduction. We have viewed ecological relationships, growth, and behavior. And we have studied the history of evolution. Now it is time to look directly at the organisms we have been analyzing and discussing.

But where shall we begin, and how shall we proceed? Authors of children's alphabet books have found one solution: they simply proceed from "A is for Aardvark" to "Z is for Zebra." Classification systems based on alphabetical order are important, as all users of dictionaries, encyclopedias, and telephone directories know. Because so many different species of organisms exist on our planet (about 2 million have been discovered so far), biologists need some classification system. But one based on alphabetical order would be of little use, because the alphabet has nothing to do with the important biological goals of classification. The biologist wants to place organisms in an orderly system that (1) groups similar organisms together and separates dissimilar ones, and (2) provides as much information as possible about the relationships between the organisms so ordered. These requirements have all been met, with varying degrees of success, in the classification systems biologists have developed over the years.

Biologists seldom agree on every detail of classification. But they do agree that any system of classification must be as natural as possible—that is, it must reflect as accurately as possible the evolutionary relationships among organisms. (Classification by alphabetical order would be artificial classification, as would be a system that classifies flowers by their colors.)

As we noted earlier, this book is based on a classification system of four kingdoms, Monera, Protista, Metaphyta (plants), and Metazoa (animals). Although this system may not represent the exact pattern in which life has evolved, it seems more natural than the older systems which recognized only plant and animal groups, and for this reason it is widely used today. The justification for the system based on four kingdoms involves two main considerations. First, many present-day organisms do not fit neatly into either the plant or the animal category. And second, life did not originate as "plant" or "animal." As we saw in Chapter 2, the early stages of organic evolution probably saw many "experiments in nature" whose outcomes were organisms with varieties or mixtures of moneran and protistan characteristics as well as those of animals and plants. The fossil record shows this also.

Organisms were first classified on the basis of their gross (large-scale) anatomical characteristics. These were the only characteristics that were known in the early years of biology. With the development of the microscope and other instruments, it became possible to use other characteristics for classification as well, including microscopic structures, chromosome comparisons, and protein and serum analyses.

The four-kingdom system, like all modern biological classification systems, is hierarchical in its arrangement. In these classification systems, the general term for a hierarchical level is usually category, or, more formally, taxon (plural taxa). The formal term for "biological classification" itself is taxonomy. We have generally avoided the terms taxon and taxonomy in this book because category and classification serve perfectly well. But you may see the more formal terms frequently in the biological literature.

As we have already indicated, the broadest, most inclusive category in biological classification is the kingdom. Kingdoms are divided into phyla (singular phylum), each of which is in turn divided into classes. Classes are divided into orders, orders into families, families into genera (singular genus), and genera into species (singular also species). Phyla whose members are many and varied may have additional subcategories, such as subphyla and superorders. Examples of classification of two organisms, a plant and an animal, are shown.

	Organism I
Kingdom	Metaphyta
Phylum	Tracheophyta
Subphylum	Pteropsida
Class	Gymnospermae
Subclass	
Order	Coniferales
Family	Pinaceae
Genus	*Pseudotsuga*
Species	*menziesii*
Common name	Douglas fir

	Organism II
	Metazoa
	Chordata
	Vertebrata
	Mammalia
	Primates
	Hominidae
	Homo
	sapiens
	Human

Chapter 22

Monera and Protista

In this concluding portion of the book, we are going to look at one of the oldest—and certainly the most far-ranging—subjects in modern biology. The diversity of species was one of the first areas of the living world to be systematically studied by "natural scientists" and "natural philosophers," starting approximately in the early eighteenth century.

Until the theory of evolution, the study of diversity was little more than a cataloging process. We will see in these next three chapters the impact of the theory in giving these lists and descriptions an organizing *rationale*.

In these chapters, we have the ultimate example of the value of the "simple to complex" path we have followed in many topics in this book. For example, we start with the two kingdoms that include the single-celled and "simple" organisms. **Primitive Organisms: Kingdom Monera** include the **Bacteria** and the **Blue-Green Algae.**

The Viruses: Classification Misfits are one of the major taxonomic question marks.

Not only is it difficult to comfortably place them in a single category, but the debate still continues over whether viruses fit our "standard" definitions of living systems.

The **Diverse "Simple" Organisms** that make up the **Kingdom Protista** include the different kinds of algae (excluding the blue-greens), distinguished here by color. The **Flagellates** include species that move by whiplike flagella.

As we move toward the **Slime Molds** and the **Fungi,** we will see a deviation from plant-like characteristics even though older classification systems considered these organisms plants. The **Amoebae, Sporozoans, Ciliates,** and **Suctorians**—which conclude the chapter—have traits that make them more animal-related. However, the protist classification spares us having to place these organisms in less than appropriate categories. Thus we can concentrate on their characteristic ways of obtaining food, moving, reproducing, and adapting to their environments.

The final step across the nonlife/life boundary was the formation of primitive cells. As we saw in Chapter 2, this final step was also a first step, the beginning of life's diversification. These first, structurally simple cells eventually gave rise to more complex cells and, still later, to multicellular organisms. Many biologists think that these early forerunners of modern cells were very much like the "primitive" *moneran* cells we know today.

PRIMITIVE ORGANISMS: KINGDOM MONERA

The most fundamental distinction we make about living systems is that between *procaryotic* and *eucaryotic* organisms. In Chapter 5 we saw that the cell structure of procaryotic cells is less specialized than that of eucaryotic cells. The genetic material of the procaryotes is not organized into distinct chromosomes coated with protein; they lack a nuclear membrane; they contain no mitochondria, chloroplasts, Golgi apparatus, lysosomes, centrioles, or endoplasmic reticulum. And if they possess flagella, these consist of a single fibril which differs markedly from the $9 + 2$ arrangement found in flagellated eucaryotic organisms.

As we noted in Chapter 5, the procaryotes have a kingdom all to themselves—the kingdom *Monera*. The eucaryotes are apportioned among the kingdoms *Protista*, *Metaphyta* (plants), and *Metazoa* (animals).

All monerans are small; most are microscopic. Since many monerans exist as single cells and the rest form aggregates (colonies) of similar cells, they may be defined as *unicellular*. Thus they are distinct from true *multicellular* organisms whose cells are organized into differentiated tissues. The kingdom Monera contains just two phyla: the bacteria and the blue-green algae. Organisms of both types are found in most environments where there is some moisture.

The general characteristics of Monera may be summarized as follows:

1. They are microscopic and unicellular.
2. They contain nuclear material—DNA and RNA—but no well-defined chromosomes.
3. They lack a nuclear membrane.

4. They may have simple chromatophores but lack complex chloroplasts.
5. Nutrition is accomplished by photosynthesis, chemosynthesis, or absorption.
6. They reproduce by binary fission or fragmentation.

Bacteria: Phylum Schizophyta
Approximately 2000 identified species

These tiny organisms, often associated with disease, are classified according to their individual and collective shapes: rod-shaped (bacilli), spherical (cocci), and spiral (spirilli) (Figure 22–1, on color plate following p. 592). Bacilli and cocci often occur in chains or clumps. The growth characteristics of bacteria in various culture media are also used to distinguish among species. Many of us have at one time or another been victims of streptococcal and staphylococcal forms that cause sore throat and boils (Figure 22–2).

Like plants, bacteria have cell walls. But unlike those of plants, these cell walls consist of amino acids and amino-containing sugars. Penicillin, the first truly effective antibiotic discovered, kills bacteria by inhibiting the forma-

FIGURE 22–2   Normal chains of *Streptococcus pyogenes* ($\times 4850$). (Courtesy David Greenwood.)

tion of their walls during division. Since plant and animal cells differ in structure from bacteria, they are immune to penicillin's destructive action. Bacteria can, however, wall off a portion of their contents to produce dormant *endospores* that are able to withstand conditions that would destroy normal bacteria. The tetanus bacillus, for example, has been known to exist in spore form for more than 50 years and still be infective.

Although bacteria are known principally for their harmful effects, many forms are essential to the health of higher organisms. For example, the bacteria in our intestines help us to digest plant fibers and to synthesize several vitamins. Bacteria also decompose organic wastes. They recycle carbon, nitrogen, sulfur, and iron back into the environment in usable form. Yogurt, cheese, buttermilk, and vinegar are familiar food products formed by controlled bacterial action.

Metabolism in bacteria shows many variations. Many species are *aerobic*; that is, they must live in the presence of free oxygen. Other species are *anaerobic*, which means that they can metabolize without oxygen. The presence of oxygen actually kills some anaerobic bacteria by interfering with certain enzyme systems. Food poisoning and gangrene are caused by anaerobic species. Certain types, including some found in vertebrate intestines, can switch from the aerobic to the anaerobic mode to suit their needs.

Several species of bacteria use primitive types of sexuality. Although they do not form true sexual gametes, these bacteria exchange parts of their genetic material. There are three exchange mechanisms, *conjugation*, *transformation*, and *transduction*. In conjugation, two bacteria come together and form a tube from one to the other. A bit of genetic material is then passed through this tube from the donor ("male") to the recipient ("female"). This donor DNA must then combine with the recipient's genetic material in order to be functional. Transformation apparently occurs when DNA from one bacterium is absorbed by another through its cell wall. DNA extracted from dead bacteria has been observed to change the characteristics of recipient bacteria. In transduction, a virus carries genetic material from one bacterium to another. Certain viruses called *bacteriophages* parasitize bacteria; in the process of duplicating themselves, these viruses may pick up part of the host bacterium's DNA. The viral offspring then inject this DNA into another bacterium, thus transferring bacterial DNA.

GENERAL CHARACTERISTICS OF BACTERIA

1. Some are autotrophs, producing nutrients by photosynthesis or chemosynthesis.
2. Many are parasitic or saprophytic (feeding on dead organisms).
3. Some produce toxins pathogenic to higher organisms. For example, bacteria cause diphtheria, pneumonia, food poisoning, strep throat, venereal disease, tetanus, and many other diseases.
4. Many use simple flagellae for locomotion.
5. All contain free ribosomes in the cytoplasm.
6. They may be aerobic, anaerobic, or both.

Blue-Green Algae: Phylum Cyanophyta
Approximately 2500 identified species

Although this group is called the blue-green algae, many species contain red or yellow pigments. They occur as single cells, in colonies, or as filaments of many cells. The water of lakes and ponds is often colored by "blooms" of these organisms. The name *cyanophyta* is derived from the Greek *kyanos*, "dark blue," and *phyton*, "plant"; the blue pigment involved is *phycocyanin* (Figure 22–3).

Blue-green algae are well adapted to aquatic life because they float near the surface and synthesize their own nitrates from atmospheric nitrogen. During the summer they may reproduce so rapidly that they form a scum on the surface of ponds and lakes. This overpopulation blocks light from deeper water, killing many algae of all types. Fish may be killed if their gills become clogged by the algae or if bacterial decomposition of dead algae depletes

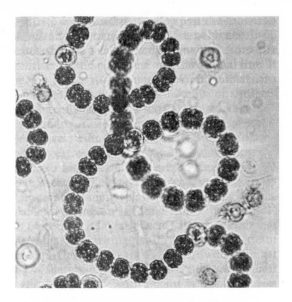

FIGURE 22–3   The blue-green alga *Nostoc,* showing several heterocysts (×1000).

the oxygen in the water. These algae can withstand temperatures from ice water to nearly boiling water. Blue-green algae do not possess flagella; some move by gliding or oscillating, the mechanism of which is not understood. These forms show no evidence of sexual reproduction.

Many blue-green algae possess large nonphotosynthesizing cells called *heterocysts.* These cells are important for two reasons: (1) They are the cells that "fix" nitrogen into usable nitrates; and (2) they are the spots at which filaments can break to produce new filaments.

GENERAL CHARACTERISTICS OF BLUE-GREEN ALGAE

1. Most forms are aquatic and single-celled, colonial, or filamentous.

2. They may contain any of a variety of pigments: green, blue, orange, or red.

3. They are autotrophic and serve as a food source for small aquatic animals.

4. Some contain large, nonphotosynthesizing cells called heterocysts that function in fragmentation and nitrogen fixation.

VIRUSES: THE CLASSIFICATION MISFITS
Approximately 500 identified varieties

Our definition of living systems: *cellular structures capable of self-perpetuation* rules viruses out of a formal place in most classification systems, including the four-kingdom classification used in this book. Viruses are excluded because they are not cellular structures and because they cannot reproduce themselves without help from the cells they infect.

Of course, denying viruses a place in the classification systems is not to deny them a place in biology. Viruses are the subject of intense study by biologists for at least three reasons. First, viruses share several structural and functional characteristics with living systems. Second, their structural simplicity makes them easier to study in some respects than living systems. Study of viruses in turn advances our understanding of the structures of living systems. For example, viruses are helping to provide answers to the complex problems of heredity. Third, all viruses are parasites that infect living systems and some are known to cause cancer. The better we understand them the more successfully we can control them.

Viruses and monerans have some characteristics in common. Although viruses lack cell structure, they contain genetic information in the form of either DNA or RNA. Viruses that attack bacteria (called *bacteriophages* or simply *phages*) possess DNA, as either a single or a double strand (Figure 14–21). This DNA may be arranged in a complete circle (Figure 14–22).

Viral DNA or RNA is surrounded by a protein capsule or shell. While in their "free" stage—that is, outside their hosts—individual virus particles are called *virions.* Virions vary greatly in shape; they may be polyhedral, cuboidal, round, or elongate. Many types have well-defined, angular heads and protruding tails like the T4 phage in Figure 22–4.

DIVERSE, "SIMPLE" ORGANISMS: KINGDOM PROTISTA

This large kingdom consists of eucaryotic organisms with widely varying characteristics. The criteria for inclusion in the kingdom Protista

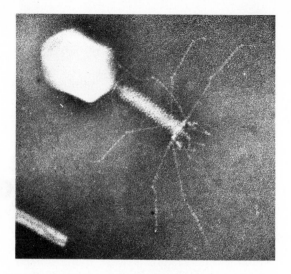

FIGURE 22–4   Electron micrograph of a T4 bacteriophage, showing angular head and rodlike tail. (Courtesy Robley C. Williams, Virus Laboratory.)

vary among biologists; its boundaries are thus rather vague. Algae and fungi, for example, may or may not be placed in this kingdom, depending on who is doing the classifying. Older taxonomic schemes attempted to classify all the organisms we now call protists as either plants or animals. Thus small green flagellates such as *Euglena*, were long an enigma for zoologists and botanists alike (Figure 22–5, on color plate following p. 592). *Euglena* can be classified unambiguously as a protist because members of Protista may or may not have chlorophyll— some are plantlike and others are animallike. The use of the kingdom Protista has helped biologists to solve such classification problems.

The following general characteristics of protists help to differentiate them from monerans, plants, and animals:

1. Cells are eucaryotic, with definite chromosomes and a nuclear membrane.

2. Cell division occurs by mitosis.

3. They may be unicellular or multicellular with a "simple," undifferentiated body.

4. Reproductive cells or structures are primarily unicellular, that is, they are or they arise from single cells.

5. Most forms are aquatic.

Green Algae: Phylum Chlorophyta
Approximately 6000 identified species

The term *algae* has been used generally to describe a large, diverse group of photosynthetic organisms, all of which contain chlorophyll *a*. Although most algae are single-celled or composed of simple filaments, some large forms, such as seaweeds, have multicellular structure (except for reproductive parts, which are always unicellular). We have already discussed blue-green algae; those are placed in Monera rather than Protista because they lack nuclear structure and cytoplasmic organelles. All protistan algae have eucaryotic cells.

Members of this group have complex chloroplasts with chlorophylls *a* and *b*, similar to Metaphyta (plants). They are found in most bodies of water and in moist soils. Algae may have any of three basic structural plans: the single cell, filamentous colonies, and aggregate colonies. Colonies do not exhibit a high degree of differentiation (division of labor among cells), but some produce flagellated reproductive cells (gametes) and undergo both asexual and sexual reproduction.

In the green alga *Ulothrix* (Figure 22–6), reproduction may be accomplished simply by fragmentation of the filament; when this occurs, each piece continues to divide, forming many new individuals. On the other hand, a cell may also divide several times within itself to produce swimming *zoospores*, which are then released to reproduce new organisms. *Ulothrix* can also reproduce sexually: vegetative cells divide internally many times to form motile gametes. When released through a pore in the cell wall, these gametes fuse with gametes from other filaments. The fusion of gametes from various filaments provides for new combinations of genetic information. Unlike typical sperm and eggs, these gametes are of equal size. This condition is called *isogamy* (*iso*, "same" or "equal") as opposed to *heterogamy*, in which gametes of different sizes are involved. The resulting *zygote* then undergoes meiosis to form four new haploid organisms. The vegetative filament cells of *Ulothrix* are haploid, so gametes can be produced by mitosis. The fusion of these haploid

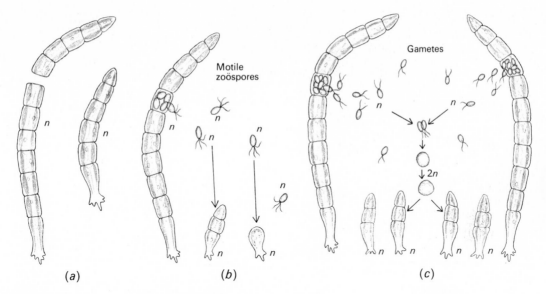

FIGURE 22-6 Three types of reproduction occurring in the green alga *Ulothrix* (Chlorophyta). (*a*) Fragmentation. (*b*) Zoospore formation. (*c*) Haplontic sexual reproduction. Note the production of isogametes.

gametes produces a diploid zygote in which meiosis must occur. This pattern of sexual reproduction is called *haplontic*, since normal cells of the alga are haploid (see Figure 15–3).

Sexual reproduction in the filamentous green alga *Spirogyra* was discussed in Chapter 15. The process is called *conjugation* (Figure 15–2) and, as in bacteria, provides a mechanism for the exchange of genetic material.

In the life cycles of these green algae (and many other protists) we see the beginnings of a two-generation life cycle: a stage containing one set of chromosomes (haploid) alternates with a stage having two sets of chromosomes (diploid). The haploid phase produces gametes; it is called the *gametophyte* generation. The diploid phase produces spores and is called the *sporophyte* generation (Figure 15–4). In the green algae the sporophyte, or diploid, generation is generally represented by only a zygote, but in other protistans and land plants the main organism is generally a sporophyte. In some plants each generation may be a separate organism, as we shall see in Chapter 23.

GENERAL CHARACTERISTICS OF GREEN ALGAE

1. They live mostly in aquatic or moist habitats.
2. They reproduce sexually through gametes; some undergo conjugation.
3. They contain chlorophyll a and b as well as other pigments.
4. They possess complex chloroplasts.

Golden-Brown Algae
Phylum Chrysophyta
Approximately 10,000 identified species

The golden-brown algae are a very diversified group containing many different forms. They usually contain large amounts of yellow and brown pigments (carotenoids) as well as chlorophyll. Many of the golden-browns have flagella, which occur in different patterns. An important characteristic of this phylum is the type of food storage utilized—oils and a polysaccharide called *chrysolaminarin*.

The diatoms are a large and important group

Bio-Topic: Sex in Small Dimensions

When a diatom divides, each of the two new cells retains one half of the silica shell that encased the parental cell. The new cell that retains the larger half of the parental shell forms a new shell that fits inside its half of the parental shell. The new cell that retains the smaller half of the parental shell forms a new shell that also fits inside its half of the parental shell. This new shell is smaller than either half of the original parental shell. The result is that each successive asexual generation of diatoms contains a few shells—and cells—that are smaller than those in the previous generation.

The formation of successively smaller diatoms cannot continue indefinitely.

Eventually a size is reached below which the new cells would be too small to function. The solution to this geometrical limitation in many diatoms is a change to sexual reproduction.

Sexual reproduction occurs in different ways in different species. In some, two cells crawl out of their respective shells and fuse to form a zygote. In others, male cells undergo meiosis and form flagellated sperms. Female cells of these species undergo meiosis and form a single large egg. The sperms swim to and fertilize the eggs and the result is a zygote. When the zygote germinates, the resulting cells form full-sized shells. And then the cycle repeats.

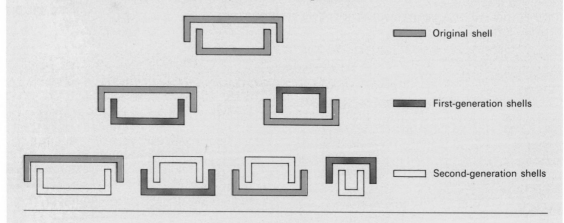

Original shell

First-generation shells

Second-generation shells

that serve as a primary food source in both fresh and marine waters (Figure 22–7). Diatoms may be single-celled, filamentous, or colonial. Each cell is enclosed in a two-part silicon shell called a *test;* one half (or *valve*) fits into another, slightly larger, half. The valves, radially or bilaterally symmetrical and characteristically marked with sculptured lines, are often used in the identification of species. Diatoms come in a great variety of shapes: disk, rod, triangle, star, and ellipse, to name a few. Great diatomaceous deposits found throughout the world, some of which are more than 3000 feet thick, attest to the large numbers of these organisms in the ancient seas. Diatomaceous earth is used as an abrasive (it serves this purpose in some toothpastes), in filter systems, and as insulation.

GENERAL CHARACTERISTICS OF GOLDEN-BROWN ALGAE

1. They occur in both fresh and salt water.
2. They may form tests (shells) containing silicon.

FIGURE 22–7   Freshwater diatoms. The symmetrical shells contain a silicon compound. (Grant Heilman, Runk/Schoenberger.)

3. They reproduce asexually or sexually by producing free gametes.

4. They contain yellow and brown pigments in addition to chlorophyll *a* and *b*.

5. They store food as oils or a polysaccharide other than starch.

6. They form the first link in most aquatic food chains.

Brown Algae: Phylum Phaeophyta
Approximately 1200 identified species

All brown algae are multicellular, and most are large enough to be easily observed. Most live in marine environments, living anchored to rocks in fairly shallow water. Kelp beds composed of large brown seaweeds occur in and around rocky shoals, where they provide a warning to boaters (Figure 22–8). The kelps are large and complex examples of this group. A limited amount of cellular differentiation can be recognized in the specialized structures of kelp—the holdfast ("anchor"), stipe ("stem") and blade ("leaf"). However, this rudimentary algal cellular differentiation does not appear to have given rise to the support and vascular tissues of higher plants. Rather, the brown algae evolved structures and life cycles independently that parallel those of land plants.

Another member of this phylum is the brown "rockweed," *Fucus*. This form lives at-tached to rocks in the high-tide zones and has an efficient reproductive pattern similar to that of animals. Unlike the cells of the green algae, the body (called a *thallus*) of *Fucus* is a diploid sporophyte. This thallus contains cuplike structures called *conceptacles*, which produce haploid gametes (Figure 22–9). The diploid sporophyte is thus not dependent on another, separate plant (the gametophyte), for successful reproduction. Eggs and sperm unite in the water to form a new sporophyte generation. In contrast, other brown algae such as *Laminaria* have separate sporophyte and gametophyte generations.

GENERAL CHARACTERISTICS OF BROWN ALGAE

1. They contain chlorophyll *a* and *c* as well as the yellow-brown pigment *fucoxanthin*.

2. Most are large, leaflike marine forms.

3. They have a conspicuous diploid sporophyte generation.

FIGURE 22–8   The brown alga *Sargassum natans*. (Grant Heilman, Runk/Schoenberger.)

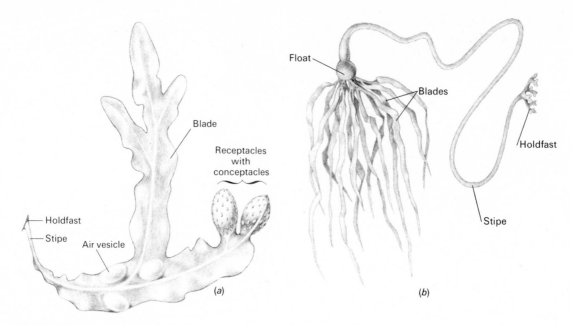

FIGURE 22–9   Two common genera of kelp. (a) *Fucus* (rockweed kelp). (b) *Nereocystis* (bullwhip kelp).

4. They undergo alternation of generations.

5. Their bodies show some differentiation into specific parts: holdfast, stipe, and blade.

Red Algae: Phylum Rhodophyta
Approximately 3000 identified species

All red algae are attached marine species. Most are multicellular seaweeds; a few are single-celled forms. The red algae have provided humans with the most diverse products of all the algal groups: agar growth media for bacteria, soups (at least in Japan), food supplements for animals, seasonings, and emulsifiers for dairy products such as ice cream. An important characteristic of this phylum is their storage of food as floridean starch, similar to glycogen in animals.

Perhaps the most important distinguishing characteristic of the red algae is the presence of both red (phycoerythrin) and blue (phycocyanin) pigments in addition to chlorophyll *a* and *d*, xanthophylls, and carotenoids. Phyco-erythrin and phycoacyanin absorb blue-green light that penetrates deepest into water. Red

algae can thus live in deeper water than other algae can—down to 600 feet.

GENERAL CHARACTERISTICS OF RED ALGAE

1. Most are attached, marine seaweeds.

2. They contain chlorophyll *a* and *d* as well as accessory pigments (carotenes, xanthophylls, phycoerythrin, and phycocyanin).

3. Red and blue pigments permit photosynthesis to depths of 600 feet.

4. Gametophyte and sporophyte generations alternate; some also have a third generation.

5. Some species reproduce through vegetative spores asexually.

6. Coralline species secrete calcium carbonate around their cells and thus contribute to building of reefs.

7. They store food as floridean starch.

Flagellates: Phylum Mastigophora
Approximately 4000 identified species

This large, varied phylum consists of unicellular and colonial organisms that possess one or more flagella. Some are free-living; others, like the trypanosome that causes sleeping sickness, are parasitic. The phylum consists of three classes: Phytomastigina (autotrophic), dinoflagellata (autotrophic or heterotrophic), and zoomastigina (heterotrophic).

Class Phytomastigina

The common green flagellates *Euglena* and *Volvox* (Figure 22–10) are prominent members of this class. Each cell possesses one or more flagella, chlorophyll *a* and *b*, and, in many cases, a red-pigmented "eye spot." The pigmented area does not itself sense light, but it shields a light-sensitive area within the cell. This area enables the organism to orient itself toward a light source.

Class Dinoflagellata

These important freshwater and marine plankton possess two flagella, one longitudinal and one transverse (encircling the cell). Most species are photosynthetic, but a few are colorless and heterotrophic. Some species cause "red tide" in which the organisms are concentrated in shellfish and are toxic to fish and other vertebrates.

Class Zoomastigina

Members of this class possess one or more flagella and commonly form symbiotic relation-

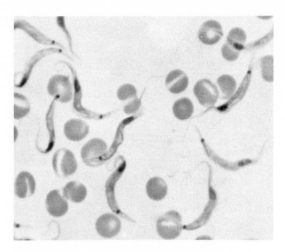

FIGURE 22–11   *Trypanosoma gambiense* in human blood. These parasitic flagellates cause sleeping sickness (×1000).

ships with other organisms. *Trichonympha*, a multiflagellate species, lives mutualistically in the guts of termites. These flagellates digest wood cellulose eaten by the termites, producing nutrients both for themselves and for their hosts.

One parasitic form is *Trypanosoma gambiense* (Figure 22–11), which causes African sleeping sickness. The trypanosome, spread among mammals (including humans) by the bite of the tsetse fly, lives and reproduces in the blood. It eventually passes into the cerebrospinal fluid; when this occurs the host lapses into unconsciousness, coma, and eventually death.

Slime Molds: Phylum Myxomycetes
Approximately 450 identified species

Many characteristics of slime molds place them between true fungi and animallike protists to be discussed later in this chapter. The *plasmodial* stage of their life cycle is much like that of a large amoeba, whereas another stage produces spores, much like a plant. Therefore several approaches to the classification of this group have been tried.

Slime molds possess no chlorophyll and thus cannot photosynthesize. They are heterotrophs, feeding by phagocytosis on bacteria and rotting

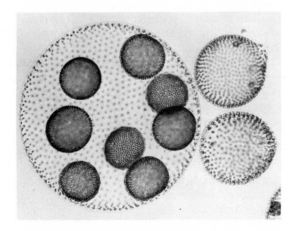

FIGURE 22–10   *Volvox*, a colonial autotrophic flagellate. (Courtesy Carolina Biological Supply Company.)

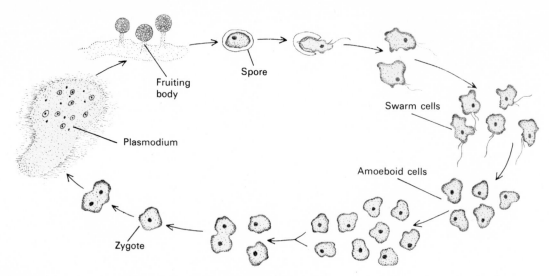

FIGURE 22–12   Life cycle of a typical slime mold. The actively feeding, multinucleate plasmodium produces fruiting bodies. Spores germinate into flagellated swarm cells, which lose their flagella and become amoeboid. Two of these amoeboid cells fuse to produce a zygote, which finally develops into a new plasmodium.

organic matter. In their plasmodial stage, they are often seen on rotting logs.

During the plasmodial stage of the life cycle (Figure 22–12), the plasmodium moves about, feeding for several days. Then it stops and forms stalked fruiting bodies called *sporangia* that produce many haploid spores. These spores are shed into a moist environment, where they germinate into biflagellated swarm cells. After a period of intense cell division, these swarm cells lose their flagella and come to resemble small amoebae. After further division, these swarming amoeboid cells pair and fuse to form zygotes, each of which develops into a plasmodium, thus completing the life cycle.

GENERAL CHARACTERISTICS OF SLIME MOLDS

1. Their life cycle has four stages: an amoeboid plasmodium, stalked fruiting bodies that produce haploid spores, biflagellate swarm cells, and amoeboid cells that fuse to produce a new plasmodium.

2. They feed heterotrophically on bacteria and organic matter.

Fungi: Phylum Eumycophyta
Approximately 100,000 identified species

In older classification schemes, the fungi were placed with the plants. Although they lack chlorophyll, fungi do have some plantlike characteristics. In classifications that include the kingdom Protista, the fungi constitute a phylum of protists. But some recent classification systems designate the fungi as a separate kingdom. This group may well represent a specialized side branch in the evolution of living systems.

The fungi include bread molds, cup fungi, mushrooms, and puffballs. Certain mushrooms and other fungi are prized as food, and several antibiotics (including penicillin) are produced by molds. But other fungi can cause serious problems for higher plants and animals. Fungal blights and rusts damage food plants; animals, including humans are commonly plagued by troublesome skin disorders caused by fungi. Along with bacteria, fungi are important in the recycling of organic matter through decay.

Most fungi consist of strings of elongate cells in long, white filaments called *hyphae*. A mass

Bio-Topic: Fungus Gardens

Cellulose is one of the most abundant natural polymers on our planet. Wood, leaves, and most other plant tissues are largely cellulose. Yet relatively few kinds of organisms can digest cellulose and make use of this enormous reservoir of carbohydrates. Most fungi are able to digest cellulose, and many other kinds of organisms have evolved mechanisms to exploit this ability. At least three groups of insects—beetles, termites, and ants— have evolved mutualistic relationships with cellulose-digesting fungi.

The "fungus-growing" beetles carve tunnels in the wood or under the bark of various trees. The beetles bring with them, often in pouches that serve no other purpose, the spores of their fungal associate. The fungus infects and digests the wood, converting the nutrients into its own cells. The beetles eat the fungus and obtain indirectly nutrients that would otherwise not be accessible to them. Female beetles infect their larvae with the fungus, thereby maintaining the association from generation to generation. For its part, the fungus benefits by being cultivated by the beetles and by being transported to new trees each year.

The social termites have evolved a somewhat different association with their fungi. These termites build within their hives large corallike combs that are assembled from their wastes. In and on these combs grow the hyphae of fungi, but the hyphae are not a large part of the termite diet. Instead, young termites feed on the combs and become infected with the fungus which becomes established in their intestines. Wood eaten by these termites is digested by the enzymes produced by the intestinal fungi. Many nonsocial termites have intestinal protozoa (which also digest cellulose) that function in a similar way.

Species of fungus-growing ants actually cultivate, fertilize, and weed elaborate gardens of specific fungi. When a queen establishes a new colony, she brings with her a wad of the fungus associated with her species. Workers gather bits of fresh plants and chew these into pulpy masses. (Some species also gather wood, dead insects, and other materials.) The pulp is mixed with the fungus wad, which grows into a garden that provides food for the nest, especially the larvae. Workers weed the garden by removing foreign fungi and fertilize it by adding their own wastes. The association is so close that the ants have evolved special anal secretions that contain protein-digesting enzymes that their fungi have lost the ability to make. The fungi have also lost the ability to form spores and rely entirely on their ant farmers for their dissemination.

of hyphae, such as the mushroom fruiting body, is termed a *mycelium*. The cell walls of some fungi contain cellulose, but most fungi have tough walls made principally of chitin, a polysaccharide. Fungi have no roots, stems, or leaves; they anchor themselves by filamentous projections called *rhizoids*. Hyphal filaments release enzymes into whatever they attach to and absorb the food these enzymes digest. Fungi never contain chlorophyll; they are always either saprophytic (living on dead matter) or parasitic. Like other protists, fungi show little cell differentiation.

Some true fungi (*ascomycetes* and a few *basidiomycetes*) enter into a mutualistic symbiosis with green or blue-green algae. Such combinations, as we saw in Chapter 6, are known as *lichens*. Lichens are extremely hardy organisms that can inhabit very cold and dry environments.

GENERAL CHARACTERISTICS OF THE FUNGI

1. Most consist of extensive filaments called *hyphae* (yeasts are an exception).

2. Nutrition is saprophytic or parasitic; fungi possess no photosynthetic pigments.

3. Most forms have cell walls composed mainly of chitin.

4. Many are parasitic on plants and animals.

5. They are essential decomposers of organic matter.

Algal Fungi: Class Phycomycetes

Common bread molds with long hyphal filaments are the best-known examples of this group. The filaments have no cross-walls and thus are multinucleate. Fruiting bodies (sporangia) arise from the hyphae on tall stalks and produce nonmotile spores that are carried away by air or water. These spores develop into new mycelia. The bread mold *Rhizopus* has two different strains that are similar to the male and female forms in higher organisms (Figure 22–13); since it is impossible to tell the strains apart visually, they are simply denoted + and −. When + and − strains come together, conjugation can occur. Two haploid hyphal filaments fuse, and many nuclei are produced by mitosis at the tips of the filaments. The wall between the hyphae then breaks down, and the nuclei fuse in pairs. This diploid (2*n*) multinucleate zygote is then released from the parent mycelium; after a dormant period it gives rise to a new hyphal filament. Since meiosis occurs in the zygote, this is the only diploid stage in the life cycle; the new hyphal filaments are haploid.

Algal fungi thrive in water and damp places. One special characteristic of some forms is the ability to produce and liberate flagellated, non-

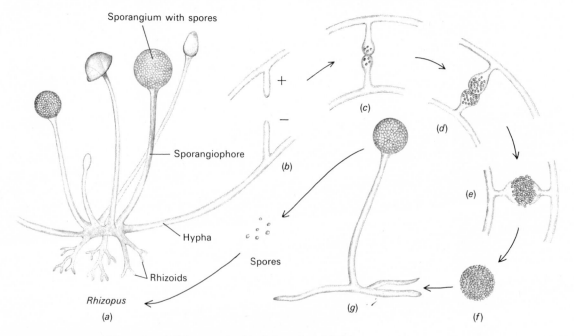

FIGURE 22–13 Life cycle of *Rhizopus,* the black bread mold. (*a*) Portion of a mycelium, showing hypha with fruiting bodies. (*b* and *c*) Hyphae of different strains (+ and −) come together in conjugation. (*d* and *e*) The filament walls break down and the haploid nuclei fuse in pairs. (*f*) A multinucleate zygote forms. (*g*) Meiotic cell division gives rise to a new hyphal filament, which produces a fruiting body with haploid spores.

sexual *zoospores* (motile spores) in the water. These spores are an excellent means of distributing the species.

Sac Fungi: Class Ascomycetes

The hyphae of sac fungi consist of individual cells with distinct cross-walls or *septae*. A unique characteristic of these fungi is the production of nonmotile *ascospores* after sexual conjugation. The cylindrical, saclike structures that produce these spores are called *asci* (singular *ascus*). Generally, each ascus contains eight ascospores (Figure 14–3).

Among the diverse members of this group are yeasts, molds, powdery mildews, red cup fungi, and the edible morel "mushrooms."

Club Fungi: Class Basidiomycetes

Members of this class, called club fungi because of their small, club-shaped spore-producing structures, include the familiar mushrooms, bracket fungi, and puffballs as well as rusts and smuts (Figure 22–14). Basidiomycetes are most common in rich organic soil, but some are found on both living and dead trees.

Like the sac fungi, the basidiomycetes have septate hyphae and generally produce a conspicuous fruiting body. Spores are formed by meiosis after a sexual merging of haploid nuclei. The structures that generate spores are called *basidia*, and the spores are termed *basidiospores*.

Mushrooms are widely distributed and are probably the most familiar of fungi (Figure 22–15, on color plate following p. 592). The mycelium of a mushroom grows underground as a spreading mass of branched hyphal filaments. Some mycelia may extend hundreds of feet through the soil. In the spring or in the fall, characteristic fruiting bodies emerge to produce and disseminate spores.

Amoebae: Phylum Sarcodina
Approximately 15,000 identified species

Amoebae are single-celled and contain no chlorophyll. Although we generally think of an amoeba as a simple, amorphous blob, many sarcodinans are highly structured organisms with beautiful shells of calcium carbonate, silicon dioxide, or chitin (Figure 22–16). Amoebae move by forming temporary cellular projections called *pseudopods* ("false feet"). Besides providing locomotion, pseudopods serve to en-

FIGURE 22–14 The basidiomycete *Polyporus squamosus,* a bracket fungus. (Courtesy Department of Plant Pathology, Cornell University.)

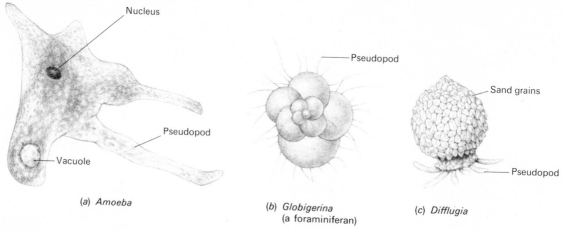

(a) *Amoeba*

(b) *Globigerina*
(a foraminiferan)

(c) *Difflugia*

FIGURE 22–16   Representative sarcodinians. (a) *Amoeba*. (b) *Globigerina*. (c) *Difflugia*.

gulf food particles by phagocytosis. Most amoebae feed on small flagellates, ciliates, or algae. A few species are parasitic in the intestine of animals, causing the debilitating and often fatal *amoebic dysentery*.

The foraminiferans, which form shells of calcium carbonate, and the radiolarians, which use silicon dioxide in forming their shells, are abundant in the oceans. For millions of years these forms have left their shells in the oceanic ooze (Figure 22–17). Geologists today can estimate the age of sedimentary rock strata and even predict the presence of oil deposits by identifying particular species of foraminiferans or radiolarians. Foraminiferans constitute a large portion of chalk and limestone deposits. The white cliffs of Dover on England's east coast are an outstanding example of an uplifted ocean bottom containing foraminiferan shells.

GENERAL CHARACTERISTICS OF SARCODINIANS

1. They move by extending pseudopods.
2. They trap food with pseudopods and engulf it by phagocytosis.
3. Their nutrition is heterotrophic.
4. Some forms produce shells of debris, chitin, calcium carbonate, or silicon dioxide.

Sporozoans: Phylum Sporozoa
Approximately 500 identified species

Sporozoans are parasitic forms that lack organelles for locomotion during most of their life cycle. The best-known are members of the genus *Plasmodium* that cause malaria. Carried by the female *Anopheles* mosquito, they undergo a complex series of transformations during their life cycle, both in the mosquito and in the human host.

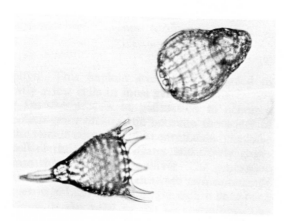

FIGURE 22–17   Radiolarian shells are composed of silicon and show many symmetric variations. Sticky pseudopods for catching prey extend through the hole in the shells. (Courtesy Carolina Biological Supply Company.)

The infective form of the parasite is generally produced in the gut of the mosquito and concentrated in its salivary glands. When an infected mosquito penetrates the skin of a human to draw blood, it injects anticoagulants from its salivary glands; some of the infective *sporozoites* then enter the bloodstream.

After they undergo further changes in the human liver and bloodstream, the organisms invade millions of red blood cells. The rupture of these cells releases toxins that produce the symptoms of malaria—chills and high fever. After many asexual cycles the parasites produce gametes in the bloodstream, and a feeding mosquito sucks them into its gut. There the gametes fuse to produce hundreds of encysted sporozoites. When the sporozoites are released, they migrate to the mosquito's salivary gland, thus completing the life cycle.

GENERAL CHARACTERISTICS OF SPOROZOANS

1. They are parasitic.
2. At some stage of the life cycle, they bear spores.
3. Their life cycle may involve a carrier such as the mosquito.
4. They possess no specialized organelles for locomotion.
5. Reproduction proceeds by alternate sexual and asexual stages.
6. They infect blood and tissues of animals and humans.

Ciliates and Suctorians: Phylum Ciliophora
Approximately 6000 identified species

The members of this large phylum are unicellular aquatic organisms that possess cilia at some stage during their life. Individuals vary in structure, including the location of cilia; the suctorians are forms that possess cilia only during their larval stage. All ciliophorans have two types of nuclei: large (macronuclei) and small (micronuclei). The micronuclei appear to contain the essential genetic information that is retained from generation to generation because they always divide by mitosis or meiosis, thereby providing equal distribution of chromosomes. Macronuclei, on the other hand, do not divide by mitosis or meiosis and even disintegrate and are lost into the cytoplasm during conjugation.

GENERAL CHARACTERISTICS OF CILIOPHORANS

1. They have cilia at some stage of their life cycle.
2. They possess both macronuclei and micronuclei.
3. They are covered with a transparent, elastic cuticle.

Ciliates: Class Ciliata
As we learned in Chapter 4, cilia are organelles with a 9 + 2 arrangement of contractile microtubules. In the most complex ciliates, several cilia may be grouped to form larger organelles called *cirri.* In some species, cirri may be used to "crawl" along a submerged substrate. Ciliates may be free-moving such as *Paramecium*, or attached by a stalk, as with *Vorticella* (Figure 22–18). Stalked species are capable of detaching themselves and swimming freely about until they find a new attachment site.

Ciliates are classified according to the complexity of their structure and the placement of their cilia. Of all the protists, the ciliates possess the most complex array of organelles: they may have contractile vacuoles for regulating water balance, dartlike stinging organelles called *trichocysts* for defense and seizure of prey, and, in some, a cell mouth (*cytostome*) and an anal pore (Figure 22–19).

Suctorians: Class Suctoria
In members of this class cilia are present only in motile young stages. Mature suctorians are attached, nonciliated cilophorans that use their unique tentacles to trap prey. The tentacles of some species are sharp and can penetrate the body of the prey; other species' tentacles have knoblike extensions. It appears that the cytoplasm of the prey is sucked into the tentacles and transported around the cell.

Moneran and protistan living systems are sometimes called "simple" (as well as "primi-

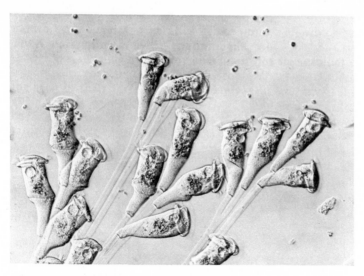

FIGURE 22–18   The ciliate *Vorticella*. (Courtesy Carolina Biological Supply Company.)

tive") organisms. But, as we have seen, moneran and protistan cells may be quite complex. Structural complexity above the cellular level, however, is a hallmark of plants (kingdom Metaphyta) and animals (kingdom Metazoa). In the following chapter we consider the plants.

SUMMARY

Monerans—bacteria and blue-green algae—are the most primitive living organisms on earth. These procaryotes have no organized nucleus, mitochondria, Golgi apparatus, lysosomes, centrioles, endoplasmic reticulum, or chloroplasts. Most monerans are microscopic; they reproduce by binary fission or fragmentation. Nutrition may involve photosynthesis, chemosynthesis, or absorption. The kingdom Monera contains two phyla: Schizophyta (bacteria), and Cyanophyta (blue-green algae).

Viruses are tiny, nonliving parasites that are difficult to place in a classification system of the living world. They are not cellular and can reproduce only inside a living cell. Viruses, do however, possess genetic information in the form of DNA or RNA surrounded by a protein shell. Once inside a host cell, the viral nucleic acids take over the protein synthesis machinery and reproduce themselves.

The simplest eucaryotic organisms occur as single cells, colonies, filaments, or a differentiated body. These organisms, called protists, have a well-defined nucleus with a double membrane, chromosomes that contain both

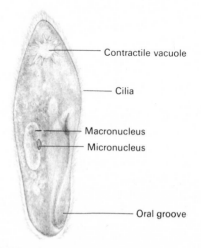

FIGURE 22–19   Some of the specialized organelles of ciliates, shown in *Paramecium*.

Contractile vacuole

Cilia

Macronucleus
Micronucleus

Oral groove

DNA and protein, and organelles. In addition, they undergo mitosis and may form sexual gametes. Many protists have complex chloroplasts, and some possess organelles for locomotion, such as flagella and cilia. The kingdom Protista contains 10 phyla: Chlorophyta (green algae); Chrysophyta (golden-brown algae); Phaeophyta (brown algae); Rhodophyta (red algae); Mastigophora (flagellates); Myxomycetes (slime molds); Eumycophyta (fungi); Sarcodina (amoebae); Sporozoa (sporozoans); and Ciliophora (ciliates and suctorians).

Many protists, including the algae and green flagellates, are important members of aquatic food chains. Some are parasitic, causing diseases in both plants and animals. Such diseases include fungus infections, malaria, and amoebic dysentery. Other protists produce harmful toxins; these include the "red tide" dinoflagellates and poisonous mushrooms.

REVIEW QUESTIONS

1. What basic characteristics distinguish monerans from protists?

2. Why is it difficult to include viruses in a natural classification system? How are viruses similar to bacteria?

3. What does the brown alga *Fucus* have in common with animals?

4. What uses have humans made of red algae?

5. What is the survival value of the pigments phycoerythrin and phycocyanin, found in red algae?

6. Diagram the four-stage life cycle of a slime mold. What stages are animallike? Which are plantlike?

7. Why does moldy bread take on a fuzzy, greenish, or sooty appearance?

8. How do radiolarians differ from foraminiferans? Of what use have these organisms been to humans?

9. How does the malarial parasite *Plasmodium* cause chills and fever during its life cycle in the human?

10. How can members of the class Ciliata be distinguished from organisms of the class Suctoria?

SUPPLEMENTARY READINGS

Alexopoulos, C. J. and H. C. Bold, *Algae and Fungi*, Macmillan, New York, 1967. This booklet provides excellent coverage of the classification, structure, reproduction, and economic importance of these very common protists.

Berg, Howard C., "How Bacteria Swim," *Scientific American*, August 1975. Flagellate bacteria move by the rotation of their flagella in a propellerlike motion. Changing course is achieved by reversing the direction of the rotation.

Goodheart, Clyde R., *An Introduction to Virology*, W. B. Saunders, Philadelphia, 1969. A general reference on viruses that discusses their size, structure, classification, and contribution to our understanding of life and molecular biology.

Litten, Walter, "The Most Poisonous Mushrooms," *Scientific American*, March 1975. The deadly toxins of *Amanita* mushrooms are ring-shaped molecules composed of amino acids. These poisons destroy tissues of the liver, kidneys, and intestinal tract by inhibiting the production of RNA in cell nuclei or disrupting membrane structure.

Rosebury, Theodor, *Life on Man*, Viking Press, New York, 1969. A delightful historical, scientific, and social commentary about the interaction between humans and microbes. Most of the bacteria that live in, on, and around humans are discussed in a witty dialogue that challenges many modern ideas about germs and cleanliness.

Chapter 23

Plants: Kingdom Metaphyta

In this chapter we trace the adaptation to life on land by following the sequential development of the metaphyta, the plants.

The "interim" phylum, the bryophytes *Mosses, Liverworts, and Hornworts,* are true plants that are heavily dependent on a moist environment. They cannot readily absorb and distribute water within their tissues.

The single most important development in the water-land transition of plants is dramatically shown in the *Vascular Plants: Phylum Tracheophyta.* The development of vascular tissues, the thin tubes that conduct water and nutrients through the organism, made possible the establishment of true plants on land. We follow the development of vascular plants chronologically. The oldest of the *Early Vascular Plants* are the *Primitive Vascular Plants: Subphylum Psilopsida.* There are only three species of them identified today. The *Club Mosses and Horsetails: Subphyla Lycopsida and Sphenopsida,* like the Psilopsida, are no longer as prevalent as they were millions of years ago. However, they were the most significant portion of the vegeta-

tive materials that became coal and other fossil fuels.

The concluding portions of this chapter deal with those plants that are particularly well known to us. The *Ferns: Subphylum Pteropsida,* are a familiar part of our landscape, particularly in the warmer temperate areas and the tropics.

The *Seed Plants: Subphylum Spermopsida* are the dominant form of plant life today. Our agriculture is exclusively based on seed plants. Why have seed plants been so evolutionarily successful? The seed, the self-contained reproductive unit that can carry and support the developing plant, gives seed plants an exceptional advantage. Seed plants can disperse their offspring over a wide geographical area, producing independent organisms that are protected against many environmental hazards.

The *Conifers: Class Gymnospermae* include the evergreen trees prominent in our northern forests. The *Flowering Plants: Class Angiospermae* are the most recent and the most successful members of the kingdom Metaphyta.

Life continued to develop past the moneran and protistan types. The evidence indicates that two large groups emerged from the protistans: the plant line and the animal line. It seems likely that metaphytes and metazoans came from protistan stock because of similarities in cell structure: protists, metaphytes, and metazoans are all composed of eucaryotic cells. Moreover, amoeboid, flagellated, and ciliated cell types, which are common among protists, are also found in plants and animals. But unlike most of their protistan ancestors and contemporaries, many plants and animals are capable of living on land.

It is their adaptations for life on land that provide the distinguishing characteristics of metaphytes. For example, land dwellers must have the ability to transport water to all their cells, because the entire plant is not bathed in water. Large land plants have specialized vascular tissue, discussed in Chapter 5, to conduct water throughout the body. Organisms which are not buoyed up by water also require structural support. This mechanical support which must be extremely strong in trees, is furnished by the woody stem. Specialized collenchyma and sclerenchyma tissues help to provide this support in some plants. Subsurface structures are needed both to anchor the plant and to absorb water; soil-penetrating rhizoids or roots perform these functions in plants. Whereas in an aquatic organism all parts may contain chlorophyll and therefore manufacture food, this is not usually the case with land plants. Specialized structures—leaves—are the principal sites of photosynthesis in plants, and vascular tissue is needed to transport food from the leaves to the other parts of a plant.

Still another problem faced by terrestrial plants is loss of water by evaporation. The waxy cuticles and hairy surfaces of a plant's epidermal tissue greatly reduce water loss without blocking the passage of light. Atmospheric gases needed in photosynthesis cannot penetrate the waxy cuticle, but they enter through special openings in leaves called *stomata*, discussed in Chapter 5.

The reproductive structures of plants are a good example of this protection against drying out. These reproductive organs are multicellular, as opposed to the unicellular reproductive structures of protists; they have a protective outer layer of cells surrounding the reproductive cells themselves. In addition, the union of gametes in land-dwelling metaphytes is far more complex than in the aquatic protistans, where swimming gametes can simply unite. In their reproductive structures, such as cones and flowers, plants reach their highest and most complex development.

So we see that organs—stems, roots, leaves, flowers—have been essential developments in the evolution of the metaphytes. Another characteristic distinctive of plants is the plant life cycle, introduced in Chapter 15. This cycle, inherited from protists, involves the alternation of an asexual, spore-producing stage, the *sporophyte*, with a sexual, gamete-producing stage, the *gametophyte*, (Figure 15–4). This basic pattern is known as the *alternation of generations*.

The evolutionary progression from the simplest plants (mosses) to the most complex (seed plants) is marked by ever greater development of the sporophyte. In the mosses the dominant stage of the life cycle is the green, leafy gametophyte. The sporophyte is usually unable to make its own food and is therefore dependent on the gametophyte. Fern gametophytes and sporophytes are both capable of making food, although the sporophyte is much larger. In the seed plants, however, the gametophyte is reduced to a structure, often only a few cells in number, that cannot photosynthesize and is retained on the sporophyte. Figure 23–1 diagrams the relationships between the gametophyte and sporophyte generations of four major plant groups.

The general characteristics of the Kingdom Metaphyta may be summarized as follows:

1. Nutrition is autotrophic by photosynthesis using chlorophyll *a* and *b*.

2. They are composed of organs or organlike structures.

3. Their life cycle alternates between gametophyte and sporophyte generations.

4. Vascular tissue is present in all but bryophytes.

5. They possess multicellular reproductive organs.

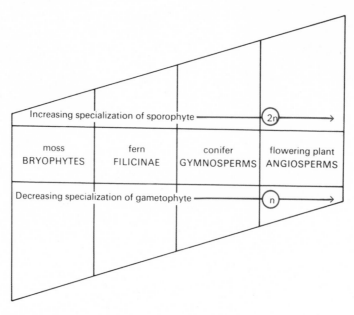

FIGURE 23–1   Relationships between the gametophyte and the sporophyte generations in four plant groups.

6. They produce multicellular embryos.

7. They contain meristematic (growth) tissue at the tips of stems and roots and in lateral positions.

MOSSES, LIVERWORTS, AND HORNWORTS: PHYLUM BRYOPHYTA
Approximately 25,000 identified species

Although metaphytes are thought of as land organisms, the bryophytes have not completed the transition from an aquatic environment. Most species do live on land, but they occur in such moist environments as shady forests and stream banks (Figure 23–2, on color plate following p. 592). These plants must remain close to water, both because they lack vascular tissues to conduct water throughout their bodies and because their flagellated sperm cells need water to reach the egg cells and fertilize them. Bryophytes are small, generally not more than an inch or two in height. They lie closely pressed to the ground because they lack the supporting structure provided by the xylem

tissue of vascular plants. Since bryophytes lack vascular tissue, their structures are described as root*like* or leaf*like* to distinguish them from the true stems, roots, and leaves of vascular plants.

Mosses and liverworts can play important roles in the ecology of an area. For example, mosses often settle in crevices on bare, rocky hillsides. Through their growth and metabolism they contribute to the breakdown of rock to form soil. In this respect mosses are often the pioneers in an area. They may later be crowded out after they have prepared the way for other inhabitants. But this tends to happen to pioneers in any environment; as we saw in Chapter 7, it happens to various species of trees in the process called *forest succession*. Since mosses can take in water through their leaflike structures and retain it, they also form a moist mat on the forest floor, conserving water for other plants. Most of us are familiar with peat moss (genus *Sphagnum*), which forms bogs and which is used by gardeners to maintain a moist medium around growing plants. Although mosses lack the advantages of vascular tissue, they are abundant, contributing members of the biosphere.

The life cycles of the various bryophytes are slightly different, but the moss life cycle is typical of this group. When we examine this reproductive pattern closely, we see that the life cycle actually involves two plants: the green, leafy gametophyte and the stalklike sporophyte (Figure 23–3). Male and female gametophytes both have sex organs at the tips of their branches. The male sex organ, the *antheridium*, produces motile sperms; the female structure, the *archegonium*, produces an egg.

During a rain or heavy dew, sperm move to the archegonium of a female plant, where one sperm fertilizes an egg. The resulting zygote divides repeatedly to form a new 2n generation, the sporophyte. At the tip of the sporophyte a swollen organ known as the *sporangium* develops. Usually part of the old female archegonium, called the *calyptra*, is still present at the top; this remnant soon dries out to give the appearance of a hairy cap. Certain cells within the sporangium, *spore mother cells*, divide by meiosis to produce many haploid spores. The spores are released when they are mature; the

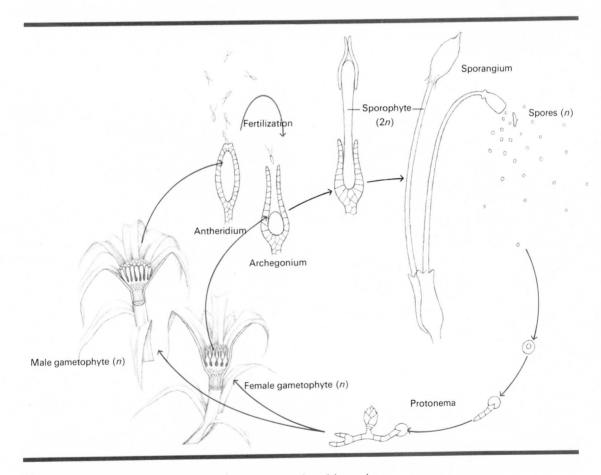

FIGURE 23–3 Life cycle of a moss. Spores are produced by meiosis in the sporangium and germinate as protonema. Gametes produced by the gametophytes fuse to form a sporophyte. (2n). Colored arrows represent haploid stages.

top of the sporangium pops off at that time. The spores germinate in the soil and develop into long threads called *protonema* which resemble a green alga. This fact supports the belief that mosses developed from filamentous green algae. Buds develop from the protonema to produce new male or female gametophytes. Some branches form rootlike structures called *rhizoids* that grow into the ground; they anchor the gametophyte and absorb water and nutrients from the soil.

Thus the complete life cycle of the moss involves two interdependent generations. The gametophytes however, may also spread by continuous growth or reproduce by asexual buds. The reproductive pattern in mosses is an example of a *diplohaplontic* life cycle, showing alternating diploid and haploid generations.

GENERAL CHARACTERISTICS OF BRYOPHYTES

1. The gametophyte generation is dominant.
2. The sporophyte is dependent on the gametophyte.
3. They lack true roots, stems, and leaves.
4. Water is necessary for the life cycle.

This phylum contains three classes: liverworts, mosses, and hornworts (a small group of about 100 species). Representative organisms are shown in Figure 23-4.

VASCULAR PLANTS: PHYLUM TRACHEOPHYTA
Approximately 250,000 identified species

The dominance of the tracheophytes in the land environment is an example of successful evolutionary adaptation. Botanists have classified the tracheophytes in five groups:

Subphylum Psilopsida: primitive vascular plants
Subphylum Lycopsida: club mosses
Subphylum Sphenopsida: horsetails
Subphylum Pteropsida: ferns
Subphylum Spermopsida: seed plants

It will be helpful to refer to geologic time as we discuss these plants. Figure 2-14 showed the geologic eras superimposed on a vertical cut through the Grand Canyon. It will be helpful to refer to another form of geologic chart (Figure 23-5) as we discuss the evolution of plants. As a group, the tracheophytes (vascular plants) share these characteristics:

1. They possess vascular tissues (xylem and phloem).
2. They have true roots, leaves, and stems.
3. The sporophyte is the dominant generation of the life cycle.

The fossil record indicates that plants moved from the water onto the land more than 400 million years ago, probably during the Silurian and Devonian periods (Figure 23-5). The evidence further shows that bryophytes as well as a variety of vascular plants—psilopsids, lycopsids, horsetails, and ferns—were present at that time. From this great variety of prehistoric forms, only the ferns and the bryophytes remain as important plant groups today. We shall therefore consider the first three subphyla of vascular plants as a single group and then concentrate more closely on the ferns and seed plants.

Early Vascular Plants: Psilopsids, Lycopsids, Sphenopsids

These three plant groups are of great evolutionary importance, but their place in the contemporary biosphere is modest. Psilopods are the simplest and perhaps the oldest vascular plants; the club mosses and horsetails were among their successors.

Primitive Vascular Plants: Subphylum Psilopsida
3 identified species

The psilopsids are represented today by only two living genera: *Psilotum* (two species) and *Tmesipteris* (one species). Most psilopsids became extinct after the Devonian period. Although they are not much more complex than some algae, these plants have aerial shoots and the other characteristics of vascular plants. However, they lack true roots (Figure 23-6). Psilopsids are leafless or have small, simple leaves; an underground portion of the stem, with rhizoids, serves the function of roots.

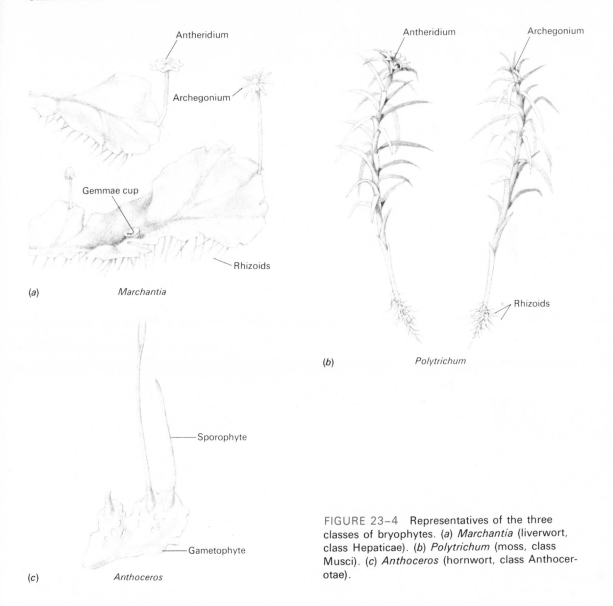

FIGURE 23–4 Representatives of the three classes of bryophytes. (*a*) *Marchantia* (liverwort, class Hepaticae). (*b*) *Polytrichum* (moss, class Musci). (*c*) *Anthoceros* (hornwort, class Anthocerotae).

Club Mosses and Horsetails: Subphyla *Lycopsida* and *Sphenopsida*

Approximately 900 identified species of Lycopsida; approximately 25 identified species of Sphenopsida

An examination of plants living today would not reveal the once vast abundance of the lycopsids and sphenopsids or their prominent place in the history of plant life. Fossils, how-ever, clearly indicate that these two groups were among the dominant plant forms during the Devonian, Carboniferous, and Permian periods, some 250 to 400 million years ago (Figure 23–7). These two groups reached the peak of their dominance in the great "coal forests" of the Carboniferous, about 350 million years ago. Some now-extinct lycopsids and sphenopsids were trees that attained heights of more than 120 feet and diameters of 6 feet. The first seed

Eras	Periods	Years Ago	Biological Events
Cenozoic	Holocene	10,000	Extensive radiation of humans
	Quaternary	2 million	Periods of glaciation. First humans and their civilizations
	Tertiary	60 million	Modern mammals and early primates appear, angiosperms become dominant land plants. Radiation of modern birds.
Mesozoic	Cretaceous	135 million	Angiosperms develop as gymnosperms decline. Radiation of mammals. Dinosaurs become extinct.
	Jurassic	180 million	Primitive mammals appear. Age of Dinosaurs. Flying reptiles and birds in evidence.
	Triassic	240 million	Gymnosperms dominant land plants. Origin of dinosaurs. Decline of seed ferns and lycopsids.
Paleozoic	Permian	280 million	Rapid evolution of reptiles. Modern types of insects appear. Lycopsids, sphenopsids, seed ferns, and conifers abundant.
	Carbonifer-ous	350 million	Seed-bearing plants (conifers) appear. Large tropical forests that produced coal. Amphibians became dominant.
	Devonian	405 million	First amphibians, ferns, and gymnosperms. Age of fishes.
	Silurian	425 million	Vascular plants move onto land. Mollusks and brachiopods.
	Ordovician	500 million	Primitive, jawless fishes appear. Marine algae abundant.
	Cambrian	600 million	Radiation of most marine invertebrates. Trilobites abundant.
Proterozoic	Precam-brian	Over 600 million	Poor fossil record. Some evidence of marine invertebrates.
Archeozoic			No direct evidence.

FIGURE 23–5   Relationships of events in the development of life to time. This geological time table assists in the understanding of the history of life on earth.

plants appeared during the Carboniferous. By the end of the Permian period, approximately 235 million years ago, the lycopsids and sphenopsids had declined and the seed-bearing plants were dominant. The principle of natural selection was certainly operating in this case, as we will see more clearly when we consider the adaptations of seed plants.

Thus the forerunners of today's relatively unimportant club mosses and horsetails provided one of our most important energy sources: billions of tons of coal, most of which

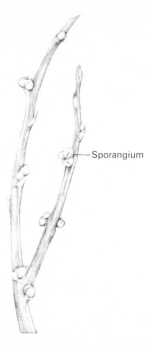

—Sporangium

FIGURE 23-6 *Psilotum,* a member of the Psilopsida. Early vascular plants of this type were probably the first to inhabit a land environment.

is yet unmined. What are contemporary club mosses and horsetails like? We might overlook them as we scan the flora of a modern landscape, because the species of the five surviving genera are dwarfed by many of the modern seed plants.

In general, living lycopsids have a more complex body plan than the psilopsids, (Figure 23-8, on color plate following p. 592). Lycopsids also have true roots and leaves. Some lycopsid leaves, *sporophylls,* have sporangia on their surfaces. When these sporophylls are clustered together they form a structure called a *strobilus* that resembles a club; from this the name *club moss* is derived.

This subphylum provides an excellent opportunity to note the two basic types of life cycles found among vascular plants: *homosporous* and *heterosporous.* In homosporous plants, sporangia produce only one kind of spore, which develops into a gametophyte. Sporangia in heterosporous plants produce two types of spores: a *microspore* which develops into a male gametophyte and a *macrospore* which produces a female gametophyte. *Lyco-*

FIGURE 23-7 Reconstruction of a forest of the Carboniferous period, which contained lycopsid and sphenopsid trees. (Courtesy Field Museum of Natural History.)

podium, or ground pine, is a homosporous lycopsid: it produces only one kind of spore. Each spore in turn produces a gametophyte that contains both archegonia and antheridia.

Although now-extinct sphenopsids were important large trees of the coal-forming forests more than 300 million years ago, their living representatives are generally less than 3 feet tall; they are known as horsetails or scouring rushes. Since horsetails are commonly found in sandy soil along streams and roads, their stems contain silica, and people have long used them for scouring and polishing. The single living genus, *Equisetum*, is homosporous. The sporophyte phase is represented by two different structures—the leafy vegetative shoot and the fertile shoot containing the strobilus (sporangia).

Ferns: Subphylum Pteropsida
Approximately 10,000 identified species

Ferns probably appeared first during the Devonian period, about 400 million years ago. They were prominent members of the Carboniferous and Permian flora. Even though some ferns produced seeds, these species were declining during the Triassic, about 240 million years ago, as were the lycopsids. Both were giving way as the more efficient seed-bearing trees developed. But the ferns are still common in our landscapes; they grow only a few feet tall in the temperate zones, but tree ferns in the tropics may attain considerable heights.

Most familiar ferns have rather large, subdivided (compound) leaves, often called *fronds*, with horizontal or underground stems (*rhizomes*) from which roots extend. In many species the sporophylls, which carry sporangia, appear as regular leaves. In some species, however, sporophylls are modified into spikelike structures. In either case, most ferns are homosporous, producing independent green gametophytes. Flagellated sperm produced from antheridia on the underside of the gametophyte require water through which to swim to reach eggs in archegonia. In this respect the ferns are no better adapted to life on land than are the mosses (Figure 23–9).

The life cycle of a fern is frequently studied in general biology classes. Several species may

FIGURE 23–9   Three ferns—goldie, narrow-leaved spleenwort, and maidenhair. (Courtesy of the American Museum of Natural History.)

be used, the most common of which are *Pteridium* (bracken fern), *Polypodium* (licorice fern), *Polystichum* (sword fern), and *Adiantum* (maidenhair fern). The life cycle involving alternation of generations, common to all plants, is well illustrated by the fern. This cycle in the fern is similar to that of the moss, but in the fern the dominant generation has shifted from the gametophyte to the sporophyte (Figure 23–10).

The fern's familiar green leaf is part of the sporophyte generation. Spores are produced by meiosis in small sporangia located in brown clusters, *sori*, on the undersides of some leaves. When the spores are mature the sporangium dries and opens, literally throwing the spores to the winds. Small heart-shaped gametophytes develop from these spores. These plants possess both male and female organs in antheridia and archegonia. When water is available, flagellated sperm cells swim to the eggs in the archegonia and fertilize them. A sporophyte then grows from the fertilized egg. Although very small, the gametophyte is an independent, photosynthesizing organism; the sporophyte that grows from it is also independent and photosynthesizing. In contrast, the gametophyte generation in seed plants is *not* an independent structure.

GENERAL CHARACTERISTICS OF FERNS

1. Large compound leaves arise from underground stems (rhizomes) or from upright stems.

2. In most ferns clusters of sporangia (sori) occur on the underside of leaves.

3. Most forms are homosporous.

4. The gametophyte (called a prothallus) is green and independent but the sporophyte is the dominant generation.

Seed Plants: Subphylum Spermopsida
Approximately 250,700 identified species

Although ferns are quite successful and abundant, their adaptation for life on land is not

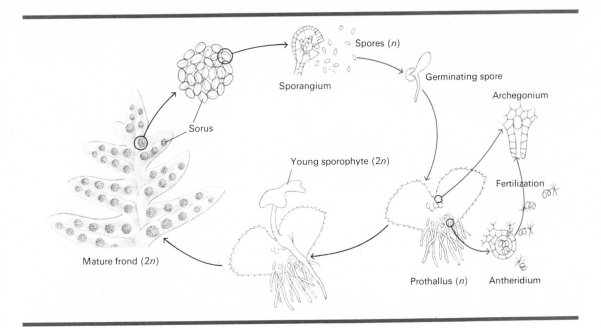

FIGURE 23–10 Life cycle of a typical fern. The sporophyte (2*n*) is the predominant generation. In contrast to that of the moss, the fern gametophyte is much reduced in size. Colored arrows represent haploid stages.

complete. If we wish to study plants that have truly adapted to a land environment, we must look to the seed plants, whose success is evident in their dominance in practically every land community. Indeed we often characterize living communities by the names of the dominant seed plants, as with a spruce-fir forest. The fossil record (Figure 23–5) indicates that seed plants appeared during the Carboniferous period, about 350 million years ago; their evolutionary development was so successful that they became dominant during the Triassic, more than 240 million years ago, and they are still dominant today. Although the chief innovation of the spermopsids was the production of seeds, an examination of this group's subdivisions shows a number of adaptive variations on the seed-bearing theme.

Why have seed plants been so successful? One of the most important reasons lies in the nature of the seeds themselves. These reproductive units enclose an *embryo* (young plant), provide it with a food supply, and surround it with a protective coat. These tiny new sporophytes have a distinct advantage in most environments.

Bio-Topic: Seed Power

A seed is little more than a dormant embryo surrounded by a mass of stored food and enclosed in a protective covering. Natural selection has produced seeds that are intricately designed for efficient dispersal and for germination only under favorable conditions. In fact, the versatility of seeds accounts for much of the success of the higher plants.

The adaptations that ensure efficient dispersal—hooks, barbs, wings, parachutes —are well known. Those that ensure efficient germination are less familiar but more fascinating. Many seeds have tough coats that prevent the entry of water and thus maintain the dormancy of the embryo. Some conifer seeds will not germinate until after the seed coat is cracked by the heat of a nearby fire. At the next rain, such seeds germinate in a bed of mineral-rich ashes and without competitors that block the sun. Other thick-coated seeds germinate only after being rotted by soil fungi that require high moisture, as the seedlings will. Others germinate only after being attacked by the digestive juices of vertebrates and will be fertilized by the animal's droppings. The variety is endless.

The seeds of many desert plants contain, in the surface layers, chemicals that inhibit germination. The built-in inhibitors are washed out only after several substantial rains. This ensures that the seeds remain dormant until there is sufficient moisture in the soil to support the seedlings. Other seeds will germinate only after prolonged exposure to freezing temperatures, ensuring that the seeds germinate after, not before, a winter that would kill the seedlings.

Perhaps the most impressive aspect of seeds is the force generated as the starches in the endosperm cells absorb water. This earliest phase of germination causes the endosperm to swell to several times its dry volume, provides water for the embryo, and loosens the soil for the young seedling. The force exerted during this swelling is so great that the ancient Egyptians are thought to have split rock with germinating seeds. A series of holes was drilled along the desired fracture plane. Each hole was filled with dry seeds and water, and the hole sealed with a tight wooden stopper. The force exerted as the seeds absorbed water and swelled was sufficient to split the rock.

Whereas the Spermopsida can be subdivided into as many as six or seven classes, only two—the *gymnosperms* (plants with naked seeds) and *angiosperms* (plants with enclosed seeds)—are prominent enough for detailed discussion here. The minor spermopsid classes, which resemble gymnosperms, include, among others, the pteridospermae, or seed ferns, which thrived approximately 300 million years ago but are now extinct; the Cycadae, mostly fossil plants but with nine living genera in tropical and subtropical regions; and the Ginkgoae, including the familiar ginkgo tree, practically extinct in the wild but growing very well when cultivated.

Conifers: Class Gymnospermae
Approximately 700 identified species

This group of woody trees and shrubs, most of which are evergreen, includes the oldest and largest plants known. Common conifers include firs, pines, cedars, hemlocks, spruces, redwoods, junipers, and cypresses (Figure 23–11). As we saw in Chapter 7, these trees dominate many temperate-zone forests. The conifers are extremely important as a source of timber. Gymnosperms became dominant more than 200 million years ago, but they held this position of dominance only temporarily; by the end of the Cretaceous period some 60 million years ago, they had given way to another group of seed-producing plants which were apparently better adapted to most land environments. In order to compare these two successful classes of seed producers, we shall describe the life cycle of each (Figures 23–12 and 23–14).

Some gymnosperms, including pines, require two years to complete a reproductive cycle (Figure 23–12). Many other conifers, including spruces and firs, complete their reproductive cycles in one season.

We shall describe the life cycle of the pine as an example. We may begin with *staminate* (male) cones and *ovulate* (female) cones. The staminate cones produce winged pollen grains that are carried by the wind to the larger, ovulate cones. Each leaflike scale of the female cone develops two *ovules*, each of which contains a *megasporangium*. One cell in each meg-

FIGURE 23–11   The gymnosperm *Sequoia sempervirens,* coast redwood. (National Park Service Photo.)

asporangium divides by meiosis to produce four haploid *megaspores*. Three of these megaspores disintegrate leaving one megaspore that divides by mitosis to produce a multicellular female gametophyte. Each female gametophyte (*n*) produces several archegonia and each archegonium produces an egg.

Each cone scale (called a microsporophyll), on the staminate (male) cone bears a pair of *microsporangia*. The microsporangia each produce microspore mother cells, which undergo meiosis to produce four haploid *microspores*. Each microspore develops into a pollen grain. In this development two functional cells are produced, a generative cell and a tube cell; two other cells of the microspore soon degenerate. A thick coat develops around the outside of the pollen grain and two wing-like structures form. A pollen grain, then, is actually a male gameto-

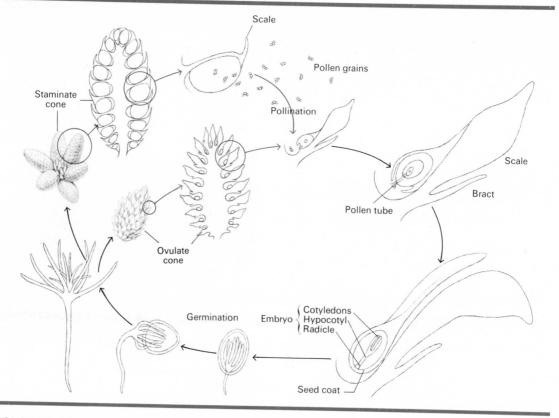

FIGURE 23–12   Life cycle of a typical conifer. Whereas pines require two years to produce a mature seed, the cycle in such conifers as fir and spruce is completed in one season. Colored arrows
represent haploid events.

phyte. This haploid structure is reduced to
only a few cells in most gymnosperms.

For the process of pollination to occur, a
pollen grain must settle between the scales of
the female cone, near its central axis. The tube
cell of the pollen elongates and slowly grows
into the female gametophyte. The generative
cell of the pollen divides into two nonmotile
sperms, which enter the tube cell to be carried
along in the tube to the archegonium. The
pollination process requires approximately one
year to complete. When the tube reaches an
egg, it bursts to release the sperms. One sperm
fertilizes an egg, forming a new sporophyte
generation (2n). The tissue of the surrounding

ovule then develops into a hardened coat, and
the fertilized egg divides to produce a multicellular *embryo*. The developing embryo is nourished by food stored in the cells of the old
female gametophyte. The embryo, with its associated food and the hardened coat, is known
as a *seed* (Figure 23–13). Such a structure gives
conifers a distinct survival advantage over
plants that do not form seeds. If the seed is
released from the plant during a dry period it
can remain dormant until water becomes
available for germination. Furthermore, a
newly formed individual already developing
(an embryo) with a source of food and a protective coating has a definite survival advantage

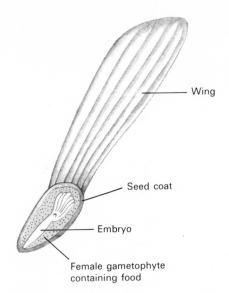

— Wing

— Seed coat

— Embryo

Female gametophyte
containing food

FIGURE 23–13 Section through a pine seed,
showing embryo, seed coat, and food source (female gametophyte).

over spores and other newly produced plant
forms in most environments. This is one reason why seed plants dominate on the earth
today.

The female pine cone dries during the second year, and the scales finally open to release
the mature seeds. In many conifers including
pines, part of the seed coat forms a thin wing,
which aids in dispersal. The mature embryo
within the seed has embryonic leaves called
cotyledons and an embryonic root, the *radicle*.
The portion of the seed between these structures, which elongates to carry the cotyledons
to the surface, is called the *hypocotyl*.

GENERAL CHARACTERISTICS OF CONIFERS

1. Seeds are exposed on the scales of cones.
2. Seeds develop on the old sporophyte and
are released for later germination.
3. Most conifers are trees with small, needle-
like leaves and woody stems.
4. Sperm cells are generally not flagellated.
5. Gametophytes are greatly reduced: the
male gametophyte is reduced to a pollen grain,
the female gametophyte consists of a group of
haploid cells.

Flowering Plants: Class Angiospermae
Approximately 250,000 identified species

Flowering plants, or *angiosperms*, represent the
most complex development in the plant kingdom, and the fossil record confirms their dominance during the last 100 million years or so.
As the angiosperms increased in prominence,
the gymnosperms declined. This reversal was
doubtless related to the more efficient reproductive process of the flowering plants. Angiosperms, like conifers, are a useful source of
wood, but they are more important as our chief
food sources: vegetables, fruits, cereals, and so
on. As in gymnosperms, the diploid sporophyte
generation of angiosperms has assumed complete dominance over the haploid gametophyte.
The gametes are produced by gametophytes, as
in other plants, but angiosperm gametophytes
are reduced even more than those of the gymnosperms. Moreover, the gametophytes (and
gametes) are produced in highly specialized
structures called *flowers*. Flowers that contain
both staminate (male) and pistillate (female)
structures are termed *perfect* flowers (Figure
23–14); if a flower has organs of only one sex, it
is called *imperfect*.

The small green *sepals* and the fragile, often
brightly-colored *petals* are attached to the
flower base, or *receptacle*. If the *pistil*, which
contains the basal ovary, sits above the receptacle, the arrangement is called a superior ovary;
if the pistil is embedded in the receptacle it is
an inferior ovary. The apple is a fruit that
develops from an inferior ovary. The outer
flesh of the apple is formed from the floral tube
which results from the fusion of the basal parts
of sepals, petals, and stamens. *Stamens* have
anthers containing microsporangia that produce microspores. The microspores then develop into pollen grains; each pollen grain contains two haploid nuclei, or sperms. When they
are mature, the pollen grains are released from
the anther of one plant and carried to the pistil
of another, usually by wind or insects. Some
pollen grains land on the *stigma* of the pistil.
Next, a long pollen tube grows down through
the *style* of the pistil to the ovary, where fertilization occurs. At the same time pollen formation occurs in the anthers, megaspores develop

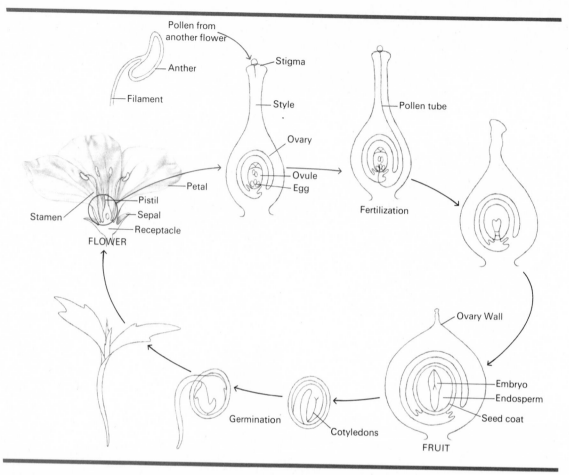

FIGURE 23–14   Longitudinal section through a perfect flower (one that contains both male and female organs.) The fruit develops from the structures indicated. Colored arrows represent haploid events.

in the ovary. As a result, each ovule contains eight haploid nuclei, three of which are functional—an *egg* and two *polar nuclei* (Figure 23–15, on color plate following page 592).

When the pollen tube reaches the ovule, the sperms are released. One sperm unites with the egg to form a diploid zygote; the other sperm fuses with the polar nuclei to form a triploid (3*n*) nucleus. This triploid nucleus gives rise to the seed *endosperm* that provides food for the developing *embryo*. The resulting embryo and endosperm, along with the seed coat that is formed from the ovule wall, constitute the angiosperm seed. In addition, the ovary wall usually develops into a thickened structure that may be hard or fleshy. This developed ovary wall with seed or seeds inside is known as a *fruit* (Figure 23–16). Some fruits assist in the dispersal of seeds: animals eat certain fruits and the hard-coated seeds pass undigested through their alimentary canal, or sticky fruits become attached to fur or clothing. The flower and the fruit, along with the seeds that contain nourishment for the developing embryo, pro-

Bio-Topic: Carnivorous Plants

There are more than 500 species of flowering plants that are carnivorous in the sense that they trap animals, usually small insects. The best known of these is the Venus' flytrap. The leaf tips of this plant are formed into a folding trap that is hinged along the midrib. On the inner surface of each half of the trap are three sensory spines. When an insect touches any two of these spines, the trap snaps shut, imprisoning the insect.

Sundews use an entirely different strategy. The leaves of these plants are thin spines that are often brightly colored. At the tips of each leaf is secreted a drop of sticky fluid that attracts insects. An insect that lands on a sundew becomes trapped in the sticky fluid and cannot escape.

A third strategy is used by the pitcher plants. The leaves of these plants are modified into various cylindrical or tubular shapes. The open end of the tube is often brightly colored, the inner surface is covered with downward-pointing hairs, and the base contains a layer of accumulated rainwater. Insects that enter the tubular leaves are often trapped by the hairs and cannot crawl or fly out. Eventually, the exhausted insect falls into the water at the base of the trap.

What is the point of these elaborate modifications? Why should three distinct lines of plants evolve devices to trap insects? The answer is simple and has to do with nutrition. All three groups of carnivorous plants are found in swamps and bogs. The soil and water in these communities are invariably deficient in nitrogen, an essential building block of proteins. The traps bring insects within reach of protein-digesting enzymes that each of these plants also produce. The enzymes reduce the trapped insects to a pool of amino acids which satisfy the plants' nitrogen needs. The traps and the enzymes are means of obtaining what the soil and water cannot provide.

vide the angiosperms with a very highly efficient method of reproduction. In the seeds of gymnosperms, we saw a reproductive capability superior to that of plants which are not seed producers. But angiosperms with their seeds and fruits have achieved even more efficient reproduction. The triploid endosperm provides a richer food source for the developing embryo, and the fruits surrounding seeds greatly enhance seed dispersal.

Seeds may remain dormant for long periods. This can be particularly important if a seed is in an unfavorable environment. When a seed germinates, it takes in water; metabolic activity, which remains at a very low level in the dormant condition, greatly increases. The resulting cell division and embryonic growth begin the development of a new plant.

GENERAL CHARACTERISTICS OF ANGIOSPERMS

1. They produce flowers.
2. Seeds are enclosed in a fleshy or dry fruit.
3. They produce herbaceous or woody stems.
4. Gametophytes are still more reduced than in the gymnosperms.
5. Fertilization is double: one fertilization produces an embryo; the other produces endosperm, the triploid food source for the developing embryo.

The angiosperms evolved into two large subclasses: *Monocotyledonae* and *Dicotyledonae*. The monocots have been a rich source of food for many civilizations, providing such seeds as wheat, rice, barley, and corn. Other common

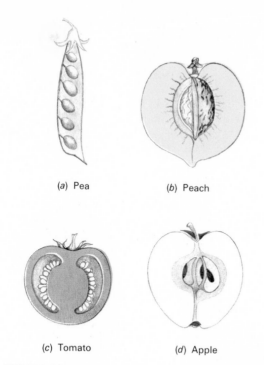

(a) Pea

(b) Peach

(c) Tomato

(d) Apple

FIGURE 23–16   Some common fruits. (a) Pea.
(b) Peach. (c) Tomato. (d) Apple.

monocots include grasses, lilies, irises, and
palms. Some familiar dicots are dandelions,
maples, oaks, potatoes, pumpkins, willows,
roses, carrots, and buttercups. The best way to
compare these two subclasses is to note differences in their characteristics (Figure 23–17).

This completes our overview of one of the
two large groups of organisms that dominate in
the world today—the plants. In the following
chapter we turn to the other prominent
group—the animals.

SUMMARY

The distinguishing characteristics of plants,
which probably evolved from protistan ancestors, are their adaptations for life on land.
These features include multicellular reproductive organs, specialized tissues for support and
conduction, and structures to prevent water
loss. All plants except bryophytes possess organs, including roots, stems, and leaves. In ad-

dition, plants have meristematic tissues specialized for growth in roots, stems, and buds. In
life cycle patterns from the simplest plants to
the most complex seed plants, we see an increasing dominance of the sporophyte generation over the gametophyte.

Members of the phylum Bryophyta include
liverworts, mosses, and hornworts. These plants
do not contain vascular tissues and lack true
roots, stems, and leaves. The gametophyte generation is dominant, and water is necessary for
completion of the life cycle.

The more advanced plants which possess vascular tissues and true roots, stems, and leaves
are placed in the phylum Tracheophyta. Tracheophytes are classified in five subphyla:
Psilopsida (primitive vascular plants);
Lycopsida (club mosses); Sphenopsida (horsetails); Pteropsida (ferns); and Spermopsida
(seed plants). The sporophyte generation is
most dominant in the seed plants.

Seed plants may be further separated into
two classes, Gymnospermae (plants with naked
seeds, such as conifers) and Angiospermae
(plants with seeds enclosed in fruits). The
highly specialized structure known as a seed,
contains an embryo and a food supply that
nourishes the embryo upon germination. With
a few exceptions, gymnosperms bear male (pollen-producing) and female (egg-producing)
cones. Angiosperms produce flowers. Imperfect
flowers are those that contain only male or
female sex organs; perfect flowers contain both
male and female parts. Flowering plants represent the most complex development in the
plant kingdom.

REVIEW QUESTIONS

1. Why are bryophytes commonly short or
trailing plants? Why do they flourish in wet or
humid environments?

2. What is the adaptive purpose of waxy
cuticles on leaves?

3. What is meant by alternation of generations in plant life cycles? Give an example from
mosses, ferns, and seed plants.

4. What adaptations must land plants have?
Explain why they must have each one.

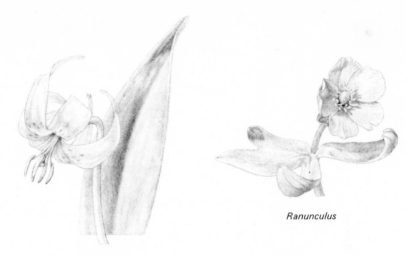

Ranunculus

Lilium

Characteristic	Subclass Monocotyledonae	Subclass Dicotyledonae
Cotyledons (embryonic leaves)	One embryonic leaf at germination	Two embryonic leaves at germination
Leaf venation	Parallel veined leaves	Net-veined leaves
Cambium	No vascular cambium	Distinct vascular cambium present
Vascular bundles	Vascular bundles scattered	Vascular bundles in rings
Flower parts	Flower parts in threes or multiples of three	Flower parts in fours or fives or multiples

FIGURE 23–17   Comparison of monocot and dicot characteristics.

5. What plants are represented in the great coal deposits of the Carboniferous period?

6. What is the function of the tiny sori or "rust spots" on the under surface of a fern leaf?

7. Why have seed plants been so successful?

8. Describe the processes of pollination, fertilization, and seed production as they occur in an angiosperm.

9. Of what economic importance are gymnosperms?

SUPPLEMENTARY READINGS

Gottlieb, Joan E., *Plants: Adaptation through Evolution*, Reinhold Book, New York,

1968. This brief softback stresses the classification, evolution, structure, and physiology of the bryophytes, ferns, and seed plants.

McMahon, Thomas A., "The Mechanical Design of Trees," *Scientific American*, July 1975. Tree trunks and branches increase in diameter and length as trees grow. Several physical models are suggested to explain the interrelationships of elasticity, strength, and natural frequency of vibration in this proportional growth.

Northen, Henry and R. Northen, *Ingenious Kingdom: The Remarkable World of Plants*, Prentice-Hall, Englewood Cliffs, NJ, 1970. A comprehensive treatment of the successful adaptations of plants to their environments.

Chapter 24

Animals: Kingdom Metazoa

We conclude our survey of living systems by looking at the huge kingdom that includes us and all other animals, the Metazoa. Probably the dominant factor in animal evolution is the need to obtain food supplies from the environment. Unlike plants, animals cannot convert energy from the sun into energy-laden biomolecules. Most animals have some nervous system or other mechanism for detecting stimuli in their environment. Most animals show some form of movement. Both of these traits are directly related to the dependence of animals on their environment for energy.

In this chapter we will study twelve phyla that contain the animals most familiar to us. We will organize the animal phyla according to the absence or presence of an internal cavity called a coelom. A body cavity is advantageous because it provides a space for free movement of internal organs in the fluid present in the cavity. A true coelom contains the internal organs of the organism and is lined with a tissue called a peritoneum. Organizing the animal phyla in this way relates directly to the size and patterns of development of each phylum. The **Acoelomata** are the phyla without

internal cavities of any kind. They include the **Sponges: Phylum Porifera,** the **Phylum Coelenterata** (which includes jellyfish, anemones, and corals), and the **Flatworms: Phylum Platyhelminthes.** All of these organisms are basically solid collections of differentiated cells and organs.

Moving along the evolutionary scale, we come to the **Pseudocoelomata.** These organisms have a body cavity, but it is not lined with a special tissue. This group includes a wide range of wormlike organisms, including several species that are parasitic organisms.

By far the largest group is the **Eucoelomata,** those organisms with true coeloms. This group includes the mollusks, the segmented worms, animals with jointed appendages (including insects), and starfish. Further, it also includes the **Phylum Chordata,** which is of particular interest to us. Why?

Among the approximately 45,000 species of chordates, we find the animals that seem to dominate our natural landscape: the birds, fish, reptiles, and amphibians. And of course, there is one final class among the chordates—the mammals, among them *Homo sapiens.*

When we survey the other large group of living systems that developed from protistan stock—the animals or *Metazoa*—the absence of chlorophyll is quite apparent. As we now know, chlorophyll enables plants, and the monerans and protists that have it, to make their own food. Animals are *heterotrophic:* they cannot manufacture their own food but must obtain it from their environment. If we compare the animal way of life to that of plants, we will note two other major differences between the two, both related to the heterotrophic nature of animals.

First, most animals are *motile:* they can move about. Even those animals whose adult stages are *sessile* (attached to another object, such as a rock) are motile in some other stage of their life cycle. Muscle tissue, discussed in Chapter 5, provides this ability to move. Only animals have muscle. The second difference is that animals are much more responsive to their environments than plants are, and their behavioral patterns are more complex. Muscle tissue, together with nervous tissue—another kind of tissue unique to animals, and also examined in Chapter 5—is responsible for these important characteristics. Motility and responsiveness enable animals to seek out the food they need—and to make the attempt (not always successful) to avoid becoming the food that predator animals seek.

There are other differences between plants and animals as well. One is in reproductive patterns. Plants have a reproductive cycle that alternates between gametophyte and sporophyte generations, but the animal pattern is quite different. Most animals are always diploid, a state comparable to the sporophyte phase of plants. In some animal groups, however, individuals do exist in the haploid state. And some aquatic animals have an "alternation of generations" life cycle, but both phases are diploid.

Furthermore, plants and animals differ radically in structure and body organization. As we saw in Chapter 4, plant and animal cells show basic differences. Moreover, organ development is generally much more complex and varied in animals; animal organs tend to form functional organ systems. Plants have fewer organs and do not form organ systems. Plants are capable of an almost indefinite type of growth: they can add new leaves, branches, and reproductive structures. Animals generally lack this capability; their forms are fixed early in their development.

To summarize, the metazoa have these general characteristics:

1. They lack the ability to make food.
2. They contain muscle and nervous tissue; they thus show greater movement and response than plants.
3. Their tissues form organs which make up organ systems.
4. Their cells, unlike plant cells, have centrioles but no cell walls, chloroplasts, or central vacuoles.
5. They have a fixed form determined in early development.

CLASSIFICATION OF ANIMALS

All modern classification systems use structure as their primary basis; the fundamental taxon, or category, is the phylum, which we used in discussing the kingdoms Monera, Protista, and Metaphyta. All the organisms placed in a particular phylum have similar structure and are thought to be related in their evolution. We will use phyla in this chapter, but we will also use another standard grouping system. This system distinguishes animals according to the presence or absence of a body cavity between the internal organs and the body wall. A body cavity has several advantages:

1. It provides more space and freer movement for coiled or folded internal organs.
2. It gives some protection to internal organs that are not connected directly to the body wall.
3. Fluid present in the cavity can assist in the circulation of gases and foods and help to remove wastes.
4. It facilitates physiological and anatomical adaptations necessary for larger animals, such as greater surface area and movement.

There are two types of body cavities: *coelomate* and *pseudocoelomate*. A *coelom* is a cav-

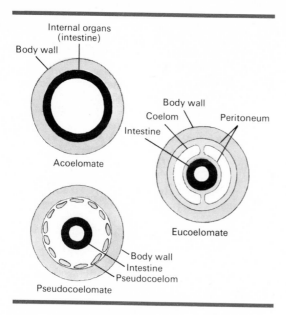

FIGURE 24–1   The three major coelomic plans: acoelomate, pseudocoelomate, and eucoelomate. The diagrams represent cross sections of generalized animal bodies.

ity in which the internal organs and the inside surface of the body wall are lined with an epithelial tissue. This tissue, known as the *peritoneum*, not only serves as a lining but also forms part of the thin sheets of connective tissue (mesenteries) that hold the internal organs in place. The peritoneum forms from the embryonic tissue called the *mesoderm*, discussed in Chapter 16. A cavity that is not completely lined with mesodermal tissue is called a *pseudocoelom*. Animals that lack a body cavity or coelom are called the *Acoelomata*; animals with a body cavity but without a true coelom are the *Pseudocoelomata*; and animals with a coelom are the *Eucoelomata* (Figure 24–1). Eucoelomic animals can be further classified according to the manner in which the coelom develops from the mesoderm.

The acoelomate condition is thought to be the most primitive. In the pseudocoelomates, which are intermediate in complexity, the straight intestinal tract lies free in the body cavity. Neither the tract or the cavity is com-

pletely lined with a peritoneum. The eucoelomate body plan is considered as the "highest" level of development.

Another important characteristic in the animal kingdom is *body symmetry*. Some animals, such as encrusting sponges, have no definite body shape and are thus classified as *asymmetrical*. Bodies that appear to radiate from a central area, like the spokes of a wheel, are said to be *radially symmetrical*; the jellyfish is a good example. Most animals are *bilaterally symmetrical*: if the body were cut in half along one certain plane, the two halves would be mirror images.

Although specialists recognize as many as 30 animal phyla, we shall limit our discussion to 12 of the most familiar. These 12 are also those most commonly encountered in natural communities. Their evolutionary relationships are shown in a treelike diagram in Figure 24–2.

ACOELOMATA

These are animals without a body cavity.

Sponges: Phylum Porifera
Approximately 4500 identified species

Compared to other animals, sponges have only a very simple organization. Their structure is reminiscent of some of the cell types and colonial organizations found among the Protista, from which animals are thought to have evolved. Sponges are considered to be a "side line" in the evolutionary development of animals; they are thought to have developed independently from the main animal branch (Figure 24–2).

Sponges are aquatic, mostly marine, forms with porous bodies. The familiar adult form may be found attached to rocks, sticks, logs, or shells; the larva, on the other hand, is free-swimming until it settles down to develop. In general, the body of a simple sponge is arranged like a globose tube. It has many pores in the body wall through which water enters, a cavity (*spongocoel*) inside, and an opening (*osculum*) at the top for water to leave. The body wall has three layers: an outside layer of thin, flat cells; an inner layer of flagellated collar cells; and,

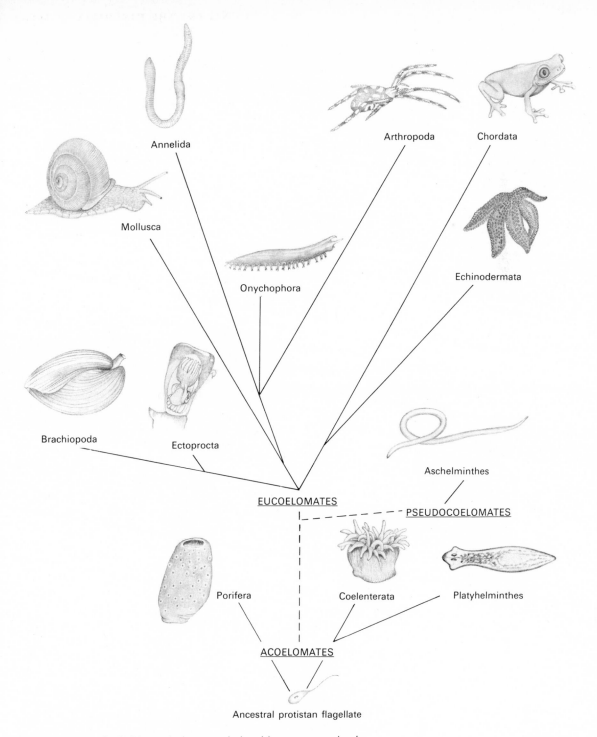

Annelida

Arthropoda

Chordata

Mollusca

Onychophora

Echinodermata

Brachiopoda

Ectoprocta

Aschelminthes

EUCOELOMATES

PSEUDOCOELOMATES

Porifera

Coelenterata

Platyhelminthes

ACOELOMATES

Ancestral protistan flagellate

FIGURE 24–2 Probable evolutionary relationships among animals, based on body cavity development. Dashed lines indicate uncertain ancestral relationships.

between these, a jellylike matrix that contains free-moving amoeboid cells and many small *spicules* of calcium carbonate or silica, which provide support for the soft body.

Sponges may reproduce either sexually or asexually. Asexually, they can *regenerate* lost or damaged regions, or they can add new parts to a colony or new individuals by *budding*. Some species can also form special structures called *gemmules* which can withstand unfavorable conditions. Although sponges do not have gonads (sex glands), sperms and eggs form in the sponge body. After fertilization, flagellated larvae form. These larvae swim some distance from the parents, attach themselves to rocks and other substrates, and develop into new individuals.

GENERAL CHARACTERISTICS OF SPONGES

1. Body organization is cellular, with some differentiation of cell types; but no organs. Body may show radial symmetry or no symmetry.

2. Food is collected by collar cells from water currents passing through the porous body.

3. Body is composed of an exterior epidermal layer, an interior collar-cell layer, and a thin jellylike intermediate layer.

4. Skeleton consists of spicules, organic fibers, or both.

5. Sponges reproduce both sexually and asexually (buds and gemmules); larvae are free-swimming.

Hydra, Jellyfish, Anemones, and Corals: Phylum Coelenterata

Approximately 10,000 identified species

Members of this phylum show organization of cells into tissues. Their bodies are composed of two tissue layers, an outer epidermis and an inner *gastrodermis*. A rudimentary nerve tissue is also present: a network of nervous cells that makes possible simple coordination.

Two body forms often alternate in this aquatic group: attached, elongate *polyps* and free-swimming *medusae*, which resemble jellyfish. These forms may appear to be dissimilar, but close inspection shows that their structure is basically the same. The body consists of a hollow tube closed at one end, somewhat like an elongated sac. The open end forms the mouth; there is no anus. The outer epidermis and the gastrodermis are separated by a thin, gelatinous layer called the *mesoglea*. The digestive cavity is known as a *gastrovascular cavity* because both digestion and circulation of materials occur there.

The medusa stage produces gametes by meiosis; these unite to form a new polyp generation. In organisms without a medusa stage, sexual reproduction is accomplished by sex organs in the polyp. In either case an oval, flattened, ciliated larva (*planula*) is produced following fertilization. It swims about and then settles down and develops into a new polyp.

Coelenterates have modified epithelial cells called stinging cells or *cnidoblasts* (Figure 24-3). These cells, often concentrated on the tentacles surrounding the mouth, are used in capturing prey, clinging to substrates, and defending against predators. Within the cnidoblast is a chitinous, capsulelike stinging organelle called a *nematocyst*.

(a)　　　　(b)

FIGURE 24-3 (*a*) A cnidoblast containing a nematocyst. (*b*) Discharged nematocyst. These threadlike structures, everted from the cnidoblast, can penetrate prey and release a paralyzing secretion.

GENERAL CHARACTERISTICS OF COELENTERATES

1. They show development at the tissue level.

2. The mouth may be surrounded by tentacles containing stinging cells (cnidoblasts).

3. They have no anus.

4. Reproduction may be asexual (budding) or sexual (by gametes).

5. Two body forms may alternate: an attached polyp and a sexual medusa, or jellyfish.

6. All species are aquatic; most are marine.

Hydralike Forms: Class Hydrozoa

In most members of this class, the polyp stage predominates. Some species, like the freshwater *Hydra*, are solitary, but most are colonial. Several species, such as *Velella* (the sail jelly) and *Physalia* (the Portuguese man-of-war), are floating colonies of polyps which are easily mistaken for medusae (Figure 24–4).

True Jellyfish: Class Scyphozoa

The bodies of jellyfish resemble inverted cups. Typically, they have fringing tentacles with nematocysts, an elongated oral tube, and a large amount of gelatinous mesoglea. In order to keep the pulsating bell oriented in the water, 4 to 16 small balance organs are situated around the periphery. Pigmented light-sensory organs called *ocelli* are often present; they probably help the jellyfish to remain in lighted water areas where plankton are more abundant. The sexually mature, swimming medusa stage is predominant; with few exceptions, it alternates with rather inconspicuous polyps. The life cycle of *Aurelia*, a comon marine jellyfish, is representative of this class (Figure 24–5).

Anemones and Corals: Class Anthozoa

This class is one of the best-known groups of seashore animals. Anemones are mostly large, solitary polyps, often beautifully colored because of the presence of symbiotic algae. Some anemones, such as *Anthopleura*, are easily seen in tide pools; others may be often hidden in deeper water. The white or orange sun anemone, *Metridium* (Figure 24–6, on color plate following p. 592), commonly attains a height of

FIGURE 24–4   *Physalia,* the Portuguese man-of-war, is a floating colony of individual polyps. (Grant Heilman, Runk/Schoenberger.)

3 feet. Other anemones are so tiny that they live on the backs or claws of hermit crabs.

Corals are of two types: the stony, or hard, varieties and the softer varieties. Stony corals are the most conspicuous inhabitants of coral reefs; they usually appear as small polyps encased in calcium carbonate.

Flatworms: Phylum Platyhelminthes
Approximately 13,000 identified species

The flatworms may have arisen from the same ancestors as the coelenterates, since many ciliated, free-living flatworm species closely resemble the ciliated planula larvae of coelenterates. If so, several new features have developed in flatworms: bilateral symmetry, a head with sense organs including a ganglionic brain, and

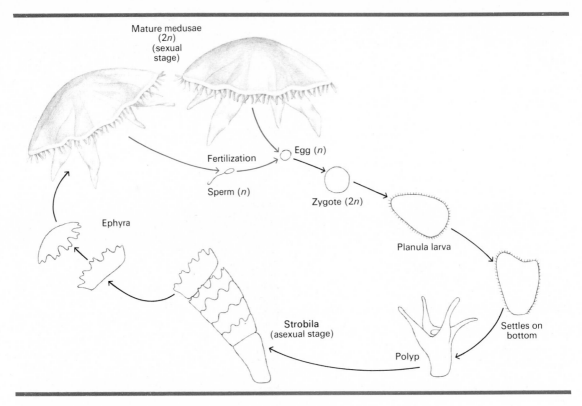

FIGURE 24–5   Life cycle of the scyphozoan jellyfish *Aurelia.*
Colored arrows represent sexual stage. The two body plans,
medusa and polyp, alternate in the life cycle.

an excretory system for the disposal of toxic wastes. These characteristics are most easily observed in free-living species such as the common planarian (Cl. Turbelaria). In parasitic forms many of these features may be modified; cilia and sense organs may be absent. These forms have also developed parasitic features, including suckers, hooks and exceptionally well-developed reproductive systems. These parasites may infect many areas of the human body, including the liver, lungs, blood, bladder, and intestine. Flukes (Cl. Trematoda) and tapeworms (Cl. Cestoda) are in this phylum.

Flatworms can regenerate lost portions of their anatomy. A planarian cut in half will often regenerate two complete worms: the head piece will grow a new tail and the original tail piece will produce a new head.

Flatworms possess an incomplete digestive tract (except when the digestive tract is absent as in tapeworms), with a mouth and an intestine but no anus. Free-living species feed mainly on small live or dead invertebrates by engulfing them and digesting them in the cells lining the intestine. A primitive excretory system, consisting of tubules and ciliated flame cells, removes waste organic matter and helps to regulate body water. The rapidly beating ciliary tufts of the flame cells create a water current that moves wastes out through several dorsal pores (see Chapter 11).

The freshwater planarian (*Dugesia*, Figure 24–7) has captured the interest of many biology students. The eyes cannot form images; they are simply pigmented cups that contain light-sensitive cells. Light enters the cups from

PLATE XIII

FIGURE 22–1 The bacterium *Spirillum volutans*, showing flagella (× 450). (Runk/Schoenberger, for Grant Heilman.)

FIGURE 22–5 The protist *Euglena* (× 1000). (Runk/Schoenberger, for Grant Heilman.)

FIGURE 22–15 The basidiomycete *Boletus felleus*. (Ward's Natural Science Establishment, Inc.)

FIGURE 22–15

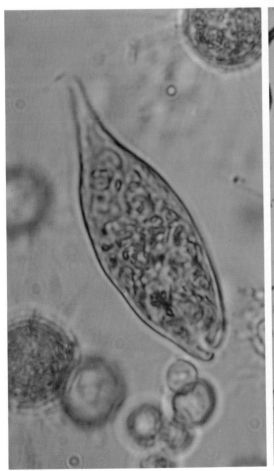

FIGURE 22–5

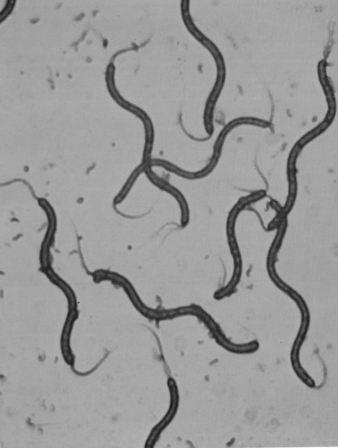

FIGURE 22–1

PLATE XIV

FIGURE 23–2   A liverwort, *Marchantia* (Grant Heilman.)

FIGURE 23–8   A wood horsetail, *Equisetum sylvaticum.* (Grant Heilman.)

FIGURE 23–15   An angiosperm, Clappertonia. (Richard Gross.)

FIGURE 24–6   The orange sun anemone *Metridium dianthus.* (Runk/Schoenberger, for Grant Heilman.)

FIGURE 24–12   The common garden snail. (Richard Gross.)

FIGURE 24–14   The tubeworm or featherduster worm, *Sabellida.* (Runk/Schoenberger, for Grant Heilman.)

FIGURE 24–16   (*a*) A spider in its web. (Richard Gross.) (*b*) The scorpion *Urotocnus mordax*, photographed in La Cañada, California. (Ward's Natural Science Establishment, Inc.)

FIGURE 23–2

FIGURE 23–8

FIGURE 24–14

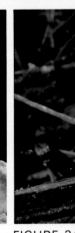

FIGURE 24

PLATE XV

E 23–15

RE 24–6

FIGURE 24–16a

FIGURE 24–16b

PLATE XVI

FIGURE 24–17 A common crustacean — the spider crab, *Lithodes*. (Ward's Natural Science Establishment, Inc.)

FIGURE 24–22 The sea urchin *Strongylocentrotus*.

FIGURE 24–27 A cuban tree frog. (Richard Gross.)

FIGURE 24–29 An iguana. (Richard Gross.)

FIGURE 24–30 California sea gulls. (National Park Service.)

FIGURE 24–17

FIGURE 24–22

FIGURE 24–29

FIGURE 24–27

FIGURE 24–30

FIGURE 24–7   The common freshwater flatworm, *Dugesia doroto-cephala* ($\times 3\frac{1}{2}$). (Grant Heilman, Runk/Schoenberger.)

the open side, and in some still unknown manner the animal determines the direction of the light source in order to flee from it. Planaria are generally found under the edges of stones in creeks. The ear-like extensions, or *auricles*, on their head end are sensitive to chemicals; a planarian can orient itself toward a piece of liver with amazing accuracy.

GENERAL CHARACTERISTICS OF PLATYHELMINTHES

1. Development includes simple organ systems such as an incomplete digestive system (if any).
2. Bodies show dorsoventral flattening and bilateral symmetry.
3. Respiratory and circulatory systems are absent.
4. Bodies have a definite head with a "brain" and sense organs.
5. Most species are parasitic, passing through complex life cycles.
6. Lost body parts can be regenerated.

PSEUDOCOELOMATA

These are animals with a body cavity that is not fully lined with mesoderm.

Wormlike Animals: Phylum Aschelminthes

Approximately 12,000 identified species

This phylum includes animals with diverse body structures. They all lack a circulatory system but possess a complete digestive system. In fact organ systems are characteristic of this phylum. Nematodes, intestinal roundworms, and the small rotifers common in lakes and ponds are included in this group. In general, the muscular bodies of these animals are not segmented and are covered by a cuticle; the digestive tract is a simple tube that does not contain muscle.

GENERAL CHARACTERISTICS OF ASCHELMINTHES

1. Organ-system level of development.
2. Circulatory system is absent.

FIGURE 24–8 A common freshwater rotifer, *Philodina*. The corona serves both for locomotion and for filter feeding.

3. Digestive system is complete, with mouth and anus.

Wheel Animals: Class Rotifera

Rotifers, common in pond water, are easily confused with the larger ciliates by observers of the microscopic life of ponds (Figure 24–8). Two conspicuous ciliated bands make up a *corona* that serves both for gathering food and for locomotion. Each species of rotifer has a

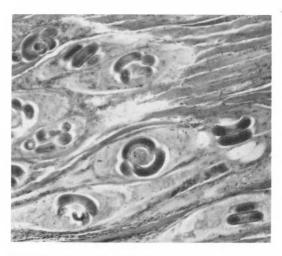

FIGURE 24–9 Trichinella larvae encysted in the skeletal muscle of a pig (×450).

unique coronal structure; and this organ forms the basis for classification of the group. Some species are colonial and sessile, but the majority are free-swimming. Most rotifers are filter feeders whose coronal cilia produce water currents to bring food into the mouth. A muscular organ located in the pharynx grinds the food.

Roundworms: Class Nematoda

These cylindrical unsegmented worms are frequently encountered by pet owners, farmers, and ranchers. Intestinal roundworms inhabit all vertebrate species; roundworms may also be found in the lungs and muscle of most types of domestic animals. Parasitic roundworms seriously deplete the energy of their hosts; unless cattle, sheep, and horses are frequently "wormed," they are almost certain to be killed by these parasites. But not all nematodes parasitize vertebrates. Small, free-living nematodes are found in almost all habitats: freshwater, salt water, soil, and plant foliage. A few forms are plant parasites, feeding by piercing the root system of a plant and sucking out juices.

The best-known species parasitic to humans are those that cause hookworm disease, trichinosis, and elephantiasis. In trichinosis, caused by the pork roundworm *Trichinella*, humans are infected by eating incompletely cooked pork in which larvae are encysted (Figure 24–9).

EUCOELOMATA

These are the animals with a true coelom, completely lined with epithelial tissue of mesodermal origin.

Moss Animals: Phylum Ectoprocta
Approximately 4000 identified species

These tiny animals, sometimes mistaken for seaweeds, are principally marine; they live in branching, mosslike colonies on rocks, shells, animal or plant bodies, or any suitable piece of debris. Microscopic examination shows that the filaments bear small, individual organisms called *zooids* (Figure 24–10). In marine species such as the encrusting *Membranipora* often seen on sea shells, the zooids are composed

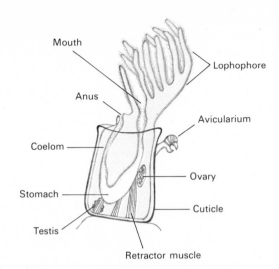

Mouth

Lophophore

Anus

Avicularium

Coelom

Ovary

Stomach

Cuticle

Testis

Retractor muscle

FIGURE 24–10 *Bugula,* a marine ectoproct. The ciliated, retractable lophophore serves for filter feeding. The pinching action of avicularia (modified zooids) keep the colony free of debris and other organisms.

largely of chitin or are calcified. Freshwater forms usually have gelatinous zooids.

A typical zooid feeds by extending a circlet of ciliated tentacles called a *lophophore* from an apical opening. If danger—such as a grazing snail—approaches, the lophophore may be retracted into the zooid for protection. The mouth at the center of the lophophore leads to a U-shaped digestive tract composed of a pharynx, stomach, intestine, and an anus which opens outward to one side of the lophophore. Ectoprocts increase colony size by frequent budding, but sexual reproduction is possible.

GENERAL CHARACTERISTICS OF ECTOPROCTS

1. Food is obtained with a circlet of ciliated tentacles called a *lophophore.*
2. Reproduction may be asexual (budding) or sexual; individuals also may be monoecious or dioecious.
3. Digestive tract is complete and U-shaped.
4. Respiratory and circulatory systems are absent.

5. Some species have specialized zooids to ward off intruders.
6. Most species are marine, but some occur in fresh water.

Lamp Shells: Phylum Brachiopoda
Approximately 300 identified living species

Of interest to both biologists and geologists, these strictly marine species have persisted in much the same form for more than 300 million years. More than 30,000 fossil species of these animals were present in the ancient seas, and their bivalved, calcareous exoskeletons have been exquisitely preserved. The valves of a lamp shell, unlike those of a clam, fit over the animal in a dorsal-ventral orientation; clam shells enclose the clam laterally. Furthermore, lamp shell valves are of unequal size: the smaller dorsal valve fits into the larger ventral valve.

GENERAL CHARACTERISTICS OF BRACHIOPODS

1. All species are marine.
2. Bodies are housed in hinged calcareous valves with a dorsal-ventral orientation.
3. They collect food with a scroll-shaped lophophore.
4. Circulatory system is complete, with a heart and blood vessels.
5. They have excretory organs called metanephridia.
6. Most are attached to a substrate by a fleshy stalk.

Snails, Clams, Octopuses: Phylum Mollusca
Approximately 100,000 identified species

This large phylum contains some familiar human food sources. The phylum Mollusca is also important and interesting from a purely biological standpoint. Through the process of adaptive radiation, discussed in Chapter 20, mollusks have come to occupy practically every type of habitat on earth. Most members are marine, but many live in brackish or fresh water, and some are terrestrial. Whereas most mollusks are burrowers (clams) or creepers (snails), some (squids) are vigorous swimmers.

The general molluscan body plan has three parts: (1) a ventral, muscular *foot;* (2) a soft body region called the *dorsal visceral mass;* and (3) a *mantle* surrounding the soft body, which in many species secretes a shell (Figure 24–11). The dorsal visceral mass contains the internal organs for digestion, circulation, reproduction, and excretion. The circulatory system is "open" like that of the arthropods (Chapter 11). Respiration is usually accomplished by gills in the mantle cavity, although some members have lungs and others utilize the mantle for gas exchange. In most species the sexes are usually separate, but some species are monoecious. Nervous systems vary widely in this phylum, from three simple pairs of ganglia in some burrowing forms to a more complex system with well-developed eyes, as found in squids and octopuses.

GENERAL CHARACTERISTICS OF MOLLUSKS

1. Bilaterally symmetrical body plan consists of three parts: ventral foot, dorsal visceral mass, and mantle (which may secrete a shell).

2. Circulatory system is open.

3. The nervous system typically consists of ganglia, but it is much better developed in some classes, often with sense organs such as eyes.

4. A wide variety of forms occupy marine, freshwater, and terrestrial habitats.

5. Respiration may be by gills, lungs, or mantle.

Chitons: Class Amphineura

The basic features of the molluscan body plan are evident in the chitons, generally considered as a primitive class. These animals are commonly seen creeping along on rocks at low tide, devouring algae from the rock surface. An efficient chitinous rasping organ, the *radula*, with crossrows of tiny "teeth" extends from the mouth cavity to assist in feeding. A chiton's body is covered with eight overlapping calcareous plates, the sides of which are covered by a fleshy girdle. Chitons are sluggish animals with a primitive nervous system.

Snails, Slugs, and Limpets: Class Gastropoda

The gastropods are the largest group of mollusks—some 40,000 known species—and one of the most diverse assemblages of animals. The most common members of this class are snails. But some gastropods, such as the unpopular garden slug and the often beautiful nudibranches, have no shells. Most gastropods live in salt water, but there are many freshwater snails, and some live on land (Figure 24–12, on color plate following p. 592).

Clams and Other Bivalves: Class Pelecypoda

Mollusks of this group have two shells, or valves. Most forms are nearly symmetrical and have bodies that are compressed from side to side. Although not so varied or numerous as the gastropods, the bivalves are a large and diverse group. They include the familiar "shellfish"—clams, oysters, mussels, and scallops—and the teredo, or shipworm, which burrows into wood, damaging pilings and boats. Most bivalves are marine but some, such as the freshwater mussel or clam, *Anodonta*, live in freshwater habitats.

Squids, Octopuses, and Nautiluses: Class Cephalopoda

Unlike other mollusks, most members of this group are swift, active animals. The body structure and adaptations of the cephalopods show that a modification of the basic molluscan plan has occurred in this class, which differs greatly from the other mollusks. The most familiar members, octopus and squid, have a well-developed head with a mouth surrounded by arms, which are a modification of the foot region (*cephalopoda*, means "head-foot"). The brain is well developed, and the eyes, like those of vertebrates, form images. The characteristic shell of most mollusks, absent in octopuses, is represented by only a small internal structure in the squid (Figure 24–13).

Segmented Worms:Phylum Annelida
Approximately 7000 identified species

We have already discussed several groups of worms, but none were segmented. Annelids are

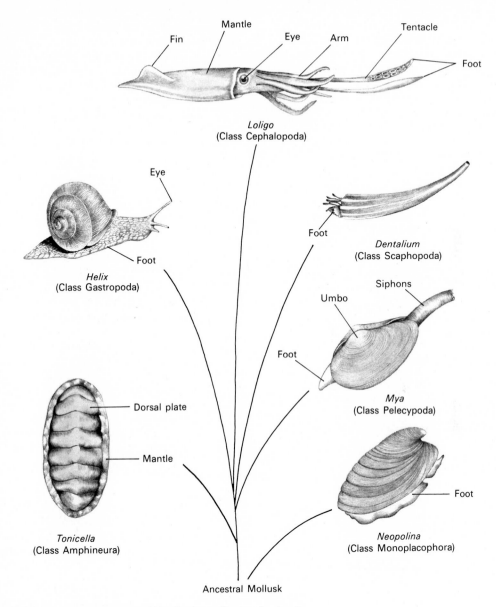

FIGURE 24–11 Modifications of the basic molluscan body plan. The six classes of the phylum Mollusca show variations of the same basic structures: ventral muscular foot, dorsal visceral mass, and a mantle which in most species secretes a shell. Chitons are believed to represent closely the ancestral mollusk from which this phylum evolved. Two classes not discussed in the text are shown: Monoplacophora and Scaphopoda.

elongated, segmented tubular animals with a mouth at one end and an anus at the other. They all require a moist environment. Although the annelids have many characteristics in common, they are best studied by considering each of their three classes separately. One characteristic by which the three classes may be distinguished is the occurrence of bristles or *setae:* one class has few (oligochaeta), one has many (polychaeta), and the third has no setae.

GENERAL CHARACTERISTICS OF ANNELIDS

1. Their elongate bodies show bilateral symmety and segmentation.

2. Body is covered by a moist cuticle through which respiration occurs.

3. Circulatory system is closed, with arteries, capillaries, and veins.

4. They live in marine, freshwater, and moist land habitats.

5. Head region is often well developed.

6. Excretory organs (nephridia) are present, typically one pair per segment.

7. Many forms possess small chitinous appendages (*setae*).

Earthworms: Class Oligochaeta

Earthworms have four pairs of small bristlelike setae on the ventral and lateral surfaces of each

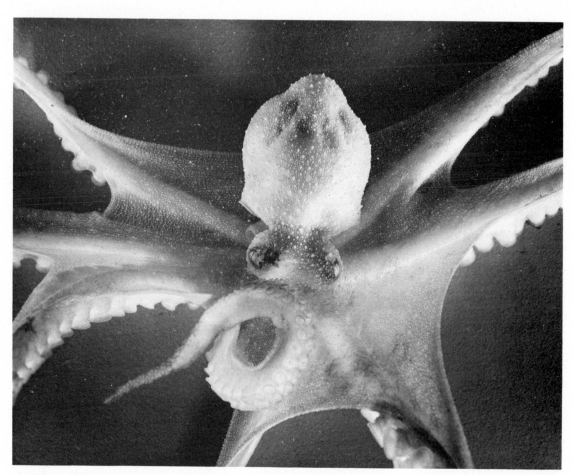

FIGURE 24–13 A cephalopod, *Octopus vulgaris.* (Grant Heilman, Runk/Schoenberger.)

segment. These assist the worm in crawling along a surface or burrowing through the ground. Earthworms prefer moist, humus-rich soils, because they pass the soil through their alimentary canal and extract nutrients as they burrow. In this way earthworms "turn over" soil, loosening it, aerating it, increasing its permeability to water, and generally increasing its productivity.

Marine Worms: Class Polychaeta

Although earthworms are often considered as the typical annelids, polychaetes are much more numerous (Figure 24–14, on color plate following p. 592). These marine worms have many stiff setae located on lateral appendages, *parapodia*, on each body segment. These parapodia, which vary in size among species, are used for both locomotion and gas exchange. Polychaete worms also differ from earthworms in three other ways: (1) sexes are usually separate (dioecious); (2) they have a free-swimming trochophore larval stage (as in some mollusks); and (3) the head is well developed, with sensory organs. Some polychaetes live in tubes or burrows; others swim or crawl about actively in the sand and under rocks. The tube dwellers are among the most beautiful organisms in tide pools and under docks: their plumelike gills wave about, assisting the respiratory process or helping to draw water into their tubes.

Leeches: Class Hirudinea

Leeches may be aquatic or terrestrial. They live as ectoparasites or as predators of other small invertebrates. Their adaptations for parasitic existence include large suckers at each end for clinging to their host, sucking ability, and a large crop for storage of blood. When a leech feeds, it attaches to its host by the suckers, pierces the skin painlessly, and sucks a huge quantity of blood. It secretes an anticoagulant (hirudin) to prevent the host's blood from clotting while it is feeding. One feeding may nourish the leech for months.

Walking or Claw-Bearing Worms: Phylum Onychophora
Approximately 65 identified species

This small tropical phylum is represented by

the genus *Peripatus* (Figure 19–4). These animals have many annelid characteristics, and some biologists consider them as a possible link between the Annelida and Arthropoda (see Chapter 19). These animals have internal segments and nephridia similar to annelids. But, like arthropods, they have clawed, jointed appendages and respire by tracheal tubes.

Joint-footed Animals: Phylum Arthropoda
Approximately 1,000,000 identified species

Our daily lives often include contact with conspicuous representatives of this phylum. Spiders, ants, and flies, for example, seem to turn up almost everywhere. We consume crab, lobster, and crayfish as food. Honeybees pollinate flowers and produce honey; silkworm larvae make silk.

Some arthropod species spread serious diseases: Rocky Mountain spotted fever (tick), sleeping sickness (tsetse fly), malaria (Anopheles mosquito), and bubonic plague (rat fleas), to name a few. Grasshopper plagues may destroy entire crops, moth larvae strip leaves and buds from vegetables and trees, and boll weevils ruin acres of cotton. Many arthropods, such as bees, scorpions, wasps, and certain spiders and centipedes, can inflict painful and even deadly stings or bites.

All arthropods possess a protective, supporting *exoskeleton* (external skeleton). This covering, which is jointed to permit movement, is composed primarily of chitin. In species such as crabs and crayfish, the exoskeleton is hardened by calcification except at the joints. Because the exoskeleton is external, in most species it must be shed and replaced in a series of *molts* as the organism grows. The hard exoskeletons preserve well, so the fossil record of the arthropods is extensive, going back more than 500 million years to the Precambrian trilobites.

The arthropod body is commonly composed of three major regions: head, thorax, and abdomen. In forms such as crabs, however, the head and thorax may be fused and the segmented abdomen tucked up underneath the main body. All arthropods possess paired, jointed appendages, which may be adapted for such functions as locomotion, sensation, eating, food capture, or defense. Another important feature of arthropods is striated muscle tissue that can contract rapidly. This feature gives them their great agility. The head of most arthropods is well equipped with sense organs. Large, many-faceted (compound) eyes that form mosaic images, chemical- and touch-sensitive antennae, and balance organs are found throughout the phylum. Compound eyes do not form sharp images as our own single lens eyes do, but they are well adapted for detecting slight movements.

There are several types of respiratory and excretory systems in this phylum, but all arthropods have an open circulatory system that includes a dorsal heart, arteries, and blood-collecting sinuses (see Chapter 11). An open circulatory system contains no capillary vessels; returning blood drains into body cavities (sinuses) before it is recirculated by the heart. With few exceptions, reproduction is sexual, the sexes are dioecious, and fertilization is internal. All arthropods lay eggs; many carry their eggs on or inside their bodies until they hatch.

Dealing with this large, diverse group is easier if we divide it into subphyla. We will use two subphyla—the *Chelicerata*, which possess no jaws, and *Mandibulata* which have crushing jaws.

GENERAL CHARACTERISTICS OF ARTHROPODS

1. They live in practically every world habitat.

2. Bodies segmented, with paired, jointed appendages.

3. A chitinous exoskeleton, which may be calcified, covers the body.

4. Head is highly developed with many sense organs.

5. Body is divided into head, thorax, and abdomen (although fusion of these parts occurs in some forms).

6. Circulatory system is open, with arteries and blood sinuses.

7. Sexes are dioecious; fertilization is internal, with a few exceptions.

8. Striated muscles are present.

Subphylum Chelicerata

These are forms with no jaws.

Horseshoe Crabs: Class Merostomata

Horseshoe crabs (Figure 24–15), which number only five species, abound on the sandy Atlantic and Gulf coast beaches of the United States and in the Far East. They lie partially covered by sand while they search for practically any kind of organic food. Like the long-extinct trilobites, horseshoe crabs are important members of the fossil record, dating back approximately 500 million years to the Ordovician seas. These jawless marine scavengers have both compound and simple eyes. Respiration takes place on sheetlike gills.

Spiders, Mites, Ticks, and Scorpions: Class Arachnida

Members of this class have four pairs of legs and no antennae. Spiders, mites, and ticks are

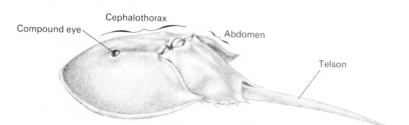

FIGURE 24–15   The horseshoe crab, *Limulus,* reaches a length of nearly 2 feet. It lives partially buried in sand on the Atlantic coast.

all capable of biting; some, like the black widow spider, inflict toxic bites that may be fatal to humans. Spiders are carnivorous; web-spinning species capture prey with intricately spun silken nets (Figure 24–16a, on color plate following p. 592). Other spiders, such as wolf spiders and tarantulas, actively hunt for prey. Spiders inject digestive enzymes into their prey and then suck out the liquified food. Gas exchange in spiders and scorpions takes place through a series of leaflike membranes known as "book lungs" on the underside of their abdomen.

Mites and ticks are small and generally oval in shape. Certain mites cause mange in dogs, and the larval forms of red mites are the notorious biting pests called *chiggers.* Several species of mites suck plant juices. Ticks are blood-suckers; some burrow deeply into the skin in quest of a meal.

Scorpions possess a unique, conspicuous postabdominal tail bearing a venomous sting. All scorpions are predatory carnivores (Figure 24–16b, on color plate following p. 592). They seize their prey with their large pincers and paralyze it with a sting delivered by the forward-arching tail. All scorpion stings are painful, and some may be lethal.

Subphylum Mandibulata

These are arthropods with jaws for crushing.

Crabs, Lobsters, etc.: Class Crustacea

Most of the conspicuous members of this class, such as crabs (Figure 24–17, on color plate following p. 592), crayfishes, lobsters, and barnacles, have hard exoskeletal shells. Others, such as the microscopic waterfleas and copepods, have more flexible exoskeletons. All crustaceans possess two pairs of antennae. Crustaceans are principally aquatic, but a few species, such as sow bugs, live in moist soil. The freshwater crayfish has several types of appendages serving different functions. In general, each body segment of the crayfish possesses one pair of appendages. The circulatory and excretory systems of the crayfish were discussed in Chapters 10 and 11.

Insects: Class Insecta (Hexapoda)

The most numerous of all animals (nearly 1 million species), the insects are perhaps the most successful metazoans on earth. Not only are there more species of insects than of any other group of organisms, but they have radiated into the most varied habitats. Insects all have three pairs of jointed legs; most have a definite head, thorax, and abdomen. The legs, all of which extend from the thorax, may be greatly modified for jumping, running, digging, or grasping. Insects have one pair of antennae and both simple and compound eyes. They breathe by tracheal tubes and have Malpighian tubules for excretion of nitrogenous wastes (Chapter 11).

Many insects can fly at some stage of their life cycle; one or two pairs of wings may occur as extensions of the exoskeleton. The membranous flying wings of beetles are protected by hardened outer wings; in grasshoppers, the flying wings are covered by a leathery outer pair. Flight is powered by sets of antagonistic muscles that alternately bulge and flatten the thoracic covering.

Most insects go through a life cycle that includes major structural and physiological changes (*metamorphosis*) from one developmental stage to another. The complete metamorphosis of butterflies and moths includes four stages: egg, caterpillar larva, pupa (cocoon or chrysalis), and adult (Figure 24–18). In grasshoppers and some other forms, development is more gradual. Newly hatched individuals resemble the adult in most body features. At each molt in this gradual metamorphosis the individual grows larger; near the end of development wing buds and sexual appendages appear.

Social behavior is a striking characteristic of certain insect types. Ants, termites, and bees are familiar examples of social insects; some of their behavioral adaptations were discussed in Chapters 17 and 18. This social behavior has evolved independently of that among "higher" animals, but a number of parallels are obvious: social ranking, division of labor within communities, and communication.

Insects are divided into approximately 25 orders, primarily on the basis of mouth parts,

Bio-Topic: Mosquitoes and Repellants

Mosquitoes are annoying and sometimes dangerous pests. Although some species transmit diseases such as malaria or yellow fever, most North American species are merely annoying. The development of effective repellants would alleviate one of life's small annoyances here, but could have important public health applications in tropical areas.

It is the female mosquito that bites. Blood from the host supplies protein needed for laying eggs. When the female senses and flies toward a host, she follows a preprogrammed attack pattern. The pattern begins when she senses carbon dioxide exhaled by a nearby potential host. She responds by flying more actively. Her flight is initially random, until she encounters a warm, moist air current of the kind that would rise from the skin of a warm-blooded host. When the mosquito senses such an air current, she turns into it and flies upstream to the skin of the host. The attack program depends on a sequence of essentially automatic responses to a sequence of stimuli. Any disruption of either sequence destroys the program. And that is how repellants work.

The ability to sense carbon dioxide and moisture depends on two sets of sensory hairs on the mosquito's antennae. One set is sensitive to carbon dioxide, the other to moisture. Repellants disrupt the attack pattern by making these hairs insensitive to the normal stimuli. Repellants seem to block pores in the hair surface that normally admit the stimulating molecules. Spherical molecules of medium molecular weight are among the best mosquito repellants.

Applying repellant to the skin turns the mosquito away just before she lands. Dispersing repellant in the surrounding air makes mosquitoes unable to follow the moist air current that leads to the host. The possibility of preventing mosquito bites by area dispersal seems promising and is being investigated. So are chemical studies of effective repellants. An understanding of the chemistry of effective repellants may lead to the development of even more effective compounds. It may even be possible to develop a repellant that can be swallowed and then be released through the skin, conferring long-term protection against bites.

leg structures, and number and types of wings. Examples of the common insect orders of North America are shown in Figure 24–19.

Starfish and Their Relatives: Phylum Echinodermata
Approximately 6000 identified species

This exclusively marine phylum has three distinct characteristics: (1) locomotion by a *water-vascular system;* (2) an endoskeleton of limy plates and, typically, spines protruding

from the skin (*echinoderm* means "spiny skin"); and (3) radial symmetry, with the body generally divided into five parts. The five-part body plan is apparent in all echinoderms when observed closely (Figure 24–20). Although the adult body is radial and has no head, these animals begin their lives as bilaterally symmetrical *bipinnaria* larvae (Figure 16–8). Some close chordate relatives, the hemichordates, also produce larvae of this type—a fact that indicates an evolutionary relationship between the two phyla.

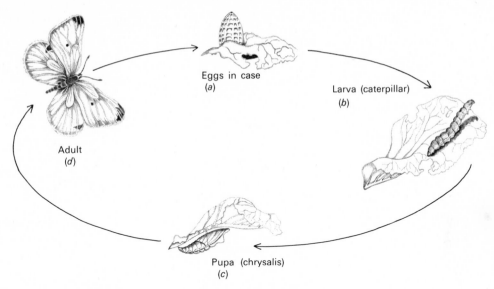

FIGURE 24–18 Metamorphosis in the cabbage butterfly. (*a*) Eggs in case. (*b*) Larva (caterpillar). (*c*) Pupa (chrysalis). (*d*) Adult.

GENERAL CHARACTERISTICS OF ECHINODERMS

1. The endoskeleton consists of separate or fused calcareous plates embedded in the skin.

2. Locomotion takes place by means of a water-vascular system.

3. A well-developed coelom is derived from the same embryonic region as that of chordates.

4. Adult forms have no head.

5. Symmetry is radial in adults, but bilateral in bipinnaria larvae.

Starfish: Class Asteroidea

In starfish anatomy we can differentiate the central *disc* from the radiating *rays* (arms). The unique water-vascular system by which the starfish moves is essentially a system of canals through which water moves to numerous *tube feet* on the lower surface of the starfish (Figure 24–21). Water first enters a *ring canal* in the central disc of the animal through a sievelike structure, the *madreporite*, on the upper surface. Five radial canals extending from this ring canal carry fluid out to the arms. Side branches from these radial canals run to the hollow tube feet that project from the lower side (or oral surface) and are in contact with a surface. Each tube foot is attached internally to a muscular, saclike *ampulla* which can contract and force fluid into the tube foot. Extended by fluid pressure, the tube foot, which terminates in a suction cup, is pressed against a surface and attaches. Next, muscles in the tube-foot wall contract, pulling the animal along and forcing fluid back into the ampulla. By repeating this process or varying it in different arms, a starfish can move about, hold its position on vertical surfaces, or cling to the underside of a rock.

Serpent or Brittle Stars: Class Ophiuroidea

These close relatives of starfish have a small oral disc with five long, flexible arms. They have no grooves beneath the arms and no anus. These organisms move by serpentlike motions of the arms.

Sea Urchins and Sand Dollars: Class Echinoidea

In these forms, the calcareous plates are fused into a hollow test, which has many movable calcareous spines (Figure 24–22 on color plate

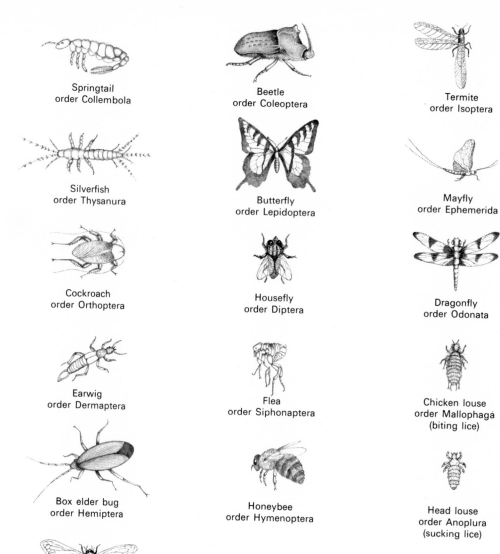

Springtail
order Collembola

Beetle
order Coleoptera

Termite
order Isoptera

Silverfish
order Thysanura

Butterfly
order Lepidoptera

Mayfly
order Ephemerida

Cockroach
order Orthoptera

Housefly
order Diptera

Dragonfly
order Odonata

Earwig
order Dermaptera

Flea
order Siphonaptera

Chicken louse
order Mallophaga
(biting lice)

Box elder bug
order Hemiptera

Honeybee
order Hymenoptera

Head louse
order Anoplura
(sucking lice)

Cicada
order Homoptera

FIGURE 24-19   Examples of some common North American insect orders.

following page 592). Tube feet extending from small pores in the test assist in food gathering and locomotion. A five-toothed structure called "Aristotle's lantern," located in the oral opening, functions to shred food as it enters the mouth.

Sea Cucumbers: Class Holothuroidea

Sea cucumbers have an elongated, muscular body that contains extremely small calcareous plates. Five double rows of tube feet run the length of the soft cylindrical body. These tube feet are used primarily to anchor the body

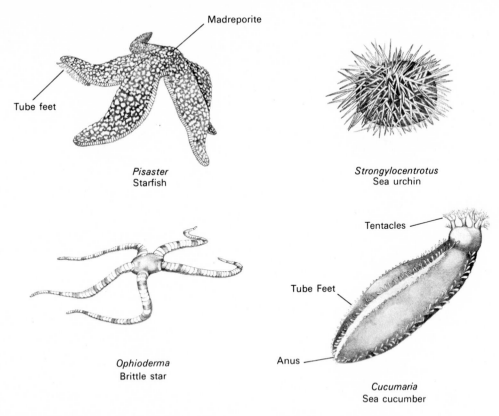

Madreporite

Tube feet

Pisaster
Starfish

Strongylocentrotus
Sea urchin

Ophioderma
Brittle star

Tentacles

Tube Feet

Anus

Cucumaria
Sea cucumber

FIGURE 24–20 Basic body plans of echinoderms. All have radial symmetry, tube feet, and an endoskeleton of calcareous plates.

while feeding is accomplished by a circlet of retractile, branching tentacles surrounding the mouth.

Phylum Chordata
Approximately 45,000 identified species

Although this phylum contains some primitive forms, it also contains some of the most highly developed animals, including our own species. Three distinctive characteristics, present at some developmental stage, unite these diverse animals into a phylum and separate them from others: (1) a dorsal tubular nerve cord; (2) a notochord (a rodlike supporting structure); and (3) pharyngeal gill clefts with gill slits.

Chordates are often divided into three subphyla: Urochordata, Cephalochordata, and

Vertebrata. Of these three, the first two are invertebrate groups; only the Vertebrata have vertebrae (backbones).

Subphylum Urochordata: Tunicates or Sea Squirts

These common, marine invertebrate chordates reveal their chordate characteristics most clearly in their larval stage. The free-swimming larvae, which resemble tadpoles, have a notochord, a dorsal nerve cord, and gill slits. After they change to adults, only the gill slits remain of these chordate characteristics (Figure 24–23). Adult tunicates can be found at low tide in most marine habitats, attached to rocks, wood, or shells. Both solitary and colonial types are common.

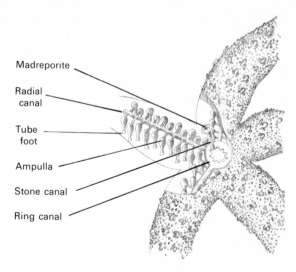

FIGURE 24–21   Water vascular system of a starfish.

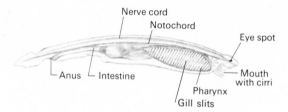

FIGURE 24–24   *Amphioxus*, often called a "lancelet" because its shape resembles a scalpel, shows three distinct vertebrate characteristics: a dorsal, tubular nerve cord; a notochord; and pharyngeal gill slits.

Subphylum Cephalochordata: Lancelets

Members of this group, commonly called *amphioxus*, are slender, translucent marine organisms. The three characteristics of the chordates—notochord, dorsal nerve cord, and gill slits—are prominent in the adult amphioxus. The segmented body, which lacks a well-defined head, is about 2 inches long (Figure 24–24). Although these animals are capable of

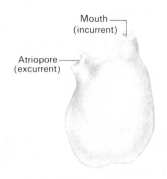

FIGURE 24–23   Adult tunicate, *Molgula*. This sessile filter feeder is covered by a nonliving "tunic." Its larva is free-swimming.

swimming, they typically burrow in the shallow waters along a shore with only the head end protruding. Water enters through the mouth and passes out through the gill slits; food particles are filtered out for digestion in the intestine. To biologists, the greatest significance of these animals is that the three fundamental chordate characteristics can readily be observed in them.

Subphylum Vertebrata: Fish, Amphibians, Reptiles, Birds, and Mammals

For various purposes, biologists commonly divide the animal kingdom into "invertebrates" and "vertebrates." All the animals of all phyla discussed up to this point are invertebrates. Vertebrates have a backbone, or spinal column, made up of bony, segmented units called *vertebrae*. The backbone supports the body and protects the spinal (nerve) cord. In most vertebrates the vertebrae replace the notochord as the organism develops past its embryonic stages. Another characteristic of this subphylum is a brain case (cranium). In most vertebrates the vertebrae, cranium, and other skeletal structures are composed of bone, but some, such as sharks, have cartilaginous skeletons. Vertebrates are usually subdivided into eight classes; four of these are fish and therefore aquatic, and four are terrestrial, although they may have aquatic members. Vertebrates show a wide range of adaptations and are found in

Bio-Topic: Dinosaurs Are Alive and Well

Most of us think of dinosaurs as dull-witted, cold-blooded reptiles that have been extinct for millions of years. Recent research suggests that this image of the dinosaur may be wrong in at least two important respects.

Three new lines of evidence suggest the dinosaurs were warm-blooded. The first has to do with the structure of their bones. Cold-blooded animals have dense bones that often show annual growth rings that reflect slower growth during cold seasons. Warm-blooded animals have a more open bone structure with no annual rings, even when the animal passes through very cold winters. Dinosaur bones are of the warm-blooded type.

A second line of evidence comes from new information about the earth's climate at the time the dinosaurs flourished. It is now clear that many dinosaurs lived at latitudes with cold winters. These winters would have been fatal to all but the smallest cold-blooded dinosaurs (which could hibernate), yet the fossil record shows that quite large dinosaurs lived at latitudes with cold winters.

It is now recognized that early dino-saurs were covered with dense growths of hairlike or scalelike structures that appear to be the forerunners of modern feathers. The evolution of such insulating layers would have been adaptive only for warm-blooded animals. This is the third line of evidence that the dinosaurs were indeed warm-blooded.

Evidence that dinosaurs may not be extinct comes from new interpretations of so-called flying reptiles such as Archaeopteryx. These small, fully feathered carnivores are now known to have been warm-blooded dinosaurs, not primitive reptiles. And they couldn't fly—the feathers were insulation; the structure of their shoulder joints did not permit the flapping motion necessary for flying. But in most other respects, these small, feathered dinosaurs were extremely birdlike. Scientists now think that, as the larger dinosaurs became extinct, some of the smaller ones evolved shoulder joints suitable for wing-flapping and adapted to a life style that included flight. It seems reasonably certain that today some dinosaurs are alive and well and living among us disguised as birds.

most environments. Their evolutionary histories have been studied in great detail (bones make good fossils), and the general evolutionary relationships among the classes have been worked out in some detail (Figure 24–25).

GENERAL CHARACTERISTICS OF VERTEBRATES

1. Bony or cartilaginous backbone composed of vertebrae is present.

2. The notochord is usually replaced by the vertebrae during development.

3. A cranium encloses a brain.

4. Most forms have two pairs of appendages.

5. Internal, jointed skeleton consists of cartilage or bone.

6. Gill clefts and slits are often modified for functions other than respiration.

Lampreys and Hagfishes: Class Agnatha

This group of jawless fishes is the most primitive vertebrate group; fossil representatives date back some 500 million years. The notochord is present in the adult, and the skeleton is cartilaginous (Figure 24–26a). Some lampreys are

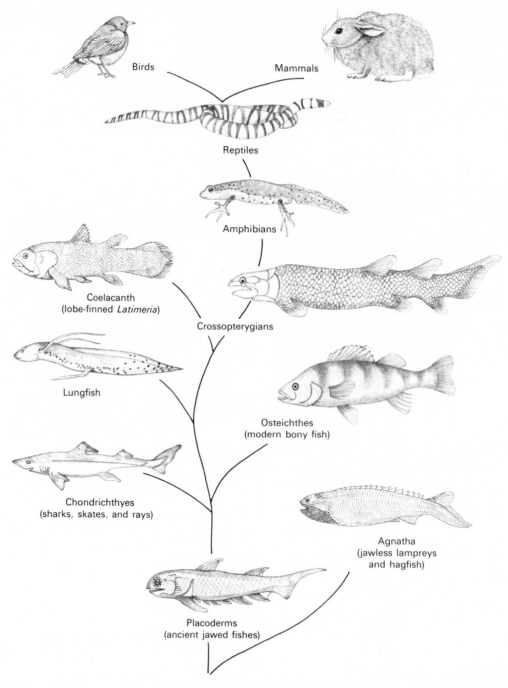

FIGURE 24–25 An evolutionary tree showing developmental relationships of vertebrates.

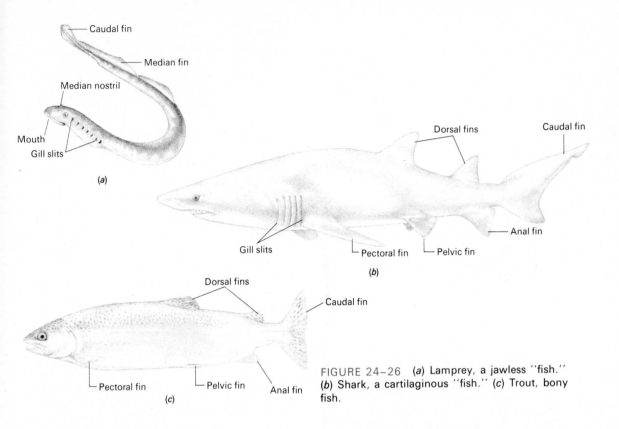

FIGURE 24-26   (a) Lamprey, a jawless ''fish.''
(b) Shark, a cartilaginous ''fish.'' (c) Trout, bony
fish.

free-living, but the species most often discussed
are parasitic on bony fish. After attaching itself
to a fish by its suckerlike jawless mouth, a
lamprey rasps a hole in the host with its teeth
and sucks fluid (Chapter 6). Hagfishes, on the
other hand, live at greater depths in marine
waters. They scavenge on worms and dead fish.

Primitive Jawed Fish: Class Placodermi

Placoderms are known only from the fossil
record. They were quite abundant throughout
the Devonian period, about 400 million years
ago, but they have been extinct for nearly 250
million years. They are important for two reasons: (1) they possessed hinged jaws which
permitted a different means of feeding from
that employed by the lampreys and hagfishes;
and (2) they gave rise to the two classes of fish
we know today.

Cartilaginous Fishes: Class Chondrichthyes

The most familiar representatives of this group
are sharks (Figure 24–26b), rays, and skates.
Their skeletons are entirely cartilaginous, their
vertebrae are well-developed, and the jaws are
movable. All are marine predators. Small tooth-
like scales cover the body (a characteristic
which agnathans lack).

Bony Fishes: Class Osteichthyes

The bony fishes are the dominant fish group
today, with members living in all types of
aquatic habitats throughout the world (Figure
24–26c). The osteichthyes have bony skeletons
(oste, ''bone,'' and ichthyes, ''fish''). Most are
covered with scales, have a terminal mouth
with well-developed jaws, and are good swimmers. The heart is two-chambered (see Figure
24–28), as it is in the other classes of fish. Most
bony fish have a swim bladder that contains a

variable quantity of air to permit movement to various depths.

One group of bony fishes differs substantially in structure and habit. These are the lobe-finned lungfishes, which can use their thickened, lobed fins for movement along muddy surfaces. The swim bladders of modern fish developed from the primitive lungs of these fish.

Frogs, Toads, and Salamanders: Class Amphibia

Amphibians are a significant advance in vertebrate development: they are capable of living on land, even though they spend some part of their life in water and, in most cases, depend on a watery environment to complete their life cycle. Salamanders (Figure 24–27, on color plate following p. 592) are the most primitive members of the group, and probably the closest structurally to the fishlike ancestors from which all modern amphibians developed. Amphibians were apparently the dominant vertebrates during the Carboniferous period, about 350 million years ago, when the cartilaginous fishes were dominant in the seas.

Frogs and toads have an aquatic larval stage, the familiar tadpole. The fishlike tadpole has gills which are later lost in metamorphosis. The moist skin of frogs and other amphibians contains mucous glands that assist in maintaining the moisture. Moreover, the eggs of amphibians, laid in water or other moist areas, are usually covered with a gelatinous substance. Thus amphibians remain dependent on aquatic (or at least wet) environments in many ways.

This group also shows adaptations for living on land. Most importantly, adults have lungs adapted for air breathing and are therefore no longer dependent on water for gas exchange. (It can occur through the skin when amphibians are in water.) Furthermore, the two nostrils are connected to the mouth cavity to facilitate breathing through the lungs. Almost all amphibians have two pair of jointed appendages that permit locomotion both on land and in water. Frogs and toads also have sound-sensitive membranes ("external eardrums") on their bodies; such specialized sense organs are essential for land dwellers, because air does not transmit sound waves as efficiently as water. Finally, amphibians have a more efficient type of circulatory system than fish, including a heart with three chambers rather than two. This heart is a better pump than a two-chambered heart would be for moving blood to and from the lungs in the quantities necessary to provide sufficient gas exchange (Figure 24–28).

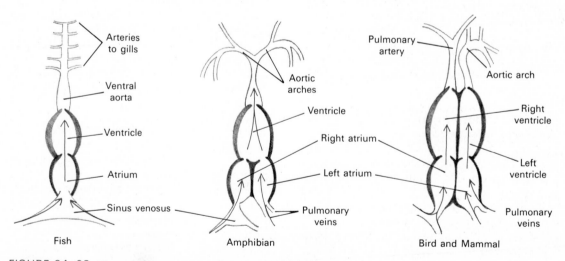

FIGURE 24–28   Two-, three-, and four-chambered hearts. Hearts are shown schematically to illustrate evolutionary development.

Snakes, Lizards, etc.: Class Reptilia

But more thorough adaptations than those made by the amphibians were necessary if vertebrates were to become completely terrestrial. The first vertebrates to make these additional adaptations were the reptiles. The modern members of the class Reptilia include snakes, lizards, alligators, crocodiles, turtles, tortoises, and the tuatara, a primitive form found only in the New Zealand area (Figure 24–29, on color plate following p. 592).

Reptiles apparently evolved from amphibian stock during the Carboniferous period. They experienced a period of great development and even dominance for approximately 200 million years. One geological era, the Mesozoic, is often called the Age of Reptiles.

Reptiles were able to assume dominance over amphibians because they could live completely on land, whereas amphibians could not. Perhaps the most important adaptation reptiles developed for terrestrial life is the reptilian egg. These eggs, laid on land, have a hard, limy shell or a leathery covering to provide protection against drying out. The eggs also contain food (*yolk*) for the developing embryo, which hatches as a young adult rather than going through a larval stage. Moreover, fertilization is internal, accomplished by *copulation*. In amphibians and aquatic forms fertilization is usually external; the male generally fertilizes the eggs after they have been released into the water by the female.

Certain respiratory and circulatory features also contribute to the adaptation of reptiles as land dwellers. For example, the reptilian heart shows the beginning of a partition in the ventricle (Figure 24–28). This feature partially separates oxygenated blood, which comes to the ventricle from the lungs, from nonoxygenated blood, which comes from other parts of the body. (In birds and mammals a complete separation occurs, creating a four-chambered heart; this separation has also occurred in one reptilian group, crocodiles.) Another reptilian adaptation for land life is dry skin, usually covered by scales. The jointed limbs, absent in some reptiles, have claws on the toes. These limbs can lift the body off the ground to permit running.

Birds: Class Aves

Vertebrate evolution continued beyond the reptiles in a reasonably clear pattern. Birds and mammals both developed from reptilian stock, but they arose from two different ancestral lines of reptiles.

In Chapter 19, we described *Archaeopteryx* as a form intermediate between birds and reptiles, since it had teeth and a tail (reptilian characteristics) and feathers (a distinct bird characteristic). In addition to wings and feathers, birds added other adaptations that increased their efficiency and led to the extremely diverse, active bird groups we observe today (Figure 24–30, on color plate following p. 592).

Foremost among these adaptations is the complete four-chambered heart that allows the organism to maintain a constant, warm internal body temperature. (We saw in Chapter 3 that metabolic chemical reactions occur at a faster rate when temperatures are increased.) A four-chambered heart makes possible the separation of oxygenated from nonoxygenated blood, so that only oxygenated blood is pumped to the body tissues (Figure 24–28). Whereas birds and mammals are "warmblooded," other vertebrates are "cold-blooded" (meaning that their body temperatures change, partly in response to environmental conditions). The "warm-blooded" condition is more accurately called *homeothermy* and the "cold-blooded" condition, *poikilothermy*. Feathers are an important aspect of the homeothermal adaptation, since they provide insulation.

Another advance of birds over reptiles is their well-developed brains and keen senses. These features enable birds to engage in more complex behavior, such as orientation, vocal communication, and more elaborate patterns of care of the young (described in greater detail in Unit VII). Birds also have strong, hollow bones, very light to facilitate flight. Their breathing efficiency is increased by the thin-walled air sacs that extend from the lungs throughout the body. Reproduction in birds is similar to that in reptiles, but some modifications may be seen in the structure of the bird egg.

Mammals: Class Mammalia

Mammals are perhaps the most familiar group of animals. They live in practically all habitats and provide us with food and clothing. Most of our pets are mammals—and we ourselves, of course, are mammals. The name of the group refers to the presence of *mammary glands* which, in the female, provide milk for the young. Like birds, mammals are homeothermic ("warm-blooded") and possess complete four-chambered hearts. Unlike birds, their outermost insulation is provided by hair or fur. Note that homeothermy and external insulation work together to provide for more efficient metabolism and regulation.

Mammalian adaptations for reproduction are especially noteworthy. Fertilization is internal, as in birds. But mammalian embryos develop internally, in the uterus of the female (except in the small egg-laying group), where they are nourished through a placenta in most cases. Embryonic membranes (Chapter 16), also found in reptiles and birds, are modified in mammals for internal development of the embryo.

Another outstanding feature of many mammals is the well-developed brain—especially the cerebral cortex, which permits memory, rational behavior, intelligence, and more complex behavior generally. Other mammalian adaptations include a muscular partition, the *diaphragm*, that separates the lungs and heart from the intestines and makes breathing more efficient; a ventral orientation and further development of the limbs, permitting a greater variety of activity; a lower jaw with only one bone (other vertebrates have several bones in the lower jaw); a middle ear with three bones instead of one, as in reptiles and birds (Figure 19–2); and various types of teeth associated with the varied eating habits of mammals.

Mammals may be divided into three subclasses on the basis of reproductive characteristics: the egg-laying mammals, pouched mammals (marsupials), and placental mammals.

Subclass Prototheria consists of the egg-layers, also known as the *monotremes*. This subclass is represented among living mammals only by the duck-billed platypus and the spiny anteater, both of which live in Australia (Figure 24–31).

FIGURE 24–31   The duck-billed platypus, an egg-laying mammal. (Australian News and Information Bureau.)

Egg-laying is of course a primitive characteristic in mammals, but like other mammals the monotremes do have mammary glands and produce milk.

Subclass Metatheria are the *marsupials*, or pouched mammals. Most forms are restricted to Australia; opossums, however, are found in other parts of the world, especially in North and South America. Marsupial young leave the uterus at a very immature stage and move to a pouch, where they receive milk from the mammary glands and develop further. Marsupials have followed an evolutionary development similar to placental mammals, occupying similar habitats (Figure 20–17).

Subclass Eutheria, the *placental* mammals, have been the dominant mammals for the last 100 million years or so; this period is often called the Age of Mammals. In placental mammals the developing embryo (later, the fetus) receives nutrients through a membrane, the *placenta*, in the uterus of the female. Ten of the most common orders of placental mammals are listed below with examples and Figure 24–32 illustrates the diversity of this group.

Insectivora (insect-eaters): shrews, moles

Chiroptera (forms with wings): bats

Lagomorpha (forms with hind legs for jumping): rabbits

Rodentia (gnawing mammals): rats, beavers, squirrels

Cetacea (aquatic mammals with dorsal nostrils): whales, dolphins, porpoises

Carnivora (meat eaters): cats, dogs, weasels, bears, seals

Proboscidea (forms with a long proboscis): elephants

Perissodactyla (hoofed, odd-toed mammals): horses, rhinoceroses

Artiodactyla (hoofed, even-toed mammals): deer, pigs, camels, cattle

Primates (forms with five digits with nails): monkeys, apes, humans

SUMMARY

Major differences exist between plants and animals, related to the fact that animals cannot make their own food. Animals adapt through movement and responsiveness to their environments. The presence of muscle and nervous tissue in animals facilitates these adaptations. Most animals have organs that operate together in systems and have a fixed form established early in development. In addition, animal cells differ from plant cells.

Animals are classified primarily on the basis of structure. They can be categorized on the basis of whether or not they have a body cavity (coelom); we therefore recognize acoelomate, pseudocoelomate, and eucoelomate conditions. Body symmetry (asymmetry, radial symmetry, or bilateral symmetry) is also important in classification. Most classification systems are organized to take into consideration similarities in structure and apparent ancestry.

The following classification system is followed in this chapter:

Acoelomata

Phylum Porifera: sponges

Phylum Coelenterata: hydra, jellyfish, anemones, corals

Phylum Platyhelminthes: flatworms

Pseudocoelomata

Phylum Aschelminthes: rotifers, roundworms, horsehair worms

Eucoelomata

Phylum Ectoprocta: moss animals

Phylum Brachiopoda: lamp shells

Phylum Mollusca: chitons, snails, clams, octopuses

Phylum Annelida: segmented worms

Phylum Onychophora: peripatus

Phylum Arthropoda: insects, crustaceans, spiders, millipedes, and centipedes

Phylum Echinodermata: starfish and sea urchins

Phylum Chordata: sea squirts and vertebrates

REVIEW QUESTIONS

1. In what major structural and functional ways do animals differ from plants? In what ways are animals generally more complex than plants?

2. What is the primary basis for classifying animals? How does our modern classification system reflect evolutionary relationships?

Myotis (bat)
order Chiroptera

Tursiops (bottlenosed dolphin)
order Cetacea

Sciurus
order Rodentia

Vulpes (red fox)
order Carnivora

Cercopithecus (grass monkey)
order Primates

FIGURE 24–32 Some examples of placental mammals. These five types show the diversity of form and habitat attained by placental mammals.

3. Describe the digestive systems of coelenterates, flatworms, and aschelminthes. What changes in complexity have occurred among these systems?

4. How are the life cycles of flukes and tapeworms similar? What specialized structures do these animals have for parasitic life?

5. What common characteristics are found among the classes of the aschelminthes? How are they more complex than platyhelminthes?

6. Review the structural characteristics of each class of the phylum Mollusca. Describe the changes that have occurred in the foot, mantle, shell, and sense organs throughout this phylum.

7. What structural features have enabled arthropods to live in practically all areas of the earth? What are the basic differences between crustaceans and insects?

8. List three characteristics that would identify an organism as an echinoderm. What similarities are there between echinoderms and chordates?

9. Describe some structural and functional adaptations made as vertebrates moved onto land. What advantages do reptiles have over amphibians for life on land?

10. What particular adaptations have made mammals the dominant land animals? In what ways are mammals similar to birds?

SUPPLEMENTARY READINGS

Amos, William H., *The Life of the Seashore*, McGraw-Hill, New York, 1966. This beautifully illustrated book describes in detail the communities of animals that live along the coastlines of the United States. It deals with sandy beaches, marshes, and rocky coasts.

Helm, Thomas, *Dangerous Sea Creatures*, Funk & Wagnalls, New York, 1976. This guidebook to the mysteries and dangers of sea life is a fascinating account of how to identify dangerous animals, how to prevent accidents, and how to apply first aid when necessary.

Morris, Desmond, *The Mammals*, Harper & Row, New York, 1965. This illustrated inventory of 300 of the world's mammals provides an accurate classification and a brief description of each species. Family trees and world distribution maps are provided for each family.

Orr, Robert T., *The Animal Kingdom*, Macmillan, New York, 1965. A comprehensive survey of the animal life of the world with hundreds of photographs of interesting species.

Romer, Alfred S., *The Procession of Life*, World, Cleveland, 1968. All the major groups of animals are discussed, including their structure, physiology, and evolutionary relationships.

"The Bugs are Coming," *Time Magazine*, July 12, 1976. This article provides an excellent and easily understood summary of insect evolution, adaptation, and physiology. In addition, hormones, pheromones, DDT, and other topics covered in preceding chapters are discussed.

Glossary

abiotic denotes the nonliving aspects of the community.

acetylcholine one of the chemical substances that transmits nerve impulses across synaptic junctions.

acid a compound that produces hydrogen ions in a solution.

ACTH *see* adrenocorticotropic hormone

action potential the bioelectric potential that changes along a nerve membrane as a result of the propagation of an impulse.

activation energy the amount of energy necessary to initiate a chemical reaction.

active sites specific structural areas in an enzyme molecule that combine with specific reactant molecules.

active transport the movement of materials across cell membranes against a concentration gradient, thus requiring the expenditure of energy.

adaptation the ability of an organism to alter its structure, physiology, or behavior to meet the requirements of a particular environment.

adaptive radiation the divergence of organisms into separate ecological niches where further adaptation and speciation occur.

adenosine triphosphate (ATP) an organic molecule composed of an adenine nucleotide that has three phosphate ester groups attached to the ribose; this molecule is the principal source of energy for all living organisms.

adenyl cyclase an enzyme that converts ATP to cyclic AMP; cAMP is a second messenger in the action mechanism of some hormones.

ADH *see* vasopressin.

adrenocorticotropic hormone (ACTH) a hormone secreted by the anterior lobe of the pituitary which stimulates the adrenal cortex.

adrenalin *see* epinephrine.

aerobic requiring air or oxygen for life.

agglutination the clumping or massing together of red blood cells under the influence of specific antibodies during incompatible transfusion.

albinism a recessive genetic condition (*aa*) in which the organism cannot produce pigments.

alcaptonuria a metabolic disease evidenced by the absence of homogentisate oxidase in the liver; apparently caused by the action of one gene.

aldosterone a hormone secreted by the adrenal cortex that causes retention of sodium by the kidneys.

alkali *see* base.

allantois an extraembryonic membrane with varying functions; in birds and reptiles it has a respiratory and excretory function, whereas in mammals it forms part of the blood vessel connection between embryo and mother.

alleles alternative forms of a gene for a particular trait (for example, tall or dwarf are alleles for height in peas).

allergy the result of an antigen-antibody reaction that requires specific capability within an organism.

alveoli the small air sacs of the lungs where gas exchange occurs.

amino acid an organic acid containing a carboxyl and an amino group on the same carbon; there are approximately 23 amino acids.

aminopeptidase an enzyme secreted by the intestine that breaks peptide bonds adjacent to free amino groups.

ammonotelic describes the excretion of ammonia as the principal form of nitrogenous waste.

amniocentesis the process of taking fluid and cells with a hypodermic needle from the amniotic fluid surrounding a fetus.

amnion the fluid-filled sac surrounding the embryo.

amphetamines drugs used as mood elevators; similar in structure to epinephrine or adrenalin.

amylase an enzyme that hydrolyzes complex carbohydrates.

anaerobic capable of living in the absence of air or oxygen.

analogous structures structures having similar functions but different evolutionary origins.

anaphase a stage of mitosis in which the chromosomes move to opposite poles; they appear to be pulled by spindle fibers.

androgen a general term for male hormones (testosterone).

angiosperms taxonomic class of flowering plants.

anther the part of a stamen that produces pollen; often called the male part.

antheridium the sperm-producing organ of a gametophyte.

anthropomorphism the explanation of animal or plant behavior in terms of human behavior.

antibody a specific substance produced by cells that reacts with a specific antigen.

anticodon three unpaired nitrogen bases in transfer RNA that are complimentary to three nitrogen bases of a messenger RNA codon.

antigen a substance, usually a protein, foreign to an organism which stimulates the formation of specific antibodies in the organism.

archegonium the egg-producing organ of a gametophyte.

archenteron the cavity in the gastrula that later becomes the intestinal tract.

atherosclerosis narrowing and hardening of the arteries due to fatty deposits.

atom the modern term for the basic unit of any element, proposed by John Dalton in 1808.

atomic number a number equal to the number of protons in an atomic nucleus.

atomic weight the sum of the number of protons and neutrons in an atomic nucleus.

ATP *see* adenosine triphosphate.

autonomic nervous system an involuntary system closely associated with, but not under direct control of, the central nervous system; it controls secretions of various glands and smooth muscle contractions; it consists of two antagonistic divisions, the sympathetic and the parasympathetic.

autosomes chromosomes other than the sex chromosomes.

autotrophic describing an organism that can produce its own food from inorganic materials.

auxins hormones that regulate the growth of roots and stems.

back cross *see* test cross.

bacteriophage a virus that parasitizes bacteria.

barbiturates drugs that depress physiological activities and act as mood depressants.

basal metabolic rate (BMR) the metabolic rate of an organism theoretically in a state of complete rest; usually expressed as Calories produced per kilogram of body weight per hour.

base (or alkali) in general, a compound in solution that can take up or accept hydrogen ions; often a substance that dissociates to release hydroxyl ions (OH^-).

behavior any externally observable action or activity of a living system.

bilateral symmetry a body plan that can be halved in only one plane so that each half is a mirror image of the other.

bile a substance secreted by the liver that emulsifies fats for digestion.

binary fission asexual reproduction in which the daughter cells are approximately the same size as the parent cell.

bioethics an area of study dealing with the effects of modern biology on human values.

biofeedback the process of "feeding back" biological information to an organism about a visceral function so that the organism may attempt to control that function.

biomes the major terrestrial regions of the earth characterized by the dominant plant and animal life; these include tundra, northern coniferous forest, deciduous forest, tropical forest, grassland, and desert.

biosphere the region of the earth and its atmosphere that contains all living organisms.

blastula the stage in animal development when a single layered ball of cells is formed; it is usually hollow, containing a blastocoel or blastula cavity.

blood the fluid that circulates in the principal vascular system of humans and other vertebrates; in humans consisting of colloidal plasma in which cells and cell fragments are suspended; blood components function in gas exchange, ingestion of foreign substances, and blood clotting.

BMR *see* basal metabolic rate

Bowman's capsule the structure of a nephron in which the glomerulus or capillary network is contained; filtration products are collected here.

Brownian motion the random movement of particles in liquid or gas due to molecular bombardment.

budding a type of asexual reproduction whereby a complete, new individual grows from an organism.

buffer a substance that moderates the hydrogen-ion concentration of a solution, thereby preventing excessive pH changes.

calorie the amount of heat necessary to raise one gram of pure water by one degree Celsius.

capillary the smallest vessel of the closed circulatory system which connects the arteries and veins.

carbohydrates compounds composed primarily of carbon, oxygen, and hydrogen, such as sugars, starches, glycogen, and cellulose.

carbonic anhydrase an enzyme found in the red blood cell which catalyzes the formation of H_2CO_3 and its breakdown into H_2O and CO_2.

carboxypeptidase an enzyme that breaks peptide bonds adjacent to free carboxyl (acid) groups.

carcinogen any substance that can produce cancer.

carnivore an animal with a primarily meat diet; for example, cats and dogs.

carotenes generally orange-red colored pigments closely associated with chlorophyll in the chloroplast.

carotid bodies nerve receptors in the carotid arteries that are sensitive to increased levels of CO_2 and decreased levels of O_2; this causes an increase in respiratory rate.

carrying capacity the number of individuals that a specific ecosystem can support; involves availability of food and shelter.

catalyst a substance that causes an increase in chemical action but is not itself consumed or permanently altered.

cell all living organisms are composed of individual units called cells, which are divided into two main regions—the cytoplasm and the nucleus; the cytoplasm includes the cell membrane, centrioles, Golgi apparatus, mitochondria, endoplasmic reticulum, lysosomes, and ribosomes; nuclear cell parts are the nuclear membrane, chromosomes, and nucleolus.

cell membrane the fat-protein structure between the cell and its environment.

cell wall the outer, nonliving structure of a plant cell composed of cellulose, lignin, and pectin.

central nervous system (CNS) the brain and spinal cord.

centrioles self-replicating bodies that form the spindle for cell division in animals and some protists.

centromere the area of a chromosome to which the spindle fiber attaches at cell division.

cerebellum connected hemispheres between the cerebrum and brain stem; functions in equilibrium and coordination of voluntary muscles.

cerebrum the largest hemispheres of the brain; concerned with conscious, sensory, and motor functions.

chief cells cells located in the stomach lining which secrete pepsinogen (inactive pepsin).

chitin a tough carbohydrate-nitrogen substance found in the exoskeleton of insects and crustaceans.

cholecystokinin a hormone released by the intestinal lining that activates the release of bile from the gallbladder.

cholinesterase an enzyme that breaks down acetylcholine at nerve synapses.

chorion the outermost extraembryonic membrane that forms part of the placenta in some mammals.

chromatid each half of a duplicated chromosome.

chromosome map a diagram of the positions of genes along a chromosome based on the percent of crossover occurring among the genes.

chromosomes long filaments in the cell nucleus composed primarily of DNA and protein.

cilia short, whiplike structures specialized for locomotion in some protists; cilia also occur on certain tissues of higher animals.

circadian rhythms cyclic behavior patterns that occur approximately every 24 hours.

circannual rhythms annual behavioral cycles.

cistron the individual functional units of a gene locus; perhaps involving many nucleotides.

classical conditioning a process in which a neutral stimulus can replace a natural stimulus and bring about a response.

climax the final successional stage in an area which is stable and self-reproducing.

cloaca the canal in some vertebrates where the digestive, excretory, and reproductive tracts come together.

clone a group of cells that has arisen by mitosis from a single parent cell; also the production of a colony of identical organisms from cells of a single parent.

codon a series of three nucleotides which code the position of a specific amino acid in a protein.

coelom a body cavity in animals between the visceral organs and the body wall which is completely lined with mesoderm (this lining is called a peritoneum).

coenzyme a complex molecule containing

the vitamin pantothenic acid which combines with pyruvic acid as it enters the Krebs cycle.

coenzymes small organic molecules that activate enzymes and can transport intermediate products such as hydrogen in specific enzyme reactions.

cohesion the attraction of like molecules for each other.

collenchyma cells thickened at corners that provide support in the stem region of plants.

colloid the suspension of small particles (usually larger than molecules) in a medium; it can exist as a sol or a gel; in a cell the particles are protein and the medium is mainly water.

commensalism two organisms living together in which one organism is benefited and the other is not harmed.

community all the organisms living and interacting within a particular area.

complement a substance found in blood plasma which in the presence of antibodies causes the rupture and destruction of foreign cells.

compound the chemical combination of two or more elements.

conditioned reflex behavior in which a response is made to a specific stimulus which is different from the stimulus that naturally elicits the response; acquired through experience.

conjugation the process in which genetic material is exchanged between two protists or two monerans.

connective tissue provides intercellular support and cohesion among all types of tissues; cartilage and bone are dense connective tissues specially adapted for support.

consumers organisms that feed on other species, either producers or other consumers.

contractile vacuole a specialized organelle in some protozoans which functions in water balance and excretion.

convergence the development of similar characteristics in two or more groups of organisms that are not closely related.

corepressor a metabolic end product that unites with a repressor substance to inhibit an operator gene.

corpus callosum a band of nerve fibers that interconnects the two cerebral hemispheres.

cotyledon embryonic leaflike structures of a seed plant.

covalent bond the bond formed when two atoms share a pair of electrons, such as the bond between carbon and hydrogen.

cretinism a condition caused by lack of thyroxin during development; characterized by low mentality, retarded growth, and impish face.

crossover the breaking and exchange between homologous chromatids during meiotic prophase (observed at tetrad stage); the microscopical observations are termed chiasmata.

cutaneous breathing gas exchange that occurs across moist skin such as found in amphibians.

cytochrome a tetrapyrrole ring molecule containing an atom of iron; the iron functions in the transport of electrons through alternate oxidation and reduction.

cytokinesis division of the cell cytoplasm to form daughter cells.

cytology study of cells.

cytoplasm the region of a cell between the nuclear membrane and the cell membrane.

Darwin-Wallace theory the theory of evolution based on changes in species due to natural selection.

deamination the removal of an amino group (NH_2) from an amino acid.

decomposers bacteria and fungi that break large organic molecules of dead organisms into smaller reusable molecules.

deletions parts of chromosomes that are lost.

deme small breeding group within a population.

denaturation a permanent structural change in a protein which alters its function in the cell.

denitrifying bacteria bacteria that convert ammonia, nitrites, and nitrates into free nitrogen.

deoxyribonucleic acid (DNA) a nucleic acid containing deoxyribose, found chiefly in the nucleus of cells, that functions in the transference of genetic characteristics and in the synthesis of protein.

diaphragm the muscular separation between the chest and abdominal cavities; functions in respiration and elimination.

diastolic pressure the blood pressure resulting from relaxation of the atria and ventricles of the heart during a heartbeat cycle.

differential reproduction organisms better suited to their environment give rise to more and better adapted offspring than those less suited.

differentiation a process of change in the developing organism in which nonspecialized cells become specialized.

diffusion the movement of gas or solid particles from a region of high concentration to a region of low concentration.

dihybrid cross a genetic cross involving two characteristics; for example, height and seed color in peas.

dioecious the condition in which male and female or staminate and pistillate structures are in separate individuals.

dipeptidase an enzyme that splits double amino acids into single amino acids.

diplohaplontic describes an organism with alternating haploid and diploid generations; haploid spores are produced by meiosis.

diploid the number of chromosomes formed by the union of two gametes ($2n$); 46 in humans.

diplontic describes a life cycle with diploid adults; gametes produced by meiosis.

disaccharases enzymes that split double sugars into simple sugars.

disaccharides twelve-carbon sugars such as maltose.

distal convoluted tubule the region of the nephron where further reabsorption occurs, especially of water and some ions.

divergence the development of different characteristics in two or more groups of closely related organisms.

DNA *see* deoxyribonucleic acid.

dominant gene a gene that always produces its characteristic when it is present.

dorsal referring to the back region of a body.

Down's syndrome often called mongolism; evidenced by a third chromosome in pair 21.

duodenum the first ten inches of the small intestine.

dynamic equilibrium a balance due to the active coordination and regulation of all the chemical and physical interactions occurring in an organism.

ecology the study of the relationships of organisms to one another and to the environment.

ecosystem a living community and the physical environment associated with it.

ectoderm the outside germ layer in the developing embryo; the skin and nervous system develop from this layer.

effectors structures that react to stimuli to bring about a counterchange.

electrocardiogram (ECG) recordings picked up by surface electrodes of the electrical events occurring during the cardiac cycle.

electroencephalogram (EEG) recordings of the electrical activity of the brain made by placing electrodes on the skull.

electrolytes ionically bonded compounds that dissociate into charged particles in water and will conduct an electric current; for example, sodium chloride.

electron a tiny, negatively-charged particle located outside the atomic nucleus.

electron-transport series a series of reactions among electron-transfer compounds which serves to produce ATP and water; occurs in the mitochondrion; NAD, FAD, and cytochromes are important members of the series.

electrovalent (or ionic) bond a bond formed by the transfer of one or more electrons from one atom to another; for example, sodium chloride.

element a substance that contains atoms of only one type.

embryo the multicellular beginnings of an organism before germination, hatching, or birth.

endergonic describing chemical reactions that require energy.

endocrine glands ductless glands that secrete hormones directly into the bloodstream.

endoderm the inside germ layer (formed during gastrulation) in the developing embryo; forms the lining of the intestinal tract and the lining of several other internal organs.

endoplasmic reticulum the membranous structure in the cytoplasm.

endosperm the food material in the seeds of flowering plants.

energy the ability to do work; in living organisms, energy is required to perform the chemical reactions necessary for life.

enterocrinin the hormone secreted by the intestinal lining that initiates the flow of intestinal enzymes.

enterokinase a nondigestive enzyme secreted by the intestinal mucosa which activates trypsinogen to trypsin.

entropy a measurement of the degree of disorganization in a chemical system.

enzyme a protein molecule capable of bringing specific reactants together to speed up a biochemical reaction.

enzyme induction the synthesis of an enzyme due to the presence of a specific inducer substance.

epidermal tissue the protective tissue covering many plant parts; in the leaf, special guard cells surround openings (stomata) to permit gas exchange.

epilimnion the region of a body of water above the thermocline.

epinephrine (adrenalin) a hormone secreted by the adrenal medulla which increases respiration, heartbeat, and blood sugar.

epistasis the effect of one gene influencing the expression of another nonallelic gene.

epithelial tissue tissue that covers or lines the organs of the animal body and sometimes forms glandular tissue; generally specialized for protection, absorption, or secretion; specific types include squamous, cuboidal, and columnar.

estrogen the female hormone produced by the

egg follicle; responsible for female secondary sex characteristics.

estrus a cycle of events in most female mammals in which the female is receptive to the male; the egg is released at this time.

ethology the study of behavior under natural conditions.

eucaryotic describes cells possessing a nuclear membrane, DNA-protein chromosomes, and cytoplasmic organelles.

eugenics the study of genetics with particular emphasis on ways of improving the health and quality of humans.

euthanasia the act of putting an organism to death in a painless manner.

eutrophic describing a body of water that contains a large number of organisms and organic products.

evolution the theory that all existing plants and animals were derived from preexisting forms; also includes the concept that the changes occurring in organisms are due to slight genetic variations through successive generations.

excretion generally the release of waste products from a cell or an organism.

exergonic describing chemical reactions that release energy.

exobiology the search for life on other planets.

extracellular digestion digestion that takes place outside the cells in a cavity such as the stomach or intestine.

extraembryonic membranes a group of membranous sacs associated with the embryos of most reptiles, birds, and mammals; these membranes are the chorion, amnion, and allantois, and they function in protection, respiration, nutrition, and waste disposal.

FAD see flavine adenine dinucleotide.

fats compounds composed of glycerine and fatty acids.

feedback a mechanism by which the output of a reaction may act to modify that reaction.

ferredoxin an iron-containing protein that acts as an electron acceptor in system I of photosynthesis.

fetus a stage of early development in humans and other mammals; generally, in humans, from the third month of pregnancy until birth.

flagella whiplike appendages similar to cilia in structure and function but much longer; flagella also occur as the locomotor organelles of sperm.

flame cells specialized ciliated cells that function in excretion and water balance; for example, in flatworms.

flavine adenine dinucleotide (FAD) a hydrogen-transporting coenzyme.

follicle-stimulating hormone (FSH) a hormone secreted by the anterior lobe of the pituitary; it stimulates the production of an egg in the ovary.

food chain the flow of energy from one trophic level to another based on which organisms eat other organisms.

food web a complex of food chains involving many different species.

fossilization the process of preserving the form or actual structures of an organism.

free energy the energy in a biological system that is available to perform useful work.

fruit a mature ovary with seeds enclosed.

FSH see follicle-stimulating hormone.

fundamental tissue various kinds of cells that function in support, food making, or food storage; the three types are parenchyma, collenchyma, and sclerenchyma.

galaxy a group of stars such as the Milky Way.

gametophyte the haploid generation of a plant that produces gametes.

ganglion a collection of nerve cell bodies; for example, dorsal root ganglia.

gastrin a hormone secreted by the stomach lining which causes the secretion of pepsin.

gastrovascular cavity a cavity in some lower animals that serves the functions of both digestion and circulation (coelenterates).

gastrula the stage in animal development when a two-layered (and later, three) structure is formed; a new cavity, which will become the intestinal tract, forms and replaces the blastocoel.

gene the fundamental unit of heredity; a small segment of a chromosome defined according to its functional characteristics.

genetics the study of heredity.

genetic engineering the manipulation of the genes in gametes or a fetus for purposes of treatment of disease or improvement of phenotype.

gene pool the total possible genotypes in an interbreeding population.

genotype the actual genetic composition of the alleles resulting from a cross.

gills small membranous structures found in many aquatic animals which function in gas exchange.

glomerulus the blood capillary network of a nephron.

glucagon a hormone produced by the alpha cells of the islets of Langerhans which stimulates the conversion of glycogen into blood glucose.

glucocorticoids a group of hormones secreted

by the adrenal cortex which tend to increase blood glucose.

glycogenesis   the synthesis of glycogen from glucose.

glycogenolysis   the enzymatic hydrolysis of glycogen to glucose.

glycolysis   the breakdown of glucose or glycogen to pyruvic acid; this series of reactions occurs in the cell cytoplasm and involves the removal of hydrogen and the synthesis of ATP.

glyconeogenesis   the conversion of noncarbohydrate molecules into glycogen (amino acids and fats).

goiter   an overgrowth of thyroid gland tissue sometimes caused by inactive thyroxine due to iodine deficiency.

Golgi apparatus   smooth, membranous sacs in the cytoplasm that seem to function in the storage and transport of cellular secretions.

gonads   the male and female sex glands.

gram-atomic weight   the atomic weight of a substance expressed in grams.

granum   a structure composed of alternate layers of protein-lipid membrane in the chloroplast and containing all the pigments and enzymes necessary for photosynthesis.

green glands.   excretory organs found in the head region of crayfish.

gymnosperms   the taxonomic class of naked seed, coniferous plants.

habitat   the specific physical area in which an organism lives.

habituation   the decreased response to stimuli that is not associated with positive reinforcement.

haploid   the basic chromosome number for an organism abbreviated as (n); generally the number of chromosomes in gametic cells; 23 in humans.

haplontic   having only one set of chromosomes per cell in the adult organism; meiosis follows gamete fusion.

Hardy–Weinberg principle   in a biparental, sexually reproducing population, genotype frequencies will remain constant if the following conditions are met: no mutations, random mating, and a relatively large and isolated population.

hemocoel   a part of a body cavity that collects blood in open circulatory systems.

hemocyanin   a blue, copper-containing pigment found in the blood of some arthropods and molluscs.

hemoglobin   the respiratory pigment of humans, other vertebrates, and some invertebrates; a complex of iron porphyrin and protein.

hemophilia   a sex-linked genetic disease in which the blood does not clot normally; commonly known as bleeder's disease.

hepatic portal vein   an accessory venous system that carries nutrient-laden blood from the intestines to the liver.

herbivore   an animal with a diet of only plant material; examples of herbivores are cow, sheep, and rabbit.

Hering–Breuer reflex   a nerve reflex that inhibits inspiration when the alveoli are filled with air.

heterogamy   gametes of different size, usually micro (male) and macro (female); gametic union occurs only between the two different forms; includes sperm and egg.

heterotrophs   organisms that cannot synthesize their own food (consumers).

heterozygous   describes the situation in which the alleles for a particular trait are different on homologous chromosomes (R,r).

histamine   an amine substance produced by tissues that causes dilation of blood vessels and inflammation in allergic responses.

histology   the study of tissues.

histones   small proteins attached to nuclear DNA of eucaryotic cells.

homeostasis (steady state): the concept that all processes in an organism must be controlled within certain limits or death will result.

homeothermy   maintenance of a constant body temperature (warm-blooded).

homologous chromosomes   chromosomes occurring as pairs following fertilization, one member of each pair coming from the mother and the other from the father; homologous chromosomes are similar in size, shape, and genetic content.

homologous structures   structures that have similar origins; for example, the forelimb bone structure of birds and humans.

homozygous   describes the situation in which both alleles on homologous chromosomes are the same (RR or rr).

hormone   a chemical substance secreted by specific cells in one part of an organism and capable of stimulating cells in other regions.

hybrid   the offspring resulting from the crossing of two genetically different parents.

hydrogen bond   the attraction of the hydrogen proton for negatively charged chemical groups.

hydrogen ion   the positive ion produced when hydrogen is separated from its electron.

hydrolysis   a chemical process in which large molecules are split into smaller molecules; this usually involves the addition of water (hydrolytic cleavage).

hydroxyl ion   when a hydrogen ion is removed from water, the resulting charged radical is called a hydroxyl ion (OH^-).

hyperosmotic a solution on one side of a membrane which has more dissolved particles (therefore a lesser water concentration) than the solution on the other side.

hypha an individual, threadlike structure composing the body of a fungus.

hypocotyl the embryonic root or radicle of a seed plant.

hypolimnion the region of a body of water below the thermocline.

hyposmotic a solution on one side of a membrane which has fewer dissolved particles (therefore a higher water concentration) than the solution on the other side.

hypothalamus the area of the brain beneath the thalamus; it is connected to the pituitary gland and regulates body temperature and some hormone secretion from the posterior pituitary.

hypothesis an educated guess as to the explanation of an observed event.

iliocecal valve the muscular constriction between the small and large intestine.

immunity resistance to infection.

immunization the process of producing immunity in an organism by injection or ingestion of weakened microbes, toxin, serum, or antibodies.

imprinting a type of learning, occurring early in life, in which an individual learns to recognize an object and becomes attached to it.

incomplete dominance describes the situation in which one member of a pair of alleles is not dominant; each allele expresses itself and contributes to the phenotype.

independent assortment genes on different chromosomes separate independently of one another during gamete formation; Mendel's second law.

induction the developmental process in which a group of cells or tissues brings about the differentiation of neighboring cells; thus the position of cells in a developing organ is an important determiner of what they will become.

inhibition a situation in which the product of an enzymatic reaction restrains or checks the action of an enzyme necessary for the formation of that product.

innate describes a type or a component of behavior in which the pattern is essentially inherited.

instinct a series or pattern of successive reflexes producing an often elaborate type of behavior which appears to be mainly inherited.

insulin a hormone produced by the beta cells of the islets of Langerhans in the pancreas which converts glucose into glycogen.

interferon a protein substance released by animal cells upon stimulation by certain viruses; this substance produces resistance to viruses in neighboring cells.

intermedin a hormone secreted by the intermediate lobe of the pituitary which controls pigmentation in some animals.

interphase a stage of mitosis in which the chromosomes are extended and uncoiled; DNA is replicated.

intracellular digestion digestion that occurs inside the cell.

inversion an event in which a portion of a chromosome breaks and reunites on the same chromosome in such a way that the genetic order is reversed.

ion a charged atom or group of atoms resulting from the gain or loss of electrons.

ionic bond *see* electrovalent bond.

islets of Langerhans isolated patches of endocrine tissue found throughout the pancreas.

isogamy the fusion of gametes of similar size and shape to form a diploid cell.

isosmotic refers to equal concentrations of water and dissolved substances on either side of a membrane.

isotope any atom of an element that has a different number of neutrons and consequently a different atomic weight.

karyokinesis division of the nuclear material; in some cases nuclear division occurs without cellular division.

kinetic theory the theory that all matter is in constant motion in the universe.

kingdom the most fundamental category for classification of the living world; examples of kingdoms are Monera, Protista, Metaphyta, and Metazoa.

Klinefelter's syndrome a condition in humans in which the offspring receives a double X and a single Y chromosome because of nondisjunction.

Krebs cycle a cyclic series of chemical reactions that occurs in the mitochondrion; pyruvic acid is oxidized to produce ATP, carbon dioxide, and water.

lactase an enzyme that hydrolyzes lactose into glucose and galactose.

lacteals small vessels found in the intestinal villi which absorb emulsified fat.

larva immature form of an animal that differs from the adult.

law a theory with a high degree of probability based on experimentation.

law of mass action the rate of a chemical reaction is directly proportional to the concentration of the reactants.

learning a modification of behavior as a result of experience.

leucocytes　white blood cells (WBCs).

LH　*see* luteinizing hormone.

lichen　fungus and green algae living together in a mutualistic manner.

linkage groups　genes on the same chromosome which are inherited as a group.

lipase　an enzyme that hydrolyzes fats to glycerol and fatty acids.

lipid　fatty substances including fats, fatty acids, and phospholipids.

luteinizing hormone (LH)　a hormone of the anterior pituitary which causes the formation of corpus luteum from the egg follicle after ovulation.

lymphatic system　a network of vessels that carries emulsified fat and lymph to the veins near the heart.

lysis　the dissolution or destruction of cells; a breaking down or decomposition.

lysosomes　membranous bags containing enzymes that digest proteins, fats, and nucleic acids.

Malpighian tubules　long, thin excretory structures connected to the digestive tract of insects.

maltase　an enzyme specifically for the hydrolysis of the double sugar maltose to two molecules of glucose.

mechanism　the concept that all natural phenomena can be explained in terms of physics and chemistry.

medulla oblongata　the anterior portion of the spinal cord which controls heartbeat and respiration; it is the origin of many cranial nerves.

medusa　the sexual jellyfish stage of certain coelenterates.

megasporangium　the structure that produces megaspores which will develop into female gametophytes.

meiosis　the process of gamete production in which the chromosome number is reduced from diploid to haploid.

menstruation　the monthly shedding of the uterine lining by human females.

meristematic tissue　cells responsible for growth in plants; these cells can form other tissue later.

mesentery　thin sheets of tissue that hold the internal organs together and to the body wall; composed primarily of connective tissue.

mesoderm　the middle germ layer (between ectoderm and endoderm) in the developing embryo; most parts of the animal body come from this layer—for example, muscles, bone, excretory system, and reproductive system.

messenger RNA (mRNA)　soluble RNA synthesized by DNA in the nucleus into specific nucleotide sequences that convey information for protein synthesis to the cytoplasmic ribosomes.

metabolism　the total of all the chemical reactions occurring in an organism; the breakdown of food to produce the fuel molecules for energy is an important part of metabolism.

metamorphosis　the change in body form following embryonic development; often the change from larva to adult.

metaphase　the stage of mitosis in which the chromosomes align on the equatorial plate prior to division.

Metaphyta　the kingdom name for plants.

Metazoa　the kingdom name for animals.

microsporangium　the structure that produces microspores which will develop into male gametophytes.

migration　the movement of species from one area into another.

mimicry　the imitation of one organism by another which serves for protection.

mineralocorticoids　steroid hormones secreted by the adrenal cortex which regulate the reabsorption of mineral ions by the kidneys.

mitochondria　membranous organelles in the cell cytoplasm that contain enzyme systems for energy production (Krebs cycle and the electron-transport series).

mitosis　an orderly sequence of nuclear and cytoplasmic events that produces two daughter cells exactly like the parent cell.

models　generally synonymous with the term theory; models are formulated from existing evidence and subjected to more experimentation.

mole　the amount of substance equal to its molecular weight in grams.

molecular weight　the sum of the protons and neutrons in all of the atoms of a molecule.

molecule　a group of atoms held together by mutual attractions called chemical bonds.

Monera　the kingdom name of the procaryotic bacteria and blue-green algae which have no true nuclei, no cytoplasmic organelles, and no protein in their chromosomes.

monoecious　the condition in which male and female or staminate and pistillate structures are present in the same individual.

monohybrid cross　a genetic cross involving only one characteristic—for example, tallness in peas.

monosaccharides　simple sugars such as glucose which may unite to form more complex carbohydrates.

motor (efferent) pathway　nerve tracts carrying impulses from the spinal cord to effect a response (muscle contraction).

mRNA　*see* messenger RNA.

mucin a complex polysaccharide protein that is the major constituent of mucus secreted along the digestive tract.

multiple alleles describes the situation in which more than one set of alleles contribute to the expression of a particular trait.

mutation any stable change in the genetic constitution of an organism.

mutualism two organisms living together in which both are mutually benefited.

mycelium a collective mass of hyphae that forms the body of a fungus.

NAD see nicotinamide adenine dinucleotide.

NADP see nicotinamide adenine dinucleotide phosphate.

natural selection the effect of different reproductive rates in a population due to the influence of the environment upon the different genetic types in that population. A more classical definition is: a process in nature resulting in the survival and perpetuation of only those forms of plant and animal life having certain favorable characteristics that enable them to adapt to a specific environment.

neo-Darwinism the modern development of Darwin's theory of evolution which incorporates the theories of mutation and gene action.

nephridium a tubular excretory organ found in some invertebrates such as the earthworm.

nephron the individual, minute excretory unit of the vertebrate kidney.

nerve tissue a tissue composed of cells specialized for the functions of irritability and conductivity; the fundamental nerve cell is called the neuron.

neutron a component of the atomic nucleus that contributes one unit of mass but has no charge.

niche the functional place of an organism in the community; sometimes called its "occupation."

nicotinamide adenine dinucleotide (NAD) a coenzyme that transports hydrogen.

nicotinamide adenine dinucleotide phosphate (NADP) a coenzyme that transports hydrogen.

nitrogen fixing the production of usable nitrate from atmospheric nitrogen by certain bacteria; $N_2 \rightarrow NO_2 \rightarrow NO_3$.

nondisjunction a situation in which homologous chromosomes do not separate during meiosis; one gamete receives an extra chromosome and one receives none.

nonelectrolytes compounds that do not dissociate in water and do not conduct electricity; for example, covalent compounds like sucrose.

norepinephrine (noradrenalin) the synaptic transmitter substance secreted by the postganglionic fibers of the sympathetic division of the ANS.

notochord a supporting rodlike structure occurring at some stage of development in all chordates.

nucleic acids macromolecules composed of long chains of nucleotides; the two types are RNA and DNA.

nucleotide the basic unit of nucleic acids composed of a nitrogen base, a five-carbon sugar, and phosphoric acid.

nucleus the structure in most cells that contains the chromosomes (carriers of heredity) and the nucleoli (storage centers for ribosomal RNA).

oligotrophic a body of water that contains little organic material in ratio to the volume of water.

omnivore an animal that eats both plant and animal material.

oögenesis the meiotic process in the ovary which produces eggs.

operant conditioning learning through a program of reinforcement, such as a reward of food, for a certain behavior; the animal's behavior is instrumental in producing the learning.

operator gene a gene that controls the function of a series of structural genes by turning the structural genes off or on.

operon an operator gene and the associated structural genes that it controls.

organ a group of tissues, united structurally, that performs a specific function in a multicellular organism.

organism a living unit in nature.

ornithine cycle see urea cycle.

oscilloscope an electronic instrument somewhat similar to a television set which allows visualization of electrical events such as the movement of a nerve impulse.

osmoregulation the ability to maintain constant concentrations of body fluids despite changing conditions in the environment.

osmosis the movement of water across a semipermeable membrane from a region of high concentration of water to a region of low concentration of water.

oviparous describes the development of an organism within an egg that has been laid outside the mother's body.

ovoviviparous the type of reproduction in animals in which eggs are incubated and hatched in the mother's body prior to live birth.

ovule the structure of the seed plant in which the egg or ovum is contained.

oxidation the addition of oxygen to a compound or the loss of electrons (removal of hydrogen).

oxytocin a hormone secreted by the posterior lobe of the pituitary which stimulates contraction of smooth muscle.

pancreozymin a hormone secreted by the intestinal lining which initiates the flow of pancreatic enzymes.

pangenesis the theory that small "pangenes" were collected into the gametes from all parts of the body.

parallelism the evolutionary development of similar characteristics in two groups of closely related organisms.

parasitism two organisms living together in which one is benefited but the other is harmed.

parathormone the hormone secreted by the parathyroid glands which regulates the metabolism of calcium and phosphorus in the blood.

parenchyma thin-walled cells that often contain chlorophyll and hence are sites of food making; they may also be sites for food storage in the stem or root.

parietal cells cells in the stomach lining that secrete hydrochloric acid.

parthenogenesis the development of an unfertilized egg.

peck order a social ranking system by which a definite hierarchy is established within a group; commonly observed in birds.

pepsin an enzyme released into the stomach which breaks down complex proteins.

peptide linkage the bond formed between two amino acids.

periodic chart a table of all the known elements in which the elements are organized according to their chemical properties.

peripheral nervous system (PNS) a nerve network that includes the 12 pairs of cranial nerves and the 31 pairs of spinal nerves.

peristalsis the rhythmic muscular contractions that move food along the digestive tract.

petals the generally thin, leaflike, colored structures of the flower.

pH *see* pH scale.

phagocytosis the engulfment of solid particles into the cell.

pharyngeal gill slits slitlike openings that appear in the pharynx of the embryonic stages of all chordates.

phenotype the visible characteristics resulting from a genetic cross.

phenylketonuria (PKU) a metabolic disease that produces mental retardation and is caused by the inability of the organism to convert phenylalanine to tyrosine; phenylpyruvic acid is accumulated due to the absence of an enzyme.

pheromone chemicals secreted by an organism which influence the behavior of other members of the same species.

phloem food-conducting tissue of the plant that consists of sieve tubes and companion cells; it composes much of the bark of a tree.

photolysis the separation of $2OH^-$ into H_2O + $\frac{1}{2}O_2$ + $2e^-$ through the action of light and chlorophyll; sometimes called the light reaction of photosynthesis.

photoperiod (ism) response of an organism to the relative lengths of light and dark.

photosynthesis the process of trapping light energy with the aid of chlorophyll to combine water and carbon dioxide to form carbohydrate.

phototrophism a growth response toward light in plants.

pH scale a numerical scale that indicates the relative amount of hydrogen ion in a solution; a pH value between 0 and 7 is acidic and between 7 and 14 is alkaline (7 represents neutral).

phylum a major classification category of organisms with similar characteristics; phyla are subcategories within each kingdom.

phytochrome a pigment system in plants that participates in timing of light and dark periods related to seasonal flowering.

pinocytosis the engulfment of water into the cell.

pistil the egg-producing portion of a flower, consisting of a stigma, style, and ovary; often called the female part.

pituitary gland the "master" endocrine gland attached by a short stalk to the hypothalamus of the brain.

PKU *see* phenylketonuria.

placenta the structural and functional connection between the mother and the embryo in most mammals; it is formed from parts of the chorion membrane and the lining of the uterus.

planet a solid body of matter that orbits about a star and reflects light.

plankton organisms that characteristically float with wind and tide; they provide food for larger consumers.

plasma cells cells developed from lymphocytes capable of producing antibodies.

plasma membrane the outermost living membrane of a cell.

plasmolysis the shrinkage of a cell's cytoplasm due to the removal of water by a hypertonic solution.

plastids bodies found in the cytoplasm of plant and some protist cells; the three kinds are leucoplasts, chromoplasts, and chloroplasts.

plastoquinone an organic compound that contains a carbon-ring structure which can take up and release electrons; it is important in photolysis of photosynthesis.

pneumotaxic center the area in the medulla oblongata of the brain that functions in the nervous control of breathing.

PNS *see* peripheral nervous system.

poikilothermy animals whose body temperatures are dependent on the environment (cold-blooded).

pollination the process in which the pollen grain comes in contact with an ovule and, ultimately, the egg.

polymorphism the occurrence of two or more phenotypes in a population of a species.

polypeptide a molecule composed of several to many peptide linked amino acids.

polyploidy the condition of having more than two complete sets of chromosomes.

polyribosome complex in the cytoplasm of a cell consisting of functional ribosomes and messenger RNA.

polysaccharides long chains of monosaccharide units; for example, starch, glycogen, and cellulose.

population a group of one species of organisms.

population genetics the genetics of a breeding group or population.

porphyrins a class of compounds composed of four pyrrole rings and a metallic ion; the fundamental structure of chlorophyll, hemoglobin, and cytochromes.

predation a relation between animals in which one species (predator) hunts down and kills another species (prey) for food.

probability the chance, often expressed as a percentage, that a specific event will occur; a probability of 1 (or 100 percent) represents certainty.

procaryotic cells lacking a nuclear membrane, DNA-protein chromosomes, Golgi, mitochondria, lysosomes, and chloroplasts (bacteria and blue-green algae).

producers primarily the photosynthetic members of the ecosystem.

productivity generally the amount of carbon (as glucose or starch) made available by producers.

progesterone a hormone secreted by the corpus luteum which promotes the vascularization of the uterine lining prior to the implantation of the fertilized egg.

prolactin a hormone secreted by the anterior lobe of the pituitary gland which stimulates the production of milk.

prophase a stage of mitosis in which chromosomes shorten, centrioles move to poles, asters form, nucleoli disappear, and the nuclear membrane breaks down; in meiosis homologous chromosomes synapse.

prostaglandins a group of hormonelike substances produced in various tissues with a wide spectrum of action; they are thought to function in regulating hormone action.

proteins complex compounds composed of amino acids connected by peptide linkages.

Protista the kingdom name for organisms that cannot be classified as true plants or animals.

proton a component of the nucleus of an atom which has one unit of mass and a positive charge.

protonema the "first thread" or filament of a germinating moss spore.

proximal convoluted tubule the region of the nephron near the glomerulus where reabsorption of glucose, water, and some ions occurs.

pseudocoelom a body cavity incompletely lined with mesoderm.

pyloric valve the muscular constriction between the pyloric stomach and the small intestine.

pylorus the lower portion of the stomach which passes digesting food into the small intestine.

quantitative inheritance when more than one set of alleles appear to influence the expression of a trait; sometimes called additive inheritance.

radial symmetry a circular body plan that can be halved in two or more planes so that each half is a mirror image of the other.

radicle the embryonic root or hypocotyl of a seed plant.

radioactivity spontaneous changes in the nuclei of certain atoms to emit electromagnetic waves or particles.

reasoning application of prior learning to new situations.

receptors structures, often specialized, for the detection of chemical or physical changes both internal and external.

recessive gene a gene that produces its characteristic only when two of the same type are present, that is, in the absence of a dominant gene.

reduction the addition of electrons (or hydrogen) to a compound.

reflex an involuntary response to a stimulus.

reflex arc the reflex pathway that commonly involves sensory (afferent), internuncial, and motor (efferent) neurons; occurs across the spinal cord from dorsal root to ventral root.

regeneration the process of producing a new structure to replace a lost part.

regulator gene a gene that exerts a controlling action on other genes; acts on the operator gene.

reinforcement reward for a specific type of behavior.

releaser a structure, chemical, sound, or action

that acts as a stimulus to trigger specific behavior patterns.

rennin an enzyme present in the stomach of young mammals which causes the curdling of milk.

repression a situation in which the product of an enzymatic reaction interferes with the synthesis of an enzyme necessary for the formation of that product.

repressor a protein that inhibits the synthesis of messenger RNA when combined with an operator gene.

respiration the release of energy in the form of ATP from organic fuel molecules which can be used by cells; hydrogen atoms are removed in a sequence of reactions with the liberation of carbon dioxide and water.

respiratory quotient (RQ) the ratio of carbon dioxide produced to oxygen used in the oxidation of foods ($RQ = CO_2/O_2$).

resting potential the electrical potential between ions inside and outside a nonconducting nerve cell membrane.

Rh factor a group of antigens found in the red corpuscles of many humans that react with antibodies formed against rhesus monkey cells.

ribonucleic acid (RNA) a nucleic acid that contains ribose, found chiefly in the cytoplasm of cells; in comparison to DNA, it is generally single stranded and contains the pyrimidine uracil; the genetic material of many viruses.

ribosomes small particles of RNA and protein in the cell cytoplasm which are the sites of protein synthesis.

ribulose diphosphate a five-carbon sugar ($C_5H_8O_7P_2$) that combines with carbon dioxide in the first step of the dark reaction (carbon fixation) of photosynthesis.

RNA *see* ribonucleic acid.

root pressure the pressure produced by water moving into root hair cells which helps move water upward in the plant.

RQ *see* respiratory quotient.

rugae the ridgelike folds of the interior stomach wall.

salt the product formed in the reaction between a strong acid and a strong base.

saprophyte an organism that obtains its nutrition from dead organic material.

science an organized study of the material universe; scientific methods involve procedures that provide an orderly and systematic approach to problems dealing with matter.

sclerenchyma cells with thick, hardened walls which provide support and rigidity to plant stems.

secretin a hormone secreted by the intestinal lining which stimulates the flow of sodium bicarbonate from the pancreas.

seed an embryo with associated food and a hardened coat.

segregation the random separation of genes during meiosis when each gamete receives a complete set of alleles; Mendel's first law.

sensory (afferent) pathway the nerve tract bringing sensory impulses into the spinal cord.

sepals the green, leaflike structures that protect the flower bud and are located at the base of an open flower.

serosa the extraembryonic membrane formed by the apposition of the chorion and allantois.

sex chromosomes a pair of chromosomes distinguishable from other chromosomes in the cell; they are often different in male and female.

sexuality the capability of some organisms to exchange genetic materials as a part of their reproductive process; also includes the condition of male and female.

sickle-cell anemia an anemia (impaired oxygen transport) caused by the production of an inefficient hemoglobin and deformed sickle-shaped red blood cells.

smog an undesirable pollution of the atmosphere generally by industrial or automobile smoke and fog.

somatostatin a hormone secreted by the hypothalamus that suppresses production of insulin and glucagon.

somatotropin a hormone secreted by the anterior lobe of the pituitary which stimulates growth and metabolism.

speciation the process by which new species are formed; when sufficient changes have occurred in the genotypes of certain populations due to physical or biological barriers so that the organisms cannot interbreed, a new species is formed.

species a group of actually or potentially interbreeding organisms.

spermatogenesis the meiotic process in the testes which produces sperm cells.

spiracles the small outside openings of the tracheal tube respiratory system in insects.

sporangium the spore-producing structure of the sporophyte.

sporophyte the diploid generation of a plant which produces spores.

stamen the organ of a flower consisting of a pollen-producing anther and a supporting filament.

star a self-luminescent collection of matter in the universe.

steady state *see* homeostasis.

stimulus any internal or external change that can cause a biological reaction.

stroke a loss of blood supply or hemorrhage in the brain often causing paralysis and loss of sensation.

structural gene the gene that codes messenger RNA for the production of a specific protein.

succession the progressive changes in vegetation in an area.

sucrase an enzme that hydrolyzes sucrose into glucose and fructose.

symbiosis the living together of two dissimilar organisms, especially when the association is mutually beneficial.

symmetry the shape of the body of an organism with respect to a particular plane or point of reference; radial, spherical, or bilateral symmetry.

synapse the junction between two neurons.

synapsis the pairing of homologous chromosomes in the first prophase of meiosis.

synthesis a chemical process in which small molecules are joined to form larger molecules; this usually involves the loss of water (dehydration).

systolic pressure the blood pressure resulting from contraction of the atria and ventricles of the heart during a heartbeat cycle.

taxis movement of an organism in response to a stimulus.

telophase a stage of mitosis in which the cell membrane constricts (in animals) or cell wall develops (in plants) and daughter cells are formed; chromosomes and nucleus return to interphasic condition.

territoriality the phenomenon whereby a specific number of animals mark and defend a particular area against intruding species.

test cross (back cross) a test for determining whether a parent is homozygous or heterozygous dominant; the doubtful genotype is crossed back to the recessive character.

testosterone the male hormone secreted by the interstitial cells of the testis which is responsible for male secondary sex characteristics.

tetrad the result of duplicated homologous chromosomes following synapsis; it is thought that crossover occurs at this stage of meiosis.

thalamus a portion of the forebrain beneath and posterior to each cerebral hemisphere; provides relay connections between spinal cord and cerebrum.

theory an explanation of an observed event based on extensive experimentation or testing.

thermocline a zone in a lake or ocean in which there is a rapid drop in temperature related to depth.

thoracic duct the large duct of the lymphatic system in mammals which transports fats and lymph from the lacteals to the superior vena cava.

thorax the chest cavity containing the heart and lungs; in insects, the mid-region of the body bearing the wings and legs.

thromboplastin a substance produced by injured tissues that, along with calcium ions, initiates clotting reactions.

thymosin a hormone secreted by the thymus gland responsible for the full development of antibody-producing ability of lymphocytes.

thyroid gland a two-lobed endocrine gland located on each side of the trachea, the secretion of which regulates the rates of metabolism and body growth.

thyrotropic hormone (TSH) also called thyroid-stimulating hormone; a hormone secreted by the anterior lobe of the pituitary which stimulates the thyroid gland to produce thyroxine.

thyroxine the hormone secreted by the thyroid gland which contains iodine and increases metabolism.

trachea the windpipe leading to the lungs.

tracheal tubes a system of small tubules in insects which supply air directly to the tissues.

transamination the exchange of an amino (NH_2) group between an amino acid and a keto acid or between two amino acids.

transcription the process by which DNA in the chromosomes produces a sequence of complementary bases in messenger RNA necessary for protein synthesis.

transduction the result of the transfer of DNA from one bacterium into another through the agency of a bacterial virus.

transfer RNA (tRNA) RNA synthesized by DNA in the nucleus which has two areas of unpaired bases—one area attaches to a specific amino acid and the other recognizes the mRNA code on the ribosomes.

transformation the result of the direct transfer of DNA from one bacterium into another.

translocation the movement of food materials in plants from the leaves to other areas for storage or respiration; also the breaking off of a segment of a chromosome followed by a reunion of that segment with a homologous or nonhomologous chromosome.

transpiration the release of water to the atmosphere from the leaves and stems of plants.

triploblastic an animal body composed of

three embryonic germ layers: ectoderm, mesoderm, and endoderm.

tRNA   *see* transfer RNA.

trophectoderm   the outer layer of cells surrounding the inner cell mass of developing primate eggs.

trophic levels   the various energy levels in an ecosystem beginning with the producers and ending with the decomposers.

tropism   a movement in plants caused by a growth response to a stimulus.

trypsin   a pancreatic enzyme that hydrolyzes proteins into amino acids in the intestine.

TSH   *see* thyrotropic hormone.

Turner's syndrome   a human condition in which the offspring receives only a single X chromosome because of nondisjunction in the female; the single X chromosome comes from the male.

umbilical cord   the cord that contains blood vessels and connects the embryo to the placenta; the navel is the point of attachment on the embryo.

urea cycle (ornithine cycle)   a cyclic series of chemical reactions that combine carbon dioxide and ammonia into urea.

ureotelic   describes the excretion of urea as the principal form of nitrogenous waste.

uricotelic   denotes the excretion of uric acid as the principal form of nitrogenous waste.

valence   the bonding potential of an atom; valence is determined by the number of electrons in the outer shell.

vasectomy   the cutting and tying off of the vas deferens for contraceptive purposes.

vasopressin (ADH)   an antidiuretic hormone (ADH) secreted by the posterior lobe of the pituitary which causes constriction of blood vessels and reabsorption of water in the kidney tubules.

ventral   referring to the front or the anterior side of a body.

vestigial   describes anatomical structures that have been retained in an organism but are no longer of functional significance.

villi   fingerlike projections of the lining of the intestine; they greatly increase the absorptive surface area.

virion   virus existing in a free state outside a living cell.

virus   extremely small noncellular particle composed of a protein coat and a nucleic acid core that must invade a living cell to reproduce.

vitalism   a philosophy that holds that events of unknown cause are produced by supernatural forces.

vitamins   organic compounds necessary for the proper functioning of specific enzymes, usually forming a vital part of a coenzyme.

viviparous   indicates the development of an organism within the mother's body.

xylem   plant tissue that conducts water upward in the plant and consists mainly of tracheid and vessel cells and fibers; it forms the woody part of a tree.

yolk sac   the food source for embryos of reptiles and birds but practically nonfunctional in most mammals.

zero population growth (ZPG)   the limitation of a population to a particular size because the birth rate equals the death rate.

zoöspores   flagellated, motile spores that develop directly into new plants.

zygote   the result of the union of two gametes; a fertilized egg ($2n$).